MISTER ROGERS' PLAN & PLAY BOOK

Activities from
Mister Rogers' Neighborhood
for Parents & Child Care Providers

FIFTH EDITION

Family Communications, Inc.
  Mister Rogers' Plan & Play Book

Family Communications, Inc. is a nonprofit company dedicated to children, their families and those who support them. Through the production of materials in all media, we encourage open and honest communication. Respect for healthy emotional, social, and intellectual development is at the core of what we do.

THE MISTER ROGERS' NEIGHBORHOOD CHILD CARE PARTNERSHIP is designed to help child care providers incorporate the Mister Rogers' Neighborhood television program into their schedule and plan activities based on its developmental and educational themes using the Plan & Play Book and other materials including:

"Extending Mister Rogers' Neighborhood to Child Care" Video
"Around the Neighborhood" Newsletter
"Going to Day Care" Book
"When Parents Are Away" Mister Rogers' Home Video
The Mister Rogers' Neighborhood "National Broadcast Schedule"

For more information about these and other materials call or write to:

Family Communications, Inc.
4802 Fifth Avenue
Pittsburgh, PA 15213
Phone: (412) 687-2990
Fax: (412) 687-1226

ISBN 1-885950-00-4

Printed in the United States of America

Dear Parents and Child-Care Providers,

It's now over 35 years that I've been trying to use television to help young children grow in healthy ways. The opportunity to develop this book gave all of us at Family Communications a great deal of pleasure because it allowed us to find ways to make our work helpful in new directions.

I've talked with many parents and caregivers, and I know how much of a person's self goes into caring for children. Planning the day, thinking of activities to do, and just dealing with day-to-day happenings all take lots of time. That's why we tried to make this book as easy as possible for you to use. We also tried to include activities that would be fun and simple to do. As you well know, caring means much more than preparing meals and having a place for children to play…much more! In fact, we like to think that this book is one way we have of caring for you as you care for the children. We really trust that it'll be helpful.

We originally wrote PLAN & PLAY for child-care providers, but over the years we have heard from so many parents who enjoyed using it at home that we decided to make this book available for families as well. Although the activities were developed for children in groups, we believe they are easily adaptable for family situations.

Those of you who are child-care providers become partners with parents. You work together by learning each other's needs and hopes, and by talking about the things that please you, as well as the things that concern you, about each child. That way, you are better able to give the children in your care the truly important things their parents aren't there to give them during the working day: love, support, understanding, comfort, limits, an excitement in their growing abilities, a healthy curiosity about their world, an eagerness to learn, a belief that they are valuable, and a feeling that life is worth the effort to live.

That's what we, at Family Communications, have tried to do all these years in our own way. From our work directly with children and with the help of many teachers and consultants, we have learned that children at certain ages all seem to need help in understanding certain things about themselves and their world. They need help, for instance, in understanding their bodies and their feelings—and what to do with those feelings. They need help in understanding what is real and what is pretend. They need help in coping with times of separation from their parents…and from other caregivers as well. They need help in understanding that while they have some things in common with every other human being, they are also different from any other person in the world, and that those differences are part of what makes them special to the people who love them.

Helping each child grow — inside and out — at his or her own pace is one of the most important jobs of a child-care provider. Some days, of course, will seem to be easier than others. We all have times when we are irritable or just plain tired. That's true for children as well as for us. When I began working with children at a family and child-care center many years ago, I would sometimes feel that a play session hadn't been the least bit helpful. I remember after one particularly difficult time with a child I told my supervisor how badly I thought I had done. "Fred," my supervisor told me, "an hour with a child in which you've given your attention and tried to understand that child as well as you knew how — that hour is never wasted." I now believe that to be true. Even on hard days, the relationship between a child and a caregiver can grow, and it's that relationship, more than anything else, that helps the child. Being there with consistency, supporting the child's own unique ways of growing: that's what's essential.

"You are special" is something I often tell my young television friends, but children's caregivers such as you are truly special, too. If you feel like letting us know how you used this book, we'd certainly be grateful to hear from you. We're always interested in the ways that adults and children make the best of life together.

Fred Rogers

SIX HELPFUL SUGGESTIONS

1 EACH ACTIVITY HAS A NUMBER THAT MATCHES THE TELEVISION PROGRAM NUMBER.

The one-page National PBS Broadcast Schedule in the back of this book shows the number of the program broadcast from PBS each day. A local station chooses when in the day to show that program and may also repeat it later in the day, on the weekend, or during the following week at another time. You can also find the program number at the end of each program.

Some of the programs in the series are no longer being shown, but we've left the activities in the book to give you a larger selection.

If you have trouble finding out which program is going to be on, we suggest you call your local PBS television station and talk with the Instructional Television Director or the Program Manager.

2 WATCHING THE PROGRAMS WITH THE CHILDREN.

If you're not familiar with MISTER ROGERS' NEIGHBORHOOD, we suggest you watch it a few times before using it with your children. That way you'll understand more about the themes and characters on the program.

We strongly urge you to watch with the children, so that you can talk with them about what they've seen. Watching can also help you use the activities to build on the ideas offered during the program.

3 SOMETIMES CHILDREN MAY NOT FEEL LIKE DOING AN ACTIVITY.

It can be hard to know why a child doesn't feel ready to join in any particular play, but there's usually a good reason. It's fine for a child just to watch or have some quiet, private play.

4 HOW YOU USE THIS BOOK IS UP TO YOU AND YOUR CHILDREN.

You may want to do one activity each day, or you may choose to use the activity book only two or three times a week.

Some days you or the children may not feel like doing an activity we've suggested. If you want an alternative activity, you can refer to the index. You and your children may come up with ideas of your own after watching the programs, and you may find those are the best activities of all.

CHILDREN ARE MORE COMFORTABLE WHEN ADULTS LET THEM KNOW WHAT THE LIMITS ARE.

It's a good idea to let children know in advance your rules about using materials. For example, you may want to limit some of the messy activities to the kitchen.

Some of the activities are not suitable for very young children. Rather than spending your time trying to set limits they can't manage, you may find it's better to offer these activities to older children when younger ones are napping.

THE WORDS TO MANY OF THE SONGS ARE PRINTED IN THE APPENDIX.

Music is an important part of MISTER ROGERS' NEIGHBORHOOD. The songs on each program often express concerns and feelings that most young children have. You may want to use them whenever those concerns and feelings arise naturally during the day.

The Importance of

CREATIVE PLAY

"Child's play" is one of the most misleading phrases in our language. We often use it to suggest something easy to do, something trivial, but it's not—not by any means. When children play, they're *working*. For them, play is both a serious and a necessary business, and it's one of the ways children learn and grow.

Some play is just for the fun of it; like all of us, children need a relaxing time-out.

Some play helps children work out things going on in their own development. For example, as they deal with feelings about their parents' leaving, it can help children feel reassured about their parents' return when they can make their toy trucks go away...and *come back*.

Some play can help children rehearse events that may be difficult or anxiety-producing, like going to the hospital or getting a shot. We all feel more comfortable when we know what to expect in a new situation and talk about or play about it first.

Pretending is a particularly important part of children's play. Dressing up in grown-up clothes can help children feel big and powerful and to feel in charge of things for a change. Even little children need to *feel* in control of their world from time to time...without the scary responsibility of actually *being* in control. On the other hand, particularly at stressful times, they may need to feel smaller and younger than they really are; and then they can pretend to be a baby again. Whatever it is that children are pretending, it's usually a way for them to work on their feelings about their world and their place in it. It's a way for them to grow on the inside, which is every bit as important—probably even *more* important than growing on the outside!

Responding to Creativity

Children's drawings, paintings and sculptures, and their use of toys and puppets can tell us so much about the way children are feeling. In fact, those are often the best ways children have to let their feelings out.

Showing approval of our children's creative efforts tends to encourage their creativity; little children want the approval and love of the people they care most about. Often, sincere interest means more to a child than extravagant praise. Asking a child what a picture is about, and then sitting down and really listening, may say a lot more than a rave review, like "Boy, are you a great artist!" It's also easy for grownups to misunderstand children's artwork: Saying, "That's really beautiful!" may not be what's called for when the splashes of reds and yellows and blacks are the expression of angry feelings. As most caregivers know, just displaying a picture on a refrigerator or at the office can make a four year old as proud as an artist at a gallery opening.

We certainly don't have to understand all of a child's creative efforts. What's important is that we communicate our respect for children's attempts to express what's on their minds at the moment.

No matter how children choose to express themselves, they can know, as we do, the pleasure of creating something unique from inside ourselves. Encouraging children to discover that uniqueness and helping them develop its expression can be one of the greatest gifts we can ever give.

SPECIAL NEEDS

We often hear heartwarming stories about children with special needs or disabilities who have appreciated MISTER ROGERS' NEIGHBORHOOD and used the messages to help them cope with their feelings and concerns. That naturally leads us to believe that in early childhood settings, children with challenges can benefit in many ways from watching MISTER ROGERS' NEIGHBORHOOD with an adult and doing many of the activities suggested in this book.

The activities themselves can be helpful because they are based on universal childhood themes. The activities and discussions we've included can help children find ways to express joys, cope with frustrations, and calm fears that are a natural part of childhood.

Also, the conversations or comments from the children as they do the activities may give you some insight into what is important to them — what they especially like, as well as what may be difficult for them.

At the same time, we recognize that children with disabilities and special challenges have unique needs and abilities, and so it is with your creativity that the activities in this book can be adapted for them.

One good starting point for adapting is to look at the variations we've included in the description for many of the activities. (We noted those because we recognize that all children bring unique and special needs to an early childhood setting.) Some variations offer ideas for modifying the activity for younger children, and those suggestions may be useful for children who have developmental delays. There are also comments about changes you may want to make for children who have different learning styles and temperaments.

Adjustments need not be elaborate. You can address special learning needs simply by modifying the environment. For instance, it might be more helpful for a particular child to sit on the floor or on a chair at a table. Perhaps a child in the group could sit next to another child for help with an activity. This support could be helpful to both children.

Varying color, size, and texture can also help make the activities more successful for children with special needs. Most children prefer colorful materials, but materials that are too colorful can distract some children from the purpose of the activity. You may also want to offer larger materials and more working space for children who do not have fine motor control. For matching games, you may want to compare on the basis of texture, as well as shape or color.

Sometimes at the end of an activity we've listed an alternative, and that might work better for a particular child. You could also look for options in the index, where we have arranged the activities by type and by topic.

Even under the best circumstances, you may find that some children are too challenged by some of the activities we've suggested. If you need additional help, you might want to consult with an early intervention specialist. If you want to find more information about early intervention, you could contact your local school district or disabilities agencies.

Since you know the children best, you can probably find ways to make your own adjustments and adaptations for the children in your care. As with everything else you do with the children, it's *your* genuine care for them as unique individuals that makes an activity successful.

Thoughts For The Week

Whenever we move away from a place where we've lived for a while, it can be really hard. We often feel like we're leaving a little bit of ourselves behind— even if we know the move will bring new opportunities and experiences. For children, play can be a way to work on feelings like this. One child I know spent weeks rehearsing his move to a new house. He was quite concerned that some of his favorite toys would be left behind. Each day he "practiced" moving by packing all his toys in a box. Then he taped the box closed and used a wagon to pull it to the front yard where he unpacked everything and pretended that he had arrived at his new home. His play seemed to help him feel ready for what lay ahead.

This week in the Neighborhood of Make-Believe, the Frogg family is moving to the Westwood Children's Zoo because Dr. Frogg has a new job there. The Frogg's son, Tad, is unhappy about leaving his friends in the Neighborhood of Make-Believe. In real life, thousands of families move to new homes each year, and the move can be stressful for everyone. But moving can also be a time for both children and grownups to learn and grow. One thing children need to hear and to know is that when they move the people who take care of them will move with them. They will always have someone to care for them.

Fred Rogers

Songs On The Programs This Week

1002 *"You've Got to Do It"*
      "You're Growing"

1003 *"Museum Wares"*

1004 *"I'd Like to Be Like Mom"*
      "To Go to Some Place Else"

1005 *"Everybody's Fancy"*
      "I'm Glad I'm the Way I Am"

Your Notes For The Week

1001

Mister Rogers talks about things that are round and shows a film of round objects. Then he starts a Shape Sculpture with a circle.

"Things That Are Round" can help children:
- learn to recognize likeness and difference;
- learn more about their world;
- learn to look carefully.

Things That Are Round

Materials
- a box with assorted round objects inside such as a paper plate, ball, ring, coin, etc. (If you have very young children, be sure the objects are not so small that they may be swallowed.)
- round scrap materials (buttons, paper circles, round stickers)
- one piece of paper for each child
- a round object to use for tracing (plate, pot or pan lid)
- pencils, crayons or markers
- paste or glue

Can any of the children think of something that's round? Show the children several objects from the box and encourage them to feel the round edges. You could take a tour of the house and look for other objects that are round, things like:
- clocks or other dials;
- pots and pans;
- balls and other round toys;
- cabinet and door knobs;
- baskets, flower pots or trays.

If the weather is pleasant, you could take a walk and look for round things outside, too! You might see things like tires, wheels, windows and round signs. Would there ever be a round cloud? The children could practice tracing around pot lids (or whatever) to make circles on pieces of paper. They might like to decorate these circles with bits of scrap material and turn them into collages.

1002

The Froggs have been invited to move to the Westwood Children's Zoo, and Tad is unhappy about the move because he has to leave his friends. Lady Aberlin helps him talk about these feelings, and then they pretend about visiting each other.

"Moving Day" can help children:

- develop their imaginations;
- use play to work on feelings.

Moving Day

Materials

- boxes of many different sizes
- toys, dress-up clothes, etc.
- tape
- markers

If you ever had to move to a new house, you might want to tell the children how you felt about the move. Have any of the children ever had to move to a new house? Can they tell you how they felt about:

- packing their toys and clothes;
- leaving friends and neighbors;
- seeing the old house when it was empty;
- unpacking at the new house?

What are some of the things they liked about the old house? How about the new house? If none of the children have ever moved to a new house, perhaps they moved to a new room, or said good-bye to a friend who moved. Encourage the children to pretend about moving day by setting out the props—empty boxes and toys or clothing to pack. Help them tape the boxes and label the contents. After they have "moved" to the new house, you could help them unpack the boxes, returning all the toys to their proper places.

(Or, 1391 "Where I Live"; 1434 "Unhappy Feelings.")

1003

Someone must learn to do Mrs. Frogg's job as caretaker of the Museum-Go-Round before the Froggs can leave the Neighborhood of Make-Believe. To everyone's surprise, Lady Elaine turns out to be the one who wants to try. Miss Emilie's poem, "Be the Best of Whatever You Are," helps Lady Elaine decide to be the best museum caretaker she can be.

"A Job to Do" can help children:

- learn to do things independently;
- practice making choices.

A Job to Do

Materials

- large piece of paper or cardboard
- name tags
- tape

On the paper or cardboard, list some jobs the children could do and hang it for the children to see. Here are some suggestions:

- wash the table(s);
- put away toys;
- water the plants;
- pass out juice and crackers;
- set the table.

Who would like to do what? You can tape the children's names next to the jobs they choose. They may need your help for a while as they learn what it is you want them to do, but this activity can become an everyday way for the children to help you out. Do any of them have regular jobs they do at home? Do they know that one of your jobs is taking care of children?

1004

Today is moving day in the Neighborhood of Make-Believe. Lady Elaine is moving into the Museum-Go-Round and the Froggs are moving to Westwood. Mister Rogers pretends that a family of dolls is moving to a new doll house—but one of the dolls doesn't want to move.

"A New Doll House" can help children:

- talk about feelings;
- use play to work on feelings;
- develop creative play.

A New Doll House

Materials

- two large cardboard boxes
- small boxes or doll furniture (see page B-3)
- toy people or little dolls

How do the children think Lady Elaine and the Froggs felt about moving? If any of your children have moved recently, how did they feel? For some children talking about a recent move might be too painful. They might want to tell you about it some other day...some other month. Using two cardboard boxes as doll houses, pretend the dolls or toy people have to move from one to another. Older children could paint the boxes and (with your help) cut out doors and windows. Simple furniture can be made from little boxes or folded cardboard. You might want to ask the children how they think the dolls feel about moving into their new house. What are some of the things the dolls need to do to settle into their new home?

- unpack boxes?
- arrange the furniture?
- choose bedrooms?
- meet the neighbors?

What other play ideas do the children have?

1005

Mister Rogers has two baby ducks on his front porch. He puts them in a pool of water and, later in the program, shows two plastic ducks. He talks about the differences between the real ducks and the plastic ducks.

"Things That Are Alive" can help children:

- learn more about their world.

Things That Are Alive

Materials

- a sheet of paper
- old magazines
- glue or paste

Can any of the children tell you some things that are alive? What about plants? You could play a game by asking the children to say "yes" or "no" to the question, "Is this alive?" as you point to objects and people in the room. It can be a good outside game, too. If you have some old magazines, the children could look for pictures of things that are alive, cut them out, and paste them into a collage to hang on the wall.

(Or, 1168 "Playing about Animals.")

Thoughts For The Week

This week in the Neighborhood of Make-Believe, everyone is waiting for King Friday to make a very important announcement. Seeing how the neighbors feel about waiting can help children begin to understand their own feelings about having to wait. Waiting isn't very easy for anyone—and it's especially hard for young children. One thing that makes waiting easier is to talk about what's going to happen and help children learn to find things to do right now while they have to wait.

Fred Rogers

Songs On The Programs This Week

1006 "We Welcome You Today"
1007 "Let's Be Together Today"
"I Like to Be Told"
1008 "Today Is a Very Special Day"
1009 "Everybody's Fancy"
1010 "Days of the Week"
"Sometimes People Are Good"

Your Notes For The Week

1006

An important visitor is coming to the Neighborhood of Make-Believe today. Her name is Sara Saturday and King Friday is busy with his welcoming plans. He has invited a trumpet player to play when Sara arrives and Lady Aberlin will play the triangle. In reality, Mister Rogers visits a trumpet player who knows how music can be used to express feelings—happy, sad or angry. "Cardboard Trumpets" can help children:

● express feelings through music;
● develop creative play.

Cardboard Trumpets

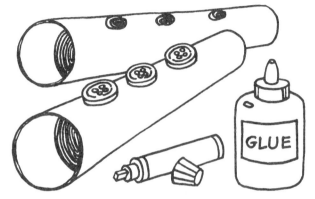

Materials
● cardboard tubes from paper towel or toilet paper rolls
● markers or crayons
● paste or glue
● aluminum foil (optional)
● buttons

Help the children draw or paste buttons on the cardboard tubes to make pretend finger stops. (They could make shiny horns by first covering the tubes with aluminum foil.) When the horns are done, the children can hum through the tubes to make a kazoo-type sound. Encourage them to "play" music that expresses different feelings. You could ask them:

● Can you make happy music?
● How about sad music?
● What would the music sound like if you were angry?
● What if you felt lonely?

Then you might want to "play" a song together—one of Mister Rogers' songs, or another familiar tune they all know.

(Or, 1212 "Ringing Spoons"; 1404 "Sandpaper Blocks.")

1007

Mister Rogers is painting his porch swing. He opens and closes the paint can to show what the words "open" and "closed" mean. In the Neighborhood of Make-Believe, the castle is closed today because of an important meeting between King Friday and Sara Saturday. It will be open tomorrow for King Friday's special announcement.

"Open and Closed" can help children:

- learn more about their world;
- learn to use words.

Open and Closed

Materials

- a box with a lid, or a small suitcase
- blocks or toys

What kinds of things can you find—inside or outside—that open and close (doors, lids on boxes, jars, milk cartons, cans, mailboxes, garbage cans)? What do they look like when they're open and when they're closed? Has anyone thought of people's mouths? Or eyes? They open and close. If you have a box with a lid, or a small suitcase, the younger children can practice opening and closing it, filling and emptying it. They might enjoy doing this with a lower kitchen cupboard where you keep pots and pans or canned goods.

1008

Mister Rogers continues painting today. He is careful to wash up when he is finished. In the Neighborhood of Make-Believe everyone is finding it hard to wait for King Friday's announcement. Lady Elaine decides to paint the Museum-Go-Round to make the time go faster.

"Painting Boxes" can help children:

- develop their imaginations;
- develop creative play.

Painting Boxes

Materials

- boxes of various sizes
- non-toxic paint and brushes or fingerpaint
- aprons or paint shirts
- plastic or newspapers

Let each child pick a box to paint and cover a work area with newspaper or plastic. On a nice day you could do this activity on your porch or in the yard. (You may want to set a few limits before giving out the paint, like being sure the children know where they can paint and where they cannot, and reminding them that they will have to share the different paints.) Do any of the children want to make something from the box? (A car? House? Rocket?) Or work on a large box together? Or glue several small boxes together when the paint has dried? You can have a lot of fun with this activity, but as you can tell by now, it's a really messy one! If you have very young children around, you might want to do a different activity today.

(Or, 1080 "While You Wait"; 1311 "Talking about Waiting.")

1009

There's going to be a wedding in the Neighborhood of Make-Believe. Newspaper and television reporters interview the King and Sara about their wedding. In the "real" neighborhood Mister Rogers shows a film of children dressing up as kings and queens and pretending to have a wedding.

"Kings and Queens" can help children:
- develop their imaginations;
- try out different roles.

Kings and Queens

Materials
- paper crowns
- fancy hats or scarves
- junk jewelry
- pieces of flowing material for capes and robes
- mirror

Your children might want to plan a royal wedding, or make up their own ideas about kings and queens. You could help them make paper crowns, or use hairpins to fasten old necklaces and pieces of junk jewelry in their hair. Old curtains or towels or just about any pieces of cloth can be pinned or tied to make wedding gowns or head coverings. If you have a big mirror, the children will probably enjoy parading around in front of it.

(Or, 1267 "Headbands That Fit.")

1010

There is excitement in the air in the Neighborhood of Make-Believe today as the neighbors attend a fashion show of wedding clothes. Sara Saturday looks at samples of materials for her wedding gown.

"Making Doll Clothes" can help children:
- develop creative play.

Making Doll Clothes

Materials
- scraps of material
- ribbon or string
- scissors
- facial tissue or paper towels
- clear plastic tape
- dolls or stuffed animals

Here's how old scraps of material can be turned into simple doll clothes:
- Fold a rectangular piece of material in half and help the children cut a small opening along the fold for the doll's head.
- Make a short slit down the front or back so the dress (or shirt) will slip on easily.
- Help the children fasten the material by tying a ribbon or string around the doll's waist.

Capes or veils can be made by taping a tissue or paper towel around a doll's shoulders or head.

Thoughts For The Week

*Weddings hold a great deal of interest for most children. This is partly because the ritual, ceremony, and festivities of weddings are interesting, but there may be more to it than that: At one time or another, most children have had fantasies about marrying their moms or dads. Pretending about "getting married" can be a way for children to express these feelings and, through play, come to a better understanding of both family relationships and what their lives may **really** be like when they grow up.*

Fred Rogers

Songs On The Programs This Week

1011 "I Like You As You Are"
1012 "You Can Never Go down the Drain"
1013 "One and One Are Two"
"Because"
"Trolltalk"
1014 "You've Got to Do It"
1015 "Going to Marry Mom"
"Peace and Quiet"

Your Notes For The Week

1011

Mister Rogers has a carpenter's measuring rule with him today. He uses it to make different shapes. In the Neighborhood of Make-Believe, Robert Troll uses a measuring stick to make letters and a pretend house.

"Stick Designs" can help children:

- develop their imaginations;
- develop creative play.

Stick Designs

Materials

- popsicle sticks, or
- strips of heavy paper (one-half inch wide and several inches long)
- cardboard (use the inside of cereal boxes that have been cut apart)
- glue (dilute it by adding one part water to one part glue)

See what the children feel like doing with the sticks or strips when they're just spread out on a table or on the floor. After a while (five minutes or so) you might ask the children to show you some things they could make. If you have toddlers in care, you could help them make simple designs while the other children make:

- fancy designs;
- shapes;
- letters;
- outlines of houses, wagons, cars, etc.;
- their names.

Some of the children might like the idea of gluing their pictures or designs onto cardboard. The sticks or paper strips that are left over can be kept in a special box for the children to use whenever they want.

1012

Mister Rogers washes his hands before trying on several pairs of mittens and gloves. He sings the song "You Can Never Go down the Drain." In the Neighborhood of Make-Believe, King Friday has ordered everyone who comes to the wedding to take a bath and wear purple gloves.

"Bathing the Dolls" can help children:

- try out different roles;
- use play to work on feelings.

Bathing the Dolls

Materials
- dishpan
- washable dolls or animals
- soap
- wash cloths
- towels

Do any of the children want to pretend that the dolls are going to King Friday's wedding and have to take a bath first? They could just pretend that it's bedtime and the dolls need to have baths. Encourage the children to help plan the bath time. Can they tell you some of the things they would need? You might want to cover the floor or table with a large towel before filling the dishpan with water, but you could use the sink or bathtub if you prefer. The children can take turns bathing the dolls, or they could bathe the same doll if you only have one washable doll. You may find the children are very interested in watching the water go down the drain when you are finished. Some of the children might want to dress the dolls for bed and pretend about bedtime—or they could dress them for attending the Royal Wedding and pretend about that. It could help for the children to see that not even dolls can go down the bath drain—only water and suds go down the bathtub drain—never ever people!

(Or, 1009 "Kings and Queens"; 1380 "Going down the Drain.")

1013

There is a Variety Show in the Neighborhood of Make-Believe today. Being busy with the performance makes it easier for everyone to wait for the Royal Wedding. Mister Rogers pretends to put on a pair of purple gloves before the Variety Show begins.

"Getting Dressed" can help children:

- develop their imaginations;
- learn different ways people communicate.

Getting Dressed

Materials
- none

Can the children pretend to put on a pair of gloves? See if they'd like to pretend to put on other clothes. How would they put on things like:

- a shirt?
- shoes?
- socks?
- a jacket?
- jeans?

Then encourage them to pretend about:

- tying shoes;
- buttoning a sweater;
- zipping a jacket.

You could play a game by asking one child to pretend to put on a piece of clothing. Can the others guess what that child is pretending to do? No matter what somebody is wearing that person is still inside. Even if gloves are covering your hands, your hands are still there.

(Or, 1281 "Variety Show.")

1014

Mister Rogers builds a house from blocks and shows a film of a real house being built. In the Neighborhood of Make-Believe, Lady Elaine and Handyman Negri use magic to build a new castle large enough to hold all the wedding gifts.

"Making a House" can help children:

- develop their imaginations;
- develop creative play;
- practice working cooperatively.

Making a House

Materials

- blocks and toy people
- boxes
- table and blanket
- laundry basket

Ask the children to help make a pretend house for the play area today. Can any of the children tell you what kinds of materials might be needed to build a pretend house? For instance:

- blocks or boxes to build a doll house for the toy people;
- a table and a blanket for a tent-like house;
- a laundry basket upside down for small dolls;
- some chairs, pillows, and baskets to set off an area for pretending.

See what the children can think up. What kinds of things could they use in their pretend house?

- furniture?
- dress-up clothes?
- toy dolls?

What do people do inside of houses? Let the chldren tell you...and you'll have a unique opportunity to know what is important to them.

(Or, 1391 "Where I Live.")

1015

Chef Brockett bakes a wedding cake and Mister Rogers helps decorate it. In the Neighborhood of Make-Believe, all the neighbors turn out in their best clothes for the Royal Wedding of King Friday and Sara Saturday.

"A Wedding Cake" can help children:

- practice working cooperatively;
- learn more about foods.

A Wedding Cake

Materials

- your favorite cake recipe and ingredients
- measuring cups and measuring spoons
- mixing bowls and spoons
- cake pans or cupcake pans

If you feel like it, you and the children can celebrate the Royal Wedding by making your own cake or cupcakes. Children usually like to help or at least watch adults cook. When you're baking or cooking, maybe the children could do a few things to help you. This activity can be used for other special events too, like birthdays or holidays. Use your own cake recipe or try the pound cake recipe that can be found on page 319. You might want to begin by making a list of the jobs that the children could do. For example:

- everyone wash hands;
- fill the measuring cups;
- add ingredients;
- mix the ingredients;
- grease the pans;
- beat the eggs;
- clean up.

Do any of the children want to decorate the room for celebrating? Balloons and streamers are nice, but the children might have more fun making their own signs and pictures. Some children might know about a real wedding they could tell everyone about. There's lots for children to wonder about at weddings.

Thoughts For The Week

We all know that we can learn a great deal by doing. But it's only natural that in learning to do something we are bound to make mistakes. Children need to know that everyone makes mistakes once in a while. Even grownups make mistakes. Not everything I do on television is perfect, not by any means. I might button my sweater the wrong way or drop something by accident. Talking about our own frustrating experiences can help children see that making mistakes can be a part of learning and growing.

Fred Rogers

Songs On The Programs This Week

1016 *"You're Growing"*
1017 *"Everybody's Fancy"*
1018 *"Just for Once"*
"We Welcome You Today"
1019 *"Sometimes People Are Good"*
1020 *"I'm Taking Care of You"*

Your Notes For The Week

1016

Dr. and Mrs. Duckbill Platypus arrive in the Neighborhood of Make-Believe today. They are looking for a new home and decide they can build one at the frog pond.

"My Home" can help children:

- understand and accept individual differences;
- recognize likeness and difference.

My Home

Materials

- paper
- crayons or markers
- children's books (Your local library is a good place to find them.)
- housekeeping toys

What are the things children think about when they think of their own homes? Can they tell you what they like to do when they go to their homes after day care? They might be able to tell you how their homes are different from the day care home and what about them is alike. See if the children would like to draw pictures of their homes or pictures showing some of the special things they like to do at their homes. Younger children might want to sit with you and look through your children's books for pictures of houses where people might live. Would any of the children like to use the housekeeping toys for make-believe today?

1017

Today Mister Rogers talks about vegetable plants. He shows different seeds—beets, carrots, onions, and radishes. All the seeds are different, and they grow into different vegetables. All people are different, too.

"Vegetable Prints" can help children:

- recognize likeness and difference;
- learn more about foods.

Vegetable Prints

Materials

- different vegetables (onion, potato, carrot, pepper, radish, etc.)
- non-toxic paint
- shallow dish or tray
- knife
- cutting board
- paper

Can any of the children tell you the names of the vegetables you have? How are the vegetables alike? Can they find any differences? You could cut the vegetables in half, or cut them crosswise in several pieces so the children can see the inside part of the vegetables. Here's how the children can make vegetable prints using the pieces of vegetables:

- First pour a little paint into a shallow tray.
- Show the children how to dip the cut end of the vegetable in the paint.
- Use the vegetable to make prints on the paper.

Encourage the children to make their own designs or patterns with the vegetables and paint. Can they tell you how the prints are different from each other? Some of the children may be able to match the vegetable to its print. On your next trip to the store, see if the children can name the vegetables they see.

1018

Mister Rogers uses moving boxes to talk about the meaning of "full" and "empty." The Platypus family is moving into the Neighborhood of Make-Believe with boxes that are full of their possessions.

"Pouring Rice" can help children:

- develop coordination;
- learn more about their world;
- learn about conservation.

Pouring Rice

Materials

- rice (popping corn or dried beans)
- plastic bowls or dishpan
- measuring cups or plastic containers of different sizes
- a large towel
- large pan

It's probably best to cover the table with a large towel or two for an easier cleanup. The children can use measuring cups and spoons to practice pouring rice (or whatever). Can the children show you a cup that is full of rice? Where is an empty cup? Encourage them to use different-sized containers. When the activity is over, let everyone empty his or her container into a large pan. You might want to prepare rice for lunch today, or, if you use popcorn, make some for a snack.

(Or, 1353 "Water Play.")

1019

Mister Rogers shows pictures of a boat and a film of himself and several young friends riding in motor boats.

"Playing with Boats" can help children:

- develop creative play;
- learn more about their world.

Playing with Boats

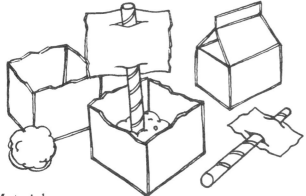

Materials

- toy boats
- milk cartons (pint or quart size)
- modeling dough or clay
- straw or stick
- paper (tissue paper may work best)

You may have toy boats for the children to use, but you can also help them make a sail boat for water play. You can make a simple boat from a milk carton:

- Use a small milk carton (pint or quart) and cut off the top so the bottom of the carton is about three inches high.
- One of the children could cut or tear a paper sail from tissue paper and fasten it to a stick or straw.
- Place a piece of clay or modeling dough in the bottom of the milk carton and put the straw in the clay.

The children can sail the boats in the sink, bathtub, or in a dishpan or wading pool outside. What happens when they blow on the sail? If the boat falls over they can "right" it and try again.

1020

The people in Make-Believe are working hard shoveling earth. They need a cool drink when they are finished. In the "real" neighborhood Mister Rogers shows Joe Negri how to make popsicles.

"Making Popsicles" can help children:

- learn more about their world;
- learn more about foods.

Making Popsicles

Materials

- small paper cups or an ice cube tray
- popsicle sticks or plastic spoons
- unsweetened fruit juice
- a small pitcher

If you pour the juice into a small pitcher, each child may be able to fill his or her own cup with juice. (Fill the cups about three-quarters full.) Then put the cups in the freezer until the juice becomes slushy enough for a popsicle stick or plastic spoon to stand up in it (one or two hours, depending on your freezer). Return the popsicles to the freezer until they are frozen—four or five hours at least, or leave them overnight and serve them to the children the next day. Once the popsicles are frozen, the children can tear off the paper cups to eat their popsicles.

(Or, 1244 "Melting Ice Cubes.")

Thoughts For The Week

*Children are often concerned about broken things—a stuffed animal whose stuffing comes out, or a doll's arm that falls off. When young children are learning about their bodies, it's easy for them to think that **their** arms could fall off or that their insides will spill out through a cut or a skinned knee. No wonder children are easily upset about cuts and bruises! It's at times like these when they need the comfort and reassurance of a trusted grownup. All children need to hear that their bodies won't fall apart the way that toys and other objects sometimes do when they break. People are different from toys because a person's body is all one piece.*

Fred Rogers

Songs On The Programs This Week

1021 "What Do You Do?"
1022 "B-O-X Spells Box"
1023 "We Welcome You Today"
1024 "You've Got to Do It"
"One and One Are Two"
"I'm a Man Who Manufactures"
1025 "Parents Were Little Once Too"
"Days of the Week"

Your Notes For The Week

1021

In the Neighborhood of Make-Believe, the neighbors are helping to dig a new home for the Platypus family. "Digging a Hole" can help children:

- develop their imaginations;
- develop muscle control;
- express strong feelings in appropriate ways.

Digging a Hole

Materials

- old spoons
- plastic shovels
- small metal shovels or garden tools
- plastic containers or pails

Is there a place in your yard where the children could dig a hole? Maybe along the edge of the house or in a corner of the yard? Or is there a park nearby with a sandbox? The children can use plastic shovels and metal spoons if the ground is loose, or they could use small metal hand tools and a small-sized shovel to dig in earth that is hard. The digging could have a purpose such as:

- digging a garden in the spring or early summer;
- pretending to dig for hidden treasure;
- digging a home for pretend animals.

If it's winter and you have snow, you might let the children dig in that instead. Many children may want to dig just for the fun of it. If you are comfortable with mud play (and if extra clothes are available), you could let them use water to mix with the earth to make mud pies or mud sculptures. Mister Rogers sings the song "What Do You Do?" (with the mad that you feel) today. You could point out that shoveling earth or digging in a sandbox or snow is one thing a person could do when he or she feels angry...something that doesn't hurt yourself or anyone else.

1022

In the Neighborhood of Make-Believe, everyone is talking about who gets to keep the magic kite. The magic kite itself gives the answer—take turns and share.

"Taking Turns" can help children:

- practice sharing;
- practice taking turns;
- practice waiting.

Taking Turns

Materials

- a tricycle or other riding toy

Sharing and taking turns are often very hard for a young child. Can any of the children tell you something they have to take turns to do? You might want to ask questions like:

- What does "taking turns" mean?
- Why do we sometimes have to take turns?
- How can we decide when someone else gets a turn?

Often the riding toys are limited in number and require "turn-taking." Using a tricycle or other riding toy, practice taking turns. Let the children help decide about:

- the order in which each child has a turn;
- how to decide when each one's turn is over;
- other activities the children could do while waiting for a turn.

Then ask the children how they feel about taking turns. Can they think of things to do to make waiting for a turn easier?

- Is there a picture book to look through?
- Some modeling dough to use?
- Some blocks for building?

1023

Mister Rogers shows a film about looking for things that resemble letters, and then he recites the letters of the alphabet. "You could look for letters wherever you are," he tells his television friends.

"Looking for Letters" can help children:

- recognize and use symbols;
- learn to look carefully.

Looking for Letters

Materials

- old magazines, catalogues, newspapers
- paper
- paste
- scissors

Your older children may be able to recognize certain letters. Encourage them to look through the old magazines, catalogues or newspapers to find the letters of their names, or their favorite letters. Do any of the children want to paste their letters on a paper to hang up or take home? If the younger children don't seem interested in looking for letters, maybe they can go through the magazines looking for other things, like cars, animals, or airplanes. If the weather is nice, you could take a walk outside and spend some time (not all of the time) looking for letters on signs, car license plates, stores, and other places.

(Or, 1349 "Alphabet Soup"; 1371 "Modeling Dough Letters.")

1024

Mister Rogers repairs a chair for Officer Clemmons. Pretending is fine, Mister Rogers says, but you can't pretend that a chair has been fixed. You have to really do it.

"You've Got to Do It" can help children:

- understand wishing can't make things happen;
- understand the difference between real and pretend;
- develop the ability to keep on trying.

You've Got to Do It

Materials

- puzzles, blocks, other toys in the play area

Have any of the children ever wished something would happen by magic? Can any of the children tell you some things they wish would happen magically? For instance:

- cleaning up the toys;
- fixing a broken toy;
- putting a difficult puzzle together;
- balancing a tower of blocks.

The children might want to use a "magic" wand to pretend about making something happen. But did it *really* happen? Encourage them actually to do the thing they wished would happen by magic. Point out ways to make the jobs seem easier. For example:

- turn all the puzzle pieces right side up so they can all be seen;
- divide the toy area into small sections and tidy up one part at a time;
- find a way to make a sturdy base for a tower of blocks.

Even though you might suggest these ways, the children may find their own ways, too. You might want to sing or say the words to Mister Rogers' song, "You've Got to Do It."

(Or, 1259 "Fixing Things.")

1025

Mister Rogers finishes making a globe that a friend gave him. He explains that a globe is a map of the world and shows how it resembles an orange. Then he peels a real orange. In the Neighborhood of Make-Believe, X the Owl enjoys eating an orange.

"Oranges" can help children:

- learn more about their world;
- learn more about foods;
- practice working cooperatively.

Oranges

Materials

- orange
- knife
- large piece of paper (a grocery bag cut open will work just fine)
- orange paint and brushes or crayons
- paste or glue
- several three-inch circles cut from paper

What can the children tell you about oranges? You might ask:

- Where do we get oranges?
- What color are they?
- What shape are oranges?

Then you could peel or cut up an orange for the children to eat. Are there any seeds? How does it taste and smell and feel? Is the peel thick or thin? Can the children think of other fruits that are round? You could all work together to make an orange tree. On a large piece of paper draw a trunk and branches of a tree. See if the children want to color or paint paper circles orange and paste them on the branches of the tree. You might want to add some green leaves. Did the children know that oranges grew on trees? Can you help them name other fruits that grow on trees? Perhaps you could find a book in the library about fruits to share with the children.

Thoughts For The Week

*Pretending is important play for all children. It's one of the ways they learn how they feel about themselves, their own little world and the grownup world around them. When a child pretends to be a firefighter or storekeeper, he or she is trying to understand more about what it means to be "grown up" and what adult life is like. Pretend play is also a way for children to imagine about things they **can't** ever be—kings and queens, witches and wizards, monsters and giants. Grownups have a big role to play in helping children learn what is **real** and what is only **pretend**.*

*Enjoying pretend things is fine but it's also important for children to enjoy being themselves. They learn self-confidence by succeeding at things—by practicing and getting better and trying. Yet they also need to know that nobody is perfect at everything, not even their parents or their day caregiver. We can help children feel good about themselves when we recognize what they do well and accept them and enjoy them for who they **are**.*

Fred Rogers

Songs On The Programs This Week

1026 *"Everything Grows Together"*
      "To Go to Some Place Else"

1027 *"What Do You Do?"*

1028 *"Children Can"*
      "I'm a Man Who Manufactures"

1029 *"Just for Once"*
      "I Like You As You Are"

1030 *"We Welcome You Today"*
      "Tree, Tree, Tree"

Your Notes For The Week

1026

Chef Brockett "talks" to Mister Rogers without using words. He uses gestures to offer Mister Rogers some of the cupcakes he made.

"Messages" can help children:

- learn different ways people communicate.

Messages

Materials

- mirror (optional)

The children might enjoy sending messages without using words. How about:

- Come here.
- Go away.
- I don't know.
- Hold my hand.
- Yes.
- No.
- I'm sorry.
- My stomach hurts.
- I love you.
- I'm hungry.

If the children have difficulty with the message, you might trying using a mirror. Sometimes seeing their own expressions can be helpful. Or, you could ask the children to guess some messages you make up. Then maybe they can make up some of their own for everyone else to guess.

(Or, 1259 "Fixing Things"; 1260 "Puzzles.")

1027

Lady Aberlin is playing a sad song on the xylophone—she's missing King Friday and Queen Sara. Robert Troll is playing with blocks and he knocks them over because he's afraid that Queen Sara will never come back.

"How Do You Feel?" can help children:

* express strong feelings in appropriate ways.

How Do You Feel?

Materials

* non-toxic paint
* brushes
* paper
* modeling dough

Can the older children in your group tell you how Lady Aberlin was feeling today? Why do they think Robert Troll knocked over all the blocks? Give each child paper, paint, and a brush and encourage them to paint a picture showing how they feel when they are sad. They might want to paint another picture showing how they feel when they are happy, or just how they feel right now. The children could also use modeling dough to show how they feel when they are angry at someone. They might want to pound, punch, or break the dough—or mold an angry creature. And of course they might not want to. Angry activities are best when you're really *feeling* angry. Do any of the children want to make up a song or a little poem about how they feel when they are sad? Angry? Happy?

1028

Mister Rogers listens to a song and paints a picture that shows how the music makes him feel. He explains that everyone's picture of the same song would be different, because everyone's feelings—and expressions of those feelings—are different.

"String Painting" can help children:

* develop their imaginations;
* develop creative play.

String Paintings

Materials

* non-toxic paint
* paper
* string (foot-long pieces)
* crayons or markers
* newspapers

For this activity, you'll probably want to cover your work area with plenty of newspapers. Let each child dip a piece of string into the paint and arrange it on one half of a piece of plain paper, leaving an end of the string hanging off the bottom. Fold the other half over onto the string, press firmly on the paper, and let the child pull out the string. When the papers are opened again, do the designs suggest anything to the children? After the paint has dried, the children could use markers or crayons to add to the patterns they see or to make the designs into pictures.

(Or, 1420 "Paint to Music"; 1423 "Fingerpainting Designs.")

1029

Mister Rogers shows a film of children playing dress-up in grownups' clothes, and Mr. McFeely visits Mister Rogers with masks from the mask-maker.

"Paper-Plate Masks" can help children:

- develop their imaginations;
- try out different roles.

Paper-Plate Masks

Materials
- paper plates
- markers or crayons
- scrap materials (yarn, buttons, paper, cloth, etc.)
- glue
- popsicle sticks or unsharpened pencils
- tape

Younger children may be able to draw a simple face on a paper plate, while older children could use scrap materials to make fancier masks with yarn hair and button eyes. They could even cut holes for eyes so that they can see through their masks. If you tape a stick to the back of each mask, the children can hold them in front of their faces while they act out a role. You may need to show the younger children how easily the mask can be taken away and reassure them that the person behind the paper plate is the person they know. If the masks are too frightening for any of the children, encourage everyone to use the paper-plate faces as puppets, or put the masks on a teddy bear or doll. (A person's face is very important to babies and very small children; a mask of any kind may be frightening.)

(Or, 1261 "Dress-up.")

1030

King Friday and Queen Sara return from their honeymoon. King Friday thinks he's looking in a mirror when he is greeted by Lady Aberlin and Joey Hollingsworth. They are dressed in costumes that make them look like the king and queen.

"Looking in the Mirror" can help children:

- use play to work on feelings;
- recognize likeness and difference;
- practice taking turns.

Looking in the Mirror

Materials
- dress-up clothes or a costume
- mirror

Lady Aberlin and Joey Hollingsworth were dressed up like the King and queen. Ask the children if they were *exactly* like the king and queen. How did Robert Troll know the queen was really back? (He recognized her troll talk.) See if any of the children want to try on a costume or some of the dress-up clothes. Encourage them to take turns trying on the same outfit and looking at themselves in the mirror. Even though several children might wear the same outfit, did any child look *exactly* like another child? What are some ways they were different:

- size?
- hair?
- faces?
- voices?

And just as important: What are some ways they were alike?

Thoughts For The Week

*New experiences are hard for anyone to face. Children especially need the support of a trusted grownup when they face things that are new and different. One way we can be really helpful to them is to let them know what to expect. When children know ahead of time what's going to happen, they can prepare themselves for the experience. And they can also learn the kinds of things that will **not** happen. Often the fear of the unknown is more frightening to them than the actual experience is likely to be.*

Fred Rogers

Songs On The Programs This Week

1031   *"Children Can"*
       "You're Growing"

1032   *"Everybody's Fancy"*

1033   *"I'd Like to Be Like Mom"*

1035   *"I Like You As You Are"*
       "I'm Taking Care of You"

Your Notes For The Week

Monday

1031

Mister Rogers matches picture frames to pictures of the right size and shape. King Friday and Queen Sara brought a wonderful gift to the Neighborhood of Make-Believe—a magic moving picture frame.

"Picture Frames" can help children:

- recognize likeness and difference;
- develop their imaginations.

Picture Frames

Materials

- a framed picture (photograph or painting)
- paper
- paper frames to fit each piece of paper
- scrap materials
- crayons or markers
- glue or paste

See if the children can tell you what a frame is. You might have a framed photograph or painting that you could show them. You could let the children use the paper and supplies to make a picture. You might be able to make the paper frames while the children are working, or you could make the frames ahead of time. Here's how:

- From papers the same size as the children's papers, cut out the center part leaving a one-inch frame. (Save the cut-out part for another activity.) Be sure you have a frame to fit each child's paper.

Show the children the paper frames. Can each one find a frame that fits his or her picture? You may need to help the children fasten the frame around the pictures with paste or tape. Of course some may prefer their picture without a frame. That's fine too. (Many paintings nowadays don't use any frames.) They might want to display their art work on the wall or a door.

(Or, 1022 "Taking Turns.")

Tuesday

1032

Plans continue for a carnival in the Neighborhood of Make-Blieve. Lady Aberlin is dressed as a tightrope walker.

"Tightrope Walking" can help children:
- develop coordination;
- develop the ability to keep on trying.

Tightrope Walking

Materials
- two six-foot pieces of string or masking tape
- tape to fasten the string

You can make a "tight rope" by taping a long piece of string or masking tape on the floor. Show the children how to walk on the line by placing one foot in front of the other (heel to toe). They might need to hold your hand at first. If any of the children have trouble staying on a single line, you could place another piece of tape or string about four inches from the first one. See if the children can walk between the two lines. Balancing takes practice. If you try this activity several times on different days, you'll probably find the children get better and better at it—something you can point out to them. When they feel ready, some of the children might want to try walking backwards on the string, or even playing "Follow the Leader."

Wednesday

1033

Today Mister Rogers talks about the Neighborhood character, Robert Troll, who sometimes likes to speak in nonsense words. Mister Rogers points out that Robert Troll is like a young child learning to speak and who enjoys playing with words.

"Nonsense Rhymes" can help children:
- learn to use words;
- learn to listen carefully.

Nonsense Rhymes

Materials
- none

Ask the children if they remember how Robert Troll talks. Is he hard to understand? Does it help to watch his body? Or listen to the way his voice goes up and down? Can any of the children imitate the way he sounds? The children might want to practice rhyming by making up nonsense words or phrases. You could begin this game by telling them a word (nonsense word or real word). Then see how many ways they can rhyme. Here are a few suggestions to get you started:
- purple—durple, skirpel, turple;
- cellar—pellar, kellar, dellar;
- carnival—barnival, scarnival, tarnival;
- butterfly—putterfly, tuttertye, mutterfly.

Then just make up all kinds of words, just for fun. It'll be up to you to tell the children when "back to real talk" begins...but give them due warning:
"Real talk begins in five minutes."

1034

Everyone in the Neighborhood of Make-Believe is busy getting ready for the carnival, but King Friday won't allow it because carnivals are too noisy. The neighbors convince him to change his mind by asking him to lead the carnival parade.

"It's Too Noisy" can help children:
- develop self-control.

It's Too Noisy

Materials
- the children's voices

Can any of the children think of a time when they thought something was *too* noisy? They might be able to think of times like:
- naptime when they wanted to sleep;
- a birthday party where there were loud noises;
- a celebration with fireworks;
- a parade where there was loud music.

Can they think of a time when a grownup asked them to stop making so much noise? You could begin this activity by letting the children talk loudly for several seconds. Then give the signal to stop. (It's important to agree on the signal before you begin.) Some children might be frightened of too much noise. A frightened child might want to sit on your lap and help you give the signal to stop. Other things they can do to make noise are singing loudly, shouting, clapping hands, stomping feet. When you are sure the children can stop, you can even give them a chance to do all these things at once—for a *short* time. You could end the activity by asking the children to be as quiet as possible for several seconds. Afterwards you might want to sing the Mister Rogers'song "Peace and Quiet."

1035

Today is Carnival Day in the Neighborhood of Make-Believe. Three claps will get you into the carnival.

"Clapping Rhythms" can help children:
- learn to listen carefully;
- develop the ability to keep on trying;
- develop their memory.

Clapping Rhythms

Materials
- none

Can any of the children remember the signal to get into the carnival? Let each child try to give the signal—three claps. Then see if the children can imitate other clapping rhythms.
- clap once (X);
- clap three times (XXX);
- clap twice (XX);
- repeat all this again.

When the children are able to do this well, you could vary the *pattern* and the number. For instance:
- clap once, then three quick claps (X XXX);
- clap twice, wait, then twice more (XX XX).

Can any of the children repeat the patterns? They could make up patterns for the others to repeat or they could even clap a rhythm to their names:
- Patricia (clap three times);
- Ann (clap once);
- Michael (clap twice).

You could sing a song and let the children clap the rhythm while you sing.

The series continues with program number 1041.

Thoughts For The Week

One way children can learn about themselves and the world around them is by asking questions. They usually ask questions about things that concern them at the moment. For instance, a child may wonder why a helium balloon floats away when a person lets go of the string. It can be very important for that child to learn why balloons fly away so that he or she can understand that children can't float away like balloons do. Children need simple answers that will make things clear to them. If we don't understand a child's question, maybe we can help him or her to say it in another way to help us understand. And when children ask questions we can't answer, we need to explain that we don't know, but perhaps we can find out. Maybe it's a question that can be answered by someone else—or in a book from the library.

Fred Rogers

Songs On The Programs This Week

1041   *"Children Can"*
       "Just for Once"
       "I'm Taking Care of You"

1042   *"You Are Special"*
       "To Go to Some Place Else"
       "Just For Once"

1043   *"You've Got to Do It"*
       "To Go to Some Place Else"

1044   *"Children Can"*
       "I Like You As You Are"

1045   *"You're Growing"*
       "We Welcome You Today"
       "Tree, Tree, Tree"

Your Notes For The Week

1041

Mister Rogers makes a game of finding the right-sized container for an assortment of objects.

"Outline Match" can help children:

- learn to look carefully;
- recognize likeness and difference.

Outline Match

Materials

- a large sheet of paper
- markers
- assorted objects (block, key, toy car, ruler, coin, envelope)
- pots and pans with lids, assorted plastic containers and pitchers (optional)

Some of the older children may be able to help you make tracings of various household objects on a large piece of paper. Then mix up the objects and give each child a chance to choose an object and match it to its outline on the paper. When all the objects have been matched, see if the children can think of other things that could be traced and matched. Younger children won't be able to do the tracing, but they might enjoy playing a guessing game. You could say the name of some object in sight and they could take turns finding it.

For another game, you can use pots and pans with lids. See if the children can match the lid that fits each pot or pan. You might want to try the same thing with plastic containers, plastic pitchers or empty coffee cans with plastic lids.

(Or, 1031 "Picture Frames.")

1042

In the Neighborhood of Make-Believe, King Friday doesn't like Robert Troll's noisy game. So Robert Troll goes to Some Place Else to play his noisy game.

"Some Place Else" can help children:

- practice making choices;
- develop self-control;
- practice working cooperatively.

Some Place Else

Materials

- none

When children aren't allowed to play what they want, they need encouragement to play something else, or to find Some Place Else for playing, rather than doing "nothing." Help the children think of places for noisy or active play. Or think of times when noisy play won't disturb other people. Are there times when you need quiet play? Active play? You might want to ask the children questions like:

- Where can you play when the baby is napping?
- What quiet play can you do instead? Play with a puzzle? Look at a book? Roll some modeling dough?
- Is there a special place for using large toy trucks or tricycles?
- Can you use a quiet "inside voice"? What is an "outside voice"?
- What other kinds of things can you do when it's time for quiet play?

1043

Donkey Hodie and Robert Troll wish that Lady Elaine would let them use her tents to make a community center at Some Place Else. They learn that people don't know what we're thinking unless we tell them.

"Questions" can help children:

- feel comfortable asking about what they need to know.

Questions

Materials

- none

Explain to the children that asking questions is a good way to find out what we need to know. You can play a simple version of "Twenty Questions" by having the children take turns choosing an object in the room. (The chooser could whisper it to you so you can help with the questions and the answers.) Then let the others ask questions to find out what it is. You may need to suggest a few questions to get them started. For instance:

- What color is it?
- Can we play with it?
- Does it have wheels?
- Is it big or little?
- Can we ride on it?

The idea of the game is to *help* the questioners guess, not to stump them.

(Or, 1085 "Can You See What I'm Thinking?")

1044

Mister Rogers is measuring the porch step when Officer Clemmons stops by. Officer Clemmons is on his way to Make-Believe to deliver a building permit for the new community center.

"How Long?" can help children:

- learn more about their world;
- develop healthy curiosity.

How Long?

Materials

- hands
- feet
- string
- a block

Using the materials above, the children can measure various objects around the room. You can show them that many things can be used to measure. How many "hands" long is the table? Using the string, the children could measure how tall they are, too.

You might want to encourage dramatic play about measuring today. If you set out a box with paper, pencil, tape measures and rulers, along with a carpenter's hat or a tool box with plastic tools, the children can pretend to build something—a community center, a playground, or something else. You could encourage the children to measure everything as they pretend to build.

1045

Mister Rogers shows viewers several different kinds of flowers. He explains that even though they all are flowers, they all look different.

"Tissue-Paper Pictures" can help children:

- recognize likeness and difference;
- understand and accept individual differences.

Tissue-Paper Pictures

Materials

- tissue paper in several colors
- tray or shoe box
- liquid starch or diluted glue
- cotton swabs or small brushes
- background paper

Everyone can work together to tear sheets of tissue paper into small pieces, using a tray or shoe box to hold all scraps. The children can use cotton swabs or small brushes to paint the background paper with liquid starch or diluted glue (half glue and half water) and then arrange the tissue paper scraps on the sticky paper. Let them add more starch or glue as needed and continue arranging the scraps. When the pictures are finished, some of the children may want to tell you ways their pictures are alike. How are they different? This may give you a chance for some important talk about how *people* are the same and how they are different.

Thoughts For The Week

*There's a birthday in the Neighborhood of Make-Believe this week, and the neighbors find that giving gifts isn't always easy. Sharing and giving presents can be difficult for many young children. In their early years, it's natural for children to think of their favorite toys and favorite clothes as part of themselves, almost as part of their bodies. I once observed a young three-year-old who became upset when any other child played with the toy she had just used. It took her a long time to learn that playing with a toy did not make it hers. But little by little she did learn that she was **separate** from the people and toys around her. But when children have a very special blanket, teddy bear or other special toy, we need to assure them that we know it does belong to them alone. That kind of reassurance and security can make it easier for them to share other things that don't have such a personal meaning. And when children make a gift for us, we need to show appreciation for what they have done. They often feel that things they have made are part of them, too. Appreciating our children's gifts is an important way of showing them we appreciate them for who they are.*

Fred Rogers

Songs On The Programs This Week

1046   *"It's Raining"*

1047   *"When a Baby Comes to Your House"*
         "One and One Are Two"

1048   *"You Are Special"*
         "Today Is a Very Special Day"

1049   *"Today Is a Very Special Day"*
         "I'm a Chef"

1050   *"You Have to Learn Your Trade"*
         "Today Is a Very Special Day"

Your Notes For The Week

1046

It's a rainy day in the Neighborhood of Make-Believe. King Friday is bored because he can't go outside and he thinks he's done everything there is to do inside.

"Something-to-Do Box" can help children:

- practice making choices;
- develop creative play.

Something-to-Do Box

Materials

- a large box
- assorted toys or specially interesting objects (magnets, markers, carbon paper, pencils, small notebooks, magnifying glass, small books, etc.)
- marker

A box full of toys that aren't used every day can be a help when children suddenly seem "played out" and complain that there's nothing to do. In this activity, the children can help you choose things to start off the box, but they can go on adding to it from time to time, and you can add occasional surprises of your own.

As the children help you select things, give them time to play with the toys before putting them in the box. How many different ways can they use the toys? When they're finished playing, put everything in the box and, using a marker, label it "something-to-do box." Can you find a separate, special place to keep it?

1047

In the Neighborhood of Make-Believe, King Friday wants everyone to have a house number so he can be Number One. In reality, Mister Rogers sings the song, "When a Baby Comes to Your House."

"Caring for Baby" can help children:

- develop their imaginations;
- use play to work on feelings;
- express strong feelings in appropriate ways.

Caring for Baby

Materials
- baby dolls
- facial tissues
- clear plastic tape
- doll clothes
- baby clothes

You could begin by talking with the children about babies. What can babies do? What do they need? Why do they eat and sleep so much? You could explain that all children were babies once. Even grownups were babies once. If you have an infant in your care, the children may have a lot to say about babies — and a lot of feelings about the amount of time people have to spend with babies.

Using a baby doll, encourage the children to help you take care of a pretend baby. The children could help do things like:

- change the diaper (use a facial tissue or paper towel and tape);
- feed the baby with a bottle;
- sing to the doll;
- burp the doll;
- put the doll to bed.

This all will probably have an extra special meaning for a child who has a new baby at home. When children have *very* strong feelings about a new baby, they may not feel ready for this kind of doll play or they may play it with more vehemence than some dolls can take. You'll be able to know who can and who cannot use this play well.

(Or, 1177 "I Feel Jealous When.")

1048

Mister Rogers is making a book to keep all the drawings sent to him by children who watch the program. He also makes a cookbook for Chef Brockett's birthday.

"Making a Book" can help children:

- develop their imaginations;
- practice making choices.

Making a Book

Materials
- cardboard (the backs of tablets or cardboard from empty cereal boxes)
- paper for pages (heavier paper works best)
- scraps of material
- glue
- yarn, shoe laces, heavy string or notebook rings
- old magazines or catalogues

You can make front and back covers for each child's book by cutting pieces of cardboard a little larger than the paper pages you'll be using. If you use the cardboard from cereal boxes as book covers, the children can glue scraps of material on the printed sides to make fancy covers. Put five or six paper pages between the covers, poke holes along the sides and lace the booklets together with yarn, shoelaces, or notebook rings.

The children can fill the books with anything that interests them. They could look through old magazines for pictures of their favorite things. Would anyone like to make up a poem or a song for you to write in his or her book? Some children might want to use the books for their own drawings — making pictures right on the pages. You might want to make several booklets for the toddlers to use with pictures of animals and familiar objects. The younger children can sit on your lap and look through the books, naming the objects they see, or pointing to things for you to name.

1049

Mister Rogers is baking a birthday cake for Chef Brockett. The chef helps him by giving directions but doesn't make the cake for him.

"All by Myself" can help children:

- learn to do things independently;
- develop the ability to keep on trying;
- feel proud of their accomplishments.

All by Myself

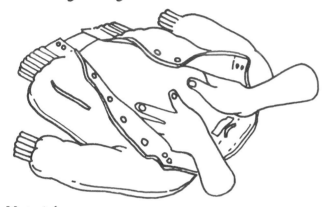

Materials

- the children's own coats or jackets
- other clothing (shoes, belts, skirts, etc.)

Can the children think of things they can do all by themselves?

- Can they walk up or down the stairs?
- Can they button a sweater?
- Can they tie or buckle a shoe?
- Can they feed themselves?

Are there some simple things you could show them how to do? For instance, here's an easy way for children to put on a jacket by themselves:

- Lay the open jacket on the floor upside down so the neck part is closest to the child.
- Show the children how to put their arms in the sleeves and lift the coat over their heads so the jacket is right side up again.

If older children can already put on sweaters or coats, show them how to buckle a belt or tie a shoe. Children's first attempts at anything will not be perfect. Point out the things they did well and reassure them that learning anything new takes practice for adults as well as children.

1050

It's Chef Brockett's birthday today. He wonders why people have treated him to so many things—an orange, a cake, a song on the bagpipes, a dance. Mister Rogers tells him it's because people like him.

"Handprint Cards" can help children:

- express feelings through art work;
- practice working cooperatively.

Handprint Cards

Materials

- one sheet of folded paper for each child
- paint
- brush
- soap and water

Making a hand print card can be a special way to tell someone you like them. Give each child a folded sheet of paper. One at a time, paint each child's hand with a thin coat of paint. If any of the children are concerned about having their hands painted, you may want to paint your own hand first and then wash it off to show how easily the paint comes off. Let them choose where they wish to put their handprint on the card. They might want to put two or three prints in different places. Wash each child's hand once they've made their prints to avoid a mess. When the cards are dry, let the children sign their names. Those who can't form letters yet could just make a mark of their own. You could then print their names on the card in another place. The children might like you to write inside the card for them, too. You could suggest:

- I love you.
- You are special to me.

Can the children think of something else they'd like to say?

(Or, 1450 "Birthday Parties.")

This series continues with program number 1061.

Thoughts For The Week

There are many different ways for children to find out about the world around them—looking carefully at things, touching and feeling the things they see, and listening carefully to the sounds they hear and the words people say.

People communicate their feelings in different ways, too. Because children can't always use words to say what they're feeling, we can sometimes discover their feelings through their drawings and paintings, by their facial expressions, and through the make-believe situations they create. Children are often aware of adults' varied expressions of feelings, especially if they're adults the children care about a lot. A four-year-old asked her mother one morning, "Well, why is Daddy so upset?" When the child's mother responded that he hadn't talked about being upset, the girl then asked, "Well, why does his face look like a stone face?" That child was able to notice her father's change in facial expression and understood that something was wrong.

Fred Rogers

Songs On The Programs This Week

1063 *"Everybody's Fancy"*
      "What Do You Do?"
1065 *"Children Can"*
      "You Are Special"

Your Notes For The Week

1061

Everyone is building something today. Mister Rogers builds a small car from wooden blocks, using the blocks to explain the meaning of "big" and "little."
"Big and Little" can help children:

- recognize likeness and difference;
- practice working cooperatively.

Big and Little

Materials

- two baskets
- an assortment of blocks, boxes, or plastic containers in two different sizes

At the beginning of block play today, you might want to talk with the children about the words "big" and "little." Can anyone show you a *big* block? Where is a *little* block? See if the children can make a tower using all the little blocks; then one using all the big blocks. Or what ideas do they have for using the blocks? If you don't have a set of blocks, try using different sized boxes or plastic containers (with lids) that will stack one on top of the other. Or make some blocks from milk cartons (see page B-1).

At the end of this activity, see if the children can help put the blocks away by placing all the big ones in one basket and all the little blocks in the other.

1062

Van Cliburn visits again today and plays the piano. Chef Brockett makes a special cake in the shape of a piano for Mr. Cliburn.

"Secret Envelopes" can help children:

- learn to look carefully;
- recognize likeness and difference.

Secret Envelopes

Materials

- crayons
- several envelopes
- assorted flat objects (penny, button, key, paper clip, toothpick, etc.)

First, show the children the assortment of objects and see if they can name them. Then slip each one into an envelope and close it. Give the envelopes to the children and let them feel what's inside. Can they guess what it is? Using the crayons, the children can rub over the object until a shape appears. Now can they guess? After the children have opened the envelopes to check for sure what's inside, you can repeat the activity by switching the objects from envelope to envelope. This time, the children can do their crayoning on the other side.

(Or, 1332 "Hide and Seek"; 1134 "Shoe-Box Harp.")

1063

Mister Rogers looks closely at leaves and tries to notice how they are the same and how they are different. Lady Aberlin has a magic leaf that makes magic when she uses the Spanish words—"una hoja." ("Una hoja" means "a leaf.")

"Una Hoja" can help children:

- recognize likeness and difference;
- learn more about their world;
- develop healthy curiosity.

Una Hoja

Materials

- a tree with leaves
- paper and paste
- a bowl of water
- crayons

If the weather permits, you might walk to a nearby tree. Encourage the children to look at the tree, touch and feel it. You could ask:

- How is the tree like you?
- How is it different?

You might be able to find two different types of trees and talk about how they are alike and how they are different. For instance:

- How does the bark feel?
- Is the tree tall or short?
- Is it straight or crooked?

Then the children could look for leaves. Do any of the children remember the Spanish word for leaf? Can they find different kinds of leaves? How are the leaves different in color, shape and size? If you take the leaves home, the children could:

- paste them on paper;
- float them in water;
- make crayon rubbings on paper.

1064

Mister Rogers demonstrates several games that can be played with buttons. In the Neighborhood of Make-Believe, Handyman Negri introduces the Royal Button Band, and Vija Vetra does the Button Dance.

"Sorting Buttons" can help children:

- recognize likeness and difference.

Sorting Buttons

Materials

- lots of buttons (some the same, some different)
- plastic containers or muffin tins
- a dishpan or shallow box

Put the buttons in a dishpan and see how the children begin playing with them. Some may use the buttons like dried beans or sand; others may begin looking for certain kinds of buttons. Did any of the children begin sorting all by themselves? Give them plastic containers or muffin tins if they want to sort the buttons. They could tell you how they are different. Encourage the children to decide how they want to sort the buttons:

- by color?
- by size?
- by two-hole, four-hole, no-hole?

(If you have toddlers around who might put the buttons in their mouths, you could play a simple hand game with them like "pat-a-cake" while the others sort the buttons.)

(Or, 1323 "Games"; 1401 "Buttoning.")

1065

Queen Sara helps King Friday to understand the way Robert Troll talks by suggesting that he first try to understand what Robert Troll is feeling.

"Feelings Show" can help children:

- recognize feelings;
- talk about feelings.

Feelings Show

Materials

- mirror (optional)
- pictures of people with different facial expressions

Sometimes we can tell how people are feeling by what they say, but there are other ways to know how people feel, too. Share a set of pictures with the children that show how people feel—happy, sad, sick, angry, excited, hurt, etc. Encourage them to tell you how they think the person feels. You could ask questions like:

- How do you think this person feels?
- How can you tell?
- Have you ever felt that way?
- What happened to make you feel that way?

See if the children can make different faces that show different feelings. Have you a mirror handy so that they can see what their expressions look like? You might want to remind the children that we can't *always* tell how someone is feeling by their facial expressions. Words are important, too.

(Or, 1048 "Making a Book.")

Thoughts For The Week

*Some people can talk about how they feel, and others prefer to sing about it. Some cry about what makes them sad, and some try to look especially brave even when they're really frightened. We all need to know that feelings are natural. Everyone feels angry, sad, happy, or frightened sometimes. When children are small, they often have trouble understanding what they feel. They may not have learned the meaning of words such as "angry," "glad," or "sad." They learn to understand what these words mean by watching the way people around them express their feelings and by hearing a trusted grownup name those feelings. There are sure to be times in the day when **you** feel frustrated and angry. It can be very helpful to you and the children to say something like, "I get angry when you dump the toys all over the floor—just when we've picked everything up." An explanation like that will help them understand how **you** feel and later, when they feel angry, they can begin to understand—and talk about—their own feelings, too.*

Fred Rogers

Songs On The Programs This Week

1066   *"Kings and Castles"*
        "Let's Be Together Today"

1067   *"Everything Grows Together"*
        "You've Got to Do It"

1068   *" A Handy Lady and a Handy Man"*

1069   *"Sometimes People Are Good"*

1070   *"I'm a Man Who Manufactures"*
        "Sometimes"
        "You Are Special"

Your Notes For The Week

1066

Robert Troll is angry because King Friday is in a meeting and doesn't have time to play. He makes up a song called "Kings and Castles" and later sings it for the king.

"Making Up Songs" can help children:

- express feelings through music.

Making Up Songs

Materials

- none

In talking about today's program, you might begin by asking:

- Do you know why Robert Troll was angry with the King?
- How did he let the King know how he felt?
- Can you remember anything about Robert Troll's song?
- Can you think of a time when someone didn't have time to play with you? How did you feel? What did you do about your feeling?

Can the children make up their own songs about anything they're thinking about? They could make up a tune— or use the tune of a familiar song, with their own words—or they could *chant* the words that say what they're thinking. It can be very useful and just plain fun to make up songs or chants of our own.

1067

In the Neighborhood of Make-Believe, X the Owl is happy to learn that wishes don't make things come true. It's people who can make things happen—by doing them.

"Three Magic Wishes" can help children:

- understand the difference between real and pretend;
- understand wishing can't make things happen.

Three Magic Wishes

Materials

- none

Children need to know that wishes don't make things come true—especially "scary, mad wishes." But it can be fun to pretend about wishing. Help the children make up a story about three magic wishes. (You could do this activity sitting on the floor, but it could also be an activity to do outside on the porch or in the yard, while taking a walk to the store or playground, or sitting around the lunch table. You can begin by saying something like:

- Once upon a time there was a group of little elves who lived deep in the forest. One day they met a magical hummingbird who was caught in the branches of a tree. The elves helped free the bird and, in return, she granted each elf three magic wishes....

Then let each child pretend to be a character in your story and tell what he or she would wish for. Remind them that it's just pretend...just a story. Older children might want to add to the story, making up how the wishes came true or what happened next. Making up stories isn't easy at first, but practice helps. You might want to spend a little time each day—after lunch or before naps—making up stories, but if they involve wishing, it could be very helpful to sing all or part of Mister Rogers' song "Wishes Don't Make Things Come True" with children.

1068

Lady Elaine has decided that she's tired of taking care of the Museum-Go-Round. She wants to be a bus driver. Handyman Negri helps her see how important her job at the Museum-Go-Round really is.

"What Could I Be?" can help children:

- try out different roles;
- understand the difference between real and pretend.

What Could I Be?

Materials

- none

Can any of the children think of a time when they wished they were someone or something else? Maybe they can tell you what they would like to be when they grow up. You might suggest they pretend about a person they could be—a truck driver, dentist, or parent. How about animals or people they could never be—such as a lion or superhero?

Some of the children might want to tell you things they like about being exactly who they are.

1069

"Sometimes the best toys are the ones you just find yourself, somewhere," Mister Rogers tells his viewers. For example, a paper towel roll makes a good toy. It can be used as a tunnel for toy cars.

"Paper Towel Rolls" can help children:

- develop their imaginations;
- develop creative play.

Paper Towel Rolls

Materials

- cardboard tubes (from paper towel and toilet tissue rolls)
- scrap materials (buttons, string, yarn, paper, etc.)
- paste or glue
- tape

You might want to set the box of cardboard rolls on the floor and just see what the children do with them. What kinds of ideas do they have? You may not have to suggest ideas, but here are some in case:

- tunnels for toy cars;
- pretend horns;
- arms and legs for cardboard people;
- telescopes;
- megaphones for talking or singing.

Some children might want to pretend with the tubes just the way they are. Others may prefer to decorate them or make them into something else by pasting or taping on buttons, ribbon, or other scrap materials.

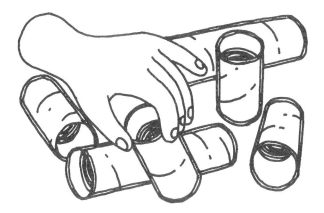

1070

Mister Rogers makes something from an ice-cream cup and explains that another person would make something different because each *person* is different.

"Paper-Cup Containers" can help children:

- develop creative play.

Paper-Cup Containers

Materials

- paper cups
- yarn
- felt scraps
- tissue paper
- liquid glue
- cotton swabs or small brushes

Do the children have any ideas about using paper cups? They might want to decorate the cups, using a cotton swab or small brush to cover the sides with liquid glue. (The cups will be steadier if they're turned upside down first.) Some children might want to add scraps of yarn, felt, or tissue paper to the sides of the cup, while others might be able to wind pieces of yarn around the outside of the cups to cover them completely. When the glue has dried, the children can use the decorated cups as containers for crayons and other small objects, or they might like to give them as gifts to their parents.

(Or, 1186 "Spoon Puppets"; 1280 "Shape Designs.")

The series continues with program number 1076.

Thoughts For The Week

It may seem to children that time goes by very slowly. They often think they'll never grow to be big or be able to do the things they want to do. To us adults it looks like the children are growing and learning quickly, going from crawling to toddling to running before we know it. We need to remind our children that they are growing day by day, not only outwardly in height and physical abilities, but also inwardly in learning self-control, becoming able to share, and to recognize and talk about their feelings. When we show our children we are proud of the way they're growing, we do so much to help them feel proud of themselves. And for children, that's the most important feeling of all.

Fred Rogers

Songs On The Programs This Week

1078 *"When a Baby Comes to Your House"*
"Children Can"
1079 *"You're Growing"*
1080 *"After the Waiting"*

Your Notes For The Week

1076

There are folk dancers at the castle today and they're performing for the neighbors in Make-Believe. Lady Elaine and Handyman Negri do the "Museum-Go-Round Twirl," and X the Owl shows everyone how to do the "Fly."

"Dancing Day" can help children:

● express feelings through movement and dance.

Dancing Day

Materials

● enough room for dancing

You might want to begin this dancing activity without music—to encourage the children to move in ways that express how *they* feel, not how the music makes them feel. Can the children make up names for their dances? Then you could suggest that they make up:

● a happy dance;
● a sad dance;
● an angry dance;
● a sleepy dance.

Turn on the music and see if the children can dance the way the music feels. Does it suggest different feelings to different children?

(Each child will need an old shoe box for tomorrow's activity. If you don't have enough, see if any of them can bring one from home.)

1077

Mister Rogers suggests some creative ways of using an old shoe box—making cars, beds, puppets, telephones. He explains that everyone could make a shoe box into something different—because everyone is different.

"An Old Shoe Box" can help children:

• develop their imaginations;
• develop creative play.

An Old Shoe Box

Materials

• one empty shoe box for each child
• scraps of paper or cloth
• yarn
• glue
• crayons or markers

See if the children have any ideas for using the shoe boxes. Encourage those who have ideas to go ahead and work on their boxes. If some of the younger children have trouble thinking of something, you could suggest:

• a wagon for toys or dolls;
• a decorated box to keep or give as a gift;
• a cradle for the dolls;
• a garage for toy cars and trucks;
• a container for a set of toys;
• a place to keep pictures of things you like.

The younger children may need your help to get started, but let them do what they can on their own. Once the projects are finished you can point out how many different things they made.

(Or, 1272 "Making Doll Beds"; 1134 "Shoe-Box Harp.")

1078

John Costa's grandson, John-John, visits with Mister Rogers today. In the Neighborhood of Make-Believe, X the Owl and King Friday enjoy remembering what they liked to do when they were little.

"Growing" can help children:

• develop their imaginations;
• learn more about their bodies;
• learn more about growing.

Growing

Materials

• none

Today's program is a good chance to pretend about growing. You could begin by all crouching down and pretending to be plants growing from the ground. How small can the children make themselves? What parts of them will grow first? How tall can they grow? You might want to talk with the children about the important things everybody needs for their bodies to grow—inside and out:

• food;
• exercise;
• sleep;
• play;
• work;
• and most important, love.

(Or, 1154 "When We Were Little.")

1079

Mister Rogers shows a film and sings the song "You're Growing." In the Neighborhood of Make-Believe, a visit to the Westwood Zoo shows that Tad is growing into a frog.

"Watching Seeds Grow" can help children:
- learn more about growing;
- learn more about their world.

Watching Seeds Grow

Materials
- three or four dried beans
- paper towels
- glass jar
- water

Help the children with the following experiment (if you soak the dried beans in water overnight, they will grow faster):
- Line a jar with damp paper towels.
- Place three or four dried beans between the towels and the jar so you can see them.
- Add a little water to the bottom of the jar each day as needed to keep the paper towels damp.
- Encourage the children to check the seeds from time to time for signs of growth.

When the plant is about two inches tall, the children could plant it outdoors (in spring or summer). Watch for the changes that take place: more leaves, blossoms, and tiny beans. If the beans grow large enough, the children could taste them—or open them to look at the bean seeds inside.

(Or, 1299 "Sweet Potato Plants.")

1080

Today Mister Rogers talks about waiting. He suggests there are many creative things to do while waiting, like making up games to play. Everyone is waiting to hear the royal secret in the Neighborhood of Make-Believe.

"While You Wait" can help children:
- practice waiting.

While You Wait

Materials
- flour
- salt shaker
- cinnamon
- ground cloves, allspice, nutmeg, etc. (optional)
- several bowls (metal or plastic)
- mixing spoons
- empty coffee can or storage container

You can use this activity to help your children wait while you're preparing a snack or a meal. Give each child a bowl with a little flour in it (about one-half cup). Let the children *sprinkle* different spices into the bowls and stir the mixtures together just for the fun of it. (Plan for the mess by spreading out newspapers, but remind the children to keep the materials in that area.) When you're finished with your meal preparations, let the children empty their concoctions into an empty coffee can or storage container. You can use the spiced flour for making nut breads or apple crisps—or let the children add a little oatmeal another time and use the mixture for making cookies.

Thoughts For The Week

There are times in the lives of most young children when they feel a powerful urge to bite. It's a natural urge, but it can be a scary one for children, all the same, because they may not be able to control it. When they are angry, for instance, they may bite someone they love and really hurt that person. Playing with things that are mouth-like—scissors, boxes with hinged lids, or puppets with mouths that open and shut, can help children learn to control what their own mouths do. That's just one way that play is really important in helping children grow.

*We all need times of privacy, no matter how old we are, and one of the most reassuring kinds of privacy is knowing that our **thoughts** are private. The trouble is there are some times when grownups seem to know everything and even be "mind readers." When doctors look into children's bodies with x-ray machines, or into their ears with otoscopes, or listen to their bodies with stethoscopes, children may really believe that the doctors can "see" or "hear" their thoughts as well. We need to help children understand that their thoughts are theirs alone, for them to share or not share as they see fit.*

Fred Rogers

Songs On The Programs This Week

1081 *"You Are Special"*
"A Lonely Kind of Thing"
1083 *"Today Is a Very Special Day"*
1084 *"Children Can"*

Your Notes For The Week

1081

Mister Rogers talks about teeth and biting. In the Neighborhood of Make-Believe, Henrietta Pussycat meets Bob Dog. She's afraid of him at first, but X the Owl and Lady Aberlin explain that Bob Dog won't bite her.

"Cutting Paper" can help children:
- express strong feelings in appropriate ways;
- develop coordination;
- learn about conservation.

Cutting Paper

Materials
- children's scissors (blunt-nosed)
- old calendar pages
- strips of construction paper (one inch by six inches)
- used wrapping paper

See if the children can tell you things they could do when they feel so angry they could bite. You might want to suggest:
- pounding clay;
- chanting "I am angry!";
- kicking a ball outside;
- tearing newspapers.

Before you give out scissors, you'll need to set some limits about their use. For instance:
- Scissors are for cutting only paper.
- When you are finished cutting, put the scissors back in the container and pick up the scraps of paper.

You could give the children old calendar pages to use for cutting and show them how to use the lines as a guide. Younger children could snip strips of paper to make the cutting easier. Children who use scissors well might want to cut out designs from used wrapping paper. You can keep all the scraps in a box to use for an art project later. When children see you saving things—conserving things—for a later use they're being introduced early in life to the importance of conservation.

1082

Mister Rogers has a visit from Bramble, the horse. Bramble and his owner visit the Neighborhood of Make-Believe, where King Friday learns that it takes a baby a long time to grow big enough to ride a *real* horse.

"What Can Babies Do?" can help children:

- learn more about growing;
- understand the difference between real and pretend.

What Can Babies Do?

Materials

- none

You might begin this activity by asking if any of the children can tell you some things a baby could do. You could ask questions like:

- What toys could a baby use?
- What sounds could a baby make?
- How could a baby move?
- How could a baby eat?

Can the children show you some toys they play with now that they couldn't play with as babies? Can anyone tell you about a toy they used as a baby that they still enjoy using? They might want your reassurance that lots of children feel like playing with toys they enjoyed as a baby once in a while — but that doesn't make a person a baby. The children could pretend to be babies for a while, but they'll need you to let them know when it's time to stop pretending.

1083

Mister Rogers talks about visiting his father's office when he was a boy, and how interested he was in the letters on the typewriter. In the Neighborhood of Make-Believe, the King and Queen watch an artist draw pictures to go with the songs they hear.

"Salt Drawings" can help children:

- develop their imaginations.

Salt Drawings

Materials

- trays, cake pans, or shoe-box lids
- salt (cornmeal, sand, or flour can be substituted)
- popsicle sticks, chopstick, unsharpened pencils (optional)
- music

Pour a thin layer of salt on whatever you use as a tray and show the children how they can draw in the salt, using a popsicle stick, a chopstick, an unsharpened pencil, or even a finger. (You could put on some music and encourage them to draw while the music is playing.) When the children have completed a picture or design, show them how to shake the box or tray to erase the picture. Then they can make another picture. There are all kinds of drawings or writings they can do. Can the children tell you what the salt feels like? Does it have any taste? It can be collected and saved for making modeling dough another day.

1084

Mime Walker visits the Neighborhood of Make-Believe and learns the King's secret. He gives the neighbors a clue by pantomiming that he is rocking a baby to sleep in his arms. Lady Elaine thinks they are bringing baby animals to the neighborhood in order to start a zoo.

"Giving a Clue" can help children:
- learn different ways people communicate.

Giving a Clue

Materials
- none

Show the children how to give a clue without using words. Then encourage the children to give pantomime clues for you and the others to guess. Give them several suggestions at first to help them get started. Some of the things you could include are:
- washing the dishes;
- sewing;
- putting on a shirt;
- brushing teeth or hair;
- sweeping the floor;
- pounding a nail;
- pouring some juice.

Can the children think of other activities they could pantomime?

1085

Lady Elaine tries to read the King's mind to find out what the royal secret is. When she can't read his mind, she tries using a magnifying glass to read Lady Aberlin's mind.

"Can You See What I'm Thinking?" can help children:
- learn more about privacy;
- learn more about their bodies.

Can You See What I'm Thinking?

Materials
- mirror

Encourage the chldren to use a mirror while they change facial expressions so they can see the ways they let people know how they feel. The children can take turns doing this activity, or if the mirror is large enough, all of them could do it together. Here are some different ways you and the children can show how you feel when you are:
- angry—make a fist, stomp your feet, glare at someone;
- happy—smile, laugh, dance, clap, jump up and down;
- afraid—huddle together, hide your eyes, lower your heads;
- surprised—open your mouths, widen your eyes, jump back as if startled;
- sad or lonely—frown, pretend to cry, walk with slumped shoulders, etc.

The children might enjoy playing a guessing game by taking turns acting out feelings and asking the others to guess what they are. But, it's important to let the children know that you know nobody can tell what somebody else is thinking. If we want other people to know what what we're thinking we have to tell them.

Thoughts For The Week

Children find security in the familiarity of routines and in knowing what to expect. Change can be hard for them. One of the ways that children may react to changes in their lives is by returning to behaviors they had when they were younger. Some children may become clinging. Others may suck their thumbs once again or forget their toilet training now and then. Such behaviors are usually only temporary, and as children become accustomed to their new situations, they will once again "act their age."

One of the most difficult changes that children experience is the separation that occurs when someone moves away. We have a farewell party in the Neighborhood of Make-Believe this week, and I hope it will give you a chance to talk with your children about when someone close to you has to move away.

Fred Rogers

Songs On The Programs This Week

1086   *"One and One Are Two"*
       "When a Baby Comes to Your House"
1087   *"You Will Not Go!"*
       "I'm Glad I'm the Way I Am"
1088   *"You Are Pretty"*
1089   *"You Are Pretty"*
1090   *"We're Thinking of You"*

Your Notes For The Week

1086

Mister Rogers brings scales with him and compares things by their weight. In the Neighborhood of Make-Believe, the neighbors hear some very good news: Officer Clemmons has a new job, and King Friday and Queen Sara announce that they are going to have a baby!

"Comparing Weights" can help children:

- learn more about their world;
- develop curiosity.

Comparing Weights

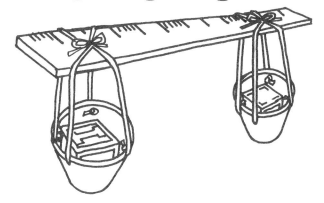

Materials

- ruler
- heavy string (six pieces, each a foot long)
- two paper cups
- objects that will fit in the cups (beans, rubber bands, coins, toy car or toy people, blocks, clay, etc.)

Make a simple weighing scale by tying the strings through three holes made around the top part of the cups. Tie the other ends of the string around the ends of the ruler. Now balance the rule on your index finger. What happens when you put one of the objects in one of the cups? Now try putting one object in one cup and a different object in the other cup. Which object is heavier? Or do they balance (weigh the same)? Experiment with all the objects you've collected. The children might enjoy pretending to be scales. With their arms stretched out at their sides, they could bend from side to side, tipping like the scales.

(Or, 1318 "What's Different?")

1087

Lady Elaine tries to keep Officer Clemmons from going to his new job until he explains that he will return to visit the Neighborhood. She learns that everyone needs to make his or her own choices and that forcing a person to do something may make that person angry.

"Make Your Own Choice" can help children:

- practice making choices.

Make Your Own Choice

Materials

- dress-up clothes
- crayons or markers
- books
- trucks and cars

Sometimes children don't want to do an activity that everyone else is doing, and often they have a good reason for not wanting to do it. At times like this, they may be able to find something else to do.

Today you could suggest three or four play activities and let them make their own choice of what to do:

- dressing up for a pretend tea party;
- using paper and crayons for drawing a picture;
- looking through books;
- playing with trucks or cars.

There are many choices children can make each day—what to eat, where to sit, what to play or work with. They need practice in making these decisions, but they also need to learn that though we may give them choices with some things, with others we don't. There are some things we all have to do whether we like doing them or not.

1088

Lady Aberlin, Henrietta, and X the Owl visit Queen Sara to talk about the baby she is expecting.

"Important Talk" can help children:

- use play to work on feelings;
- talk about feelings.

Important Talk

Materials

- baby dolls
- baby bottles
- blankets

If any of the children in your care have a new baby at home, or are expecting a new baby soon, or if a new infant is coming to day care, you can help them work through the feelings they have by talking with them about their concerns. They may be wondering:

- whether it will be a girl or a boy;
- if they can play with the baby;
- if they will lose a special place in the family;
- whether there will be enough time, attention, and love for everyone.

Set out one or two baby dolls today along with bottles and blankets. Encourage the children to pretend they are real babies. How would they care for them? They could pretend to fix a bottle for baby, give baby a bath or rock baby to sleep. Some children are more comfortable playing about their feelings than talking about them.

You could set aside a time every day for children to talk about important things that are on their minds. Because love is often associated with food, snack or meal times can be good times for this kind of sharing.

1089

Mister Rogers shows the children how to lace shoes. Everyone is busy preparing for the farewell party for Officer and Mrs. Clemmons.

"Lacing Shoes" can help children:

● develop coordination;

● learn to do things independently;

● develop the ability to keep on trying.

Lacing Shoes

Materials

● an assortment of tie shoes or lacing cards (page B-1)

● shoelaces

Lacing and tying shoes are activities that require time, patience, and practice. Most three- and four-year-olds aren't ready to learn to tie their own shoes. But the children can practice lacing and can play with the laces to get used to the feel of the laces and to become interested in learning how to tie them when they are older.

Pull the shoelaces out of the shoes and let the children try lacing them through the holes. It's not important that they lace them perfectly or even correctly—they may need practice just getting the shoelace through the hole. (If the laces are frayed, wrap the ends with a piece of tape to make the lacing easier.) Some children may become frustrated if they think they are lacing the shoes "wrong." Explain that today everyone is lacing a different way—just for the fun of it. When the activity is over, five- or six-year-olds may be able to help you put the shoelaces back in the shoes so they can be worn again.

(Or, 1352 "Yarn Designs.")

1090

Today is Party Day—a going-away party for Carole and Francois Clemmons. Chef Brockett has prepared Raspberry Delight for everyone to share.

"Instant Pudding" can help children:

● practice taking turns;

● practice waiting;

● learn more about foods.

Instant Pudding

Materials

● instant pudding mix (one box equals four servings)

● milk

● jar or plastic container with a *tight-fitting* lid

● measuring cup

● paper cups and spoons

Open the instant pudding mix and help a child pour it into a jar. (If you need two boxes, use a second jar.) Another child can pour in the milk (two cups). With the lid on tightly, let the children take turns shaking the pudding mix. You can limit each turn by watching 15 seconds pass on a clock or by counting to 15 with the children. Then pass the jar on to the next person. The pudding mix needs to be shaken for at least two minutes—that's about eight turns—so the children may be able to have a second turn. It's more important to see that each child has the same number of turns, than to worry whether the pudding has been mixed too long. When the shaking is done, the children can help pour the pudding into paper cups. Let it sit at least five minutes before eating.

Who can think of something to help pass the waiting time? Can the children:

● help clean up the work area?

● set the table with spoons and napkins?

Thoughts For The Week

This week of programs is about looking carefully and listening carefully. For a child, every day is full of opportunities to look and listen as well as to learn the names of things around them. It's important for us to take the time to help children observe their surroundings and talk with them about the things they see and hear. We help them learn the names of things when we talk about the different foods we eat or pictures we see or objects we play and work with. I know of a very talented preschool teacher who always sits with the children during their snack time, using that time to talk with the children about whatever interests them. The parents of the children in her group began to comment about how freely their children had learned to express themselves and ask questions. That teacher realized how important talking time can be in helping young children grow!

Fred Rogers

Songs On The Programs This Week

1901   "You've Got to Do It"
         "Let's Be Together Today"

1092   "Let's Be Together Today"
         "Everybody's Fancy"

1093   "What Do You Do?"

1094   "You're Growing"

1095   "Children Can"
         "Let's Be Together Today"
         "Won't You Be My Neighbor?"

Your Notes For The Week

1091

Mister Rogers explains the differences between a unicycle, a bicycle, and a tricycle. Mr. McFeely is having trouble with his bicycle and a repairman fixes it for him. In the Neighborhood of Make-Believe, Bob Dog is afraid of things with wheels and barks at the trolley and Mr. McFeely's bicycle.

"Wheel Toys" can help children:

- learn to look carefully;
- develop healthy curiosity.

Wheel Toys

Materials

- riding toys with two wheels, three wheels, and four wheels
- toy cars or trucks
- plastic tools

One way to begin this activity is to walk through the house or yard together, looking for all the toys that have wheels. Can they show you a toy with two wheels? How about a three-wheel toy? Which toys have four wheels? Can they name the toys?

If weather permits, this might be a good time to play with the riding toys outside. Can anyone ride a two-wheel bicycle? How about a tricycle? What about a four-wheel toddler's riding toy? Some children might be interested in the way wheels move. You could put a tricycle on its side and let the children spin a wheel. Do you have a friend who knows how to repair wheel toys? Could that friend come to visit and show some real tools?

1092

Different musical instruments make different sounds. Mister Rogers makes up a game with some musical instruments and a tape recorder to help his viewers recognize different sounds.

"Familiar Sounds" can help children:

● learn to listen carefully;

● recognize and use symbols.

Familiar Sounds

Materials

● keys

● paper

● pencil

● ball

● measuring spoons

● water

● pitcher

The children might enjoy playing a guessing game the way Mister Rogers did. Collect a few simple items that can be used to make noises. Stand behind a piece of furniture so the children cannot see you make the noise. Make sounds such as these and ask the children to tell you what they hear:

● knocking on a door;

● rattling keys;

● clapping hands;

● stamping feet;

● cutting or tearing paper;

● bouncing a ball;

● snapping fingers;

● jingling a set of measuring spoons;

● pouring water.

1093

Mister Rogers explains that he feels frustrated today. Last night he pushed the wrong button on the tape recorder and erased all the music he recorded. In the Neighborhood of Make-Believe, Lady Aberlin feels frustrated, too. The scarf she's knitting doesn't look right.

"Fishing" can help children:

● develop the ability to keep on trying;

● practice taking turns;

● practice waiting.

Fishing

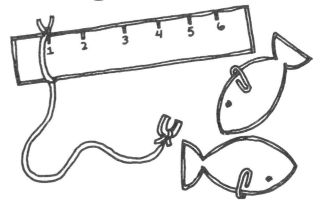

Materials

● magnet

● string

● pencil or ruler

● bucket or dish pan

● fish shapes cut from heavy paper

● paper clips

● scissors

Older children may be able to help draw or cut fish shapes from heavy paper and place paper clips on them. By tying a magnet to a piece of string and fastening the string to a pencil or ruler, you can make a fishing rod for the children to use. Encourage them to take turns using the rod to catch the fish from a bucket or dishpan. You might want to write directions on the fish that tell the children to do something: for instance, "jump three times," or "hop on one foot." Can they follow the directions?

1094

Mister Rogers talks about words that begin with the "B" sound. He shows different kinds of balls—a basketball, football, and a baseball. All of them are balls, but each one is different.

"Playing with Balls" can help children:

● develop coordination.

Playing with Balls

Materials

● several balls
● laundry basket

Sometimes children like to play with a ball by themselves—throwing and catching it alone. Other times it can be fun to play with other people. Set some limits about playing with balls before you begin. For example:

● No hitting people with balls.
● Bounce them on the floor, not on walls or furniture.
● Keep the balls in the yard if you're playing outside.
● Never go in the street after a ball.

Trying to toss a ball into a laundry basket can be a challenging game for four-, five- and six-year-old children. As the children get better and better at hitting the basket, you might want to move it farther away. Younger children might prefer to roll the balls back and forth to you...or try to bounce or balance the balls.

1095

Mister Rogers makes a window out of paper. In the Neighborhood of Make-Believe, Lady Elaine uses magic to fix a window that is broken.

"Paper Windows" can help children:

● develop their memory.

Paper Windows

Materials

● two pieces of paper for each child
● crayons or markers
● tape
● scissors

Give the children one sheet of paper each and see if they can make several "windows" by drawing squares on the paper. Using the scissors yourself, cut around three sides of each "window" and help the children fold the paper back. The windows can open like doors, or they can fold up or down. With your help, the children can tape the paper onto a second sheet of paper. Now the children can draw or paste a picture on the paper under each window. When they are finished, the children can play a "peek-a-boo" type game by opening and closing the windows. They can try to remember which picture is behind which window.

Thoughts For The Week

Children learn about time by talking with you each day. When you say "It's almost twelve o'clock. We need to get ready for lunch," or, "Your mom will be back at five o'clock," they begin to learn about the passage of time. Young children can be very interested in clocks and watches, but most children learn to tell time only after they are old enough to start school. Preschool children may find it hard to understand terms such as "today," "yesterday," and "tomorrow." It can help when you ask question like "Can you find the book we read yesterday?" or, "What will we do at the zoo tomorrow?" And of course the song from MISTER ROGERS' NEIGHBORHOOD that many children like to sing—for any special occasion—"Today Is a Very Special Day."

Fred Rogers

Songs On The Programs This Week

1096   "Just for Once"
      "I'm a Chef"

1097   "I'm a Man Who Manufactures"

1098   "Everybody's Fancy"
      "A Handy Lady and a Handy Man"

1099   "I'd Like to Be Like Mom"

1100   "It's Such a Good Feeling"
      "Be Brave, Be Strong"
      "I'm Taking Care of You"

Your Notes For The Week

1096

Lady Elaine receives two letters today. The first letter tells of a boomerang contest at Some Place Else. The second letter says she must bring a friend who also has to throw the boomerang. Chef Brockett agrees to go with Lady Elaine.

"Working Together" can help children:

- practice working cooperatively.

Working Together

Materials

- toys that require two people (swing, ball, wagon, seesaw)
- paper
- markers, crayons or non-toxic paint and brushes

Friends can help each other in many ways. Encourage the children to work together with a friend on a project today. Some children might be able to take turns pulling each other in a wagon or pushing each other on a swing. (Be sure they know how to push a swing safely.) Using a seesaw is another activity where children need to cooperate with one another. Some children might enjoy rolling a ball back and forth. Other children might want to work together on a drawing or painting, taking turns choosing and adding colors. Younger children might enjoy playing alongside another child at the sandbox. If a child wants to play alone, help him or her find a play activity that is suitable. Perhaps that child will choose to play with a friend on another day.

(Or, 1109 "Cooperation.")

1097

Chef Brockett, Robert Troll, and Lady Elaine are all at Some Place Else practicing for the boomerang contest.

"Flying Discs" can help children:

- develop creative play;
- develop coordination.

Flying Discs

Materials

- cardboard (you could use empty cereal or cracker boxes)
- scissors
- crayons or markers
- paint and brushes (optional)

Cut different-sized circles from pieces of cardboard to make patterns. Older children may be able to draw around the patterns to make their own circles on another piece of cardboard. The circles don't have to be exact, so it doesn't matter how accurate the drawing is. With your help, the older children can cut out their own circles and decorate them, while the younger children can use the cardboard patterns *you* cut out. If you cut a thin pie slice out of each circle, the disc will fly better, and the children can practice tossing them outside and watching them spin through the air. You might want to save your plastic lids from coffee cans or shortening; they make good flying discs, too.

1098

Mister Rogers shows a variety of eggs in different shapes and sizes. Later in the program he shows a picture book of animals that lay eggs. In the Neighborhood of Make-Believe, Elsie Jean Platypus lays an egg that will hatch in ten days.

"Eggshell Pictures" can help children:

- develop their imaginations.

Eggshell Pictures

Materials

- eggshells
- food coloring and water mixture
- paper towels
- paper
- glue

The children might be able to help you tint the eggshells ahead of time by dipping them into water mixed with a few drops of food coloring. Spread the broken shells out to dry on several sheets of paper towels, and once they've dried you can all crumble them up. The children can then put liquid glue on pieces of paper and sprinkle the eggshell fragments on top to make designs.

You might want to make egg salad (see 1255 "Egg Salad Sandwiches") from your hard-boiled eggs for lunch.

(Or, 1393 "Comparing Sizes.")

1099

Chef Brockett and Mister Rogers talk about wanting to be first...and in the Neighborhood of Make-Believe, King Friday is upset because the platypus baby will arrive before the royal baby comes.

"An Award for Everyone" can help children:

- feel proud of their accomplishments.

An Award for Everyone

Materials

- props for pretending
- awards made of construction paper

Contests are always hard for children because some win and others don't. You can have a Festival of Pretending contest and give an award to *everyone*. Encourage the children to take turns pretending to be someone or something. When everyone is finished, awards can be given for the shortest pretend, the silliest, the scariest, the slowest or the happiest. Children who don't feel like pretending can be made to feel important as helpers. You can give out a Helper Award to a child who helped you distribute the awards or helped another child make a prop or costume.

1100

Queen Sara helps King Friday understand that their baby will be special because it will be the first human baby in the Neighborhood of Make-Believe, and the platypus baby will be the first animal baby. Mister Rogers shows a book of animals and talks about the kind of babies each would have.

"Parents and Babies" can help children:

- learn more about growing;
- recognize likeness and difference.

Parents and Babies

Materials

- magazine pictures of adult animals and baby animals
- construction paper, cardboard or notecards
- paste

Before you begin today's matching game, you'll need to cut out pictures or drawings of animal babies and adult animals. The children could help you look for the animal pictures. Paste them on small pieces of heavy paper so the children can handle them more easily. Let them choose a picture of a baby animal and match it with its parent. Can they name the animal? You can tell the children the correct names of the young animals, but they may prefer to name them "horse and baby horse." That's fine, too.

(Or, 1110 "Pretend Animals"; 1274 "Animal Sounds.")

Thoughts For The Week

*As a caregiver, you'll know that a child can be happy, sad, angry, and excited all in the space of a day. As children grow, they learn that other people have these same feelings, too, and it helps when we can tell them about **our** feelings. Talking about feelings has a way of making those feelings more acceptable, and children need to know that having a wide range of feelings is part of being human. But adults also need to tell children what they do with those feelings—particularly with strong ones like sadness and anger. When we talk about letting those feelings out in acceptable ways, we can help children learn that all feelings are not only mentionable but can be manageable, too.*

Fred Rogers

Songs On The Programs This Week

1101 *"Sometimes People Are Good"*
      "Some Things I Don't Understand"
1102 *"You Are Special"*
      "Let's Be Together Today"
      "A Handy Lady and a Handy Man"
1103 *"Parents Were Little Once Too"*
1104 *"Please Don't Think It's Funny"*
      "Tree, Tree, Tree"
1105 *"Ornithorhynchus Anatinus"*

Your Notes For The Week

1101

The death of one of Mister Rogers' fish leads to sensitive talk about the death of a pet dog Mister Rogers had as a child.

"When a Pet Dies" can help children:

- talk about feelings;
- express strong feelings in appropiate ways.

When a Pet Dies

Materials

- paper
- crayons, markers or paint
- favorite stuffed toys or blankets

Can you remember how you felt when a pet died? You may be able to talk with the children about the feelings you had. This might be a time of strong emotions—especially if any children have recently experienced the death of a pet or a person close to them. Some children may want to have a stuffed toy or blanket nearby to help them feel more secure. Give the children a chance to ask questions about the program today—they might have a lot to say…or they might prefer to think about things for a while and save the talking for another time.

If this discussion brings out strong feelings, the children might find it helpful to draw or paint for a while when the talk is over.

1102

Mister Rogers has a picture book with photos of familiar objects. There are two pictures of each object—a small picture and a large picture—and Mister Rogers ask if the viewers can match the bigger and smaller pictures of the same object.

"Matching Pairs" can help children:

- recognize likeness and difference;
- learn to look carefully.

Matching Pairs

Materials

- several pairs of objects (shoes, gloves, mittens, socks)
- a large box

Here's another matching game: If you have several younger children, put pairs of objects that are very different in a box—a pair of shoes, a pair of mittens, a pair of socks, a pair of slippers. Let each child pull out an object and try to find its match. Older children could match pairs that are more similar—four or five different pairs of mittens, gloves, shoes, or socks. They might enjoy taking off their own shoes and socks to use in the matching game.

When you are folding laundry, see if any of the children would like to help match the pairs of socks, or tops and bottoms of pajamas or play clothes that are sets.

(Or, 1350 "Matching Shoes.")

1103

Mister Rogers talks about how hard it is to wait for something you want to do. All the neighbors in Make-Believe are waiting at the platypus mound for Elsie Jean's egg to hatch. Most of them get tired of waiting and leave.

"Jack-in-the-Box" can help children:

- work on feelings about separation;
- practice waiting.

Jack-in-the-Box

Materials

- a toy jack-in-the-box (optional)
- a large box (large enough to hold a child)

If you have a toy jack-in-the-box, the children might like to play with it. Very young children could become frightened when the toy pops out, so you may want to keep the younger ones near you. Then, using a large box, see if anyone wants to pretend to be a jack-in-the-box. The older children could try first if the others are timid. Help a child climb into the box and hide down inside it. (If you don't have a large enough box, the children could take turns hiding behind a chair and popping out.) You and the other children can sing a short song like "Pop Goes the Weasel." At the end of the song, the child can pop out of the box. Other children may want a turn to be in the box. When the children are comfortable with this play, practice waiting without singing and let the child in the box pop out when he or she is ready to surprise the others.

(Or, 1455 "Making Bread.")

1104

Mister Rogers has a bandage put on his sprained ankle and explains to the children that even though a bandage covers a part of your body, that part of your body is still there...underneath.

"The Doctor's Office" can help children:

- develop their imaginations;
- use play to work on feelings.

The Doctor's Office

Materials

- long strips of cloth (old sheets work well cut into three-inch by four-inch strips)
- tape
- doctor's kit (optional)
- white shirts for doctor's smock (optional)

Can the children tell you what happened to Mister Rogers' leg? Do they know how the bandage helped him? This might be a time for the children to pretend about wearing bandages—and it gives them a chance to see first-hand that bandages are only wrappings that are put on to help part of the body get better. When that part does get better, the bandages can be removed.

The children may be most comfortable if they use the strips of cloth to bandage *your* leg or arm. Or encourage them to practice bandaging a stuffed animal or a rag doll. The cloth can be fastened with tape. Some of the children may want to play doctor by dressing up in old shirts and using a toy medical kit. When the children feel more comfortable with the bandages, they might want to bandage each other's arms or legs. If you have a supply of ordinary adhesive bandages, younger children might prefer to pretend with the smaller strips. Bandage play may bring on talk about accidents and hurts. It can be helpful for the children to hear how people get better after they're hurt.

1105

Johnny Costa visits Mister Rogers today. He plays the piano and accordion while Mister Rogers draws. Everyone in Make-Believe has gifts for Ana, the new baby platypus. King Friday has a portait of himself, and Handyman Negri has a song.

"Draw a Song" can help children:

- express feelings through art work;
- express feelings through music.

Draw a Song

Materials

- paper
- crayons or markers
- music

The children may be able to help you choose the music they want to draw to. Encourage them to "draw a song," showing how the music makes them feel or what the music makes them think of. Everyone has a special way of reacting to music, so each picture will be different. The children might want to find other ways to respond to music. They could:

- make up a dance;
- put words to the music;
- fingerpaint to music;
- pound clay or modeling dough in rhythm to the music.

When the activity is over, some of the children might enjoy sitting quietly—just *listening* to the music.

(Or, 1140 "Paint How You Feel"; 1264 "Seagulls.")

Thoughts For The Week

It's natural—and healthy—for children to be curious about the people and the world around them. When we express our awareness and appreciation of children's interest and wonder, we let them know that it's good to be curious. There are many ways to help a child put curiosity to good use, and one of the best ways is to respond to children's questions with honest answers. There may be times when you'll need to say "I don't know. That's a good question," or "I often wonder about that, too," or "I'll find out more about that for you." When children see that we value their curiosity and will help them find out the things they want to know, they're more likely to move through their school years and beyond with a real eagerness to learn.

Fred Rogers

Songs On The Programs This Week

1106 *"Everything Grows Together"*
1107 *"It's Such a Good Feeling"*
      "Ornithorhynchus Anatinus"
1108 *"Let's Be Together Today"*
      "Wishes Don't Make Things Come True"
1109 *"You're Growing"*
1110 *"Tree, Tree, Tree"*

Your Notes For The Week

1106

Mister Rogers shows a film of his visit to Francois Clemmons' new house. Then he visits Robert Trow and walks back to his own house with Mr. McFeely.

"Going for a Walk" can help children:

* learn more about their world;
* learn to look carefully.

Going for a Walk

Materials

* a place to walk (sidewalk or yard)

When adults go for a walk, they usually have a purpose—and keep walking at a steady pace. When children go for walks, they stop and look at things around them. This looking is often more important than the walk. You may only get to the corner and back, but the children can have a chance to explore:

* cracks in the sidewalk;
* leaves on the ground;
* tiny bugs or stones;
* different flowers or plants;
* cars, trucks, buses, etc.;
* traffic signs.

During your outing you may find the children helped you learn something, too: How to see old, familiar things in a new way. If they've widened your horizon in any way, it will really please them to hear you say so.

1107

Mister Rogers shows the children how to make a simple cardboard suitcase and shows a film on how real suitcases are made. In the Neighborhood of Make-Believe, Mr. Anybody is making up a play about suitcases to keep the King's mind off waiting.

"What's in the Suitcase?" can help children:

- develop creative play;
- develop their imagination.

What's in the Suitcase?

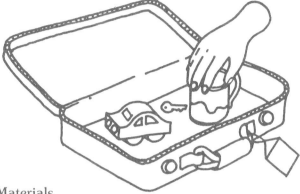

Materials

- a small suitcase (or box)
- different objects (a set of keys, a paper hat, a spoon, a napkin, a cup, a toy car.)

Fill a box with an assortment of props that children could use for pretending. Let each child choose an object, then use it to pretend about something. Would anyone like to pantomime something for the others to guess? You can help younger children participate by asking them to choose the object and then offering a suggestion for using it. For example:

- keys—Can you pretend to unlock the door?
- cup—If you had juice in the cup, how would you walk so it wouldn't spill?
- red paper hat—What do firefighters do?

1108

Betty Aberlin shows Mister Rogers and Joe Negri some magic tricks she's been practicing. In the Neighborhood of Make-Believe, Lady Elaine hides the props for the play because she's angry about not having a role.

"Hide It, Find It" can help children:

- develop healthy curiosity;
- feel comfortable asking about what they need to know.

Hide It, Find It

Materials

- a small block or toy
- box
- scarf
- paper bag
- pillow

You can begin this activity by showing the children the small toy and the hiding places: the box, scarf, paper bag and pillow. While the children cover their eyes, put the toy in the box, under the scarf, inside the paper bag, or under the pillow. Younger children might want to search the different hiding places until they find the toy, but the older children could ask questions before starting to search—questions like:

- Is it under something?
- Is it in something?
- Is the hiding place paper? Cloth? Cardboard?

The children can take turns doing the hiding, too.

1109

The neighbors in Make-Believe are working on a play, and they learn that it often takes cooperation to get something done.

"Cooperation" can help children:

● practice working cooperatively.

Cooperation

Materials

● blocks or boxes for building

Can anyone tell you what "cooperation" means? Does someone remember how the neighbors in Make-Believe worked together to get something done? Some of the children might be able to tell you things they like to do that require cooperation—pulling or pushing someone in a wagon, riding on a seesaw. By giving each child one or two boxes or blocks, and then asking the children to build something that needs lots of blocks, you can set up a play situation that will encourage them to cooperate.

You might suggest:

● a road;
● a house;
● a zoo;
● a bridge;
● a rocket ship.

Can anyone build these things alone? What if they all work together? Encourage them to see how many different things they can make by combining the blocks. Other things the children could work on together are:

● cleaning up after a snack;
● picking up toys in the play room;
● setting the table for lunch.

1110

"Let the Vet Get the Pet." That's the name of the "suitcase play" in the Neighborhood of Make-Believe. Mr. Anybody plays the vet, and Bob Dog is the pet.

"Pretend Animals" can help children:

● develop their imaginations.

Pretend Animals

Materials

● none

What can the children remember about the play, "Let the Vet Get The Pet"? Encourage them to pretend to be animals—at first, ones that are not too scary. For instance:

● kittens;
● puppies;
● rabbits;
● squirrels.

Can they all be rabbits at the same time? You could point out the ways each "rabbit" is different—the way it hops or runs. How about being squirrels? Some children may be ready to pretend about other animals such as:

● monkeys;
● elephants;
● lions.

Do any of the children have a certain animal they'd like to pretend about? Can the children tell you which animals are possible to have in your home and which are impossible to have in your home?

(Or, 1100 "Parents and Babies.")

Thoughts For The Week

One of the natural concerns that children have is about separation from their parents. Not all children show their anxiety openly. A mother once told me that her toddler adjusted to day care quite easily and seemed to have no concern about leaving her. It was only when that boy was older that he was able to tell her, "I remember when you went to work and every day I cried and cried inside." Fortunately that mother and son were able to talk about those feelings he'd had. One of the important ways we can help children cope with separations is to let them know when their parents will return. Young children may not understand the concept of hours or minutes, but it can be very reassuring for them to hear that their parents will return "after storytime" or "after snacktime," and once they learn to "tell time" they will find comfort in looking for the clock to show 5:30.

Fred Rogers

Songs On The Programs This Week

1111 *"I Need You"*
      "Ornithorhynchus Anatinus"

1112 *"Ornithorhynchus Anatinus"*
      "Who Shall I Be Today?"

1113 *"How Many Times?"*
      "You Are Pretty"

1114 *"Sometimes"*
      "I Like to Be Told"
      "It's Such a Good Feeling"

1115 *"Everybody's Fancy"*
      "Let's Be Together Today"
      "To Go to Some Place Else"
      "I'm Taking Care of You"

Your Notes For The Week

1111

Mister Rogers shows how to use seashells for paperweights. In the Neighborhood of Make-Believe Ana Platypus appears for the first time, and Robert Troll gives the baby a shell.

"Stone Paperweights" can help children:

- develop their imaginations.

Stone Paperweights

Materials

- an assortment of stones
- pan of water
- paper towels
- non-toxic paint
- brushes
- liquid glue
- paper or cloth scraps, cotton, yarn, etc.
- newspapers

You could begin this activity by taking a walk with the children to look for stones to use as paperweights. Rinse the stones, and while the children dry them with paper towels, cover your work area with newspaper. Encourage the children to decorate their stones any way they feel like it. Older children might like to use scrap materials to turn a stone into an animal paperweight—adding eyes or whiskers. Younger children may just want to paint their paperweights.

1112

Mister Rogers has an hourglass today. In the Neighborhood of Make-Believe, X the Owl and Henrietta learn that they have to wait until Ana is older before they can play with her.

"Measuring Time" can help children:

● learn more about time.

Measuring Time

Materials

● things that measure time (kitchen timer, clock with a second hand, hourglass or egg timer, etc.)

● old magazines or catalogues (optional)

● paper

● marker

See if any of the children can tell you ways we measure time. You could take a walk through the house finding things like clocks, clock-radios, watches or kitchen timers. The children might want to look through old magazines or catalogues to point out these kinds of objects, too. Explain that these things help grownups know what time it is, or how much time has passed. Can the children tell you how *they* know what time it is? You could ask questions like:

● How do you know when it's time to get up?

● How do you know when to get ready for snack?

● When do we watch MISTER ROGERS' NEIGHBORHOOD?

● When do we go outside to play?

● Do you know when your parents come to get you?

You might find it helpful to make a schedule showing what the children do during the day. Older children might want to know that nap time is one hour long, or that story time lasts about ten minutes. This will help them begin to understand about measuring time.

1113

Mister Rogers and Mr. McFeely play a card game called "How Many Times?"

"How Many Times?" can help children:

● practice taking turns;

● recognize and use symbols.

How Many Times?

Materials

● game spinner with numbers (see page B-1)

● paper or index cards

● marker

● scissors

The children could make up a "How Many Times?" game like the one Mister Rogers and Mr. McFeely played today. You'll need a game spinner with numbers on it. Cut paper into three-inch by five-inch pieces to use as direction cards. The children could help you think of directions to write on the cards. Here are a few suggestions:

● Clap your hands.

● Whisper "no, thank you."

● Turn around.

● Touch your toes.

● Shout "yes, please."

● Say your name.

● Knock on the door.

Mix up the cards and let the children take turns drawing a card. After a card is drawn, spin the spinner to see how many times to do whatever the card says. For instance, if the spinner stops on four, and the card says "Say your name," the child says his or her name four times.

1114

Betty Aberlin is off to the hairdresser. Mister Rogers shows a film about Betty having her hair washed and set. In the Neighborhood of Make-Believe, Handyman Negri tends to the King's hair and beard.

"Hair Styles" can help children:
- develop their imaginations;
- use play to work on feelings.

Hair Styles

Materials
- hair rollers (without bristles)
- barrettes
- comb
- brush
- water
- dolls with hair (optional)

Some children might like to change their own hairstyles to see how different they look. (You might want to check with the parents in the morning to see if they mind if their child changes his or her hairstyle.) The older children may enjoy adding rollers or barrettes. (Rollers without bristles don't tangle hair as easily.) Younger children may need your help even to do the combing or brushing. If children have very short hair, you could dampen it a little and let them try combing it a different way. Some children might not want to have their hair changed at all, but watching the children who do may help them feel differently about it another time. At the end of this activity, do the children want to put their hair back the way it was? Or would some like to keep their new hairstyle to show their parents? Even though their hair looks different, they are still the same persons---inside!

1115

Mister Rogers shows a mother dog taking care of her puppies, and Mister Rogers' son, John, takes care of their dog, Frisky. When the Queen's baby is born in the Neighborhood of Make-Believe, different people will be needed to help care for the baby in different ways.

"I'm Taking Care of You" can help children:
- develop their imaginations;
- try out different roles;
- learn to do things independently.

I'm Taking Care of You

Materials
- dolls or stuffed animals
- plants
- old magazines

Do any of the children have a dog or cat at home that they help care for? See if they can tell you the things they do as part of that care. Or the children might suggest ways they *could* care for a pet some day. You could suggest things like:
- feeding the animal;
- taking it for a walk;
- petting it;
- brushing it.

If the children have a pet such as a fish or frog, how do they care for *that* pet? If you have plants in your home, the children might each like to care for one plant by checking it each day to see if it needs watering. Encourage the children to use the dolls or stuffed animals to show you the ways parents take care of babies. If any of the children have a new baby at home, they may be able to show you the things *they* do to help care for the baby.

(Or, 1299 "Sweet Potato Plants"; 1273 "Planting Beans.")

Thoughts For The Week

Pretending is a way for children to work on their feelings about the world around them and their place in it. One particularly important use of play is getting ready for things that can be difficult or worrisome. Playing about going to a hospital for an operation, for instance, can often help a child learn what to expect and cope better with an actual hospitalization when it happens. The child who pretends to give an injection may be playing out a healthy feeling of being in control rather than passively accepting the hurts that go with a hospital experience.

*And it's not only playing about something **before** it happens that can be helpful: Difficult times often leave children with deep and confusing feelings, so playing about such a time afterwards can be a way of safely reliving and reworking something that was hard for them. The birth of a baby brother or sister, for instance, may bring out strong feelings of jealousy and rivalry. A friend's daughter created an imaginary baby named Danny when her new brother arrived. She sometimes pretended to care for Danny; but several times she "accidentally" dropped Danny or pretended that he was in other dangerous situations. This was her safe way of expressing the strong feelings she had toward her real brother.*

Fred Rogers

Songs On The Programs This Week

1116   *"Look and Listen"*
        "I'm Taking Care of You"
        "There Are Many Ways"
1117   *"When a Baby Comes to Your House"*
1118   *"I Did Too"*
        "A Lonely Kind of Thing"
1119   *"Look and Listen"*
        "I'm Taking Care of You"
1120   *"Please Don't Think It's Funny"*

Your Notes For The Week

Monday

1116

In the Neighborhood of Make-Believe, Henrietta Pussycat pretends to be a nurse and practices taking care of a baby in preparation for the arrival of the royal baby.

"Taking Care of Someone" can help children:

- develop their imaginations;
- try out different roles.

Taking Care of Someone

Materials

- dolls
- doll clothes
- blankets
- bottles
- beds

You might begin this activity by using dolls and asking the children what kinds of things they could do to help take care of a baby. For instance:

- holding and rocking it;
- feeding;
- changing the diaper;
- singing to the baby;
- telling it a nursery rhyme;
- playing peek-a-boo;
- showing it rattles or toys.

If there are infants and toddlers in the group, the older children might like to help take care of them today. Can they think of ways to entertain an older baby for a few minutes—perhaps while you are preparing lunch?

(Or, 1047 "Caring for Baby"; 1267 "Headbands That Fit.")

1117

Mister Rogers shows the way he used to build block towers when he was a young boy. Everyone in the Neighborhood is anxiously waiting for the birth of the royal baby.

"A Block Tower" can help children:

- develop coordination;
- practice taking turns;
- recognize feelings.

A Block Tower

Materials

- a set of small blocks or boxes

Spread out the blocks or boxes on the floor in an area where the falling tower won't hurt anything. If the blocks are small, a tabletop will do. As the children sit around the blocks, be sure they stay far enough back so the blocks won't fall on them. Put the first block in place and let each child take a turn stacking a block on top. Continue taking turns until the tower falls over. In talking with the children afterwards, see if they can tell you what feelings they had while waiting for the blocks to fall. Why do they think the tower fell over? They may want to experiment with different ways to stack the blocks and play the game again and again. They may even want to show you how to build such a sturdy building that it doesn't fall down.

1118

Mister Rogers makes building blocks from scraps of wood. He uses sandpaper to make the wood smooth so no one will get a splinter.

"Sanding Wood" can help children:

- recognize likeness and difference;
- practice working cooperatively.

Sanding Wood

Materials

- scraps of wood
- sandpaper
- markers or crayons

Do any of the children know the meaning of "rough" and "smooth"? You can probably show them a rough edge on a scrap of wood. Let them feel the rough sandpaper, too. After you have sanded a piece of wood, give them a chance to feel the difference. You might point out that building blocks need to be very smooth so children won't get wood splinters. Give each of the children a piece of sandpaper and a block of wood to sand. The children could work on this project a little at a time until all the pieces are smooth and they could use the wood blocks in the play area. What other things in the house and outside can the children find that are rough? That are smooth?

(Or, 1362 "Wooden Scuplture"; 1499 "Animal Blocks.")

1119

A watchmaker visits Mister Rogers to show him the inside of a pocket watch. Mister Rogers shows a film of what it's like inside a hospital.

"What's Inside" can help children:

● learn more about their world;
● develop healthy curiosity.

What's Inside

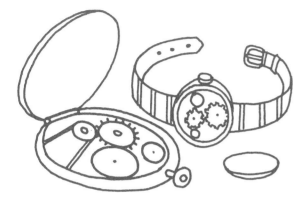

Materials

● something that can be taken apart (flashlight, battery-operated toy, old alarm clock, a radio that doesn't work)
● screw driver

See if you have a battery-operated toy or flashlight that you could take apart so the children can see what's inside. They might be able to help take out the screws. You can show them the small parts inside and try to find out how the object works. Then put it back together again. If the object is easily managed by the children, you could keep it and a small screwdriver in a special box for children to use when they want to take something apart. This might be a good time to remind them that human beings are all one piece: Everything in them grows together. You and the children could sing or say the words to Mister Rogers' song, "Everything Grows Together."

(Or, 1502 "Hospital Play.")

1120

At Betty Aberlin's Theater, Mister Rogers sees a special performance of a ballet designed for children—"The Raccoon Ballet." It's a story about bedtime at the Raccoon household.

"Pretending about Bedtime" can help children:

● develop their imaginations;
● use play to work on feelings;
● work on feelings about separation.

Pretending about Bedtime

Materials

● small blankets
● pillows
● stuffed animals
● books
● box

A large pillow, the sofa, chair, or even the floor can make a good bed for the children to use. See if the children can tell you the things they do before going to bed. For instance:

● take a bath;
● listen to a story;
● brush their teeth;
● get a drink of water;
● listen to a record.

Do they have any favorite toys that they take to bed with them? Set out a box with bedtime props such as small blankets, little pillows, stuffed animals and books. One or two of them can pretend to be the children, and the others can be grownups who help them get ready for bed and tuck them in. Later they can switch roles and continue the play...if they want to. This kind of play could remind some children (who haven't had much time away from home) of missing their parents, so they just might not want to join in this play today.

Thoughts For The Week

*Many children have a hard time accepting the arrival of a new child in the family. They sometimes think that if someone new comes, someone else will have to leave. I know of a three-year-old girl who called her parents by their first names for nearly six weeks after her new brother was born. It seemed as if she believed her parents couldn't be a mom and dad to her **and** be parents to the new baby at the same time. The idea of sharing the love of their parents with somebody new is hard for them to understand. Children may also do things that they know are "bad" to test parents and see if they will send them away. When a child comes to understand that the arrival of a new person **doesn't** change anybody else's special place in the family, those normal feelings of jealousy don't seem so overwhelming.*

Fred Rogers

Songs On The Programs This Week

1121   "Just for Once"
        "When a Baby Comes to Your House"

1122   "Days of the Week"
        "A Handy Lady and a Handy Man"
        "I'm Glad I'm the Way I Am"
        "The Clown in Me"

1123   "One and One Are Two"
        "I Need You"

1124   "It's Such a Good Feeling"

Your Notes For The Week

1121

Mister Rogers explains that babies have to cry for things because they don't have any words yet. In the Neighborhood of Make-Believe, Lady Elaine Fairchilde complains that the royal baby's crying is disturbing the peace in the neighborhood.

"Say It without Words" can help children:

- learn different ways people communicate.

Say It without Words

Materials

- none

Ask the children a few questions like:

- How does a dog tell you it wants to go for a walk?
- How does a cat say "I like you"?
- How does a baby say "I'm hungry"?
- How do you say "yes" or "no" without words?

Is there another way each of these animals or people could say the same things?

- The dog could bark or scratch at the door.
- The cat could purr or rub against you.
- The baby could cry or make sucking movements with his or her mouth.
- You could nod your head or put your thumb up or down for yes or no.

Now play a game with the children: Say or do something and see if the children can find another way to communicate the same thing. Here are a few ideas to get you started, but you'll probably come up with lots of your own.

- Give a hug to say "I like you."
- Shrug your shoulders to say "I don't know."
- Wave to say "good-bye" or "hello."

61

Tuesday

1122

Mister Rogers talks about jealous feelings children may have when a new baby comes into the family. In the Neighborhood of Make-Believe, Lady Elaine's jealousy over the attention given to the new baby causes her to create some mischief with her magic boomerang.

"Sharing Someone's Time" can help children:

- recognize feelings;
- practice sharing;
- practice waiting.

Sharing Someone's Time

Materials
- books
- puzzles
- toys, rattles, etc.
- box

See if any of the children can tell you how Lady Elaine felt today. Perhaps you can tell them how you felt when a brother or sister was born, or when you had to share someone's attention with a newcomer. What did you do about it? Can they think of a time when they felt that way, too? Help the children think of ways they can let someone know how they feel—ways that won't hurt anyone. What can they do at day care when everyone wants your attention at once?

Encourage the children to act out a pretend situation where you need to attend to something else (such as comforting a crying doll), and see if they can find something to do during that time. You might suggest:

- playing with a toy on the floor next to you;
- looking at a book;
- drawing a picture;
- helping you comfort the crying doll.

Wednesday

1123

Mister Rogers explains that machines need people; they don't work by themselves. Dr. O.K. Moore visits Mister Rogers and shows his machines that help children learn.

"A Vacuum Cleaner" can help children:

- learn more about their world;
- develop healthy curiosity;
- use play to work on feelings.

A Vacuum Cleaner

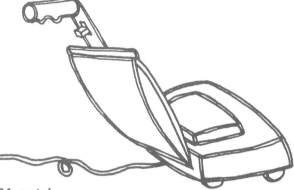

Materials
- a vacuum cleaner

Can you all take a house tour to look for helpful machines?

One machine the children can try to operate is a vacuum cleaner.

After you have plugged in the electrical cord, show the children how to turn the vacuum cleaner off and on. The children can take turns pressing the button and controlling the cleaner. Children who find the noise of a vacuum cleaner scary may be especially interested in controlling the noise by turning it on and off. Others may find its sucking action scary, and you may have to help them understand that vacuum cleaners only suck up tiny things—not people.

(Or, 1135 "Machines.")

1124

Mister Rogers explains how telephone operators do their job. He shows a film that helps explain how telephone messages travel.

"A Telephone Conversation" can help children:

- work on feelings about separation;
- use play to work on feelings.

A Telephone Conversation

Materials

- toy telephone

Encourage the children to use the toy telephone to have a pretend conversation with someone. You could encourage them by carrying on a pretend conversation yourself—perhaps telling someone in your family what you and the children have been doing today.

Then give the telephone to the children and see if they can take turns pretending to call someone. Do any of the children want to have a pretend conversation with a parent or other relative? Some children may find this reminder of separation upsetting, but others may enjoy the pretend conversation and use it as a way to feel better about the separation. If you have two toy telephones, the children could practice telephone conversations by talking with one another.

(Or, 1270 "Telephones.")

1125

It's opera day in the Neighborhood of Make-Believe. Everyone is getting ready for the production of "Pineapples and Tomatoes."

"Pineapples and Tomatoes" can help children:

- learn more about food;
- recognize likeness and difference.

Pineapples and Tomatoes

Materials

- pineapple (fresh, frozen or canned)
- fresh tomatoes (cherry tomatoes, if available)
- knife
- cutting board
- plate

If you have a fresh pineapple, the children might be interested in comparing the skin of the pineapple and the skin of the tomato. How are they alike? How are they different? If you are using frozen or canned pineapple, compare the pineapple with a cut-up tomato. How is the inside of a tomato different from the inside of a pineapple? You could point out the seeds that are inside a tomato. Help the children arrange pineapple chunks and tomato wedges on a plate or tray for snack or lunch time. As they eat their snacks, see if they can tell you how the taste is different. If the children close their eyes and eat a piece of pineapple or tomato, can they tell you which is which? How did they know (the feel, the smell, the taste)?

Thoughts For The Week

*Children grow at different rates and often in ways we can't easily see. A young child who grows taller over the summer can be proud of growing, but so can the child who learns to walk up and down stairs or to put on a sweater or jacket, or the child who learns to talk about feelings and express them in acceptable ways. Grownups play an important role in helping children feel good about all kinds of healthy growing, and children's **inside** growth is really the kind we need to appreciate most of all.*

Fred Rogers

Songs On The Programs This Week

1126 *"Look and Listen"*

1127 *"You Are Special"*
      "Let's Be Together Today"
      "You Are Pretty"

1128 *"It's Such a Good Feeling"*
      "You Are Special"
      "I'm a Man Who Manufactures"
      "You Are Pretty"
      "To Go to Some Place Else"

1129 *"Everybody's Fancy"*
      "You Are Pretty"

1130 *"I Need You"*

Your Notes For The Week

1126

Captain Kangaroo and Bunny Rabbit visit today. In the Neighborhood of Make-Believe, Lady Elaine "helps" Donkey Hodie grow carrots quickly by planting fully grown carrots. The carrots are for Donkey Hodie's friend, Bunny Rabbit.

"Carrot Top Sprouts" can help children:

- learn more about foods;
- learn more about growing.

Carrot Top Sprouts

Materials

- one carrot for each child
- shallow dish for each child (margarine containers work well)
- pitcher of water
- knife
- paint (optional)

See if the children can remember why Donkey Hodie was planting carrot seeds. How did Lady Elaine "help" Donkey Hodie's carrot seeds grow? Let the children have a chance to look at fresh carrots. You can show them where the leaves used to be. Using a sharp knife, cut off the carrot tops for the children. (You can save the rest for lunch, or use a few pieces for activity 1017 "Vegetable Prints.")

Give each child a shallow dish for the carrot tops. Using a small plastic pitcher, the children can pour water into the containers—enough to just cover the carrot tops. The tops will begin to sprout new leaves in a few days. You may need to add water from time to time. If you keep a chart showing the number of days it takes for each top to begin sprouting, this can be a chance to talk with the children about growing— different carrot tops grow at different rates, just as children grow at different speeds.

(Or, 1017 "Vegetable Prints.")

Tuesday

1127

In the Neighborhood of Make-Believe, King Friday thinks it's time for Prince Tuesday to learn subtraction; but Prince Tuesday is only two weeks old! The King learns that babies have lots of very important things to learn before they learn subtraction.

"Learning to Do New Things" can help children:

- feel proud of their accomplishments.

Learning to Do New Things

Materials

- large paper or cardboard
- marker

See if any of the children can tell you about something new they have learned to do. For instance:

- walking down stairs alone;
- tying shoes;
- putting on a jacket;
- using words instead of hitting;
- talking about feelings.

How about making a chart to show the new things your children are learning? Write each child's name along the left side of the paper. Write in at least one accomplishment for each child, and then, as the children learn something new, you can add that accomplishment as well. As you continue to use the chart, it can serve to remind the children that they are growing *inside* as well as out.

(Or, 1351 "Blowing Bubbles.")

Wednesday

1128

Mister Rogers shows that making something with your hands can be a way to express your feelings. He makes modeling dough from flour, salt, and water. "Thumbprint Pies" can help children:

- learn more about food;
- practice working cooperatively.

Thumbprint Pies

Materials

- 1 cup flour
- ½ teaspoon salt
- 4 tablespoons margarine
- 2 tablespoons water
- mixing bowl
- cookie sheet
- mixing spoon or fork

With your help, the children can measure the flour, salt, margarine, and water into a bowl. Each child can then take a turn mixing the ingredients with a fork or spoon until the dough is smooth. Give the children a chance to play with the dough before showing them how to roll it into little balls. Put the dough balls on a cookie sheet and let the children mash their thumbprints into them. Bake the pies at 350 degrees for eight to ten minutes. The thumbprints can be filled with peanut butter or jelly after the pies are cooled.

1129

Mister Rogers reassures children that their teeth come out to make room for new teeth.

"Making Toothpaste" can help children:

- learn to do things independently;
- learn more about their bodies.

Making Toothpaste

Materials

- 4 teaspoons baking soda
- 1 teaspoon salt
- 1 teaspoon flavoring (vanilla, almond, or peppermint extract)
- toothbrush
- floss
- air-tight containers

Are any of the older children beginning to get their permanent teeth? They may want to talk about how it feels to lose a tooth. Other children might be able to tell you about care of their teeth. In talking with the children about caring for their teeth, you can emphasize the following:

- teeth should be brushed in the morning and before bed;
- teeth should be brushed after meals when you can;
- flossing is important, too;
- sweet and sticky foods need to be rinsed or brushed off as soon as possible.

You and the children could make a batch of toothpaste together...or you could let each child mix up a batch in his or her own small container. Just add and mix the ingredients listed above. The children could use the home-made toothpaste for brushing their teeth after lunch or snack time. Cover the containers with tightfitting lids after each use.

(Or, 1297 "Take Care of Your Teeth.")

1130

In the Neighborhood of Make-Believe, Lady Elaine plays a mischievous trick on X the Owl—she hangs artificial oranges on his tree.

"Scented Balls" can help children:

- recognize likeness and difference;
- develop muscle control;
- learn more about foods.

Scented Balls

Materials

- oranges
- box of whole cloves
- ribbon or string

Pour a box of cloves into a shallow dish and let the children smell them. Then pass around an orange for them to smell. Can they recognize the difference? They could close their eyes and see if they can tell the difference without seeing. A fragrant air freshener can be made by poking the sharp end of the cloves into oranges. The more cloves the children use, the stronger the aroma will be. Tie ribbons around the oranges and fasten them in place with several cloves. Let the scented balls dry in the sun or near a radiator for three or four days. These make good presents for someone to hang in a closet.

(Or, 1258 "Guess What's in the Bag.")

66

Thoughts For The Week

Children take a lot of pride in being able to do things for themselves. "I want to do it all by myself," is a sentence children use again and again as they master new skills. We help children feel good about themselves and their achievements when we appreciate their efforts. Trying is a really important part of growing! There may also be times when a child feels the need to be little again. He or she may pretend to be a baby or want a grownup to fasten the coat or tie the shoelaces he or she can already manage. There are times when we all feel the need for a little extra attention, and each of us has different ways of asking for it.

Fred Rogers

Songs On The Programs This Week

1131   *"I'm Proud of You"*

1132   *"Let's Be Together Today"*
        "I'm Taking Care of You"

1133   *"Children Can"*
        "It's You I Like"

Your Notes For The Week

1131

Mister Rogers shows different ways to use construction paper—tearing it, sailing it through the air, making it "dance." He shows a film on how construction paper is made.

"Construction-Paper Mobiles" can help children:

- develop creative play;
- learn more about their world.

Construction-Paper Mobiles

Materials

- construction paper in assorted colors
- paper punch or sharp pencil
- string
- coat-hangers or wooden dowels
- crayons
- glue or paste

Can any of the children make pieces of construction paper fly? Can they make the paper "dance" the way Mister Rogers did? What other things could they do with construction paper? Encourage the children to draw different shapes on the paper with crayons. Can the children tear out the paper shapes? Some of the children might want to glue several shapes together— one on top of the other. When they've finished, help them make mobiles with their construction paper shapes:

- Poke a hole in the top of each shape.
- Tie a piece of string through the hole and fasten the other end to the coat-hanger or wooden dowel. (You could make one large mobile for the group or help each child make one to take home.)
- Cut the string varying lengths so the shapes will hang at different levels.

What happens to the shapes when the children blow on them? Or when you hang the mobiles outside in the breeze?

1132

Mister Rogers visits a doctor's office. In the Neighborhood of Make-Believe, Lady Elaine looks for a pill to make the baby prince stop crying, but the pediatrician explains that a pill isn't the answer.

"Why Is the Baby Crying?" can help children:

- learn different ways to communicate;
- try out different roles.

Why Is the Baby Crying?

Materials

- none

Can any of the children tell you why babies cry? What might they be trying to let someone know? For instance, the baby may need:

- a diaper change;
- to be fed;
- someone to play with;
- someone to be nearby.

Some of the children might want to take turns pretending to be a baby. Ask them to try to tell you and the others how they feel or what they need without using any words. They could pretend to be:

- hungry;
- thirsty;
- in need of something to play with;
- lonely;
- hurting;
- sleepy.

You could point out that as babies get older, they start to use words to tell people what they need.

(Or, 1304 "A Hospital for Toys.")

1133

Mister Rogers shows many different things that children have made from popsicle sticks and shows a film about popsicle-stick designs. In the Neighborhood of Make-Believe, Lady Elaine is poking at people with a tongue depressor. The neighbors help her learn that doctors poke only for a reason—not for the fun of it.

"Stick Sculptures" can help children:

- develop creative play;
- express strong feelings in appropriate ways.

Stick Sculptures

Materials

- popsicle sticks, tongue depressors, or straws
- modeling dough or clay

In talking with the children about the program today, you could ask questions like:

- Why do you think Lady Elaine was poking at people with a tongue depressor?
- Why do doctors need to use a tongue depressor?

The children could use tongue depressors, popsicle sticks, or straws to poke at clay or modeling dough and pretend to examine something. Or, using the sticks or straws and the modeling dough, they can make stick sculptures by poking the sticks into the clay to make different shapes. Younger children may never make a finished product—and that's fine, too.

1134

Mister Rogers shows different types of stringed instruments, and a string quartet visits the neighborhood music shop.

"Shoe-Box Harp" can help children:

- develop creative play;
- recognize likeness and difference.

Shoe-Box Harp

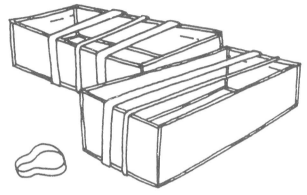

Materials

- one shoe box for each child
- different-sized rubber bands (three or four for each child)

The children might like to make an instrument like Mister Rogers…and here's a way to make another with a shoe box and different-sized rubber bands. Each child will need a shoe box (without its lid) and three or four rubber bands of different thicknesses. Help the children stretch the rubber bands across the shoe box and then show them how to pluck or strum the rubber bands. Then listen for the different sounds.

- Do different boxes make different sounds?
- Are some louder or softer?
- Do thick rubber bands make a different sound than thin rubber bands?
- How are the sounds different?

The children can form their own orchestra and try playing their instruments together. The older children might think it's funny to call themselves "The Rubber Band."

1135

In the Neighborhood of Make-Believe, King Friday is looking for a shortcut to learning to play the bass fiddle. He sends Mr. McFeely to find a machine that will play the fiddle for him, but he soon learns that using the magic machine isn't as much fun as plucking strings himself.

"Machines" can help children:

- learn more about their world;
- learn more about work;
- practice making choices.

Machines

Materials

- mixing bowl, spoon, modeling dough ingredients (page A-1)
- doll clothes, water, dishpan, soap

See if the children can tell you about some machines that help us do something. For instance:

- an electric mixer stirs ingredients faster than a person can do it;
- a vacuum cleaner sweeps the floor better than someone trying to pick up crumbs;
- an electric fan doesn't get tired the way our arms do when we fan ourselves.

You could point out that sometimes doing something yourself can be more fun than watching a machine do it. You might let the children do something by hand—something that could be done by machine. They could choose from:

- mixing cookie dough or modeling dough;
- washing doll clothes in a dishpan;
- sweeping up the floor.

When they are finished, ask the children what they liked about using their hands. Were there things they didn't like?

(Or, 1272 "Making Doll Beds"; 1078 "Growing.")

Programs 1136-1140

Thoughts For The Week

One fear that many young children have is that they might go down the drain—a bathtub drain when the plug is removed, or the toilet drain when someone flushes the toilet. It's not uncommon for these concerns to begin around the time of a child's toilet training. This is the time when they're trying to master control of the fluids inside their bodies and learning to let them go—on demand. When children see body products being flushed away, it may occur to them that the rest of their bodies could be flushed away as well. While children are learning to control the fluids within themselves, they may become very interested in learning to control fluids outside their bodies too—pouring water from one container to another or filling up the sink with water and then watching as the water swirls down the drain when the plug is removed. What children play about is often what they've been practicing to master within themselves.

Fred Rogers

Songs On The Programs This Week

1136 *"You Can Never Go down the Drain"*
        "It's Such a Good Feeling"
1137 *"Everybody's Fancy"*
        "It's Such a Good Feeling"
1138 *"Wishes Don't Make Things Come True"*
        "I'm Proud of You"
1139 *"I'm Interested in Things"*
1140 *"You Are Special"*
        "I Want to Win"
        "I Did Too"

Your Notes For The Week

Monday

1136

Mister Rogers does an experiment with water and shows that only liquids go down the drain. In the Neighborhood of Make-Believe, King Friday has a waterfall built at the castle.

"Pouring Water" can help children:

- recognize likeness and difference;
- use play to work on feelings.

Pouring Water

Materials
- small plastic pitcher(s)
- water
- plastic containers of different sizes
- several towels
- food coloring (optional)

Outdoors is the best place for this activity, but if you have to stay indoors, you'll want a large towel to catch any spills. See how well the children can pour water from a pitcher into different-sized containers. For fun, you could add food coloring to the water. Help the children to make comparisons about the amount of water in the different containers. You could ask:

- Which cup has more water?
- Which has less?
- Is there more water in the big cup or in the little cup?

The children who are most concerned about spilling may turn out to be the children who are most concerned that they'll "wet" themselves.

(Or, 1380 "Going down the Drain.")

70

1137

In the Neighborhood of Make-Believe, gymnasts perform exercises for King Friday, and Lady Aberlin learns to do a cartwheel.

"Rolling" can help children:

● develop coordination;

● develop muscle control.

Rolling

Materials

● several blankets

You might want to emphasize to the children that the gymnasts on the program today had to practice a long, long time before they could do the exercises they performed for King Friday. Some may have started as small children, doing simple tumbling exercises like rolling sideways over and over across the floor.

● Make a mat for the children to use by spreading several blankets on the floor.

● Show the children how to roll over across the length of the blankets.

● You or another child may need to stop them when they reach the end of the blanket. (They might be a little dizzy.)

This activity could be done outside on a grassy lawn, and when the children can do it well, they could try rolling down a *little* hill (if there's one nearby).

(Or, 1032 "Tightrope Walking"; 1365 "Recycle Collage.")

1138

Mister Rogers shows a cleaning tool for the aquarium that makes water go *up* instead of down. As he feeds the fish, he reminds the viewers that all living things need food of some kind to live.

"How Do Plants Eat?" can help children:

● learn more about their world;

● learn more about foods.

How Do Plants Eat?

Materials

● water

● jar or glass

● food coloring

● celery stalks (including leaves)

● peanut butter

● straws

Can any of the children tell you what makes plants grow? Do they know how plants get food? If you cut off about one inch from the bottom of a stalk of celery, show the children the little holes (veins) in the stalk. You can explain that the plant draws water up through the holes—the way we drink from a straw. And if you put the celery stalk in a jar of colored water for a few hours, the top leaves will begin to turn the same color as the water. Cut one of the celery stalks in half and the children may be able to see the colored water in the veins. How about letting the children help you spread peanut butter into fresh stalks of celery for snack today? You could give them straws for drinking their juice or milk, too.

(Or, 1270 "Telephones.")

1139

In the Neighborhood of Make-Believe, Lady Elaine causes an uproar when she takes a part from the King's waterfall without asking anyone.

"The Missing Pieces" can help children:

- understand and accept individual differences;
- recognize feelings;
- talk about feelings.

The Missing Pieces

Materials

- puzzles (or toys) that have missing pieces
- heavy cardboard
- markers or crayons
- scissors

You might begin this activity by talking with the children about the King's reactions when Lady Elaine took a piece of the waterfall machine without asking. You could ask questions like:

- Why do you think Lady Elaine took part of the waterfall?
- Why do you think the King was upset?
- Can you think of a time when something was missing that you needed? How did you feel?

Sometimes people feel angry, upset, or frustrated when something is missing. Set out several puzzles that have missing pieces and help the children put the puzzles together. Talk with the children about the feelings they have when they can't finish a project because something is missing. If possible, help the children make new puzzle pieces from heavy cardboard. Put the puzzles together over a piece of cardboard and trace the missing pieces. After you have cut out the shapes, the children could color them to resemble the missing puzzle pieces.

(Or, 1259 "Fixing Things.")

1140

Mister Rogers visits Betty Aberlin's Theater to see performers express their feelings through dance. He talks about different ways to express feelings—dancing, singing, talking.

"Paint How You Feel" can help children:

- recognize feelings;
- express feelings through art work.

Paint How You Feel

Materials

- plastic table cloth, a shower curtain, or a large garbage bag cut open
- tape
- soapsuds fingerpaint (page A-2), shaving cream or liquid starch

Cover your work area with plastic and make a space for each child to use. Define each child's space by taping a rectangle (about 18 inches by 24 inches) in front of the child. Encourage the children to use the soapsuds fingerpaint, shaving cream, or liquid starch to show different feelings. You could ask:

- Can you paint a happy picture?
- How do your fingers move when you are happy?
- Can you paint a sad picture?
- How do your fingers move now?
- What about a mad picture?
- What other kinds of pictures can you paint?

You might want to let the whole project dry, remove the tape, and hang the plastic as a mural.

(Or, 1105, "Draw a Song"; 1264 "Seagulls.")

Thoughts For The Week

Most of us have had the experience of breaking or damaging something that belonged to someone else. Children may get very upset when accidents like that happen: They work very hard at doing things carefully, but they are growing and learning and everyone makes mistakes along the way. It helps if children can see that many broken things can be repaired, and that sometimes they can help with the repairs. It's always hard to tell a person that you've broken something—but being confident that people can get angry and still go on loving you can make the telling easier.

Fred Rogers

Songs On The Programs This Week

1141   "Ornithorhynchus Anatinus"
        "There Are Many Ways"

1142   "Let's Be Together Today"

1143   "A Lonely Kind of Thing"
        "It's Such a Good Feeling"

1144   "It's Such a Good Feeling"
        "Doing Song"
        "Look and Listen"

1145   "I Did Too"

Your Notes For The Week

1141

Mister Rogers uses glue to repair a wooden bird and he fixes a doll's broken arm. He sings the song "Everything Grows Together."

"Broken Toys" can help children:

- learn more about their bodies;
- learn more about growing;
- learn more about their world.

Broken Toys

Materials

- broken toy or a toy that comes apart
- paper
- crayons

The children might be interested in looking carefully at a broken toy. In talking about the toy, you might want to explain that many toys break because they have been used a long time. Show the children how the broken parts fit together—repairing them if you want to. Many toys simply snap back together; the children could put toys like that back together again themselves. Ask the children to look at their own arms and legs. You can show them that the skin covering their shoulders or knees is all one piece: There aren't any seams like the ones you can find on toys. You and the children could sing (or say) Mister Rogers' song, "Everything Grows Together," pointing to the body parts as they are named. Do any of the children want to draw a picture of themselves—or somebody they love?

(Or, 1259 "Fixing Things"; 1260 "Puzzles.")

1142

Mister Rogers visits a doll collector to see many different kinds of dolls. In the Neighborhood of Make-Believe Dr. Bill Platypus needs a doll for his first lesson in becoming a baby doctor.

"Moms and Dads" can help children:

- try out different roles;
- develop their imaginations;
- use play to work on feelings.

Moms and Dads

Materials

- dress-up clothes
- baby dolls
- small blankets
- doll clothes
- baby bottles

Can the children tell you what they think it would be like to be a mom or a dad? You could ask:

- What would you wear?
- What would you do?

See if the children want to try on the dress-up clothes and pretend to be moms and dads. Do they want to use the dolls or stuffed animals as the children? Encourage them to show you how they would take care of the children. You might want to point out that pretending can be a way of practicing for things they might really do someday.

(Or, 1304 "A Hospital for Toys.")

1143

Mister Rogers accidentally damages a drawing that belongs to Bob Trow. He talks about what to do when accidents happen and sings "A Lonely Kind of Thing."

"When Accidents Happen" can help children:

- recognize feelings;
- talk about feelings.

When Accidents Happen

Materials

- none

Can any of the children think of a time when they accidentally damaged something that belonged to someone else? Can they tell you how they felt? Perhaps you can think of a time when that happened to you and tell the children how you felt about it. What did you do? You might ask the children what a person could do if he or she:

- spilled milk at lunch time;
- spilled paint on someone else's picture;
- dropped a glass on the floor and it broke;
- grabbed someone's doll and tore it.

You might want to emphasize things like:

- finding a grownup to help;
- helping to clean up the mess or fix the broken toy;
- saying how you feel about the accident.

The children might want to go over the words to Mister Rogers' song, " A Lonely Kind of Thing."

(Or, 1347 "When Something Breaks"; 1253 "Talking about Feelings.")

1144

In the Neighborhood of Make-Believe, Mr. McFeely has a delivery for the Platypus family—a package and letter saying Dr. Bill will continue his studies in Australia.

"Speedy Delivery" can help children:

● develop their imaginations;

● learn more about their world;

● develop creative play.

Speedy Delivery

Materials

● hats

● badges or three-inch circles for homemade badges

● envelopes and junk mail

● small packages

● tote bag

The children could pretend about delivering mail using an old tote bag as a mail satchel. Fill the bag with junk mail or old envelopes and small packages. Any kind of hat will do if you fasten a "badge" on the front. (Slogan buttons make good badges for the children to wear, or you could make a few "Speedy Delivery" badges out of cardboard circles.) One way to encourage the children to pretend about their own ideas is to get the play started with questions like:

● How would you walk with your heavy satchel?

● What kind of deliveries do you have to make today?

The children can take turns pretending to be the letter carrier while the others collect and open their "mail."

1145

Mister Rogers makes a simple airplane and shows a film of a remote-control model airplane. In the Neighborhood of Make-Believe, the Platypus family takes off for Australia—in a balloon.

"Balloons" can help children:

● develop their imaginations;

● express feelings through movement and dance.

Balloons

Materials

● balloons

● soft music (optional)

Help the children blow up the balloons and tie them closed. As you and the children toss them into the air, watch the way they move. Encourage the children to hit the balloons gently, making them rise and fall again. Turn on some soft music (if it's available) and ask the children to let the balloons fall to the floor. See if they can move like balloons—pretending to float in the air. Can they think of other things that float in the air? They might try moving like clouds, kites, airplanes, or birds. Some of the children might even want to use the balloons as part of the dance. And, of course, sometimes balloons break and that's another good opportunity to remind children how toys are different from people. Even though balloons have people's "air" in them, they still aren't alive. They're just toys.

(Or, 1307 "Going on a Trip.")

Thoughts For The Week

*Young children often feel that their lives are being completely controlled by other people: Grownups tell them what to eat, when to go to bed, and where they can play. No wonder it's so important for them to feel in control of some things! They may practice for long periods of time to pour water without spilling, to make the puzzle piece fit just right, or to control the actions and feelings of all the toys in a make-believe situation. Making decisions is another way of controlling things—deciding which toys to use or which color of paint for a picture. These kinds of play slowly help young children to feel more control themselves—to stop when it's time to stop, to stay within limits, to keep from hurting themselves or others. When children learn **self** control, they can really feel proud of themselves!*

Fred Rogers

Songs On The Programs This Week

1146 *"I'm the Merry Bird Watcher"*
"Sometimes People Are Good"

1147 *"Look and Listen"*
"I'm a Man Who Manufactures"

1148 *"It's Such a Good Feeling"*
"The Truth Will Make Me Free"

1149 *"It's You I Like"*
"Cinderella as a Princess"

1150 *"Look and Listen"*
"A Lonely Kind of Thing"
"It's Such a Good Feeling"

Your Notes For The Week

1146

Mister Rogers talks about rules and limits. In the Neighborhood of Make-Believe, Lady Elaine disregards the king's "Quiet Please" sign.

"Quiet Please" can help children:

- develop self-control;
- practice waiting;
- talk about feelings.

Quiet Please

Materials

- kitchen timer or clock with a second hand

Set the timer for 15 seconds and ask the children to sit on the floor as quietly as possible until the timer rings (or you signal that the time is up). Then talk about how they felt while waiting for the timer to ring. You could ask:

- Was it hard to sit very still?
- Did they feel like shouting or making noise?
- How did they feel when the time was up?
- Did they feel proud of themselves for staying quiet?
- What did they think about while they were waiting?

Set the timer for 20 seconds and encourage them to sit quietly again. You could increase the waiting time to 30 seconds if they seem able to wait that long. Then you could talk about the things they think or feel that help make the time pass when they are sitting quietly.

(Or, 1263 "Talking about Limits.")

1147

Mister Rogers shows a hidden-object picture and sings the song "Look and Listen."

"In the Bag" can help children:

- learn to look carefully;
- develop their memory.

In the Bag

Materials

- three identical paper bags (such as lunch bags)
- small common objects (such as paper clips, blocks, rubber bands, etc.)

Here's a game to play with a few common objects. Take three identical paper bags and while the children are watching place one object in one of the bags. Now have the children either close their eyes or turn their backs while you switch the bags around. Ask the children to look at the bags again and guess where the object is now. Can the children remember which bag you first put the object in and where it was sitting? You and the children can play the game again using different objects. You might even want to let the children take turns being the one who hides the object.

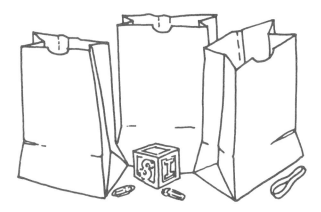

1148

The Polka Dot Players fail to arrive for their appearance in Betty Aberlin's Theater. Betty and her friends have to improvise, making up games like hide and seek and drop the handkerchief, and creating their own kind of play.

"Guess Which Hand" can help children:

- develop creative play;
- practice taking turns;
- talk about feelings.

Guess Which Hand

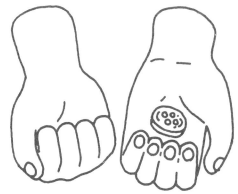

Materials

- a button, a bottle cap, a small toy, etc.

Can the children tell you about a time when they felt disappointed because someone didn't arrive, or they couldn't go somewhere as planned? What kinds of things can they do when they feel disappointed? For instance:

- listen to a story;
- draw a picture;
- tell someone how they feel;
- make up a song;
- put on a play;
- play a game.

"Guess Which Hand" is a game that is easy to play anywhere. All the children can play as a group, using one button, or let the children each find partners and give each pair a button. One child takes a button, hides it in one of his or her hands and the other child (or children) guess which hand it's in. When a child guesses correctly, he or she gets to hide the button next.

(Or, 1103 "Jack-in-the-Box.")

1149

Mister Rogers talks about children's fascination with "inside out" and "upside down." In the Neighborhood of Make-Believe, everybody tries saying the opposite of what he or she means—and Queen Sara becomes very upset.

"Upside-Down Pictures" can help children:

- recognize likeness and difference;
- develop healthy curiosity;
- learn more about their world.

Upside-Down Pictures

Materials
- paper
- markers

What would it look like if everything were upside down? Encourage the children to talk about the possibilities by asking questions like:

- What direction would plants grow?
- What would happen when you dropped a ball?
- What if you tried to pour water?

Can the children use the paper and markers to draw pictures of upside-down things? Older children may be able to draw a whole scene, but younger children may represent "upside down" with scribbles. Go through the play area and turn some of the toys upside down to see how they would look. Do the toys look different? Are the toys the same toys—even when they're upside down?

1150

Mister Rogers uses a blowing machine to keep a styrofoam ball twirling in the air. In the Neighborhood of Make-Believe, Bob Dog becomes so interested in Corney's suspended chair that he forgets to give a letter to Henrietta from Queen Sara.

"Use Your Breath" can help children:

- learn more about their bodies;
- develop the ability to keep on trying;
- develop coordination.

Use Your Breath

Materials
- styrofoam balls, ping pong balls, or clean crumpled tissues
- straws
- masking tape

Start this activity by giving the children straws and showing them how to blow out through them. (If they put their hands at the end of the straw, they'll be able to feel their breath.) Give them balls (or crumpled tissue) and let them see what happens when they blow at them. Can they make the balls move the way they want them to go? After they've practiced a bit, make a path across any smooth surface (table or floor) using two strips of masking tape. Give each child a chance to move a ball down the path by blowing it with the straw. (Younger children may not be able to stay on the path and may just enjoy blowing.) Can they move the ball across a table but keep it from falling on the floor?

(Or, 1229 "Rocket Ship"; 1351 "Blowing Bubbles.")

Thoughts For The Week

*It's hard for young children to understand that some things "belong" to other people, or that some things are to be used only in one way and not in others. They may think that whatever they see is theirs to use as they want. A child might take Dad's screwdriver—and dig with it in the yard. One four-year-old decided he needed a cardboard tube, and so he unrolled paper towels all over the kitchen floor. Grownups can get upset when these things happen, and often children don't understand why. Talking with children about belongings and what things are meant to be used for can slowly help them understand a grownup's point of view. But even more important than the words we say is the example we can set by respecting our **children's** belongings and the uses to which **they** put them.*

Fred Rogers

Songs On The Programs This Week

1151   "Everything Grows Together"
       "It's You I Like"
1152   "Hammers and Pliers"
       "Everybody's Fancy"
       "Tree, Tree, Tree"
       "It's Such a Good Feeling"
1153   "I'm Proud of You"
1154   "Lullaby"
       "It's Such a Good Feeling"
1155   "I Like to Take My Time"

Your Notes For The Week

1151

Mister Rogers shows a film about how shoes are made. In the Neighborhood of Make-Believe, Bob Dog discovers that shoes don't make a person better or more likable—it's the person inside the shoes that counts.

"Comparing Shoes and Feet" can help children:

- recognize likeness and difference;
- learn more about their bodies;
- learn more about growing.

Comparing Shoes and Feet

Materials

- baby shoes or a picture of baby shoes
- paper
- crayons or markers

Show the children the shoes and see if the children can tell you who might wear them. Talk about things babies do at different ages—crawling, standing, walking. Can the children tell you some things they can do now that they couldn't do when they were babies? Let the children who feel like it take off their own shoes and compare them with the baby shoes. They could also compare their shoes with those of an older child in the group or with a pair of your shoes. While the children have their shoes off, you could trace around their feet to show how each child's feet are different. It might be fun to turn the outlines into "foot-faces" with each child giving his or her paper foot the features you'd expect on a face.

1152

Mister Rogers talks about how parents and children both like to know their possessions won't be tampered with while they're away. When he was young, he recalls, he made a tool board to hang his tools on so he would know right where they were. In the Neighborhood of Make-Believe, Corney is upset when Lady Elaine Fairchilde borrows a tool without permission.

"Supply Depot" can help children:
- practice working cooperatively;
- learn to do things independently.

Supply Depot

Materials
- all the materials the children use for arts and crafts projects (paint, glue, scissors, paper, scrap paper, materials, yarn, etc.)
- several cardboard boxes
- marker
- place to store it all

Today might be a good day to reorganize all the arts and crafts materials you have. Begin by getting everything together on a table or on the floor. The children can probably do this themselves. You will need to label the boxes and explain what should go in each. One might be for paint and one for glue, or you might combine two or three things in a box. When all the things are sorted and put in the right containers, find a place to keep all the supplies. You might want to make a sign to hang near that place that says "Supply Depot." When everything has its own place, it's easier for children to learn to put things back after they've used them. Do any of the children know what a "depot" is? You could explain it's a place where things are stored until they're needed—like buses, trains or supplies.

1153

Mister Rogers is disappointed because a nursery rhyme poster that he ordered doesn't have pictures. He uses his imagination for the missing parts. Dancers act out nursery rhymes at Betty Aberlin's Little Theater.

"Nursery Rhymes" can help children:
- develop their imaginations;
- try out different roles.

Nursery Rhymes

Materials
- a book of nursery rhymes (optional)

Can the children tell you their favorite nursery rhymes? You might want to tell or read several of your favorites. Encourage the children to act out some of the rhymes while you and the others say the words. For instance:
- Old King Cole;
- Humpty Dumpty;
- Little Miss Muffet;
- Jack and Jill;
- Jack Be Nimble;
- Mary Had a Little Lamb.

The children might like to make up their own versions of these old favorites or think up a few new rhymes of their own, too.

1154

Mister Rogers draws a song to Japanese music. In the Neighborhood of Make-Believe, singer Yoshi Ito gives a special concert for King Friday and Queen Sara. In the real neighborhood, Mr. McFeely brings a dog to visit Mister Rogers. Mister Rogers remembers the dog when it was a puppy.

"When We Were Little" can help children:

- learn more about growing.

When We Were Little

Materials

- paper
- crayons or markers

Children usually like hearing about things that happened when they were smaller. Can the children remember something they enjoyed doing when they were younger? If you knew the children then, you could help them remember about a favorite toy or a favorite activity. Tell them what you remember about them when they first came to day care. Some of the children may be able to draw a picture of themselves as a younger child. Then they might want to draw a picture of themselves as they look now—doing something that is special to them. Other children might want to take this time to find a toy or activity they enjoyed when they were younger. Ask them to show you something they enjoy now—or the different way they now play with the same toy. Do any of the children think they'd like to be babies again? Just for a little while? Or maybe not right now?

(Or, 1105 "Draw a Song.")

1155

Mister Rogers makes a push-cart from an old baby buggy. In the Neighborhood of Make-Believe, Grandpere prepares to make homemade french fries at his Eiffel Tower. They each discover the satisfaction of "doing it yourself."

"Making Applesauce" can help children:

- learn more about foods;
- practice making choices.

Making Applesauce

Materials

- apples
- water
- sugar or honey
- pan
- spoon
- cinnamon
- paper cups and spoons

You might want to make applesauce today using the following recipe:

- Peel, core and slice four medium apples.
- Add one-half cup water and simmer for 15 minutes.
- Stir in one-fourth cup sugar or honey and a sprinkle of cinnamon.
- Serve warm or cold.

The children can all help wash and dry the apples, but you'll have to peel and core the apples yourself. Older children may be able to help you slice the apples or cut them into chunks using plastic knives. Encourage the children to participate as much as possible, but explain that there are some things that are only safe for grownups to do—like stirring on the hot burners. This might be a good time to talk about the choice between making applesauce yourself and buying it in a jar or can from the store. Which is more fun? Do all the children know where apples come from? They can take turns stirring in the honey or sugar and cinnamon and spooning the applesauce into paper cups to eat or to save for a snack.

Programs 1156-1160

Thoughts For The Week

*Visits to the doctor, dentist, or hospital can be difficult for young children, but knowing what to expect can make them feel more comfortable. Your children may have a lot of questions about such visits. We hope the programs this week can help children learn more about what might happen at a doctor's office or during a hospital stay, and understand better why people seem to be poking and pulling at them during these visits. Pretending about hospitals, doctors, and dentists can give children a chance to explore the possibilities of what **might** happen, to rehearse their own responses, or to feel in control by pretending to be the doctors, nurses, and other medical personnel. The more children learn about experiences they might have, the better prepared they can be for facing them.*

Fred Rogers

Songs On The Programs This Week

1156　"I Like to Be Told"
　　　　"I Like to Take My Time"
1157　"I Did Too"
　　　　"Exercise Your Eyes"
1158　"Sometimes People Are Good"
1159　"It's You I Like"
1160　"Pretending"
　　　　"I'm Proud of You"

Your Notes For The Week

1156

Mister Rogers narrates a film of his own hospitalization. The film shows him going through admission procedures, injections, blood tests, and anesthesia.

"Listen to Your Heart" can help children:

- develop healthy curiosity;
- learn more about their bodies;
- use play to work on feelings.

Listen to Your Heart

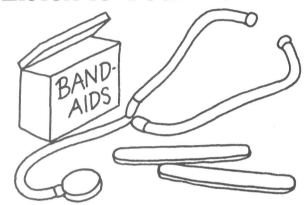

Materials

- toy stethoscope (optional)
- dress-up clothes for doctor play
- toy medical kit (bandages, popsicle sticks for tongue depressors, empty ballpoint pen for pretend needles, etc.)

Can any of the children remember visiting a doctor's office when the doctor used a stethoscope to hear their heartbeats? If you have a toy stethoscope you could let them pretend to listen to their hearts. (If you know someone who could lend you a real stethoscope, that would help!) Do the children know what a heartbeat is? You may need to explain that the heart pumps blood through the body and the heartbeat is the sound of the pumping. If the children put their hands over their hearts, they might be able to feel their hearts beating. You could show them how to feel a pulse on their wrists or neck, too. Encourage the children to pretend about doctors and hospitals by setting out dress-up materials—a white jacket, if you have one, and a shoebox full of medical supplies such as bandages and tape. In the course of this kind of play, you may find the chance to help children learn more what doctors and nurses really do...and *don't* do.

(Or, 1502 "Hospital Play.")

1157

Mister Rogers visits the optometrist's office to have his eyes examined. He talks about the need to have one's vision checked regularly and shows several eye exercises.

"Eye Exercises" can help children:

- learn more about their bodies;
- develop muscle control.

Eye Exercises

Materials

- hand puppet or hand-held toy

Encourage the children to try some of the exercises that the eye doctor suggested today—exercises such as:

- blinking;
- winking;
- looking up and down;
- looking from side to side.

You might also want to use a puppet or brightly-colored toy to see if the children can follow movements with their eyes—without moving their heads.

1158

Mister Rogers explains how a magnifying glass makes things *look* bigger but doesn't *make* them bigger. In the Neighborhood of Make-Believe, King Friday thinks that Prince Tuesday has grown when he looks at him through a magnifying glass.

"A Close Look" can help children:

- develop healthy curiosity;
- learn to look carefully.

A Close Look

Materials

- magnifying glass (if available)
- a box of assorted interesting objects (feathers, pine cones, thread, yarn, seeds, etc.)
- newspaper

This activity could easily be done outdoors, weather permitting. If you have a magnifying glass, show it to the children. Using a newspaper or magazine, let them see how different letters or pictures look when seen through a magnifying glass. Then let them use the glass to look at interesting objects. If you don't have a magnifying glass, sit down with the children and examine the objects in the box very closely. What do they see? Do they notice anything about the object that they didn't see before?

You can encourage them to look carefully at their surroundings, too. You can point out things like:

- fuzz on the carpet;
- worms in the yard;
- threads in the curtains;
- cracks in a painted toy;
- a hair;
- a leaf.

1159

Francois Clemmons sings part of a French opera. Mister Rogers tells the viewers that in an opera people *sing* words instead of *saying* them. In the Neighborhood of Make-Believe, everyone is disappointed because the platypus family's visit has been delayed.

"Singing Instead of Saying" can help children:

- learn different ways people communicate.

Singing Instead of Saying

Materials

- kitchen timer or clock

You might want to try this activity at the end of lunch or snack time — or another quiet time during the day. Set a kitchen timer for about five minutes and encourage the children to sing whatever they want to say until the timer rings. You may want to start by singing the directions. When the time is up, ask the children what it was like to sing instead of speak the words. You could explain that operas are stories that people sing. Would the children like you to set the timer so they can try it again? Do any of the children want to act out a little story — singing the parts instead of saying them?

1160

Mister Rogers has a costume party for his neighbors, and everyone tries to guess who is in the different costumes. Mister Rogers sings the song, "Pretending."

"Guess What I Am" can help children:

- try out different roles;
- learn more about work;
- develop their imaginations.

Guess What I Am

Materials

- none

Here is a guessing game you and the children can play — without wearing costumes. Acting as the leader, make movements that suggest a certain job or occupation. See if the children can guess what you are pretending to be. Once they have guessed, encourage them to pretend to do that job, too. Some movements you could do are:

- typing as a secretary would;
- directing traffic like a policeman;
- driving a truck or bus or car;
- examining a patient as a doctor would;
- giving a haircut like a barber or beautician.

The children may be able to think of others.

Thoughts For The Week

*Children find many ways to express their feelings and some of those ways are through play, dance and movement, singing, and art work. Art of all kinds gives children natural ways to work on understanding their world. Even their lines and scribbles, which may not mean much to us adults, are likely to have meaning to them. And when they draw a car with all four wheels on one side, it may look "wrong" to us, but to them it accurately "says" something they may have just understood: Cars have four wheels. We grownups don't need to criticize children's ways of portraying what they understand just because it doesn't match what we know. And we don't need to praise every mark a child makes on paper either. What we **do** need to do is to show an alert interest in our children's strivings to understand their world and let them know we're proud of all the things they are learning at their own time and at their own speeds.*

Fred Rogers

Songs On The Programs This Week

1162 "I Like to Take My Time"
"It's Such a Good Feeling"

1163 "Children Can"

1164 "It's You I Like"

1165 "I Like to Take My Time"
"I'm Taking Care of You"

Your Notes For The Week

1161

Mr. McFeely brings a pet snake to show Mister Rogers. Mister Rogers explains that not all snakes make suitable pets.

"Snake Pictures" can help children:

- develop their imaginations.

Snake Pictures

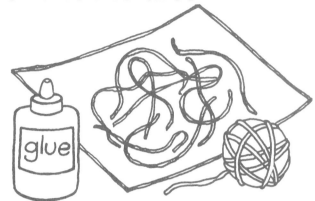

Materials

- yarn or string (cut into 12-inch to 15-inch pieces)
- glue
- water
- shallow dish
- food coloring or paint
- paper

Mix liquid glue with water (two parts glue to one part water) and add a little paint or food coloring. Help the children dip their strings into a shallow bowl filled with the glue mixture. They can create designs on paper with their colorful "snakes." Let the glue dry thoroughly before hanging the pictures or sending them home. The children might enjoy pretending to be snakes, too. Can they show you how they would "slither" across the floor?

1162

Mister Rogers finds out that it takes time to learn to hop with a pogo stick, and he talks about animals that hop. Captain Kangaroo visits the Neighborhood of Make-Believe, where Corney makes a "hopping rocking chair" which everyone tries.

"Hopping" can help children:

- develop their imaginations;
- develop coordination;
- express feelings through movement and dance.

Hopping

Materials
- music

Can any of the children show you different ways of hopping? Older children might be able to hop on one foot, then the other. Can anyone hop on all fours? See if the children can think of several animals that hop. Encourage them to try hopping the way different animals do. If you have some lively music, the children might like to move with the music. You could suggest they move like frogs, kangaroos, or rabbits, but some of the children may want to hop in their own ways. That's fine, too, but you may need to caution them not to hop into one another.

1163

Mister Rogers welcomes new neighbors — marionette-makers Bob and Judy Brown — and tours their new workshop. Mister Rogers shows and talks about signs ("shingles") and about the symbols for occupations that show up on signs.

"Jobs and Occupations" can help children:

- learn more about work;
- try out different roles;
- learn more about money.

Jobs and Occupations

Materials
- paper
- marker
- crayons
- magazines and catalogues
- paste

There are many different reasons why people work, one of the most common being to earn money. Can the children tell you why people need money? You may find they don't yet understand that grownups have to:

- pay for food;
- pay for a place to live;
- pay for clothes and toys for themselves and their families.

Talk with the children about some of the different kinds of work that people do...some of the jobs their moms and dads do. The children might enjoy making "signs" for the different jobs or occupations they've talked about. On each sheet of paper write the name of a job or occupation. Can the children think of something they could put on the paper to represent the job? If you've written "fireman," one child might draw a picture of a fire truck or fireman's hat. Or look through magazines or catalogues and find a picture to paste on the sign. Would any of the children enjoy playing about a job they might someday like to have?

1164

Ezra Jack Keates, a children's author, visits Mister Rogers. Mr. Keats shows a film about how a children's book is produced. In the Neighborhood of Make-Believe, Lady Elaine Fairchilde is pleased by a new neighbor—Brenda Joyce, a book editor.

"The Day Care Book" can help children:

- learn more about their world;
- practice working cooperatively.

The Day Care Book

Materials

- paper
- stapler or notebook rings and a hole punch
- felt-tipped markers
- paste or tape
- magazine pictures of toys and children playing
- photographs of you and the children

Can any of the children tell you different ways to make a book? They can see the work that goes into it by making a book about day care. The children can work together—each doing separate pages. Then they can help put the book together in the order they choose. Staple the book along one edge or punch holes along the side and insert notebook rings so the pages turn easily. Here are some suggestions for things to include in the books:

- photographs of you and the children at day care;
- self-portraits drawn by the children;
- magazine pictures of the toys at day care;
- drawings, art work, original songs or poems;
- a daily schedule;
- a list of the children's names, birthdates, addresses, telephone numbers, etc.;
- the words to a favorite song;
- pets in the neighborhood.

What other things do the children want to include? This might be a book that the children will want to look through again and again. (For a sturdier book, you could use an old photo album instead of loose sheets of paper.)

1165

Mister Rogers visits Bob and Judy Brown's marionette theater and watches a performance of "Jack and the Beanstalk."

"Bean Collage" can help children:

- develop their imaginations;
- develop creative play.

Bean Collage

Materials

- dried beans (several different kinds)
- heavy paper or cardboard
- liquid glue
- containers
- other kinds of seeds (optional)
- popcorn kernels or stale poporn (optional)

Can the children tell you how the different beans and seeds are alike? How are they different? Using heavy paper and liquid glue, the children can create bean collages. Younger children might prefer to make a design using liquid glue, dropping the beans onto the glue to make lines and shapes. Older children may be able to dip each bean in glue and then place it on the paper to create a picture or design. Other seeds or popcorn can add variety.

(Or, 1079 "Watching Seeds Grow"; 1273 "Planting Beans.")

Thoughts For The Week

*During this week the neighbors in Make-Believe make up a new opera. This one is about animals, a zookeeper and an organ grinder whose business isn't going well. The neighbors play and sing all the roles. Playing out different roles is a way for children to begin understanding feelings—their own and other people's. Seeing things from another point of view can be particularly hard for children, so role-playing can be a way to help them feel what it might be like to be another person for a little while. Of course role-playing can also help them discover that when we "take on" the role of another, we don't really **become** that person. As with most of our operas, this one is a problem-solving one and ends up affirming that the loving way is the best way to solve anything.*

Fred Rogers

Songs On The Programs This Week

1166   *"I'm Interested in Things"*

1167   *"You Are Special"*
       "You're a Fine Horse"

1168   *"It's You I Like"*

1169   *"I Take Care of the Animals"*

1170   *"I'm a Chef"*
       "Exercise Your Eyes"
       "It's Such a Good Feeling"

Your Notes For The Week

Monday

1166

Mister Rogers shows a film about harvesting peanuts and he makes "peanut butter" from peanuts and butter.

"Peanut Butter" can help children:

● learn more about foods;

● practice working cooperatively.

Peanut Butter

Materials

● ⅓ cup shelled peanuts (dry roasted)

● 2 tablespoons soft butter or margarine

● bowl

● wooden spoon or mallet

● rolling pin

● plastic bag

● crackers

● butter knife

Here's how to make crunchy peanut butter you can all enjoy at snack time: Pour the roasted peanuts into a plastic bag. Let the children take turns pounding and crushing the peanuts with a wooden spoon or mallet (a meat tenderizer will work). When the pieces are fairly small the children can finish crushing the peanuts with a rolling pin. Pour the crushed peanuts into a bowl and add two tablespoons of softened butter, mixing the butter and nuts together until creamy.

1167

Mister Rogers explains that changing a person's appearance with a mustache and wig can be upsetting to children. In the Neighborhood of Make-Believe, Prince Tuesday is upset when his father, King Friday, is disguised in a wig.

"Paper Mustache" can help children:

- develop creative play.

Paper Mustache

Materials

- construction paper
- blunt scissors
- crayons or markers
- tape
- mirror

Can some of the children draw a mustache on a piece of construction paper? With your help, each child can cut out his or her mustache. Roll small pieces of tape, so the tape is sticky on both sides, and help the children put the mustaches on their faces. They might want to look in the mirror to see how different they look. Some children may not want to wear a mustache, but they could draw a face on construction paper and glue the mustache in place on it. They could also make a simple beard by cutting a fringe on a piece of paper. Curl the fringe by rolling it around a crayon or marker, and use tape to fasten the beard in place.

1168

In the Neighborhood of Make-Believe, the neighbors are rehearsing an opera about animals. They try on their costumes and act out the roles of animals. In the real neighborhood, Mr. McFeely brings a mallard duck for Mister Rogers to see.

"Playing about Animals" can help children:

- try out different roles;
- develop their imaginations.

Playing about Animals

Materials

- a story about animals

You could begin this activity by talking about the duck on the program today. Can the children pretend to walk like ducks? Can they quack like ducks? Help them think of other animals they might pretend to be — monkeys, lions, rabbits, frogs. Encourage each child to take a turn pretending to be an animal and see if the others can guess what animal it is. If you have a story about animals, you might want to read or tell it to the children. They could sing a song like "Old MacDonald," and each child act out a different animal in the story or the song.

1169

Mister Rogers presents an original children's opera—"A Monkey's Uncle." Lady Aberlin pretends to be a zookeeper and sings the song, "I Take Care of the Animals."

"Make a Birdfeeder" can help children:

- learn more about their world;
- practice working cooperatively.

Make a Birdfeeder

Materials

- pine cones
- peanut butter
- popsicle stick or plastic knife
- bird seed or sunflower seeds
- string or twine

You could begin this activity by walking through the neighborhood looking for birds. (While you're walking, you could collect any pine cones there may be.) Do the children know what birds eat? You might want to explain that many birds will stay around if they can find food—especially in the wintertime. Then the children can make birdfeeders for the birds in your yard. Tie a piece of string around the pine cones and spread peanut butter into the grooves and hollows with a popsicle stick or plastic knife. Roll the pine cone in bird seed or sunflower seeds and tie a piece of string to the feeder. Hang the birdfeeders near a window if you can, so the children can watch the birds come to eat.

(Or, 1498 "An Animal Comes to Visit.")

1170

Mister Rogers discusses the importance of "exercise"—whether it's riding a bike or exercising your feelings.

"All Kinds of Exercise" can help children:

- develop muscle control;
- develop coordination.

All Kinds of Exercise

Materials

- none

See if the children can tell you about ways they exercise. Can they pantomime how they:

- ride a bike;
- push a wagon;
- run hard and fast;
- climb;
- throw or catch a ball?

You might want to help them see that there are other ways to exercise, too. You could ask:

- Can you show me a way to exercise your eyes?
- How could you exercise your voice?

And then you could do some exercises with the children:

- stretch your hands and arms high in the air, stand on your toes and reach for the sky;
- hop up and down on two feet;
- use your eyes to look up, then down, then from one side to the other;
- use your voice to sing a loud song and then a very quiet one.

Thoughts For The Week

*Learning to do anything new requires at least **some** practice. And to do something really well, we usually need to practice again and again. For children, pretending can be a way of practicing. They can practice what it might be like to be a grownup by taking care of the dolls, or acting out other grownup roles. As a caregiver, you probably see children practicing in many other ways, too— pouring water back and forth from one container to another, playing with words and sounds, buttoning and unbuttoning sweaters, or riding a tricycle around the yard without seeming to get tired. We may wonder why such simple tasks holds a child's attention for long periods of time: Children's play is the way they practice their growing understandings of what this world is all about.*

Fred Rogers

Songs On The Programs This Week

1171   *"When a Baby Comes to Your House"*
1172   *"There Are Many Ways"*
1173   *"I'm Interested in Things"*
1174   *"Sometimes People Are Good"*
1175   *"I Like to Take My Time"*
        "Sometimes People Are Good"

Your Notes For The Week

1171

Mister Rogers reads the poem "Jabberwocky" and appreciates the enjoyment children find in playing with sounds.

"Nonsense Talk" can help children:

- learn to use words;
- learn different ways people communicate.

Nonsense Talk

Materials
- hand puppet

You might begin this activity by asking the children to take turns talking the way babies "talk." Then show the children the hand puppet, pretending that this puppet talks and understands only nonsense words. Speak for the puppet in a nonsense sentence and encourage the children to answer the same way. Can they tell what the puppet is trying to say by the tone of its voice or its gestures? Or is it just having fun trying out the different sounds of made-up words?

(Or, 1033 "Nonsense Rhymes.")

1172

In the Neighborhood of Make-Believe, Lady Elaine Fairchilde and Henrietta Pussycat wonder if a new puppet has come to take their place, until they realize that this puppet is just making a friendly visit.

"Meeting Someone New" can help children:

- recognize feelings;
- express feelings through play;
- develop their imaginations.

Meeting Someone New

Materials

- hand puppets

Using a hand puppet—perhaps the same one you introduced yesterday—pretend that it is someone new who has come to day care. Ask the children how they could make the puppet feel welcome. What could they do or say? You could begin by talking to the puppet yourself. You could say:

- Would you please tell us your name?
- Are you new in the neighborhood?
- Do you ever feel shy when you meet new people?
- What are some of your favorite things?

Then encourage the children to talk to the puppet—asking questions or telling it about their day. They could mention who they are and what kinds of things they do at day care. If you have other puppets, the children could use them to introduce several more newcomers to the group.

(Or, 1409 "Sock Puppets.")

1173

Barry and Gary Nelson, college basketball players, visit Mister Rogers and talk about "teamwork." In the Neighborhood of Make-Believe, Daniel Tiger is upset because he can't play basketball—until the Nelsons help him scale down the game to his size.

"Basketball" can help children:

- develop coordination;
- practice taking turns.

Basketball

Materials

- wastebasket, laundry basket or a stiff grocery bag (double your bags)
- string
- lightweight foam or plastic ball

This basketball game is best played outdoors, although you can set it up indoors in an area where there are no breakable objects. Can any of the children tell you anything about the game of basketball? Perhaps they can help you tie a wastebasket onto a porch railing or to a nail or hook that is about the same height as they are. Show them how to toss the ball into the basket or bag. Encourage them to take turns aiming and throwing the ball into the "basket."

(Or, 1398 "Bean Bag Toss"; 1449 "Bean Bags.")

1174

Mister Rogers discusses fears of witches and frightening movies. The Neighborhood of Make-Believe is in an uproar over a witch until the neighbors discover that their "witch" is nothing more than a kite caught in a tree.

"Flying Ghosts" can help children:

- understand the difference between real and pretend;
- use play to work on feelings.

Flying Ghosts

Materials

- white facial tissues
- thread or dental floss
- felt-tipped marker
- cotton balls (optional)

Help the children make pretend ghosts by covering a few cotton balls with a white tissue. (A second tissue crumpled into a ball can be used instead of the cotton balls.) Gather the tissue to make a neck, and tie it with a long piece of thread or dental floss. Leave the thread attached for the children to hold while they "fly" the ghosts. They can add faces using a felt-tipped marker. The children could also "fly" the ghosts by tossing them through the air like paper airplanes. In talking with the children about these ghosts, you could ask:

- Are they real or pretend?
- Do they move all by themselves or does someone make them move?

1175

A tympanist demonstrates the sounds of a kettle drum. In the Neighborhood of Make-Believe, Bob Dog and Lady Elaine discover that adults can get scared. They discover that scaring people can get scary, too.

"Scary Sounds" can help children:

- express feelings through play;
- use play to work on feelings.

Scary Sounds

Materials

- pie tins, metal bowls, or cake pans
- wooden spoons

What kinds of sounds do the children find scary? Can they name the things that make those scary sounds? Using the pans and wooden spoons, can the children make scary sounds that are loud? What about soft scary sounds? How about with their voices? And what kinds of sounds can the children make that *aren't* scary?

Thoughts For The Week

Children often wonder if it's wrong to feel jealous, but everybody feels jealous from time to time. Talking about those feelings is one way to learn to manage them. When people feel jealous, it's usually because they feel that some love and affection that they want is being given to someone else. Jealousy can arise when a new person joins the family or the neighborhood—or when someone has a fancy new dress or a brand new toy that makes that person the center of attention. One of the ways we can help children cope with their jealous feelings is to reassure them that it isn't what a person has that makes him or her lovable. It's who that person is. And each person in this world can be special and lovable in his or her own way.

Fred Rogers

Songs On The Programs This Week

1176	*"Everybody's Fancy"*
	"It's You I Like"
1177	*"What Do You Do?"*
	"A Handy Lady and a Handy Man"
1178	*"A Place of My Own"*
1179	*"You Have to Learn Your Trade"*
	"Wishes Don't Make Things Come True"
1180	*"Some Things I Don't Understand"*
	"You Are Pretty"
	"I Like to Take My Time"

Your Notes For The Week

1176

Betty Aberlin invents her own fancy writing. In the Neighborhood of Make-Believe Henrietta is upset because Collette's photo is so fancy, and she tries to make herself fancy, too. In his living room Mister Rogers explains that it's the person inside that counts, and sings "It's You I Like."

"My Inside Self" can help children:

- talk about feelings;
- learn more about growing.

My Inside Self

Materials

- paper
- old magazines or catalogues
- paste
- blunt scissors

You might begin this activity by talking with the children about the differences between outside appearance and the feelings and thoughts we have inside. See if the children can describe their outside appearances. For instance:

- the clothes they are wearing;
- the way each person's hair is styled;
- the expressions on their faces;
- their size, skin, and hair color.

Then you could talk about the person inside. Can the children tell you something about their inside selves? You could suggest things like:

- the way they feel;
- the things they like and don't like;
- things that make them angry and happy;
- their favorite foods, colors, or animals.

If you have old magazines and blunt-nosed scissors, the children might like to find and cut out pictures that show something about their inside selves. The pictures might show their favorite things or the feelings they sometimes have. Encourage them to talk about the pictures while they paste them onto pieces of paper.

1177

Mister Rogers talks about jealous feelings, emphasizing that people who can talk about those feelings can often manage them. In the Neighborhood of Make-Believe, Henrietta is having trouble overcoming her jealous feelings about the arrival of Grandpere's granddaughter, Collette.

"I Feel Jealous When" can help children:

- recognize feelings;
- talk about feelings;
- express strong feelings in appropriate ways.

I Feel Jealous When

Materials
- paper
- markers or crayons

Can you tell the children about a situation from your childhood when you felt jealous? Give each child a chance to finish the sentence, "I felt jealous when …" or you could finish the sentence and then ask if anyone ever felt that way. For instance:

- when my new baby brother or sister was born;
- when the baby needed a lot of attention;
- when you were reading a story to another child;
- when someone arrived wearing a new shirt;
- when someone brought a new toy;
- when my brother or sister got to stay up late.

Here are some ideas to help the children think of things they can do when they feel jealous:

- Tell a grownup how they feel;
- Ask for a special time alone with a grownup;
- Paint a picture;
- Pound on clay;
- Start to think about the things that are special about themselves.

1178

Mister Rogers talks about "privacy." He shows his television neighbors locks and keys. Then he sings the song, "A Place of My Own."

"Key Match" can help children:

- recognize likeness and difference;
- develop creative play;
- develop their imaginations.

Key Match

Materials
- an assortment of keys
- pencil
- heavy paper or cardboard
- string

Allow the children to look at and feel the different keys. Can they tell you how they are alike and how they are different? See if they can tell you why people use keys. Do they have a special place or special belongings that they don't want other people to use? You could let the children try locking and unlocking a door, a suitcase, or a jewelry box. This might be a good time to talk about being careful not to lock a door they can't open. It's important not to frighten the children, but it's equally important for them to understand why you are cautioning them about locking doors.

Using a pencil and cardboard, trace around each key, then mix up the keys and let the children match the keys to the outlines. Point out the ways each key is different and explain that keys and locks have to match so the lock will open. When the game is over, you could cut out the key outlines and string them together to make a pretend key chain for the children to use.

(Or, 1412 "A Place of My Own"; 1327 "My Special Box.")

Thursday

1179

A cake decorator displays his artistry at Chef Brockett's Bakery. In the Neighborhood of Make-Believe, Henrietta thinks her angry wishes have spoiled a fancy cake for Collette.

"Decorating Pretend Cakes" can help children:

- develop creative play;
- develop their imaginations.

Decorating Pretend Cakes

Materials

- colored paper
- pencil
- round cake pan
- scissors
- scrap materials (yarn, ribbon, buttons, paper)
- glue or paste

The children might be able to help you trace around a cake pan with a pencil to make round circles from the colored paper. Help them cut out the circles to use for their pretend "cakes." The shapes don't have to be exact—wavy edges may make them more interesting. Set out a box of scrap materials (old buttons, dried beans, yarn, paper, cloth scraps, feathers) along with paste or glue. Encourage the children to decorate their pretend cakes.

Friday

1180

Mister Rogers talks about different parts of a newspaper and makes a newspaper hat with the help of his son, Jamie.

"Our Newspaper" can help children:

- learn more about their world;
- practice working cooperatively.

Our Newspaper

Materials

- large sheets of paper (plain shelf paper will do)
- markers
- an old newspaper

Show the children a newspaper and see if they can tell you about it. Do they know why we have newspapers? What do newspapers tell us? Encourage the children to make a simple newspaper for their parents to read today. Cut five sheets from a roll of shelf paper and fold them in half so you have about ten pages to use. Talk with the children about things you want to include in your day-care newspaper. The children can tell you what words they want you to print. For example:

- List the things you did at day care today;
- Print tomorrow's menu (or today's menu);
- Ask the children to draw pictures for the newspaper, and you can print whatever the children say about the pictures.

Help them stack and fold the pages to resemble a newspaper and save it for the parents to read when they come to pick up their children. Do the children's parents read newspapers at home?

96

Thoughts For The Week

Anything we can do to help children develop their five senses is likely to help them find out more about their world. It takes practice to look and listen carefully. Listening to the sounds around them, for changes in someone's voice, or to differences in music, can be a way to practice listening. It's the children who trust that they'll see and hear something good who are the ones who can look and listen best. What a great gift we adults give to children when we let them know— through many gentle ways—that there are countless things in the world that are not frightening to look at or listen to. There are wonderful things to see, hear, feel, smell and taste!

Fred Rogers

Songs On The Programs This Week

1181 *"I'm Interested in Things"*
      "It's Such a Good Feeling"
      "I Like to Be Told"

1182 *"You Are Special"*
      "I'm Angry"
      "There Are Many Ways"

1183 *"You Are Special"*

1184 *"Everything Grows Together"*
      "Everybody's Fancy"
      "It's Good to Talk"
      "It's You I Like"

1185 *"Look and Listen"*
      "I'm Interested in Things"

Your Notes For The Week

1181

Mister Rogers talks about traffic lights and safety rules. "Traffic Light Game" can help children:
- develop self-control.

Traffic Light Game

Materials
- construction paper (red, yellow, green)
- a three-and-one-half-inch cardboard circle
- glue
- plain paper (approximately eight inches by twelve inches, cut in half lengthwise)
- black marker
- blunt-nosed scissors
- three rulers or sticks (optional)
- music

For this game you'll need three traffic lights. Let the children take turns using the cardboard circle and have them trace:
- one circle on each piece of colored construction paper;
- three circles on each of the three half-sheets of paper.

Then the children can take turns pasting a green circle over the bottom outline for one "light," a yellow in the center for the second "light," and a red circle on the top for the third. Tape each "light" to a ruler or stick if you have one handy. Here's a game to play: Have the children move around the room or yard to music as long as you are showing the green light. When you change to the yellow light the children should begin to slow down. And when you show the red light, they must "freeze." (Sometimes it's hard for children to stop completely after moving around a lot—the yellow light will give them a chance to "wind down" before stopping.)

(Or, 1431 "Safety Rules.")

97

1182

Today Mister Rogers talks about some things that are hard and some that are soft. In the Neighborhood of Make-Believe, X the Owl cries when he is struck by something hard while he's flying. Mister Rogers points out that tears can express many feelings.

"Hard and Soft" can help children:

- recognize likeness and difference;
- practice taking turns;
- develop their memory.

Hard and Soft

Materials

- soft objects (cotton, handkerchief, tissue, stuffed animal, a pot- holder, feather, etc.)
- hard objects (block, wooden or metal toys, spoon, coin, crayon, etc.)
- pillow case or "McFeely Box" (page B-3)

Talk with the children about things that are soft and hard. You might take a walk around the house and ask the children to find things that are either one or the other. If you put all these hard and soft objects into a pillow case or "McFeely Box," the children can take turns finding the kind of object that you ask for:

- "Tony, would you please find us something that is hard?"
- "Jenny, can you find us something that is soft?"

After each child's turn, see if the others agree. Remind the children that some things need to be hard and some need to be soft.

1183

Mister Rogers visits Bob Trow's Workshop for a demonstration of how to operate shop tools safely. In the Neighborhood of Make-Believe, Cornflake S. Pecially ignores instructions on his new lathe and gets a pinched finger.

"Safety First" can help children:

- learn about limits.

Safety First

Materials

- scissors
- knives
- forks
- mirror or other things made of glass

It's important for children to understand and follow rules about things that may be sharp and dangerous for them to handle. Talk with the children about important safety rules you may have for the objects listed above:

- Never run while carrying scissors or other sharp objects.
- Always return sharp things to the safe place where they are stored after using them.
- Handle things made of glass carefully.
- If something that is glass should break, don't try to pick the pieces—call a grownup for help.

You may have more rules of your own you'll want to add to this list. Do the children have other rules they must follow at home? Let them know that mothers, dads and day caregivers make rules for safety because they love their children and don't want any of them to get hurt.

1184

Mister Rogers shows how you can tell what things are by feeling when you can't see them. Jazz saxophonist Eric Kloss performs and talks about his blindness.

"Letter Rubbings" can help children:

- recognize and use symbols;
- understand and accept individual differences.

Letter Rubbings

Materials

- letters of the alphabet cut from cardboard (the first letter in each child's name, or more letters if you like)
- cardboard (from cracker, cereal or other boxes)
- thin paper
- crayons

Show the children the letters you've cut from cardboard. Ask the children to close their eyes and give them each a letter to feel. Can anyone tell what letter it is just by feeling it? With younger children you might want to use objects or cardboard shapes instead of letters. The children might have fun making rubbings of the first letter in their name: On a flat, hard surface, place a letter under a sheet of paper. Hold the paper down with one hand and color over the sheet with a crayon. Can they tell you what letter appeared on their paper? If they want to, they could exchange letters and do it again. You may find the children have questions about Eric Kloss not being able to see. It's important for everyone to know that blindness is not something that we "catch" from somebody else. Blind people are people who don't see with their eyes, but they have other ways of telling what things look like.

(Or, 1279 "Rubbings"; 1083 "Salt Drawings.")

1185

Mister Rogers compares differences between jazz and classical music. In the Neighborhood of Make-Believe, Mr. McFeely fears he'll lose his reputation for "speedy deliveries" when he has trouble reading an address label which is smeared.

"Making Drums" can help children:

- recognize likeness and difference;
- learn to listen carefully.

Making Drums

Materials

- empty coffee cans with no sharp edges, or oatmeal boxes (you might ask the children's parents for their empty ones, too)
- music (radio or record player)

Give each child an empty coffee can or oatmeal box to use as a drum. Before turning on the music, you might want to let the children practice pounding a bit. They could practice pounding loudly and then softly. Or practice pounding out a rhythm like:

- pound, pound, pound, stop, repeat;
- pound, stop, pound, pound, stop.

While the others listen, let each child have a turn pounding his or her own rhythm. Now turn on some music and the children pound to the music they hear. You might want to change the music so they can practice changing their pounding from slow to fast, from loud to soft.

(Or, 1035 "Clapping Rhythms.")

Thoughts For The Week

It's because parents and caregivers are so important to children's growth that times of separation can be so hard to manage. You may have found that some of the children in your care may be able to talk with you quite freely about their parents and about how they feel about being away from them. But for others, the talking may be a reminder of their parents' absence—a reminder that can make the separation even more difficult. One child may ask for a parent all day long and then turn away from, or ignore, the parent when he or she finally arrives. Another child may keep the feelings inside during the day and then greet the parent's arrival with an angry, defiant outburst. Separations bring out strong feelings in most people, but children, especially, need help in sorting out these feelings and understanding that they are natural and okay...but that there are appropriate and inappropriate ways to express them.

Fred Rogers

Songs On The Programs This Week

1186 *"I Like to Take My Time"*

1187 *"I'm Taking Care of You"*

1188 *"Just for Once"*
"You're Growing"
"I Like to Take My Time"
"There Are Many Ways"

1189 *"Ornithorhynchus Anatinus"*
"It's Such a Good Feeling"

1190 *"I'm Proud of You"*
"You've Got to Do It"

Your Notes For The Week

1186

Puppeteers Bob and Judy Brown show Mister Rogers how to make puppets from household objects.

"Spoon Puppets" can help children:

- develop their imaginations;
- develop creative play;
- express feelings through play.

Spoon Puppets

Materials

- old wooden spoons or large serving spoons
- handkerchiefs or squares of material (five or six inches square)
- yarn, felt, cotton balls, paper
- glue
- markers
- ribbon or yarn

You can make these simple puppets by using ribbon or yarn to tie a handkerchief or square of material around the neck of a spoon. Faces can be drawn on the back of the spoon with markers, or glued on using bits of felt or scrap paper. Yarn or cotton balls glued to the top of the spoon can become hair. The children can move the puppets, holding the spoon handles under the handkerchiefs. One important rule: puppets (like the people who use them) aren't allowed to hit or hurt anybody else.

(Or, 1285 "Stick Puppets"; 1409 "Sock Puppets"; 1452 "Box Puppets.")

1187

Mister Rogers visits with a babysitter, who shares her experiences about caring for children. In the Neighborhood of Make-Believe, Daniel Tiger is worried about babysitting for Prince Tuesday. He is glad to know that Lady Aberlin will be around to help.

"A Caregiver" can help children:

- try out different roles;
- work on feelings about separation.

A Caregiver

Materials

- dolls
- doll clothes
- handkerchiefs or tissues (for diapers)
- tape
- blankets

Can the children tell you about times when their parents go away and someone else takes care of them? For instance:

- when the parents are at work;
- when they go shopping;
- when they go out for an evening.

What are some of the things that a good caregiver does for children?

- prepares meals or snacks;
- comforts them when they're lonely;
- makes sure they are safe;
- reminds them about limits;
- plays with them or helps them learn to do new things;
- reads to them, holds or hugs them;
- listens to their ideas.

Using the dolls, encourage the children to pretend to be caregivers. They could hold and change the baby dolls, or pretend the dolls are older children. What are some things they could do to care for toddlers or older children?

(Or, 1116 "Taking Care of Someone.")

1188

Mister Rogers recalls how important a parent's face is to a child. He shows the viewers how to make a family album and sings the song, "There Are Many Ways" (to Say I Love You).

"My Family and Me" can help children:

- develop creative play;
- work on feelings about separation;
- express feelings through art work.

My Family and Me

Materials

- photographs of the children's family members (optional — check with parents ahead of time for photographs)
- paper
- crayons or markers
- stapler

If some of the children have photographs of their family members, they might like to show them to the other children. Would they like to use the crayons and markers to draw pictures of their families? Older children might be able to draw a family portrait on one page and a picture of themselves on another. Younger children often use a whole page to draw one person, so they may need several pages. When everyone is finished, staple all their pages together to form My Family and Me books.

Here are some questions you could ask while the children are working:

- Can you tell the names of the people in your family?
- What do they look like?
- What are some of the things you like to do with them?

(You'll want to be sensitive to the feelings of children who may have only one parent, no parents or adoptive parents. You can let them know that children grow up in all kinds of different "families." Perhaps there's something special about your family which you could share.)

1189

Mister Rogers talks about different people having different preferences.

"Things I Like, Things I Don't Like" can help children:

- understand and accept individual differences.

Things I Like, Things I Don't Like

Materials

- two pieces of paper for each child
- old magazines and catalogues
- scissors
- paste

See if the children can find pictures of things they like and don't like in old magazines and catalogues. Help them cut or tear out the pictures and paste them onto paper — one paper for things they *like* and the other for things they *don't like*. When the pictures are finished, the children might want to talk about them. You could point out that some people like the same things but that often people feel very differently about the same things. Can the children find something on one person's "I Like" page that is on another person's "I Don't Like" page? You might take a survey to see which common foods some children like while others don't. And of course a child's list may change. One year he might not like spinach but the next he might. Our tastes often change as we grow.

1190

"Wee Pals" cartoonist Morrie Turner visits Mister Rogers and draws some cartoon characters. Mister Rogers shows a film on how a newspaper is put together. In the Neighborhood of Make-Believe, X the Owl wants to be a printer. His first job is making ten posters for Lady Elaine's book show.

"Carbon Paper Printing" can help children:

- develop creative play;
- learn more about their world.

Carbon Paper Printing

Materials

- carbon paper
- paper
- black crayons
- pencils or ball point pens

You could begin by showing the children how a real piece of carbon paper works. Place the carbon paper between two sheets of paper and draw a design or print someone's name. Show the children how the picture or printing is transferred to the second sheet. You could point out that it is easier and faster to make copies of something with carbon paper than to copy the second page over by hand. Here's how the children can make their own carbon paper:

- Using a black or dark-colored crayon, help the children completely cover one side of a piece of paper so that there are no empty spaces.
- Place the paper, crayoned side down, on top of a second piece of paper.
- The children can draw on the white side and see their pictures duplicated on the paper underneath.

Thoughts For The Week

Guessing games can be fun for children, but children shouldn't have to guess about the really important things in their lives. When their parents go away, children shouldn't have to guess whether or not they will ever come back. When children have to go to the dentist or to school for the first time, they shouldn't have to guess what will happen there. If a child gets a cut or scrape, he or she shouldn't have to guess whether the hurt will ever get better. At times like these, children need to be told. So often what we tell our children will be less scary than their own guesses and can help them feel prepared for both the pleasant and unpleasant changes in their lives. What's more they'll learn to trust that we'll always try to be honest with them.

Fred Rogers

Songs On The Programs This Week

1191 "It's You I Like"
         "Look and Listen"
1192 "I Like to Be Told"
1193 "Children Can"
1194 "Just for Once"
         "A Handy Lady and a Handy Man"

Your Notes For The Week

1191

Mister Rogers talks about the ways animals use camouflage for protection. In the Neighborhood of Make-Believe, Mr. McFeely delivers a chameleon to King Friday.

"Camouflage" can help children:

- learn more about their world;
- develop healthy curiosity;
- develop creative play.

Camouflage

Materials

- colored paper
- plain paper
- scissors
- glue

See if the children can draw a picture of an animal (or other object) on a piece of white paper, cut it out, and glue it on a piece of colored paper. Give each child a second piece of the same color and let them tear it into little pieces, gluing the pieces onto their white cut-out—sort of like putting the spots on a leopard. Is it harder to see the shape of their cut-out? They could continue this activity by sticking little bits of white paper all over the colored background. Is it even harder now to see the original cut-out? The children might be interested in knowing the word for this kind of hiding—camouflage.

(Or, 1357 "Purple Print Pictures.")

1192

Mister Rogers reads a book that he brought from the library and talks about how disguises and guessing games can sometimes be upsetting to children.

"What's Going on in the Picture?" can help children:

- practice looking carefully;
- learn to use words.

What's Going on in the Picture?

Materials

- a storybook that's mostly pictures

Choose a book that's not very familiar to the children. Show the children the pictures in the book without reading the words to them. You could show them all the pictures first (if the book is short) and then go back and show them again. The second time, encourage the children to tell their version of the story by the clues they've guessed from the pictures. What do they think is happening in the story? When they have had a chance to make up their own stories, you could read the words from the book, emphasizing that there are many different ways to tell a story.

1193

Mister Rogers looks at photographs of himself and pianist Van Cliburn as boys. He also makes a pretend trolley from a carton.

"Shoe-Box Trolley" can help children:

- develop creative play;
- develop their imaginations.

Shoe-Box Trolley

Materials

- shoe box for each child
- crayons or markers
- construction paper
- glue
- scissors

Cut the construction paper into several different shapes. If your children are very young, then you'll have to do the cutting for them. Set out the shapes and containers of glue and see if the children can make trolleys or buses out of the boxes to use in their make-believe play. They could cover the boxes with construction paper and decorate them with the paper shapes and crayons, adding headlights, windows, or whatever they feel like. Be sure any glue they use is dry before the children use their trolleys in the play area.

1194

Lady Elaine is upset because *everyone* is too busy to spend time with her. She asks Handyman Negri to chain up Mr. McFeely's bicycle so he will *have* to stay.

"Paper Chains" can help children:

- develop coordination;
- understand and accept individual differences.

Paper Chains

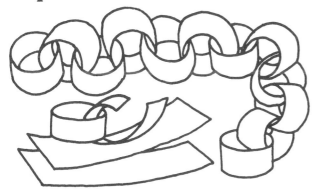

Materials

- strips of colored paper (roughly one inch by five inches)
- tape

Do any of the children know how to make a paper chain?

- Tape the two ends of one strip of paper together to make a circle.
- Put another strip through the circle and tape *its* two ends together.
- Continue looping each new strip through the last circle you've made to make a paper chain.

While the children are working on the chains, talk with them about the way Lady Elaine tried to get Mr. McFeely to stay for a visit.

- How did Mr. McFeely feel when he saw his bicycle had been chained?
- Did that make him *want* to stay and visit?
- Why did Handyman Negri come back to visit Lady Elaine?

You might want to point out that trying to force someone to do something can make that person angry. People like to visit or play because they *want* to, not because they *have* to.

When the paper chains are finished, you could use them for a party decoration by joining everyone's individual chains together. Of course, some children may prefer to keep theirs separate, hanging them up or taking them home.

1195

Mister Rogers shows how to decorate eggs. Audrey Roth brings her collection of fancy eggs from around the world to show Mister Rogers. In the Neighborhood of Make-Believe, the neighbors prepare to dye eggs.

"Fancy Eggs" can help children:

- practice waiting;
- practice taking turns.

Fancy Eggs

Materials

- one egg for each child, plus a couple extra in case one breaks
- food coloring or egg dye
- large pot and water
- vinegar
- several containers
- crayons
- newspaper

Most people think of dyeing eggs only at Easter, but it can be a fun activity any time of the year. Give each child one raw egg to examine...*carefully*. Then let them place their eggs one at a time into a pan of cold water. Boil the eggs until hard (about ten or fifteen minutes). You might want to set a timer so you and the children will know when the eggs are cooked. While you wait, the children can help cover the table with newspaper. Prepare the different containers for egg dyeing by placing one teaspoon of vinegar, 1/2 cup boiling water and enough food coloring for the desired color. You might want to talk about the fancy eggs the children saw on today's program and how they think they might want to decorate their own eggs. Once the eggs are cooked, put them in cold water, setting your timer for another ten minutes. While you and the children wait for the eggs to cool, it might be fun to make up a story about eggs, or remember the nursery rhyme "Humpty Dumpty." When the eggs are ready, the children can dip them in their favorite colors and draw designs on them with crayons. The children might enjoy taking their eggs home, or saving them for snack time or lunch the next day.

Thoughts For The Week

There are times when each of us feels the need to be alone, and that includes children. When a child needs to get away from the group, it's often hard for other children to understand why that child doesn't want to be with them. Sometimes a child may need a special hiding place, and sometimes a child may just need to know that thoughts and feelings can be kept safe inside. I believe that children who are allowed their times alone are the ones most likely to feel comfortable around other people—just as the children who know their thoughts are private are the ones who become most able to share their feelings with the people they love.

Fred Rogers

Songs On The Programs This Week

1196   "Pretending"
       "It's Such a Good Feeling"
1198   "Everybody's Fancy"
       "You've Got to Do It"
1199   "One and One Are Two"

Your Notes For The Week

1196

Mister Rogers shows a film of birds in flight and imitates their movements. He stresses the importance of pretending. Betty Aberlin and Mary Sweenie practice dancing like birds at Betty's Little Theater.

"Birds in Flight" can help children:

- express feelings through movement and dance;
- develop their imaginations.

Birds in Flight

Materials

- soft music
- scarves to use as wings

Can the children imitate the movements of the birds they saw in the film today? Encourage them to try out different ways of moving. They could use scarves or pieces of material as "wings" (or just their arms) as they pretend to float through the air. If you can put on some soft music, the children might be able to show you different ways the music makes them feel.

1197

Mister Rogers looks at the many ways people and animals communicate. He shows how to write invisibly—with soap.

"Invisible Pictures" can help children:

- develop creative play;
- develop their imaginations.

Invisible Pictures

Materials

- a bar of white soap
- white paper
- soft lead pencils
- knife

Cut the bar of soap into several strips about an inch and a half wide so the children can use a piece of it like a crayon. (Thicker soap lines show up better, so the children will need a chunky piece.) Encourage them to draw "invisible" pictures—simple ones like a face, shapes, or letters. To reveal the secret picture, rub a soft lead pencil across the paper. It works best using the side of the lead, not the point. If the picture doesn't show up at first, help them rub over the design again, making the pencil rubbing darker.

(Or, 1293 "Talking without Words.")

1198

It's Poetry Day in the Neighborhood of Make-Believe. The neighbors share their creativity and expressions of feelings. Lady Elaine Fairchilde makes fun of the nonsense sounds in X's poems until she tries them out in her poem—and likes the result.

"Poetry Day" can help children:

- learn to use words;
- recognize likeness and difference;
- talk about feelings.

Poetry Day

Materials

- a book of children's poetry or rhymes
- paper
- markers or crayons
- stapler

Help the children create their own poetry today as a way of expressing their feelings. You might begin by reading out loud from a book of children's poetry. Or you all could say favorite nursery rhymes together. The words the children use for their own poems don't have to rhyme and can even be nonsense words.

Here are some examples of children's poetry:

- "It's sundown
  And the sky is pretty."
- "Books are nice things.
  They are about different things."

If you write the words on paper, each child might like to draw a picture about his or her own poem. Staple the pages together to make a Poetry Book. If some children don't want to participate, they may enjoy listening to the poetry that someone else creates.

1199

Chef Brockett shows Mister Rogers many different kinds of bread. In the Neighborhood of Make-Believe, people are frightened when a giant loaf of bread appears in the sky.

"Tasting New Foods" can help children:

- learn more about foods;
- recognize likeness and difference.

Tasting New Foods

Materials

- different kinds of bread (rye, whole wheat, white, sourdough, muffin, banana bread, corn bread, French bread, bagels or pocket bread)
- knife
- platter
- butter

Do you have a bakery or grocery store nearby where the children could see all the different kinds of bread? Can the children point out one or two kinds they have never tasted for you to buy and serve today? At your home, cut small pieces of each kind of bread and arrange them on a platter. Encourage the children to taste each kind. They could tell you:

- ways the breads are alike;
- ways they are different;
- the ones they prefer;
- the ones they don't like.

You might serve one of their favorites for lunches this week. If you have a lot of bread left over, you could freeze the remainder for another time.

(Or, 1455 "Making Bread.")

1200

Bob Trow learns how to ride a bike—showing that grownups learn new things every day, too. Mrs. McFeely shows how to grow seeds in eggshells.

"An Eggshell Garden" can help children:

- learn more about their world;
- develop self-control;
- learn more about growing.

An Eggshell Garden

Materials

- eggshell halves
- potting soil or earth
- garden seeds (an assortment)
- empty egg carton to hold shells
- small plastic spoons
- pitcher of water

Because eggshells are delicate, this activity takes time and patience. Encourage the children to fill the shells carefully with earth or potting soil. Small plastic spoons will make the task easier. Put the filled eggshell halves in an egg carton to keep them steady while the children plant an assortment of garden seeds. Help them water the soil as needed and record the growth of each seedling. When the plants grow to several inches, you can plant them outside, shell and all.

(Or, 1078 "Growing.")

Thoughts For The Week

Young children are just beginning to learn about the world around them. Most of their concerns reflect the way they feel about themselves, their families, and the special people they have come to know. In the programs this week, we introduce the idea of conservation—reusing discarded items and avoiding pollution. I reassure my television friends that the pollution problems grownups talk about are very different from the spills and messes that children make. Spilling and making messes are a part of growing—and can be cleaned up.

Fred Rogers

Songs On The Programs This Week

1201   *"I'm Proud of You"*
      "I Like to Take My Time"
      "It's You I Like"

1202   *"Please Don't Think It's Funny"*

1204   *"It's You I Like"*
      "I'm a Man Who Manufactures"
      "Sometimes People Are Good"

1205   *"I'm a Man Who Manufactures"*
      "It's Such a Good Feeling"

Your Notes For The Week

Monday

1201

Mister Rogers makes a stick sculpture and shows a film about different things that children can make from popsicle sticks. In the Neighborhood of Make-Believe, Corney needs encouragement to keep on working at making a present for Prince Tuesday.

"Styrofoam Sculptures" can help children:

- develop their imaginations;
- develop creative play.

Styrofoam Sculptures

Materials

- styrofoam packing material (check with a local storekeeper)
- popsicle sticks, paper clips, toothpicks, hairpins, etc.

The children can help you break up styrofoam packing material into manageable pieces to use for this project. They could use several pieces of styrofoam to make a sculpture—with popsicle sticks to hold the pieces together. Younger children may prefer to stick the sticks, clips, and even pencils into one piece of styrofoam to make an interesting shape. If the children need help, you could hold the styrofoam steady for them. Would the children like to use markers or paint to decorate the sculptures? They might want to give the finished product to someone special as a gift.

(Or, 1133 "Stick Sculptures"; 1362 "Wooden Sculptures"; 1451 "Clay Sculptures.")

1202

Mister Rogers shows yo-yos and other toys that "come back." He explains that *people* come back without anything to tie them to each other. In the Neighborhood of Make-Believe, Robert Troll wants to play ball, but he's afraid to let go of his rag ball; he thinks the others might not give it back.

"A Rag Ball" can help children:

- develop creative play;
- work on feelings about separation;
- develop coordination.

A Rag Ball

Materials
- old rags
- old sock

The children might be able to help you tear old rags into inch-wide strips. As you are knotting the ends of the strips together, one child can begin winding them into a good-sized ball. Stuff the ball into the toe of an old sock, knot the end of the sock near the stuffing, and fold the excess back over the ball. The children can use the rag ball for a game of catch. If any of the children have trouble letting the ball go, you might want to make several more rag balls. Playing catch with *you* may help a child feel more secure because he or she can trust you to throw the ball right back.

(Or, 1449 "Bean Bags.")

1203

Mister Rogers shows that waiting is easier for people when they think of things to do. While he waits for a teakettle to whistle and for a model steam engine to run, Mister Rogers makes a pinwheel, sings, pretends, and suggests other ways of waiting.

"Making Butter" can help children:

- learn more about foods;
- practice taking turns;
- practice waiting.

Making Butter

Materials
- heavy cream
- container with tight-fitting lid
- butter knife
- crackers or bread

Pour a pint of heavy cream into a jar with a tight-fitting lid and let the children take turns shaking the jar. It takes a while (ten to twenty minutes) for the cream to become lumpy and the waiting can be hard for children. Do they have any suggestions for making the waiting time go faster? You could suggest:

- singing a song while they shake;
- listening to a story;
- talking about the things they'll put the butter on;
- setting the table for snack;
- drawing pictures while waiting for a turn to shake.

Once the cream forms large lumps, pour off the liquid (or drain it off through a cheesecloth) and add a little salt. Refrigerate the butter until snack or lunch time and let the children spread it on bread or crackers with a butter knife.

(Or, 1455 "Making Bread.")

1204

Mister Rogers makes a paddlewheel boat from a milk carton and explores ways to help keep streams and rivers clean. In the Neighborhood of Make-Believe, Robert Troll dumps stain in Corney's waterfall.

"Mixing Colors" can help children:
- learn more about their world;
- develop healthy curiosity.

Mixing Colors

Materials
- a jar for each child
- food coloring or water paints (four colors)
- water
- newspaper or plastic covering
- spoons or popsicle sticks

To prevent food coloring from staining the table, cover the work area with newspapers or a piece of plastic before you begin this activity. Each child will need a jar of water and a spoon or popsicle stick for stirring. Begin by letting the children choose a color from the ones available. You might want to be the one to add the food coloring at first until the children see how to shake out only one or two drops at a time. As the color is added, the children can watch it spread. Then stir the water to see what happens. They can choose another color to mix with the colored water they already have. What happens to the water? Let the children add colors, mixing them to see how the water changes. They may need to get fresh water to try new color combinations. You might talk about how easily a little food coloring spreads—even in a full jar of water.

1205

Mister Rogers makes a toy from discarded materials, showing that many things can be recycled for other uses. In the Neighborhood of Make-Believe, Lady Elaine cleans up the pollution problem with magic.

"Let's Use It Again" can help children:
- learn about conservation;
- develop their imaginations.

Let's Use It Again

Materials
- a box of discarded objects (toilet tissue rolls, empty milk cartons, bottle caps, string, rubber bands, twist ties, cash register receipts, styrofoam pieces, aluminum foil, eggshells, papers from the ends of tea bags, etc.)
- liquid glue
- paper

As you show the children each discarded object, see if they can tell you what it is and how it was used before. Do the children have any ideas for using the discarded objects to make something else? Older children might be interested in creating "something" from the materials—a pretend horn, a puppet, a telescope. Younger children might want to glue the objects onto paper to make a collage or string them from a stick to make a mobile. When everyone has finished, you could have a show of what's been made by recycling the discarded materials.

(Or, 1256 "Soapsuds Fingerpainting"; 1365 "Recycle Collage.")

Thoughts For The Week

Children sometimes wonder, "Why can't I have all the things that I see and want?" We adults need to help children understand about buying things and making choices: nobody can have everything. But it's also important to let children know that parents will take care of them and try to see that they have what they need—a place to live, food to eat, and enough clothing and toys to help them grow. Parents have the responsibility of making those kinds of decisions, and little by little, children can begin to help make choices that are appropriate for themselves.

Children may not always understand why a parent must leave them and go off to work. But they can learn that when parents work, they are saying that they care about their children—by earning the money they need to provide the things children need. There are many ways to say "I love you," and working is one of those ways.

Fred Rogers

Songs On The Programs This Week

1206   *"I'm Interested in Things"*

1207   *"You've Got to Do It"*
       "There Are Many Ways"
       "A Handy Lady and a Handy Man"

1210   *"The Truth Will Make Me Free"*
       "What Do You Do?"
       "It's Such a Good Feeling"

Your Notes For The Week

1206

At Betty's Little Theater, Susan Linn and her puppets, Audrey Duck and Cat-A-Lion, talk about buying a new television set, and about being liked for what you *are*, not for the things you own.

"Making Choices" can help children:

- learn more about money;
- practice making choices.

Making Choices

Materials

- none

Can you take the children to a nearby store to buy something for snack or lunch? Before you go, you could plan the purchase(s) you might make. Show the children a certain amount of money and explain that when we buy things, we trade the money for the things we buy. For some of the children this may be too difficult to understand, but they could help you make choices about what to buy—several choices, involving one or the other, but not both. The children could choose from:

- orange juice or apple juice;
- rye bread or wheat bread;
- jelly or honey;
- soda crackers or graham crackers;
- peanut butter or cheese.

(You might want to check the materials list for tomorrow's activity and let the children make choices about those things, too. Check with the parents to see if each child could bring in one vegetable from the list.)

Tuesday

1207

With help Mister Rogers builds a crystal radio. In the Neighborhood of Make-Believe, Handyman Negri makes a television set from a kit because the King thinks ready-made sets are too expensive.

"Homemade Soup" can help children:

- learn more about foods;
- practice working cooperatively.

Homemade Soup

Materials

- beef or chicken broth (this could be homemade from meat bones or purchased at the store)
- a variety of fresh vegetables (potatoes, tomatoes, peas, celery, beans, onions, carrots)
- noodles, rice, barley, or lentils
- large pot
- wooden spoon
- knife, peeler, scraper
- seasonings

While children help wash and dry the vegetables, you could all talk about the colors, textures, and tastes of the different vegetables. Older children may be able to help peel or scrape the vegetables before you cut them into small pieces. Let the children add their own vegetables to the pan of broth. Add a handful of noodles, rice, barley, or dried lentils. Bring the soup to a boil and let it simmer for about one hour. The children can add seasonings (salt, oregano, parsley, etc.) just before serving. It's the many *different* vegetables which make vegetable soup so special. It's the many different people who make the world (and your day care place) so special.

(Or, 1220 "Making Cookies.")

Wednesday

1208

On a visit to Negri's Music Shop, Mister Rogers explains about money and credit.

"Let's Go Shopping" can help children:

- learn more about money;
- practice making choices.

Let's Go Shopping

Materials

- coins (penny, nickel, dime, quarter)
- pretend money (page B-4)
- old purses and wallets (optional)

Have any of the children ever gone shopping with their parents or with you? Do they remember what was used to exchange for the things they brought home (paper money, coins, check, credit card)? The children can go on a pretend shopping trip today—but first they need to have something to use to pay for the things they want to buy. Help the children make pretend money. The children could use old purses and wallets—if you have some around—for carrying their money. They can exchange the money for a toy to take to their pretend home. Younger children may find it hard to give up the play money, but they could pretend to give you something in return for the toy. The play money and other props could be kept with the dress-up clothes for future pretending.

(Or, 1206 "Making Choices.")

113

1209

Mister Rogers shows how an alarm clock works and makes a sand clock. He shows a film of sand designs.

"Sand Clock" can help children:

- learn more about time.

Sand Clock

Materials

- two paper cups
- sharp pencil
- sand or salt
- magazines and catalogues

You might begin this activity by taking the children on a tour of the house to look for clocks. Or let the children look through magazines and catalogues, pointing out the clocks they see. You can make a sand clock by poking a pencil hole in the bottom of a paper cup. Pour sand or salt into the cup and show the children how the sand runs through the hole. You can explain that people can measure time by counting how long it takes for all the sand to run out. The children might want to count with you—until the sand is all in the second cup. You might use this sand timer to measure how long it takes children to do something—for instance, how many times they can jump up and down before the sand runs out. You probably won't want to use too much sand!

(Or, 1083 "Salt Drawings"; 1112 "Measuring Time"; 1338 "Sand Pictures.")

1210

Mister Rogers talks about rules and limits that restrict and protect us. When he gets a parking ticket, he goes to court to tell the judge what happened.

"Rules and Limits" can help children:

- learn about limits;
- talk about feelings.

Rules and Limits

Materials

- none

Can any of the children tell you what happened to Mister Rogers on the program today? Can they tell you why there are rules about parking a car? Can any of the children tell you some of the limits you have at day care? Can they tell you *why* you have those limits? For instance:

- throwing toys could hurt someone or break something;
- hitting and kicking can hurt people and damage things;
- small pieces of toys that are left on the floor could be swallowed by younger children or babies;
- when children run in the house, they could break something or fall and get hurt.

Do any of the children want to tell you how they feel about the rules and limits?

- How do they feel when someone reminds them not to do something? (Angry? Glad?)
- How do they feel when they stop themselves from hurting someone? (Proud? Glad?)
- What can they do if they think a rule isn't fair?

Encourage children to let you know when they feel one of your rules isn't fair. You can help them understand the rule better, or you can talk about how a rule might be changed.

Thoughts For The Week

We often take listening for granted, but careful listening—what I like to call "active" listening—is not only an important way to learn about people and things, but it can also be the source of great pleasure. For me, growing up, I found delight in listening to music. Later on, making music became one of my best ways of expressing myself. I've always used music a lot in my television programs. I suppose that's because it's an important part of who I am. But I hope, too, that hearing music will help children listen—and find joy in the many things there are to hear and the many sounds they can make.

Fred Rogers

Songs On The Programs This Week

1211   "I'm Angry"
       "I Like to Take My Time"

1212   "It's You I Like"

1213   "I'm Angry"
       "It's Such a Good Feeling"
       "It's You I Like"

1214   "I'm Proud of You"

1215   "You Can Never Go down the Drain"
       "It's Such a Good Feeling"

Your Notes For The Week

1211

Mister Rogers shows how different bell-like tones can be made by tapping a glass when it contains various amounts of water. A film shows how crystal goblets are made. Another film shows kaleidoscope patterns.

"Kaleidoscope Patterns" can help children:

●   develop their imaginations;

●   learn more about their world.

Kaleidoscope Patterns

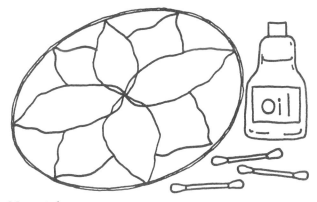

Materials

●   cardboard circle for tracing (six to eight inches in diameter)

●   thin, light-colored paper

●   pencil

●   crayons

●   blunt-nosed scissors

●   baby oil or cooking oil

●   cotton swabs

Some of the older children may be able to use a cardboard pattern to trace a circle on their papers, but you may have to help others. See if the children can draw shapes and designs on the paper circles with dark-colored crayons and fill in the spaces with bright colors. Younger children may just scribble on the paper. When the patterns are finished, use a cotton swab to coat the back of the paper with baby oil or cooking oil and you'll find you have a see-through design for hanging in a window.

(Or, 1441 "Crayon Window Hangings"; 1509 "Musical Jars.")

1212

X the Owl is feeling jealous about the bell King Friday gave Henrietta, and he decides that bell-ringing is disturbing people in the Neighborhood of Make-Believe.

"Ringing Spoons" can help children:

- recognize likeness and difference;
- learn to listen carefully;
- develop creative play.

Ringing Spoons

Materials

- four or five spoons of different sizes
- string
- stick or strip of heavy cardboard

Use the string to hang three or four different-sized spoons from a stick or a piece of cardboard so that they hang down anywhere from a few inches to a foot or so. The children may be able to help you with the tying. Take another spoon and hit the ones dangling from the strings. You'll find they make different sounds according to their size. Can the children hear the difference? They might like to combine this spoon instrument with other homemade instruments you may have.

(Or, 1509 "Musical Jars"; 1134 "Shoe-Box Harp"; 1443 "Paper- Plate Shakers.")

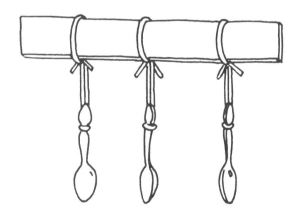

1213

Mister Rogers makes an oatmeal-box bass viola and recalls using musical sounds to express feelings of anger, sadness, and fear. Mrs. McFeely uses the oatmeal box to make a sand design.

"A Stringed Instrument" can help children:

- develop creative play;
- learn to listen carefully.

A Stringed Instrument

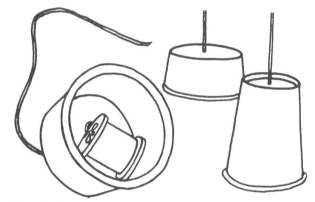

Materials

- plastic margarine, yogurt, cottage cheese containers
- strings about three feet long
- spool from thread, half a popsicle stick, or a large button
- tape

Give each child a container and poke a hole in the bottom with a sharp pencil. Help the children wrap a little tape around the ends of the strings so they can thread them through the holes. Tie a spool, stick or button on the other end to keep it from slipping through the hole. The children can play this instrument best when sitting down, resting their feet on the containers, and pulling the string tight. All they have to do is pluck the string. The sound will vary depending on how hard they are pulling the string.

(Or, 1134 "Shoe-Box Harp.")

1214

A mime group pantomimes different occupations at Betty's Little Theater. In the Neighborhood of Make-Believe, X gets the job of printing King Friday's calling cards.

"Occupations" can help children:

- learn more about their world;
- learn more about work;
- develop their imaginations.

Occupations

Materials

- none

You may want to explain that an "occupation" is the kind of work that a person does. What jobs can they think of that grownups do? For instance:

- factory worker;
- airline pilot;
- bus driver;
- firefighter;
- lettercarrier;
- cleaning person;
- child caregiver.

You might begin the activity by acting out one of the occupations they have mentioned. Can they guess what job you are pantomiming? Give the children a chance to act out occupations for the others to guess. They might like to pretend about one of the occupations later today. Help them choose one and think of the props they could use:

- doctor—medical kit and smock;
- lettercarrier—pretend letters and tote bag;
- factory worker—string, plastic nuts and bolts, plastic tools, etc.

(Or, 1276 "Name Cards.")

1215

A plumber fixes a drain for Mister Rogers and reassures children that "You can never go down the drain."

"Plumbing and Drains" can help children:

- learn more about their world.

Plumbing and Drains

Materials

- pipes and plumbing under a kitchen or bathroom sink
- spoons and plastic cups.

Children are sometimes very interested in the pipes and plumbing systems in kitchens and bathrooms. Show the children the drain in a kitchen or bathroom sink and let them look at any pipes they can see. Turn on the water and let them watch and listen as the water goes down the drain and through the pipes. They may have lots of questions about where the water goes and how it gets there. As you answer their questions as best you can, you might also want to reassure the children that people can never go down the drain...just as the plumber told Mister Rogers. Could the children help you wash the spoons or plastic cups after lunch today? When the dishes are finished, they could watch the water go down the drain, and all of you could sing Mister Rogers' song, "You Can Never Go down the Drain."

(Or, 1380 "Going down the Drain.")

Thoughts For The Week

As children grow they become better able to do things for themselves. They often take great pride in buttoning their clothing, tying shoes, or zipping a jacket. Yet young children still need to feel that someone is there to take care of them. There may be times when a child needs an adult to help button up the coat or put on the shoes—not because the child isn't able to do it alone, but because he or she has come to associate those experiences with the feelings of being well cared for. At a time like that a child may just be asking for an extra portion of your care.

Fred Rogers

Songs On The Programs This Week

1216 *"You Are Special"*

1217 *"Look and Listen"*
       "You've Got to Do It"
       "KFQSSRFFTPA"

1218 *"Let's Be Together Today"*
       "KFQSSRFFTPA"
       "It's Such a Good Feeling"
       "It's You I Like"

1219 *"When a Baby Comes to Your House"*
       "I Like to Take My Time"
       "KFQSSRFFTPA"

1220 *"KFQSSRFFTPA"*

Your Notes For The Week

1216

Mister Rogers talks about parents providing for their children. In the Neighborhood of Make-Believe, a magician needs money and thinks he will have to sell his belongings.

"My Parents Take Care of Me" can help children:

- learn more about work;
- learn more about money.

My Parents Take Care of Me

Materials

- large piece of paper (a grocery bag cut open)
- crayons or markers

Can the children think of ways their parents take good care of them? As they mention different ways, write them on a large piece of paper. For instance:

- buying food;
- preparing food;
- seeing that they have clothes to wear;
- helping them do things;
- providing a place to live;
- buying toys or other belongings;
- listening to them;
- telling them what to expect;
- looking after them when they're sick or hurt;
- giving them hugs and kisses;
- finding a good caregiver for them during work hours.

Some of these ways of taking good care require that parents earn money. Read through the list, one item at a time, and ask the children to tell you which ways of taking good care require money. You might want to use a marker or crayon and put a star or other symbol beside those items. Now go over the list again and use a different color and symbol to mark the ones that don't require money. You could hang the list on a door or wall and talk about ways of taking good care another day. As the children grow and have new experiences they will come up with more ways their parents take good care of them...and ways *they* take good care of others!

1217

Mister Rogers shows how animated cartoons are made. Film-maker Andrew N. Wyeth visits with Mister Rogers and shows his animated film, "You've Got to Do It."

"Spinning Circle" can help children:

*   develop creative play.

Spinning Circle

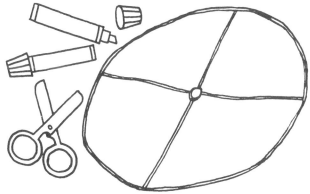

Materials

*   circles cut from heavy paper or cardboard (five or six inches across)
*   pencils or pens (one for each child)
*   crayons or markers
*   scissors

Each child will need a round piece of heavy paper or cardboard and a pencil or pen. Older children might want to cut their own circles by tracing around a pattern and cutting it out. Help the children divide their circles into four sections by marking them with a large X. Use a sharp pencil or pen to poke a hole in the center of each circle and show the children how to spin the circles on the tip of the pencils or pens. Some of the children may want to decorate the circles with crayons or markers. Suggest that they choose four different colors and fill in each section with one color. Now when they spin their circles, they will see the colors blend as the circles spin.

1218

A tailor shows Mister Rogers how he makes clothes that fit. Mister Rogers is drawing pictures by tracing numbered dots: a house, a star. He uses a yardstick to measure his height.

"Connect-the-Dot Designs" can help children:

*   develop their imaginations;
*   develop creative play.

Connect-the-Dot Designs

Materials

*   pencils
*   paper
*   crayons and markers

Make up several "dot" designs ahead of time, placing lots of dots anywhere on several pieces of paper. Or, have the children make their own dot designs in the same way. Then the children can connect the dots with a pencil, joining one to the other in any sequence, making patterns and designs. When they are finished, they can use crayons or markers, coloring the patterns however they wish. Younger children might enjoy just making scribble marks and dots on their papers while the older children make designs.

1219

Mister Rogers talks about children's concerns that a new baby in the house may take an older child's place. He sings the song, "When a Baby Comes to Your House." Later Mister Rogers and Mr. McFeely try out a hammock.

"A Cradle for the Dolls" can help children:

- use play to work on feelings;
- develop their imaginations.

A Cradle for the Dolls

Materials

- crib sheets or baby blankets
- two chairs

Help the children tie or pin the sheet between two chairs to make a swinging cradle for the dolls or stuffed animals. The children can role-play about taking care of the dolls and putting them to bed. The children might enjoy learning a lullaby to sing as they put the dolls to sleep...or they might make one up: a lullaby of their own.

(Or, 1272 "Making Doll Beds"; 1047 "Caring for Baby.")

1220

Mister Rogers makes a sand-flower painting and remembers giving ones like it to his mother. At Brockett's Bakery, he helps to make cookies with different-shaped cutters.

"Making Cookies" can help children:

- learn more about foods;
- practice waiting.

Making Cookies

Materials

- mixing bowl
- electric mixer
- cookie cutters or plastic knives
- cookie sheet
- $2/3$ cup shortening
- $3/4$ cup sugar
- 1 teaspoon almond or vanilla extract
- 2 cups flour
- $1\frac{1}{2}$ teaspoons baking powder
- 1 teaspoon salt
- egg

Today the children could help you make cookies to serve at snack time or to give as a gift to someone. Mix the shortening, sugar, almond or vanilla extract with an electric beater. Add the egg and beat the mixture again. In another bowl, mix the flour, one and one-half teaspoons of baking powder, and one teaspoon of salt. Add the dry ingredients to the creamed mixture and refrigerate for one hour. Later today the children can roll out the dough, cut it with cookie cutters or make their own shapes with plastic knives. Bake the cookies on a greased cookie sheet at 375 degrees for six to eight minutes.

(Or, 1338 "Sand Pictures.")

Thoughts For The Week

Many of the fears that appear during a child's early years are clearly associated with children's inner feelings. For instance, children may become frightened of things that bite and scratch—just at the time when they are learning to control their own biting and scratching impulses. When a child learns to control biting feelings, that child is learning about self-control. It's very frightening for children to feel out of control, so grownups need to step in until children learn to stop themselves. Little by little, children practice and learn to control themselves, and often that feeling of self-control helps them understand many things that otherwise might seem frightening. We look on other people with our own eyes, often expecting of them what we feel inside ourselves. We all need to grow in the knowledge that everybody's different... unique.

Fred Rogers

Songs On The Programs This Week

1221   "The Clown in Me"
1222   "I Like the Elephants"
1223   "I'm a Man Who Manufactures"
*   "Look and Listen"*
*   "O.C.S. Alma Mater"*
1224   "Sometimes People Are Good"
1225   "Everybody's Fancy"

Your Notes For The Week

1221

Mister Rogers explains that children often resort to tricks and clowning to gain attention—especially when they're feeling insecure. He sings the song, "The Clown in Me." Lady Elaine wants attention and flashes a light in Mr. McFeely's eyes.

"The Clown in Me" can help children:

* talk about feelings;
* learn to use words;
* develop their imaginations.

The Clown in Me

Materials

* silly hat or wig
* clown costume (optional)

Do any of the children ever feel like acting silly? Can they tell you why they act silly? (They feel like it; they want someone to laugh; they want attention.) You might help them see that *telling* someone how they feel can be a better way to let a person know what they need. Do any of the children want to act like a clown just for fun? What are some things they could do? For instance:

* make a face;
* wear a silly hat or wig;
* walk in a silly way;
* do silly tricks.

The children can take turns being a clown for the others to watch—or everyone could be a clown at the same time. If you have circus music, the children might like to listen to it while they pretend to be clowns—or they could sing Mister Rogers' song, "The Clown in Me." Some children may have seen adult clowns and have been frightened by them. They may tell you that they were too loud or they had too many "surprises."

1222

In the Neighborhood of Make-Believe, Lady Elaine makes the Museum-Go-Round into a carousel. Back in the "real" neighborhood, Elsie Neal shows Mister Rogers how to make a round bowl from clay.

"Coil Pots" can help children:
- develop creative play;
- develop muscle control.

Coil Pots

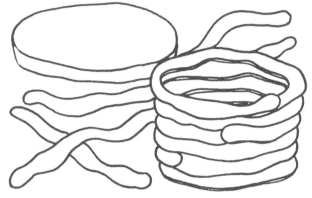

Materials
- clay or modeling dough (page A-1)
- rolling pin

Have the children take turns using the rolling pin to flatten their clay or modeling dough. Cut a circle about four or five inches across out of the flattened dough for each child to use as a base for his or her pot. Show the children how to make long coils from the rest of the clay by rolling chunks of it on the table with the palms of your hands until it forms a snake-like shape about a half-inch thick. The children can form sides of a bowl by forming the coils into circles. Stack seven or eight coils on the base, one on top of the other, piecing them together when the coils aren't long enough to fit. The result will be a clay pot. If you are using potter's clay or modeling dough, the pot will harden overnight and could be painted to give as a gift. Younger children may enjoy just rolling and manipulating the clay or dough while you help the older children make their pots.

(Or, 1371 "Modeling-Dough Letters"; 1451 "Clay Sculptures.")

1223

In the Neighborhood of Make-Believe, Handyman Negri walks around the neighborhood playing his guitar and singing favorite songs. A bouncing ball brings X's latest O.C.S. lesson. In the "real" neighborhood, Mister Rogers shows a film about a bouncing ball.

"Ball Bounce" can help children:
- develop coordination;
- develop the ability to keep on trying.

Ball Bounce

Materials
- balls

Take the balls outside, if the weather permits, and encourage the children to bounce them.
- Can they catch the ball after it bounces?
- Can they bounce it to another child?
- See if anyone can bounce fast.
- How about slow bouncing?

When the children come in from outdoor play, you could put on some music and encourage them to pretend to bounce like balls—bouncing high, bouncing low, fast then slow.

(Or, 1134 "Shoe-Box Harp"; 1035 "Clapping Rhythms.")

1224

Mister Rogers does some experiments with magnets. He talks about how children sometimes feel like being close to someone and sometimes feel like being away from someone.

"Magnets" can help children:

- learn more about their world;
- develop healthy curiosity.

Magnets

Materials

- magnet(s)
- assorted objects (some containing iron and others that are not magnetic)
- two baskets
- paper

Spread the objects on the table or floor and give the children time to look at them. Encourage them to experiment with the magnets—seeing which objects the magnets will attract. They could sort the objects into two baskets—one basket for non-magnetic items and the other for magnetic ones. They might also like to try moving an object across a piece of paper by moving the magnet back and forth *under* the paper. The object will seem to move by magic.

1225

Mister Rogers talks about cooperation and shows a film about bees working together in the hive. He and his neighbors get together to raise vegetables in their garden.

"Making a Mural" can help children:

- practice working cooperatively;
- develop creative play;
- practice making choices.

Making a Mural

Materials

- a long piece of paper (a roll of plain shelf paper)
- markers or crayons
- tape

Unroll a long piece of paper the length of your work area. You may need to use tape to hold the ends down. You can help the children decide how to work together by asking questions like:

- How can we decide where each person should draw?
- Should we each draw a part of one picture or should each of us draw his or her own pictures?
- Do we need a theme? (A vegetable garden, the circus, the children at our day care home, etc.)

Once the children have come to an agreement, set out the crayons or markers, encouraging them to talk about any disagreements that arise. Your remarking on times of cooperation can be important, too.

Thoughts For The Week

*An astronaut can sometimes seem like a superhero to a child. Children may have a lot of questions about how an astronaut really looks and what that person does in a space capsule. Our television visits this week include conversations with astronaut Al Worden, and we hope the children can see that he is **not** superhuman. Colonel Worden tells how astronauts eat, what happens when a rocket takes off, how the equipment helps them do things like walk in space or walk on the moon, and how they feel about their work. All this gives children facts and ideas they can use in pretending about things like rockets or space travel—things that will probably be a very real part of their future.*

Fred Rogers

Songs On The Programs This Week

1226   *"It's Such a Good Feeling"*
         "I'm Interested in Things"
1227   *"Everything Grows Together"*
1228   *"I'm Proud of You"*
1229   *"Pretending"*
1230   *"I Like to Take My Time"*
         "I'm Proud of You"

Your Notes For The Week

Monday

1226

It's a foggy day in the Neighborhood of Make-Believe. Bob Dog rides into the fog on his bicycle and can't see where he's going. Lady Elaine clears up the fog with her boomerang.

"What's behind the Fog?" can help children:

- learn more about their world;
- develop their imaginations.

What's behind the Fog?

Materials

- colored paper
- crayons
- white or gray paint mixed with water
- brushes

Encourage the children to make a picture using the crayons and colored paper. When the pictures are finished, see if any of the children want to make "foggy" pictures by painting over the crayon with watered-down paint. The paint will not stick to the crayon but will make the rest of the picture appear foggy. (If you mix soap with the paint, the paint *will* stick to the crayon.) Some of the children may not want to paint over their pictures, but they could experiment with another piece of paper and just make crayon marks to cover with "fog."

1227

In the Neighborhood of Make-Believe, Lady Elaine Fairchilde plans to launch a spaceship.

"Parachutes" can help children:

- develop creative play;
- develop their imaginations.

Parachutes

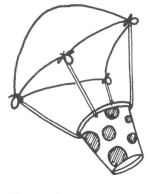

Materials

- handkerchief or square piece of cloth
- string (four eight-inch pieces for each parachute)
- small paper cups or metal nut/washer
- pencil

You can make simple parachutes by knotting an eight-inch piece of string to each corner of a handkerchief or piece of cloth. Using a pencil, poke four holes around the rim of a paper cup and fasten the end of each string to the holes. The children can put toy people or small animals inside the cups, and this will add the necessary weight to make the parachutes float properly. Another way to make parachutes is to tie the ends of the strings to a metal nut or washer. Toss the parachute in the air, and it will open and float to the ground.

1228

Astronaut Al Worden is delayed and won't arrive until tomorrow. Everyone finds something to do to help make the time go faster. In the Neighborhood of Make-Believe, Lady Elaine practices jumping to the moon. Handyman Negri holds a model of the moon, and Lady Elaine practices jumping farther and farther.

"Jumping over the Moon" can help children:

- develop coordination;
- develop the ability to keep on trying.

Jumping over the Moon

Materials

- crescent-shaped moons (cut from a circle about dinner-plate size)
- tape

How high and how far can the children jump? See if they'd like to show you. Tape a crescent-shaped moon on the floor and let the children take turns jumping over the moon. When they jump over it easily, see if they can jump over three or four (one at a time) without stopping. Space the moons so there is room to land between each moon. You can also see how many moons they can jump over at the *same* time.

(Or, 1324 "Nighttime Pictures.")

1229

Astronaut Al Worden visits Mister Rogers and talks about his trip to the moon. He shows a film of his space walk.

"Rocket Ship" can help children:

● practice taking turns;

● practice waiting;

● develop the ability to keep on trying.

Rocket Ship

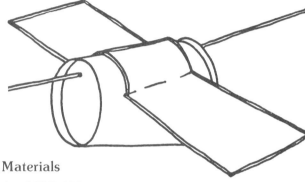

Materials

● paper cup

● heavy paper or lightweight cardboard

● glue

● scissors

● piece of string about eight to ten feet long

Here's how you can make a simple rocket ship for the children to pretend about: Punch a hole in the bottom of a paper cup near one edge. From heavy paper or lightweight cardboard, cut a wing and glue it to the cup (see illustration). Thread the string through the hole in the bottom of the cup and out the open top. Tie the string between two trees, door hinges or whatever, so that the string is at the children's head level. One child at a time can then blow into the open end of the cup to move the rocket ship along the string. The children that are waiting for a turn may enjoy pretending to be on the rocket ship. They could tell you about the things they might see on their pretend voyage. What do planets look like when you're very close to them?

1230

Astronaut Worden shows Mister Rogers some of the food he ate while orbiting the moon. He mixes hot water with the contents of one package to make a spaghetti dinner.

"Instant Oatmeal" can help children:

● learn more about foods;

● develop healthy curiosity.

Instant Oatmeal

Materials

● instant oatmeal (or any instant-type hot cereal or even hot chocolate mix)

● hot water

● bowls

● spoons

● cinnamon

The children may be able to pour their oatmeal into bowls while the water is heating. Do the children know what "instant food" is? Add the hot water according to the package directions, pouring it carefully. The children can mix the water and oatmeal with a spoon until it cools. They might like to sprinkle some cinnamon on top of the cereal. Do any of the children want to pretend they are eating this food while riding in a spaceship? Why is "instant food" helpful for astronauts? This might give you a chance to see if the children have other questions about astronaut Al Worden's visit with Mister Rogers this week.

Thoughts For The Week

*Children often like to pretend they are someone else—it's fun, and it's a way for them to learn about other people. But it's also important for them to know that although we can pretend to be someone else, we can never **be** someone else. Each person is unique and special, and adults can help children take pride in those things that make each of us different. Although people may share the same experiences or sometimes have the same feelings, each one of us has characteristics that are uniquely our own.*

Fred Rogers

Songs On The Programs This Week

1231   "O.C.S. Alma Mater"
       "Everybody Has a History"
       "It's Such a Good Feeling"
       "Everybody's Fancy"

1232   "Everybody Has a History"

1233   "You Are Special"
       "Sometimes People Are Good"

1234   "It's You I Like"

1235   "Wishes Don't Make Things Come True"
       "I'm Taking Care of You"
       "It's You I Like"

Your Notes For The Week

Monday

1231

Mister Rogers makes rubbings of different kinds of leaves. In the Neighborhood of Make-Believe, Lady Elaine gets leaves from X to make a leaf mat for flying to Jupiter.

"Leaf Rubbings" can help children:

- learn to look carefully;
- recognize likeness and difference.

Leaf Rubbings

Materials

- different kinds of leaves
- lightweight paper
- crayons

You might want to take the children for a walk to collect some leaves. When you return home, encourage the children to look at and feel the different leaves. Can they tell you how the leaves are alike and how they are different? Each child might like to pick a favorite leaf for this activity: Place the leaf under a piece of paper and show the children how to rub across it with a crayon to see the leaf outline. As you continue rubbing, the veins of the leaf will begin to show, too. Give the children paper and crayons and let them try using different leaves and different colored crayons. See if they can find the things that are alike about the leaf rubbings and the things that are different. How are the *rubbings* like the leaves and how are they different? The children could use other flat household objects to make rubbings, too.

(Or, 1279 "Rubbings.")

1232

At Brockett's Bakery Mister Rogers talks about eating foods that are made in different animal shapes. Mister Rogers shows a cookie animation film.

"Animal Cookies" can help children:

- understand the difference between real and pretend.

Animal Cookies

Materials

- animal crackers or cookies

You might want to make your own animal-shaped cookies using cookie dough and animal cookie-cutters, or use cookies you've bought at a store. In talking with the children about the cookies you might ask:

- What kind of animal did you choose?
- What can you tell us about the animal?
- Is it a real animal or does it just look like an animal?

You might mention that some children don't feel like eating cakes or cookies that are shaped like animals because they worry that the animals might get hurt. Reassure the children that the cookies are only *shaped* like animals. (If the children made the cookies, you could remind them that the cookies were made from cookie dough.) You might also find it helpful to mention to the children that cookies and cakes could never bite anybody!

1233

Mister Rogers shows a wind vane and talks about wind and flying. He shows a film of flying ducks. In the Neighborhood of Make-Believe, Lady Elaine uses a leaf mat to blast off for Jupiter.

"Space Shapes" can help children:

- develop their imaginations;
- develop creative play.

Space Shapes

Materials

- string
- liquid starch or liquid glue and water
- waxed paper
- shallow tray or bowl
- food coloring

You can add some color to your liquid starch or watered-down glue by adding some food coloring. Help the children dip pieces of string into the starch. Squeeze out the excess so the pieces don't drip, and coil the strings into different shapes on a piece of waxed paper. Let the shapes dry for an hour or two until they are stiff and then peel them off. Tie another piece of string to each dried shape and either make one large mobile with all the shapes or let each child dangle his or her own from the string. Your mobiles could even be hung outside for the wind to spin. The children might like to pretend to go on a rocket ship, and the shapes could be planets and stars they see along the way. Do any of the children think a person could ever really fly into space on a leaf mat like Lady Elaine's? Or could such a thing only happen by pretending?

1234

Mister Rogers shows several seashells. He explains how each shell is different, just as each grain of sand is different and each person is different. In the Neighborhood of Make-Believe, X the Owl has decided to *become* Benjamin Franklin, not just *pretend* to be Benjamin Franklin.

"There's No One Just Like You" can help children:

- understand and accept individual differences;
- recognize likeness and difference.

There's No One Just Like You

Materials

- plain paper
- stamp pad (or paper towels, shallow dish and waterpaints)

Everyone's fingerprints are unique. Using a stamp pad, let the children experiment by making different finger and thumbprints on their papers. If you don't have a stamp pad, you can make one using a shallow dish (meat tray), several layers of paper toweling, and a little bit of paint poured onto the towels. As the children are making their prints, let them compare the prints they make. See if they want to use the same finger to make two prints. Are the prints exactly alike? Now let them compare their prints with another child's print. Can they find the differences? Can they see the similarities? Using a separate sheet of paper, let each child make his or her thumbprint and write each child's name alongside it. You might want to hang these prints somewhere in the room so the children can look at them again and again.

1235

Mister Rogers makes a sign for Francois Clemmons' new studio. The sign has a singing mouth on it.

"Name Signs" can help children:

- recognize and use symbols.

Name Signs

Materials

- index cards or strips of paper
- markers
- stickers (optional)
- tape

As you print each child's name on a piece of paper or an index card, encourage the children to think of something they would like to use as a symbol—a star, a shape, an animal, a flower—to put on their signs as well. They could draw the symbol on the paper or choose a sticker or magazine picture to tape beside their names. They might want to have several name signs: to tape on their art work or on the boxes for their belongings, to set on the table as place cards, to hang above the hook where they hang their coats. (Use the same symbol on each sign for the same child.) Younger children, especially, will be able to recognize their signs by the symbols. Older children may be able to recognize their names, or at least the first letter of their names, as well.

(Or, 1452 "Box Puppets.")

Thoughts For The Week

Self-expression through art work is one of the ways a child shows he or she is unique. When children create something, the thoughts and feelings they express may be common ones—ones most children share—but each child expresses those thoughts and feelings in his or her own special way. Even when children start out with the same materials, each child's product will be different. When we show our appreciation of those differences, we are really showing our appreciation of that individual child. "I like what you made just the way you made it," is another way to say, "I like you just the way you are." Of course, saying those things has value only when we mean them.

Fred Rogers

Songs On The Programs This Week

1236	*"I Like to Be Told"*
	"I'm Proud of You"
1237	*"It's You I Like"*
1238	*"I'm Glad I'm the Way I Am"*
	"It's Such a Good Feeling"
	"You Are Special"
1239	*"Everybody Has a History"*
1240	*"It's Such a Good Feeling"*

Your Notes For The Week

1236

In the Neighborhood of Make-Believe, Chef Brockett believes Henrietta's rumor that Lady Elaine has found a husband, so he bakes her a wedding cake. When he learns the rumor isn't true, he turns the wedding cake into a "welcome home" cake.

"A Pretend Tea Party" can help children:

- develop creative play;
- develop their imaginations.

A Pretend Tea Party

Materials

- toy dishes and silverware
- table
- chairs
- tablecloth (optional)
- modeling dough (optional)

What do the children think you'd need to have for a pretend tea party? Who would they like to pretend is there? Parents? Friends? Favorite dolls or toy animals? You could use modeling dough for pretend food. What would they like to serve? The children may start off by following your example in pretending to eat and drink, but as the play progresses, they may have a lot of ideas of their own that they want to share with you.

(Or, 1015 "A Wedding Cake.")

1237

In the Neighborhood of Make-Believe, Lady Elaine announces she has discovered Planet Purple—a planet where everyone and everything is the same.

"Purple Paint" can help children:

- develop their imaginations;
- understand and accept individual differences.

Purple Paint

Materials

- red paint
- blue paint
- paintbrushes
- paper
- plastic margarine tubs or other containers
- spoons

Do the children know what color *purple* is? Can they find anything purple in the room? Explain that they can make purple paint by mixing two other colors together. Each one can mix his or her own in a small plastic container. Put a spoonful of red paint in each container, then a spoonful of blue paint. As the children stir the paint with paintbrushes, point out that each person's paint is a shade of purple. Are they all the same shade? They can use the paint to make Planet Purple pictures. What do they think it is like on Planet Purple where everyone and everything is the same? What would spaghetti look like? What color would toast be? Would the hamburgers be purple, too? What about everyone's clothes: Would they all be the same? Would it be any fun to be exactly the same as everybody else? All the time?

(Or, 1204 "Mixing Colors.")

1238

In the Neighborhood of Make-Believe, Lady Elaine receives a Purple Platter, then answers questions about Planet Purple. She learns that all the boys on the planet are named Paul and all the girls are named Pauline. They all wear the same clothing and eat the same foods. Lady Elaine is enthusiastic about life there, but the neighbors have their doubts—they all like being different from one another.

"Paper Dolls" can help children:

- understand and accept individual differences.

Paper Dolls

Materials

- plain paper
- scissors
- crayons or markers

What do the children think of the description of Planet Purple? Can they imagine what it would be like to be *just like* everyone else? While you are talking with the children, use the scissors and paper to cut out a series of simple paper dolls that are exactly the same. Can the children tell one from another? Encourage each child to take one and draw features and clothing. Now compare the dolls. Can they see the differences? Do those dolls seem more interesting now?

(Or, 1280 "Shape Designs.")

1239

Mister Rogers visits Francois Clemmons' music studio to watch children moving to music.

"Rhythm Exercises" can help children:

- develop coordination;
- develop muscle control.

Rhythm Exercises

Materials

- music

You can use music from a radio or record player—or you can keep a simple rhythm with a drum and a wooden spoon or by clapping your hands. You might want to try 3/4 time and tap out: *ONE*, two, three, *ONE*, two, three --; or 4/4 rhythm *ONE*, two, three, four --. Encourage the children to listen to the *rhythm* and move in different ways. Do the different rhythms make the children *want* to move in different ways. Older children may be able to skip and gallop to the rhythm. For younger children, you may want to alternate between music with a fast rhythm and a slow rhythm.

1240

Mister Rogers makes a splatter painting and learns the technique of pole dyeing from Elsie Neal.

"Pole Dyeing" can help children:

- develop their imaginations;
- learn more about their world.

Pole Dyeing

Materials

- paper towels (plain white works best)
- pencils
- string
- paint (several colors)
- brushes
- newspaper

For this activity, you'll probably want to cover your work area with newspaper. Place the point of a pencil in the center of a sheet of paper towel. Gently (but tightly) wrap the paper towel around the pencil and tie a small piece of string around it to hold the paper tight. Some of the children may be able to wrap the paper towel themselves, while others will need your help to do the wrapping and tying. Taking turns, the children can use different colors of paint on different parts of their "pole" as Elsie Neal did on today's program. Allow the paper towels to dry 30 minutes to an hour. Then take off the strings and let the children open their paper towels to see the designs.

Thoughts For The Week

*Young children may think that when they do something bad, it means they are bad **people**. They may think that good people never do bad things or have angry thoughts and feelings. Well, we know that no one is good all the time and no one is bad all the time, and that's something we need to help children understand. It can be so easy to say "bad boy!" or "bad girl!" to a child who has done something we don't like or ignored a limit we have set. But that child may really come to believe that he or she **is** bad, and that's very unhealthy. It's feeling **good** about who we are that helps us feel good about others.*

Fred Rogers

Songs On The Programs This Week

1242   "You've Got to Do It"
*1243   "Good People Sometimes Do Bad Things"
        "It's Such a Good Feeling"*

Your Notes For The Week

1241

In the Neighborhood of Make-Believe, Lady Elaine tries to make snow with an eggbeater—and she stirs up a blizzard.

"Foam Painting" can help children:

- develop their imaginations;
- develop muscle control.

Foam Painting

Materials

- soap flakes
- water
- eggbeater or electric mixer
- bowl
- dark-colored paper

You can whip up some foamy "paint" by mixing two cups of soap flakes and a cup of water. The children might enjoy taking turns using the eggbeater or watching you use the electric mixer until the foam is quite stiff. Each child can take several handfuls of foam and spread it around on dark paper. The foam will act much like fingerpaint. These paintings will have to be dried overnight before the children can hang them somewhere or take them home.

(Or, 1262 "Making Snow"; 1423 "Fingerpainting Designs.")

1242

Lady Elaine's snowstorm has covered all of Make-Believe. Reardon appears and decides to make up a winter opera. In his own neighborhood, Mister Rogers shows a way to make paper snowflakes.

"Snow Pictures" can help children:

● develop their imaginations.

Snow Pictures

Materials

● colored construction paper
● cotton balls
● liquid glue
● crayons or markers

Give each child four or five cotton balls and ask them to pull the cotton apart into little pieces. Gluing cotton pieces on colored construction paper is one way to make pictures of a snowstorm. Some of the children might want to draw a picture first and then cover it with the "snow." Can they tell you about their snow pictures? Have they ever seen real snow?

(Or, 1262 "Making Snow.")

1243

In the Neighborhood of Make-Believe, Lady Elaine decides to create a multi-colored snowstorm. She succeeds with the help of Lady Aberlin, Reardon, and Francois Clemmons, who help her make up a magic snow song.

"Multi-colored Snow" can help children:

● develop their imaginations.

Multi-colored Snow

Materials

● small pieces of sponge
● spring-type clothes pins
● shallow trays or margarine tubs
● different colors of paint
● plain paper

You can make a painting tool by clipping a spring-type clothes pin onto a little piece of sponge. By dipping the sponges into paint, the children can "print" colored snow designs on paper. Encourage the children to use each piece of sponge for one color only—exchanging with other children when they want a new color. The children might also try different ways to use the sponges: Instead of printing individual snowflakes, they could create snowstorms by smearing the sponges across the paper. Help them experiment and try out their own ideas. They may invent something we adults have never thought of.

1244

Mister Rogers shows his viewers different kinds of heaters: electric, hot water, forced-air, and an open fireplace. He also shows how an ice cube melts when placed over a heater.

"Melting Ice Cubes" can help children:

- learn more about their world;
- develop healthy curiosity;
- practice waiting.

Melting Ice Cubes

Materials

- ice cube
- small pan

Do any of the children know what happens to snow and ice when it disappears? Explain that snow and ice are really water and that when water becomes very cold it "freezes." You could mention that when it is very cold outside, the water that would normally be rain gets so cold that it freezes into snow and ice, and that when snow and ice are warmed up they become water again. To help them understand, place an ice cube in a small pan and put it on a radiator, in front of a heater, or in a sunny window. Wait about ten minutes. What happens to the ice when it is warmed up? You can put the melted ice back in the freezer for a while. What happens to it then? Add an ice cube to each child's juice at snack time today and see how much it melts.

(Or, 1020 "Making Popsicles.")

1245

The Winter Opera! Lady Aberlin plots revenge on Yoshi Ito and Francois Clemmons because they won't let her play with them. She learns the magic words for making snow and freezes them into snow people. But she can't remember how to unfreeze them. With the help of a warm pussycat she learns that even good people sometimes do bad things.

"Snow Statues" can help children:

- develop muscle control;
- develop their imaginations.

Snow Statues

Materials

- none

Yoshi Ito and Francois Clemmons were playing badminton when Lady Aberlin turned them into snow people. The children might want to pretend about various sports by acting them out. For instance:

- playing tennis;
- playing basketball;
- running a race;
- swimming in water;
- playing softball.

Let the children act out the activity until you say the word "freeze." At that time, they stop whatever they are doing and stand as still as statues. When you give the signal "unfreeze" they can continue with the pretend activity. You could do this several times and give the children a chance to imitate different sports.

(Or, 1159 "Singing Instead of Saying.")

Thoughts For The Week

To children, it may seem that machines operate on their own—starting and stopping by themselves. They may not understand that even automatic timers, clock radios, and washing machines need to be set by a person before they will operate. Children often hear the radio come on, or the washing machine change cycles, without knowing that someone had to set the dial to make the machines work. Machines that seem to work on their own can be frightening to children, so it's important to help them understand that all machines—even electronic games and computers—need a person to invent them and to make them stop and go. They're not magic.

Fred Rogers

Songs On The Programs This Week

1246 "I Like to Take My Time"
"It's Such a Good Feeling"

1247 "I'm Interested in Things"
"It's Such a Good Feeling"

1248 "It's You I Like"

1249 "What Do You Hear?"
"You Are Special"
"It's Such a Good Feeling"

1250 "Look and Listen"
"It's Such a Good Feeling"

Your Notes For The Week

1246

In the Neighborhood of Make-Believe, the telecan booth begins to go up and down by itself. X and Cousin Mary Owl put a caution sign beside it.

"Caution" can help children:

* learn more about their world;
* learn about limits.

Caution

Materials

* paper
* marker
* tape

You might begin this activity by asking the children why X the Owl and Cousin Mary put a caution sign beside the moving telecan. Can they think of objects at day care that can be dangerous at times? For instance:

* doors;
* steps;
* a stove;
* a swing set.

Make several small caution signs for the children to tape on these objects. As they do the taping, you might remind them that "caution" means they need to be very careful when they are near those objects. The children might want to place caution signs at other places where you have things that can be harmful—such as at medicine cabinets or the drawer where knives and scissors are kept.

(Or, 1431 "Safety Rules"; 1487 "Safe Toys.")

1247

Mr. McFeely doesn't feel well and is examined by a doctor. The doctor says he is just tired and needs to rest more.

"When Someone Feels Tired" can help children:

* recognize feelings;
* try out different roles.

When Someone Feels Tired

Materials

* blanket
* toy medical kit
* toy dishes
* books

Can the children think of times when they didn't feel well or were very tired? What kinds of things helped them feel better? Someone in the group could pretend to be feeling tired, and the rest of you could think of ways to help that person feel better. The children might pretend about:

* fluffing a pillow;
* covering the person with a blanket;
* reading a story;
* offering juice or toast on a tray.

What other things might help that person (no noise, soft music, being alone)? The children might want to take turns being the person who feels tired.

1248

In the Neighborhood of Make-Believe, the telecan is still not working properly. Lady Elaine prescribes magic exercises which must be performed every hour for one whole day.

"Magic Exercises" can help children:

* develop their imaginations;
* understand wishing can't make things happen;
* understand the difference between real and pretend.

Magic Exercises

Materials

* none

Lady Elaine prescribed magic exercises on today's program to get the telecan to work properly again. The children could make up their own exercises and pretend they will work magic. See what suggestions the children have. They might come up with something like:

* standing on their toes;
* clapping both hands over their heads;
* saying a magic word;
* standing on one foot;
* wishing hard;
* clapping both hands behind their backs;
* waving a magic wand.

Put the exercises together to make a simple routine and see if the children can repeat them several times. You might want to talk with the children about magic. Can these exercises really make magic? Can they think of other solutions for controlling the moving telecan in the Neighborhood of Make-Believe?

1249

Mister Rogers sets up a model of the Neighborhood of Make-Believe and asks the viewers to imagine what has happened to the moving telecan.

"Your Own Make-Believe" can help children:

- practice working cooperatively;
- develop their imaginations;
- develop creative play.

Your Own Make-Believe

Materials

- empty cardboard boxes
- tubes from paper towels or toilet paper
- art supplies (crayons, paints, markers, tape, scissors, etc.)

Encourage the children to tell you what they think has happened in the Neighborhood of Make-Believe. You might ask questions like:

- What has happened to the moving telecan?
- Did Lady Elaine's exercises help?
- How did people try to fix it?
- What is happening now?

Using the throwaways and art supplies available, help the children make a model of the Neighborhood of Make-Believe. Using the model they've made, see if the children can make up their own stories. Who's in the story? What's happening? If you have very young children they might enjoy rolling the hollow tubes or just playing nearby while you help the older children make their model.

1250

Mister Rogers looks at different kinds of mushrooms and shows a "funny-fast" film of Mr. McFeely cutting the grass.

"Funny Fast" can help children:

- develop muscle control;
- develop coordination.

Funny Fast

Materials

- music

Can any of the children pretend to do something moving quickly and jerkily like the film of Mr. McFeely? Encourage them to pretend to do something in a "funny-fast" way. For example:

- cutting the grass;
- making the bed;
- walking down the street;
- playing ball;
- eating breakfast.

See if the other children can guess what each child is doing. You could put on some music and see if the children want to pretend about "funny fast" along with the music. Ending the activity with soft music, or acting out some of the same things in very slow motion the "funny slow" way may help everyone settle down again.

Thoughts For The Week

We are all different in many ways, but sometimes children are afraid to be different because they want to be like the people they love. Some children may even come to feel there's something wrong with being different. That's why grownups need to help children learn that being different is part of what makes them special to the people who love them.

Children also need help in learning that doing something bad doesn't make you a bad person, and that the people they love can get angry at them but still go on loving them. That's a very important thing for children to know.

Fred Rogers

Songs On The Programs This Week

1251   "Look and Listen"
1252   "You are Special"
1253   "Sometimes People are Good"
1254   "I Like to Take My Time"

Your Notes For The Week

1251

Ezra Jack Keats, a writer and artist, shows Mister Rogers how he made some pages for a book. Each of his designs was an experiment, and each turned out differently.

"Food-Coloring Designs" can help children:

● develop their imaginations;

● learn to recognize likeness and difference.

Food-Coloring Designs

Materials

● a roll of white paper

● small cups or containers filled with water

● food coloring (several different colors)

● vitamin droppers or small basters

● smocks or aprons

● newspapers or other table covering

● a bowl of soapy water for cleanup

About one-half bottle of food coloring added to the water in each container makes a clear, bright color when dropped with a dropper or small baster onto a sheet of paper towel. (Some children may need your help in learning to fill the dropper.) Each child's design will be different. You might want to talk about how everyone is using the same things, but that no two people made exactly the same design. Would it be as much fun if everyone's design did come out the same?

(Or, 1280 "Shape Designs.")

1252

Mister Rogers shows some paintings drawn by children and tries to figure out what they are. He points out that children often know exactly what they plan to draw or paint, even when other people can't tell what the final picture is.

"Drawing Pictures" can help children:

- express feelings through art work;
- talk about feelings;
- learn to use words.

Drawing Pictures

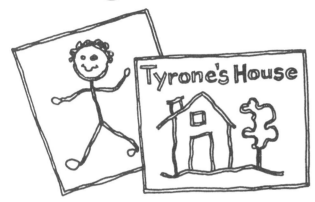

Materials

- large sheets of paper
- colored markers or crayons

Encourage the children to make drawings of their own. Not all children may want to talk about their drawings, but for those who do, write down what each child says about his or her picture. Some children might like the words on the drawings; others may want them on a separate piece of paper. Taking the time to write down what the children say about their pictures helps them feel they are being understood and makes them feel their drawings are important. You could hang the pictures up, start a looseleaf booklet for each child, or let the children take them home.

1253

Susan Linn brings her puppets to MISTER ROGERS' NEIGHBORHOOD. She is a ventriloquist who can talk for her puppets without making her lips move. She puts on a puppet show about a duck named Audrey who ruins a very special painting and is afraid to tell anyone what she did.

"Talking about Feelings" can help children:

- talk about feelings;
- understand and accept individual differences.

Talking about Feelings

Materials

- none

Audrey Duck felt afraid after she ruined the painting. Can you remember a time when you felt that way and share it with the children? It can be reassuring for children to know that adults have these feelings, too, and can talk about them. Ask them how they feel when they do something they think is bad. You could ask questions like:

- Did you ever do something that you thought was bad?
- How did you feel when you thought someone might find out?
- What did you think would happen when someone did find out?

Some children may want to talk about the bad things they've done, but you can help them remember good things they've done, too. It's important for children to learn that the very same people who do good things sometimes, are the very same people who do bad things sometimes.

1254

In the Neighborhood of Make-Believe, Bob Dog feels left out because Queen Sara spends so much time with Prince Tuesday.

"Making Modeling Dough" can help children:
- practice working cooperatively;
- practicing sharing.

Making Modeling Dough

Materials
- 2 cups flour
- 1 cup salt
- ½ cup colored water (food coloring works well)
- large mixing bowl

Children usually like to help as much as they can. In this activity, each child can have a special job: One can mix the flour and salt; another can help you color the water; all the children can take turns stirring and kneading. (Add more water as needed.) Before passing out the modeling dough, you may want to remind the children to stay at a certain table when playing with the dough. Divide the dough equally among the children, leaving none for yourself. Can the children think of ways for you to have some dough, too? A way that everyone will have some? (Of course some children may not feel ready to share.) When it's time to put all the dough back together, you can remind the children that they can use it again at another time.

Please Note: Toddlers might be tempted to eat modeling dough, so if there's a chance they may be around when the dough is used, it may be better to lower the salt content. The salt makes the texture coarse; otherwise, the flour and water mixture is like a paste. You may want to experiment to see how much salt is needed to get a consistency that works well for your needs.

1255

Mister Rogers shows that an egg changes when it is cooked, even though it is still an egg.

"Egg Salad Sandwiches" can help children:
- learn more about foods.

Egg Salad Sandwiches

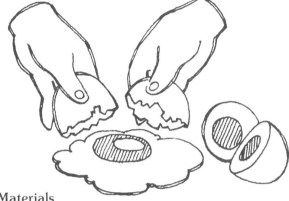

Materials
- eggs
- saucepan
- mixing bowl
- fork or potato masher
- mayonnaise
- bread
- crayons (optional)

You might start this activity by giving each child an egg that has been marked in crayon with his or her initials. When the children have put their eggs in a pan of cold water, hardboil the eggs and then cool them immediately in cold water. (You might want to crack a raw egg for comparison.) Help the children peel their own eggs, and then they can take turns mashing them all in a bowl. Add mayonnaise and mix. Each child can make his or her own sandwich. You may need some other sandwich fillings on hand for those who don't like egg salad. How do the children feel about making their very own real sandwiches?

(Or, 1098 "Eggshell Pictures"; 1415 "Egg Drop Soup.")

Thoughts For The Week

*Growing up takes time. Sometimes children get tired of waiting to be a grownup—tired of being small and not being able to do things that grownups do well. You can help them learn that there are a lot of things they **already** do well, and that with practice, they can learn to do other things well, too. Some activities, though, are only for grownups to do—like working with dangerous tools. It **is** hard to wait. Growing **does** take time. But children can do it and feel good about it, too.*

Fred Rogers

Songs On The Programs This Week

1256 *"Good People Sometimes Do Bad Things"*
1257 *"Let's Be Together Today"*
1258 *"Look and Listen"*
1259 *"A Handy Lady and a Handy Man"*

Your Notes For The Week

1256

Lady Elaine Fairchilde tries to use her magic to clean up the purple on Grandpere's french-fry sign. Her magic doesn't work, but the soap and water does. Children often make messes, sometimes purposely, sometimes by accident.

"Soapsuds Fingerpainting" can help children:

- learn to do things independently;
- practice working cooperatively.

Soapsuds Fingerpainting

Materials

- soapsuds fingerpaint (recipe on page A-2)
- food coloring
- sponges or small rags
- water for cleaning up
- cookie sheet or trays

Ordinary fingerpainting can be a messy activity, but soapsuds fingerpaint cleans up easily. The children can "paint" on cookie sheets or trays with the soapsuds. You may have to remind them to keep the "paint" on their trays. Then you can all work together to clean up the mess. Everyone can clean up his or her own space or each one can take a job to do. Encourage the children to help clean up after other activities, too:

- at snack and meal times;
- after art projects;
- whenever toys are put away;
- before going home.

You can make cleanup time a part of your daily routine.

1257

Mister Rogers talks about balancing things and watches two ballet dancers perform. When children grow, they often go through periods of feeling awkward and clumsy.

"Balancing Blocks" can help children:

- develop coordination;
- develop muscle control;
- develop the ability to keep on trying.

Balancing Blocks

Materials
- building blocks

How high can the children make a stack of blocks? When everyone has had a chance, the children can try balancing blocks in one hand. Can they balance more than one block at a time? Or make the blocks dance by moving their hands? You can try doing some balancing exercises with them:

- standing on tiptoes and counting to ten;
- standing on one foot and then on the other;
- hopping up and down on one foot and then on the other;
- jumping in the air and landing on both feet without falling.

This might be a good time to talk about practicing: To do something well, you have to "do it, do it, do it." (You might want to read or sing the words to Mister Rogers' song, "You've Got to Do It.")

1258

Mister Rogers invents a "hidden objects" game— seeing, feeling, and listening are good ways to find out about things.

"Guess What's in the Bag" can help children:

- recognize likeness and difference;
- develop the ability to keep on trying.

Guess What's in the Bag

Materials
- pillowcase or "McFeely Box" (see page B-3)
- common household objects (examples: comb, brush, pencil, toothbrush, clothespin, spoon, ball, block, crayon)

Put everything into the pillowcase. (If you have very young children, you could show them the objects first to make sure they know what they are.) Let each child reach into the case, feel an object without looking at it, and then try to guess what it is. Why do they think so?

- Did anyone think a crayon was a pencil?
- How are crayons and pencils alike?

You can remind them how Mrs. McFeely fooled Mister Rogers by leaving the wrapper on a bar of soap. (Mister Rogers thought it was something else.) What's important is for the children to think carefully about what their fingers are telling them—not whether they guess right or wrong. It's the trying that's the most important.

1259

Lady Aberlin helps Handyman Negri with his repair work. Children often like to help with grownup jobs.

"Fixing Things" can help children:

- practice working cooperatively.

Fixing Things

Materials

- anything broken that can be fixed with glue or tape (toys, books, doll furniture, small chairs, etc.)
- glue
- tape

Children can do things to help, but they like to watch grownup activities, too. In looking for things that need to be fixed, you may find some that need hammer and nails or needle and thread. This could be a good chance to emphasize that some tools are for grownups to use or to be used only with a grownup's help. For those things that can be fixed with glue or tape, you might encourage the children to help by:

- figuring out how the broken pieces might fit together again;
- holding the pieces so that another child might tape them together;
- holding the broken pieces in place while the glue dries.

1260

Mister Rogers and Elsie Neal mold a horse and rider from a piece of clay. Mister Rogers reminds the children that their bodies are all one piece and that "everything grows together."

"Puzzles" can help children:

- practice working cooperatively;
- learn more about their bodies.

Puzzles

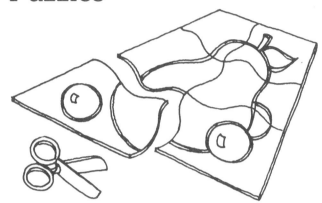

Materials

- pictures of cars, toys, or other objects
- blunt-nosed scissors
- construction paper
- glue

In making your own picture puzzle, it's best to choose pictures of cars, toys, or other objects. (Some children may feel anxious about cutting up pictures of people or animals.) Each child can glue a whole picture onto heavy paper, or you can all work together on one picture. After the glue has dried, you and the children can cut the picture into five or six pieces. Then you can mix up the pieces and let the children try to put them back together again. This might be a good time to act out the words to Mister Rogers' song: "Everything Grows Together." Puzzles can be taken apart and put together, but our bodies are all one piece.

Can the children bring you anything from home that you'll need for next week's activities? Particularly old clothing for Program 1261!

Thoughts For The Week

Children need to pretend. It's a good way for them to find out about themselves—how they're different from the people they pretend to be and how they're like those people. Most children can't use words as well as grownups, so they often use play or "pretending" to express their feelings.

Sometimes when children feel angry, they feel like cutting or tearing things. That's when grownups need to set limits! A caregiver once told me how she learned about the need for setting limits. She gave an angry child some old newspapers to tear up—thinking it would help that child let off some steam. But the child's tearing became so out of control that he began tearing everything he saw, including some of the other children's paintings. Children's destructive behavior can be very frightening to them. Setting limits for them and helping them understand the reason for those limits is one of the caregiver's best ways to help children learn self-control.

Fred Rogers

Songs On The Programs This Week

1261 "Good People Sometimes Do Bad Things"
1262 "I Like to Take My Time"
1263 "What Do You Do?"
1264 "Ornithorhynchus Anatinus"
1265 "You Are You"

Your Notes For The Week

1261

Mister Rogers tries on a Santa Claus outfit. It's a little big for him, but when Chef Brockett tries it on, it fits him just right.

"Dress-up" can help children:

- understand the difference between real and pretend;
- try out different roles.

Dress-up

Materials

- dress-up clothes
- purses, jewelry, hats (see "Recipes and How-To's" for props you can make)

Offer the children different dress-up clothes to use in their pretending. See which ones the children choose and who they want to pretend to be. What kinds of things would that person do or say? Are there other kinds of people they would like to pretend to be? (Firefighters? Doctors? Lettercarriers? Chefs? Farmers?) Maybe some of the children would like to talk about their parents' jobs. What kinds of clothes or props would they need for those jobs?

1262

Mister Rogers visits a barber and gets a haircut. He reminds the children that barbers cut *only hair*, and that cutting hair doesn't hurt. Lady Elaine Fairchilde feels like cutting Santa's beard and Prince Tuesday's hair, but Santa shows her how to cut paper instead.

"Making Snow" can help children:

● develop coordination.

Making Snow

Materials

● blunt-nosed scissors
● strips of paper
● watered-down glue
● construction paper
● brushes or cotton swabs

Lady Elaine had fun making snow with magic, and you and the children can make snow by snipping or tearing little pieces off strips of paper. The children might enjoy gluing confetti of all colors onto colored construction paper. They can paint the watered-down glue on the paper first and then sprinkle the confetti over it.

1263

Mister Rogers talks about rules and why we need them. Lady Elaine finds out why King Friday made the Mitten Rule. Children often wonder why grownups set limits that seem "unreasonable."

"Talking about Limits" can help children:

● learn about limits.

Talking about Limits

Materials

● none

Lady Elaine thought King Friday's Mitten Rule was a silly one until the hand-freezing breeze came along. What did Lady Elaine think then? Good rules are limits on behavior for health, safety, or fairness. Ask the children to tell you some of the limits you have at day care. Ask them why they think that grownups set limits about:

● using scissors and other tools;
● cutting up books or clothing;
● crossing streets;
● what things can be eaten;
● when children have to go to bed.

What are some of the limits the children have at home? You might want to point out that different families set different limits. Some limits are for children and adults as well—rules about traffic lights and crosswalks. Are there other limits or rules the children think would be good for everyone?

Thursday

1264

Mister Rogers shows a slow-motion film of animals running and flying. In the Neighborhood of Make-Believe, Lady Aberlin and Bob Dog are looking for a seagull.

"Seagulls" can help children:

- express feelings through music;
- express feelings through movement and dance;
- develop their imaginations.

Seagulls

Materials

- white paper
- blunt-nosed scissors
- string
- tape or stapler
- music

See if the children can cut or tear white paper into shapes that could represent seagulls. Any kinds of shapes will do. Using tape or staples, fasten strings to the seagulls so the children can make them fly. See what different kinds of music you can find on the radio, and encourage the children to move the seagulls with the music. Some children may want to pretend to be seagulls themselves and move their whole bodies with the music. What other birds or animals might they pretend to be? Ending this activity with soft music can help the children get the sense of real seagulls flying in a calm sky.

Friday

1265

Today is the opening of Chef Brockett's Soda Shop right beside his bakery. Eric Kloss, a gifted saxophonist who is blind, plays "You Are You," a song written by Mister Rogers for the special occasion.

"Chef Brockett's Concoction" can help children:

- learn more about foods.

Chef Brockett's Concoction

Materials

- strawberries
- bananas
- wheat germ
- milk
- butter knife
- potato masher
- eggbeater or blender
- bowl

For this activity, you'll need two cups of fresh strawberries (or one unfrozen package) for the children to mash up with a potato masher. Using a butter knife, older children may be able to cut banana slices—enough to fill one cup. Then with an eggbeater or blender, combine the strawberries and bananas, adding one-half cup of wheat germ and one cup of milk, a little at a time. The children might want to pretend about being at a soda shop while they drink their fruit concoctions.

Thoughts For The Week

One of the most important things for growing children to learn is that each person is important and valuable, and that a person's value doesn't come from possessions or even special talents or abilities. Children may be concerned, for instance, about how a particular sweater fits, especially if that sweater once belonged to someone else. A child may even wonder if wearing someone else's clothes could change who he or she is. We need to help children learn that although clothes may be important, it's the person inside that really counts.

Fred Rogers

Songs On The Programs This Week

1266   *"It's You I Like"*
1267   *"You Are Special"*
1268   *"You've Got to Do It"*
          "What Do You Do?"
1269   *"Everybody's Fancy"*
          "Good People Sometimes Do Bad Things"
1270   *"I'm a Man Who Manufactures"*

Your Notes For The Week

1266

Francois Clemmons and Yoshi Ito practice singing loudly and softly.

"Loud and Quiet" can help children:

- develop self-control;
- use play to work on feelings.

Loud and Quiet

Materials

- metal pans
- wooden spoons

Can the children think of things that make loud sounds? What sorts of things make quiet sounds? See what kinds of sounds the children can make with the pans and spoons. Can they make quiet as well as loud sounds? Ask them to try using their voices to make loud sounds, then quiet sounds. How do the children feel about the difference between loud sounds and quiet sounds? Which are easier to make? Can they think of sounds that are scary? Are they loud sounds or quiet sounds? There are some days that adults just can't stand loud noises. If you're having a day like that, save the pans and spoons (and the soft and *loud*) for another time.

(Or, 1146 "Quiet Please.")

1267

Henrietta Pussycat gives Queen Sara the hand-me-down hat that didn't fit her. It fits Queen Sara just right.

"Headbands That Fit" can help children:

● develop creative play.

Headbands That Fit

Materials

● strips of construction paper about four inches wide
● blunt-nosed scissors
● tape
● scrap materials (scrap paper, yarn, buttons, feathers, etc.)

Most children will need two strips of paper, taped together, to make a headband that fits. Each child can decorate the headband in his or her own special way, even using scissors to make points or a fringe along the top edge. When the decorations are finished, you can fit each headband to the child's head and tape the ends, overlapping as much as necessary.

1268

Mister Rogers tells about a time when he was little and he accidentally hit another child. He also talks about mad feelings and sings the song "What Do You Do?"

"Angry Feelings" can help children:

● talk about feelings;
● express strong feelings in appropriate ways.

Angry Feelings

Materials

● paper
● pencil, pen or marker

Can you share an experience that you had when you hurt someone, telling the children how you felt afterwards? What did you do about it? Some of the children may be able to tell you of a time like that that they remember.

● How did they feel afterwards?
● What did the other person do?
● How do they think that person felt?

Sometimes people hurt other people when they're angry. Ask the children to tell you some other things people can do when they're mad—things that don't hurt anybody. On your paper, list the things that the children mention. Keep the list you've made handy and go over it from time to time with the children, particularly on a day when someone is having angry feelings. (You might want to read or sing the words to Mister Rogers' song, "What Do You Do?")

1269

Mister Rogers taps rhythms on the floor, on the chairs, and on a drum.

"Drum Rhythms" can help children:

● express feelings through music;

● express strong feelings in appropriate ways.

Drum Rhythms

Materials

● coffee cans or empty boxes

Let the children experiment with drumming sounds and different rhythms. Do they remember the sounds they made with pans and wooden spoons (#1266)? Ask them to pound hard, then softly, to pound fast, then slowly. Which sounds made them think of angry feelings? Ask them how they would play the drums if they were angry. Or happy. You might want to remind them that they can also use words to *say* they're angry or happy or sad. Maybe they can think of words to go along with their drumming and use them as a chant.

1270

Corney needs X the Owl's help to make a swing for King Friday. In the real neighborhood the telephone repairman comes to fix Mister Rogers' phone and explains how a phone works.

"Telephones" can help children:

● practice working cooperatively;

● develop creative play.

Telephones

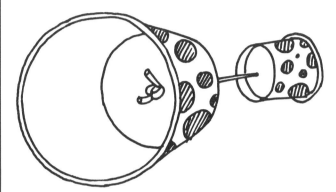

Materials

● frozen juice can or paper cups

● heavy string cut in roughly three-foot lengths

The children may be able to help hold the cans while you make holes in the bottom of each one. They could probably thread the string through the holes while you tie the knots inside the cans. You might want to make a couple of "telephones" so there will be enough to go around. (The telephones work best when the string is as tight as possible.) The most important parts of a telephone call are the people who are talking—just like the most important parts of day care are the children and you!

Thoughts For The Week

Sometimes it's hard for children to sort out what's real from what's pretend. Talking with a grownup can help them learn the difference, and then scary things like monsters may not seem so frightening. Children sometimes use imaginary friends to help them pretend—especially about strong feelings. These imaginary friends seem to appear when they're needed, stay with a child for a while, and then disappear as quickly as they came. For many children, these "friends" are a natural and healthy part of growing even though they can be perplexing for these children's caregivers!

*When children think about growing up, they sometimes feel they'd like to marry their moms or dads. That's because their moms and dads are so special to them. We can let them know that although they won't marry their moms and dads, they can grow into women and men who will find other people who are special to them in a different way. We need to let our children know we understand these kinds of feelings, just as we need to let them know what they can really expect to happen—and **not** happen—as they go on growing.*

Fred Rogers

Songs On The Programs This Week

1271	"Pretending"
1272	"Pretending"
1273	"I Did Too"
1274	"Everybody's Fancy"
1275	"Everybody Has a History" "Please Don't Think It's Funny"

Your Notes For The Week

1271

Daniel Striped Tiger's imaginary friend, Malcolm Apricot Dinko, is a source of help to Daniel when he's scared. Daniel is afraid of staying overnight at Grandpere's. He wonders if he will find monsters there, but he learns that monsters are just imaginary.

"An Imaginary Person" can help children:

- use play to work on feelings;
- understand the difference between real and pretend.

An Imaginary Person

Materials

- none

What can the children tell you about Malcolm Apricot Dinko? Is he real or pretend? Do any of the children have an imaginary friend they'd like to tell you about? See if the children would like to make up an imaginary person together. You can get them started by asking questions such as:

- Does your friend have hair?
- Is it a boy or girl?
- What are the clothes like?
- What does it use for shoes?
- How does it talk?

Ask them to think of a name for their person. Some children may want to make up stories about the imaginary person or draw a picture of it. This could be a good time to talk about other things that are only pretend.

1272

Mister Rogers pretends about bedtime. He tries on a nightshirt and shows how he used a blanket and toy animals for pretend when he was little.

"Making Doll Beds" can help children:

● use play to work on feelings.

Making Doll Beds

Materials

● dolls or stuffed animals
● boxes of different sizes
● pieces of material or old baby blankets

Folded-up pieces of material can serve as mattresses and pillows for the doll beds. While the children are making the beds, some might want to talk about what they do to get ready for bed at home. Do any of them have special blankets or toys to use at bedtime? Is there a special bedtime song or story they like? The children can play "bedtime" with their dolls and toy animals. If you have toy baby bottles, they might like to use them for pretend, too.

(Or, 1120 "Pretending about Bedtime.")

1273

Robert Troll plays the harmonica and makes Donkey Hodie's vegetables grow so fast that he needs help to pick them.

"Planting Beans" can help children:

● learn more about growing;
● practice waiting.

Planting Beans

Materials

● crayon or marker
● paper cups
● dirt
● water
● bean seeds
● spoons

Can any of the children tell you what is needed to make plants grow? What kinds of things do children need to grow? Write the children's names on paper cups, then help them:

● Spoon dirt into the cups.
● Plant the bean seeds.
● Water the seeds.

(You might want to plant seeds in an extra cup or two in case someone's seeds don't grow.)
By measuring how much their seeds have sprouted each week, the children can see that growing takes time. What kinds of changes take place as a plant grows?

● A small sprout pops out of the dirt.
● The sprout gets taller.
● Leaves begin to grow on the stem.

Can the children tell you what kinds of changes take place as a child grows?

(Or, 1078 "Growing.")

1274

Mister Rogers shows a film about different kinds of cows. He visits the McFeelys' house and watches Mrs. McFeely milk a cow. Mister Rogers and Francois Clemmons sing a song about the sounds animals make.

"Animal Sounds" can help children:

- learn more about their world;
- learn to listen carefully.

Animal Sounds

Materials

- paper
- pencil, pen or marker

Ask the children to say the names of some animals while you make a list. Let them take turns making the sound that each animal on the list makes. Are there different ways to sound like the same animal (bow-wow; woof, woof; or arf, arf)? The children might want to try talking to one another using animal sounds and words the way Henrietta Pussycat talks. ("Meow don't feel like meow meow today.") Can they guess what that kind of talk really means? This might be a good time for everyone to sing "Old MacDonald."

(Or, 1110 "Pretend Animals.")

1275

Mister Rogers arranges toy animals and matches baby animals to their mothers. He sings the song, "Everybody Has a History," and talks about growing up.

"My History" can help children:

- learn more about growing;
- develop their memory.

Everybody Has A History

Materials

- none

Ask the children if they remember anything about being babies. Can they imagine what it was like when they couldn't talk at all? What can babies do? Some of the children may be able to pretend to grow up little by little—first being babies that crawl, then stand, then walk. How about being older children—toddlers who are learning to talk and learning to run? Are there things they specially like about being their real ages? You might want to end this activity by going over the words to Mister Rogers' song, "Everybody Has a History," encouraging the children to act out the words when possible.

Thoughts For The Week

Children sometimes feel left out when a new baby comes to their house or when a new child comes to day care. They often wonder if they are still special when they see the new one getting extra attention. An important way that you, as a grownup, can help, is to find ways to let the children talk about those feelings. Some children may find talking about these strong feelings too difficult. One preschool teacher told me about a little girl who drew about her feelings. She drew a picture of her new brother called "The Hand of the Monster," showing a large hand grabbing at a little blob of paint. That was her way of communicating the feelings she had. She let her teacher know that she was pretty angry about that new baby's arrival— and also that she was struggling with the anger inside herself. Later that year she drew another picture for her little brother—a family portrait. By helping each child find out how he or she is special, you can help all the children see that everyone has a special place that no one else can take away. Each person is special for being just who he or she is.

Fred Rogers

Songs On The Programs This Week

1276 "*You Are Special*"
1277 "*Look and Listen*"
     "*When a New Baby Comes to Your House*"
1278 "*Children Can*"
     "*You Are You*"
1279 "*You are Special*
     "*There Are Many Ways*"
1280 "*Everybody's Fancy*"

Your Notes For The Week

1276

Mister Rogers talks about the similarities and differences in words. Chef Brockett shows Mister Rogers his personalized cakes with names on them. "Name Cards" can help children:

- recognize likeness and difference;
- recognize and use symbols.

Name Cards

Materials

- crayons or markers
- paper for name cards

As you write each child's name on a card, talk about the similarities and differences.

- Which names, if any, start with the same letter?
- Are other letters the same?
- Do any of the children have the same name? If so, how do they feel about it?
- Do any of the children's names rhyme?

If some first names are the same, you might want to add the last name or initial on the card and talk about how the *last* names are different. You could ask the children if they think anyone in the world might have exactly the same name that they have. Would the two of them be the same person? In what ways might they be different (likes, dislikes, parents, birthdays)? You may want to keep the name cards handy and use them often at snack or lunch time to give each child a place of his or her own.

1277

Lady Aberlin finds out that it was Lady Elaine, dressed in a purple cow costume, who ruined Harriett Elizabeth Cow's cake with a downpour of milk from the sky. Lady Elaine was jealous because Harriet was new to the neighborhood, and everyone seemed to pay more attention to Harriet than to her.

"Feeling Jealous" can help children:

* talk about feelings.

Feeling Jealous

Materials

* none

Maybe you can think of a time when you felt jealous or left out, and you could share it with the children. Some of the children may have younger brothers or sisters. How did they feel when that new baby came home? When a new child comes to day care, the children may experience similar feelings.

* How do they feel about the extra time you need to spend at first with a new child?
* Can they remember when they first came to day care?
* What feelings did they have?

The children may enjoy hearing you read or sing the words to Mister Rogers' song, "When a Baby Comes to Your House."

1278

Mister Rogers makes a box from folded cardboard and builds with wooden blocks. He shows a film about children building with blocks and sings the song, "Children Can."

"Look What I Built" can help children:

* develop creative play.

Look What I Built

Materials

* several wooden or cardboard blocks (see page B-1).

After the children have been working for a while, see if they'd like to tell you things they've built. What kinds of ideas did they have? Do they need any other toys to finish their play (little people, cars, airplanes, etc.)? Some children may want to make up a story about the things they've built, but others may not want to share their play ideas yet. Sometimes children find it hard to tear down their buildings. Taking a photograph, or encouraging them to draw what they build is a way for them to "keep" the buildings.

(Or, 1397 "Pretending with Boxes.")

Thursday

1279

Mister Rogers shows rubbings of different items and a Braille book.

"Rubbings" can help children:

● learn to look carefully.

Rubbings

Materials

● paper (thin paper works best)
● crayons
● pennies, leaves, paper clips, rubber bands, etc.

Show the children how to place the object under the paper and color over it with crayons, making the outline of the shape appear. Let them try making rubbings with all of the objects. At the end, can they match the rubbings to the actual objects?

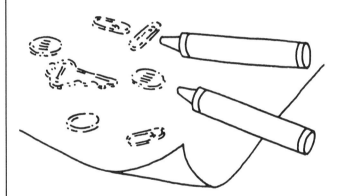

Friday

1280

Mister Rogers makes designs with pieces of felt on a flannel board, and shows a film of designs made from paper shapes.

"Shape Designs" can help children:

● recognize likeness and difference;
● understand and accept individual differences.

Shape Designs

Materials

● paper
● glue or paste
● pieces of yarn
● paper shapes (several circles, squares, triangles, rectangles, long strips—all of different sizes and colors)

You could start this activity by talking about ways the paper shapes are alike and ways they are different. Some are the same color but may be different shapes or sizes. Others are the same shape, but may be different in color or size. How many differences can the children find? While the children are gluing the shapes on paper, you might point out that everyone's ideas are different, and so each picture will be different, too.

Thoughts For The Week

*There are naturally things that children aren't able to do; but there are many things that they **can** do. Sometimes they need a grownup to remind them about the things they do well and to help them see that they can learn to do new things, too. Trying new things is hard, but with a grownup's help, children can try and can learn, each in his or her own way.*

Every child is different and all children have their own good ideas. That's why it's important for grownups to listen to children's ideas and encourage them to try out their healthy ideas by building, painting, making up stories, using a special talent.

Fred Rogers

Songs On The Programs This Week

1281 *"There Are Many Ways"*
       "Everybody's Fancy"
1282 *"I Like to Take My Time"*
1283 *"Children Can"*
1284 *"You Are You"*
1285 *"I Like to Be Told"*
       "Troglodytes Aedon"

Your Notes For The Week

1281

Today is the day of the Neighborhood Variety Show. Everyone takes part in some way—by performing in the show, helping make signs, or being a member of the audience.

"Variety Show" can help children:
- feel proud of their accomplishments.

Variety Show

Materials
- paper
- markers

You might want to talk about the Neighborhood Variety Show:
- Do the children know what "variety" means?
- Can they remember any of the performances?
- What had to be done to get ready for the show?
- What did the spectators do?

Encourage the children to think of things each of them would like to do for your Variety Show—things like singing, dancing, drumming rhythms, doing a pantomime, showing their art work, making signs, setting up chairs, or being in the audience. This could be a good time to invite parents to visit and watch the show, too. Try to plan a time when all the parents could visit. You and the children might prepare a simple snack for the visit, or you could suggest a potluck dinner and ask parents to bring a dish to eat and share after work. You might want to plan the Variety Show a week or so in advance so everyone has ample time to plan ahead. And when you do have your show, it's important for everyone to remember that it's a Variety *Show* NOT a contest. Each person's contribution is as valuable as another's.

1282

Lady Aberlin and Bob Dog are frightened at first by a new visitor from Planet Purple. When they find out it is friendly Purple Panda and learn that he's looking for Lady Elaine, Bob Dog realizes there's no reason to bark at him.

"I Used to Be Afraid" can help children:

- recognize feelings;
- talk about feelings.

I Used to Be Afraid

Materials

- none

What used to frighten you when you were a child? Can you tell the children about it and how you worked on your fear? Ask them what kinds of things used to frighten them that don't anymore. What made the difference? This kind of talk can let children know that the grownups they trust can comfort them when they're afraid, and can help them understand about things that frighten them.

(Or, 1175 "Scary Sounds"; 1123 "A Vacuum Cleaner.")

1283

Mister Rogers pretends about horses, then visits the McFeely's house where there is a *real* horse. He learns that horses are measured in hand units even though most things are measured with a yardstick or tape measure.

"How You Are Growing" can help children:

- learn more about growing;
- understand and accept individual differences.

How You Are Growing

Materials

- yardstick or tape measure
- long strip of paper (four feet long)
- tags (four inches long by one inch wide)
- tape
- pen, pencil or marker

Children's outside growing can be measured by hanging a growth chart on a wall or bringing it out every month or two to show the children how much they've grown. But it's just as important for children to see how much they are growing "inside." On the growth chart, in addition to the child's height, you could add tags marking special events. Some events you might hang tags for are:

- John can say his whole name.
- Sarah sometimes shares her toys.
- Chris caught a ball.
- Tina moved to a new house.
- Rick tied his shoelaces.
- Curtis has a new baby brother.

You and the children will think of other ways they are growing from time to time.

1284

Purple Panda breaks a Planet Purple rule by rocking in a rocking chair and is not allowed to return to Planet Purple. Mister Rogers says he's glad he doesn't live on Planet Purple where everyone's the same. He likes being different, and the people who like us best are the ones who like our differences.

"I'm Thinking of a Child" can help children:

- understand and accept individual differences;
- recognize likeness and difference.

I'm Thinking of a Child

Materials

- none

It may be best for you to lead this game—at least at the start. Think of one particular child and give clues by describing something about that child. For instance:

- age;
- hair color, eye color;
- likes, dislikes;
- kinds of things he or she helps people do.

If you mention clothes or other things that change from day to day, try also to include something that's special about the child. Add clues until the other children can guess who the person is. (Remember that children may be sensitive about unusual physical differences.)

(Or, 1238 "Paper Dolls.")

1285

King Friday has a wooden bird on a stick that he calls by its formal name, Troglodytes Aedon.

"Stick Puppets" can help children:

- develop their imaginations;
- develop creative play.

Stick Puppets

Materials

- popsicle sticks, chopsticks, small dowels cut into seven-inch lengths or unsharpened pencils
- construction paper or thin cardboard
- crayons or markers
- blunt-nosed scissors
- scrap materials
- magazine pictures of animals

Here's a way your children can make stick puppets to use in their pretending. On their paper or cardboard, older children may want to draw their own animal or person puppets. Younger children may want to choose a magazine picture of an animal to glue onto their paper or cardboard. Each child can then glue their picture onto a stick. The children might enjoy making up names for their puppets, even having their puppets sing a song.

(Or, 1169 "Make a Birdfeeder.")

Thoughts For The Week

Sometimes it's hard for children to talk about their feelings. It can be easier for them to express what they feel when they pretend that someone else has those feelings, someone like an imaginary friend or a puppet. Pretending to be someone else or making up stories are other ways to express feelings.

To do something well, you have to practice it. Children have to practice things like standing, walking, talking, running, skipping, building with blocks. Children often like to know that grownups, too, have to study and practice very hard to learn to do new things like typing on a typewriter or flying an airplane. If we want to do something really well, we all have to practice again and again.

Fred Rogers

Songs On The Programs This Week

1286　"Everybody Has a History"
　　　"Pretending"
1289　"You've Got to Do It"
　　　"Walking Giraffe"
　　　"Everybody Has a History"

Your Notes For The Week

1286

The Browns are preparing a marionette show about three little pigs. They show Mister Rogers the marionettes and the set for the production.

"Puppet Play" can help children:

- develop their imaginations;
- develop creative play;
- talk about feelings.

Puppet Play

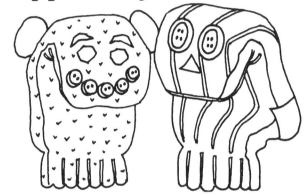

Materials
- puppets (1409 "Sock Puppets" or 1389 "Paper Bag Puppets")

It's best to begin this activity by introducing each puppet to the children before putting it on your hand. The following sequence often works well:

- First, talk to the children *about* the puppet—what it is, what it's made of, how it feels, what kind of puppet it might be.
- Then you can slip the puppet on your hand and begin talking *to* the puppet—telling it about the children or what has been happening.
- As the children become more interested in the puppet's reactions than in what you're saying, you can begin talking *for* the puppet—answering the questions you ask and turning the puppet to talk with the children as well.

Encourage the children to try on the puppets and pretend to be the puppet characters. You can support this play by continuing to talk to the puppet while the child holds it. Some children may even begin talking to one another through the puppets.

1287

King Friday is making plans to buy an airplane by looking at airplane catalogues and talking with an airplane salesman.

"Buying Groceries" can help children:

● learn more about money;

● practice making choices.

Buying Groceries

Materials

● paper

● pencil

Ask the children if they know where and how we get our food. Some of them may not understand that when we buy it at a store each item costs money. Talk about the things you need to buy at the grocery store. You might want to make a list of the foods you will need for the children's lunches and snacks. If you only had enough money to buy one or two things, can each child tell you which items they would choose to buy? If it's possible, visit a small grocery store. Let the children help select the items. They may want to show you some of the things their parents buy to eat. Are there other times when the children could help you plan about buying things (getting supplies like paper and crayons)? The older children might be interested in hearing how much money certain items cost; it may help them understand that prices of things influence the choices we make.

1288

Mister Rogers sees three live piglets at the McFeelys' house, then watches the Browns' marionette production, "The Three Little Pigs."

"Making Up Stories" can help children:

● develop their imaginations.

Making Up Stories

Materials

● paper

● pencil or marker

If some of the children have trouble getting started on a story, it might be helpful to suggest a theme — even their own version of "The Three Little Pigs" (maybe "The Three Little Carrots"). You might find a "group story" works best, with each person adding his or her ideas to the story. How about writing the story (or stories) down and making a book? The children might like to draw pictures for the book and share it with their parents. The children will be able to sense the adults' delight in their "creations." Your "Three Little Carrots" might turn out to be every bit as whimsical as "The Three Little Pigs." Younger children may enjoy activity 1410 "Homemade Marionettes."

(Or, 1153 "Nursery Rhymes"; 1390 "Let's Tell a Story.")

1289

When King Friday's Royal Airplane is delivered, he expects Handyman Negri and Edgar Cooke to be the pilots—just by reading the flight manual. Pilot Ito helps the King understand that flying an airplane takes lots of practice.

"Practicing" can help children:

- develop the ability to keep on trying;
- feel proud of their accomplishments;
- practice making choices.

Practicing

Materials

- none

Is there something that you do well? How long did it take you to learn to do it? Can you share that experience with the children? Ask them if they can remember learning something that took a lot of practice (riding a trike, going up and down stairs, feeding themselves). Can they remember how it felt when they were just learning to do it? How did they feel after they had learned it? Can they think of some things they'd like to be able to do? Talk about how much practicing it would take. (Learning to whistle may not take as long as learning to play a trumpet.) Let them choose a skill they could practice for a week.

Three and four year olds could practice:

- going up and down stairs;
- winking one eye;
- pouring from a small pitcher.

Four and five year olds could practice:

- standing on one foot;
- buttoning or zipping a jacket;
- putting on a coat.

Five and six year olds could practice:

- whistling;
- tying a shoe;
- snapping their fingers.

Next week you could talk with the children about the progress they're making.

1290

Marcel Marceau is a famous mime who visits Mister Rogers and performs for King Friday. He pantomimes walking up stairs, walking in the wind, eating french fries, chasing butterflies, and other actions.

"Pantomime" can help children:

- develop their imaginations;
- learn different ways people communicate.

Pantomime

Materials

- none

You might want to start this activity by doing several gestures all together until the children begin to feel comfortable. Here are some simple ones:

- eating an ice cream cone;
- brushing your teeth;
- going to bed;
- combing your hair;
- sweeping the floor.

Can any of the children think up their own? Each child who wants to try can perform and let the others guess what the pantomime is.

(Or, 1121 "Say It Without Words.")

Thoughts For The Week

Birthdays are meant to be special days that celebrate a person's birth into this world and times to express the joys and good feelings we have toward each other. But birthdays can often be overwhelming, especially to the child whose day is being celebrated. When children receive too much of anything at one time, for example, they may feel they can never be good enough to make up for all they have received. And we have all probably seen big, fancy birthday parties that turned into such overexciting events that there were tears and conflicts. We grownups can help keep birthdays and other holidays manageable and happy times by finding simple ways for children to feel special on those occasions. Just giving a child the chance to make some decisions that adults make—what to eat, where to go, what to do—can often be one of the best birthday presents of all.

Fred Rogers

Songs On The Programs This Week

1292 *"What Do You Do?"*
"Everybody Has a History"
"Today Is a Very Special Day"

1293 *"It's You I Like"*
"The Truth Will Make Me Free"

1294 *"It's Raining"*

Your Notes For The Week

1291

Lady Elaine Fairchilde is in charge of a catalogue of birthdays in the Neighborhood of Make-Believe. Lady Aberlin and Daniel Tiger learn from Purple Panda that there are no birthdays on Planet Purple.

"A Birthday Party" can help children:

- develop creative play.

A Birthday Party

Materials

- paper
- markers
- stuffed animal or doll
- modeling dough

See if any of the children can tell you what a birthday is. What do they like best about having a birthday? This is a good time to point out that everyone has a birthday, and you might want to make a list of the children's birthdays and see if they can tell you how old they are. How about a pretend birthday party today for one of the stuffed animals or dolls? Using modeling dough, the children could make a pretend birthday cake or other treats and gifts for the party. (You might need to remind younger children not to eat the modeling dough "food.") They might enjoy using paper and markers to make birthday cards.

163

1292

Mister Rogers shows how painting pictures can help express feelings of all kinds, even angry feelings. In the Neighborhood of Make-Believe, Purple Panda is sad because he doesn't have a birthday.

"My Favorite Color" can help children:

- understand and accept individual differences;
- talk about feelings.

My Favorite Color

Materials

- crayons
- paper

Do any of the children have a favorite color? Can they tell you the name of the color or show you something in the room that is the same color? How do their favorite colors make them feel? The children might be able to tell you how other colors make them feel, too. Show them several different-colored crayons and see if they can show you which colors they might choose to make a happy picture. How about a sad picture? Scary picture? Angry picture? Does anyone want to use the crayons to make a picture showing how they feel today?

(Or, 1204 "Mixing Colors.")

1293

Mister Rogers says there are some people who have trouble hearing, and that people who don't hear what you say sometimes watch your mouth to *see* what you're saying. He demonstrates this by whispering.

"Talking without Words" can help children:

- learn different ways people communicate.

Talking without Words

Materials

- crayons
- paper

Do any of the children know someone who is hearing-impaired? Ask the children how they think that person knows what other people are saying. How many ways can the children find to "say" something without making sounds? Encourage each child to try a way:

- reading lips;
- sign language (In the illustration is the sign for "I love you." The hand should be directed towards the intended person(s).);
- writing words;
- drawing pictures;
- changing expressions;
- making gestures.

Can the other children guess what's being "said"?

1294

It's raining in Mister Rogers' Neighborhood today. Mister Rogers shows a film about rain and talks about being afraid of thunder and lightning. It's the flash of lightning and the suddenness of the thunder that make them scary. Several musicians show how thunder-sounds can be made on violins. In the Neighborhood of Make-Believe, Lady Elaine tries to drown out the thunder with piano sounds.

"Thunder Noises" can help children:
- use play to work on feelings.

Thunder Noises

Materials
- metal pans
- wooden spoons
- flashlight (optional)

Let the children try making thunder-sounds. You could use a flashlight, turning it on and off, to make lightning. You'll want to give a signal so the children will know when to stop. How many different kinds of thunder-sounds can the children make? They might want to talk about how they feel when they hear thunder or see lightning. What kinds of things can they do if they are afraid? They may find it reassuring to know that thunder and lightning don't go on forever: They end when the storm is over.

1295

Mister Rogers looks at some beautiful rocks and visits with a man who shows how to polish stones in a tumbler. Astronaut Al Worden shows what a moon rock looks like.

"Collecting Stones" can help children:
- learn to look carefully;
- recognize likeness and difference.

Collecting Stones

Materials
- stones
- bowl of water
- newspaper
- cardboard
- paint and brushes
- glue

Can you and the children go for a walk to collect small stones? (Or ask the children to bring some stones with them from home.)

Once the stones are collected, help the children wash them in a bowl of water and spread them out on newspaper to dry.
- How are they alike?
- How are they different?
- Are they shiny or dull, large or small?
- Do they have pointed edges or rounded ones?
- What else do they notice about the stones?

Some children might like to paint stones different colors and take them home. Others might enjoy gluing them onto cardboard to make a stone picture or design.

Thoughts For The Week

*One thing we can do to help children understand more about themselves and the world around them is to encourage their healthy curiosity. Children often seem to be full of questions—wanting to know how things work or why certain things happen. They are also very curious about grownups—especially the important grownups in their lives. It's easy for us grownups to become annoyed when children ask questions we consider personal, but we need to remember that their desire to know comes from their **caring** about us. When a child feels that questions are welcome and that grownups will answer them as best they can, then he or she will sense that curiosity is something to be valued. If there's something we can't answer, or don't feel comfortable answering, then we need to say so. It can be reassuring to children to learn that, while asking questions is fine, privacy is fine, too.*

Fred Rogers

Songs On The Programs This Week

1296 *"A Place of My Own"*
"You Are Pretty"
1297 *"I Like to Be Told"*
"We Welcome You Today"
1298 *"To Go to Some Place Else"*
"Just for Once"

Your Notes For The Week

1296

Mister Rogers uses a typewriter and shows how to put in the paper and type on it.
"Washing Clothes" can help children:
- learn more about their world;
- recognize likeness and difference.

Washing Clothes

Materials
- laundry
- soap
- washing machine

Ask the children to bring an extra clean pair of socks from home. As you prepare to do a regular load of your own laundry, the children could throw the socks they are wearing into the washing machine to be washed, too. Do any of the children know how the washing machine gets the clothes clean? Some things they might want to know about are:
- setting the machine and choosing water temperature;
- measuring the soap;
- how the machine cleans the clothes;
- how the clothes look after spinning.

When the clothes are dry, the children may be able to help fold the laundry by matching the socks, finding their own socks or stacking the clothes in a basket. Are there other machines the children could learn about? You'll want to be especially careful and watch the children closely when they are around any electrical appliances. Be sure to remind the children that such machines can be dangerous and should be used *only with grownups*.

(Or, 1419 "People and Machines.")

1297

Mister Rogers visits the dentist where he has his teeth examined and cleaned. He also learns about proper brushing and flossing techniques.

"Take Care of Your Teeth" can help children:

- learn more about their bodies;
- learn more about foods.

Take Care of Your Teeth

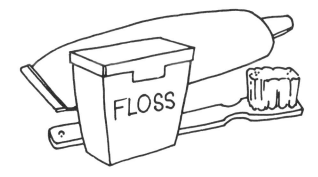

Materials

- paper
- magazine pictures of nutritious food
- paste

Ask the children if they can remember the things the dentist did when Mister Rogers went for a visit. They may talk about:

- the examination;
- cleaning the teeth;
- showing how to brush and floss.

Can the children tell you the kinds of foods that are good for their teeth? What are good breakfast foods? What are good snack foods? Can they tell you some foods that are *not* good for their teeth? See if they can choose magazine pictures of nutritious food to glue onto paper. They might want to hang the pictures on their own refrigerator to remind them which foods are healthy.

1298

Mister Rogers shows pictures of animals and their teeth, and shows a film about different kinds of animals.

"Mouth Puppets" can help children:

- use play to work on feelings;
- develop self-control.

Mouth Puppets

Materials

- animal puppets with mouths (ready-made ones or 1409 "Sock Puppets"; 1452 "Box Puppets")

You might begin this activity by using the puppet yourself. If some of the children are particularly interested in the puppet's mouth and teeth, they might want to hear from you that you wouldn't let anybody or anything bite them. Encourage the children to help create the puppet's personality. They might be able to:

- make up a name for the puppet;
- think of its favorite foods;
- describe where it lives;
- suggest things it likes and dislikes.

Later, they might want to try on the puppet themselves, but it's important that they don't frighten themselves or others by pretending to be too aggressive and biting or hitting.

(Or, 1232 "Animal Cookies"; 1334 "Animal Parade.")

1299

Plans are being made in the Neighborhood of Make-Believe for an opera about a cow who wants to be a potato bug. Mister Rogers shows the difference between sweet potatoes and plain potatoes, then looks at the roots and leaves of a sweet potato plant.

"Sweet Potato Plants" can help children:

- learn more about growing;
- learn more about foods.

Sweet Potato Plants

Materials

- sweet potatoes
- glass jars
- water
- toothpicks
- marker

Give the children a few minutes to examine the potatoes. What can they tell you about them? Have they ever eaten sweet potatoes? Fill the glass jars with water, put toothpicks in the potatoes (about four or five in each) and rest the toothpicks around the rim of the jars. See if the children want to name each potato. If they do, you can write the names on the jars. As the potatoes begin to grow, the children can compare the growing rates. Roots will reach into the water and leaves will begin sprouting from the top. After about two weeks, you will be able to plant the potatoes in soil.

1300

Today is the day of the opera, "Potato Bugs and Cows." Priscilla Cow has a good friend who is a potato bug. Priscilla wants to be like her friend and tries to become a potato bug, too. When she meets Joe Bull, she decides to remain a cow, but learns that she can still be friends with the potato bug.

"Alike and Different" can help children:

- understand and accept individual differences;
- recognize likeness and difference.

Alike and Different

Materials

- none

Can the children think of ways they are just like their friends? Do they:

- like to do some things that are the same?
- live in the same neighborhood?
- have some of the same toys?

Then see if they can tell you how they are different from their friends. Do they:

- have the same parents?
- like the exact same foods?
- wear the same clothes?
- live in the same houses?
- have the same ideas or feelings?
- look the same as their friends?

Ask the children to look carefully at the person sitting next to them. How are they like that person? How are they different?

Thoughts For The Week

***Everyone** has feelings. Learning to recognize and express those feelings in acceptable ways is one of the important parts of growing. There are times, though, when children find it hard to say how they feel. That's when a trusted adult can be a great help, recognizing and naming those feelings, making them mentionable and often more manageable. There are other ways people can say how they feel, too. Some children may find talk less comfortable than drawing or painting a picture, making up a song, or playing about their feelings. And pretending about something can be a really helpful way for children to work through **many** of the feelings they have.*

Fred Rogers

Songs On The Programs This Week

1301	"There Are Many Ways"
	"I Did Too"
1302	"Wishes Don't Make Things Come True"
1303	"I Like to Be Told"
1304	"Sometimes People Are Good"
	"Sometimes"
	"There Are Many Ways"
	"You Are Special"
1305	"I'm a Chef"
	"Just for Once"

Your Notes For The Week

1301

Mister Rogers and Bob Trow pretend to be storekeepers and customers.

"A Pretend Store" can help children:

- learn more about money;
- practice making choices.

A Pretend Store

Materials

- empty food containers
- cardboard box or small table
- pretend money (see page B-4)
- pencils or crayons

Can the children tell you what used to be in the boxes and cartons? Can they recognize any of the labels? Your older children might like to write out price tags for each item and make their own pretend money. While they work you could talk with them about making choices when they shop. If you have only a certain amount of money, you need to pick and choose carefully the items that you want to buy. For your younger children, the idea of exchanging money for groceries may be new. (They often want to keep both the money *and* the groceries.) Keeping a pretend store as part of your play area can encourage the children to make up their own ideas about buying and selling. Can you take the children with you the next time you need to go shopping?

(Or, 1206 "Making Choices.")

1302

Queen Sara is sick with a cold and is feeling irritable. Bob Dog wants her to watch him play Superdog, but Queen Sara wants to rest for a little while. Bob Dog's feelings are hurt, and Queen Sara sends a message saying she still loves him.

"Time to Myself" can help children:

- learn more about privacy;
- recognize feelings.

Time to Myself

Materials

- none

Can you remember a day when you weren't feeling well and acted a little irritable with the children? By talking about that time, you can point out that grownups do need rest or time to themselves (just like children do), but that doesn't mean they don't love the people around them.

Can the children think of a time when they didn't feel well and wanted to be left alone? What are some of the things that help them feel better when they feel that way? For instance:

- taking a nap;
- being alone in a cozy place;
- looking at books;
- listening to records.

You might want to give the children a chance to find something to do on their own—away from each other—for a short time.

(Or, 1412 "A Place of My Own.")

1303

Queen Sara has been staying in bed because of her cold. Lady Elaine Fairchilde tells Daniel that Queen Sara has gone away instead. Daniel becomes very upset, but is reassured when he's allowed to visit the Queen in her room.

"Making a Map" can help children:

- work on feelings about separation;
- learn more about work.

Making a Map

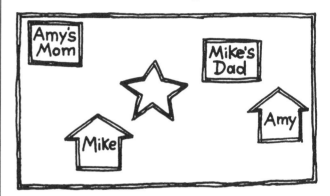

Materials

- large sheet of paper
- markers or crayons
- toy cars or people

Children may feel better about separation from their parents when they know where their parents are. Talk about where the children's moms or dads work, and draw a simple map showing where your house is, where the children live and where each of the children's parents work. You could mark your house with a star or an X. Write the children's names by their houses and their parents' names on the places where they work. (You might want to talk about what the parents do at their jobs.) Lay the map out on a table and let the children use little cars or people to trace the trips from home, to day care and work, then home again.

Younger children may enjoy moving the cars and people on a simpler map: Just a street or two on a plain sheet of paper.

1304

Mister Rogers explains why people get injections (shots), and he looks at the contents of a doctor's kit. He assures the children that doctors use a stethoscope to listen only to how a person's body is working. Nobody can use a stethoscope to hear what you're thinking. No machine can do that.

"A Hospital for Toys" can help children:

- talk about feelings;
- use play to work on feelings.

A Hospital for Toys

Materials

- strips of cloth for bandages
- adhesive strips or tape
- white shirts to use as smocks
- stuffed animals or dolls
- toy medical kit (optional)
- ball point pen (without the ink tube inside) for giving pretend shots

Have any of the children been to a hospital or a doctor's office? What happened there? Did any of them feel afraid? How did they feel afterwards? Were they able to talk with anyone about how they felt? See if the children would like to pretend that several of the dolls (or animals) are sick or hurt and need someone to help them get better.

Ask them what kinds of things they would do. How would they treat the patients? If you can store all the medical materials together in a box, the children will be able to use them on their own when they feel like it.

Would the children like to sing or say the words to Mister Rogers' song, "I Like to Be Told"?

1305

Mister Rogers makes several fruit and vegetable juices and talks about the importance of eating things that are healthy. Chef Brockett closes his eyes and tries to guess what each fruit is by feeling it.

"Fruit Salad" can help children:

- learn more about foods;
- recognize likeness and difference;
- practice sharing.

Fruit Salad

Materials

- bowl
- three or four kinds of fruit (banana, apple, orange, pear, pineapple, grapes, melon, strawberries, etc.)
- knife
- small cups or bowls
- spoons

The children can help wash and dry the fruit, but you might want to do all the cutting and slicing while they:

- separate the pieces;
- peel bananas or oranges;
- mix the fruit;
- put the salad into cups.

Share the fruit salad once it's made and talk about the fruits. How are the fruits different from one another?

- Are they soft or crunchy?
- Are the colors the same or different?
- Are they juicy or dry?
- Can you eat the peelings?
- Do any of them taste sweet?

This is a good time to remind the children that eating healthy food is one way that we take care of ourselves, and that good food helps us grow.

Thoughts For The Week

When someone they love goes away, children may think that person won't ever come back. It helps children to have ways to think about the person who went away: a calendar to show when he or she will return, or a photograph to remind them of the person. Little by little, children do come to trust that when the people close to them go away, they will come back. Most caregivers certainly know that to be so.

It can be very upsetting for children to find that people who love each other can get very angry with each other. When parents quarrel, children may worry that they don't love each other any more. Grownups need to reassure children that getting mad at people doesn't have to mean that you stop loving them.

Fred Rogers

Songs On The Programs This Week

1306   "Days of the Week"
        "Look and Listen"

1307   "It's You I Like"
        "Days of the Week"

1308   "It's the People You Like the Most"
        "There Are Many Ways"

1309   "It's the People You Like the Most"
        "There Are Many Ways"

1310   "I Like to Take My Time"
        "You're Growing"

Your Notes For The Week

1306

The McFeelys are getting ready to go on a trip. Mister Rogers shows an empty suitcase he is loaning them. He plays a hiding game by putting his sweater inside the suitcase.

"What's Missing?" can help children:

- learn to look carefully;
- develop their memory.

What's Missing?

Materials

- five or six small objects (toy car, brush, block, ball, comb, crayon, spoon)

This activity can begin with your talking about the objects you have chosen, making sure the children can name all of them. After spreading them out on the table or floor, give the children several minutes to look at them carefully. Ask the children to close their eyes, and take one thing away. When they open their eyes, can they guess what's missing? If they can't guess, ask them to close their eyes again while you put the object back. Now do they know which one it was? The children may want to take turns being the person to take the object away. End the activity by showing the children all the objects again. Can they help you return each object to the place where it belongs?

- Put the spoon in the kitchen?
- Put the comb in the bathroom?
- Put the block in the toybox?

1307

Mr. and Mrs. McFeely show how they pack their clothes carefully for a trip to see their grandchildren.

"Going on a Trip" can help children:

- work on feelings about separation.

Going on a Trip

Materials

- small box or bag with handles
- dress-up clothes
- assorted props for an overnight stay (comb and brush, toothbrush, keys, blanket, stuffed animal, etc.)

The children might enjoy helping you collect the materials. They could even bring some items from home. To get the play going, you can ask questions like:

- Where are you going on your trip?
- Is anyone going with you?
- How long will you be gone?
- What will you do?
- What do you need to take with you?
- Will you send a postcard or write a letter?
- When will you be back?

The children will most likely start using their own ideas to continue the play. Make sure they have enough time to finish the play by pretending to come back and unpack their suitcases. You might want to ask the children to tell you how they feel when they or their parents go on a real trip.

1308

Mister Rogers visits Trow's Workshop where Marianne Wion is using an electric saw to make a wooden pull-toy. She shows Mister Rogers other toys she has made and talks about how hard it is to be a working mother away from her child.

"The Working Way" can help children:

- learn more about work;
- work on feelings about separation.

The Working Way

Materials

- paper
- crayons or markers

Can the children tell you about the work their parents do when they're away all day? You may want to encourage the children to ask their parents to share more about their jobs. Some parents may even be willing to talk with all the children about their work. You can explain that parents sometimes have mixed feelings about their jobs—wanting to go to work, but also wanting to be with their children. Do the children ever feel two ways about coming to day care?

See if any of the children want to try out working roles by playing about the work their parents do. If some of the children seem angry about their parents' work, it might be because the work takes their parents away. This could be a good time to remind the children that their parents *will* return. Older children might want to draw pictures about the kinds of work their parents do.

(Or, 1303 "Making a Map"; 1431 "Safety Rules.")

1309

King Friday and Queen Sara are no longer angry with each other, but Lady Aberlin is still concerned about the argument they had yesterday. She thinks that people who love each other don't get angry with each other. She's puzzled by just what love is.

"What Is Love?" can help children:

- understand and accept individual differences;
- talk about feelings.

What Is Love?

Materials

- paper
- pencil, pen or marker

Each person in Make-Believe has different answers about what love is. What do the children think love is? You can make a list of all the things they think of…and talk about them. Have they ever been angry with someone they love? What made them angry? When they were finished being angry, did they still love that person? You may want to remind the children of the different ways you show your love for them:

- hugging them;
- cooking for them;
- listening to them;
- keeping them safe;
- reading to them.

1310

Mister Rogers looks at a Jerusalem cherry plant and its fruit. He cuts one of the berries and shows the seeds.

"Looking at Seeds" can help children:

- learn more about foods;
- recognize likeness and difference;
- learn about conservation.

Looking at Seeds

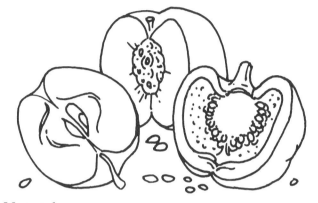

Materials

- three or four fruits or vegetables that have seeds (peppers, apples, pears, peaches, grapes, cucumbers)
- knife
- cutting board

After you cut open the vegetables or fruit, let the children find the seeds.

- Do they know why plants have seeds?
- What might happen if the seeds were planted?
- What differences do the children notice among the seeds? (Size? Shape? Color?)

End the activity by cutting up the fruits and vegetables into smaller pieces to serve for snacks so the children see that food is not to be wasted.

Thoughts For The Week

*Children often need reassurance that they **are** growing—both inside and out. Growing takes time, and the changes are sometimes so small that the waiting seems endless. We can help children understand that waiting doesn't need to be empty time by showing them that there are many things to think about and many things to do that can make waiting easier. Of course, the most important thing for all of us to remember (children and adults alike) is that no matter how much or how little we're growing at the moment, there are many things about us that are fine just the way they are.*

Fred Rogers

Songs On The Programs This Week

1311   *"We Welcome You Today"*

1312   *"You Are Special"*
       "A Handy Lady and a Handy Man"
       "It's You I Like"

1313   *"Look and Listen"*
       "What Do You Hear?"

1314   *"Children Can"*
       "I'm a Man Who Manufactures"
       "Everybody Has a History"

Your Notes For The Week

1311

The neighbors in Make-Believe are planning a joyous welcome-home party for Mr. McFeely. Lady Elaine Fairchilde gets impatient when he doesn't arrive on time and is angry with him when he does arrive—even though he's only a little late.

"Talking about Waiting" can help children:

- talk about feelings;
- practice waiting.

Talking about Waiting

Materials

- none

Ask the children about times when they have had to wait—times like:

- waiting to have a turn with a toy;
- waiting for a grownup to help them do something (tie shoes or put on coats);
- waiting for their parents to pick them up;
- waiting for a special holiday or birthday.

How do they feel when they have to wait? They might enjoy hearing about times when it's hard for you to wait, too. This is a good chance to talk about things they can do when they have to wait. You might suggest:

- looking at a book;
- drawing a picture;
- thinking about a happy time they've had.

What other things can they think of? If they have to wait for you to prepare lunch today, or to wait for someone to pick them up, encourage them to do one of the things you talked about.

(Or, 1079 "Watching Seeds Grow"; 1200 "An Eggshell Garden.")

1312

Lady Elaine Fairchilde helps Handyman Negri cement a crack in the museum wall. She asks Henrietta to help, but Henrietta doesn't want to get her new dress messy. Lady Elaine thinks Henrietta is calling her a messy person, and she calls Henrietta a sissy.

"Making Pretend Cement" can help children:

- develop creative play.

Making Pretend Cement

Materials
- sand and water
- flour, salt, and water
- containers

Making pretend cement from sand and water is a good outdoor activity. Give the children small containers to mix the "cement." They can use it in the yard or sandbox—or even use it to patch the cracks in the sidewalk or driveway. (Encourage them to help sweep up the mess when the sand dries.)

For indoor play, mix up pretend cement using Mister Rogers' recipe for homemade clay:

- 1 cup salt
- 2 cups flour
- Mix with cold water (about ½ cup) until it is right for modeling. Mix with your hands.

Help the children roll it out and make prints of their hands or fingers. After several hours this mixture will harden.

(Or, 1346 "How Would You Feel?")

1313

Henrietta is still hurt by Lady Elaine having called her a sissy. But Handyman Negri helps her see that everyone has different likes and dislikes.

"Things I Can Do" can help children:

- understand and accept individual differences;
- feel proud of their accomplishments.

Things I Can Do

Materials
- none

Encourage the children to tell you things they like to do or things they do well. These could be things like:

- getting dressed alone;
- building with blocks;
- drawing pictures;
- washing the table;
- catching a ball.

This might be a good time for you to take notes for yourself about things the children do well and things they still need to practice. From time to time you can refer back to these notes to see in what ways the children have grown. Parents like to hear about these kinds of things, too.

1314

Mister Rogers visits Mrs. McFeely and watches baby chicks hatching from eggs.

"Ways I'm Growing" can help children:
- learn more about growing;
- feel proud of their accomplishments.

Ways I'm Growing

Materials
- baby pictures (from the children's parents or from magazines)
- pictures of yourself growing up

While showing the children the baby pictures, see if they can tell you what kinds of things babies can do. How can they tell a baby is growing? Talk about things they themselves can do now that they couldn't do when they were babies:
- riding a tricycle;
- walking up and down stairs;
- playing ball;
- drawing pictures;
- running fast.

Ask them what kinds of things they would like to be able to do. You may want to emphasize that there are many ways we grow that are "inside" ways of growing—like learning to tell people how we feel or learning to express our angry feelings without hurting ourselves or anybody else.

(Or, 1078 "Growing"; 1283 "How You Are Growing.")

1315

King Friday has ordered a rocking throne, and X the Owl is very eager for it to be finished. He has to wait for Miss Paulificate to finish a special needlepoint cover for the throne.

"Make a Piñata" can help children:
- practice working cooperatively;
- practice waiting.

Make a Piñata

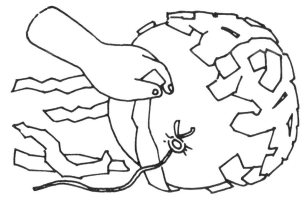

Materials
- large balloon
- strips of newspaper (one inch by 12 inches long)
- diluted paste or glue
- dishpan

A piñata is a container made of papier-mâché or clay and filled with treats for a holiday celebration. To make one:
- Blow up the balloon and tie it.
- Soak newspaper strips in a dishpan of diluted paste.
- Cover the balloon with the wet newspaper strips, making five or six layers.
- Let it dry for several days.
- Paint and decorate it once it's dry.

Then you can cut a hole in it, break the balloon and fill it with small bags of nutritious treats. The children can pass the piñata at snack time and fish out a treat from their homemade container.

Thoughts For The Week

*Coping with sudden changes is a difficult task for anyone, but it's especially hard for children. When changes occur unexpectedly, children can start wondering if **anything** will stay the same. One way we can help to prepare them for changes is by letting them know what to expect. That way, the changes may seem more manageable. Whenever we know in advance of something out of the ordinary that's going to happen, something that will affect the children, we do them a great service when we tell them about it.*

*Learning to channel angry feelings into constructive activities is another hard task, but it's one of the most important things anybody can learn to do. Children's caregivers can help children learn that angry feelings **can** be expressed—as long as the children don't hurt themselves or others. We can help them to pound on clay, **not** on breakable toys; to chomp on crunchy food **not** on another child; to kick a ball instead of kicking people or to throw a beanbag when they feel like throwing a toy. By setting firm limits, showing what's acceptable and what isn't about the expression of anger, you will be supporting them in some very important lifelong growing.*

Fred Rogers

Songs On The Programs This Week

1316 *"You Are You"*
1317 *"I Like to Take My Time"*
1318 *"Look and Listen"*
1319 *"What Do You Do?"*
      "Please Don't Think It's Funny"
1320 *"What Do You Do?"*
      "There Are Many Ways"

Your Notes For The Week

1316

The McFeelys are wallpapering their kitchen today, and Mister Rogers is going to help them. Lady Elaine Fairchilde is tired of the same old Neighborhood of Make-Believe and decides to rearrange everything— without asking anyone.

"Unexpected Changes" can help children:

- recognize feelings;
- talk about feelings.

Unexpected Changes

Materials

- none

Can you tell the children about a time when someone changed plans without warning, and you felt upset about it? Ask them how they would feel if someone made changes without asking them. You may want to ask questions like:

- How would you feel if you came home and found your parents had moved the furniture around in your room?
- How would you feel if I weren't here one day and there was someone new to look after you?
- Have your parents ever had to pick up you early (or late) without letting you know? How did you feel?

You could also talk with the children about how they'd feel if the same changes happened—but they knew ahead of time and could help with the preparations. For instance:

- moving to a new room (and helping to set it up and move the toys);
- meeting a substitute caregiver (before you leave);
- staying late at day care (knowing their parents have special needs).

1317

Mister Rogers uses scraps of wallpaper to cover an ice cream carton and to make greeting cards. As he works, he sings the song, "I Like to Take My Time."

"Paper Collage" can help children:

- develop creative play;
- recognize likeness and difference.

Paper Collage

Materials

- scraps of wallpaper, used wrapping paper, or magazine pictures
- flour-and-water paste (see page A-2)
- paper or cardboard

Encourage the children to create their own designs using scraps of wallpaper and paste. If you have younger children, you might have to show them how to put paste on the *backs* of the scraps they're using. Or let them brush paste on the background paper and arrange the scraps on that. While the children are pasting, you may want to talk about differences and similarities:

- Can they find any scraps that are the same color?
- Are there pieces that have the same design in different colors?
- If you're using wallpaper, what does it feel like? (Some pieces may be fuzzy or nubby.)

They may enjoy singing the words to Mister Rogers' song, "I Like to Take My Time" while they work.

(Or, 1376 "Fabric Cards.")

1318

Lady Elaine Fairchilde is selling her maps of the switched-around Neighborhood of Make-Believe. Back in the "real" neighborhood, Mister Rogers says it can be fun to have a change for a while, but it's nice to have old familiar things, too.

"What's Different?" can help children:

- learn to look carefully;
- recognize likeness and difference;
- talk about feelings.

What's Different?

Materials

- small furniture, toy people, cars, airplanes, etc.

Help the children set up a pretend room, village, airport, zoo, or other small setting of their choice. When they've had a good look at it, ask them to hide their eyes while you switch something around. Can they tell you what's been moved? Can they remember how things were and put them back after each turn? If some children find it hard to guess what's different, let them be the ones to do the switching. You could take this chance to talk about moving to a new room or to a new house. What changes would there be? Can they think of things that would stay the same? (Their favorite toys or blankets?)

Thursday

1319

Mister Rogers visits a glassblower to see how glass spiders are made. He talks about "fragile" things. Henrietta's glass cat gets broken, but Handyman Negri promises to fix it.

"Things That Are Fragile" can help children:

● develop creative play.

Things That Are Fragile

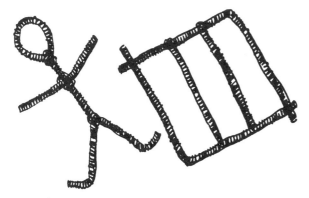

Materials
● pipe cleaners

Have you some fragile things you could show the children? How do you have to handle them? Give each child several pipe cleaners to make a pretend object. Some children may want to make spiders or bugs, but other children may choose to make something very different. When the pipe-cleaner sculptures are finished, encourage the children to pretend they are made of glass. How would they pass them to you?

You may want to talk about how some fragile objects can be fixed when they're broken, but that sometimes things are broken into too many pieces to be put back together again. Going over the song, "Everything Grows Together," would be a way to reassure them that their bodies don't break and fall apart the way glass or fragile objects can.

(Or, 1028 "String Painting"; 1352 "Yarn Designs.")

Friday

1320

The neighbors in Make-Believe still have angry feelings about the switched-around neighborhood—even though Lady Elaine put things back when she heard little Ana crying. The king plans a Festival of Mad Feelings to express some of the anger in a way that doesn't hurt Lady Elaine or anyone else.

"A Pounding Festival" can help children:

● express strong feelings in appropriate ways.

A Pounding Festival

Materials
● modeling dough
● pillows
● drums or pots and pans
● crunchy celery and carrot sticks

Before you begin this activity, you'll want to set limits you feel comfortable with, such as:
● Modeling dough is to be kept at the table.
● The children may pound on the pillows, dough, or drums only—not on any other toys or on people.
● When you give the stop signal, everyone's to stop.

Start out with short time limits for pounding (15-30 seconds) to make sure the children can stop themselves; then you can increase the limit to a minute or two of pounding. Does anyone feel like making up a mad song or chant? You could finish up with a snack of crunchy celery and carrot sticks for teeth chomping.

Other things you could try are:
● making a mad picture;
● making up a mad dance;
● showing how your face looks when you're angry.

You might want to remember this activity for a day when there are real angry feelings.

Thoughts For The Week

Ideas are so important in this world! They help us find solutions to problems, create new things, and give us ways to express ourselves. Young children's ideas may sometimes seem strange to us, but we need to take them seriously as expressions of healthy curiosity and an eagerness to make their own unique sense out of the world they are getting to know.

Some people have to overcome physical limitations such as difficulty in walking, seeing, or hearing. But we all have our limitations to live with, even if they aren't immediately apparent. Helping children accept their own limitations and the limitations of others can be one of the most helpful gifts we can give them. Children need to know we accept them as they are, limitations and all, just as they need to know we are proud of their accomplishments, however large or small they may seem.

Fred Rogers

Songs On The Programs This Week

1321   *"Sometimes People Are Good"*
         "I Did Too"
1322   *"You Are Special"*
         "I'm Proud of You"
1323   *"Everybody's Fancy"*
1325   *"Look and Listen"*

Your Notes For The Week

1321

"Wee Pals" cartoonist, Morrie Turner, is visiting today and shows how he turns an idea into a cartoon. He and Mister Rogers agree that ideas are some of the most important things you can have.

"I Have an Idea" can help children:

- develop their imaginations;
- develop creative play.

I Have an Idea

Materials

- small toys (people with cars, trucks, animals, etc.)

Do any of the children know what an idea is? You may want to point out that ideas are things we think up to do or to try out. What kinds of ideas do they have about playing (pretending) with toys? Show the children the small toys you've collected. You may want to ask questions to help them start the play:

- Who are these people?
- What are they doing?
- What do you think is going to happen?
- How do they feel?
- What might they say?

You could mention that all books and television programs started out as an idea in someone's mind. So did drawings, songs and dances, buildings, bridges and machines.

1322

Mister Rogers shows some crutches and leg braces and talks about how they can be strong sturdy supports. He visits with Mrs. McFeely and her granddaughter, Chrissie. Mrs. McFeely says that Chrissie can handle her crutches so well that she doesn't need a wheelchair. They sing the song, "You Are Special."

"Talking about Disabilities" can help children:
* understand and accept individual differences;
* feel proud of their accomplishments.

Talking about Disabilities

Materials
* none

Why do the children think some people need to use crutches or wear leg braces? Some things you may want to point out are:
* People use crutches or braces to make walking easier.
* Using crutches or wheelchairs takes practice; people who use them well can feel proud of learning how.
* People who have trouble walking or seeing or hearing became that way because of an illness or an accident — not because they saw, heard, or did something bad.
* People don't change just because they try on braces or try out crutches or a wheelchair.

What kinds of things do each of the children do well? What kinds of things do they find difficult?

1323

Mister Rogers looks at homemade games at Elsie Neal's Craft Shop. She has a pin-the-star-on-the-donkey game, a spinner game, a bean bag game and a ring toss.

"Games" can help children:
* develop creative play;
* develop the ability to keep on trying;
* develop coordination.

Games

Materials
* game spinner (use one from an old game, or make your own, page B-1)
* wastebasket
* balls or bean bags

Do the children remember the games that Mister Rogers played today? Suggest that you all make up some games together. You could make up a few games first, then encourage the children to make up their own. (Keep the emphasis on making up the games and playing them, not on who wins or who does best.) Some game ideas are:
* Spin the spinner to see how many times to jump, throw the ball, clap hands, or hop.
* Toss the ball (or bean bag) into the basket.
* Hold the basket and try to catch the ball.
* Kick a ball into a basket lying on its side.

What games can they think of? Try to keep the games simple enough for all the children to try.

1324

It's nighttime in the Neighborhood of Make-Believe. Daniel, Grandpere, and Lady Aberlin are working on a star-shaped prize for Donkey Hodie. Daniel falls asleep and wakes up to find he has spent the whole night away from his clock. He feels very proud of himself.

"Nighttime Pictures" can help children:

- learn more about their world;
- develop their imaginations.

Nighttime Pictures

Materials

- paper
- star shapes cut from construction paper
- moon shapes cut from paper
- glue or paste
- black or gray paper (gray cardboard from the inside of cracker boxes)
- crayons, markers, or white chalk

How does the sky look at night? Encourage the children to paste one moon and many star shapes anywhere on the paper. Some children may want to draw nighttime pictures. Crayons or markers won't show up very well on dark paper, and you can use this chance to talk about how hard it is to see clearly at night. Can the children tell you anything about their pictures? It's surprising to think that the stars are always in the sky but we don't see their light until the sky is dark at night!

You might want to borrow a children's book about nighttime from your local library to read with the children.

1325

A barbershop quartet performs today, and Mister Rogers looks at several different music boxes. The Make-Believe Sweethearts—Lady Aberlin, Harriett Cow and Lady Elaine—sing enthusiastically in the Neighborhood of Make-Believe.

"A Songfest" can help children:

- express feelings through music;
- develop their memory.

A Songfest

Materials

- records or tapes with children's songs (optional)

Start the songfest with simple songs the children are likely to know:

- "Old MacDonald";
- "Twinkle, Twinkle, Little Star";
- "Row, Row, Row Your Boat."

Ask what favorite songs they want to sing. The words to many of Mister Rogers' songs can be found in the back of this book.

Thoughts For The Week

Children may sometimes feel overwhelmed by the size of everyday things: A table can seem huge to a child who can walk under it, and silverware and plates must seem twice the size they do to us. I like to reassure small children that small things are very important in life. A small paintbrush can handle corners that a large one can't. A small pan or spoon is just as important in the kitchen as a big one. Children need to be reminded that even though they are small, there are lots of things they can do particularly well.

Fred Rogers

Songs On The Programs This Week

1326 "Children Can"

1327 "Come On and Wake Up"

1328 "You've Got to Do It"
      "I'm Proud of You"
      "Tree, Tree, Tree"

1329 "Let's Be Together Today"
      "O.C.S. Alma Mater"
      "What Do You Do?"

1330 "You Are Special"

Your Notes For The Week

1326

Mister Rogers is painting his house. He shows how little brushes can get into places that big brushes can't. Mister Rogers sings his song, "Children Can," and shows a film about things children can do best.

"Children Can" can help children:

- learn to do things independently;
- feel proud of their accomplishments.

Children Can

Materials

- none

You might begin this activity by singing or saying the words to Mister Rogers' song, "Children Can," and by acting out some of the words. Ask the children if they can think of something they do well that a bigger person has trouble doing—things like:

- turning a somersault;
- sitting under a table;
- playing hard all day;
- climbing a jungle gym.

What do they have trouble doing that they'd like to learn to do? You could take this chance to talk about the difference between things people can learn to do and things they can't ever learn to do—like flying all by themselves, or becoming a superhero. What are the children's favorite kinds of pretending? Are they things that people could really do?

1327

A curious Prince Tuesday opens Miss Paulificate's purse and does some exploring. Queen Sara understands that Prince Tuesday is at the age when he's interested in what is inside things. She gives him a special box to keep things in.

"My Special Box" can help children:

- learn more about privacy.

My Special Box

Materials

- shoe box for each child
- scrap materials
- glue or paste
- markers or crayons

How do the children feel when babies or younger children mess up their toys? Reassure them that they don't have to share everything unless they want to: Some things are special and for them alone. Do their moms or dads have things they put in special places, too? In this activity, each child can decorate a shoe box in his or her own way and keep it as a place for special possessions that *don't* have to be shared. After the children have decorated their boxes, print each child's name so there won't be any confusion about ownership. The children may want to talk about the things they plan to keep in the boxes and why they want to keep them safe.

1328

Mister Rogers shows how a pizza-cutting wheel works and watches a pizza being made at Brockett's Bakery.

"Making Pizza" can help children:

- learn more about foods;
- practice working cooperatively.

Making Pizza

Materials

- 1 package yeast
- 1¼ cups warm water
- 3½ to 4 cups flour (white or whole wheat)
- tomato sauce
- grated cheese (mozzarella or any kind will do)
- bowl
- mixing spoon
- cookie sheet

You may want to give everyone a job as you prepare the pizza:

- Mix the yeast and warm water.
- Add half the flour, beating until smooth.
- Stir in the rest of the flour and knead.
- Let rise in a bowl for a half-hour; then knead again.

Give each child a piece to make his or her own little pizza. You can flatten the dough with a rolling pin or your hands. Top with tomato sauce and cheese. Bake the pizzas on greased cookie sheets at 425 degrees for 20 minutes.

If you want to make this activity easier, you could make a pizza bagel or a pizza English muffin. Split the bagel or muffin, add the sauce and let the children tear the cheese into shreds for the topping.

1329

Mister Rogers shows two model-railroad crossing signals and talks about how the signals go down when a train passes. Stop and go lessons are seen on a film about children riding tricycles.

"Stop and Go Game" can help children:

- learn about limits;
- develop self-control.

Stop Sign Game

Materials

- paper
- markers
- yardstick or old broomhandle

Make a large stop sign out of paper and tape it to a yardstick;then make a go sign and tape it on the other side. When the go sign is facing them, the children can move; when the stop sign is facing them, they must stop. Keep the periods of time to 15-20 seconds. You may want to try this game while the children are:

- riding tricycles;
- playing with cars or trucks;
- moving to music.

You might even use the stop sign alone as a permanent marker for an area that is off limits—like a driveway or the edge of the yard.

(Or, 1245 "Snow Statues.")

1330

Lady Aberlin announces that the circus is coming to the Neighborhood of Make-Believe. When X asks her when it will be coming, she realizes she has been only wishing the circus would come. There's a difference between wishing about something and making it happen.

"Wishing and Doing" can help children:

- understand wishing can't make things happen.

Wishing and Doing

Materials

- paper
- pencil, pen or marker

Was there ever a time when you wished something would happen so much that you began to believe it would happen? Can you tell the children about it? Ask them about things they wish would happen and make a list of their wishes. Could any of them come true? What would someone have to do to make them happen? Point out that wishing doesn't make things happen; someone has to *do* something to make a wish come true.

(Or, 1067 "Three Magic Wishes.")

Thoughts For The Week

*People coming and going is an important theme this week. As you know, children often find it hard to say good-bye to their parents. They may be wondering when (or even **if**) their parents will return, even though you may have assured them again and again that their parents **will** be coming back. And many day caregivers have found that it helps for children to have a good-bye routine with their parents, one they can use every day, like waving from the window, giving a hug, or throwing kisses. No one really likes people to leave unexpectedly, adults no more than children. It may sometimes seem easier for you when parents slip away unnoticed, but children are likely to feel much more secure when they've had a chance to say good-bye and are told when to expect their parents back. They may cry and protest for a while, but deep inside they're learning to trust that what you say is true.*

Fred Rogers

Songs On The Programs This Week

1331   *"Everything Grows Together"*
1332   *"You Are Special"*
1333   *"Please Don't Think It's Funny"*
1334   *"It's You I Like"*
       "I'm Proud of You"
1335   *"There Are Many Ways"*

Your Notes For The Week

1331

It's Circus Week in the Neighborhood of Make-Believe. Mister Rogers shows a circus toy—a clown riding a bike. Elsie Neal makes a clown face using a paper plate, stars and a balloon.

"Paper Plate Pictures" can help children:

- develop their imaginations;
- develop creative play.

Paper Plate Pictures

Materials

- paper plates
- scrap materials (buttons, yarn, fabric, paper, twigs, beans, etc.)
- paste or glue

How did the clown face look that Elsie Neal made? Happy? Sad? Angry? What else can the children think of to make with a paper plate? Looking through the scrap box may help them decide what they want to make—another clown face, an animal, or maybe a picture or just a fancy decoration.

1332

Oliver, the Circus Clown, searches through the Neighborhood of Make-Believe looking for his friend, Purple Panda. Purple Panda is lonely for his circus friends. When they find each other, there is a joyous reunion.

"Hide and Seek" can help children:

- work on feelings about separation;
- practice taking turns.

Hide and Seek

Materials

- none

You'll need to set some boundaries for hiding so the children will know which areas are off limits. It's best to keep the play in one or two rooms so you can see who goes where. (You may find some children don't like being "It"—the seeker—and some may not want to play at all.) Those who do want to be seekers should leave the room at the beginning of their time while the others find safe hiding places. You may want to help the seeker by giving hints when he or she is getting close to a hiding place. Try to keep the emphasis on the reunion, not on who remains hidden the longest. For instance, the hiders could pretend to be sheep, and the seeker the sheepdog who has to bring the sheep back safely to the shepherd—you.

1333

Mister Rogers shows several "peek-a-boo" games today. In the Neighborhood of Make-Believe, Oliver Circus Clown has left the Neighborhood without saying good-bye. Miss Paulificate is disappointed because she just baked a special welcome cake for him.

"Can You Find the Toy?" can help children:

- work on feelings about separation;
- develop the ability to keep on trying.

Can You Find the Toy?

Materials

- box of sand (cornmeal or popcorn may be substituted)
- small toys (car, person, spoon, shovel, block, etc.)

After you have shown all the toys to the children, hide one in the sand. Encourage the children to take turns trying to find the toy by feeling. Then you can hide two toys at once. Can the children guess which toys they have found by the way they feel? This activity can be done in pairs: One child hides a toy in the sand and another feels around trying to find it.

(Or, 1258 "Guess What's in the Bag.")

1334

Daniel Striped Tiger is afraid of the circus animals. He's able to overcome his fears with the help of his friends, and they all watch the great circus parade.

"Animal Parade" can help children:
- develop their imaginations;
- develop creative play.

Animal Parade

Materials
- lively music for marching
- metal cake or pie pans
- wooden spoons

You can all organize the parade together by planning ahead:
- what animal each child will pretend to be;
- where the parade will go;
- how the parade will know when to stop.

If some children seem afraid of pretending to be animals, they might like to be part of the band instead (playing on metal cake or pie pans with wooden spoons), or they might just want to be spectators.

(Or, 1274 "Animal Sounds.")

1335

The circus is over and Purple Panda is leaving with it. Queen Sara gives Panda a going-away gift—his favorite blanket to help him with the move.

"Saying Good-Bye" can help children:
- work on feelings about separation;
- talk about feelings.

Saying Good-bye

Materials
- none

Have there been children who have had to leave your day care? You might try asking the other children:
- Do you remember friends who used to be here but are gone now?
- What do you remember best about them?
- How did you feel when they had to leave?
- How do you think they felt?

Were there any special things you did to say good-bye that the children can remember? Some children may want to talk about times when other people they know have gone away. Remind them that it sometimes helps to:
- call them on the phone;
- write them letters;
- draw pictures for them;
- keep a photograph of the person who went away.

Thoughts For The Week

Learning to share is a difficult task for human beings. Toddlers often feel anything they touch is theirs, a part of themselves. No wonder it's so hard to learn that some things are for other people to use, too! It's easier for children to learn about sharing when they can talk about the difference between things that are theirs only—like a special blanket or stuffed toy—and things that everyone uses. Perhaps hardest of all is sharing a favorite grownup. Children want to have that special person all to themselves, but learning to share a grownup's time is an important part of growing. It can come little by little...but only when a child learns to be sure of a grownup's love.

Fred Rogers

Songs On The Programs This Week

1337 *"Sometimes People Are Good"*
1338 *"Please Don't Think It's Funny"*
1340 *"Peace and Quiet"*

Your Notes For The Week

1336

Daniel goes over to Some Place Else to see the Washer-Dryer-Sorter-Dumper. While he is away, his clock mysteriously disappears. There is a new visitor in the Neighborhood of Make-Believe—Mr. Allmine. In his "real" neighborhood, Mister Rogers misplaces his watch but finds it in his coat pocket.

"Find the Timer" can help children:

- learn to listen carefully;
- work on feelings about separation;
- practice working cooperatively.

Find the Timer

Materials

- kitchen timer or a loud-ticking alarm clock

Can you remember losing something that you can tell the children about? Were you able to find it again? Can some of the children remember times when they lost something?

- How did they feel about losing it?
- Were they able to find it again?
- If so, how did they find it?
- If not, what do they think happened to it?
- What do they think happened to Daniel's clock?

Set the timer or alarm clock to ring in about five minutes. Then hide it someplace in the room. Ask the children to listen carefully as they try to find the timer. Can they discover it before the bell rings? You might want to encourage working together to find the timer—rather than stressing the competition about *who* finds it. The object of the game is to find the clock or timer before the alarm goes off. If they work together, they might find it faster.

Tuesday

1337

When Mr. Allmine appears, bragging about his many possessions, Lady Aberlin begins to suspect he may have taken Daniel's clock. In the "real" neighborhood, Mister Rogers wonders if Mr. Allmine thinks that everything belongs to him and that he doesn't have to share anything.

"Talking about Sharing" can help children:

• practice sharing;

• learn more about privacy.

Talking about Sharing

Materials

• none

Ask the children how they feel about having to share toys at day care.

• What are some of their favorite toys?

• How do they feel when they see someone else playing with them?

• What toys do they like to share? Why?

• Are the toys only for them to use?

• How can we decide who plays with what and when?

You may want to point out that sharing toys means taking turns playing with them. It doesn't always mean they have to give up a toy just because someone else wants it. It's okay to finish playing with it first. Take time to talk about things they don't have to share, like special toys or blankets from home. Point out that thoughts are something else that belong to them alone: They can always decide if they want to share their thoughts and feelings.

Wednesday

1338

Mister Rogers shows a film about an American Indian sandpainting.

"Sand Pictures" can help children:

• express feelings through art work.

Sand Pictures

Materials

• construction paper or cardboard

• liquid glue

• sand

• brushes

• newspapers

Dilute the glue with water—about half and half—so the children can paint designs on the paper with paintbrushes dipped in the glue. (Be sure to cover the work area with newspapers!) After they've painted their designs, help them sprinkle sand over the paper. Let the glue dry, then shake off the extra sand into a container. The sand will stick to the glue to make a sand picture.

(Or, 1083 "Salt Drawings.")

1339

Mister Rogers shows what a pillow looks like without its cover and looks at a film about how foam pillows are made. In Make-Believe, Edgar Cooke is afraid Mr. Allmine will take his pillow, so he's holding onto it tightly.

"Making Pillows" can help children:

- learn more about privacy;
- work on feelings about separation.

Making Pillows

Materials

- fabric (they may be able to bring this from home)
- needle and thread (or sewing machine)
- stuffing (old stockings or other washable filling)

You'll need to do the sewing, but the children may enjoy watching as you sew.

- Place the two pieces of fabric (nap sides facing) together.
- Stitch around three of the edges.
- Turn the case right side out and let the children put the stuffing into the pillow through the open end.
- Make a small hem and sew the pillow closed.

While the children are stuffing the pillows, you may want to talk about these pillows, pointing out that:

- each pillow belongs to only one child;
- they don't have to share the pillows.

Can you set up a special pillow box or pillow cupboard where the children can find their pillows when they want them?

1340

Mister Rogers visits with an old friend, and they make up a pretend "tag" story—one person starts a tale, and when a second person is tagged, he or she adds to it.

"Tag Stories" can help children:

- develop their imaginations;
- learn to listen carefully.

Tag Stories

Materials

- none

You'll want to keep these stories simple. They might be about:

- a child and a pet;
- three magic wishes;
- monsters;
- whatever the children have been talking about that day.

You may find it works better to make up the story yourself, leaving out key words for the children to fill in ("Once upon a time there was _____ who went to the forest where he met a _____.")
You might even want to use a story the children already know, and as you re-tell it, leave out certain words. As you practice tag stories more with the children, at snack or lunch time, they will begin to contribute more.

Thoughts For The Week

Getting to know more about ourselves is one of the themes for this week. As children are learning about the world around them, they're also finding out who and what they are—where the boundaries of their bodies are, and what their bodies look like. Grownups help children learn about themselves through simple body games like "This little piggy went to market," "Where's your nose?" or "Show me your eyes." Reflections, shadows, snapshots and statues are other ways for children to find out more about themselves and their bodies, too. All human beings have things in common and things that are different. In some ways we're all alike and in other ways we're each unique.

Fred Rogers

Songs On The Programs This Week

1341 *"You're Growing"*

1343 *"You Are You"*

1344 *"Look and Listen"*

Your Notes For The Week

1341

Mister Rogers visits the McFeelys and listens to some old-time records. They see a film about the day the McFeelys bought their record player and brought it home on a trolley.

"Remember When" can help children:

- learn more about growing;
- develop their memory.

Remember When

Materials

- a collection of old things (photographs, clothing, shoes, dishes, tools, etc.)
- crayons or markers
- paper

Most children like to hear grownups talk about the days when they were little. Show the children the old things you've collected, telling them something about each one. You might want to tell about some experiences you had when you were little. Can the children remember anything that happened when they were younger—things like:

- the first time they came to day care?
- the birth of a baby brother or sister?
- a vacation or a special visit?

Would some of the children enjoy drawing a picture about their special happening? Are there old things at home the children can tell you about (baby shoes, baby clothes, rattles or other baby toys, baby pictures)? Older children may prefer to draw a picture of a favorite toy or piece of clothing. Perhaps they could bring something from home to show everyone on another day.

1342

Mister Rogers shows pictures of some animal tracks, and then welcomes his son, John, who shows a set of cat tracks in mud. They make plaster casts of the cat tracks and of their own handprints.

"A Handprint Mural" can help children:

● practice taking turns;

● learn more about their world.

A Handprint Mural

Materials
● roll of plain shelf paper (or a cut-open grocery bag)
● newspaper
● paint (washable and non-toxic)
● brush
● bowl of soapy water

Cover your working area with newspaper and unroll a long piece of shelf paper. You might want to explain that a mural is a big painting, sometimes painted by more than one person. This activity is likely to go more smoothly if you work with the children one at a time:

● Paint a child's hand with paint. (Or, put a little paint in a shallow pan and let the child dip his or her hand into the paint.)

● Let each one make handprint designs any place where the paper is blank.

You can write the child's name beside one of his or her handprints. A bowl of soapy water at the table for handwashing can help make sure the children don't touch anything else with their painted hands.

1343

Mister Rogers shows a film about different kinds of reflections and talks about how important it is for us to know who we are. In Make-Believe, Prince Tuesday is fascinated with his mirror reflection.

"Mirror, Mirror on the Wall" can help children:

● learn to listen carefully;

● learn to look carefully;

● practice taking turns.

Mirror, Mirror on the Wall

Materials
● mirror

Encourage the children to take turns looking at their reflections in the mirror (but don't insist if a child doesn't want to). You or the other children could ask:

● Can you point to your nose?
● Can you cover your eyes?
● Where is your forehead?
● Where are your teeth?
● Can you touch your feet?
● Can you raise your arms?
● Can you show us how your face would look if you were happy? Sad? Mad?

Can the children think of (and perhaps even find) other places where they can see their reflections:

● the side of a toaster?
● windows?
● rain puddles?
● shiny doors?

1344

Mister Rogers shows a painting that was made with dots of paint. Then he tries making his own painting the same way. In the Neighborhood of Make-Believe, Henrietta shows Mr. McFeely the name signs she made with needlepoint.

"Paper-Punch Designs" can help children:

- develop muscle control;
- develop creative play.

Paper-Punch Designs

Materials

- colored strips of paper (about two inches wide)
- paper punch (several, if you can borrow them)
- plain paper
- glue or paste

As the children punch the colored paper, you'll want to keep the punched-out pieces from falling over the floor: A tray or a shallow box is a good way to catch most of these dots. The children will have to take turns with the paper punch, so you might find it necessary to limit the use of the paper punch to a few minutes each. By painting the glue on the plain paper first, the children can make designs by sprinkling their dots over the sticky surface.

(Or, 1352 "Yarn Designs"; 1305 "Fruit Salad.")

1345

The Make-Believe neighbors are gathered together to see the unveiling of the statue of King Monday IX. Everyone congratulates Elsie Neal on her fine creation. Prince Tuesday is fascinated by the big statue of his famous ancestor.

"Body Outlines" can help children:

- understand and accept individual differences;
- understand the difference between real and pretend.

Body Outlines

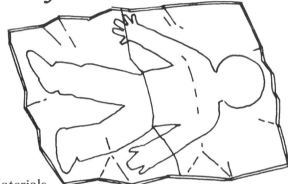

Materials

- large sheets of paper (or several grocery bags taped together)
- markers or crayons

Here's a way to make paper "statues" of the children:

- Trace the outline of each child's body on a big sheet of paper.
- Encourage the children to draw in their own faces, clothing, etc.
- Cut around the outlines and hang them up.

Can the children find their own outlines? How is each one different? How are they alike? The children may enjoy putting name cards under their paper outlines. You may want to remind the children that statues are not real people; they are just made to show what the real person looks like.

(Or, 1451 "Clay Sculptures.")

Thoughts For The Week

*Part of what children need to learn about themselves is what they're feeling. It's a big step for a child to be able to say how he or she feels, and it's a still bigger one for a child to find constructive ways to express that feeling. When grownups talk about their own feelings, children learn something else that's important: We all have many of the same feelings. We **all** feel happy, sad or mad from time to time. In fact, having those feelings is a very special part of what makes us human beings.*

There is something else we all share: We all have accidents. We spill things by accident, drop things by accident and break things by accident. When children have accidents, grownups sometimes get mad—and that can be scary for a child. Times when something goes wrong and someone gets mad are really important times for talking about feelings! The same is true when something goes well and someone gets pleased!

Fred Rogers

Songs On The Programs This Week

1348   *"Everything Grows Together"*
        "A Handy Lady and a Handy Man"

1349   *"I Like to Take My Time"*
        "O.C.S. Alma Mater"

1350   *"I'm Proud of You"*

Your Notes For The Week

1346

A magician performs in the Neighborhood of Make-Believe and turns a pretend tear into a glistening jewel. Mister Rogers stresses the importance of being able to talk about your feelings.

"How Would You Feel?" can help children:

- talk about feelings.

How Would You Feel?

Materials

- paper plates (one for each child)
- face features cut from construction paper
- tape

Pretending how we feel, or might feel, at certain times can be a good way to talk about feelings. Using a paper plate for a face, and paper shapes to represent features, show the children different facial expressions and see if they can tell you the feelings the faces express. Encourage the children to arrange a set of paper features on their own plates as you ask, "How would you feel if:

- you were getting ready to open a present?
- you were riding a trike and someone pushed you off?
- you threw a ball in the house and broke a vase?
- you were going to get a new puppy?
- your parents called and said they would be late picking you up?
- you were alone in a dark room?"

The children might not all make the same expression at the same time. You might want to talk about the range of feelings a person could have in each situation.

1347

Prince Tuesday is hammering on the royal statue—and breaks it. King Friday is very angry with him, but Lady Elaine brings some glue and helps to repair the statue. The king takes Prince Tuesday to the Pounding Room where his hammer won't hurt anything.

"When Something Breaks" can help children:

- recognize feelings;
- talk about feelings.

When Something Breaks

Materials

- building blocks or small cardboard boxes

Ask the children to work together using blocks or boxes to build a tower or castle. While you and the children are building, talk with them about the broken statue on today's program. You may want to ask them questions like:

- What was Prince Tuesday doing when the statue broke?
- Why do you think he was hammering on it? (Was he angry? Was he pretending to make a statue?)
- How do you think he felt when the statue broke? (Surprised? Afraid? Sad? Or all three?)
- How do you think he felt when Lady Elaine fixed the statue?

Lady Elaine understood how Prince Tuesday felt because she could remember breaking things, too. Can any of the children remember a time when they broke something? As you've been building your tower:

- Has anyone accidently knocked it over?
- Has anyone purposely knocked it down?

How do they feel about what happened? Can the tower be built again?

(Or, 1259 "Fixing Things"; 1260 "Puzzles"; 1320 "A Pounding Festival.")

1348

At the bakery today, there's a special sale on all the round items. Mister Rogers helps Chef Brockett sort out the round cookies from the other shapes.

"Sorting Shapes" can help children:

- recognize likeness and difference.

Sorting Shapes

Materials

- a set of cardboard or heavy paper shapes (circles, squares, triangles in different colors and different sizes)
- shoe boxes or small containers

Spread the shapes out on the floor or table and see what the children do with them. You can encourage sorting by asking them to find the ones that are alike. Some of the children may separate the shapes by color (all the reds, all the blues, all the yellows); others may separate them by size (big ones, little ones, middle-sized ones); and still others may sort them by shape. Can the children tell you how the objects they sorted are alike? Are they the same color? Same size? Same shape? Keep the shapes in a box for the children to use again.

1349

X the Owl is searching for letter shapes in the Neighborhood of Make-Believe.

"Alphabet Soup" can help children:

- recognize and use symbols;
- learn more about foods.

Alphabet Soup

Materials

- chicken broth
- alphabet noodles
- saucepan

Sit around a table and give each child a handful of dry alphabet noodles. (You might want to give them a bowl or plate in which to keep their noodles.) Encourage them to look for letters they recognize. Older children may be able to find the letters of their names. You or one of the older children might help the younger ones find the first letters of their names. When everyone's had a good look, you can all put your noodles in the chicken broth. Cook the noodles and serve the alphabet soup for lunch or a snack. What letters can the children find in their bowls now?

(Or, 1371 "Modeling-Dough Letters.")

1350

Mister Rogers attends a performance of "The Elves, the Shoemaker, and the Shoemaker's Wife."

"Matching Shoes" can help children:

- recognize likeness and difference.

Matching Shoes

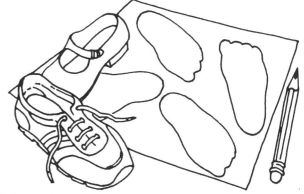

Materials

- a box with four or five pairs of shoes (baby shoes, children's shoes, grownup's shoes, sneakers, slippers, etc.)
- shoes from each of the children
- pencil
- paper

Ask the children to take off their shoes and add them to the box of shoes you've collected. You might want to add yours to the box, too. Now, spread out the shoes on the floor and talk about who might wear each pair. Mix up all the shoes and give each child a chance to find two shoes that match. Once all the shoes are matched, the children could try some of these activities:

- Arrange the shoes from smallest to largest.
- Put all the big shoes in one place and the small ones in another.
- Sort the shoes by color.
- Can the children find their own shoes? Their friends' shoes? Your shoes?

How about tracing around each child's foot and letting the children match their shoes to their paper tracings? Or even cutting out the tracings and putting them *in* their shoes?

Thoughts For The Week

*Children often enjoy playing with water, and water play can be important play because it helps children learn how to keep water where it belongs. Many caregivers have told me that they avoid water play because it makes such a mess. Other caregivers have told me that they have learned to control the mess by setting strict limits about water play **before** the play begins. This week we'll be talking about on and off switches for waterfalls, turning faucets, squirting water, and putting out fires. Children need to know how to turn water off and on, what the limits are for splashing, what things can be sprayed with water and what can't, and how to clean up water that has been spilled. Learning to control water through play can be a big help in a child's effort to learn **self**-control.*

Fred Rogers

Songs On The Programs This Week

1351   *"O.C.S. Alma Mater"*
       "Good People Sometimes Do Bad Things"
1352   *"I'm Taking Care of You"*
       "It's the People You Like the Most"
1353   *"Parents Were Little Once Too"*
1354   *"Sometimes People Are Good"*
1355   *"Sometimes"*
       "Look and Listen"
       "It's You I Like"

Your Notes For The Week

1351

Mister Rogers uses a piece of flexible tubing and pretends he is playing a musical instrument. He shows how to make a waterfall by controlling the water from a faucet.

"Blowing Bubbles" can help children:

- develop creative play.

Blowing Bubbles

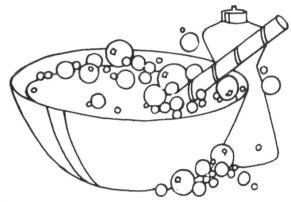

Materials

- straws
- bowls
- dish soap
- bubble wands or pipes (optional)

Children can make mounds of bubbles by blowing through straws into a bowl of soap suds. They will need to understand that they have to blow *out* through the straw, so let them practice blowing through the straws first. (They can hold their hands near the ends of their straws to feel the air coming out.) Then give each one a bowl of plain water for practicing, then a bowl of soapy water to use for blowing suds into bubbles. Can you play outdoors today and show the children how to make bubbles that float in the air? If you don't have a bubble wand or pipe, you could try using the fingerholes in a pair of blunt-nosed scissors as a way to launch the bubbles.

Tuesday

1352

Audrey Cleans Everything, her daughter, Holly, and her granddaughter, Maggie, visit with Mister Rogers. Holly shows some needlepoint creations. In the Neighborhood of Make-Believe, Miss Paulificate has a magic needlepoint "on and off" sign. Mister Rogers enjoys the music of a Vietnamese sitar player and stresses the importance of practice in learning.

"Yarn Designs" can help children:

• develop the ability to keep on trying;
• develop muscle control.

Yarn Designs

Materials

• cardboard or styrofoam tray
• yarn
• tape
• sharp pencil or paper punch

Before you begin the activity, wrap the ends of the yarn with tape to make a hard tip that will thread easily. Then, using a paper punch or sharp pencil, make holes in the tray or piece of cardboard. Show the children how to thread the yarn through the holes to make designs. They may want to use several colors of yarn if you have them available. Encourage them to try out different ways of overlapping the yarn. They may find the threading a little difficult at first, but you can reassure them that learning something new takes time and practice. This might be an activity that they could do again on other days to see how much easier it becomes.

Wednesday

1353

Mister Rogers talks about controlling fluids. He shows how to turn a spigot off and on and uses a squirt bottle to spray water into the tub. There's a fire in the Neighborhood of Make-Believe, and the fire is put out with squirt bottles.

"Water Play" can help children:

• develop self-control.

Water Play

Materials

• dish pan or plastic tub
• measuring cups or small plastic pitchers
• funnel

The children might like to help you fill a dishpan or plastic tub with lukewarm water. Add measuring cups, plastic pitchers and funnels for the children to use for pouring, filling and emptying. You may need to set limits about things like:

• keeping the water in the tub;
• wearing aprons or plastic smocks;
• the number of children playing with water at one time.

If weather permits, you could fill squirt bottles for outdoor water play. Children can use the bottles for:

• spraying plants with water;
• cleaning up the sand toys;
• pretending about fires.

You might have to emphasize that water is not for spraying at people. Also point out to them how well they're able to keep their squirts in the tub or the pan. They really can *control* their fluids. If any of the children were frightened about the Make-Believe fire, you might want to talk with them about how the people in Make-Believe felt.

200

1354

Lady Aberlin and Bob Dog talk about yesterday's fire. Henrietta was crying, and Bob Dog says some people cry when they're scared and mad.

"Why Do People Cry?" can help children:

- express strong feelings in appropriate ways;
- talk about feelings.

Why Do People Cry?

Materials

- none

Crying is a way to express our feelings. Why do the children think Henrietta is crying? How do they think she felt? Can they tell you about something that made them feel like crying? What are some of the feelings people can show when they are crying?

- sadness?
- loneliness?
- anger?
- fear?
- pain?

Can any of the children think of a time when someone they know cried because they were happy:

- When he or she received a special present?
- At a friend's wedding?

Sometimes people cry when they're happy because they are so full of special feelings. Crying doesn't always mean a person is sad, but it's only the person inside who knows why he or she is crying. Other people can guess, but they don't know for sure unless that crying person tells them.

1355

Mister Rogers begins reading "The History of Planet Purple." People in the Neighborhood of Make-Believe are cleaning up after the fire with soap and water.

"Washing Toys" can help children:

- learn to do things independently.

Washing Toys

Materials

- plastic bowls or buckets
- soapy water
- cloths or sponges
- old toothbrushes, nailbrushes or scrub-brushes
- washable toys

If the weather permits, this could be an outdoor activity. Otherwise, the toys could be washed on a plastic tablecloth, on the kitchen floor, or in the bathtub. (Only washable toys of course.) You'll probably need to find a place for some of the toys to dry before returning them to the shelves. The children may also be able to help you wash plastic spoons or dishes. Each child could wash his or her own, or one could wash while others dry and put away.

(Or, 1357 "Purple Print Pictures.")

Thoughts For The Week

*Being different from one another is part of what makes each of us special. Children, though, often want to be **like** other people, particularly the people they love. They need time to learn both about the ways we are alike and about the ways each of us is different. It may take a lot of reassurance from grownups before they really understand that the people who love us are the ones who like us to be different.*

Something else that's often hard to learn is that people will love us for who we are whether we win or lose. Small children often lose when they compete with people who are older. Older children seem to run faster or play games better! When they're young, children need a grownup's help to see that they are getting better at doing things as they get older. Most of all, they need grownups to let them know they are acceptable and lovable just the way they are right now.

Fred Rogers

Songs On The Program This Week

1356 *"Everybody Has a History"*

1357 *"You Are You"*

1358 *"Everybody's Fancy"*
"You Are Special"

1359 *"A Handy Lady and a Handy Man"*
"It's the People You Like the Most"

1360 *"The Clown in Me"*

Your Notes For The Week

1356

Mister Rogers continues reading "The History of Planet Purple." He reads about the changes that are taking place and reminds viewers that when people have a chance to hear and see different things, they may start to make changes themselves.

"My History" can help children:

- learn more about their world;
- understand and accept individual differences.

My History

Materials

- paper
- stapler
- tape
- glue
- magazines pictures of babies, baby toys and baby clothes

You can make a "history" book for each child by stapling several blank pages of paper together. Things you might then include in the books are:

- date of birth;
- city of birth;
- names of parents;
- names of any older brothers or sisters or other relatives;
- baby pictures;
- favorite foods, colors, animals, etc.

The children could draw pictures of themselves as babies, then as older children, or paste pictures of favorite toys they had as a baby, then as an older child. Can they tell you about important things that happened as they were growing up—things you could jot down for them in their books? The things that children remember as "important" could give you some extra clues to special relationships in their lives.

<table>
<tr><td>

Tuesday

1357

In the Neighborhood of Make-Believe, Paul and Pauline arrive for a visit from Planet Purple. They announce that the new laws on Planet Purple allow everyone to be different.

"Purple Print Pictures" can help children:

- recognize likeness and difference;
- understand and accept individual differences.

Purple Print Pictures

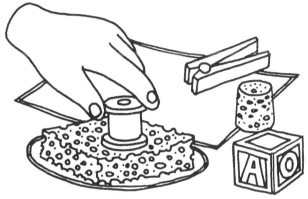

Materials

- purple paper
- light-colored paper
- purple paint or purple food coloring (mix red and blue)
- sponge(s)
- plate(s)
- several small objects for printing (spools from thread, blocks, corks, clothespins, etc.)

You and the children can make one or more stamp pads by pouring a little diluted paint or food coloring onto a sponge. (If you place the sponge on a plate it may help to avoid a messy table.) Then the children can use the small objects you've collected for print pictures. Allow the children to do some printing on the purple paper first. How well can they see the prints they've made? You could point out that it's hard to see the prints when everything is one color. Can the children tell you several ways that the people on Planet Purple are alike? For example:

- all men and boys are named Paul;
- all women and girls are named Pauline.

Then ask the children what changes Paul and Pauline have made. (One is that they wear a different color sash.) Let the children make prints on the light-colored paper. Can they see the prints more easily?

(Or, 1191 "Camouflage"; 1276 "Name Cards.")

</td><td>

Wednesday

1358

Among the changes that are taking place on Planet Purple is a name change: Planet Purple Fairchilde. Lady Elaine is overjoyed to hear that the planet has been named for her. Mister Rogers talks about the different names one person can have.

"What Do You Call Me?" can help children:

- learn more about their world.

What Do You Call Me?

Materials

- none

The idea of one person having several names can be a hard one for children to understand. As their caregiver, what name do the children call you? Have they ever heard anyone call you something else?

- What do your own children call you?
- What do your day care children's parents call you?
- What names do other adults or children use for you?

Point out that a person can have several different names:

- Mrs. Smith;
- Barbara;
- Aunt Barb;
- Grandma;
- Mom, Mother.

Some children may be able to talk about the different names they have. Do any of the children have names for a favorite doll or stuffed animal?

</td></tr>
</table>

1359

Lady Elaine wants to change the name of the Neighborhood to "Neighborhood of Make-Believe Fairchilde." Handyman Negri takes a survey and the vote is "No." Lady Elaine feels rejected because she lost, but she soon realizes that nobody wins all the time.

"Winning and Losing" can help children:

- practice making choices;
- understand and accept individual differences.

Winning and Losing

Materials

- none

Can you plan a time today when you all can take a vote on something? For instance:

- apple juice or orange juice at snack time;
- modeling dough or painting at the kitchen table;
- playing in the yard or walking to the park.

Not all the children will get their preferences, and you could talk with them about winning and losing. How did they feel if their choice did not get the most votes? Is it hard to go along with the group decision when it's different from their own? (Younger children may need your reassurances that the other snack or activity will be available another time.) Can any of the children remember a time when they lost in a game like running a race, catching a ball, playing a board game? How did they feel? You could point out that winning games can seem more fun than losing, but the playing of the game is what's meant to be the most fun of all.

1360

Purple Panda teaches Lady Elaine Fairchilde the "purple" way to travel—just think where you want to be and that's where you are.

"Ways to Travel" can help children:

- understand wishing can't make things happen;
- understand the difference between real and pretend.

Ways to Travel

Materials

- magazine pictures of people walking or running
- magazine pictures of vehicles (children on bikes and riding toys, as well as trains, buses, cars, airplanes, rockets)
- paper
- paste

Ask the children about Purple Panda's quick way to travel:

- Is that a real way to travel or a pretend way?
- What are some real ways that people can go somewhere?
- How could you really travel to another planet?

Let the children look through the magazine pictures to choose the ones they want to paste on their paper. Do any of the children want to draw their own pictures of ways to travel? Have they ever traveled in a plane? A train? A bus? A trolley? The children might enjoy making a travel display. Encourage them to find all the toy cars, trucks, planes, trains, buses, and wagons you may have and put them all in one place. They might like to show the display to their parents at the end of the day.

Thoughts For The Week

Helping grownups with household tasks is one way that children can feel useful and important. There are many things you do around the house that children can do with you. Cooking and baking, for instance, give children a chance to learn about tastes, smells, textures, and changes that take place. Children use lots of energy when they mix, knead, pound, or beat ingredients, and they may need to practice persistence and concentration, too. When we encourage children to work along with us in our daily chores, we help them realize how many things they can accomplish.

Fred Rogers

Songs On The Programs This Week

1361 *"There Are Many Ways"*
     "I'm a Chef"
1362 *"It's You I Like"*
1363 *"A Handy Lady and a Handy Man"*
1364 *"I Like to Take My Time"*
     "Tree, Tree, Tree"
1365 *"I Like to Take My Time"*

Your Notes For The Week

1361

Mrs. McFeely and Chef Brockett ask Mister Rogers to help make waffles today. Mister Rogers makes a list of what he needs and finds the ingredients in the kitchen. When the waffles are done, they all try different toppings (peanut butter, honey, jam).

"Pancakes or Waffles" can help children:

- learn more about foods;
- try out different roles;
- practice taking turns.

Pancakes or Waffles

Materials

- skillet or waffle iron
- your favorite pancake or waffle recipe (there's one on page C-1)
- pancake turner
- bowl
- measuring cups and spoons
- mixing spoon
- syrup or honey

As you make the pancakes or waffles, the children can take turns doing things like:

- beating the eggs;
- adding the flour;
- mixing the ingredients.

Children usually like to help grownups with cooking activities, but they also like to *pretend* about cooking and preparing meals. Today might be a good day for pretending about cooking, too. All you'll need are props like plastic bowls, cups, cooking utensils and aprons. A chef's hat pattern can be found on page B-2.

1362

Mister Rogers repairs a leaky bucket, then visits Bob Trow's workshop and watches a cooper making a wooden bucket. The cooper tells Mister Rogers that he always enjoyed working with wood, even when he was a child.

"Wooden Sculptures" can help children:

- learn more about their world;
- develop creative play.

Wooden Sculptures

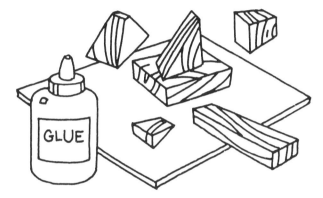

Materials

- small wood scraps (lumber yards often have an assortment of small throwaway pieces)
- liquid glue
- brushes (optional)
- sandpaper

In an area protected by newspapers or plastic sheets, the children can arrange the wooden pieces and glue them together to make wooden sculptures. (Be sure the wood scraps are free of splinters.) When the glue has dried, some children may want to paint their finished sculptures. Can the children find things around the house that are made of wood? Take them on a tour and let them feel the texture of wooden furniture.

1363

An American Indian family visits Mister Rogers and shows him several Indian dances. Mister Rogers joins them in a "Friendship Dance."

"Friendship Dances" can help children:

- express feelings through movement and dance.

Friendship Dances

Materials

- drum (an oatmeal box or empty coffee can will work)

One way to begin this activity is for you to be the drummer and beat out a steady rhythm. Encourage the children to clap along if they wish. Then see if they can move their feet to the rhythm, making up a dance. If they want to try a friendship dance, they could all join hands in a circle and dance together to the drumming sounds. Some of the children might want a turn being the drummer.

(Or, 1269 "Drum Rhythms"; 1338 "Sand Pictures.")

1364

Mister Rogers listens to tape-recorded sounds from the Neighborhood—a dog barking, a cat meowing, a cow mooing, a canary, and a whippoorwill.

"What Do You Hear?" can help children:

- learn to listen carefully.

What Do You Hear?

Materials

- none

Ask the children to close their eyes and be as quiet as possible. What kinds of sounds do they hear? Listen for things like:

- the refrigerator motor;
- cars outside (engines, horns);
- dogs barking;
- water dripping;
- footsteps.

Try making other sounds for them to identify—like snapping fingers, bouncing a ball, etc. This is a good activity to do over and over again. Listen for different sounds when you're:

- taking a walk;
- in the yard playing;
- waiting for parents to come at the end of the day.

Remind the children that listening carefully takes practice. If by any chance you should have a child who is hearing-impaired in your group, that child could show everyone the "signs" for the different sounds the others discover. Then that child can be a teacher for a while.

(Or, 1274 "Animal Sounds.")

1365

Mister Rogers shows a film of the Watts tower in Los Angeles—a tower made from discarded things.

"Recycle Collage" can help children:

- practice working cooperatively;
- learn about conservation.

Recycle Collage

Materials

- box of discarded objects (plastic caps, pieces of styrofoam, cardboard tubes, rubber bands, paperclips, twist ties, popsicle sticks, soap wrappers, etc.)
- cardboard (cut off the side of a large box)
- glue

The children can make a collage by gluing discarded objects on a piece of cardboard. There may be lots of discussion about where to put things. This can be a chance for you to help them cooperate and work together to make some decisions by asking questions or making suggestions like:

- How should we do this?
- Could each person work on a different side?
- Would you rather work as partners on each side of the cardboard?
- Maybe one of you could arrange all the paperclips and someone else could glue the soap wrappers.

If some of the children find a group project too difficult, you might need to provide separate pieces of heavy paper or cardboard for each to use alone.

Thoughts For The Week

1366

This week, John Reardon of the Metropolitan Opera Company joins the neighbors in Make-Believe in planning an opera for children. During the week-long process that leads to the opera, viewers are exposed to much more than the opera itself. There's the thinking and planning and helping and making…and the willingness of everyone to stick with the project even though much of the work seems routine or tedious. Even the children watching at home are contributing to our opera as they become our spectators or as they sing along with the songs they'll hear again and again this week. Watching our opera gives children the chance to see people acting and singing about things they're thinking about. With your encouragement, your children may find their own ways (musical and otherwise) to express their thoughts and feelings, too.

Fred Rogers

Songs On The Programs This Week

1366 "When a Baby Comes to Your House"
"It's Such a Good Feeling"
1368 "Just for Once"
1369 "Everybody's Fancy"

Your Notes For The Week

Mister Rogers visits with his sister, Lanie, and her two children. He talks about relationships like brother, sister, nephew, and uncle. In the Neighborhood of Make-Believe, plans for the opera begin.

"All about Families" can help children:

- learn more about their world;
- work on feelings about separation.

All about Families

Materials

- paper
- markers or crayons
- photographs of family members (optional)

Families come in many different shapes and sizes. Sometimes our "family" is made up of people who aren't related to us by blood at all, but they're still our family because they're the ones who love us and care for us when we need it. You may have to help some children understand that even when mommies and daddies don't live together, they still go on being mommies and daddies. It's important in this activity that all the children feel part of a loving "family" of grownups and friends who care about them. See if the children can tell you the names of the people in their families. Here are some questions you might want to use:

- Who are the people in your family?
- How are they related to you?
- Do families always live in the same house?
- What makes a person part of your family?

Encourage the children to draw pictures of their families and tell you the names of the people in their pictures. Or, ask the parents to send in photographs of the people in their families, and see if the children can name them. How are they related to each other? Older children may be able to think of different names for the same person. For instance:

- your mother's *sister* is your *aunt*;
- your father's *mother* is your *grandmother*;
- your aunt's *daughter* is your *cousin*.

1367

Mister Rogers shows an old-time washboard and pantomimes washing clothes on it. He and Mr. McFeely see a demonstration of a wringer washing machine. In the Neighborhood of Make-Believe a setting for the opera has been chosen: It will take place in a laundry.

"Washing Doll Clothes" can help children:

- learn to do things independently;
- learn more about their world;
- practice taking turns.

Washing Doll Clothes

Materials

- wash-basin or sink
- soapy water
- doll clothes
- large plastic container with a tight-fitting lid (optional)

Can the children think of different ways to clean clothes? For example:

- washing them by hand;
- rubbing them on a washboard;
- using an automatic washing machine at home;
- going to a laundromat.

How do their parents do laundry:

- Do they go to a laundromat?
- Is there a washer and dryer in the building for everyone to share?
- Do they wash clothes by hand?
- Do they have their own washing machine?
- Do they hang clothes on a line to dry or do they use a dryer?

The children can wash the doll clothes by hand in the sink or create their own homemade "washing machine" by putting water, soap and doll clothes in a plastic container with a tight-fitting lid. The children can take turns shaking the container to clean the clothes. They will need to rinse the clothes in clean water, squeeze out the excess water (they could roll them in a dry towel) and hang them to dry.

(Or, 1296 "Washing Clothes.")

1368

Francois Clemmons has taken several photographs with his new camera—photographs of the fronts and backs of people. Mister Rogers tries to guess the neighbors from the photographs of their backs. Francois plans to be Philip Photographer in the opera.

"Front and Back" can help children:

- learn to look carefully;
- learn more about their bodies.

Front and Back

Materials

- large mirror
- hand mirror
- paper
- markers or crayons
- scissors
- paste
- magazines

Talk with the children about objects in the room that have fronts and backs. These could be things like books, furniture, dolls, or toy cars and trucks. Using a doll, show the children its front and then its back, talking about the ways the doll looks different and the ways it looks the same. When one child stands with his or her back to the group, can the others tell who it is? How? If you have a large mirror, the children could take turns standing with their backs to it and holding a hand mirror in front of them. Can they see their backs? Some of the children may be able to draw a picture of themselves from the front on one side of a piece of paper, and then from the back on the other side. Can they find pictures of people's backs in old magazines? Are these people male or female? Grownups or children? How can you tell?

1369

Mr. McFeely arrives with two rare diamonds, one of which is black and very expensive. At Bob Trow's workshop, Mr. Kaplan is visiting and has brought with him an array of sparkling diamonds. In the Neighborhood of Make-Believe, Lady Aberlin polishes a stone to make a pretend diamond for the opera. Back in the "real" neighborhood, Mister Rogers shows a film about things that sparkle in the wintertime.

"Sparkle Paintings" can help children:

- develop creative play.

Sparkle Paintings

Materials

- flour
- salt
- water
- food coloring (optional)
- containers
- brushes
- cardboard or heavy paper

You might start by talking with the children about different things that sparkle. Can they remember some of the things they saw in the film. You could ask questions like:

- What does "sparkle" mean?
- Can you think of some things that sparkle?
- Do you know what makes something sparkle?
- How do you feel when you see something sparkle?

By mixing equal parts of flour, salt, and water, you and the children can make a white sparkle paint to use on different-colored papers. You can add food coloring to this mixture, too. When the paint dries, the salt gives the picture a glistening quality. The children might want to tell you about their paintings and imagine what the sparkles could be.

1370

The opera, "All in the Laundry," is presented today. Lady Elaine is the mean owner of a laundry. She forces Reardon to do all the dirty work. Lady Aberlin, who sings the part of a rich woman, falls in love with a photograph of Reardon's back, but doesn't know where to find him. Chef Brockett and Pilot Ito, two handball/football players, recognize Reardon's photo and tell Lady Aberlin who he is. Reardon, for his part, has already fallen in love with a photograph of Lady Aberlin, so when the two meet, they plan to be married. Lady Aberlin buys both the laundry and X the Owl's apartment house—for 23 quadrillion!

"Attending the Opera" can help children:

- develop their imaginations;
- try out different roles.

Attending the Opera

Materials

- none

Today would be a good time to be sure all of you watch MISTER ROGERS' NEIGHBORHOOD together. Talk with the children about what it means to be part of the audience (listening quietly, no loud talking, sitting in one place, etc.). Then, when the program is over, talk with them about the opera. What do they remember? They might want to make up their own opera—maybe an opera about your day care place. See if anyone would like to make up a story and sing the words instead of saying them. That's what making an opera is all about.

Thoughts For The Week

One theme that we talk about again and again in our television programs is that everyone is different and that those differences make each one of us unique and special. Accepting differences in other people is not always easy, and sometimes the differences may even frighten us. Our special guest on the programs this week is Tim Scanlon of the National Theater for the Deaf, a talented actor, artist, and teacher of pantomime. I explain to the children that at first I had a hard time understanding some of the things Tim said. But a person's voice isn't the most important thing—it's the person himself that's important. Each time I saw Tim, I understood him better, and the more I understood, the better I liked him. That's true for most of us. The more we understand people, the better chance we have of liking them.

Fred Rogers

Songs On The Programs This Week

1371 *"It's You I Like"*
1373 *"Everybody's Fancy"*
1374 *"Look and Listen"*
       "I'm Taking Care of You"
       "I'm Proud of You"

Your Notes For The Week

1371

Mister Rogers visits a doughnut-maker who shows him how to make doughnuts by forming the dough, shaping and twisting it, then frying it in hot oil. In the Neighborhood of Make-Beieve, the Trolley delivers doughnuts shaped like alphabet letters to X the Owl.

"Modeling-Dough Letters" can help children:

- recognize and use symbols.

Modeling-Dough Letters

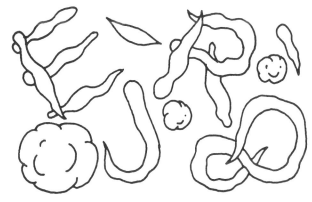

Materials

- modeling dough (recipe on page A-1)

You might want to begin this activity by giving the children time to knead, poke, punch, and roll the modeling dough. Then see if any of the children can roll pieces of the dough between their hands to make long strands. Can they loop and shape them to make letters? Start with easy letters like O, C, S, X, T, E, L, and W. (You might want to show the children how a C can become an O or how an F can become an E.) If the younger children find this activity too difficult, they may prefer to continue pounding, punching, and rolling the dough while they watch you or the older children make letters. Do any of the children want to make their names from dough letters? If you let the letters dry overnight, the children could paint them or take them home.

1372

Mister Rogers tries on a set of headphones that go with a stereo. He can't hear sounds around him with them on, and so he talks about how feeling left out can make a person feel mad or sad. The neighbors in Make-Believe meet Tim Scanlon, X's new teacher. Tim is deaf, and the neighbors have trouble understanding him because at first his voice sounds strange.

"Lip Reading" can help children:

- learn different ways people communicate;
- talk about feelings.

Lip Reading

Materials

- none

Can any of the children tell you how being able to hear helps them? What kinds of things can they hear? For instance:

- friends talking;
- sounds around them;
- music;
- the telephone or doorbell;
- a radio or television.

How do they think it would feel if they couldn't hear at all? See if the children can read your lips as you form words without your voice. You could use a simple sentence like, "How are you?" or name each child in the group. Can they tell you how they feel when they can't understand you? Say the words out loud for them, then let them try to read your lips again. Was it easier the second time? You might point out that people who can't hear have to practice a long time to learn to "read" lips well. If you have a hearing-impaired child in your group, that child can "teach" some of the other ways of "hearing" that he or she has learned.

(Or, 1293 "Talking without Words"; 1364 "What Do You Hear?")

1373

The Neighborhood of Make-Believe is covered with decorations and signs—all the work of X the Owl and his new teacher, who is a master printer.

"Making Signs" can help children:

- recognize and use symbols;
- learn more about their world.

Making Signs

Materials

- notecards or strips of paper
- markers or crayons
- tape

Talk with the children about the signs in the Neighborhood of Make-Believe. Can they remember what any of the signs said? Ask them to look around the room and try to name the things they see. As they name each object, print the word on a card and hang it up near the object. Some things you could label are:

- stove, refrigerator, sink, etc.;
- chair, sofa, table, etc.;
- objects on the toy shelf;
- objects on the book shelf;
- floors, walls, doors, closets, etc.;
- television, radio, clocks.

The children might want to decorate the signs with markers or crayons before you hang them, and you could leave the signs up for a while to let the children practice "reading" them. On a nice day, you might want to take the children for a walk through the neighborhood and look for other signs.

(Or, 1276 "Name Cards.")

1374

Mister Rogers talks about ways that people who don't hear well can find out about things with their hands and their eyes. They can understand a lot by watching people.

"Pantomime Feelings" can help children:
- learn different ways people communicate;
- learn more about their bodies.

Pantomime Feelings

Materials
- paper
- hand mirror
- markers or crayons

See what kinds of feelings the children can name for you. Then pantomime different feelings, using facial expressions, and ask them to guess the feelings you are showing them. Encourage the children to try out different facial expressions. How would they look if they were:
- happy?
- sad?
- afraid?
- surprised?
- angry?

If you have a small mirror, you could let the children look at themselves while they change facial expressions. Do any of them want to draw faces that show different feelings? Do any of them feel like making a funny face?

1375

King Friday invited everyone to a dinner party in honor of Professor Scanlon. Unfortunately, he didn't tell anyone about it until the last moment, and Professor Scanlon had to leave before the party began. The King says he learned a lesson about planning parties in advance, and all the neighbors agree they learned many things from Tim Scanlon.

"Planning a Party" can help children:
- practice working cooperatively.

Planning a Party

Materials
- paper and pencil
- scrap materials
- scissors
- glue, tape, or string

You could plan a party as part of a holiday or birthday celebration. Or, plan your own festive occasion, such as a day for parents to stay for a before-dinner snack of cheese and crackers. Talk with the children about the things that should be done ahead of time. Things like:
- setting the date;
- making invitations;
- planning the menu;
- making decorations and welcome signs;
- making placecards or placemats with people's names.

Encourage all the children to take part in the planning by finding a special job for each one to do. On the day of the party they might want to:
- help serve the food;
- show where to hang coats;
- introduce their parents and friends;
- sing a song together.

(Or, 1281 "Variety Show.")

Thoughts For The Week

Learning to play is one of the most important tasks of childhood. Through play, children are able to explore their inner feelings and play out ideas with toys and imaginary people. They can put the toys and people in different situations and control them in a way they can't control real people or big things around them. Some children need encouragement to create pretend worlds. Others need only the props—dress-up clothes; little cars, people, and furniture; or a set of blocks. Providing plenty of time and space for playing is a gift many of us give children without realizing what an important gift it is!

Fred Rogers

Songs On The Programs This Week

1376 "Be Brave, Be Strong"
1377 "Children Can"
1378 "It's You I Like"
       "Pretending"
       "What Do You Hear?"
1379 "I Like to Take My Time"
       "I Like to Be Told"
       "I'm a Man Who Manufactures"
1380 "You Can Never Go down the Drain"

Your Notes For The Week

1376

Elsie Neal gives Mister Rogers a shirt she has made. He matches the pattern on the shirt to a piece of fabric she has in the shop and helps her cut out another shirt.

"Fabric Cards" can help children:

- develop creative play;
- feel proud of their accomplishments.

Fabric Cards

Materials

- small scraps of fabric
- yarn, ribbon, or lace
- liquid glue
- old greeting cards (optional)
- heavy paper folded to make a card

Encourage the children to look at the scraps and feel them, calling their attention to things like:

- different colors;
- textures;
- patterns.

After they have covered the outside of the card with scraps, let them make up a message for you to write inside. Or, if you have any old greeting cards, you could help them cut out the messages to glue inside their own cards. When they are finished, talk about how they feel when they make something special to give to people they love.

(Or, 1240 "Pole Dyeing.")

1377

Lady Elaine misunderstood something Lady Aberlin said, and now she thinks that Corney loves her best. When he gives her a baseball bat that she admires, she considers it an engagement present and rushes to tell Elsie Jean that she is engaged.

"Misunderstandings" can help children:

● learn to listen carefully.

Misunderstandings

Materials

● none

Can you share with the children a time when a person said something to you, and you thought that person meant something else? How did you feel when you found out what that person really meant? (Disappointed? Sad? Glad?) Older children might enjoy this game about misunderstandings: Whisper a rhyme or silly phrase into the ear of one child, and tell that child to whisper it to the person next to him or her. Continue around the group, and then ask the last person to say the phrase out loud. How close was the phrase to the one that you whispered at the beginning? Younger children might be able to play this game in pairs. Tell one child to whisper something to the other one. Can he or she repeat the phrase out loud? If they're not sure what was said, can they try to guess? You could point out that sometimes things people say are misunderstood by others. Listening carefully is one way to try to understand.

1378

Mister Rogers shows an assortment of hats, including a silk top hat that is too big for him. He shows a film of children getting dressed up in grownups' clothing. Lady Elaine is busy planning her wedding day, but she hasn't told Corney yet. (He's supposed to be the groom, but he doesn't know anything about it.)

"Trying on Hats" can help children:

● try out different roles.

Trying on Hats

Materials

● an assortment of hats, or
● pictures from magazines or books of people in different kinds of hats

See if the children can bring in any old hats from their homes. Add to the collection by making several hats from construction paper. As the children try on the various hats, encourage them to think of a person who might wear the hat. Here are some ideas:

● a cap for a baseball player;
● a large hat or a silky scarf for a bride or bridesmaid;
● a top hat (see page B-2);
● a fancy hat for going to a party;
● a red hat for a firefighter;
● an old military hat for a lettercarrier or policeman;
● a helmet to wear when riding a bike.

Set aside time for them to try out their roles. They may be able to play out a story or a theme. For instance, a wedding, directing traffic, or going to a party. Or you might want to just look at pictures of people in different kinds of hats. What might those people be doing? Where might they be going?

1379

Mister Rogers shows how to set a table using a placemat, napkin, fork, knife, spoon, and cup.

"Setting the Table" can help children:

- learn to do things independently.

Setting the Table

Materials

- placemats (paper towels work well)
- plates or bowls
- silverware
- cups
- napkins

Can any of the children tell you what things you need to set the table for a meal? For example:

- Do you need plates, cups, forks?
- What about napkins?
- Can any of the children tell you how many of each thing they would need for setting the table at day care? What if they were setting the table at their own home?

When it's time to set the table, help them get started by setting out the correct number of placemats, or arrange the exact number of chairs around the table. Each child can have a job to do. You might also want to find a set of toy dishes for the play area—or make a set of dishes from cardboard. Then the children can practice setting the table on their own and can pretend about mealtimes.

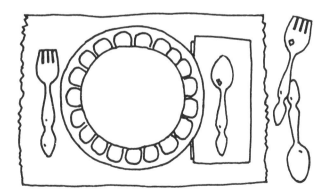

1380

Mister Rogers shows how a sand sifter works, letting small pieces of sand fall through the screen. Then he shows how water runs through the sifter, too. He talks about how very young children may be afraid of going down the drain along with the water, and sings "You Can Never Go down the Drain."

"Going down the Drain" can help children:

- use play to work on feelings.

Going down the Drain

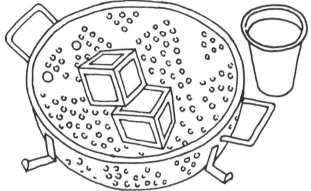

Materials

- collander or sand sifter
- sand (salt may be substituted)
- water
- several small toys
- dishpan to catch sand and water

Show the children how sand will go through the collander or sifter easily. They might want to try putting their fingers into the holes. Can their fingers fit through? Let each one have a chance to pour sand into the collander. Can they tell you why the sand goes through but their fingers can't?When everyone has had a chance to use the sand, place several toys into the collander and pour water over them. (You'll want to do this in a dishpan or over the sink or bathtub.)

- Did the water go through?
- What about the toys?

Explain to the children that a drain is like the holes of a collander—it allows water to go through but not people. Toys that are smaller than the drain opening *might* go through, but children's bodies are too big. If you can find an old collander, you might want to make it available for sand or water play so the children can keep on experimenting.

Thoughts For The Week

Children often need a grownup's help to understand the difference between reality and fantasy. That's one reason why, in our programs, we keep the Neighborhood of Make-Believe very separate from our "real" neighborhood. In Make-Believe, we pretend about many things that couldn't ever happen in real life, and we encourage children who are watching to pretend whatever they want to pretend when they're making up their own play. Pretending about their feelings and their world is one of the most important ways that children can play. At the same time, children need to know where pretend stops. They need to know, for instance, that in the real world it isn't magic and wishes that make things happen, but real live people like themselves who learn and work and try and keep on trying as they attempt to make their hopes and wishes come true.

Fred Rogers

Songs On The Programs This Week

1381 "Everybody's Fancy"
"You Are You"
1382 "Pretending"
1383 "It's You I Like"
"You Are Special"
1384 "Pretending"
1385 "I'm a Chef"

Your Notes For The Week

1381

In the Neighborhood of Make-Believe, Lady Elaine continues to plan her wedding, even though some of the neighbors doubt that there's really going to be a wedding. In the "real" neighborhood, Mister Rogers talks about how important it is to know when we're pretending.

"Pretending" can help children:

- understand the difference between real and pretend;
- develop their imaginations.

Pretending

Materials

- none

Do the children think Lady Elaine's wedding will really take place? Why or why not? You could point out that people sometimes get confused about real and pretend. Can they think of a time when they weren't sure if something was real or pretend? They might think of things like:

- someone dressed up at Halloween time;
- another child pretending to be a tiger or a monster;
- a puppet on someone's hand;
- a clown at a parade or circus;
- a scary dream.

Would any of the children like to pretend to be an animal or another person? Is it real or pretend? Then everyone could pretend to be:

- elephants;
- clowns;
- birds;
- airplanes.

Do the children have any other ideas for pretending? You might want to give them a "five minutes more" warning before it's time to stop.

(Or, 1271 "An Imaginary Person.")

1382

Corney finally learns of Lady Elaine's wedding plans. He's going on a business trip and tells Lady Elaine that he's too busy to play wedding. Lady Elaine then realizes that the engagement was all in her imagination. Lady Aberlin takes her to talk with King Friday about her disappointment.

"Disappointments" can help children:

● understand wishing can't make things happen;

● understand the difference between real and pretend.

Disappointments

Materials

● paper

● crayons or markers

Can any of the children tell you how Lady Elaine felt when she realized that Corney never intended to marry her? Someone might be able to tell you of a time when he or she hoped something would happen and then felt disappointed when it didn't. You could ask questions like:

● What were you disappointed about?

● How did you feel? (Angry? Sad?)

● What helped you feel better?

You may need to explain that Lady Elaine was disappointed because she had imagined things would be very different than they turned out, but she was able to talk with King Friday about her feelings. Remind the children that it can be fun to imagine and pretend as long as we remember that our pretending isn't what makes things happen. Encourage the children to talk about some imaginary things that could never happen, like a dog driving a car, or a horse being able to talk. Some of the children might want to draw a picture of the wedding Lady Elaine imagined, or of something they've imagined themselves doing. When the pictures are finished, you could ask the children if they would like to tell you and the others what their pictures are about.

1383

Mister Rogers shows the difference between a picture of something and the real object. Then he talks about scary things on television that are only pretend.

"Pictures of Things" can help children:

● recognize likeness and difference;

● learn more about their world.

Pictures of Things

Materials

● real objects to show the children (furniture, toys, clothing, food, etc.)

● magazine photos of similar things

See if the children can name the real objects as you point out each one. Then show them the magazine pictures. Can they name the things they see in the pictures? You might want to give each child a picture and see if he or she can match it to the real object. Ask the children how the pictures are different from the real thing. This might be a good time to talk about television pictures. Although Mister Rogers is a real person, he can't see the children because the television set only shows a moving picture of him. What are some other things they see on television?

● cartoons?

● monsters?

● wild animals?

You'll want to reassure the children that the things they see on television cannot come out of the television set. They may not be able to understand this fully at first, but they do need to hear your reassurances until they know for themselves that it's so.

1384

Mister Rogers brings his puppet collection and shows how he moves them and speaks for them. He stresses the make-believe aspects of his television programs. And in the Neighborhood of Make-Believe, Lady Elaine makes an important announcement—she is starting her own television station.

"A Television Program" can help children:

● develop creative play.

A Television Program

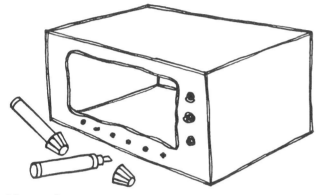

Materials
● large cardboard box
● markers
● paint and brushes (optional)
● puppets, dolls, and other toys for props

How about making a pretend television program today? Cut one side out of a large cardboard box. Cut a hole, the size of a television screen, out of the opposite side. The children might enjoy painting the pretend television set. When the paint has dried, they can add knobs and dials with a marker, or different-colored paint, or wood scraps. Using puppets and other toys for props, the children can take turns putting on television programs. They might enjoy:

● pretending about a favorite television program;
● acting out a simple story with the puppets;
● singing a song.

Some of the children could pretend to be the people at home, watching the television performance. If you keep the props together in a special place, the children could initiate television play at another time and try out new ideas.

1385

King Friday is annoyed because Lady Elaine started a television station without his permission. He tells her she must have a license from him before she continues to broadcast. Mister Rogers explains that getting a license is like getting permission to do something.

"Getting Permission" can help children:

● learn more about their world;
● learn more about work.

Getting Permission

Materials
● a driver's license or other kind of license

If you have some kind of a license to show the children, tell them what it allows you to do (drive a car, operate a day care home, etc.). Can any of them think of other things that require a license? You could mention things like:

● driving a school bus;
● working as a doctor, dentist, nurse, etc.;
● opening a school;
● flying an airplane;
● being a barber or a hairdresser.

Point out that a license usually shows a person has worked hard to learn to do special things. What kinds of things do they need permission to do?

● Go outside to play?
● Visit a friend?
● Use messy art supplies?

You'll want to point out that these things don't need a license, only your permission. Then you could give out pretend tricycle driving licenses to the children who want them. Ask each child to show how to:

● get on a tricycle;
● ride forwards;
● stop the tricycle;
● get off carefully.

Those are things which could qualify them for their tricycle driving license.

Thoughts For The Week

A caregiver once told me that she could tell when a certain child was developing new fears because he always played about them. When he was struggling with nightmares about monsters and giants, his play was full of monsters, too. Even as a toddler, this child chose to play about things that frightened him—like pretending to use a vacuum cleaner and pretending to bite the stuffed animals with a toy alligator. This kind of play can help children overcome fears, but sometimes even the play becomes too scary. Children need to know that a grownup will help them keep their play within comfortable limits and will stop play that is frightening to themselves or other children.

One of the new experiences that faces all children is starting school for the first time. During our television visits this week, we'll spend some time talking with teachers and showing school rooms and the things that children do in kindergarten and first grade. Most children have mixed feelings about any new situation, but everyone reacts to newness in his or her own special way. Perhaps this week you will find your children "playing" school as a way of getting ready for what could happen there.

Fred Rogers

Songs On The Programs This Week

1386   *"Speedy Delivery"*
1387   *"You Are Special"*
        "A Handy Lady and a Handy Man"
1388   *"What Do You Do?"*
        "It's You I Like"
1389   *"You've Got to Do It"*
1390   *"I'm Proud of You"*

Your Notes For The Week

1386

Mister Rogers shows a film about kindergarten and talks about why children go to school. He discusses different ways children may feel about going to school. "Talking about School" can help children:

- use play to work on feelings;
- talk about feelings.

Talking about School

Materials

- magazine pictures of things you would find in a school
- large piece of paper or cardboard
- paste

Ask the children if any of them know someone who goes to school. What do they think children do at school? (Perhaps you have a school-age child in the group, or one who attends kindergarten, who would be willing to tell the others what school is like.)

Give the children a chance to look through the pictures you have that show something they might see at a school. Can they tell you what the object is or what the children are doing? You might want to point out that some children might be afraid to go to school for the first time. What things might be scary to them? (New place? New people? Not knowing what to expect?) See if they can remember coming to day care for the first time. Can they remember how they felt? Are there any other first-time situations they'd like to talk about? For instance:

- the first haircut;
- a visit to the doctor;
- a visit to the dentist;
- staying away from home overnight;
- going to the hospital.

Maybe some of the children can tell you how they felt at times like these. How do they feel about them now?

1387

Mister Rogers talks about things that children like to do on their own. He points out that *everyone* needs help sometimes, *even* grownups.

"Help Me, Don't Help Me" can help children:

- learn to do things independently;
- understand and accept individual differences;
- recognize feelings.

Help Me, Don't Help Me

Materials

- none

See if the children can tell you things they can do alone. For example:

- putting on shoes;
- zipping a jacket;
- buttoning a sweater;
- combing their hair;
- brushing their teeth.

They might like to demonstrate some of these abilities. Then ask if they can tell you some things they need help to do. The younger children probably need help with buttoning, tying, zipping, etc. Older children might need help taking a bath or washing their hair.

You might want to reassure them that sometimes people don't feel like doing things — even things they know how to do. You could remind them of the song, "Sometimes Isn't Always."

1388

In the Neighborhood of Make-Believe, Bob Dog's witch costume frightens Henrietta. In a televised interview, the King assures the neighbors that witches are not real; they are only pretend.

"Things That Are Scary" can help children:

- talk about feelings;
- understand and accept individual differences.

Things That Are Scary

Materials

- paper
- crayons or markers

Henrietta was frightened because she thought there was a real witch in the Neighborhood. Do any of the children want to tell you about a time when they were startled or afraid? Were the things that frightened them real or pretend? You might encourage the children to draw a "scary" picture, and then talk about their pictures when they've finished. You could point out that things that are scary for one person may not be scary for another, and that pretending about things that scare us can often make them less frightening.

(Or, 1286 "Puppet Play"; 1409 "Sock Puppets.")

1389

Henrietta is able to overcome her fear of witches by playing with a witch puppet and singing a song about what frightens her.

"Paper-Bag Puppets" can help children:

- use play to work on feelings;
- develop creative play.

Paper-Bag Puppets

Materials

- paper bags (lunch bags are a good size)
- scrap materials (yarn, paper, fabric, buttons, etc.)
- crayons or markers

Before you begin making puppets, talk with the children about people or animals they find scary. Can any of the children tell you what it is about the person or animal that frightens them? (Some children are afraid of the teeth; others may be afraid because of size, sound, or unusual appearance.) Allow the older children to make their own puppets out of paper bags, using the scrap materials. Younger children might prefer drawing scary features with crayons or markers, or be able to tell you how to decorate their paper bags for them. When the puppets are finished, let the children take turns telling about their puppets and encourage them to pretend with them. You'll need to keep the play within bounds, reminding them often that this is all pretend. Can they think of ways to tame the scary puppets? Maybe they're scary, those puppets, because they're sad about something. The children could try to help the puppets feel better about themselves…and then they might not be so scary any more.

1390

Mister Rogers attends the puppet show Chrissie and Terri Thompson are staging as a surprise for their grandparents, Mr. and Mrs. McFeely. They made up their own version of "The Princess and the Pea."

"Let's Tell a Story" can help children:

- develop their imaginations;
- learn to listen carefully.

Let's Tell a Story

Materials

- a children's book with lots of pictures (optional)

Storytelling can be a good way for children to express themselves. It can also be a quiet, relaxing time for both you and the children—a time to hold an infant or toddler, and a time to listen to the ideas, feelings and thoughts of the children in your care. Storytelling could become a part of each day. If this is your first storytelling time with the children, you'll probably want to use a book with lots of pictures or a familiar story like "The Princess and the Pea." Later, as you get more confident in storytelling, and the children join in more and more, you may not need a book, just your imagination. To begin the story, you could use "once upon a time," or come up with a beginning of your own. Make up the story as you go along, using experiences from your past and parts of other stories you know. It's important for you to leave time for the children to join in, but never demand that the children contribute to a story. If a child does want to add something, be sure to take the time to be an interested listener. Once you have had several storytelling times, you might just find that the children will become the storytellers. Storytime can also happen when you're busy working with your hands—rolling clay or painting or drawing. Any time can be a storytime.

(Or, 1288 "Making Up Stories.")

Thoughts For The Week

The feeling of fear can be useful in helping us recognize a dangerous situation. For instance, fear of being hurt can keep children from touching something hot or running out into a busy street. For children, talking with a special grownup about things that scare them is a way to understand what kinds of things they need to fear and what kinds of things they don't. For instance, when a grownup helps children see that monsters or giants are only in their imaginations, they can start learning to control the fears that go with any sort of scary pretending.

Fred Rogers

Songs On The Programs This Week

1392 "I'm Taking Care of You"
1395 "Everybody's Fancy"

Your Notes For The Week

1391

Audrey Cleans Everything gives Mister Rogers a tour of her new mobile home and office. Later, they see a film of mobile homes and people who live in them.

"Where I Live" can help children:

- learn more about their world;
- recognize likeness and difference.

Where I Live

Materials

- paper
- crayons or markers
- magazine pictures of places where people live (optional)

Ask the children what they remember about Audrey's mobile home. What was it like? See if any of the children would like to tell about their homes. Some questions you might ask are:

- What do you call the place where you live?
- Who are the people in your family?
- Do other families live in the same building?
- What kinds of things are the same in everyone's home?
- How are some homes different from others? Are they different colors? Different sizes?

Would the older children like to draw pictures of the places where they live? Or they could use the magazine cut-outs to make a collage of houses like their own...the outsides and the insides.

1392

Barbara B. Frisbee brings a giant-sized Frisbee to the Neighborhood of Make-Believe. Daniel is frightened because Lady Elaine says that a giant is coming. Lady Aberlin helps him talk about scary things. In the "real" neighborhood, Mister Rogers says it's good to have someone nearby to talk with you when you're feeling scared.

"Scary Things" can help children:

- recognize feelings;
- talk about feelings.

Scary Things

Materials

- none

How did Daniel feel today? Why was he scared? Some very tall people are called "giants," but they're not the scary, pretend kind; they're just tall *people*. How did Lady Aberlin help make Daniel feel better? Can the children tell you about a time when they were afraid of something?

- Why were they afraid?
- What or who helped them not to be so scared?

Do you remember things that scared you when you were a child? What was a help to you? Most children like to know that grownups once felt the same way they do, and that those grownups found ways of growing and feeling better.

1393

Lady Elaine still believes a giant owns the big Frisbee—and that he's coming to get it. In his "real" neighborhood, Mister Rogers thinks Lady Elaine is feeling very small compared to a giant. He recalls how small he felt when he was a child next to his parents.

"Comparing Sizes" can help children:

- recognize likeness and difference.

Comparing Sizes

Materials

- household items such as silverware, dishes, empty food boxes, furniture, toys

Here are some ideas for games of comparison. Start with something simple, such as comparing your shoe to a child's shoe. Ask the children to tell you which one is bigger and which is smaller. Other things to compare are:

- teaspoon and soupspoon;
- dinner plate and saucer;
- cereal box and pudding box;
- large bowl and small bowl;
- toy car and actual automobile;
- your coat and a child's coat.

Can they think of more? Now choose an item you find around the house, such as a pencil. Can the children find something bigger than a pencil? Show something else. Can they find something smaller than that? You might also ask the children if the things they find are a *lot* bigger or smaller or just a *little* bigger or smaller. You might try arranging four or five objects from biggest to smallest. Shift them around while the children turn their backs, and then see if they can put the objects back in order.

1394

Mister Rogers shows a series of inkblots on paper and asks his viewers to guess what they look like. Then he tries making some blots with food coloring. Audrey Cleans Everything uses spot remover to clean Mister Rogers' shirt cuff.

"Paint Blots" can help children:

● develop their imaginations.

Paint Blots

Materials

● non-toxic paint
● paper
● crayons or markers

Give each child a piece of paper and show how to fold it in half. When they've opened the paper, help them put a small blob of paint on the inside. (You could use two colors of paint.) Fold the paper and rub gently to spread the paint. Open the paper and look at the blots. What do the blots suggest? Do they suggest other things if they're turned upside down? Can different people see different things in the same blot? When the blots are dry, the children can use markers or crayons to add to their blots and make even more elaborate pictures.

1395

Mister Rogers decides to clean out his closet, sorting out some things his sons may be able to wear now. In the Neighborhood of Make-Believe, X the Owl learns that wearing someone else's clothes doesn't change who you are.

"Trying on Clothes" can help children:

● use play to work on feeling;
● talk about feelings.

Trying on Clothes

Materials

● dresses
● shirts
● ties
● shoes
● hats
● mirror

Let the children take turns trying on clothes and looking at themselves in the mirror. Do they think they look different in the dress-up clothes? Are there any ways they look the same? Do they feel like someone else? They may feel like it, but they are still themselves. Do any of the children ever wear clothing that used to belong to someone else? How do they feel about getting hand-me-down clothes? Who gets *their* hand-me-down clothes? Some of the children may have strong feelings about clothes they've outgrown. They may be able to tell you what happens to old clothing in their family. Wouldn't it be fun if there were some kind of clothes that grew as the person grew? But that would be pretend, because clothes don't grow by themselves.

Thoughts For The Week

Children don't always understand that people can be angry with someone and still love that person. Much of adults' anger with children stems from a deep concern for children and their safety. When we do get angry with our children, it's very helpful if we tell them why. That can help them to realize that the reason we feel so strongly about them is that we love them. We want them to take good care of themselves, and when they don't we get angry...and sometimes scared, too.

Fred Rogers

Songs On The Programs This Week

1396 *"I'm Angry"*
      "The Truth Will Make Me Free"
      "Everybody's Fancy"
1397 *"Pretending"*
1398 *"You're Growing"*
1399 *"Everything Grows Together"*
      "It's You I Like"
1400 *"Please Don't Think It's Funny"*

Your Notes For The Week

1396

Mister Rogers reads a book, *Lost Little Boy*, about a child's fear of being lost. In the Neighborhood of Make-Believe, Prince Tuesday is missing. When he is found, King Friday and Queen Sara are very upset and angry. They were frightened when they couldn't find him.

"Feeling Angry" can help children:

- recognize feelings;
- talk about feelings;
- express strong feelings in appropriate ways.

Feeling Angry

Materials

- none

See if any of the children can tell you why King Friday and Queen Sara were upset and angry today. Some of the children might be able to tell you what kinds of things make them angry — for instance:

- when it's time to go to bed, and they want to stay up;
- when someone breaks a favorite toy;
- when it's time to come in for dinner, and they want to stay outside and play;
- when it's time to clean up, and they don't want to help;
- when another child hits them.

When King Friday and Queen Sara were upset and angry, they took Prince Tuesday to a room to talk. Can the children think of things they can do when they're feeling angry? Things like:

- pounding clay;
- drawing an angry picture;
- singing a mad song;
- banging on a saucepan;
- running hard and fast;
- saying "I'm mad!";
- talking with someone they love about how they feel.

(Or, 1320 "A Pounding Festival.")

1397

Mister Rogers builds a tower of large and small blocks. He compares his height to that of the tower and reminds his viewers that towers can fall over, so it's best not to build them near other people. Then he makes a street from blocks and shows a film of children pretending to be firefighters, using blocks for a fire engine.

"Pretending with Boxes" can help children:

● develop their imaginations.

Pretending with Boxes

Materials

● large and small cardboard boxes (try to include at least one box big enough to hold a child)

● crayons or markers

● yarn or heavy string

You might begin by asking the children to think of things they could do with the boxes. Here are some suggestions:

● Build a tall tower.

● Make a playhouse from one large box or several small ones.

● Use a large one for a fire engine, car, or truck.

● Tie several small ones together to make a train for dolls or stuffed animals.

● Use string to make a wagon without wheels for pulling toys.

You could suggest using crayons or markers to add things like doors, windows, or headlights on cars.

1398

Mister Rogers and Bob Trow make a horseshoe-tossing game at the workshop. Mister Rogers sings "You're Growing" and shows a film of children doing all kinds of things such as riding bikes, playing Frisbee and kickball, and more.

"Bean Bag Toss" can help children:

● develop coordination;

● develop the ability to keep on trying.

Bean Bag Toss

Materials

● bean bag or small ball

● large box or basket (laundry basket)

● masking tape

Place the basket in an area that is clear of breakable items. About three or four feet from the basket, place a piece of masking tape on the floor. Show the children how to stand on the tape and toss the bean bag into the basket. It could be helpful, if you miss hitting the basket, to say something like, "Nobody gets the bag in the basket every time." That gives your children the right to miss the basket, too. This might be a good time to talk with the children about other games they like that take practice. If you have younger children (three or four years old) in your care, you could let them stand as close as they need to, so they'll have a better chance at hitting the basket.

(Or, 1281 "Variety Show"; 1314 "Ways I'm Growing"; 1449 "Bean Bags.")

1399

Mister Rogers plays an autoharp, explaining how it works. He compares the autoharp with a regular harp and meets a harpist who plays in a symphony orchestra.

"A Pretend Orchestra" can help children:
- try out different roles;
- learn to listen carefully.

A Pretend Orchestra

Materials
- radio (a station playing instrumental music)
- record player and records
- tape recorder and tapes of music

See if the children can pantomime playing different musical instruments. For instance: guitar, violin, drums, piano, harp or trumpet. You can make a pretend orchestra with a "conductor" to tell the children when to start and stop. Put on some music so the children can "play" their instruments as if they were making the music. Now encourage the children to sit quietly and listen carefully to the music. Can you help them begin to tell what instruments are playing?

(Or, 1134 "Shoe-Box Harps"; 1404 "Sandpaper Blocks"; 1443 "Paper-Plate Shakers.")

1400

Mister Rogers reads a new book, *Speedy Delivery*, about Mr. McFeely. Mister Rogers explains that even when children learn to read, they sometimes like to have grownups read to them. Then he sings the song, "Please Don't Think It's Funny."

"Bookmarks" can help children:
- develop their imagination;
- learn more about their world.

Bookmarks

Materials
- strips of cardboard or heavy paper (about two inches wide and five inches long)
- crayons, paint, or markers
- fabric scraps, yarn, etc.
- glue

The children might like to tell you about their favorite books.
- Why do they think they like them so much? Because of the story? Because of the pictures?
- Do they have favorite parts of the favorite books?
- How can they find their favorite parts when they want to?
- Or find the place where they—or someone reading to them—stopped until the next time?
- Can some of the children read page numbers?

You can explain how bookmarks help us find places in books. (Perhaps you are reading a story to the children little by little and can use one, too.) Encourage the children to make fancy bookmarks for their own books or for presents to their families— Valentine bookmarks, Halloween bookmarks, Christmas or Chanukah bookmarks, or "any-old-time" bookmarks. They can decorate the cardboard strips any way they wish. (A thin coat of clear fingernail polish or hairspray will help seal the colors so they don't rub off on the pages of the book.)

Thoughts For The Week

Having guests in one's home can be fun, but it can also be difficult, especially for children. This week, we pretend about how a character in Westwood feels when Prince Tuesday comes for a visit and becomes the center of attention. When someone new gets all the attention, it's possible to feel left out at first. When we talk with children about their feelings of jealousy or feeling left out, we let them know that it's all right to have those feelings. At the same time, we can assure them that the special place they have in our lives—at home or in a day care group—is a place no one can ever take away.

Fred Rogers

Songs On The Programs This Week

1401   *"You Are Special"*
1402   *"We Welcome You Today"*
        "It's You I Like"
1403   *"It's the People You Like the Most"*
        "Everybody's Fancy"
1404   *"Look and Listen"*
1405   *"We Welcome You Today"*

Your Notes For The Week

1401

Mister Rogers talks about different ways clothing stays together—zippers, Velcro tabs, and buttons. Then he shows an assortment of buttons and a film about how buttons are made. He recalls how hard he worked as a child learning to button his coat buttons.

"Buttoning" can help children:

- develop muscle control;
- develop the ability to keep on trying.

Buttoning

Materials

- clothing that has buttons for fasteners

See if the children can think of different ways that clothes are fastened—snaps, zippers, ties, and buttons.

- What different kinds of fasteners do the children have on their clothing?
- How many have buttons on their clothes?
- Are some children already able to button and unbutton by themselves?

You, and the children who already know how to button, can help the others learn by practicing on their own buttons or on a piece of clothing you have at hand. Children who already know how to button could practice tying or zipping.

(Or, 1064 "Sorting Buttons"; 1399 "A Pretend Orchestra.")

1402

In the Neighborhood of Make-Believe, the Royal Family arrives in Westwood for a visit. King Friday receives the key to the city, and Queen Sara is glad to be back in her native land.

"Visiting" can help children:

- develop their imaginations;
- learn more about their world.

Visiting

Materials

- none

Have any of the children been away on visits to friends or relatives? Would they like to tell you and the other children about one special visit? You might begin by telling the children about a special visit *you* remember. The children might want to pretend about going for a visit. To encourage the play or to keep it going, you may want to ask questions like:

- Where are you going?
- Who will you see there?
- What kinds of things will you do or see?
- How long will you be gone?
- When will you be coming home?

Would it be possible for you to take the children for a real visit—to see a neighbor or to visit another caregiver who lives nearby?

(Or, 1307 "Going on a Trip.")

1403

In the Neighborhood of Make-Believe, Tad is jealous of all the attention Prince Tuesday is receiving during his visit to Westwood. This leads to a fight between Tad and Prince Tuesday, with Bob Dog and Mayor Maggie intervening. Mrs. Frogg comes and helps Tad deal with his feelings of jealousy.

"Having Guests" can help children:

- talk about feelings.

Having Guests

Materials

- none

See how the children felt about the way Tad acted. They could talk about similar situations and perhaps act them out. For instance:

- A new child joins the group for day care. How do the children think the new child feels? Can they remember how they felt? How could they make that child feel welcome? See if one child would like to pretend to be a newcomer in the group. The others could practice introducing themselves.
- How would they greet a grownup family friend who came to visit at home for the first time? Can they act it out?
- How would the children welcome a visitor to their day care home? Would they be able to show the visitor around and explain what goes on?

(Or, 1277 "Feeling Jealous.")

1404

In Westwood, all the friends are gathered, ready to perform in the neighborhood orchestra. They practice playing a march, then the king plays a solo on his bass viol.

"Sandpaper Blocks" can help children:
- develop creative play;
- express feelings through music.

Sandpaper Blocks

Materials
- blocks of wood
- glue
- coarse sandpaper
- markers
- scissors

Using felt-tipped markers, the children could trace the outlines of wooden blocks onto pieces of sandpaper. They may not be able to cut the sandpaper themselves, but after you have cut it for them, they could spread the glue on one side of each block and put the sandpaper in place. Once the glue is dry, rub two blocks against each other or knock the wooden sides together. Do any of the children want to "play" the blocks while singing a song or listening to music?

(Or, 1134 "Shoe-Box Harps"; 1212 "Ringing Spoons"; 1443 "Paper-Plate Shakers.")

1405

Lady Aberlin is waiting for the Royal Family to come back from Westwood. She is joined by Francois Clemmons, and together they create a catchy saying. When the Royal Family returns, everybody joins in welcome-home kissing.

"Making Up Poems" can help children:
- learn to use words;
- express strong feelings in appropriate ways.

Making Up Poems

Materials
- paper
- pencil, pen, or marker

You may have some poetry for children handy, which you could read to your group, or you may know some nursery rhymes or nonsense verses you can recite. You may also find that some of the children already know some simple poems they would like to share with you.
- Today Francois Clemmons made up the following poem:
  "When you miss somebody
  You can kiss somebody
  As soon as he comes back."

Are some of the words in Francois' poem exactly alike?
- Do some sound *almost* alike?
- How about in the verses you or the children know?

You can help the children understand "rhyme" by playing a rhyming game in which you say a simple word and the children think of a word that rhymes. Together you and the children might make up a simple poem which you could write down and put up on a wall. The children might feel like adding to it from time to time.

(Or, 1256 "Soapsuds Fingerpainting.")

Thoughts For The Week

*One of the fantasies in fairy tales and in the play of young children is the magic of wishes that come true. Pretending that we can wish things just the way we'd like them to be can be a way of coping with the frustrating realities of everyday life, but children need to learn that wishing doesn't make things happen. Most children, at one time or another, have wished something scary—that a new baby would just disappear, or that a parent would get sick or even die. And sometimes, by coincidence, these scary things **do** happen...and a child can be overwhelmed with the guilt of feeling responsible. This week we try to emphasize that wishes cannot make things happen. Wishing is fun, it's part of dreaming, imagining and pretending, but part of our job as adults is to help children understand that in reality it is people, not wishes, that make things happen.*

Fred Rogers

Songs On The Programs This Week

1407   *"We Welcome You Today"*
       "You've Got to Do It"
1408   *"Wishes Don't Make Things Come True"*
1409   *"It's You I Like"*
1410   *"Pretending"*

Your Notes For The Week

1406

In the Neighborhood of Make-Believe, Prince Tuesday wishes the Froggs would visit and is excited to hear they will be coming. Dr. Bill gives Lady Aberlin a checkup, reassuring her that nobody can look into her eyes and tell what she is thinking.

"I Am Thinking of..." can help children:

- learn more about privacy;
- practice taking turns;
- learn to use words.

I Am Thinking of...

Materials

- none

Here's a simple guessing game you all could play: Somebody, perhaps you at first, could think of something and say what kind of thing it is—fruit, vegetable, animal, color, etc. Everybody gets one guess. If no one guesses right, the thinker gives a clue, and everyone takes another guess. Once someone guesses correctly, another person gets to be the thinker and the game continues. Your example may help the children, when one of them is the thinker, to approach the game in the spirit of wanting someone to guess *right* and offering clues as a way to be *helpful*. It's best to avoid making the game a competitive one with winners and losers. The chance to be thinker can pass in order around the circle, rather than being a reward for guessing right.

(Or, 1284 "I'm Thinking of a Child"; 1304 "A Hospital for Toys.")

1407

Mrs. Frogg brings a blanket for Prince Tuesday when she arrives for a visit. This is the second time his wish has come true, and he is afraid he can make things happen by wishing about them.

"Can Wishes Come True?" can help children:

● understand wishing can't make things happen.

Can Wishes Come True?

Materials

● none

Can some of your children remember something they wished hard for? Did their wish come true? If a wish did come true, what made it happen? Did someone make it happen? What sorts of wishes do they have now? Could they come true? How? This would be a good time to let your children know that most people have "scary, mad wishes" from time to time—wishes that something bad or sad would happen. It's important for young children to hear from a grownup they trust that wishes can never make such things happen. People or accidents make those things happen, but never our wishes. You might want to go over the words to Mister Rogers' song, "Wishes Don't Make Things Come True."

1408

Mister Rogers talks about anger and ways to express angry feelings. He shows how to make modeling clay from flour, salt, and water. In the Neighborhood of Make-Believe, Prince Tuesday is hiding once again. Daniel thinks Prince Tuesday is frightened about his "scary, mad wishes."

"Dough Play" can help children:

● express strong feelings in appropriate ways;
● express feelings through art work.

Dough Play

Materials

● modeling dough

There are lots of ways to use modeling dough, and children can express a wide range of feelings as they use it. You might want to make homemade modeling dough (recipe on page A-1). When children are angry and feel like pounding or punching, they can pound on modeling dough, or a pounding bench, or a punching bag, but they *can't* pound on people or breakable toys. And when children feel really good about themselves, they can turn the modeling dough into many imaginative things.

Thursday

1409

At the Browns' Marionette Shop, plans are underway for their production of "Little Red Riding Hood." In the Neighborhood of Make-Believe, Lady Aberlin stages her own version of this classic fairy tale.

"Sock Puppets" can help children:

- express feelings through play;
- develop their imaginations.

Sock Puppets

Materials

- one sock for each child
- scrap materials (buttons, paper, fabric, yarn, etc.)
- glue
- needle and thread (optional)

Show the children how to slip a sock over their hands and make a mouth by tucking the toe end into their fingers. Encourage them to add decorations such as:

- buttons for eyes;
- yarn for hair;
- fabric or paper for ears;
- a row of buttons for teeth, etc.

The children can glue on their own decorations, or you can sew them on in the places that they suggest. See what ideas the children come up with all by themselves. Some children might like to make puppets of their favorite storybook characters. Others might want to make something totally original. When each child has a puppet, you might be able to help them create a puppet play in which the characters meet. Using a puppet yourself, show the children how they might make one puppet talk to another.

(Or, 1340 "Tag Stories"; 1285 "Stick Puppets.")

Friday

1410

Mister Rogers and Mr. McFeely attend the Browns' marionette production of "Little Red Riding Hood."

"Homemade Marionettes" can help children:

- develop creative play.

Homemade Marionettes

Materials

- stuffed animals
- string
- stick, ruler, or tube from paper towels
- different kinds of puppets, if available

If you have some different kinds of puppets handy— or even some pictures of different kinds—you could explain how they work. You can make simple marionettes for the children to play with by attaching (tying tightly or sewing) strings to the heads, arms, and legs of the stuffed animals that you have. Attach the other end of the strings to a stick, ruler, or tube. (If the animals do not have parts that move, strings attached to the front and back ends of the body will do.) Let each child take a turn pulling the strings and making your homemade marionettes move. If you have several, the children can make them move and talk to one another. See what stories they invent on their own and what feelings the children choose to express in their play. Sometimes it's easier for a child to express a real feeling through a puppet than it is to say it straight out.

(Or, 1286 "Puppet Play.")

Thoughts For The Week

"I like to have a place of my own." Those are the words from a song I sing on the programs this week. Everyone likes to have a place of his or her own—a place to be alone or somewhere to hide "treasures." Maybe it's a shoe box, a special drawer or a secret hiding place. Whatever it is, it is personal and private, and children as well as grownups have a need for privacy.

In the Neighborhood of Make-Believe this week, when Lady Aberlin and Daniel Tiger leave the neighborhood without telling anyone, everyone becomes concerned. Many grownups like to provide safe, private spaces for children—behind a sofa, under a blanket-draped table, or inside a large box. Then children can have a "place of their own" to go when they feel like being alone.

Fred Rogers

Songs On The Programs This Week

1411　*"A Place of My Own"*
　　　 "I Like to Take My Time"
1412　*"Please Don't Think It's Funny"*
1413　*"It's You I Like"*
　　　 "Everybody Has a History"
　　　 "You've Got to Do It"
　　　 "Please Don't Think It's Funny"
1414　*"Some Things Belong to You"*
1415　*"Some Things Belong to You"*

Your Notes For The Week

1411

Mister Rogers shows a sea captain's old-time wooden writing desk with many compartments, including two secret drawers. In the Neighborhood of Make-Believe, Lady Aberlin helps Lady Elaine Fairchilde find the secret way to open a mystery box.

"Boxes inside Boxes" can help children:

- learn more about their world;
- develop creative play;
- practice taking turns.

Boxes inside Boxes

Materials

- five or six boxes of graduated sizes so that each one will fit into the box of the next size larger (e.g. small ring box, long necklace box, shirt box, dress box, cardboard carton)
- a small toy that will fit into the smallest box

Before you begin this activity, and without the children knowing, place a small object in the smallest box and then place each box inside the other. Place the set of boxes on the floor and give each child a turn to open one box at a time. After the smallest box has been opened, see what they would like to do with the boxes. They may want to:

- put them back together with a different surprise in the smallest box;
- build with them;
- use them for houses in their play;
- do something adults might not think of.

You may find it interesting to see the different choices the different children make.

1412

Mister Rogers shows a tent outside in his front yard and talks about having "a place of your own." Then he shows how to make a tent using two chairs and a blanket, and says he sometimes likes to pretend he's in a boat.

"A Place of My Own" can help children:
- learn more about privacy;
- practice taking turns.

A Place of My Own

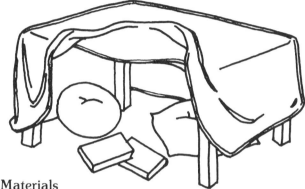

Materials
- blanket or sheet
- two chairs or a small table
- pillows, books, etc. (optional)

Perhaps some of the children can tell you about times when they feel like being alone. For instance:
- when everything around them is too noisy;
- when they are missing someone;
- when they want to think about something important;
- when they feel really happy and want to keep it to themselves for a while.

Are there any special places in your house where a child can go to be alone? You might want to mention these places, and then you can help them make an added special place for them to use today. They can set up the chairs and hold the blanket while you arrange things. You'll want to set some ground rules about things like:
- the number of children allowed in;
- the kind of play permitted;
- ways to see that everyone has a turn to try it out...alone.

If you have a lot of space, some children may want to make a more permanent structure by decorating a large carton (television box or refrigerator box), making windows and doors. Adding a small rug or several pillows can make it really cozy.

1413

Mister Rogers works with seven wooden blocks, grouping them, turning them on their sides, and building different things. He reminds the viewers that everyone is different and sings the song, "Everybody Has a History."

"Blockbuilding" can help children:
- develop creative play;
- develop their imaginations.

Blockbuilding

Materials
- wooden blocks, milk-carton blocks (page B-1), or cardboard boxes.

Encourage the children to try different ways of building with blocks by asking questions like:
- What could you make if you put them end to end? Side by side?
- Could you stack them one on top of another?
- Can you make a shape that is closed (circle, triangle, square)?
- What other ideas do you have?

Then give them time to use the blocks any way they choose. You might want to point out that each one has his or her own ideas. Some children might want to combine blocks and ideas to work together making more complex buildings and roads, but others just might want to do it alone.

(Or, 1278 "Look What I Built.")

1414

Handyman Negri is busy searching for Daniel and Lady Aberlin. They went to the Land of Allmine without telling anyone where they were going. Lady Elaine thinks Mr. Allmine has taken them away.

"Missing Persons" can help children:
- recognize feelings;
- learn about limits.

Missing Persons

Materials
- none

Can any of the children tell you of a time when someone went away without telling them? How did they feel? Talk with them about how grownups feel when they can't find a child. Can *you* remember a time when someone was missing and you didn't know where he or she was? This might be a good time for storytelling, and you might begin by setting the story in a department store or a shopping mall. A child sees a fancy toy, wanders towards it, and gets lost from Mom or Aunt Susie. Build the story by adding more people as Mom looks for her child and others help her search. The children may enjoy adding what the child might do or be feeling. End the story happily with Mom and the child together again. Emphasize the mother's concern and feelings (even though one feeling was probably anger). You might want to point out that grownups want to be sure that children are safe, and that they need to know where children are at all times. Some of the children might want to talk about times when they need to let a grownup know where they have gone—times like:
- when they feel tired and want to lie down;
- when they need to be alone in a special place.

Can they think of times at home when they should be sure to tell their parents where they are?

(Or, 1332 "Hide and Seek"; 1427 "Going Away and Coming Back.")

1415

Mister Rogers visits Brockett's Bakery and meets David Yee, who shows how to make egg drop soup by beating an egg in a bowl and dropping it into boiling chicken broth. The hot soup cooks the egg.

"Egg Drop Soup" can help children:
- learn more about foods.

Egg Drop Soup

Materials
- chicken broth
- egg
- saucepan
- spoon
- small bowl
- fork or eggbeater

Have any of the children ever eaten egg drop soup? You may want to point out that it's a kind of soup that is Chinese in origin, but lots of people enjoy it. Can the children remember the ingredients that Mister Rogers and David Yee used? See if anyone can tell you the steps to making the soup:
- Heat the broth in a saucepan.
- Beat the egg in a small bowl.
- Add the egg to the hot broth.
- Serve the soup when the egg has been cooked.

Encourage the children to take part as much as they can, being sure that they understand some things are for you to do because they are not safe for children to do.

(Or, 1098 "Eggshell Pictures"; 1255 "Egg Salad Sandwiches.")

Thoughts For The Week

There are many ways to say "I love you," whether you are an adult or a child. Helping children find ways to express affection is a natural outgrowth of our own loving concern for them and an important part of helping them develop their capacity to love. By providing a loving environment while their parents are away, you are expressing your concern for the children in your care, and it's only natural for them to develop a strong affection for you as well. Helping them express their love in natural ways can be a wonderful thing for them... and for you.

Fred Rogers

Songs On The Programs This Week
1417 "There Are Many Ways"
1418 "I'm Taking Care of You"

Your Notes For The Week

1416

Mister Rogers emphasizes the importance of proper tooth care when he visits a dentist's office to watch a neighborhood friend, Brian, having a dental examination. Then he talks about using dental floss and shows how he flosses his teeth. In the Neighborhood of Make-Believe, when Daniel Tiger loses a baby tooth, Edgar Cooke pretends to be the Tooth Fairy and exchanges money for the tooth he takes away.

"Playing Dentist" can help children:
- try out different roles;
- use play to work on feelings.

Playing Dentist

Materials
- an old white shirt for a smock
- tongue depressor or popsicle stick for a dental instrument
- toothbrushes
- dental floss

You might want to ask the children if they can remember what the dentist did during Brian's examination. See if they can remember things like:
- using a mouth mirror and toothpick to look at Brian's teeth;
- cleaning the teeth;
- applying fluoride to the teeth;
- X-raying Brian's teeth.

If you feel comfortable letting the children look in your mouth, you could pretend to be the patient and let the children pretend to be the dentists. (Remind them that dentists always wash their hands before examining a patient's teeth.) Or you may prefer to help the children set up a dentist's office, using dolls as patients. The children can take turns playing the roles of dentist, dental assistant, receptionist and parents.

If you have five- and six-year-old children who are beginning to lose their baby teeth, this might be a good time to encourage talk about losing a tooth. (You may need to remind them that the Tooth Fairy doesn't bring teeth; teeth grow in a person's mouth.) And when a child's tooth comes out, a new one is growing in that same place.

1417

In the Neighborhood of Make-Believe, Henrietta would like to tell astronaut Al Worden that she likes him, but she is too shy to say so. X pretends to be Colonel Worden, and Henrietta practices telling him how she feels. That way, she's able to overcome her shyness and tell the real Al Worden.

"Saying What You Feel" can help children:

- talk about feelings;
- use play to work on feelings.

Saying What You Feel

Materials

- none

You could begin this activity by telling the children about a time when you wanted to tell someone that you liked him or her, but felt too shy to do so. Can any of the children remember a time when they felt that way, too? What did Henrietta do to get over her shyness? See if the children can think of different ways to let someone know how they feel—things like:

- giving a smile;
- drawing a picture;
- giving a hug;
- making a present;
- making up a song;
- cleaning up your room;
- making something to eat;
- finding a flower;
- sharing a toy.

You could read or sing the words to Mister Rogers' song, "There Are Many Ways."

(Or, 1309 "What Is Love?")

1418

There's an energy crisis in the Neighborhood of Make-Believe. The waterfall has stopped; Edgar Cooke's television doesn't work; the machines at Corney's factory won't start; and none of the cameras or lights at the television station are operating.

"An Energy Crisis" can help children:

- learn more about their world.

An Energy Crisis

Materials

- flashlight
- new batteries
- old, worn-out batteries
- magazines (optional)

Have any of the children ever tried to use a flashlight or a toy with a worn-out battery in it? What happened? You might want to show them the light from a flashlight with worn-out batteries, and then the amount of light that comes from a set of good batteries. Older children may be able to understand that during power shortages there isn't enough electricity, and everything works the way the flashlight did with the old batteries in it. Can they remember a time when the electricity went off at your house or at their own homes? Maybe they can tell you what happened. The children might want to look through magazines, pointing out things that use electricity (an iron, a toaster, a vacuum cleaner, a lamp, a fan, etc.) and things that don't (candles, fireplace, etc.).

1419

The energy problem in the Neighborhood of Make-Believe is solved with a solar power system. Mister Rogers explains that people are different from machines—we make our own energy from the food we eat, and we can move ourselves.

"People and Machines" can help children:
- learn more about their world;
- recognize likeness and difference.

People and Machines

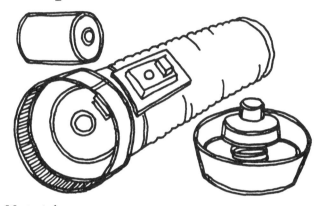

Materials
- flashlight
- vacuum cleaner
- light switch
- television

See if the children can tell you ways that people and machines are different. You might want to suggest a few ways:
- people eat food, machines don't;
- people have feelings and machines don't;
- people can move by themselves, but machines need power from somewhere else.

You might want to show the children the batteries inside a flashlight or a battery-operated toy. Then let them turn it on and off using the swtich. You can point out that people make machines work—they don't work by themselves. Other interesting switches might be:
- light switches in the house;
- vacuum cleaner switch;
- record player, radio, or television on/off button.

Remind the children that even though you're letting them try the switches, they are not to play with them unless they ask you or another adult.

1420

At the McFeely's, Mrs. McFeely and Mister Rogers play a flute-like-instrument called a recorder. Later in the program, Mister Rogers thinks it might be fun to paint to music, so he uses a tape recorder for music and "paints" on paper at the easel.

"Painting to Music" can help children:
- develop their imaginations;
- express feelings through music.

Painting to Music

Materials
- paper
- non-toxic paint
- brushes
- music

Mister Rogers talked about "drawing a song." You could encourage the children to listen to music and think about how they want to paint. Remind them that each person's painting will be different because each person will have different feelings about the music. When the paintings are finished, you could hang them on a door or a wall for everyone to enjoy. When children draw or paint, the things they make often have special meaning to them, even though grownups see only scribbles or blotches. Can the children tell you anything about their music paintings? If possible, you may want to repeat the music after the children have finished, so they can look at everybody else's paintings and see how that music made them feel.

Thoughts For The Week

In our children's opera this week, we show that many different ideas can be brought together to create a story. A lost key, a taffy factory, swans, beavers, and a wicked witch become connected as Betty Aberlin unlocks a magic door and visits a dream-like place called Otherland. As the plot of our opera takes shape, we try to show that many people can contribute to a story—each in his or her own special way.

Fred Rogers

Songs On The Programs This Week

1421   "Be the Best of Whatever You Are"
        "It's You I Like"
1422   "Love Is People"
1425   "Key to Otherland" Opera

Your Notes For The Week

1421

Mister Rogers shows the *Guinness Book of World Records* and talks about biggest and smallest. He says it doesn't really matter if you are the largest or smallest; what counts is being the best of whatever you are.

"The Best of Whatever You Are" can help children:

- feel proud of their accomplishments;
- understand and accept individual differences.

The Best of Whatever You Are

Materials

- none

You might begin this activity by pointing out that every person is special and can be the "best" of something. Encourage the children to tell you about several things that they do well. They might be able to think of things like:

- sharing;
- running, hopping, skipping or going up and down stairs;
- comforting others;
- zipping a jacket, tying shoes, or putting on a coat;
- building with blocks, riding a trike, or bouncing a ball;
- singing a song, painting a picture, or dancing to music.

Can they demonstrate something they do well?

(Or, 1393 "Comparing Sizes.")

1422

Mister Rogers listens to a special machine that reproduces the sound of the ocean. Then he shows a film about waves and plays a "which is which?" game with a bell and the ocean machine.

"Which Is Which?" can help children:

- learn to listen carefully.

Which Is Which?

Materials

- spoon
- piece of wood
- metal pan
- two glasses

Could the children tell the difference between Mister Rogers' bell sound and the ocean machine? Encourage them to listen carefully as you first clap your hands, then knock on wood. Can they hear the difference? Then ask them to turn their backs while you either clap your hands or knock on wood. Can they tell you which is which? Try it several more times. Do they improve with practice? Then, while they're watching, tap the spoon on a piece of wood, then on a metal pan. Again, can they hear the difference? When they turn their backs, can they still tell you which is which? Now try using two glasses, one empty and one filled with water. While the children watch, tap each with the spoon. Can they hear the difference? When their backs are turned, can they tell you which is empty and which is filled with water?

1423

Mister Rogers tries fingerpainting, talking about the different designs he creates. He says the best part of fingerpainting is the feel of it while you're doing it.

"Fingerpainting Designs" can help children:

- develop their imaginations.

Fingerpainting Designs

Materials

- glossy shelf paper cut into foot-long strips
- liquid starch
- powdered paint (optional)
- newspaper or plastic
- old shirts or aprons

This can be a very messy activity, and you'll want to set it up in an area protected by a plastic covering or by newspaper. When you've given each child a piece of shelf paper, help them all sponge over the glossy side with water before starting to fingerpaint. The children can experience the "feel" of fingerpainting with the liquid starch alone, but adding paint makes it more interesting. Mixing several colors together makes it more interesting still. Encourage the children to use different techniques to move the paint around. They could use:

- the palms of their hands;
- fingernails;
- knuckles;
- sides of their hands;
- fingertips.

Do they want to talk about their paintings when they're finished? (Some children may not want to do this activity — they may not like the feel of the paint or may have strong feelings about getting messy. For those children, you could have some blocks for building, or a book, or crayons and paper in another part of the room.)

1424

Mister Rogers looks at an assortment of locks and keys. He matches keys with the proper locks and shows how combination locks work. Lady Aberlin is thinking about keys and doors to another land as she gets ready for the opera in the Neighborhood of Make-Believe.

"Keys" can help children:

● learn more about their world;

● develop their imaginations.

Keys

Materials

● keys

● locks

Perhaps some of the children can tell you what keys are for. For instance:

● locking and unlocking doors;

● locking or unlocking boxes, trunks, etc.;

● starting a car, truck, or motorcycle.

Show the children several keys and see if they can tell you how they are alike and how they are different. You could show them the ragged edges and explain that each lock has a set of matching edges. Every key is different, and most keys fit only one lock. If you can, show the children what the keys are for—the front door, back door, a trunk, suitcase, etc. Older children might be able to try out the keys (if you feel comfortable having them do so). It might be a good idea to make a set of cardboard keys, or give the children a set of plastic keys for pretending. If you have an old set of keys that you don't need, label them "play keys," or put a special color tape or string on them so the children don't get them confused with a set of other keys.

(Or, 1178 "Key Match.")

1425

Today Mister Rogers pretends about the opera: "The Key to Otherland." Lady Aberlin finds a key that opens the door to Otherland, where she encounters a swan, beavers, and a wicked witch. When she returns to the beach, she buries the key in the sand for another person to find.

"An Imaginary Land" can help children:

● develop their imaginations;

● practice taking turns.

An Imaginary Land

Materials

● a key made out of cardboard

See if the children can tell you what happened in the opera. What were their favorite parts? Encourage them to create their own fantasy by pretending that the cardboard key opens a door to an imaginary land. As you give each child a turn to use the key to open an imaginary door, you could ask questions like:

● What do you see when you open the door?

● Who might you meet in this imaginary land?

● What could happen there?

Some of the children might like to act out their own stories about the imaginary land, or they could all join together to create one story. Do they understand the meaning of the numbers of the combination lock: 12-15-22-5 (L-O-V-E)? And, of course, love is the key to any land, any relationship.

Thoughts For The Week

For a young child, separation may feel like a loss of love, as punishment for something the child has said or done or wished. Children may then feel responsible for the absence of the loved person. This week in the Neighborhood of Make-Believe, we pretend that someone is going away. It gives us a chance to talk about ways to handle the feelings that arise when someone we love does go away. We hope you can use this opportunity to help the children in your care handle the feelings they sometimes have about the daily separations that take place when they come to day care and when they go home.

Fred Rogers

Songs On The Programs This Week

1426   "There Are Many Ways"
1427   "Once Upon Each Lovely Day"
1428   "Children Can"
        "Everybody's Fancy"
1429   "It's You I Like"
1430   "I'm Taking Care of You"

Your Notes For The Week

1426

King Friday is upset because John Reardon wants to return home. The king tries to get him to stay by appointing him Royal Opera Chamberlain. In the "real" neighborhood, Mister Rogers talks about how hard it is for children to understand why people have to go away.

"When Someone Goes Away" can help children:

- work on feelings about separation;
- talk about feelings;
- try out different roles.

When Someone Goes Away

Materials

- none

How do the children feel about leaving their parents in the morning? Here are some questions you could ask:

- Do you know where your parents are?
- What are they doing there?
- How do you feel when you see them leave?
- Do you ever miss them while they are gone?
- What can you do to help yourself feel better?(Find a grownup or a favorite toy?)
- How do you feel when your parents come back? (Sometimes children feel happy, but sometimes they're still angry because their parents left.)

Encourage the children to pretend being the grownups who go to work, and let them practice saying good-bye to their "children." To get the play started, you could ask questions like:

- Where do you work?
- What time are you leaving?

Or make statements like:

- Be sure to tell your little girl where you are going;
- I'll take care of her while you're gone.

Do any of the children want to try out the role of caregiver?

(Or, 1303 "Making a Map.")

1427

Mister Rogers talks about going away and coming back by having Mr. McFeely show a movie of his seaplane ride.

"Going Away and Coming Back" can help children:

- work on feelings about separation.

Going Away and Coming Back

Materials

- bell or whistle (optional)

Reardon enjoyed his stay in the Neighborhood of Make-Believe, but now he wants to return home. Can you think of a time when you had mixed feelings about going home? If so, tell the children about that time and then see if any of them ever felt that way, too. You could suggest situations such as:

- coming home from a vacation;
- going home after playing at a friend's house;
- leaving day care at the end of the day.

You might be able to help them see that people often have mixed feelings— that sometimes it's hard to decide if you want to go or stay. You could tell the children that so many people feel two ways about the same thing that there's even a word for it. That word is "ambivalent." It sometimes helps to have a word for the way we feel. Here's a game you could play about going away and coming back. (Be sure to set some boundaries like: no one leaves the yard; or don't go upstairs.) Begin by gathering everyone around you. When you give the signal, with a bell or whistle, everyone should leave the group. When the children hear the signal again, they should come back to you. Repeat the game a few times and then let each child who wants to, be the signaler while you join the others in being one of the ones who "goes away and comes back."

(Or, 1332 "Hide and Seek.")

1428

Mister Rogers talks about a storyteller who will be visiting later. It can be hard to wait.

"When You Have to Wait" can help children:

- practice waiting.

When You Have to Wait

Materials

- kitchen timer or alarm clock
- a snack

Show the children your timer or clock and tell them that in 15 minutes they will have a snack. You could do this before your regular snack time or plan a special snack for the children. Show them how you set the timer or clock and tell them what to expect when the 15 minutes is up (the bell will ring or the alarm will go off). See if the children can tell you about other times when they have to wait:

- waiting in a doctor's office;
- waiting for parents to pick them up;
- waiting for a friend to arrive;
- waiting for a grownup's help;
- waiting for a bus.

What kinds of things can they do when they have to wait? While you wait until it's time for a snack, you might make the time pass by:

- looking at a book;
- drawing a picture;
- playing with blocks or clay.

1429

Mister Rogers shows different types of uniforms and explains that what really matters is the person inside the uniform. Betty Aberlin is having her hair styled at the Beauty Parlor.

"You Look Different" can help children:

● recognize likeness and difference.

You Look Different

Materials

● a hat, scarf, or bandana
● mirror
● dress up clothes
● sunglasses

Perhaps you have had the experience of having a child look at you suspiciously after getting a haircut or a new pair of glasses. Young children, especially, can become upset by changes in a grownup's appearance. Today's activity is a way for you to let them practice seeing changes. Use a hat, scarf, or bandana to cover your hair, and wear a pair of dark glasses. Do the children still recognize you? Can they tell you what is different? Does it make you a different person? Then encourage the children to try the things on a doll or stuffed animal. Now they might want to take turns trying the scarf or hat or glasses on themselves. Do they want to look into a mirror to see how they look?

1430

Mister Rogers talks about parades and how they are a kind of grownup way of pretending. He shows a film of people marching in parades.

"Let's Have a Parade" can help children:

● develop creative play;
● express feelings through music.

Let's Have a Parade

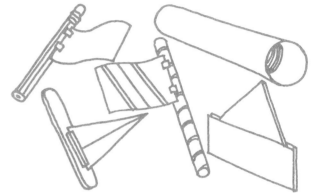

Materials

● pie tins and wooden spoons for drums
● tubes from paper towel rolls for horns
● marching or lively music (optional)
● parade hats (optional)
● straws, popsicle sticks or unsharpened pencils (optional)
● colored paper (optional)
● crayons or markers (optional)
● tape or glue (optional)
● scissors (optional)

Have any of the children ever been to a parade? What can they tell you about it? If you can find some rousing music on the radio or on a record, encourage the children to move with the music. They could even make their own music with pie-tin drums and cardboard horns as they march through the house or around the yard. For some extra fun, help the children make parade hats or flags. Flags for the parade can be made by:

● cutting pieces of paper into squares, rectangles or triangles;
● decorating them with designs, if you like;
● taping or gluing the shape to a straw, popsicle stick or unsharpened pencil.

Directions for making parade hats are on page B-3.

Thoughts For The Week

As children grow, they discover that people who care about them also set limits for them. As they learn more about safe limits, children can learn to set these limits for themselves. It's important for children to learn that limit-setting is one way that grownups show love and concern.

Moving to a new house, giving up old familiar toys, or parting with outgrown clothing can all be unsettling experiences for children. We find comfort in familiar surroundings, and security in having our favorite people and objects nearby. In the programs this week, we talk about how it feels to give up old things, even when we replace them with new things. Perhaps you can use these programs to encourage your children to talk about growing, moving, and changing.

Fred Rogers

Songs On The Programs This Week

1431 *"What Do You Do?"*
1432 *"You Are Special"*
1433 *"It's You I Like"*
   "Good People Sometimes Do Bad Things"
1434 *"I Did Too"*
   "You're Growing"

Your Notes For The Week

1431

At his workshop, Bob Trow is making a wooden jigsaw puzzle. He and Mister Rogers talk about safety rules in the workshop.

"Safety Rules" can help children:

* learn about limits.

Safety Rules

Materials

* large piece of paper (a cut-open grocery bag)
* marker

You might want to point out that some safety rules are about things that must be done to be safe; other safety rules are about things a person must *not* do to be safe. Can any of the children think of safety rules that are things people must do to be safe? Things like:

* wearing a seatbelt when riding in a car;
* wearing protective eye goggles in the workshop;
* wearing a lifejacket in a boat;
* wearing mittens on a very cold day;
* asking a grownup to use a knife to cut meat for you;
* wearing boots when it's wet or cold.

What are some safety rules that mean a person must *not* do something? For example:

* not running into the street after a ball;
* not leaving the yard without permission;
* not putting things in their mouths;
* not touching a stove or furnace.

At the top of your large piece of paper, write "Safety Rules." Ask the children to name some safety rules you have at day care and write them down. You might want to keep the list to go over every so often with the children.

(Or, 1260 "Puzzles.")

1432

When Corney gets a new saw, he can't decide what to do with his old one. He is reluctant to give it up, but there isn't room for two saws. Just the same, Corney feels more comfortable with the old saw nearby.

"Giving Up Old Things" can help children:

* talk about feelings;
* learn more about growing.

Giving Up Old Things

Materials
* none

Maybe you can remember a time when you had to give away some old clothing or a favorite old toy. Share that experience with the children, and encourage them to tell you about a time when they outgrew a favorite piece of clothing and had to give it up. Here are some questions you could ask them:

* Did you ever want to keep on wearing something even though it was too small?
* What could you do with clothing that no longer fits?
* How would you feel if you saw someone else wearing your favorite shirt or dress?
* Do any of you like to keep old clothes or shoes or toys even when you've outgrown them? What do you do with them?
* Where do you get new clothes when the old ones are too small? (From a store? From an older friend, relative, brother or sister?)

You may want to remind the children that even when a person wears something that belonged to someone else, he or she is still the same person. Wearing someone else's clothes doesn't change that.

1433

Mister Rogers visits the McFeely's to see how tacos are made. Their grandchildren help with grating the cheese and preparing the tacos.

"Making Tacos" can help children:

* learn more about foods.

Making Tacos

Materials
* corn tortillas or taco shells
* ground beef
* lettuce
* tomatoes
* cheese
* green pepper
* hot sauce (optional)

Can any of the children remember how the McFeelys made tacos? Encourage them to help you prepare the ingredients. You'll have to cook the ground beef in a skillet and cut the tomatoes and peppers yourself, but the children could tear lettuce into small pieces and perhaps grate the cheese. They could then prepare their own tacos by filling the tortillas or taco shells with their favorite ingredients. A taco salad is a simpler version of tacos. Add a little tomato or taco sauce to the ground beef, and substitute corn chips for tacos. Toss all the ingredients together in a large bowl, pouring the hot ground beef and sauce over the salad.

1434

It's moving day for Mrs. Baker and her children. Mister Rogers talks about what a moving van does. Joe Negri uses his music-shop truck to help move the Bakers. Mister Rogers talks about some of the feelings people have when they have to move away from friends.

"Unhappy Feelings" can help children:

- talk about feelings;
- express feelings through art work;
- express strong feelings in appropriate ways.

Unhappy Feelings

Materials

- mirror
- crayons
- paper

See if the children can think of times when they felt unhappy about something. You might want to encourage them to think about ways they let people know they are unhappy. For instance:

- crying;
- going off to be alone;
- saying they feel unhappy;
- looking sad.

Can they show you how they look when they feel unhappy? You could use a mirror to let the children see their own expressions. Some of the children might want to use crayons and paper to make a picture of the way they feel when they are unhappy. You might want to help the children think of ways to manage sad feelings. What kinds of things could they do that might help to make them feel better? For instance:

- talking with a grownup;
- drawing or painting;
- making up a song;
- holding onto a favorite toy.

(Or, 1391 "Where I Live"; 1002 "Moving Day.")

1435

Mister Rogers says that lots of people have old things they don't need anymore, but that maybe other people could use them. It's Flea Market Day on MGR-TV with Lady Elaine as host.

"Flea Market" can help children:

- practice making choices;
- learn more about money.

Flea Market

Materials

- old toys, clothing, jewelry, etc.
- popsicle sticks, stones, shells, or other interesting objects.

Check with the parents ahead of time to see if each child can bring in one or two old toys or a piece of clothing that no longer fits. If that's not possible, the children can make things to sell or trade at the flea market. They could help you make modeling dough and package small portions in airtight plastic bags. Or they could make pictures, cards, and other art projects. The children can arrange the objects on the floor or tables by putting things together that are similar. For instance, clothing, toys, art objects, etc. They could use pretend money or homemade money (page 320) or simply trade objects.

(Or, 1301 "A Pretend Store.")

Thoughts For The Week

Games like hide and seek, lost and found, and the many variations of peek-a-boo have a universal appeal to young children. These games are ways that children can pretend about separation and return. Often when children protest about parents' leaving, it's because they don't fully understand that their favorite people will ever come back. Young children need the reassurance that people **do** *return. One way for them to learn that is through playing about things like going away and coming back, hiding objects and discovering them again, hiding from someone and being found. When the children themselves can control the coming and going, they can see that people leave for a reason and that they come back because they* **want** *to come back.*

Fred Rogers

Songs On The Programs This Week

1436   "Look and Listen"
1437   "Wishes Don't Make Things Come True"
1439   "I Like to Take My Time"

Your Notes For The Week

1436

Mister Rogers meets the members of an African dance ensemble, who play a song about learning to count. Then he watches a marionette performance about a turban, and sees how a turban is wrapped around the head, using one piece of cloth. Lady Aberlin is wearing a fancy African turban on her head today—and everyone wonders what's underneath it!

"What's under the Turban?" can help children:

- feel comfortable asking about what they need to know.

What's under the Turban?

Materials

- a long strip of cloth (about one foot wide and three or four feet long)
- bath towel

Have any of the children ever seen someone wearing a hat or clothing that seemed out of the ordinary? Your older children might be able to recall what happened when Lady Aberlin wore a turban in the Neighborhood of Make-Believe. Here are several questions you could ask:

- What did the neighbors think Lady Aberlin had underneath the turban (a gift for King Friday, hair curlers, an aching head)?
- How did they find out that only her hair was underneath?

  (Robert Troll finally asked her.)
- Have you ever seen someone wearing a turban?

You might want to explain that a turban is a kind of hat that some people wear to protect their heads from the hot sun and the blowing sand. You can make a turban out of a long strip of cloth or get the same effect using a bath towel. Place the towel around the back of your head, twist the loose ends at your forehead and tuck them into the material around your head. Would any of the children like to try wearing the turban?

1437

A magician visits Mister Rogers and does several tricks for him. Balls, cups, and sticks appear and disappear — but those things don't *really* disappear: It's the magician's skill with fast hand movements that fool the eye. In the Neighborhood of Make-Believe, X and Henrietta practice a disappearing trick. When Bob Dog becomes upset by Henrietta's disappearance, X shows him how to practice disappearing behind his cape.

"Peek-a-Boo" can help children:
- use play to work on feelings;
- work on feelings about separation.

Peek-a-Boo

Materials
- scarf or soft blanket

There are many different ways to play peek-a-boo, ways for all children to join in — even infants or toddlers. One way to begin is to use a doll or stuffed animal. Cover it with a scarf or soft blanket. Wait several seconds and then pull it off.

Now try covering your own head. You might want to say something like "Where am I?" while you are hidden, and "Here I am" when you remove the scarf. You could cover your head several more times, letting the children take turns pulling off the scarf to find you.

Do any of the children want to cover their own heads? Younger children may want to pull off the scarf when they are ready, but older children might like the surprise of having you pull off the scarf unexpectedly. Can any of the children tell you other ways to play peek-a-boo?

(Or, 1103 "Jack-in-the-Box.")

1438

Using a set of blocks, Mister Rogers shows the difference between ramps and steps. He shows that wheels can go up and down ramps easily, and then talks about ways people use ramps. He also shows a film about different kinds of ramps. In the Neighborhood of Make-Believe, Lady Elaine Fairchilde turns everything upside down with her magic boomerang.

"Playing with Ramps" can help children:
- develop creative play;
- learn more about their world.

Playing with Ramps

Materials
- pieces of heavy cardboard or strips of wood
- blocks or empty boxes
- toy cars
- toy people
- doll furniture

Using the blocks, strips of cardboard, and a few toy cars, show the children how a ramp makes it easy for the cars to drive up onto higher blocks. Can the children think of other uses for ramps? (For instance, making it easier for people in wheelchairs, or children in strollers, to go up or down a set of stairs.) You could explain that ramps are sometimes used to slide heavy furniture or boxes up or down stairs. How would they use the ramps to move doll furniture? Can the children think of other ways to use the ramps in their block play?

(Or, 1149 "Upside-Down Pictures.")

1439

Mister Rogers talks about getting excited before a big event and how hard it is to wait until everyone's ready. He builds with blocks while he waits for his wife, Joanne, whose piano recital is tomorrow, and sings "I Like to Take My Time."

"Take Your Time" can help children:

- practice waiting;
- develop the ability to keep on trying.

Take Your Time

Materials

- blocks or boxes
- sweaters, shirts, or other clothing with fasteners
- paper
- crayons or markers

Can any of the children think of a time when it was hard to wait for you to do something? For instance, when you had to prepare lunch or snacks? You might explain that it's important to take your time to do a job well. What are some things the children like to do carefully? Buttoning or zipping? Building with blocks? Making a picture? What would happen if they hurried too much? The children could try doing something—first hurrying and then taking their time to do it carefully. You could suggest something like:

- building a tower of blocks or boxes;
- buttoning a sweater;
- drawing a picture with crayons or markers.

Maybe they can talk about the results. What happened when they hurried? Was it different when they did it carefully? Of course there are times when people *have* to hurry...but they can ask for help if they need it.

(Or, 1428 "When You Have to Wait.")

1440

Tim Scanlon returns to the Neighborhood of Make-Believe with a new friend. X is upset about having to share time with Professor Scanlon and expresses his jealous feelings to Handyman Negri. But X enjoys the magic tricks that Tim and his friend, Darren, perform, and he feels a lot better having talked about his feelings.

"Expressing Feelings" can help children:

- talk about feelings;
- express strong feelings in appropriate ways.

Expressing Feelings

Materials

- paper
- non-toxic paint
- modeling dough
- crayons or markers
- dolls or puppets

Do any of the children know why X was feeling jealous? What did X do that made him feel better? Maybe the children can think of a time when talking about their feelings helped them feel better. You might point out that it's sometimes hard to *say* what we feel, but that there are other ways to show our feelings. Let each one choose one of the ways below to express the feelings he or she has right now:

- painting a picture;
- drawing with crayons;
- pretending with dolls or puppets;
- playing with clay or modeling dough;
- making up a song;
- telling a story.

There are some days some people just don't want to talk about their feelings. For those people "there's always another time."

Thoughts For The Week

*Sharing seldom comes easily to children, but there are two notions about sharing that may make it easier for them. One is that when people share, everyone has more to play with, more things to enjoy. The other is that no one has to share everything. There are some special things that are ours alone—not only things but thoughts, too— and thoughts are for sharing only when and if we **want** to share them.*

Fred Rogers

Songs On The Programs This Week

1441   *"You Are Special"*

1443   *"I Like to Be Told"*
        "Everybody's Fancy"

1444   *"Please Don't Think It's Funny"*

1445   *"Some Things Belong to You"*

Your Notes For The Week

Monday

1441

Mister Rogers sees a demonstration of stained-glass window making. The artist is using multi-colored glass to make a rainbow window. In the Neighborhood of Make-Believe, King Friday learns that Prince Tuesday has never seen a rainbow, and he sends Mr. McFeely on a Royal Quest to bring one back.

"Crayon Window Hangings" can help children:

- develop creative play.

Crayon Window Hangings

Materials

- old crayon pieces
- crayon sharpener or a plastic knife
- waxed paper
- iron
- picture of a rainbow or draw one yourself

Have any of the children ever seen a rainbow? Can they describe what it looks like? You might want to show the children several pictures of rainbows. Some of the older children may be able to name the colors they see. Here's a way you can help the children combine colors to make a window hanging: With a crayon sharpener or plastic knife, shave off small slivers of crayon onto a piece of waxed paper. Help the children cover the crayon shavings with another piece of waxed paper. Then you can press the sheets together with a warm iron.
The crayon will melt and run together, making interesting-looking designs. If you hang the designs in a window, the light will shine through the designs, as if through stained glass. Did you know that there is a definite sequence to the colors of a real rainbow? They go in this order: red, orange, yellow, green, blue, indigo and violet.

(Or, 1251 "Food-Coloring Designs.")

1442

Mister Rogers shows a picture book with photographs of different kinds of exotic birds. Lady Elaine is hosting a television program called "Feathered Friends" and invites the king and his wooden bird, Troglodytes Aedon, to be guests on the program.

"Same but Different" can help children:

- recognize likeness and difference.

Same but Different

Materials

- old magazines that contain pictures of birds
- glue or paste
- large sheet of paper or cardboard (a grocery bag cut open)
- scissors
- marker
- soft music

Can the children tell you how all birds are alike? What are some ways they are different? See if the children can find pictures of birds in your old magazines and help them tear or cut out the pictures. When you have a collection of bird pictures, the children can paste them onto a large piece of paper or cardboard. What else do they know about birds? For example:

- Where do young birds live?
- What do they eat?
- What does a bird's nest look like?

The children might want to pretend to be birds as they move to soft music. Or you could all take a walk and look for real feathered friends.

(Or, 1169 "Make a Birdfeeder.")

1443

Mister Rogers attends a jazz session at Negri's Music Shop and looks at different kinds of saxophones. Then he makes his own musical instrument with a piece of waxed paper folded over a comb.

"Paper-Plate Shakers" can help children:

- develop creative play;
- learn to listen carefully.

Paper-Plate Shakers

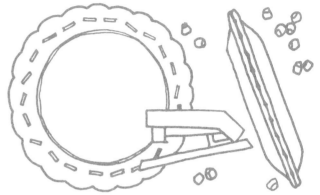

Materials

- two paper plates for each child
- dried beans, popcorn, or rice
- stapler or tape
- crayons or markers
- tape recorder (optional)

A simple rhythm instrument can be made from two paper plates fastened together and filled with dried beans, popcorn kernels or rice. Use a stapler or tape to fasten the plates together, leaving a small opening to pour in the beans. The children can fill the shakers and decorate them by drawing with crayons or markers on the outsides. Would the children like to use the shakers while they sing a favorite song? Show them how to use the shakers like tamborines to keep the beat of the music. You might want to add metal pans and wooden spoons and see if the children want to pretend to be in a marching band.

If you have a tape recorder you could tape the jazz session on today's program and play it back to the children. They could add their "shaker" music to the jazz music.

(Or, 1404 "Sandpaper Blocks"; 1185 "Making Drums.")

1444

Mister Rogers shows a film of a caterpillar making a cocoon, then growing, changing, and emerging as a butterfly. In the Neighborhood of Make-Believe, Lady Elaine wants a visiting butterfly to return to a cocoon and become a caterpillar again — to entertain her television audience. Lady Aberlin convinces her that it's not possible to grow backwards.

"Caterpillars and Butterflies" can help children:

- learn more about growing;
- develop their imaginations.

Caterpillars and Butterflies

Materials

- scarves and bath towels in assorted colors.

What can the children tell you about caterpillars? Can anyone show you a way to move like a caterpillar? Suggest the children try out different ways of crawling as if they were caterpillars. Then ask them to pretend to be in a cocoon — being very still. You might want to throw a scarf over each child as a pretend cocoon. Wait for a moment and then encourage them to come out of their "cocoons" and move like butterflies. Some children might want to use the scarves as wings while they "fly" around.

What other things change as they grow?

- Seeds turning into plants?
- Babies growing to be children?

Do any of the children want to pretend to be growing plants or growing children? You might see some beautiful dances evolving with this kind of play.

(Or, 1078 "Growing.")

1445

It's raining in the Neighborhood of Make-Believe, and everyone is eagerly looking for a rainbow. When Mr. McFeely finally finds one near the castle, Prince Tuesday claims it for his very own. Queen Sara explains that rainbows belong to everyone. Lady Elaine promises to share the movies she took of the rainbow whenever Prince Tuesday wants to see them.

"Some Things Belong to Everyone" can help children:

- practice sharing.

Some Things Belong to Everyone

Materials

- paper
- paint, markers or crayons

Can the children think of some things at day care that have to be shared with everyone — such as:

- the toys;
- the books;
- the furniture;
- the day care provider?

Perhaps they can tell you about things at home that belong to everyone — things like:

- the dishes;
- the television;
- their parents' attention.

See if anyone can think of something that belongs to everyone in a neighborhood. For example:

- a playground;
- the sidewalk.

Children sometimes find it easier to share things when they know there are certain things they *don't* have to share. Help them think of something that is all theirs — a favorite blanket or stuffed toy. To finish up, they could all share the paint, crayons or colored markers — to make their very own picture of a rainbow or something else with many colors.

(Or, 1305 "Fruit Salad.")

Thoughts For The Week

Giving gifts is an important theme in the Neighborhood of Make-Believe this week. It's King Friday's birthday, and each character in the neighborhood finds his or her special way to wish him a "Happy Birthday." But Lady Elaine doesn't want to give a present to the king. Her difficulty in giving a present may give you a chance to talk about the way people feel about giving gifts. Children sometimes find it hard to part with a toy their parents have purchased for them to give to another child. They want to keep it themselves. Not because they're mean or "selfish." They find it interesting and want to make good use of it for a while. Human beings "grow" into the understanding of giving. And when a special gift children have made and given is overlooked or not appreciated by the person who gets it, children may feel overlooked themselves.

*I think it's helpful to young children when we allow them to make their own decisions about what sort of gift they want to give someone or whether they want to give a gift at all. Children certainly need to know that people should give presents because they **want** to give them—and the greatest present is the one that's given in love.*

*Day caregivers give so much. If someone isn't able to receive what you have to give, that doesn't mean that your gift isn't valuable. Any gift given with care **is** of real value.*

Fred Rogers

Songs On The Programs This Week

1446　"You're Growing"
　　　"It's You I Like"
　　　"Sometimes"
1447　"Everybody Has a History"
1449　"Let's Be Together Today"
1450　"I'm Angry"
　　　"Love Is People"
　　　"You're Older Today"

Your Notes For The Week

1446

Marilyn Barnett shows Mister Rogers several exercises, and dancer Vija Vetra demonstrates the art of Indian dancing, using hand gestures to make lotus flowers, snakes, waterfalls, and tigers. Mister Rogers talks about different ways to express ourselves.

"Let's Dance" can help children:
* express feelings through movement and dance;
* develop coordination.

Let's Dance

Materials
* music
* long scarves or strips of soft cloth

What do the children remember about the exercises or dances they saw today? Can anyone show you the hand gestures that Vija Vetra used in her dances? The children could make up their own dances by moving to music. Some of the children may feel comfortable dancing as soon as you turn on the music, but others may need encouragement—or they might just prefer to watch. You could suggest:
* holding scarves or strips of cloth while they are moving;
* pretending to be birds, butterflies, elephants, or other animals;
* making up different kinds of dances to show different feelings.

Dancing and movement are very natural ways for many children to express themselves. This kind of activity can be used again and again.

1447

Mister Rogers looks at the number book, *Numbers of Things*, showing pictures and corresponding numerals. Lady Aberlin tells people that Friday will be the king's birthday.

"Looking for Numbers" can help children:

- recognize and use symbols.

Looking for Numbers

Materials

- old calendars
- scissors
- paste
- paper

One way to begin this activity is to ask if the children can tell you how old they are. Can they show you by holding up the right number of fingers? Then you could show the children the old calendar pages and see if any of them can point out their favorite numbers. Some of the children might want to cut out the numbers and paste them on paper to make a number collage. Older children could make a number booklet by pasting a numeral on each page and then drawing or pasting in pictures that show that same number of objects.

Today might be a good day to practice counting things around you—such as:

- buttons on a shirt;
- blocks in a tower;
- children at day care;
- chairs at the table.

(Or, 1356 "My History.")

1448

Mister Rogers brings in an array of baskets and a book that shows different kinds of baskets. He visits a basket maker. In the Neighborhood of Make-Believe, Corney is making a new basket for the king's party.

"All about Baskets" can help children:

- recognize likeness and difference.

All about Baskets

Materials

- baskets in assorted sizes and shapes

Show the children the different baskets you have. Can some of the children tell you how the baskets are alike? How are they different? Do any of the children have an idea for using the baskets? How many different ways could the baskets be used today? You could suggest:

- serving a snack in one;
- arranging fruit or flowers in another;
- playing bean bag toss with a basket as a target;
- making up a story about a basket;
- using baskets for pretending with dress-up clothes.

You could point out that no two baskets are exactly alike even though they are all baskets—just the way each of us is different even though we are all people.

1449

Mister Rogers shows three different bean bags and asks viewers to look at them carefully for differences. At Elsie Neal's Craft Show a man is making and selling bean bags. In the Neighborhood of Make-Believe, Daniel Tiger makes three bean bags for the king's birthday present.

"Bean Bags" can help children:

- develop creative play;
- develop muscle control.

Bean Bags

Materials

- dried beans
- measuring cups and spoons
- dishpan or large pan
- scraps of material
- scissors (preferably pinking shears)
- needle and thread or a sewing machine
- cardboard tracing pattern (four-inch circle or square)

The older children may be able to trace around the cardboard pattern onto scraps of material to make the front and back sides of a bean bag. With your help (and pinking shears, if you have them), they could cut out the shapes. After you have stitched three sides of the bag, the children could spoon or funnel beans into the bags until almost full. As you sew the tops closed, the children may be able to think of ways to use the bean bags. Some children may not be interested in making bean bags, but they might want to play with the dried beans in a pan while you help the others. You could give them plastic measuring cups and spoons to use and remind them to keep the beans in the pan. Some children might pretend to be preparing a meal; others might enjoy filling and emptying the cups and spoons or even just listening to the sound of the beans or feeling them. (Be sure the younger children don't put the beans in their mouths.)

(Or, 1398 "Bean Bag Toss.")

1450

Mister Rogers shows a sign that says "Happy Birthday, King Friday," and Mr. McFeely stops by with many party favors: rattles, whistles and horns. Today is the day for King Friday's birthday party. Daniel Tiger is crying because the king forgot to open the present Daniel brought.

"Birthday Parties" can help children:

- develop their imaginations.

Birthday Parties

Materials

- old party hats and favors (or paper to make hats and favors)
- tape, string, or ribbon
- old wrapping paper or newspapers to wrap pretend presents
- modeling dough to make a pretend birthday cake
- straws cut into pieces to use as pretend candles
- toy dishes
- a box of odds and ends to use for pretend presents (stones, shells, cars, blocks)

Can any of the children tell you what birthday parties are like? What do they like about parties? Are there things they *don't* like about parties (the noise, strangers, etc.)? See if anyone can tell you why Daniel Tiger was crying at the king's party. What happened to make him feel better?

You might want to put all the materials you've collected in a big box or in one corner of the room and see what ways the children can think of to use them for a pretend party. You might help them get started by asking:

- What could we use to make a cake?
- Does anyone want to wrap some presents?

Encourage the children to continue playing out their own ideas, adding some of your own when necessary to keep the play going.

Thoughts For The Week

*One task of growing up is learning to use our teeth to chew—but **not** to bite other people. Most small children are likely to have angry times when they feel like biting other children and grownups, but, little by little, they can tame these biting feelings, often letting them out in play. Toddlers may be particularly interested in things like pliers, because pliers have "mouths" with "teeth." When children first learn to use scissors, their own mouths sometimes open and close as they cut paper, because the scissors seem like a mouth that is biting. Pretending can be a way to master the biting, too. For example, children often like to play that they are dogs or cats and even tigers that growl, pretending to bite lots of things. But the only lasting way to tame our urges to bite is to come to the realization that we want people to love us, and biting them doesn't help them to do that.*

Fred Rogers

Songs On The Programs This Week

1451 *"You're Older Today"*
1452 *"Everybody's Fancy"*
       "What Do You Do?"
1453 *"Let's Be Together Today"*
1455 *"You're Growing"*

Your Notes For The Week

1451

Mister Rogers shows a picture of a friend, Frederick McFalls, who is a doctor and a sculptor. Then he shows a film of Dr. McFalls making a clay statue. Mister Rogers gives a recipe for homemade modeling dough and mixes up a batch.

"Clay Sculptures" can help children:

* develop creative play.

Clay Sculptures

Materials

* clay or modeling dough
* cookie cutters, popsicle sticks, rolling pin, or other "tools"

If you don't have clay or modeling dough on hand, you and the children could begin this activity by making modeling dough (page A-1). Some of the older children might want to make clay sculptures of animals or people — snakes, lizards, dinosaurs.

Sculptures of people are more difficult, but the children could use a ginger bread-man cookie cutter (if you have one) to make a clay person. Younger children may not be able to make a clay sculpture, but they could make things like balls, pancakes or pretend cookies. Even the toddlers in your group can use the clay for pounding, poking, flattening, rolling, or just *feeling*.

Would any of the children like to let what they've made harden overnight, paint it tomorrow, then take it home?

1452

There are many lizards on the program today. Daniel Tiger is still frightened about meeting King Friday's lizard friend. He wonders if it will bite. And Lady Elaine wonders if it is a regular lizard or one that changes into other things. King Friday answers the questions: Princess Margaret H. Lizard is a *special* kind of lizard, and she only eats vegetables.

"Box Puppets" can help children:

• use play to work on feelings.

Box Puppets

Materials

• small empty boxes (pudding, gelatin, or individual-sized cereal boxes)
• knife or scissors
• tape
• non-toxic paint and brushes
• scrap materials (buttons, paper scraps, yarn, etc.)
• glue

Can any of the children tell you how Daniel Tiger felt about meeting Princess Margaret H. Lizard? What was scary to him? The children can help make box puppets by taping down the lids of small boxes and then giving them to you to cut in half on three sides. Fold the box so the children can put their fingers in the top part and their thumbs in the bottom part. The folded part of the box will be the mouth. The children can paint the boxes and decorate them with buttons or other scrap materials to make puppets. If any of the children want to pretend about biting, you may need to set some limits about not biting people—and not scaring younger children by even pretending to bite them. If you cut one or two extra boxes, your toddlers might enjoy just playing with the boxes—opening and closing them like mouths.

1453

Margaret Hamilton, the actress who portrayed the mean witch in "The Wizard of Oz," visits Mister Rogers. She tells how, as a little girl, she liked to pretend she was a witch for Halloween. She tries on a witch's costume and explains that witches are only pretend.

"Playing about Witches" can help children:

• use play to work on feelings;
• understand the difference between real and pretend.

Playing about Witches

Materials

• witch's hat (see page B-2)
• black cape or a piece of black material to use as a cape
• dress-up skirt
• magic wand made from cardboard
• mirror

Do any of the children want to try on a witch's outfit? You could help them pretend about being a witch by asking questions like:

• How does a witch talk?
• Can you laugh like a witch?
• Can you make your face look like a mean witch?

Let the children see themselves in a mirror and then encourage them to pretend about witches. They could act out things a witch might do. For instance, pretending to make things disappear by waving a magic wand.

The children might want to use other dress-up clothes to make up a story. What ideas do they have? You might want to be part of the audience, along with any children who don't feel like playing. If you keep the witch costume in a specially marked box, the children can use it for dramatic play at other times, too.

Thursday

1454

Mister Rogers shows an array of old videotapes that are highlights of past programs. In the Neighborhood of Make-Believe, everyone is preparing for the "Festival of Remembering."

"Remembering" can help children:

• develop their memory.

Remembering

Materials

• paintings, drawings and objects that were made by the children when they were younger

• toys that may have been their favorites when they were younger

• any old photographs of the children

If the children are new in your group (or if you have nothing they made or used when they were younger), you could check with their parents to see if the children could bring something from home — a photograph or a baby toy. If you have old drawings the children made several months ago (or even a year ago), spread them out on the table or floor and let the children look at them. Can they recognize the ones they drew or painted?

See if the children can each remember one thing that happened when they were younger. You could help them remember by recalling situations such as:

• someone's birthday celebration;

• a special trip;

• an activity they liked to do when they were younger.

You could talk about how they've grown — outside ways like getting taller or looking older, and inside ways like being able to say how they feel or thinking up more and more ways to play.

Friday

1455

At Brockett's Bakery, Mister Rogers watches Mrs. Costa make bread from her own recipe — mixing the dough, kneading it, and waiting for it to rise.

"Making Bread" can help children:

• learn more about foods.

Making Bread

Materials

• your favorite bread recipe (or the whole wheat bread recipe on page C-1)

• ingredients to make bread

• bowls

• measuring spoons and cups

• mixing spoons

It takes several hours to make bread (but most of the time is spent waiting for the dough to rise), so you might want to start this activity early in the day. The children can all participate by measuring or mixing ingredients. For instance:

• adding yeast to water and mixing it;

• scooping flour into a bowl with a measuring cup;

• pouring water into measuring cups;

• stirring the batter until it gets firm.

Each child can knead a piece of dough, or they all can take turns kneading one large piece. Then put the dough in a bowl and let it rise. You could set a timer to show the children how long you have to wait. Some children may not understand how long one hour is, but you could tell them the dough will be ready — "when we come in from outside play," or "after lunch," or "after snack." The children can then punch out the air bubbles and knead the dough again. This time each child can form a small loaf of bread. Put the loaves on a cookie sheet or in small bread pans and let them rise again before baking.

(Or, 1080 "While You Wait"; 1408 "Dough Play.")

Thoughts For The Week

*Children want so much to be loved by the people they love, and when those people get mad, it can be very scary. A child may wonder, "Have I stopped being loved?" Accidents and messes often bring on adults' anger, and when they happen, we need to be careful to explain why we're angry. "I'm really mad you spilled the juice," we might say, "because now I've got to clean the floor all over again!" That kind of talk is much more understandable to a child than shouting, "Bad boy! You spilled the juice!" After all, **he** isn't bad, it's just what he's done that's bad. A caregiver once said to me, "But when the third cup of milk hits the floor, I feel so angry that I yell at the child. And then I'm sorry that I yelled." Well, most of us lose our tempers once in a while, and it's quite understandable that cleaning up messes can make a person angry. And children can understand that people sometimes get so angry that they say and do things they're sorry for later. They learn a lot about angry feelings when they hear you say "I'm sorry I yelled at you; I just lost my temper." Children need to know that we all have accidents—adults and children alike. All we can do when accidents happen is fix what we can and then go on again, trying to be as careful (full of care) as we know how.*

Fred Rogers

Songs On The Programs This Week

1456 *"You're Growing"*
1457 *"A Handy Lady and a Handy Man"*
1458 *"Pretending"*
       "Everybody's Fancy"
1459 *"Everybody's Fancy"*

Your Notes For The Week

1456

There's a crystal ball in the Neighborhood of Make-Believe that shows the future. Mister Rogers wonders if his "television friends" like to pretend about the future.

"Pretending about the Future" can help children:

- develop their imaginations;
- learn more about growing.

Pretending about the Future

Materials

- ball
- scarf
- dress-up clothes and accessories

Any fairly large ball can serve as a "crystal ball" which the children can cover with a scarf the way Lady Aberlin did to make the "magic" work. Ask the children to tell you what they "see" in the ball. You could ask questions like:

- What do you see yourself doing when you grow up?
- Will you have little children to care for?
- Will you go to work or do your work at home?

The children could play about the future by dressing up in old clothes and pretending to be grownups. They could use dolls or stuffed animals as the children. But they need to know that no ball—crystal or otherwise—is really going to show the future. People grow and change and make choices and do things. That's how the future develops.

1457

Betty Aberlin mixes up some gray paint to cover a chipped area on the tree model and later paints a windowsill for Mister Rogers. In the Neighborhod of Make-Believe, Lady Elaine is painting the crystal ball to make the future come sooner—but the crystal ball won't work until the paint is removed.

"Painting with Water" can help children:

● develop their imaginations.

Painting with Water

Materials

● water
● buckets
● brushes
● something to paint (the porch, railings, doors, or chairs)

Children often like to help grownups with tasks such as painting and fixing things. But house paint is not safe for children to use—and can't be removed easily when spilled. But you could let the children pretend to paint, using only water. Give them buckets of water and old paintbrushes to use on things like the porch, steps, railings, or other washable surfaces. If the weather doesn't permit outdoor play, you might let them paint a kitchen chair (placed on newspaper) or a kitchen counter. Do any of the children want to pretend to be housepainters? They could dress up in caps, aprons or old coveralls. Even though the pretend paint (water) doesn't paint anything, you could tell the children how much cleaner the thing they "painted" looks.

1458

King Friday is upset because the paint won't come off the crystal ball. He scolds Lady Elaine for painting it without permissionand consults Princess Margaret Witch for a solution. She suggests knocking three times on the ball. When nothing happens, she promises to come tomorrow for on-the-spot aid.

"Cleaning Up a Mess" can help children:

● talk about feelings;
● learn to do things independently.

Cleaning Up a Mess

Materials

● none

Can you think of a time when you tried to help someone—and accidentally spilled or broke something? Tell the children what happened and how you felt about it. Can they tell you how Lady Elaine felt today? You could ask questions like:

● Why do you think she painted the crystal ball?
● How did King Friday feel when he found out?
● How might they get the paint off?

There are lots of times during the day when children make a mess by spilling something or putting paint or crayon marks somewhere they shouldn't. Sometimes these things are done on purpose, but many times they are accidents. Talk with the children about what they could do if:

● someone spilled a glass of milk;
● a toddler marked on the wall with crayon;
● the box of blocks was knocked over;
● paint spilled on the table.

You can point out that often the mess can be cleaned up, and show them where sponges or small rags are kept. Encourage children to clean up things they spill—not as a punishment but as a way to put things in order again.

(Or, 1256 "Soapsuds Fingerpainting"; 1261 "Dress-up.")

1459

Mister Rogers gathers up things for a project he will do at the Garage Workshop. Using construction paper, glue, and pieces of torn paper, he makes a collage and then sprinkles sand on it for texture. A flour-and-water paste is used in the Neighborhood of Make-Believe to remove the paint from the crystal ball.

"Torn Paper Pictures" can help children:

* develop their imaginations;
* develop muscle control.

Torn Paper Pictures

Materials

* easy-to-tear paper (tissue paper, magazine pages or newspapers—the comic pages of the Sunday paper will add some color)
* flour
* warm water
* bowl
* whisk or fork
* background paper

To make a sticky paste, put one-half cup of warm water in a small mixing bowl. Add flour in small amounts (a tablespoon or two at a time), whipping after each addition. Continue to add flour until the mixture becomes thick and creamy. Set the paste aside while the children tear up pieces of brightly-colored paper. Even the toddlers could participate by helping with the tearing. Give each child a piece of background paper and a small amount of paste, and let everyone create his or her own designs with the torn pieces of paper.

1460

Today Mister Rogers talks about remembering special times on MISTER ROGERS' NEIGHBORHOOD.

"Let's Do It Again" can help children:

* develop their memory.

Let's Do It Again

Materials

* pencil or pen

The activities in this book were written to help in planning your day. But we hope that the activities can be done again and again—whenever you or the children want to do them. Today might be a time when you could encourage the children to remember some of the activities they have enjoyed doing. Can the children tell you something they would like to do again? You could make a list of these activities and try to include them in your plans for the next few weeks. If the children have trouble remembering, you might ask if they can think of specific activities such as:

* an art project they did (painting, drawing, pasting, fingerpainting);
* a favorite story or song;
* a pretending activity (playing dress-up, hospital, puppets, etc.);
* a dance or music activity;
* an important talking time.

If you have materials on hand for one of the activities they remember, you could let them do it today. See if anyone can remember the supplies you need or how to get ready for the play activity. They could even try closing their eyes and trying to picture something they've made (or drawn) and telling you about it. If there's something they remember, it may have been quite important to them.

Thoughts For The Week

Most children are naturally eager to learn and join the world of the "bigger kids" who go to school. But like other important times in our lives, starting school can bring mixed feelings. If going to school will mean leaving you and the day care setting, at least for a large part of the day, the prospect of that separation may bring particular stress. When children feel uncertain about a new experience, they sometimes behave in ways they did when they were younger. They may cling more to you or to their parents. Some may suck their thumbs again. Others may forget their toilet training now and then. At times like this, children often need some extra attention and reassurance. Encouraging children to talk about what they might be thinking and feeling is one of the best ways to help them prepare for the changes that will take place.

Fred Rogers

Songs On The Programs This Week

1462 "One and One Are Two"
1463 "Everybody's Fancy"
1464 "Did You Know?"
1465 "I'm Proud of You"

Your Notes For The Week

1461

Mister Rogers talks about home and school today. He visits a kindergarten teacher who shows them what a school is like. In the Neighborhood of Make-Believe, the trolley is pretending to be a school bus.

"A Pretend School Bus" can help children:

- develop their imaginations;
- use play to work on feelings.

A Pretend School Bus

Materials

- chairs or boxes to sit on
- schoolbooks, crayons, etc. (optional)
- toy steering wheel (optional)

Are any of the children in your group getting ready to go to school? Even children who won't be going for a year or two may enjoy pretending about it. How will they get to school—walk, ride a bus, go in someone's car? If some of the children will be riding a bus, you could ask them what they think the school bus will be like. Then you could help them pretend about a school-bus ride. Set up chairs or boxes in rows to be used as seats in the bus. You could be the bus driver first and explain to the children that real bus drivers are always adults who know how to drive big buses very well. Does anyone want to pretend to be the bus driver? If you have more than one volunteer, the children can take turns. You might suggest they act out:

- waiting for the bus;
- getting on the bus;
- riding to school;
- getting off the bus at school;
- pretending to be at school;
- riding home;
- getting off the bus and meeting you or their parent.

If the children have their own ideas about a school-bus ride, encourage them to act them out. Your pretend "school bus" could be a car, a train or an airplane, too.

1462

Mister Rogers sings the song, "One and One Are Two." In the Neighborhood of Make-Believe, Daniel is excited about the delivery of study cards—one set with numbers and the other with letters. He wonders how he can play with them.

"Card Sorting" can help children:

- recognize likeness and difference;
- recognize and use symbols.

Card Sorting

Materials

- an old deck of cards

Becoming familiar with numbers—noticing the numbers on houses or perhaps on a clock—is one of the first ways children begin to learn about numbers. Four- and five-year-old children can play different sorting games with an old deck of cards. They can:

- sort the cards by color;
- sort the cards by the shapes on them—hearts, diamonds, clubs, spades;
- sort them by number;
- trade cards to make sets (all the fours, all the hearts, etc.).

You might find that even the toddlers enjoy the feel of cards and want to have a few to spread out on the table or pass back and forth. They won't be able to sort them, but perhaps they can pretend or just enjoy being part of the activity.

1463

Mister Rogers brings a chalkboard today. In the Neighborhood of Make-Believe, Lady Elaine is scaring all the children about going to school by telling them they already have to know their numbers and alphabet. Lady Aberlin talks with her about the importance of play as well as learning in school.

"Chalk Drawings" can help children:

- learn more about their world.

Chalk Drawings

Materials

- colored chalk and white paper
- dark paper and white or yellow chalk
- hair spray (optional)

Have any of the children seen a chalkboard at a school? Do they know what a chalkboard is for? If you have a small one, you could show it to them. Or a child who has one at home could tell the others about it. The children might be interested in how easily the chalk erases on a chalkboard. Then give the children paper and chalk to use for drawing. Once the drawings are finished, you can spray them with hair spray (preferably outside and away from the children) so the chalk doesn't rub off. Encourage the children to tell you about their pictures. Some of the children may not want to tell you right away about what they've drawn but might feel like it later.

1464

Ana Platypus and Prince Tuesday are ready for their first day at school. Daniel Tiger is still frightened about school and brings along his toy dump truck to make him feel more "at home."

"Take Something Along" can help children:

- talk about feelings;
- use play to work on feelings.

Take Something Along

Materials

- none

Can any of the children tell you how Daniel felt about going to school? See if they know why he was frightened. Have they ever felt that way before a new experience like:

- going to a new day care home;
- visiting a friend's or relative's home;
- going to the doctor or dentist;
- riding a bus or airplane for the first time?

What kinds of things helped Daniel? Do any of the children have favorite objects they bring to day care? They might want to show the others their favorite toy, stuffed animal or blanket. Encourage the children to pretend to go to school for the first time (or to day care for the first time, if the children are younger). What could they take along that would help them feel comfortable? Children find it very hard to share the favorite toys they bring from home, and it's important to them that they know *they don't have to* share them. You might want to set aside an area with hooks or boxes for the children to use as safe places for their own special belongings.

1465

Mister Rogers puts a name tag on a picture of Francois Clemmons and a name tag in the Trolley School Bus. In the Neighborhood of Make-Believe, children in Some Place Else find their own desks at school with a name tag for each of them.

"Name Tags" can help children:

- recognize and use symbols.

Name Tags

Materials

- index cards or heavy paper cut into tags (approximately three inches by five inches)
- marker

Today you could make name tags for each child to use at snack or lunch time. Can anyone tell you the first letter of his or her name? As you print the name cards, say the person's name and give the card to the child to hold while you make the others. Can some of the children match their cards with their names printed in other places—on pictures they have done or on their special boxes? Set out the name cards at lunch or snack time and help each child find his or her own place. If you have younger children, perhaps the older ones could help them find their places. You can also make symbols beside the names of younger children to help them recognize their own—for example, colored circles, squares and triangles.

(Or, 1373 "Making Signs.")

Thoughts For The Week

*The adult world can seem overwhelmingly large to children. As a result, children often pretend they have super powers and strength that will make them superbig, superfast, and superstrong, even stronger than adults! Television superheroes can be very appealing to young children, but they can also be very frightening. We need to help children realize that the superheroes and monsters they see are either pictures that someone has drawn, or people dressed up in costumes and make-up. They're not real, but they often scare people because they **look** so real.*

Fred Rogers

Songs On The Programs This Week

1466 *"You Are Special"*

1467 *"Did You Know?"*

1468 *"What Do You Do?"*

1469 *"You've Got to Do It"*

1470 *" It's You I Like"*

Your Notes For The Week

1466

Queen Sara is worried because Prince Tuesday is having bad dreams about a dinosaur wearing a large crown. Prince Tuesday is feeling stronger than anyone else because of his "superfunnel." In school Ana tells of her superskirt and Daniel is afraid to hear of such scary things.

"Super Capes" can help children:

- use play to work on feelings;
- understand the difference between real and pretend.

Super Capes

Materials

- soft blankets, pieces of material, etc.
- safety pins or diaper pins

You will need to be very clear about limits for children's "super" play and let them know:

- they must not hurt anyone while pretending;
- jumping, knocking things over and the like is not allowed;
- toys are not to be thrown or broken;
- the minute anyone says "stop" the super play must stop.

Help those children who want capes to tie or pin what material you have around their shoulders. You might want to encourage superhero play outside where they can run. Remind the children that they cannot really fly—even with a super cape! Some children have trouble keeping their play within safe limits during this kind of pretend. It's up to you to decide if this activity is appropriate for your group of children. If not, you can encourage the children to use the capes as royal robes for a different kind of make-believe.

(Or, 1392 "Scary Things.")

1467

Mister Rogers shows two dinosaur models and explains that dinosaurs don't exist anymore. In the Neighborhood of Make-Believe, Daniel is frightened by Purple Panda—dressed as a dinosaur wearing a golden crown. Back in the "real" neighborhood, Mister Rogers meets Dr. Mary Dawson who takes him on a tour of the Dinosaur Room at Carnegie Museum of Natural History.

"Dinosaur Models" can help children:

- use play to work on feelings;
- develop their imaginations.

Dinosaur Models

Materials

- modeling dough (recipe on page A-1) or clay
- paper
- markers or crayons

One way to begin this activity is to ask the children to tell you what they know about dinosaurs. You could ask:

- What did they look like?
- Do they live anywhere today?
- How do we know about dinosaurs?

You might explain that there were many different kinds of dinosaurs. Then encourage the children to mold dinosaurs from the clay or modeling dough. They could make realistic looking dinosaurs or dinosaurs from their imaginations. Dinosaurs may seem too scary for some children—in which case they can use the clay or modeling dough in other ways. Would any of the children prefer drawing a picture about dinosaurs? You might be able to find a book about dinosaurs at your local library to share with the children, or even visit a museum as Mister Rogers did.

1468

Mister Rogers talks about dreams not being real—only thoughts in our heads. In the Neighborhood of Make-Believe, Prince Tuesday learns that it helps to talk about his fears.

"A Picture of a Dream" can help children:

- express feelings through art work;
- learn to use words.

A Picture of a Dream

Materials

- paper
- crayons or markers
- non-toxic paint
- brushes

See if any of the children would like to talk about a recent dream. Some children may want to tell you a dream, others may not be able to remember a dream, or may not want to share it. Encourage those who do to make a picture of a dream, using crayons, markers, or paint. The pictures can be representations of people, or dinosaurs, or anything that might be in a dream…or they can be designs and combinations of color on paper. If the children don't want to draw their own dreams, can they create a picture showing how they might think a dream could look? This might give you a chance to talk about dreams as being a way people have of thinking about things in our sleep. What do the children do when they have a bad dream? You might want to remind them that it helps to talk with someone we love about things that frighten us.

1469

Mister Rogers visits "The Incredible Hulk" set and watches Lou Ferrigno ("The Hulk") put on his costume and make-up.

"Make-Up" can help children:

- understand the difference between real and pretend;
- use play to work on feelings.

Make-up

Materials

- old make-up or Halloween make-up
- cold cream or petroleum jelly
- wig or yarn
- wash cloths
- soap and water

If you have old make-up (or Halloween make-up), the children could use it to change their appearances. You could suggest they make clown faces or pretty faces, but some may really need to make ugly monster faces. The younger children in your group may need your comfort if these "monsters" look scary. For children who don't want their faces painted, you could suggest painting their hands instead. And if some just want to watch, that's okay, too. Remind all the children that the changes they see don't change the person under the make-up. Add an old wig, or make a mop of hair from yarn for the children to try on. When they've had enough, help them remove the make-up with soap and water, cold cream, or petroleum jelly. You could take this chance to remind the children that television monsters are created with make-up, too. Can they tell you how the "Hulk" was created on the program today?

(Or, 1029 "Paper-Plate Masks.")

1470

Mister Rogers shows a film of a backhoe and points out that the machine does not go by itself. It takes a person to make it work.

"Mechanical Monsters" can help children:

- learn more about their world;
- use play to work on feelings.

Mechanical Monsters

Materials

- magazine or catalog pictures of trucks and construction equipment
- scissors
- toy trucks (cement mixer, backhoe, fork-lift, etc.)
- construction site (optional)

You could begin this activity by sitting with the children and looking through old magazines for pictures of construction equipment. See if the children can point them out. You can tell them the names if you know what they are. If a person is operating the machinery, remind the children that people make machines go. Do any of the children want to cut out or tear out the pictures and save them? If you have trucks and construction toys, the children might like to use them for pretending today. You could point out that the toys don't move unless the children move them—just like real machinery needs to be driven by people. Do you know of a construction site in the neighborhood where the children could safely watch the workers use trucks, a backhoe, or steam shovel? Some children can watch that kind of work for long periods of time. And they like to go back often to see how the building has progressed. If there is no construction site near, you might want to get a children's book from your local library about construction equipment and building.

Thoughts For The Week

In this opera, as in others, I've tried to show children that projects can be satisfying—not just what you make or do, but the actual making and doing as well. Something else I hope children will learn as they watch our operas taking shape is the importance of cooperation. Making and doing something with several other people is a very different kind of experience than working by yourself. It brings its own problems of sharing and giving in to other people's ideas...but it brings its own rewards, too. Watching the puppets and neighbors of Make-Believe work together to create a story, make up songs and learn their parts can, I hope, help young children put value on cooperation—and on themselves.

Songs On The Programs This Week

1471 *"Look and Listen"*
     "It's You I Like"
1472 *"To Go Some Place Else"*
1475 *"Windstorm in Bubbleland" Opera*

Special Visits

1471 *Storyteller, Jay O'Callahan*
     Opera Star, John Reardon

Your Notes For The Week

Monday

1471

Storyteller Jay O'Callahan makes up a story about bubbles. In the Neighborhood of Make-Believe, opera star John Reardon offers to write a new opera. "Bubble Play" can help children:

- develop creative play;
- express feelings through movement and dance.

Bubble Play

Materials

- water
- dishwashing liquid
- string (foot-long pieces)
- dish pan or plastic bowl
- soft music (optional)

To make soap bubbles, combine a cup of mild dishwashing liquid and a quart of warm water in a plastic bowl or dishpan. After tying foot-long pieces of string into loops, let the children dip them into the soapy water. Blowing through the loops of string or holding them up in the wind will produce lots of bubbles. (If you have difficulty making bubbles, add more soap to the water.) When the bubble play is over, the children might want to create a bubble dance. Can they show you how a bubble floats in the air? Can anyone pretend to be a bubble that pops and then all the pieces come back together? Encourage the children to try out different ways to move. If you have soft music, they might like to be bubbles that float to the music.

(Or, 1340 "Tag Stories"; 1351 "Blowing Bubbles.")

1472

Mister Rogers shows a photo album of the sweaters his mother has made as a way of showing her love.

"Ways to Say 'I Love You'" can help children:

- talk about feelings;
- understand and accept individual differences.

Ways to Say "I Love You"

Materials

- old magazines and catalogues (optional)
- scissors
- paper
- stapler or string
- crayons or markers

Can the children tell you how they know that you or their parents love them? What are some things parents and caregivers do to show their love for children? For instance:

- preparing meals;
- buying clothes;
- making toys;
- reading stories;
- setting limits;
- talking;
- giving a hug or a kiss;
- saying "I love you";
- working to earn money.

Can they think of things *they* can do to show a grownup how they feel? You could suggest things like:

- saying "I love you";
- cleaning up a room;
- talking about feelings;
- drawing a picture;
- helping prepare meals;
- hugging;
- singing a loving song.

The children could make a booklet of different ways people express love by finding examples in pictures in old magazines or catalogues. They could tear or cut out the pictures they find and paste them in their booklets. Do any of the children want to draw their own pictures of people doing things that show their love? Have any of the children learned Mister Rogers' song, "There Are Many Ways"? They could make up new verses to it.

1473

Chef Brockett shows how to make different things with bananas.

"Banana and Peanut Butter Sandwiches" can help children:

- learn more about foods.

Banana and Peanut Butter Sandwiches

Materials

- bananas
- peanut butter
- toothpicks
- butter knives

Show the children how to peel one or two bananas. (While they're peeling, you might want to explain how the skin protects the fruit inside.) Give each child half a banana and ask everyone to slice the banana halves into several pieces. Then spread some peanut butter on one banana slice and put another banana slice on top. If the bananas get a little slippery and messy, you can put the peanut butter and banana slices between two pieces of bread and cut the sandwiches into several pieces so everyone can have a taste. As with all food activities, you may want to have some alternative things to eat for children who don't like bananas, or peanut butter, or either!

1474

Mister Rogers explains that even though we don't see the wind, we can see what it does. In the Neighborhood of Make-Believe, the neighbors are preparing for the opera, "Windstorm in Bubbleland."

"Straw Painting" can help children:

- learn more about their world;
- develop healthy curiosity.

Straw Painting

Materials

- paper
- non-toxic paint
- straws
- crayons or markers
- facial tissue
- ping-pong ball (or styrofoam ball)

You might begin the activity by giving the children straws and showing them how to blow. If they put their hands at the ends, they will be able to feel the air coming out through the straws. Give each child a piece of smooth paper, and spoon a little paint onto each child's piece. Then the children can move the paint by blowing through the straws. You can point out that although we cannot see the wind, we can see the way wind can move things. Ask the children to tell you about things outside that the wind moves, like leaves, clouds, your hair, your clothes, etc. When the paint has dried, crayons or markers can be used by the children to add details to their designs. Do any of the children want to talk about their designs? They could also use the straws to move other things. For instance:

- a facial tissue;
- a small styrofoam ball (or a ping-pong ball);
- small pieces of paper.

(Or, 1229 "Rocket Ship"; 1351 "Blowing Bubbles.")

1475

The performance of "Windstorm in Bubbleland" takes place today in the Neighborhood of Make-Believe. Hildegarde Hummingbird saves the Bubbleland residents from the windstorm. The Bubbleland residents learn that friends, not bubbles, are the truly important things in life.

"Windstorm" can help children:

- use play to work on feelings;
- express feelings through movement and dance;
- express feelings through art work.

Windstorm

Materials

- scarves, capes, or soft fabric
- crayons or markers
- paper

What can the children tell you about today's opera? How do they feel about Handyman Negri pretending to be the wind? Do any of them want to pretend to be a windstorm by flapping around with scarves, capes, or pieces of soft material? Encourage the children to make blowing sounds as they move. Can they show you the difference between a soft breeze and a gusty wind? You might need to set some limits about this windy play: For instance, be sure the children know they can't knock over toys or scare the other children with their windiness. To help quiet everybody down, you could suggest they pretend to be leaves that flutter about in a gentle breeze...maybe even leaves that take a trip. When the pretending is over, the children might like to use markers or crayons to make a picture of a windstorm. Can they draw about the way they feel on a very windy day or when the wind has stopped blowing?

Thoughts For The Week

*Almost every child is likely to be touched by divorce. Even though a child's own family may be together, he or she may know relatives, friends, or classmates whose families are separated. That can lead to a lot of wondering. We have developed the programs for this week to help children think about divorce and separation in ways that could make the wondering less frightening. It's especially important that children understand that when grownup relationships go wrong, children are not to blame. When parents do get a divorce, they still go on being their children's mothers and fathers. And it's also important for children to realize that people who live together are never happy **all** the time. When parents quarrel, it does **not** necessarily mean they are going to get a divorce. The children may have questions this week that they would like to ask you or their parents. It's not easy to talk about divorce, but we need to keep in mind that the reality of such hard things is so often less scary to children than the fantasies they may have about them.*

Fred Rogers

Songs On The Programs This Week

1476   *"Please Don't Think It's Funny"*
1477   *"Look and Listen"*
        "I Like to Take My Time"
1478   *"It's You I Like"*
1479   *"I Like to Be Told"*
1480   *"The Truth Will Make Me Free"*

Special Visits

1480   *Going on an Airplane*

Your Notes For The Week

1476

On a picnic with his family, Prince Tuesday meets a new friend and her mother. The Prince's friend explains that her father doesn't live with them—because her parents are divorced.

"Different Kinds of Families" can help children:

●   learn more about their world;

●   understand and accept individual differences.

Different Kinds of Families

Materials

●   paper

●   crayons or markers

There are many different kinds of families. Some children may live with two parents, but other children may live with only one parent or with another relative. Families can live in different homes or they can all live together in the same house. A good way to prepare for this activity is by thinking about the things you already know about the families of the children in your care. You might want to prepare yourself beforehand for the kinds of answers they're likely to give to questions about their own families. In talking with the children, you could ask questions like:

●   Who are the people in your family?

●   What are their names?

●   How are they related to you?

●   What are some of the special things you do with your family?

Encourage the children to draw pictures of their families. Even three year olds may be able to "draw" people with scribbles or circles. Encourage them to tell you about the people in the pictures even if it's hard for you to recognize them as people.

(Or, 1188 "My Family and Me.")

1477

In the Neighborhood of Make-Believe, King Friday and Queen Sara argue because King Friday wants to buy a fancy jet plane.

"Wanting and Needing" can help children:
* learn more about money;
* practice making choices.

Wanting and Needing

Materials
* none

Can any of the children tell you why King Friday and Queen Sara were arguing? Maybe you can think of a time when you or someone in your family wanted to buy something and another person didn't agree. How did you settle the problem? Do any of the children want to tell about a time when they wanted to buy something and a parent said "No"? For instance:
* a certain kind of cereal at the grocery store;
* an expensive toy at a shopping center.

Do any of them understand why we can't always buy the things we want? This might be a chance for you to reassure the children that parents—even parents who get a divorce—care about their children...and that care includes making sure that there is a place to live, food to eat, and clothes to wear. Even though we can't have *everything* we *want*, parents will try to see that children have the things they *need*.

(Or, 1301 "A Pretend Store"; 1287 "Buying Groceries.")

1478

Prince Tuesday has disappeared, and Handyman Negri organizes a search.

"Let Me Find You" can help children:
* work on feelings about separations.

Let Me Find You

Materials
* a safe hiding area (part of the house or a fenced-in yard)

One way that children learn to deal with separations is by playing about them in situations that are comfortable and safe. And sometimes children like to be the ones that do the "going away" for a change. Ask the children to find safe hiding places in the house or yard—while you turn your back and count to 20. Then try to find the children—one by one. Children enjoy the game even more when you pretend you *can't* find them at first. You can say things like:
* Where's Tommy? I can't find him.
* Is he under the chair? No....
* Is he behind the tree? No....
* Where could he be?

As the children are found, let them help you go on searching for the others. Even *pretending* about separations can make children feel a need to be close to a favorite grownup. You could end the activity by sitting down for a special quiet time—singing a song or telling a story together...holding hands for a minute so everyone's physically "connected."

1479

In the Neighborhood of Make-Believe, Queen Sara and King Friday come to an agreement about the new jet plane. The compromise solution is to buy an electric car-plane that won't use so much gasoline.

"Working Out Problems" can help children:

- learn to use words.

Working Out Problems

Materials

- one toy (a riding toy, a favorite doll, a ball, etc.)

The King and Queen's argument was finally settled. Can the children tell you how they came to a solution? Maybe you can help the children remember a familiar problem—like taking turns with a toy everyone likes. Have the toy handy while you're talking and see if the children can come up with several solutions—ways that seem fair to everyone. For instance:

- We could take turns playing with the doll and measure the time for each turn on a clock or kitchen timer.

- We could use the doll for pretending—together.

- We could count a certain number of ball throws or ball bounces to see when someone's turn is over.

- We could play ball together—one person throwing and the others trying to catch—or toss the ball from one person to another around a circle.

- We could count turns on a tricycle by the number of rides around the yard and make a list of the order for our turns.

When children have disagreements, we help them best by encouraging them to settle their own differences by using words—rather than fists or teeth. But, of course, there are times when adults must step in and firmly insist on safety for all.

1480

Because some children of divorced families might have to travel alone, Mister Rogers takes his viewers on a commercial airliner to help them feel at home when traveling by air. King Friday's electric car-plane is delivered today.

"An Airplane Ride" can help children:

- learn more about their world;
- develop their imaginations;
- develop creative play.

An Airplane Ride

Materials

- boxes or chairs
- tote bags or small suitcases (you could make a simple suitcase by tying a string handle on an old box for a dress or shirt)

Have any of your children ever traveled on an airplane? If so, perhaps they can tell what it was like. What do the other children think an airplane ride would be like? Encourage the children to sit in rows as in an airplane. They could sit on the floor, or on chairs, boxes or pillows. You could spend a little time talking about what it was like when you went somewhere on an airplane. Or ask the children to recall what the airplane was like on today's program. You may find the children come up with their own ideas about what an airplane ride is like, and if so, you can help them understand what parts of their play could really happen and what parts are just pretend. You might also want to give them a "snack" as they're sitting in their airplane seats.

Thoughts For The Week

Competition can be hard for young children, and it's likely to become a part of their lives from the moment they realize that parents' love and attention have to be shared with others. In fact, I've come to think that a fear of losing love is what makes "losing" difficult for many of us our whole life long: Deep down inside we feel that winners are the ones people love the best. If we can help young children feel that it is they, themselves, we love, not their winning or their losing, then we will be giving them a healthy start in coping with the many competitions that lie ahead.

Fred Rogers

Songs On The Programs This Week

1481 "You've Got to Do It"
       "You Are Special"
1482 "Look and Listen"
1483 "When a Baby Comes to Your House"
1484 "It's You I Like"
1485 "What Do You Do?"

Special Visits

1481 *How People Make Crayons*
1482 *Carnegie Museum of Art*
1483 **Sesame Street's** *Big Bird Visits*
1484 *Football Player, Lynn Swann*

Your Notes For The Week

1481

Mister Rogers suggests drawing a picture of the Neighborhood of Make-Believe. He points out that each person's picture will be different. He shows a film about how crayons are made.

"Draw the Neighborhood" can help children:

- practice making choices;
- develop their imaginations.

Draw the Neighborhood

Materials

- crayons
- paper

Older children may be able to draw the whole Neighborhood of Make-Believe (or even make a cardboard model of it), but younger children may just choose one or two favorite things to draw—Daniel Tiger's clock, Lady Elaine's Museum-Go-Round, Henrietta Pussycat's house, X's tree, or Corney's factory. Before the drawing begins, see what the children can tell you about the Neighborhood of Make-Believe. You could ask questions like:

- Who lives in the Neighborhood of Make-Believe?
- Are the things that happen there real or pretend?
- What are some of the places in the Neighborhood?

Can any children tell you what is in their pictures and the reason for their choice? They might like you to help them write some words on their pictures to go along with what they've drawn.

1482

Mister Rogers visits the Carnegie Museum of Art. In the Neighborhood of Make-Believe, King Friday has decided to have a drawing contest, and X the Owl receives a letter from Big Bird of *Sesame Street* saying he is bringing his entry.

"An Art Show" can help children:

- feel proud of their accomplishments.

An Art Show

Materials

- paper
- markers or crayons
- non-toxic paint
- brushes
- paste
- scrap paper

Let the children choose from several possible art projects—drawing, painting, or pasting. Encourage them to work carefully to do the best they can. (You might want to sing or go over the words to Mister Rogers' song, "I Like to Take My Time," while the children are creating.) Find a special place to hang the day's art projects—on a door or on the wall. When the art work is finished, the children can help you arrange the pictures wherever you've decided to put them. Be sure the children's names are on their pictures so they can find them. This might be a time for you to invite the parents to take a few minutes to look at the children's art display...not as judges, simply to enjoy them.

1483

Chef Brockett tells Mister Rogers that he has just come back from a cake-decorating contest which he didn't win. In the Neighborhood of Make-Believe, Big Bird from *Sesame Street*, arrives amid much excitement and reassures Henrietta that X the Owl will still be her best friend.

"Cookie Decorating" can help children:

- practice taking turns;
- practice working cooperatively;
- practice sharing.

Cookie Decorating

Materials

- your own cookie recipe or the recipe from activity 1220 "Making Cookies"
- rolling pin
- cookie cutters or plastic knife
- cookie decorations (sprinkles, carob chips, or a little cinnamon mixed in sugar)

You can include the children in this cookie-baking activity by letting them measure, mix and stir the ingredients. They can also use the rolling pin and cookie cutters to make their own cookies. (If you don't have cookie cutters, you can help the children use a plastic knife to cut the dough into square, round and triangular shapes.) Before baking, let each child decorate three or four cookies. The children could use their thumbs and fingers to make impressions in the cookies, or use the handle of a spoon or fork tines to make a design. While the cookies are baking and cooling, ask the children whether they enjoyed mixing the dough and doing the decorating. You can serve the cookies as a special snack or dessert.

1484

Mister Rogers goes to a dance studio to watch Lynn Swann, a famous football player, practicing ballet with a dance company. Lynn Swann tells Mister Rogers how dancing has helped him play football. In the Neighborhood of Make-Believe, Lynn Swann and Bob Dog have just come back from losing a football game and are feeling disappointed.

"Dancers" can help children:

- understand and accept individual differences;
- express feelings through movement and dance.

Dancers

Materials
- music
- three-inch circles cut from paper
- tape

Play some music and suggest the children dance any way they want to. You could dance, too—and it might encourage the others to do so. When everyone is finished, you might ask each child what kind of dancer he or she was trying to be, writing their responses on individual badges for them to wear. It's important that you have one badge for each child— even ones saying "Dancing Watcher" for the children who didn't join in the activity.

(Or, 1421 "The Best of Whatever You Are.")

1485

In the Neighborhood of Make-Believe, King Friday announces the winner of the "Draw the Neighborhood" contest and awards a very unusual prize—a rainbow. Mister Rogers talks about feelings of winning and losing and how the *doing* was the real fun of the contest.

"A Rainbow for Everyone" can help children:

- practice working cooperatively;
- practice sharing.

A Rainbow for Everyone

Materials
- three or four grocery bags cut open
- tape
- crayons or colored marker

Before the children begin this activity, cut open some grocery bags to make large sheets of paper and tape them together. With your marker, draw the outline of a rainbow. Before showing the children the paper, *see* what they know about rainbows.

- Has anyone ever seen one?
- What colors are in a rainbow?
- What makes a rainbow happen?

Have you a picture of a rainbow to show? If you can't find one in a book or magazine, you could draw a small one and color it in. (For the correct order of colors in a real rainbow see activity 1441 "Crayon Window Hangings.") Lay the large rainbow outline on a hard flat surface (a table or floor or porch) and let the children color it any way they feel like. They may need your help in sharing the crayons and in finding their own places to work. When it's finished, cut out the children's rainbow and hang it on a wall for everyone to enjoy.

Thoughts For The Week

One of the most misleading phrases in our language is "child's play." We use it to suggest something that's easy to do, something trivial. But it's not—not by any means. When children play, they're **working.** *I once heard a four year old at nursery school tell his mother, "You can leave now; I have work to do." For children, play is both a serious and necessary business: a way for them to try on different roles, pretend to be bigger than they really are, stronger than they really are, or even, at times, smaller than they really are. And playing gives children a chance to rehearse for events that may be worrisome to them—a visit to the doctor, a first haircut, or the first day of school. By pretending about such things, children can find out how they feel about them. When grownups are alert to children's play and pretending, they can often help children with their fears by letting them know what* **will** *happen in the course of a new experience and, just as important, what* **won't.**

Fred Rogers

Songs On The Programs This Week

1486 *"Please Don't Think It's Funny"*
      "Pretending"
1487 *"You've Got to Do It"*
      "I Like to Be Told"
1488 *"Everybody's Fancy"*
      "Perfectly Beautiful Day"
1489 *"Sometimes People Are Good"*
1490 *"You're Growing"*
      "Children Can"

Special Visits

1487 *How People Make Toys*

Your Notes For The Week

1486

Mr. McFeely shows Mister Rogers a "walker" that he is delivering to someone who just came home from the hospital after an accident. Mister Rogers demonstrates the walker and shows that learning something new takes practice. In the Neighborhood of Make-Believe, Bob Dog falls from a ladder while trying to get a ball that's stuck in a tree. When King Friday hears about the accident, he bans all play in the neighborhood!

"Stilts" can help children:

- develop coordination;
- develop the ability to keep on trying.

Stilts

Materials

- plastic margarine tubs (two for each child)
- long pieces of heavy string
- sharp knife or scissors

After turning the margarine tubs upside down, use a knife or sharp scissors to punch holes on two sides of each container. See if the children can thread a piece of string through the holes in each tub. With the tubs upside down on the floor, tie the ends of the strings together making loops that are about waist high for each child. Can the children stand on the tubs and, keeping the string tight, walk around as if on stilts? You could point out that learning to walk a new way takes practice. Some of the children might want to practice using just one stilt at first.

(Or, 1502 "Hospital Play.")

1487

Mister Rogers visits a toy factory to show the thought and care that go into making playthings for children.

"Safe Toys" can help children:

- learn about limits;
- practice making choices.

Safe Toys

Materials

- a box full of toys (or all the toys on the shelves)
- marker
- two baskets or boxes

Most of the toys in your home are probably safe for preschool children, but you may have some playthings of your own that you don't allow the children to use — a baseball bat or a golf ball. Can you explain to the children why these grownup "toys" aren't safe for children? If you have infants or toddlers in your care, you could ask the older preschool children to help you sort out the toys that are safe for the little children to use. What makes a toy safe or unsafe? For instance:

- a stuffed toy;
- crayons;
- tiny plastic animals or puzzle pieces;
- cars or trucks.

See if the children can sort the toys into two baskets or boxes—one "For Babies" and the other "*Not* for Babies." Encourage the children to save the "Not for Babies" box for play times when the infants and toddlers are sleeping, or to use them at a table where the younger children can't reach them.

1488

Mister Rogers talks about the importance of imagination in play. Everything is very gloomy in the Neighborhood of Make-Believe because the king's "no-play" rule is still in effect.

"Let's Imagine" can help children:

- develop their imaginations;
- develop creative play.

Let's Imagine

Materials

- none

Can the children think of times when they are not allowed free play (riding in a car with the seatbelt fastened)? Today you might be able to help the children learn to use their imaginations during those times when they can't have toys or engage in active play. You may have to suggest themes at first. Here are a few suggestions:

- Imagine you're on a rocket ship—going to Planet Purple. Ask the children to imagine what it would be like. What do they see? Can the children tell about the planet once they've pretended to arrive?
- Play a game about the things they can see around them. As each child describes an object, the others can try to guess what it is.
- Encourage the children to take turns telling their own versions of a fairy tale or other familiar story.

Try to help the children understand that imagining is a kind of playing that they can do when they need to be quiet or cannot move around.

1489

In the Neighborhood of Make-Believe, the king is reconsidering his "no-play" rule. When he understands everyone's angry feelings, he decides that the playing can go on — as long as it is *safe* play.

"Safe Play" can help children:

- develop self-control;
- learn about limits.

Safe Play

Materials

- blocks
- outdoor play toys
- balls
- toy cars and trucks

Can the children remember why King Friday made the "no-play" rule? Can they think of a time when a grownup had to tell them to stop playing something because it wasn't safe? Talk with the children about the kinds of play they enjoy, and see if they can tell you how to be sure the play is *safe* play. For example:

Block Play

- telling everyone before they knock down a tower they've built;
- not throwing blocks.

Outdoor Play

- staying in the yard at all times;
- knowing how to *stop* the tricycles and wagons;
- keeping sand in the sand box — not throwing it into the air;
- using balls away from windows.

Toy Cars and Trucks

- keeping them on the floor or in your hand — not throwing them;
- watching out for babies' fingers when they roll a car along the floor;
- stopping the trucks from running into things.

1490

Bob Dog helps persuade Lady Elaine Fairchilde to return to the Neighborhood of Make-Believe. A big play celebration follows with everybody joining in, even King Friday.

"A Play Celebration" can help children:

- learn to use words;
- practice making choices.

A Play Celebration

Materials

- several different play options (art projects, dress-up, blocks, toy cars, etc.)

What seem to be the play activities each child enjoys most? If possible, let each child do the activity he or she suggests — within reason, of course. You may prefer to limit the choices by making available one art project, one active play project, and one quiet play project. Can the children tell you *what* they like about the play activity they chose? Here are a few suggestions for activities that would be easy to set up quickly:

Art Activities

- crayons and paper; or
- clay or modeling dough (if available); or
- paper and paste; or
- blunt-nosed scissors and paper.

Quiet Play

- puzzles; or
- books; or
- games; or
- listening to music.

Active Play

- blocks; or
- cars and trucks; or
- dress-up clothes; or
- inside riding toys.

Thoughts For The Week

*Discipline means different things to different people, but I like to think of it as a way adults help children develop **self**-discipline. Developing self-control is a gradual process for children, and when we set limits on their actions and behavior, we're slowly teaching them to set those limits for themselves.*

It can be very frightening for children to have no limits—to feel that no one will stop them from hurting themselves or other people. Discipline doesn't have to mean punishment. It can just as well mean a grownup's loving way of controlling children's behavior until they can exercise that control by themselves.

Fred Rogers

Songs On The Programs This Week

1492 *"Everything Grows Together"*
"I Like to Take My Time"

1493 *"You've Got to Do It"*
"What Do You Do?"

1494 *"The Truth Will Make Me Free"*

1495 *"Sometimes"*
"Sometimes People Are Good"

Special Visits

1492 *How People Make Dolls*

1493 *Where Mister Rogers Swims*

1494 *Ice Skating Star, Peggy Fleming*

1495 *How People Make Blankets*

Your Notes For The Week

1491

Mister Rogers demonstrates a player piano and talks about how important it is to have the holes on the piano roll in exactly the right places to make the music. In the Neighborhood of Make-Believe, there's trouble ahead as Corney tries to manufacture too many things at once and gets his chairs and his pretzels all mixed up.

"Everything in Its Place" can help children:

- learn to do things independently;
- develop self-control.

Everything in Its Place

Materials

- all the things the children use;
- containers for sorting them.

Do the children understand why toys and play materials need to be put away in special places? Sometime today when everything is a mess, ask the children to sit down with you and see if they can find certain things. You could ask:

- Can anyone find the medical kit?
- Where is the blue tractor?
- Who can find the fire truck?

You can point out how hard it is to find things when everything is all mixed up and scattered, and how easy it is for the toys they use to get lost or damaged when they're left lying around. Help the children organize their playthings on shelves or in boxes by sorting out the toys that are the same or are used together.

Older children might help you make picture-and-word labels for the shelves and boxes, showing where the toys belong. Encourage the children to put a toy or toys back before other toys are used for play.

(Or, 1152 "Supply Depot.")

1492

Mister Rogers shows how dolls are made and explains that dolls are *made* and people are *born*.

"Newspaper Dolls" can help children:
● recognize likeness and difference;
● practice working cooperatively.

Newspaper Dolls

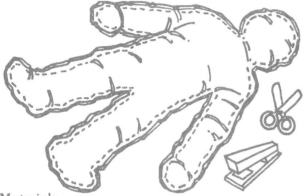

Materials
● lots of newspaper
● tape
● stapler
● markers or paint and brushes
● scissors

Tape two or three sheets of newspaper together to make one sheet that's large enough for a child to lie on...and then make three more layers of the same size. With the four layers one on top of another, trace the outline of one of the children in your group. Cut around the outline through all four layers. Staple or tape the four layers around the edges, leaving one side open, and letting the children help wherever they can. Gently stuff the outline with more sheets of newspaper crumpled up small, leaving two layers of paper on either side of the stuffing so the doll won't tear so easily. When the outline has been stuffed, staple or tape shut the open side. The child who "posed" for the outline should be the one to decide what to do with the doll, because in some respects that child might feel that the doll represents him or her. That child might want the others to help draw or paint features and clothes on the doll or choose to do it alone...or not at all. Talk with the children about how the doll and the child are alike. How are they different?

(Or, 1238 "Paper Dolls.")

1493

Mister Rogers gets his daily exercise by swimming, and today he takes his television friends along. In the Neighborhood of Make-Believe, Lady Elaine Fairchilde thinks the King Friday dolls should look like *her* and changes them all into Lady Elaine Fairchilde dolls. King Friday summons the Chief of Discipline to deal with the mischief maker.

"Exercise Every Day" can help children:
● develop muscle control.

Exercise Every Day

Materials
● none

Just about *every* day, children run and jump and hop and exercise their bodies in many ways. Starting today, set aside five or ten minutes when you and the children can do some *organized* daily exercises. Here are some exercise suggestions:

Standing in place with legs slightly apart:
● put your hands on your hips and twist from side to side;
● stretch your arms out in front of you and pretend to swim.

Lying on the floor:
● legs straight, open and close legs in a scissor fashion;
● legs straight, and arms at your sides, roll to one side and then to the other.

Repeat each exercise three or four times. If you can go outdoors, you'll have lots of fresh air and room to move. When you have to stay inside, try exercising to music.

(Or, 1495 "Walk, Crawl and Hop.")

1494

Mister Rogers goes to visit ice-skating star Peggy Fleming, who is practicing for an ice show. They talk about how doing something well takes a lot of practice. In the Neighborhood of Make-Believe, Lady Elaine Fairchilde must work in Corney's factory for two days as punishment for turning King Friday dolls into Lady Elaine Fairchilde dolls. She goes to work organizing the factory, and soon everything is running smoothly for the first time. She's making the most of her punishment.

"It Takes Practice" can help children:
- develop the ability to keep on trying;
- develop their memory.

It Takes Practice

Materials
- words to a poem or song

Have you ever tried to remember the words to a song or poem? Did you have to go over each line lots of times before you remembered all the words? Pick a favorite song or poem or choose one of the songs in the back of this book. The first song you try should be short and familiar to the children. Go over the words a few times, encouraging the children to repeat them after you. (Do only one verse if the song is long.) Practice *singing* it if you like. Repeat this activity again, today and on other days, perhaps while the children are:
- rolling clay;
- painting a picture;
- washing up for lunch;
- waiting for parents to arrive.

Talk with the children about how much practice it takes to learn the words. Is it fun to know the whole song? Once they've learned the first song or poem, would they like to choose another to work on? Do they ever sing songs or say poems that they've learned at day care when they get home (for the people who love them there)?

1495

Mister Rogers shows a film of a factory where people manufacture blankets, and talks about how some young children like to have their very own blankets. In the Neighborhood of Make-Believe, X the Owl makes a mistake, and Lady Elaine Fairchilde wants to spank him. She learns that the best discipline makes everybody feel better, and that something good can come from something bad.

"Walk, Crawl and Hop" can help children:
- learn about limits;
- develop coordination;
- develop the ability to keep on trying.

Walk, Crawl and Hop

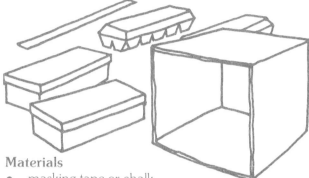

Materials
- masking tape or chalk
- large cardboard box
- two or three shoe boxes
- two egg cartons

Helping children understand why grownups set limits and have rules about certain things is a way we can help children learn self-discipline. Here's a game with definite rules—an obstacle course you can set up in your back yard or in a room with lots of space. You'll need:
- masking tape or a chalk line to make a pretend tightrope on the floor;
- shoe boxes far enough apart for the children to step over them;
- a large cardboard box with open ends for a tunnel;
- egg cartons for hopping over (if your children are very young, they could hop over a piece of masking tape instead).

Once you've set up the course, tell the children the rules they have to follow:
- walk along the tightrope;
- step over the boxes;
- crawl through the tunnel;
- hop over the egg cartons.

Let the children go through the course one at a time. Can they follow the rules? Do they get better each time they go through? Later on, or on another day, switch the things around to make a new course to try.

Thoughts For The Week

*Pets can play an important role during a child's early years. They often serve as trustworthy listeners for a child's secrets and feelings of loneliness, sadness, fear or joy. When grownups don't have time to play or listen, when a parent has scolded a child, or when a child is frightened by something (the dark, a thunderstorm), the pet is often there—available and comforting. A pet can also teach children important things about responsibility, caring and discipline. By helping care for a pet, children can learn that pets are living creatures, not just toys, and that **all** living creatures need to be treated with consideration.*

Fred Rogers

Songs On The Programs This Week

1496   "There Are Many Ways"

1497   "Everybody's Fancy"

1498   "Perfectly Beautiful Day"
       "I'm Interested in Things"

1499   "I'm Taking Care of You"
       "Waiting"

1500   "There Are Many Ways"

Special Visits

1496   *How a Friend Makes Stuffed Animals*

1500   *National Zoological Park, Washington, DC*

Your Notes For The Week

Monday

1496

Mister Rogers visits a friend to see how she makes stuffed animals for her children. In the Neighborhood of Make-Believe, the neighbors are making presents for Ana Platypus's birthday.

"Softee" can help children:

•   practice working cooperatively.

Softee

Materials

•   old pillow case(s)
•   stuffing materials (clean rags, old clothes, or worn-out nylon stockings)
•   yarn or string
•   buttons, fabric scraps, etc.
•   glue, or needle and thread

You and the children can make a "softee" together by filling an old pillowcase with soft stuffing materials. When the children have helped you fill the pillowcase, tie the end closed with a piece of yarn or string. You might want to tie some around the middle to make a "waist," or around the corners to make "ears" or "feet." Do the children have any ideas for decorating the stuffed toy? Buttons? Scraps of fabric? Yarn? When it's finished, "softee" will make a good cuddling toy.

1497

In the Neighborhood of Make-Believe, Ana Platypus wants a pet for her birthday—one that she can hug and love. The neighbors have very definite ideas about the pet she should have.

"If I Had a Pet" can help children:
- develop their imaginations;
- learn to use words.

If I Had a Pet

Materials
- paper
- crayons or markers

If any of the children have a pet, they might like to tell you and the others about it. Ask them to describe their pet or, for those who don't have one, a pet they would like to have. You could ask questions like:
- Does it have long fur or short fur?
- How many legs does it have?
- Is it big or little?
- What do you (or would you) do to care for it?
- Where does it (or would it) sleep?

Then see if any of the children want to draw a picture of their pets. They could be real or imaginary ones. Do they have names for the pets they've drawn?

(Or, 1274 "Animal Sounds.")

1498

Bob Trow brings his dog, Barney, to stay overnight with Mister Rogers.

"An Animal Comes to Visit" can help children:
- learn to do things independently;
- learn more about their world.

An Animal Comes to Visit

Materials
- a pet
- water dish
- food for an animal
- leash (if appropriate)

If you have a pet in your home, take this chance to let the children share in the care of the pet. Can they tell you how to care for it? They could help you by doing things like:
- filling its water dish;
- feeding it;
- playing with it;
- helping you take it for a walk;
- helping you to clean the place it lives.

If you don't have a pet, you might see if anyone could bring a pet—just for the day. Or maybe you have a friend or neighbor who could bring an animal for a short visit.

If an animal can't visit you, you might want to arrange a field trip so the children can see a live animal. You could take them to the zoo, a pet store, an aquarium, or a nearby farm.

(Or, 1168 "Playing about Animals.")

1499

Lady Elaine Fairchilde is very busy planning a big birthday parade for Ana with a whale, apes, and Purple Panda. Ana decides what she'd really like for her birthday is a kitten.

"Animal Blocks" can help children:

- develop creative play.

Animal Blocks

Materials

- animal pictures (cut from old magazines)
- tape
- blocks of wood, empty food boxes, or small milk cartons
- scissors

Ask the children to help you find pictures of animals in old magazines. Cut out the animal pictures for the children and help them tape them to the sides of blocks, cartons, or boxes so the picture will stand up. (If you are using empty food boxes, you can cover the printing with a piece of paper first so the animal picture can be seen better.)

The animal blocks can be used in different ways. For example:

- See if the children can name each of the animals.
- Encourage them to use the animal pictures to pretend about what animals do.
- Does anyone want to have a pretend animal parade like the one Lady Elaine is planning?

You may already have a set of toy animals for make-believe play. If so, the children could take their animal blocks home to use.

(Or, 1334 "Animal Parade.")

1500

Mister Rogers visits the National Zoological Park in Washington, D.C., where he helps prepare the food for the giant pandas.

"Let's Make a Zoo" can help children:

- develop creative play;
- develop coordination.

Let's Make a Zoo

Materials

- set of blocks or boxes
- toy animals (or animal blocks from yesterday)

Can the children tell you what animals they might see at a zoo? Using toy animals or animal blocks, the children might like to put together a zoo. They could make different sections for animals that are the same, and separate them from the others with pieces of cardboard. Can the children tell you why zoo animals need to be separated from each other and from the people who visit? Some animals live in or near water, and paper (blue or colored blue) can make lakes and ponds for their zoo.

How about using the blocks and toy animals for other kinds of pretending? For instance:

- making a farm;
- building a pet store;
- making up a story about an animal.

On another day, you might want to set out the blocks and animals in the play area and see what other ideas the children have for playing with them.

(Or, 1110 "Pretend Animals.")

Thoughts For The Week

*Creative work and play come from **within** a person. Creativity can be many things—finding new solutions to old problems, making up a simple song, dressing up, pretending. It may be as simple as using an old curtain for a bride's veil, a cast-off pair of adult shoes for pretending to be a mother or father, or a discarded spoon for digging a river bed in the dirt. Each child's expressions of creativity will be different, and by encouraging those differences we adults let our children know that we value the unique person each child is—and the unique adult he or she will become.*

Fred Rogers

Songs On The Programs This Week

1502 *"I Like to Be Told"*

1504 *"Tree, Tree, Tree"*
     "Waiting"

1505 *"Spoon Mountain" Opera*

Special Visits

1501 *How People Make Spoons*

1502 *Hospital Emergency Room*

1503 *How People Install Seatbelts*

Your Notes For The Week

1501

Mister Rogers shows a film about how people manufacture spoons.

"Using Silverware" can help children:

- learn more about foods;
- learn to do things independently.

Using Silverware

Materials

- spoons, forks, and butter knives
- a food that is best eaten with a spoon (applesauce, soup, yogurt)
- a food that is best eaten with a fork (chunks of meat, green beans or other chunky vegetables or fruits)
- bread
- soft butter or margarine
- plates, bowls, etc.

This is a snack or meal-time activity. Your children are probably quite good at eating with spoons, but how do they handle foods best eaten with a fork? You can also let them practice using a table knife or butter knife for spreading. (Lightly toasted bread won't tear as easily as soft bread.) As they become better spreaders, they'll be able to make their own peanut butter or cheese-spread sandwiches for snack or lunch on other days.

1502

In the Neighhborhood of Make-Believe, the neighbors use their creativity to build a mountain for King Friday. In the "real" neighborhood, Mister Rogers visits a hospital emergency room.

"Hospital Play" can help children:

- use play to work on feelings;
- try out different roles.

Hospital Play

Materials

- white shirt for a doctor's smock
- ball point pen without ink insert (to use for giving pretend injections)
- box to use as an X-ray machine
- material and tape for bandages
- doctor's kit (optional)
- umbrella or yardstick for a pretend cane

After watching this program, the children might feel like pretending about the hospital. Someone could pretend to be the patient, or the children could use a stuffed animal. They could pretend about the things they saw during Mister Rogers' visit to the hospital emergency room:

- the doctor's examination;
- taking a temperature;
- measuring height;
- taking a blood-pressure reading.

Or they might pretend about other hospital experiences such as:

- taking an X-ray;
- giving an injection;
- bandaging an arm or leg;
- walking with a cane.

The most important time for a child who is hospitalized or has to go to the emergency room is the going home time. The children might want to pretend about that, too. If you keep the hospital play props in a special box, the children can use them for hospital play again.

1503

Mister Rogers talks about seatbelts and how important they are. He shows a film of factory workers installing seatbelts in a car.

"Going for a Ride" can help children:

- develop their imaginations;
- practice taking turns.

Going for a Ride

Materials

- chairs
- belts
- dress-up clothes and accessories

Help the children set up chairs to use as seats in a car. Put a belt on each chair as a pretend seatbelt—any kind of belt will do.

Encourage the children to take turns sitting on the chairs and remind them to fasten their seatbelts. This can be a chance for children to practice fastening buckles, too. Going for a ride might be only a part of the pretend play. The children might want to pretend about where the ride will take them:

- to a picnic;
- to work;
- on a vacation;
- to the grocery store.

You might want to ask them what they will do when they get there.

1504

In the Neighborhood of Make-Believe, Chef Brockett makes popcorn balls, and the king decides to have popcorn at the opera tomorrow.

"Making Popcorn" can help children:

- practice waiting;
- learn more about foods.

Making Popcorn

Materials

- heavy pan (holds about three quarts)
- ⅓ cup popcorn
- 2 tablespoons oil
- large bowl

Give the children a chance to examine the corn kernels before popping. Then use a heavy saucepan or an electric popper and add the oil and popcorn. Is it hard to wait for the first kernel to pop? What is different about the corn after it is popped? Serve the popcorn as soon as it cools (or save it for a snack or for lunch). King Friday will be having popcorn at the opera tomorrow. You could make an extra batch of popcorn, and when it's cool, store it in a plastic bag for your children to eat then, too.

1505

The "Spoon Mountain Opera" is performed today—Wicked Knife and Fork is holding Purple Twirling Kitty captive on Spoon Mountain. Prince Extraordinary and Betty Green from the Park Service must climb the mountain to rescue the kitty. They finally learn the reason for Wicked Knife and Fork's nasty behavior and are able to help him change.

"Spoon Puppet Opera" can help children:

- learn different ways to communicate;
- express feelings through music.

Spoon Puppet Opera

Materials

- spoon puppets (see activity 1186) or other puppets

Once everyone has a puppet, the children might enjoy acting out their own version of "Spoon Mountain." They could use their puppets as the different characters and sing any words they feel like to tell the story. If they would rather, the children might choose another story that is familiar to them. Perhaps you'd like to make snack time or lunch time an opera time, encouraging everyone to sing any words they would normally say. When you call the children for lunch or snack, you could do it as a song and ask them to answer in song, too. Sometimes it's easier to *sing* something you're feeling than say it.

Thoughts For The Week

For a child, friendship is a way to begin learning about people who aren't family members. Early friendships can be close ones for a child, and often, as friends come and go, these friendships lead to painful separations. I know of a four year old who moved to a new house and had to leave several close friends. In talking with his parents at the time, he expressed a lot of anger about being taken away from them, and when he visited his old neighborhood a year later, he broke into tears again when it was time to leave. Learning to cope with the many good-byes in our lives takes time— and help.

Friendship is also a way for children to learn about managing strong feelings like anger, love and jealousy. Every friendship has its ups and downs. When friends, early in life, have a chance to work through problems and difficulties, they can learn that part of friendship is coming together after a disagreement to build a relationship that is even stronger than it was before.

Fred Rogers

Songs On The Programs This Week

1506   *"It's You I Like"*
1507   *"A Handy Lady and a Handy Man"*
1508   *"There Are Many Ways"*
        "What Do You Do?"
1509   *"Tree, Tree, Tree"*
1510   *"Let's Be Together Today"*

Special Visits

1506   *A Shoe Store*
1507   *How People Prepare Food in a Restaurant*

Your Notes For The Week

Monday

1506

Mister Rogers buys a pair of shoes at his friend Buzz Wagner's shoe store.

"Trying on Shoes" can help children:
- develop creative play;
- learn more about money.

Trying on Shoes

Materials
- four or five pairs of shoes
- shoe boxes
- chair
- ruler
- paper or plastic bags
- play money (see page B-4)

The children might be able to bring some old shoes today—dress-up shoes or an extra pair of their own shoes. Encourage the children to pretend about getting a new pair of shoes by playing with the dress-up shoes and other old ones. The children might enjoy playing about:
- selecting shoes they like;
- having their feet measured;
- trying on the dress-up shoes or their own shoes.

One child could pretend to be the shoe salesman and the others could be customers. Using play money, the children can "purchase" any of the dress-up shoes. Do the children remember a time when they went to the shoe store and shoes were bought for them or another member of their family? Can they tell you what was given to the salesman so that the shoes could be taken home and worn?

1507

Mister Rogers and Mr. McFeely go to Betty Aberlin's house to watch Betty's friend, Mary Jo Barron, teach a group of children some games and songs.

"Simon Says" can help children:

- learn more about their bodies;
- learn to listen carefully.

Simon Says

Materials

- none

Acting as the leader, give the children simple directions such as "Simon says:

- Touch your nose.
- Touch your toes.
- Where is your tongue?
- Show me your knees.
- Where are your eyes?"

As the children get better at this game, you can make the directions more difficult. For example, "Simon says:

- Put your finger on your knee.
- Touch your elbow on the floor.
- Stand on one foot.
- Place your hands over your ears."

Older children could try doing several things at one time. For instance, "Simon says:

- Put one knee on the floor and two hands on your head.
- Stand on one foot and put your other foot on your knee.
- Pat your head and jump up and down."

You and the children could sing Mister Rogers' song, "Everything Grows Together," and point to each part of the body as it is named.

1508

Mister Rogers goes to a restaurant and shows his viewers how food is prepared. He watches while the cook makes a cheese sandwich for him to take along when he leaves.

"Making Your Own Sandwich" can help children:

- practice making choices;
- learn more about foods.

Making Your Own Sandwich

Materials

- bread
- cheese slices
- other fillings such as lunch meat, egg salad or tuna salad
- lettuce leaves
- mayonnaise or mustard
- waxed paper
- butter knife

The children might be able to help you arrange the sandwich ingredients on plates or platters. You could use two different kinds of bread if you have them, and a small variety of fillings for the sandwiches. Help the children make their own choices and their own sandwiches. (Older children might be able to help the younger ones do some spreading with a butter knife.) You could eat the sandwiches right away, or wrap them in waxed paper to eat later in the day, maybe for a picnic in the yard.

Remember, it's important for everyone to wash their hands before handling the food.

1509

Mister Rogers shows how to make different sounds using bottles filled with water.

"Musical Jars" can help children:

- learn to listen carefully;
- recognize likeness and difference.

Musical Jars

Materials

- five or six glass jars
- pitcher of water
- spoon or pencil

See if the children can manage a pitcher of water well enough to fill the glass jars, putting a different amount of water in each one. Show the children what happens when you tap the glass with a spoon or pencil. Let them take turns tapping the jars to make different sounds. Can they tell you how the sounds are different? Compare the sounds of two jars. Which one has the higher sound? Which has the lower sound? What happens if they pour out some of the water or add more water to a jar?

Can any of the children match the sounds they hear with their voices? They might be able to make up a song by playing a simple tune on the glass jars.

1510

Mister Rogers uses empty milk cartons, an oatmeal box, and other household containers to create a miniature sandbox village. He makes buildings, bridges, and tunnels in the sandbox.

"A Toy Village" can help children:

- develop their imaginations;
- develop creative play;
- practice working cooperatively.

A Toy Village

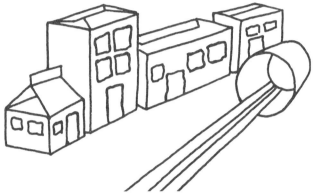

Materials

- an empty oatmeal box or milk carton
- empty food boxes
- masking tape
- little toy cars, people, animals
- tape
- construction paper
- scissors

Place the collection of materials on the table and see if the children have ideas for using them. You might want to suggest:

- cutting the top and bottom off an oatmeal box or milk carton and using the box as a tunnel for toy cars;
- covering empty food containers with construction paper and drawing pictures of houses and other buildings on the paper;
- taping a strip of masking tape on the floor to use as a road; two or three strips side by side for wider roads.

The toy village can be put together in the sandbox, in the grass, or on the floor. Set out a box of little cars, people, and animals for the children to add to the village. Very young children might just enjoy running a car up and down a masking-tape road, stacking the empty food containers, or rolling an oatmeal box back and forth with you.

Thoughts For The Week

Games are one of the ways children begin to understand about the reasons for rules and limits. When children first learn the rules of a game, they sometimes become very rigid about them and won't allow them to be changed or altered in any way. This can be difficult when older children play with younger children who can't yet follow rules and who just want to "play." It's no wonder that even a simple game of tag can sometimes end in arguments and tears!

It can be hard for some people to lose at games. Young children, especially, may feel that losing means more than just losing the game: It might mean losing love because winners always seem to get the most attention. Helping our children cope with the disappointment of losing is an important job for grownups, and it can be an easier one if we let them know from the beginning that win or lose, we still love them for trying and for doing the best they can.

Fred Rogers

Songs On The Programs This Week

1511 *"Please Don't Think It's Funny"*
"It's You I Like"

1512 *"You're Growing"*
"I'm a Man Who Manufactures"
"I'm Taking Care of You"

1513 *"You've Got to Do It"*

1514 *"Everybody's Fancy"*

1515 *"You Are Special"*

Special Visits

1511 *How People Make Towels*

1513 *How People Make Robots*

1514 *Brockett's Bakery*

1515 *Folk Singer, Ella Jenkins*

Your Notes for The Week

1511

Mister Rogers visits a towel factory. In the Neighborhood of Make-Believe, all the neighbors are invited to participate in the Make-Believe Olympic Games. Everyone agrees to the games, but before Lady Elaine Fairchilde agrees she wants to be assured that she will win.

"What's under the Towel?" can help children:

- learn to look carefully;
- feel comfortable asking what they need to know;
- practice taking turns.

What's under the Towel?

Materials

- five to ten medium-sized items (cereal box, sauce pan, baby doll, ball, plastic pitcher, cup, empty milk container, etc.)
- bath towel

Show the children each of the items you've selected for the game and ask them to tell you the name of each. Now hide all the items behind a chair, in a box, or somewhere else out of sight. Show the children the towel and explain that while they hide their eyes, you are going to place one of the items under the towel. The children could first try to guess just by looking at the shape of the item while it is under the towel. If they can't, let them take turns asking questions about the item under the towel. Once they have caught on, the children can take turns doing the hiding. You may need to help the younger children both ask questions *and* answer them when it's their turn to be the hider. You could also allow them to feel through the towel or even reach under it to figure out what the hidden thing might be.

1512

Bob Trow and Mister Rogers finish making a rocking chair. In the Neighborhood of Make-Believe, Lady Elaine Fairchilde uses magic to make rocking chairs *keep* rocking, interrupting a Stop and Go game between Bob Dog and Lady Aberlin. Lady Aberlin assures Daniel that he won't have to play games he doesn't want to play, or doesn't know how to play, no matter what Lady Elaine says.

"Stop and Go Game" can help children:

*   develop muscle control;
*   develop self control.

Stop and Go Game

Materials

*   music

The rules for this game are simple:

*   Play some music for the children to move and dance to.
*   After about 30 seconds, stop the music.
*   The children should stop and stay in the position they stopped in until the music begins again.

Continue the game as long as you like.

1513

Mister Rogers talks about inventions and visits a robot factory with Mr. McFeely. In the Neighborhood of Make-Believe, a robot comes to measure the Neighborhood of Make-Believe for the Olympic Games. The neighbors find out that machines don't feel, think, or care—only people can do those things.

"Machine Collage" can help children:

*   learn more about their world.

Machine Collage

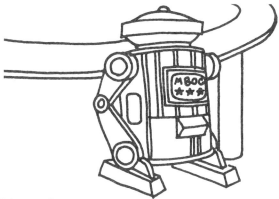

Materials

*   magazines and catalogs
*   large piece of paper
*   glue or paste
*   common machines (television, washing machine, sweeper, etc.)

How do the children think machines are different from people? Take a tour of the house and see if the children can identify the machines they see. As they name a machine, you might explain what that machine does and how it helps you. Be sure to mention that machines work for *people* and it's *people* who make them operate. The children might enjoy making a machine collage. By finding pictures of machines in catalogs and magazines, you can show them machines you might not have in your home. They could cut or tear the pictures of machines out and paste them on the paper. They also might enjoy adding pictures of things the machine is used for:

*   clothes, by a washer or dryer;
*   food, near a blender or stove or refrigerator;
*   carpet, by a vacuum cleaner.

(Or, 1419 "People and Machines.")

1514

Mister Rogers visits Brockett's Bakery and plays electronic arcade games. In the Neighborhood of Make-Believe, the neighbors prepare for the Make-Believe Olympic Games and practice several events. Lady Elaine Fairchilde still wants to control the outcome of the games so that she will win. She makes it snow.

"Toss Game" can help children:

● practice taking turns;
● develop coordination.

Toss Game

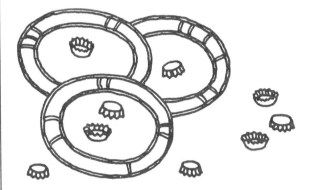

Materials

● two or three plates (preferably paper plates)
● several bottle caps

Put two or three plates close together on the floor. Stand a couple of feet away from the plates and take turns tossing the bottle caps one at a time onto the plates. After a couple of practice rounds, it might be fun to count the caps that land on the plates and on the floor after each child's turn. Younger children may need to stand close. As the children get better, they could move farther away to make it more difficult.

1515

In the Neighborhood of Make-Believe, the Olympic Games proceed...but only after the neighborhood children stop a snowstorm. In the "real" neighborhood, folk singer Ella Jenkins visits Mister Rogers and Mr. McFeely. They play different harmonicas together.

"Humming a Song" can help children:

● express feelings through music;
● learn to listen carefully.

Humming a Song

Materials

● music

Instead of a singing activity, here's a humming one. See if the children can practice humming along with some music on the radio or stereo. Now, without the help of background music, you and the children could try humming a favorite song. (You might even try one as familiar as "Happy Birthday.") You can make this a game by humming a few bars of a familiar song and seeing whether the children can guess what song it is. Would any of the children like to be the hummer? If you and the other children can't guess a tune, you might ask the child who's humming to sing a word or two of the song to help you guess.

Thoughts For The Week

*It can be confusing for children when someone outside the family becomes one of their major caregivers. That's why it's so important for caregivers and parents to develop a partnership with one another. Sharing information about the children, understanding one another's caregiving styles, traditions, cultures, and expectations, can help you better understand your new "partners" and their children. There may be mixed feelings in a caregiving partnership—love, guilt, anger, competition, trust **and** mistrust. But it's important to remember that the healthier the relationship is between parent and caregiver, the easier the caring situation becomes for the child.*

Fred Rogers

Songs On The Programs This Week

1516   "I'm Proud of You"
1518   "It's You I Like"
1519   "Everybody's Fancy"
1520   "There Are Many Ways"

Special Visits

1516   Visit to a Day-Care Home
1517   How People Make Zippers
1518   How People Make Balloons
1520   How People Make Graham Crackers

Your Notes For The Week

Monday

1516

Mister Rogers visits a day-care home and takes along a special treat from Brockett's Bakery. In the Neighborhood of Make-Believe, the King and Queen plan to go away for three days without Prince Tuesday. "My First Day" can help children:

- talk about feelings;
- develop their memory.

My First Day

Materials

- none

Talk with the children about how Prince Tuesday feels about his mom and dad going away. Can they tell you how they felt when they first came to day care? (Try not to comment on their remarks; sometimes it's important just to be a good listener.) Some children may not want to share their feelings right now, but it's good for them to know that you are concerned and will listen if and when they are ready to share.

- Do they remember if you looked the same? Was your hair longer? Shorter? The same?
- Do they remember the other children who were there that day?
- Do they remember what they had for a snack or lunch?
- Do they remember a favorite toy they had? Can they point it out or tell you about it?
- Do they remember what they did when they went home that first day?

You might want to share some of the memories you have about the first time each of the children came to day care.

(Or, 1473 "Banana and Peanut Butter Sandwiches.")

1517

Mister Rogers visits a zipper factory. In the Neighborhood of Make-Believe, the King and Queen leave to teach a course at the Royal School of Castle Management. Prince Tuesday is left with his "night and day caregiver," Mr. Aber.

"The Hoagie Factory" can help children:

- learn more about work;
- practice working cooperatively.

The Hoagie Factory

Materials

- sandwich rolls or bread
- luncheon meat
- cheese
- lettuce
- tomato
- plastic wrap or waxed paper

Were the children surprised to see how zippers were made by people? Have any of the children ever visited or seen pictures of other factories? Can they tell you about other things that are made in factories?
How about setting up a "hoagie factory" in your kitchen? Give each child a job to do, like on an assembly line, and produce enough sandwiches for everyone to have one for lunch (or save them for tomorrow). Explain to the children that when they finish their job on one hoagie, they should pass it along to the next child and begin working on the next hoagie.

- One child could butter the bread.
- One could add a piece of luncheon meat.
- One could add the cheese.
- One could add the lettuce.
- One could add the tomato.
- One could wrap the sandwich.

1518

Mister Rogers visits a balloon-making factory. In the Neighborhood of Make-Believe, Prince Tuesday and Mr. Aber visit the new balloon room at Lady Elaine Fairchilde's Museum-Go-Round.

"Balloon Faces" can help children:

- express feelings through art work.

Balloon Faces

Materials

- one balloon (preferably round) for each child
- scrap materials (paper, cloth, yarn, cotton, etc.)
- one strip of construction paper, about two inches wide, for each child
- glue

Blow up a balloon for each child (unless they can blow them up for themselves), and then make a stand to hold each balloon by taping or gluing the ends of each strip of construction paper together to make a circle. The size of the circle will depend on the size of the balloon. Put out the scrap material and glue, and see what kinds of faces the children want to make. The paper stands will hold the balloons still while they're being decorated and will also let you keep them on display.
Remind the children that balloon faces are just pretend, toy faces. When the air goes out of them they can be blown up again and discarded. People aren't like balloons.

Thursday

1519

It is nighttime in the Neighborhood of Make-Believe, and Prince Tuesday has a scary dream about a fish in a big ocean not being able to find its mother.

"Dreaming" can help children:

- talk about feelings.

Dreaming

Materials

- paper (optional)
- crayons or markers (optional)

Talk with the children about the dream Prince Tuesday had. His was a scary dream, but all dreams aren't scary. Can you share with the children a dream or dreams you've had? Explain that sometimes dreams seem real, but that they are only thoughts in pictures. Do any of the children want to share a dream with you? (Dreams may sound funny when they're told slowly, but of course they're not anything to make fun of.) Most children know what night dreaming is, but have any of them heard of daydreaming? Explain that daydreaming is a time when people sit and think about:

- things that have happened;
- things that might happen;
- places they would like to go;
- people or things they would like to be.

You could encourage the children to sit for a few minutes and daydream about something or somewhere. When you say that daydreaming time has ended, it will help your children if you have a suggestion of what they can do now. Who would like to draw about a daydream?

Friday

1520

Mister Rogers visits a graham cracker factory. In the Neighborhood of Make-Believe, Prince Tuesday's mother and father return from their trip and the Prince has to say goodbye to his "night and day caregiver." King Friday tells Prince Tuesday that he is proud of him for coping with their time when they were away.

"Graham Cracker Treats" can help children:

- learn more about foods.

Graham Cracker Treats

Materials

- graham crackers
- peanut butter
- honey
- non-fat dry milk
- rolling pin
- bowl
- plastic bag

If you put two or three graham crackers into a plastic bag, you can let the children take turns crushing them with a rolling pin. You may need to repeat this several times until you have a full cup of graham cracker crumbs. Combine the crumbs with a cup of peanut butter, $\frac{1}{4}$ cup honey and $\frac{1}{2}$ cup instant non-fat dry milk to make a kind of dough that the children can roll into little balls. Refrigerating these graham cracker treats for about a half hour will make them firm.

Thoughts For The Week

Children often have lots of questions about things like wars and bombs or tornadoes and earthquakes. Children are curious about things they hear grownups talking about, but many times, a young child's questions may really be an expression of concern for his or her own safety. A teacher once told me about the reactions of her children to a series of tornadoes in the area. Every day the children asked questions about them, and at first the teacher thought she could use this opportunity to help children learn about tornadoes. But as they became more and more anxious, she realized that they were not asking for information but were wanting to know if a tornado could ever hit the day-care center. After reassuring the children that the teachers would take them to a safe area any time there was danger, the anxiety lessened, the questions stopped, and the children were able to concentrate again on their play activities.

We seldom know the consequences of a war or the likelihood of a natural disaster, but it's not helpful for children to have to share our uncertainty and anxiety. What children really need is a sense of security—the security that comes from knowing that adults will take care of them and will do whatever possible to protect them from being hurt. When we reassure children that we will try to keep them safe, we allow them to concentrate on concerns that are more suitable for their age.

Fred Rogers

Songs On The Programs This Week

1521 *"You've Got to Do It"*
1522 *"What Do You Do?"*
1523 *"I'm Proud of You"*
1524 *"What Do You Do?"*
1525 *"You Are Special"*

Special Visits

1521 *Negri's Music Shop*
1523 *Ancient Writings in a Cave*
1524 *How People Make Marbles*

1521

Mr. McFeely delivers a coin bank that Mister Rogers ordered. They drop coins into the bank and take off the lid to find the coins again. At Negri's Music Shop, Mister Rogers sees a collection of many different kinds of banks.

"Coin Banks" can help children:

- learn more about money.

Coin Banks

Materials

- margarine tubs and lids (one for each child)
- knife or scissors
- glue
- paper scraps
- yarn
- coins

Using a knife or scissors, carefully cut a slit large enough for a coin in the center of each margarine tub lid. The children can then put the lids back on the containers. They might enjoy trying out the banks, using several pennies or coins that you may have. Encourage the children to decorate the tubs and lids by gluing on scraps of paper and pieces of yarn. When the glue has dried, you might want to let each child have a penny to keep in his or her bank. (Be sure the coins stay in the banks so younger children can't put them in their mouths.) The children might want to save pennies toward a small toy or a box of crayons.

1522

There's a big misunderstanding in the Neighborhood of Make-Believe. Corney is manufacturing something secret for the people of Southwood, and the neighbors of Make-Believe think that Corney is building something frightening.

"Shadow Play" can help children:

● develop their imaginations;

● use play to work on feelings;

● talk about feelings.

Shadow Play

Materials

● bright light (such as a desk lamp)

Can you think of a time when you saw something that turned out to be very different from what you thought it was? You might be able to tell the children about that experience. You could point out that things may seem frightening when we don't understand what they are. Shine a bright light on the wall and let the children take turns using their hands, fingers, or bodies to make shadows. Can the children imagine what these shapes could be? If any of the children are afraid, you can reassure them that you wouldn't let anything hurt them. This might be a chance to remind the children that they can talk to you about things that frighten them.

1523

Mister Rogers shows a machine that types Braille and talks about different ways of writing. He visits a cave to look at ancient writings and learns that it took a long time for people to learn to understand the writing.

"Picture Stories" can help children:

● learn different ways people communicate;

● recognize and use symbols.

Picture Stories

Materials

● paper

● markers or crayons

Most of the children in your care may not be able to read or write words, but you can help them see there are other ways to read. Draw a simple set of pictures—for instance, a seed beginning to sprout, the sprout growing a stem, leaves appearing, and finally a flower. Can the chiildren tell you what the pictures say? Encourage them to draw a picture about something and then "read" it to you, explaining what the picture means. Some children might even want to add "words" by scribbling what they want to say along the bottom of the picture.

(Or, 1197 "Invisible Pictures.")

1524

Mister Rogers shows a film of children playing a game of marbles and visits a factory to show how marbles are made. In the Neighborhood of Make-Believe, Lady Elaine discovers that the people of Southwood are using the secret parts from Corney's factory to build a bridge.

"Marble Modeling Dough" can help children:

- learn more about their world;
- develop creative play.

Marble Modeling Dough

Materials

- modeling dough in two or three colors (recipe on page A-1)

The children can make "marble" modeling dough by combining dough of different colors and rolling small pieces together between the palms of their hands. Can any of the children think of a name for the shapes they make? How are they like the glass marbles Mister Rogers had? How are they different? The children might want to use the marble shapes to make something—a bridge or a tower. Or they could let the round balls of the dough dry overnight and use them for rolling. Can they think of other things to do with the marble dough?

1525

The neighbors of Make-Believe are celebrating Peace with people from Southwood.

"A Peaceful Solution" can help children:

- practice working cooperatively;
- practice taking turns.

A Peaceful Solution

Materials

- plastic milk jug (with a narrow opening)
- clothes pins (not spring type)
- string

Can the children think of times when conflicts arise at day care? What are some of the ways they solve those problems? For instance, what can they do if two people want the same cup? What if two people want to sit in the same chair? Or want to play with the same toy? Older children might be able to play this game about cooperation: Tie pieces of string onto clothespins (one for each child), and put the clothespins inside the milk jug with only the strings hanging out (three or four at a time). Then see if the children can pull out the clothespins. What happens if they all try to pull at the same time? Can they think of a way to get all the clothespins out again? Can they do it more easily by working together and taking turns?

Thoughts For The Week

When a child's parents are away at work, he or she may have a lot of questions about what they do all day—and why they have to be gone. It can be helpful for children to know not only what their parents do, but also that working for money can be a part of caring for children: With the money they earn, parents can buy the things that children need. But parents can't always buy everything that a child wants. None of us can have everything we want! We all have to learn to make choices about the way we spend our time, our money, and our other resources.

One of the ways that children begin to learn about choices is by making decisions in their play— deciding how to use the blocks or what to do with the playdough or finding the best way to make a mountain of sand. Play is so often the way children learn about the world around them.

Fred Rogers

Songs On The Programs This Week

1527   *"Did You Know"*
1528   *"You've Got to Do It"*
       "I'm Taking Care of You"
1529   *"There Are Many Ways"*
1530   *"It's You I Like"*
       "I Like to Take My Time"
       "I'm Taking Care of You"

Special Visits

1526   *How People Make Stamps*
1527   *Dairy Farm*
1529   *Grocery Store*

Your Notes For The Week

1526

Mister Rogers shows a canceled postage stamp and visits a postal service building where he sees how a stamp is made, from design to completion.

"Mail a Letter" can help children:

- work on feelings about separation;
- learn more about the world;
- learn more about money.

Mail a Letter

Materials
- paper
- markers, pens
- envelopes
- stamps

When children are away from their parents, they sometimes like to make a special picture or dictate a special letter for their moms and dads. See if any of the children want to mail a picture or letter to their parents at work. Give the children paper and markers to use for their drawings and let them tell you the words they would like to say. You can write these words on a separate page, or on the drawing paper if the children prefer. When the drawings are finished, the children can put the papers into envelopes and seal them. (You might find it easier to address the envelopes ahead of time, but you can still read the addresses to the children). Can the children tell you why they need to put a stamp on the envelope? You might want to take the children to a post office to buy the stamps and then mail the letters. Or you could buy the stamps ahead of time and let the children pretend to buy them from you. Does your letter carrier come to your home? You could look out for that person's arrival.

(Or, 1457 "Painting with Water.")

1527

Mister Rogers visits a dairy farm to see how milk gets from cows to stores where other people buy it.

"Milk Shakes" can help children:

- learn more about food;
- learn more about work.

Milk Shakes

Materials

- ice cream
- scoop or spoon
- milk
- jar or plastic container with tight-fitting lid
- paper cups
- straws (optional)

See if the children can help you scoop ice cream into a jar or plastic container. (About four large scoops in a one-quart jar works well.) Add milk until the jar is nearly full. Once the lid is on tightly, they can take turns shaking the milk and ice cream until the lumps are dissolved. You can limit each turn by counting to 10 or 15. Each one can take a turn counting if the children want to or you could use a kitchen timer and "listen for the bell to ring." When everyone has had the same number of turns to shake, the children can pour the milk shakes into paper cups and add straws if you have them. You might talk with the children about the "work" they had to do to make milk shakes. Can they think of other ways to get a milk shake? For instance, paying money to buy one, or using a machine to make the work easier. Which way seems like more fun to them?

1528

Mister Rogers needs a new washer for the faucet in his kitchen. In the Neighborhood of Make-Believe, everyone wants a new swimming pool. The neighbors are trying to save money by doing the digging themselves, and they see big changes as everyone works together.

"Make Some Changes" can help children:

- learn more about work;
- practice working cooperatively.

Make Some Changes

Materials

- none

Can the children tell you ways the work they do changes things?

For instance:

- changing the way the room looks by picking up the toys;
- changing the way a plate of food looks by eating it;
- changing the way the blocks look by building with them;
- changing the look of paper by painting on it.

Encourage the children to work together with you to make some changes today. You might want to let them rearrange the toys on the shelves or straighten up the books and puzzles. If the weather permits, they could clean up the yard or sidewalk by picking up papers, sweeping, or shoveling snow.

(Or, 1021 "Digging a Hole"; 1208 "Let's Go Shopping"; "Plumbing and Drains.")

1529

Mister Rogers makes a shopping list and then visits a grocery store. In the Neighborhood of Make-Believe, water pipes have broken and the neighbors learn that it will cost a lot of money to fix them.

"A Shopping List" can help children:

- practice making choices;
- learn more about money;
- learn more about their world.

A Shopping List

Materials
- paper
- marker

Would any of the children like to help you make a shopping list today? Using paper and a marker, list the days of the week and see if the children can make suggestions for the nutritious snacks. This is a good time to help the children learn about making choices. You might explain that you can't buy everything they name, but that they can make choices that include a variety of foods. When the menus are finished, make another list of the items you need to buy. The children might be able to help you check the supplies you already have.

If possible, plan a trip to the grocery store and let the children help select the items. Older children might ask them if the taste or flavor of a certain brand-name product is worth the extra money you may have to pay for it.

(Or, 1215 "Plumbing and Drains"; 1301 "A Pretend Store.")

1530

Mister Rogers talks about the work he does making television programs and writing songs. He shows a film of children working and talks about play as being a kind of work that children do.

"There's Work to Do" can help children:

- learn more about work;
- develop creative play.

There's Work to Do

Materials
- blocks, cars, trucks, toy people
- modeling dough, plastic dishes, plastic utensils
- books, paper, pencils, markers

Can any of the children tell you what jobs they think they would like to do when they grow up? Encourage the children to pretend about that kind of work today. (Their work ideas may change from day to day, but that's fine. That helps them "experiment" in their play.) Here are a few suggestions:

- builders, construction workers, people who repair things;
- child caregivers, nurses, doctors, dentists;
- office workers, librarians, teachers;
- bakers, cooks, restaurant or store owners;
- firefighters, police and letter carriers.

Thoughts For The Week

"Everybody has a history" are words from one of the songs I sing on Mister Rogers' Neighborhood. In all of our histories there are parents, grandparents, and great-grandparents who came before us. Learning about these generations can help young children understand more about what "families" are. Grandparents often play a very special role in the lives of children: They do many things to help children grow and learn and they often have more "free" time to give to children than parents do. When children and grandparents live far away from each other, letters and telephone calls can still be ways of sharing closeness and caring. Even grandparents who are no longer alive influence a family—with handed-down traditions and memories that parents can share with their children. As we help children understand more about the people who came before them, we also help them learn more about who they are themselves as well as the many different ways they grow to be.

Fred Rogers

Songs On The Programs This Week

1531 "Let's Be Together Today"
1533 "Did You Know?"
      "Then Your Heart is Full of Love"
1534 "I'll Think of You"
1535 "A Granddad for Daniel"
      (Opera)

Special Visits

1531 Trolley Museum
1532 How People Make Straws
1534 A Public Aquarium

Your Notes For The Week

Monday

1531

Mister Rogers visits a trolley museum where people collect and repair real trolleys. In the Neighborhood of Make-Believe, a very special pretend trolley is able to fly as well as ride along the tracks. The trolley brings a message from Grandpere's granddaughter, Collette.

"Trolley Tracks" can help children:

- develop creative play;
- develop their imaginations;
- develop coordination.

Trolley Tracks

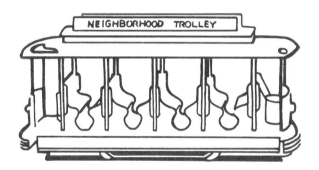

Materials

- several large grocery bags or an old sheet
- blocks or boxes
- cardboard circles to use as wheels
- tape
- markers

You can make a large mat for trolley play by taping several large grocery bags together or by spreading an old sheet on the floor. With a marker, draw a set of trolley tracks on the paper or sheet. Older children might be able to help with the drawing. Small boxes or blocks can be used as pretend trolleys by taping cardboard wheels on the sides. See if the children can drive their pretend trolleys along the tracks. Do any of the children want to draw roads for cars and trucks? What about making buildings from blocks or boxes to place along the trolley tracks?

(Or, 1193 "Shoe-Box Trolley"; 1510 "A Toy Village.")

1532

Mister Rogers uses straws and small bells to make a windchime decoration and shows a film about how people make straws. In the Neighborhood of Make-Believe, Daniel Tiger is feeling a little sad because he doesn't have a grandfather.

"Straws" can help children:

- develop creative play;
- develop their imaginations.

Straws

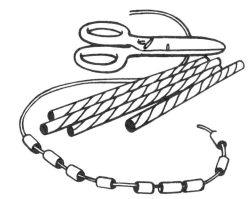

Materials
- straws
- blunt-nosed scissors
- yarn
- tape
- paper
- glue

The children might enjoy using straws to drink their juice or milk today. Afterwards, they can rinse out the straws to use for an activity. Can they think of different ways to use the straws? Here are a few suggestions:

- Make necklaces by cutting the straws into pieces and string them on yarn. If you wrap tape around one end of the yarn the stringing will be easier.

- Create design pictures by gluing straw pieces on paper. The children could help cut up the straws with blunt-nosed scissors.

- Pretend the straws are pipes or drains and use them with blocks or in sand for creative play. The children could pretend about fixing pipes or replacing drains.

What other ideas can the children suggest?

(Or, 1351 "Blowing Bubbles"; 1474 "Straw Painting.")

1533

Mister Rogers talks about his grandparents today. He remembers how his grandparents used to answer his questions and help him with things. Mister Rogers sings the song, "Did You Know?" and talks about importance of taking time to wonder about things.

"I Wonder" can help children:

- develop healthy curiosty;
- feel comfortable asking about things.

I Wonder

Materials
- paper
- marker

Today might be a special time for you to encourage the children to ask questions about things they would like to know. Try to give each child a chance to finish the sentence, "I wonder..." You might need to start this activity yourself by wondering about something. For instance:

- I wonder how straws are made.
- I wonder what happens to the snow when it melts.
- I wonder where milk comes from.
- I wonder how letters are delivered.

Encourage the children to give their own explanations. (Remember to keep your explanations simple.) Some things the children wonder about may be hard to answer, and you might want to plan a trip to the library to find more information. Or show the list to parents and see if they can help their children find answers to share with the others. Do any of the children want to ask a grandparent to help them find the answers?

(Or, 1341 "Remember When.")

1534

Mister Rogers talks about different names children call their grandparents and shows photos of his own grandparents. He recalls that it was his "Nana" who taught him to feed fish just a little bit at a time. He visits the Neighborhood public aquarium where there are many different kinds of fish.

"Aquarium Pictures" can help children:

- develop creative play;
- learn more about their world.

Aquarium Pictures

Materials

- paper
- fish shapes cut from construction paper
- paste
- water
- food coloring (blue or green)
- paper cups
- brushes
- markers or crayons

After you have cut a large variety of fish shapes, spread the shapes on the table and let the children select the ones they would like to paste on their papers. Younger children may need a little help with the pasting, but try to let them choose where they want to place the fish. Encourage the children to add personal touches using crayons or markers. They might want to add seaweed, stones, or just draw colored lines on their pictures. Then let the children paint over the pictures, using a mixture of food coloring and water to complete their aquarium pictures. When the papers are dry, the children can hang their pictures or take them home. Do any of the children have a special grandparent who might enjoy the picture?

1535

There's a little opera in the Neighborhood of Make-Believe today. It's about finding a grandfather for someone who wants one very much.

"Grandparents' Day" can help children:

- learn more about their world;
- understand and accept individual differences.

Grandparents' Day

Materials

- paper
- markers

If possible, share something with the children that came from one of your grandparents. It might be a picture, an object, a song or game, or something that you learned to do. What can the children tell you about their grandparents? Do they have special names for their grandparents? It's sometimes fun to hear all the different names children call their grandparents. You might make up a song using just names for grandparents. If any of the children are feeling left out because they don't know their grandparents, you might reassure them that everyone has grandparents—even if he or she doesn't know them. If you have time you could draw a simple family tree for each child showing that each child has a mother and father and four grandparents. The children might want to take these family trees home and ask their parents to tell them more about their grandparents.

(Or, 1356 "My History"; 1370 "Attending the Opera.")

Thoughts For The Week

*For most of us, the giving and receiving of food is closely associated with the giving and receiving of love. That's not really surprising when you think that children's earliest experiences with nourishment are also among their first indications that someone cares for them. Mealtimes can take on a deep signficance for children. And when they're separated from their parents at mealtimes, they may feel **especially** lonely because food may remind them of their parents' loving care. Helping children talk about those lonely feelings can be very helpful to them.*

Fred Rogers

Songs On The Programs This Week

1537 *"A Lonely Kind of Thing"*

1538 *"Let's Be Together Today"*

1539 *"It's You I Like"*
       "I Like To Be Told"

1540 *"I'm Proud of You"*
       "There Are Many Ways"

Special Visits

1536 *How People Make Applesauce*

1537 *How People Make Tofu*

1539 *How People Make Vegetable Soup*

Your Notes For The Week

Monday

1536

Mister Rogers visits a factory where applesauce is being made. In the Neighborhood of Make-Believe, X the Owl has a hard time waiting for the delivery of the Speedy Seeds he ordered. Mister Rogers reminds viewers that everything and everybody takes time to grow.

"Dried Apple Rings" can help children:

- learn more about food;
- practice waiting.

Dried Apple Rings

Materials

- cookie sheet
- three or four apples
- knife
- apple corer (optional)
- vegetable oil
- paper towel

While you core and slice the apples into one-fourth inch slices, the children could lightly grease the cookie sheet with vegetable oil and a paper towel. Afterwards, they can arrange the apple slices on the cookie sheet. Drying the apple slices takes about six to eight hours in the oven with the lowest possible setting. (In a gas oven, the pilot light will provide enough heat for drying.) This activity makes a good overnight project, and it gives you a chance to help children learn that waiting takes patience. Can they think of ways to measure the time they have to wait? What kinds of activities will they be doing while they wait? The apple rings make good snacks for breakfast, and you can store the unused portion in an airtight container.

(Or, 1079 "Watching Seeds Grow"; 1090 "While You Wait"; 1155 "Making Applesauce.")

1537

Mister Rogers mixes some granola and puts it in bags to give to his friends and visits a factory to see how tofu is made. In the Neighborhood of Make-Believe, the neighbors' gardens are disappearing!

"Granola Gifts" can help children:

- learn more about food;
- practice sharing.

Granola Gifts

Materials

- plain packaged granola (or make your own from the recipe on page C-2)
- raisins
- chopped dried fruit
- sesame seeds
- chopped nuts
- bowls
- spoons
- small plastic bags
- ribbon or yarn
- paper
- tape

If you have enough bowls to go around, let each child mix his or her own batch of granola, adding chopped fruit, nuts, raisins, and seeds. Once the mixing is done, the children can spoon the granola into small plastic bags, saving a little for themselves. Bright yarn or ribbon tied around the top of each bag makes a festive package. Can the children think of people who might enjoy receiving their granola gifts? They could write those names on pieces of paper and tape them to the granola packages. You might want to use this time for talking about the feelings we have when we give something to someone else, suggesting to the children that we are really fortunate when we have enough to eat and enough to share with others.

(Or, 1199 "Tasting New Foods.")

1538

Mister Rogers goes to see Chef Brockett and learns how to make a nutritious snack. When the "garden guards" discover the culprit who has been taking their food, the Neighbors of Make-Believe decide to make an all-out effort to help their friends in Southwood who have no food.

"Chef Brockett's Nutritious Snack" can help children:

- learn more about food;
- understand and accept individual differences.

Chef Brockett's Nutritious Snack

Materials

- nonfat dry milk
- peanut butter
- margarine
- chopped nuts
- raisins
- dates (optional)
- graham cracker crumbs (optional)
- banana (optional)
- bowl
- spoon

The children might want to taste each of the ingredients before combining them to make Chef Brockett's nutritious snack. Here are the directions:

- Combine one tablespoon of margarine and one cup of peanut butter.
- Add ¾ cup nonfat dry milk and mix thoroughly.
- Add raisins, nuts, and dates.
- Shape into balls and roll in cracker crumbs if desired.

If any of the children have a dislike for a particular ingredient in today's snack, you could try making several variations for the children to taste. Does anyone want to try the variation Mister Rogers liked: peanut butter on a banana?

1539

Mister Rogers visits a food processing company to see how vegetable soup is made. Daniel Tiger is excited because he thinks his vegetable soup can has grown into a vegetable soup tree. Bob Dog worries that he hasn't helped Daniel by fooling him.

"Vegetable Soup" can help children:

- learn more about food;
- understand the difference between real and pretend.

Vegetable Soup

Materials

- vegetable soup (homemade or canned)

You might begin today's activity by talking with the children about how vegetables grow. Have the children ever seen a vegetable plant? You could ask questions like:

- What made Daniel think vegetable soup cans really grow?
- How did Bob Dog make them *appear* to grow?
- What's likely to happen if Daniel plants more soup cans?
- How can Bob Dog tell Daniel the truth?

See if the children can tell you how vegetable soup is made. You might be able to make vegetable soup today (1207 "Homemade Soup"), or serve canned vegetable soup and see if the children can tell you the names of the vegetables they see in the soup. Can the children tell you the names of other healthy foods they like to eat?

1540

Mister Rogers visits John Costa, Jr. and watches him make homemade spaghetti. When Old Goat arrives to thank everyone for the food, the Neighbors of Make-Believe agree that "friendship" is a special kind of food.

"Homemade Noodles" can help children:

- learn more about food;
- practice working cooperatively.

Homemade Noodles

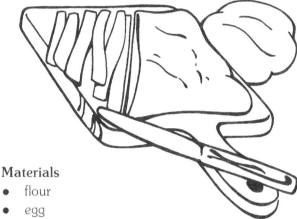

Materials

- flour
- egg
- water
- bowl
- large pan
- chicken or vegetable broth
- rolling pin
- carrots, onion, celery, potatoes (optional)
- plastic knife

Using John Costa's recipe for homemade spaghetti, the children can make noodles. In a large bowl, combine two cups of flour, one egg, and 1/3 cup of lukewarm water. The children can take turns mixing the ingredients and kneading the dough into a smooth ball. You might give each child a piece of dough to roll out like pie crust dough. With plastic knives, the children can cut strips of noodles to add to the boiling broth. Cook until the noodles are tender. If you want to add chopped onion, celery, carrots, or potatoes, they should be cooked in the broth *before* adding the noodles.

Thoughts For The Week

Children grow by testing limits, especially when caring adults are close by to help them find out what can and cannot be. Nobody says "yes" all the time, and nobody says "no" all the time. The times of testing can be hard on children—on parents and caregivers, too—but we all need to learn that life is a mixture of what is and is not possible. Coping with disappointment and accepting necessary limits are both important to children's healthy emotional growth.

Fred Rogers

Songs On The Programs This Week

1541　"Everybody's Fancy"
　　　 "It's You I Like"

1542　"Look and Listen"

1543　"What Do You Do?"

1544　"Going To Marry Mom"
　　　 "You Are Special"

1545　"You Are Pretty"
　　　 "I'm Proud of You"

Special Visits

1541　Artist, Dianne Dengel

1544　Brockett's Bakery

Your Notes For The Week

Monday

1541

Mister Rogers visits the home of an artist who is painting a portrait for him. In the Neighborhood of Make-Believe, an artist gives King Friday an "Exactly-Like-Me" portrait—with the help of a mirror.

"Self-Portraits" can help children:

- learn more about their bodies;
- understand and accept individual differences.

Self Portraits

Materials

- paper
- markers or crayons
- mirror

To begin this activity, let each child who wants to have a chance to look at his or her own reflection in the mirror. Can they identify their own features: eyes, nose, mouth, etc.? You could explain that King Friday saw his reflection in a mirror when he looked at his "Exactly-Like-Me" portrait. When everyone has had a chance to look in the mirror, the children could draw their own self-portraits with paper and crayons or markers. Some children might want to look back in the mirror from time to time while they draw. Children's drawings of themselves may not always look the way we think they should, but what they draw often represents the way children feel about themselves. Do any of the children want to hang their drawings on the wall for all to see? Some children may prefer to keep their portraits private—and that's fine, too.

1542

Mister Rogers talks about YES and NO. He reminds viewers there are some things we are allowed to do and other things we are not allowed to do. In the Neighborhood of Make-Believe, Daniel Tiger is practicing his role as ring bearer for the upcoming wedding.

"Balance The Ring" can help children:

- develop coordination;
- develop the ability to keep on trying.

Balance The Ring

Materials

- aluminum foil rings
- napkins

Have any of the children ever been in a wedding? Maybe they can tell you what a wedding is like. Can anyone show how a ring bearer carries the rings? Aluminum foil can be molded into small rings for the children to carry on folded napkins or small pillows. Can they walk from one side of the room to the other without dropping the rings? (You could remind them how hard it was for Daniel Tiger to balance the ring without dropping it.) How about making larger foil rings for the children to balance on their heads? These could make good crowns for pretend play later on. If you have very small children around, be sure to keep the small foil rings out of reach so that they won't be swallowed.

1543

Mr. McFeely's granddaughter, Chrissie Thompson, visits Mister Rogers. They talk about how it feels when someone says "no." In the Neighborhood of Make-Believe, Ana has to accept that she cannot be in the wedding, but she can attend along with her parents.

"Yes and No" can help children:

- develop self-control;
- express strong feelings in appropriate ways.

Yes And No

Materials

- none

Can any of the children tell you how they feel when someone says "no" to them? You might want to ask the children to tell you things they cannot do. For instance:

- riding a tricycle in the street;
- throwing balls near the windows;
- hitting other children.

Then you could help them think of things they *can* do. For instance:

- riding a tricycle in the yard;
- throwing the balls in the basement;
- using words to say you're angry.

Can the children tell you any other things they can do when they feel angry because someone said "no"? You could suggest:

- pounding on clay;
- drawing an angry picture;
- making up a "mad" song or dance.

1544

In the Neighborhood of Make-Believe, Queen Sara and Lady Aberlin decide to sprinkle rose petals at Betty's wedding, instead of throwing away rice. At Brockett's Bakery, Jose serves Mister Rogers a cup of Arroz Con Leche (rice with milk).

"Arroz Con Leche" can help children:

- learn more about food.

Arroz Con Leche

Materials

- one cup rice (cooked)
- cinnamon sticks
- raisins
- peeling of one orange
- one large can evaporated milk
- 1/2 can condensed milk
- vanilla flavoring
- saucepan
- spoon
- small cups
- bananas (optional)

You can boil the rice ahead of time (following package instructions) along with one or two sticks of cinnamon and orange peeling. Remove cinnamon sticks and peeling. The children can help combine the rice, evaporated milk, and condensed milk in a saucepan. Add a dash of vanilla, and see if the children can take turns stirring the mixture. Cook the ingredients on the stove top to a pudding-like consistency. Just before it is finished, add raisins. Let the mixture cool slightly so the children can serve it into small cups for lunch or a snack. For variation, you can substitute toasted coconut, apples or apricots in place of the raisins. Cinnamon, nutmeg, or sliced bananas can be added for toppings.

1545

There's a wedding in the Neighborhood of Make-Believe! Betty Okonak Templeton and James Michael Jones are getting married with King Friday presiding. Daniel Tiger makes a wonderful ring bearer.

"A Pretend Wedding" can help children:

- develop creative play;
- use play to work on feelings.

A Pretend Wedding

Materials

- dress-up hats and scarves
- fancy dress-up clothes (optional)
- red or pink paper
- small basket
- small pillow
- aluminum foil rings

Do any of the children want to pretend about weddings today? They might be able to help you gather materials to make a few props. You could also:

- make paper rose petals by tearing small pieces of red or pink paper for the flower girl to carry in a small basket;
- tape aluminum foil rings to a small pillow for the ring bearer to carry;
- make a top hat (directions on B-2) for the groom to wear;
- use scarves or dress-up hats for the bride and bridesmaids to wear.

Encourage the children to pretend, using their own ideas about weddings. Whenever possible, let the children select their own roles. If they don't want to be a part of the wedding party, they could pretend to be the guests.

(Or, 1222 "Coil Pots.")

Thoughts For The Week

Music is sometimes called the beginning of language. Early communication between children and parents often includes soft lullabies and rhythmic lap games like pat-a-cake. Music has always been an important part of my life; the adults around me encouraged me to appreciate and play music. As a child, I found that music was one of my best ways to express how I felt. And that's one reason why music is such an important part of MISTER ROGERS' NEIGHBORHOOD. The songs I sing on the programs are songs about the way people feel—when they're happy, angry, sad, or just unsure. I hope that songs like "Did You Know (That It's All Right to Wonder)?" and "What Do You Do (With the Mad That You Feel)?" will help children talk with you about things that are important to them.

Fred Rogers

Songs On The Programs This Week

1546   *"Did You Know?"*

1547   *"Tree, Tree, Tree"*

1548   *"The Truth Will Make Me Free"*
         "Be Brave and Be Strong"

1550   *"Let's Think of Something to do While We're Waiting"*
         "What Do You Do?"

Special Visits

1547   *Cellist, Yo-Yo Ma*

1548   *Folk Singer, Ella Jenkins*

1549   *Empire Brass Quintet*

Your Notes For The Week

1546

Mister Rogers shows the way the television studio musicians play the opening music for the program. In the Neighborhood of Make-Believe, King Friday wants to have a bass violin festival but he is the only one who plays the bass violin. The neighbors would rather have a festival where everyone could participate, so Lady Elaine disguises her accordion as a bass violin.

"Homemade Instruments" can help children:

● express feelings through music;

● understand and accept individual differences.

Homemade Instruments

Materials

● paper towel tubes

● pots and pans

● wooden spoons

● metal spoons

● string

● rubber bands

● margarine containers

● paper plates

● dried beans or small stones

● sandpaper

You might want to take some time to look through the *Plan & Play Book* ahead of time for the directions to make various kinds of instruments. Some suggestions are listed here:

● 1006 Cardboard Trumpets

● 1134 Shoe-Box Harp

● 1185 Making Drums

● 1212 Ringing Spoons

● 1213 A Stringed Instrument

● 1404 Sandpaper Blocks

● 1443 Paper-Plate Shakers

● 1509 Musical Jars

After you've gathered the necessary materials, let the children choose which instruments they want to make. They will probably need a little help from you to make the instruments. Encourage the children to try out their instruments, playing together as an orchestra or performing separately. Some children might not want to participate, but they could look and listen for now. If you make the instruments available throughout the week, the children can try them out when they are ready.

1547

Cellist Yo-Yo Ma visits the neighborhood, tells about himself and his family and plays cello for Mister Rogers. In the Neighborhood of Make-Believe, King Friday insists that *everyone* learn to play the bass violin, but the neighbors are having difficulty with his request.

"Listening to Music" can help children:

- express feelings through music;
- express feelings through movement and dance;
- express feelings through art work;
- understand and accept individual differences.

Listening to Music

Materials

- paint and brushes
- scarves or streamers
- paper
- markers
- radio or record player and records

Using records or a radio, try out several different kinds of music for the children. (The selections might include children's songs, country music, rock, or classical.) Do the children like certain types of music and not others? Do they have preferences that are different from the others? Does any of the music make them feel sad, happy, angry or silly?

Let the children help you choose some music to play for a longer period of time and encourage them to think of something they'd like to do while they listen. Be sure to give them a variety of choices so they can see that different people can have different interests and can participate in different ways. Here are a few suggestions:

- painting to music;
- moving to music;
- making up words to go with the music;
- drawing pictures that show how the music makes them feel;
- daydreaming while the music plays;
- or, just plain listening.

When the music is over, you could spend some time talking with the children about the music and the different ways they played or listened. Would the children like to sing "Tree, Tree, Tree"?

They could try making up other words to the song. (Maybe their own names would fit the notes.)

1548

Folk singer Ella Jenkins visits and teaches Chuck Aber and Mister Rogers a hand-clapping game. In the Neighborhood of Make-Believe, the neighbors are thinking of ways to include bass violins in whatever *they* do best so they can participate in the Bass Violin Festival. Lady Aberlin is planning to do a dance with her bass violin rather than play it, and she feels better when she tells King Friday the truth about her plans.

"The Truth Will Make Me Free" can help children:

- recognize feelings;
- talk about feelings.

The Truth Will Make Me Free

Materials

- none

Lady Aberlin had a hard time telling King Friday that she couldn't learn to play the bass violin in three days. Can you think of a time when it was hard for you as a child to tell someone the truth? If you feel like it, share the experience with your children and see if they can tell you times when they have been afraid to tell someone how they felt. They might tell you about things like:

- feeling afraid about a trip or visit to someone;
- not wanting to give a kiss to somebody;
- making a mess and feeling afraid someone will be angry;
- not liking a food that someone prepared;
- being afraid of the dark and not wanting to say so.

You'll want to be sensitive to children's feelings about having done something they consider naughty or "bad." Children find it very hard to "tell on" themselves, so if they don't feel they want to share any information, you might be able to talk about how *some* children feel when they're afraid grownups will be angry with them. The biggest help could be if *you* would be willing to tell *them* about something you once did that you considered naughty or bad, and how you grew to see that it wasn't naughty or bad to have negative feelings. Can anyone think of a time when he or she felt that way, and it turned out the grownup didn't get angry after all?

1549

Mister Rogers listens to members of a brass quintet as they practice their instruments. Even though all five musicians play together, each instrument can be heard separately, if people listen carefully.

"Each One is Separate" can help children:

- understand and accept individual differences;
- work on feelings about separation;
- practice taking turns;
- practice working cooperatively.

Each One is Separate

Materials

- none

One of the important ideas in today's program is that each of us is unique and different, even when we're part of a group. To help the children understand more about this idea, encourage them to listen carefully as each person talks or sings separately.

Then all of you can sing a song or say a rhyme together. Let the children take turns listening to the song or rhyme. Can they hear one person's separate voice while the group talks or sings together? They'll have to listen very carefully. If it's too difficult, let the children talk in pairs while the others listen for each person's separate voice.

Older children might like to play a word game in which each person says a different word in a sentence. For instance:

- 1st child: Let's
- 2nd child: sing
- 3rd child: a
- 4th child: song

This may take a lot of practice. What would happen if everyone tried to talk at once, saying different words? Let them try it.

What happens when they speak together saying the same words? You could end this activity by singing a favorite song together.

There's joy in being separate and different, and there's joy in being like others and part of a group.

1550

In the Neighborhood of Make-Believe, the music festival is a grand success! Even though everyone can't play the bass violin, each person participates by using a bass violin in his or her own special way.

"Many Ways" can help children:

- understand and accept individual differences.

Many Ways

Materials

- scarves (one for each child)

Can the children tell you some of the different ways the neighbors in Make-Believe used bass violins in today's festival (playing it, dancing with one, dressing up like one, making bass violin puppets)? You might want to point out that people have different ideas about using things, and that we don't have to do everything the way someone else does it. Hand out the scarves you've collected and talk about different ways someone could use a scarf. Encourage the children to give you their ideas. They might think of things like:

- dancing while using it as a streamer;
- wearing it as part of a dress-up outfit;
- wrapping a doll in it;
- using it to play peek-a-boo;
- hiding toys under it.

As you give each child a chance to demonstrate his or her idea, you can reinforce the uniqueness of each person's way of using the scarf. Or they might think of ways to use a bass violin that those in the Neighborhood of Make-Believe didn't think of (like living in one?).

Thoughts For The Week

Families come in all different shapes and sizes. Even people who are not related by blood at all can make up a family—because they love and care for each other. And that's what is really important about families. When people care for one another, they have a sense of belonging—of being related to each other even if they are not blood relatives. There are many ways to become a member of a family. Being born into a family is one way. Marrying into a family, or being adopted are other ways to become part of a family. When children are adopted, they sometimes need reassurance that adoptive families are like other families and that their moms and dads care for them, the same way other parents care for their children, and that adoption is forever.

There are joys and sorrows that come with being part of any family. In one of the songs, I sing: "It's the people you llike the most...who make you feel maddest." One child wrote us a letter telling us all about his "bother," misspelling the word "brother." That mistake told us something about the feelings he had toward the other boy in his family. The people we love and care for can also make us happy. The tough times and the easy times are part of everyone's family no matter how we are related.

Fred Rogers

Songs On The Programs This Week

1551 *"Let's Think of Something to do While We're Waiting"*
"What Do You Do?"

1552 *"Everybody's Fancy"*

1553 *"I Like to Be Told"*
"You Are Special"

1554 *"Please Don't Think It's Funny"*

1555 *"It's You I Like"*
"There Are Many Ways to Say I Love You"

Special Visits

1551 *How People Make Orange Juice*

1552 *An Aviary*

1553 *A Pediatrician's Office*

Your Notes For The Week

1551

While planting an orange seed, Mister Rogers talks about how long it takes for plants to grow. He also shows a film on how orange juice is made. In the Neighborhood of Make-Believe, Lady Aberlin is serving orange juice to her friends to show them that she cares about them.

"Orange Juice and Conversation" can help children:

- work on feelings about separation;
- learn more about foods.

Orange Juice and Conversation

Materials

- several juicy oranges
- orange juice squeezer (optional)
- sieve
- paper cups
- knife

Preparing and giving food is one way that parents care for their families. When children are away from their parents, times with food can be times that make that separation difficult. Today as you help the children squeeze their own orange juice, you can be extra sensitive to the strong tie between food and home.

Let the children touch and handle the oranges as you pass them around. What can they tell you about the oranges? Do they know how we get orange juice? What kinds of juice do their parents buy to drink at home? (Frozen concentrate? Cartons? Bottles?)

Have they ever tried making their own juice? Cut the oranges in half and let the children squeeze some juice into paper cups and taste it. Does it taste like the juice they have at home? If you have an orange juice squeezer, show the children how to use it to squeeze out the rest of the juice. Pour the juice through a sieve to remove the seeds and serve the rest of the juice at snack time. This could be a good time to talk about where their parents are, what they might be doing, and when they will return.

Can the children think of special things parents do to show children they love them?

1552

Mister Rogers visits an aviary and talks about different kinds of families—families of birds, families of trees, and families of people.

"Family Members" can help children:

- learn more about their world.

Family Members

Materials
- paper
- markers

You might begin this activity by talking about your own family.

Do the children know any of your family members? They might like to hear about family members they have never met—but who are still related to you. Children want to know more and more about the people they love. Then encourage the children to talk about *their* families. Do they have any brothers or sisters? What are their parents' names? Do they know their grandparents' names? Write each child's name on a sheet of paper and list the names of family members underneath. You'll need to be especially sensitive to the feelings of children who come from divorced or adoptive families. This might be a good time to talk about belonging to a family, emphasizing that families come in all shapes and sizes. What makes a group a family is a sense of belonging and caring that they all share. As children talk about people in their families, encourage them to tell about ways those people are important to them.

- What kinds of experiences do they share?
- What do they enjoy most about the person?

Some children might want to use the markers and paper to draw a picture of the people they've talked about. Or, they might want to draw pictures to give to someone special in their families.

1553

Mister Rogers visits a pediatrician's office where children are getting a medical check-up. In the Neighborhood of Make-Believe, Dr. Bill examines Carrie Dell Okonak Templeton Jones, the adopted baby of Betty Okonak Templeton and James Michael Jones.

"A Medical Play Kit" can help children:

- use play to work on feelings;
- express feelings through play;
- try out different roles.

A Medical Play Kit

Materials
- smock or old white shirt
- tongue depressors
- bandages (strips of cloth)

The children might have a lot to say about Mister Rogers' visit to the pediatrician's office. Can they remember a time when they went to see the doctor? What was the examination like? If it hurt, were they able to talk about it with someone they love?

The children could help you collect the materials to make a medical kit. A yardstick or tape measure to see how tall they've grown, along with a set of scales can be possible contents. See what things they feel they need for their medical play. If you have a toy medical kit, that can be a starting place. There are a number of things you can use from around the house. For instance:

- an old ball-point (without the ink cartridge) for giving pretend injections;
- lightweight radio headphones worn upside-down can serve as a pretend stethoscope;
- a plastic bubble wand can substitute for an instrument to check eyes or ears.

The children will need some time to explore and try out the objects you've collected. Then they may be ready to pretend about their own doctor visits.

By playing about new or scary experiences, children can learn to cope with the strong feelings these experiences may bring. If you make the medical kit available on a regular basis, children can play about a doctor's visit whenever they feel it's important to them.

1554

Mister Rogers talks about different kinds of families and shows a film about families in his neighborhood. He talks about human families and animal families, ways families are similar and how they are different. Although each of us is different, we can still love each other and be loved by them.

"Animal Family Posters" can help children:

- recognize likeness and difference;
- understand and accept individual differences.

Animal Family Posters

Materials

- magazines
- paste
- large paper cardboard
- scissors

As the children look through the magazines for pictures of animals, you could talk about ways the animals are alike and how they are different. Help the children cut or tear out the pictures and encourage them to sort the pictures.

Can they find all the horses, cows, dogs, cats, people, etc.? Do the children know that mother dogs always have puppies (baby dogs), that cats always have kittens (baby cats), and that humans always have baby humans?

For younger children, looking through the magazines and talking about the pictures may be all that interests them. Older children, though, might want to paste the pictures on large sheets of cardboard or paper to make animal family posters. While the children are pasting, you might talk with them about ways they are like the other people in their families. How are they different?

1555

In the Neighborhood of Make-Believe, a Cousin Reunion is being held—everyone who is a cousin or has a cousin is invited to attend. Bob Dog feels left out because he has no cousin, so Ana Platypus suggests they *adopt* each other as cousins. Daniel Tiger is worried that he may have to kiss all the cousins at the reunion. Lady Aberlin reassures him that there are many other ways to say "I love you."

"What Is Adoption?" can help children:

- feel comfortable asking about things;
- learn different ways people communicate.

What Is Adoption?

Materials

- none

The children may have some concerns or questions about what it means to be "adopted." If any children in your care are from adoptive families, or know adoptive families, you'll want to be especially sensitive to their feelings. Children need to be reassured that adoptive families are real families, and that the family members in them love one another just the way other families do. Children may have many fantasies about adoption—some of which are inaccurate. If you listen carefully, you may be able to find out about the things they don't understand.

For instance, sometimes children think that "adoption" means going to the store to buy a baby. You might want to reassure them that all babies are born in the same way and explain that when birth parents can't care for a child, they find a way for the child to get the love and care he or she needs. Sometimes children think that adopted children will be given back if they're naughty, and you may be able to reassure them that adoption is forever and that adoptive families will always love and care for their children just as parents in other families do.

Can the children tell you some of the ways people in their families show love for one another? Some children might want to pretend to adopt each other as cousins and have their own cousin reunion today. Can they think of ways to show their "adopted cousins" that they care about them?

Thoughts For The Week

Being creative is part of being human. Everyone is creative and each of us has his or her own unique way of expressing that creativity. When children pretend about how they would like things to be, they are trying out creative alternatives to life's experiences. The three year old who misses her mother can pretend to talk to her on the phone and creatively keep her mother with her through make-believe. Making and doing is another way that children express their creativity. Painting a picture, completing a project, building a block city all require creative problem-solving. Feeling good about things they have made can help children develop a sense of pride in themselves as unique and worthwhile individuals. Children's projects might not always turn out the way we adults expect, but they still reflect a child's own expression of creativity.

Fred Rogers

Songs On The Programs This Week

1556   *"It's You I Like"*
1557   *"Children Can"*
       "I'm a Man Who Manufactures"
1558   *"You Are Special"*
       "How Do You Help A Friend To Know
       That You Like Him?"
1559   *"Did You Know?"*
1560   *"Are You Brave and Don't Know It?"*

Special Visits

1557   *Brockett's Bakery*
1558   *How People Make Wooden Rocking Horses*
1560   *A Special Playground*

Your Notes For The Week

1556

Mister Rogers shows a film of children constructing a miniature golf course with dirt, using marbles, tubes, and other obstacles. In the Neighborhood of Make-Believe, Lady Elaine Fairchilde creates a "cover" that makes the Neighborhood Trolley look like a car.

"Marble Roll" can help children:

- develop creative play;
- develop coordination;
- practice working cooperatively.

Marble Roll

Materials

- cardboard tubes from paper towel rolls
- small milk cartons
- marbles, pingpong balls or crushed aluminum foil balls

You might begin this activity by talking with the children about the film of children playing in the dirt. You could ask questions like:

- Do you remember what the children were doing?
- What do you think they were playing about?
- Did their play give you any ideas about things you could do?
- Do we have anything around this house that you could use to play about your ideas?

See if the children would like to try using similar materials to make their own "mini-golf" courses or to try out their own ideas. Set out a carton full of things like cardboard tubes, empty milk cartons, and marbles for the children to use. (If you have very young children in your care, you can substitute pingpong balls or crushed foil balls for the marbles. That way you won't have to worry about someone swallowing a marble.)

(Or, 1069 "Paper Towel Rolls.")

1557

At Chef Brockett's bakery, Eva Kwong's grandmother makes special Chinese dumplings, and Mister Rogers talks about how children can learn from adults about making things. In the Neighborhood of Make-Believe, everyone is making some sort of cover.

"Covered Milk Cartons" can help children:

- develop creative play;
- develop imagination;
- feel proud of accomplishments.

Covered Milk Cartons

Materials

- empty milk cartons
- construction paper, pre-pasted wallpaper scraps, or adhesive-backed shelf paper
- tape or glue
- scraps cut in the shape of windows, doors, wheels, headlights, etc.

Ask the children to think of different kinds of ways they could cover the cartons. You might suggest making one look like:

- a trolley;
- a building;
- a bus;
- a truck;
- or doll bed.

Help the children select the materials they will need to cover the milk cartons and turn them into playthings. Younger children might just want to paste pictures or pieces of paper all over the cartons to cover them. At the end of the day when everyone has finished his or her projects, try to set aside time to look at and talk about the different kinds of covers.

1558

Mr. McFeely shows a film about his visit to a factory where people make wooden rocking horses. In the Neighborhood of Make-Believe, there are many interesting covers, including a set of pyramid covers in graduated sizes.

"Working With Wood" can help children:

- learn more about work;
- feel proud of accomplishments;
- learn to do things independently.

Working with Wood

Materials

- small pieces of wood (scraps from a lumber yard or woodworker)
- sandpaper
- white glue
- paint (optional)
- scrap materials (buttons, ribbon, fabric, yarn, etc.)
- hammer, nails, screwdriver, screws (optional)

The children might want to spend some time talking about the rocking horse factory. Can each child tell you something he or she remembers? If you have older children, you could write down the things the children recall and ask them to help you put them in order in which they happened.

After the discussion, spread the wood pieces out on a newspaper-covered work space for the children to make their own wooden creations. You might have to show them how to sand the rough edges so they won't get any splinters. With your supervision, older children can assemble the pieces with screws or nails. Younger children could use liquid glue to hold the pieces together. After the glue has dried (possibly the next day), the children can paint and decorate their creations.

(Or, 1411 "Boxes Inside Boxes.")

1559

In the Neighborhood of Make-Believe, Daniel Tiger becomes frightened when he sees Chuck Aber disguised as a large King Friday.

"Trying On Masks" can help children:

- understand the difference between real and pretend;
- try out different roles;
- learn more about growing.

Trying on Masks

Materials
- assorted masks (1029 "Paper-Plate Masks")
- a collection of hats (Directions for making hats are on pages B-2 and B-3.)
- mirror

Have any of the children ever been frightened at Halloween time when they saw people dressed up in costumes and masks? Sometimes children think that masks change a person. Daniel Tiger was frightened when he saw a large King Friday because he was afraid he would grow to be big too soon and have to do grown-up things. Have any of the children ever felt afraid about growing up or facing new experiences? See if they want to talk about those experiences. You might talk with them about a time you felt afraid.

When the children have finished talking, they can try on different masks and look at themselves in the mirror. You might have to reassure them that people don't change when they put on a mask. You can show them that masks are a kind of cover—a face cover. If any of the children feel afraid, they could try on an assortment of hats (head covers) to see differences in appearance. Are they still the same children underneath?

1560

Mister Rogers invites viewers to visit a special new playground designed and built by adults and children. In the Neighborhood of Make-Believe, Daniel Tiger learns that even brave people are sometimes afraid.

"A Block City" can help children:

- develop creative play;
- develop imagination;
- feel proud of accomplishments.

A Block City

Materials
- set of blocks (You could use milk cartons and cereal boxes or oatmeal containers.)
- miniature cars, animals, people

You might spend time talking with the children about planning and remind them of the planning that went into the playgrounds Mister Rogers visited. Then ask them to think about plans for making a block city. You could ask things like:

- How much space would you need?
- How many buildings can you make?
- What kinds of buildings do you want?
- Where would the roads be?
- Would you need any bridges or tunnels?

Older children could sketch out a simple plan with your help. As they work together to make their block city, the younger children might find it hard to stick with their original plans. If you let them experiment with creative arrangements, you can always talk with them later about the changes they made and the ways their city is alike and different from their plans. Did the final arrangement turn out better after all? When using small cartons or blocks, the children could make the city on a large piece of wood or a card table and leave it standing to use again at another time.

Thoughts For The Week

Celebrations are special times. Human beings have unique ways of celebrating events that are important to us. Sometimes we like to have people celebrate with us, but other times our celebrations are more private. When children celebrate things like birthdays or holidays, they sometimes become so overwhelmed with feelings that they need a trusting adult to help them manage the strong feelings they have. They sometimes wonder, "Will no one remember my birthday?" or "Will this celebration be everything I expected?"

As we help children manage the feelings of doubt as well as the feelings of joy, we show them that it's all right to have feelings—and to tell people about them, even if the feelings aren't those they expect to have on joyous occasions.

Music has always been an important part of celebrations. Through music, children often find ways to express a whole range of feelings—from sadness and anger to joy and peace. The programs this week feature music and a new opera—our way of celebrating with our television friends.

Fred Rogers

Songs On The Programs This Week

1561   "What Do You Do?"
"A Handy Lady and a Handy Man"
1562   "You Are Pretty"
1563   "You Are Special"
1564   "Happy Birthday, Happy Birthday"
1565   "A Star For Kitty"

Special Visits

1561   How People Make Trumpets
1562   A Planetarium
1563   Trumpeter, Wynton Marsalis
1564   How People Make Candles

Your Notes For The Week

Monday

1561

Mister Rogers talks about trumpets and watches a film about Mr. McFeely's visit to a trumpet-making factory. In the Neighborhood of Make-Believe, King Friday declares that an approaching comet belongs to him and decrees a week of celebrating.

"Planning A Celebration" can help children:

- practice working cooperatively;
- practice making choices.

Planning a Celebration

Materials

- large sheet of paper
- marker

You might want to talk with the children about different ways they like to celebrate special occasions such as birthdays, holidays, or other special events. Do any of the children know what the word "celebration" means? Can they think of something they would like to celebrate this week? Maybe someone is having a birthday. Or perhaps they want to celebrate about things they've learned to do well. They could set aside a day to celebrate the fun they have together and call it A Celebration of Friendship.

As you and the children make the celebration plans, keep a list of things that have to be done this week to get ready for the celebration. Your list might include things like:

- making a snack;
- writing invitations;
- making banners;
- hanging balloons.

Let the children decide when they want to have the celebration and plan your activities accordingly. If it's possible, the children could go along with you to buy the necessary supplies for your celebration.

1562

Mister Rogers and Chuck Aber play a short game of basketball and talk about the importance of trying. Playing well (not just winning) can give us reason to celebrate. Mister Rogers visits a planetarium and sees a sky show. There are pictures of the moon, constellations, and a comet!

"Connect the Stars" can help children:

- develop muscle control;
- learn more about their world;
- develop imagination.

Connect the Stars

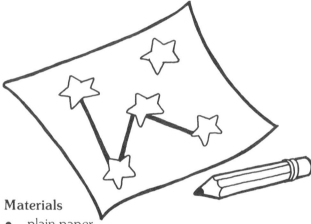

Materials
- plain paper
- marker or crayons
- foil stars (optional)

You might want to talk with the children about things people like to imagine when they look up at the sky. Can they tell you what a constellation is? If you make simple dot-to-dot designs, using stars instead of dots, children can connect the dots (stars) with crayon or marker to make their own constellations. You could arrange the stars to form shapes such as squares or rectangles, the first initial of a child's name, or place them randomly so children can connect the stars any way they want. Or, children could stick foil stars on paper and connect the stars to make designs or constellations.

(or, 1173 "Basketball"; 1359 "Winning and Losing.")

1563

Trumpeter Wynton Marsalis visits Joe Negri's Music Shop, talks with Mister Rogers about music feelings and plays two compositions including "It's You I Like." In the Neighborhood of Make-Believe, people are still looking for a comet.

"Comet Collage" can help children:

- express feelings through art work;
- develop imagination.

Comet Collage

Materials
- dark background paper
- paper shapes to represent comets, stars, full and crescent moons, meteors, etc.
- foil, self-stick stars (optional)
- glue
- glitter (optional)

Can any of the children tell you what they see when they look up at the sky at night? See if they want to close their eyes and imagine a sky full of stars. They could sing "Twinkle, Twinkle, Little Star" while they pretend. Can they imagine what King Friday's comet might look like? You could describe a comet for them and tell them that a comet is a ball of ice and rock—a rocky ice ball that leaves a trail of dust as it melts.

The children can look through the assortment of shapes you've prepared to choose the ones they want to use to make collages. Encourage them to arrange the shapes any way they want. It's not really important that the pictures actually look like the night sky— some children may choose to use five moons instead of just one.

Do any of the children want to add glitter to the finished pictures? They can create interesting effects like meteor showers or streams behind the comets by dribbling glue onto the paper and sprinkling glitter all around. When the glue has dried, you or the children can shake off the excess glitter.

1564

Mister Rogers has a celebration today to honor his television friends. He visits a factory to see how candles are made. In the Neighborhood of Make-Believe, the comet arrives with a special message and the neighbors celebrate Henrietta's birthday.

"All to Myself" can help children:

- recognize feelings;
- talk about feelings;
- express strong feelings in appropriate ways.

All to Myself

Materials

- none

King Friday wanted to have the comet all to himself, but he learned that no one can own a comet and no one can own someone else. Can the children think of a time when they wanted someone all to themselves? You might want to spend some time talking with the children about the way they feel when that happens. Even though no one can "own" another person, it's only natural that children want to have an adult all to themselves now and then. It can be particularly difficult for young children to share adult attention with several other children, so they might need your reassurance from time to time to know that you can be available to them individually as well as to the whole group. If you can arrange it, try to set aside some time today to spend alone with each child, even if only for a few moments. Let each child tell you how he or she would like to spend the time. For instance, children might select activities like:

- looking at a book with you;
- sitting on your lap;
- helping you with a task;
- pretending to be a star or a comet;
- or singing the words to Mister Rogers' song, "Just For Once (I Want You All to Myself)."

(Or, 1179 "Decorating Pretend Cakes.")

1565

Mister Rogers brings a pair of opera glasses today. In the Neighborhood of Make-Believe, everyone is celebrating while they enjoy the birthday opera, "A Star For Kitty."

"Magic Telescopes" can help children:

- develop imagination;
- understand the difference between real and pretend.

Magic Telescopes

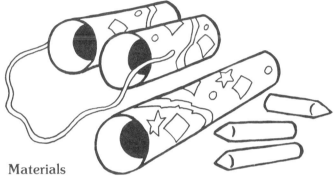

Materials

- paper towel tubes
- aluminum foil (optional)
- paper or fabric
- crayons or markers

Encourage the children to decorate the tubes with paper or aluminum foil. Some of the children might want to have you cut the tubes in half and tape each half side by side to make binoculars or opera glasses instead of telescopes. When the projects are finished, ask the children to look through the telescopes or glasses and imagine they are looking out at distant stars and planets. What kinds of things would they see on a clear, starry night? You can help them imagine by talking about the things you pretend to see. For instance, you could say things like:

- I see a comet. Can you see one? What does it look like to you?
- Oh, look, there's the moon with lots of stars around it. Do you see it?

Encourage the children to tell you what else they imagine while looking through their magic telescopes. They might want to draw pictures of the things they imagined.

Thoughts For The Week

Some people talk about play as if it were a relief from serious learning; but, for children, play is serious business. It provides a way for them to express strong feelings about important events in their lives. Play gives children a chance to work out problems on their own, to cope with anxieties, and to prepare for life as an adult by pretending about being grown up. Through play, children discover the world and learn more about themselves.

When given the opportunity, children tend to choose playthings that suit their developmental needs. You may have seen a young child put aside a newly acquired toy in favor of the empty carton or the brightly colored wrapping paper. A child may spend a long time playing happily with an empty cereal carton, or banging on a metal pot with a wooden spoon. That's because young children's imaginations are engaged by almost everything they see. In the same way, it's often rewarding for older children to make their own playthings out of everyday household things. That way they can be imaginative and involved in making the toys as well as in playing with them.

Fred Rogers

Songs On The Program This Week

1566 *"Let's Think of Something To Do While We're Waiting"*

1567 *"You've Got To Do It"*

1568 *"Pretending"*
      "I Like To Take My Time"

1569 *"You've Got To Do It"*

1570 *"I'm Proud of You"*

Special Visits

1566 *Gymnast, Chainey Umphrey*

1567 *Folk Singer, Ella Jenkins*
      How People Make Toy Wagons

1568 *Airport Control Tower*

1569 *Negri's Music Shop*

1570 *Toy Lending Library*

Your Notes For The Week

1566

Mister Rogers introduces his television neighbors to a young proficient gymnast, Chainey Umphrey. The Neighbors of Make-Believe learn of a rare top that does somersaults. Unfortunately, it is locked in a special room in the Museum-Go-Round, and no one has the key! Mr. McFeely visits Mister Rogers and brings along a set of wooden letters. They talk about toys they used to play with when they were young.

"My Favorite Toys" can help children:

● learn to use words;

● recognize and use symbols;

● talk about feelings.

My Favorite Toys

Materials

● paper

● crayons

You can begin this discussion by talking with the children about toys you especially liked when you were a child. Then see if the children can tell you about some of their favorite toys.

Do any of the children want to bring in a favorite toy to show the others? You could help the children make notes to their parents asking if they could bring in a favorite toy. Let the children dictate the words as you write them down. They might enjoy decorating the notes by coloring around the edges of the paper or by drawing on the reverse side. They could even make pictures of their favorite toys on the note, or on a separate sheet of paper.

Because favorite toys are so special, the children might need your reassurance that they don't have to let others play with the toys unless they feel ready to share.

(Or, 1023 "Looking for Letters," 1371 "Modeling Dough Letters," 1170 "All Kinds of Exercises.")

1567

Mister Rogers visits a toy factory to see how people design and manufacture toy wagons. Folk singer, Ella Jenkins, visits the Neighborhood and shows Mister Rogers her collection of spinning tops.

"Things That Spin" can help children:
● develop healthy curiosity;
● learn more about the world;
● develop creative play.

Things That Spin

● tops
● coins
● pencils
● spoons
● cardboard
● markers
● pen or pencil

You might begin this activity by talking with the children about the collection of tops they saw on the program today. Which ones did they like best? If you have a top, the children could take turns spinning it. Can they think of other things they could spin? For instance:
● pencils;
● coins;
● spoons;
● small cars.

Do they want to try out some of their ideas?

The children could make simple cardboard spinners by cutting out cardboard circles, decorating them with markers, poking holes in the center, and spinning them on the tip of a pen or pencil.

As the children spin the cardboard discs, you could show them how the colors blend together when the circle spins faster.

1568

Mister Rogers sees a film of Mr. McFeely's visit to an airport control tower. In the Neighborhood of Make-Believe, the neighbors are looking for a mysterious shiny key that flies in the air.

"Pretend Keys" can help children:
● use their imagination;
● develop creative play.

Pretend Keys

Materials
● cardboard (from cartons or cereal boxes)
● scissors
● pencil
● aluminum foil
● string
● old keys (optional)

Young children are often fascinated with keys, doors, and locks. If you have an old set of keys and are comfortable having the children pretend with them, you could label them "Play Keys" and make them available for pretend play.

You could also make pretend keys for children to use. Simply cut out key shapes from cardboard and cover them with aluminum foil to make them shiny. You can give each child his or her own pretend key, or make a set for each child by stringing several keys together.

Encourage the children to think up uses for the keys. How about:
● pretending to lock and unlock the doors;
● opening a magic box;
● pretending to start a car.

Older children might want to make key rubbings and compare different shapes and styles of keys. Can you explain how locks work? Show how the shape of each key matches the shape of the lock.

(Or, 1178 "Key Match," 1145 "Balloons," 1480 "An Airplane Ride.")

1569

Mister Rogers shows how empty containers plus some imagination can create a whole Neighborhood. In the Neighborhood of Make-Believe, Ana Platypus is jealous of Prince Tuesday's new bike and angry because her parents aren't buying one for her. At Joe Negri's Music Shop, three friends have fun making music on real and toy instruments.

"Our Neighborhood" can help children:
- develop creative play;
- develop imagination.

Our Neighborhood

Materials
- empty food cartons
- paper towel tubes
- construction paper
- glue or tape
- markers
- toy cars and people

It could be helpful to talk a little about Ana's jealous feelings about Prince Tuesday's new bike. Can anyone remember a time when someone they knew got a new toy and they were angry because they couldn't have one, too? Can the children think of things they can do when they feel angry about not getting a toy—things like:
- playing with a favorite old toy;
- making a toy from things around the house;
- using their imaginations in make-believe play.

You could let the children look through your collection of materials to find things they could use to create a pretend neighborhood. Talk with the children about their neighborhoods and label the various boxes to represent places the children know. Then, using miniature people, encourage the children to play about the things they like to do and places they go in their own neighborhoods. Children could make streets from strips of paper and drive toy cars around the Neighborhood.

(Or, 1399 "A Pretend Orchestra.")

1570

Mister Rogers visits a toy lending library and talks about the different kinds of toys children like to play with. When the Neighbors open the locked room, they find something unexpected and learn a wonderful lesson about imagination.

"Clothes-Pin People" can help children:
- develop creative play;
- use their imagination.

Clothes-Pin People

Materials
- wooden clothes pins (not snap-type)
- yarn
- markers
- fabric scraps
- glue

An important way children can pretend is by using miniature life figures to play about their experiences with people who are important to them. Simple figures can be made from wooden clothes pins by drawing faces on the tops, adding yarn for hair, and wrapping or gluing on fabric scraps for clothing. Encourage each child to make several figures. It can take time for children to learn to play with new toys, but if you make a set of figures for yourself, your pretending can serve as a playful model for children as you encourage them to use the figures they've made.

(Or, 1285 "Stick Puppets," 1381 "Pretending.")

Thoughts For The Week

Dancing is one of the most natural ways people have to express our feelings to the world. Even before children can talk they can communicate how they feel by the way they move their bodies in response to the tone and rhythm of voices and sounds around them. Through the gestures and expressions of this earliest of "dances" babies tell their caregivers a lot about fear, pleasure, anger, and curiosity.

Older children tend to find movement both a pleasure and an outlet for self-expression. They can take delight in their growing ability to control their bodies, and many even enjoy the discipline and effort that goes with learning a new skill. But even as their dances become more intricate and precise, you can sense their continuing pleasure in movement. By encouraging young children to express their feelings through movement, we can often provide them with opportunities for self-expression that can last a lifetime.

Fred Rogers

Songs On The Programs This Week

1571 *"Let's Think of Something To Do While It's Raining"*

1572 *"Everybody's Fancy"*

Special Visits

1572 *Sea World*

1573 *Dancer, Sam Weber*

1574 *Dance Theatre of Harlem*

1575 *Weaver, Ann White*

Your Notes For The Week

1571

It's raining in the Neighborhood today. As Mister Rogers watches the rain, he notices that the raindrops look like they are dancing. He suggests that there are many things to do when it's raining, such as reading a book, or drawing a picture, or just watching the dancing drops of rain. In the Neighborhood of Make-Believe, Corney has invented a new chair called a Dancerockit. It's a chair you dance in while you are sitting.

"Dancerockit" can help children:

- express feelings through movement and dance;
- develop creative play;
- develop coordination.

Dancerockit

Materials

- radio or records and record player
- small rocking chair or child-sized chair

What do the children think of Corney's latest invention? Has anyone ever tried to dance while sitting down? You could pretend you have a dancerockit in your home today and see if the children want to try it out. Any chair will do, but if you have a small rocking chair, the children could try rocking and dancing at the same time. Put on a record or music from the radio and let the children take turns dancing without getting out of the chair. You might want to talk with them about the music they hear and the different ways they feel like moving. If you want, you could try out different kinds of music and see if everyone can dance at the same time, sitting in chairs or just sitting on the floor. Some children may want to dance only with their eyebrows! Later the children might want to move their whole bodies while dancing. How is this kind of dancing the same? How is it different? Do any of the children want to pretend to be dancing raindrops as they move to the music?

You might want to end this activity by talking with the children about things they like to do on rainy days. What do they like about the rain? What do they dislike?

1572

Mister Rogers visits Sea World to see the animals that live in water, and he watches a film of a whale whose movements remind him of dancing in the water. In the Neighborhood of Make-Believe, Corney's Dancerockit is missing. Lady Elaine is opening a Dance Studio and has taken the Dancerockit because it has the word "dance" on it.

"Sea Mural" can help children:

- develop creative play;
- express feelings through art work.

Sea Mural

Materials

- roll of plain shelf paper
- construction paper in various colors
- crayons
- water colors or diluted tempera paint
- brushes
- glue
- scissors
- straws (optional)

You might want to set aside some time to talk with the children about the different shapes, sizes, and colors of fish they have seen on television, in books, or in real life. You could point out that no two fish are exactly alike—just as no two people are exactly the same. Some of the children might want to draw different fish shapes on construction paper and cut them out. After they have had a chance to play with the fish, you could suggest working together to make a sea mural for the wall.

If you let each child choose the section he or she wants to work on, the children will have a better sense of the boundaries and won't be as likely to interfere with the others' work. For instance, one or two children could use the crayons to draw seaweed or sea creatures. Others could paint the background using blue or green water colors. (The paint won't stick to crayon so the drawings will show through the paint.) Then everyone could glue fish shapes anywhere on the mural. When the project is finished, you could hang the mural where parents can see it when they arrive.

If you find some of the children have difficulty working together or waiting for their turns, you might want to consider giving each child his or her own sheet of paper to make individual sea pictures. For very young children, paper, glue, and an assortment of fish shapes may be enough for them to handle. Left-over fish shapes can be taped to drinking straws to make fish puppets for the children to use on another day.

1573

Mister Rogers visits the Dance Workshop where Sam Weber is teaching a class. He shows Mister Rogers how he dances when he is happy, and how he dances when he is sad. He tells Mister Rogers that dancing often helps him feel better. Mr. McFeely visits Mister Rogers and shows a film about how shoes are made.

"Dancing Feet Mobiles" can help children:

- learn more about body parts;
- understand and accept individual differences.

Dancing Feet Mobiles

Materials

- construction paper
- pencil or marker
- scissors
- straw
- string

You could begin this activity by asking the children to show you different ways they use their feet. They might think of things like:

- walking;
- running;
- kicking a ball;
- jumping.

Can the children use their feet to show you how they feel? You could let them stamp their feet to show you how they'd feel if they were angry. How would they move their feet if they were happy? Afraid?

Dancing feet mobiles can be made by tracing around the children's feet (with their shoes on or off) and hanging the cut-out shapes from sticks, straws, or hangers suspended from the ceiling. Children can make the feet seem to dance by blowing gently on the mobiles.

As you talk with the children about the mobiles, you can discuss differences in the sizes and shapes of children's feet. You can point out that everyone's feet are different because no two people are exactly alike.

(Or, 1151 "Comparing Shoes and Feet"; 1350 "Matching Shoes"; 1506 "Trying on Shoes.")

1574

Mister Rogers tells how his parents helped him learn to dance when he was young. He visits Arthur Mitchell at the Dance Theatre of Harlem who talks about how much he enjoys helping people learn to dance. In the Neighborhood of Make-Believe, Lady Elaine changes the name of her "Always Happy Dance Studio" to the "Sometimes Happy Dance Studio." She even admits that men can learn to dance well.

"Dancing Puppets" can help children:

- talk about feelings;
- express feelings through movement and dance;
- develop coordination.

Dancing Puppets

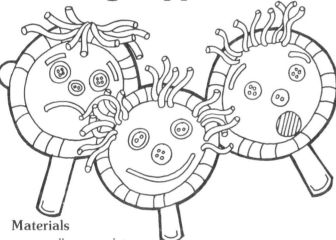

Materials

- small paper plates
- crayons or markers
- straw, popsicle sticks, or tongue depressors
- yarn, buttons, fabric scraps
- glue

Can the children show you different ways they would dance if they were happy? How about sad? What would an angry dance look like? Can the children think of other kinds of feelings to show through their dances? How would they look if they were afraid? Lonely? Disappointed?

Today you could make paper plate puppets for the children to use in their play. A simple way is to draw faces on small paper plates and then decorate any way you wish—for instance, with buttons for eyes and yarn for hair. Some of the children might want to make several puppets with different facial expressions that show different feelings. By attaching the paper plates to straws, tongue depressors, or popsicle sticks, the children will have puppets they can hold. They might like to make up a story about a troupe of dancing puppets.

1575

Mister Rogers visits a weaver and sees how cloth is made. In the Neighborhood of Make-Believe, a group of folk dancers perform at the "Sometimes Happy Dance Studio." Mister Rogers talks about the many different ways people dance.

"Rainbow Dance" can help children:

- express feelings through movement and dance;
- develop coordination.

Rainbow Dance

Materials

- scarves
- music (optional)

You can select some music for today's dance, but you can also try dancing without music, or hum or sing a song the children know. Waving bright-colored scarves can create a rainbow effect, and the children will probably come up with other ways to use the scarves while dancing. When the children have had a chance to dance individually, you could try a group dance. The children could form a chain and move around the room like a giant caterpillar, or join hands to do a circle dance, moving into the center of the circle and back out again. Or, they could take turns weaving in and out through the "windows" formed by the circle of children holding hands.

Thoughts For The Week

*It can be hard to learn that making mistakes is a part of growing. Yet none of us learns to do anything well without making some mistakes along the way. Sometimes young children feel that they're the only people who make mistakes, and it can help them to know that all people—even adults—make mistakes now and then. What really matters is what we do after the mistake, and how we try to make things right again. Sometimes that means cleaning up the spilled milk or saying "I'm sorry" to a friend. Other times, it may just mean trying again, being more careful, or simply learning what went wrong so we can change it the next time. Children's caregivers play an important role in helping children learn about mistakes, and **what** they learn from their caregivers will affect how children approach both success and failure in life.*

Fred Rogers

Songs On The Programs This Week

1576 *"You Are Special"*

1578 *"There Are Many Ways"*
      "Sometimes I Wonder If I'm a Mistake"

1580 *"I'm Taking Care of You"*
      "She'll Be Coming Around the Mountain"
      "This Little Light of Mine"

Special Visits

1577 *How People Make Books*

1578 *How People Make Erasers*

Special Visits

1576 *Ventriloquist, Susan Linn*

1577 *How People Make Books*

1578 *How People Make Erasers*

1579 *Concert Pianist, André Watts*

1580 *How People Make Erasers*

Your Notes For The Week

Monday

1576

Mister Rogers helps children understand that everyone makes mistakes once in a while. Ventriloquist Susan Linn shows how she uses puppets to help people talk about their feelings. In the Neighborhood of Make-Believe, X the Owl makes a mistake and writes a note to Audrey Duck that says "I am sorry." Audrey Duck accepts his apology and writes a poem about her feelings.

"Saying I Am Sorry" can help children:

- talk about feelings.

Saying I Am Sorry

Materials

- none

You might talk with the children about times when they have made a mistake that hurt someone's feelings. Children may find it difficult to "tell on themselves," but you could begin by telling about a time when *you* made a mistake. For instance, you could say, "Remember when I got angry about...and I found out that it was an accident?" You might talk about how they feel when someone makes a mistake and hurts their feelings. This could lead into discussion about what it means to feel sorry. How do the children feel when they are truly sorry about something? What kinds of things do they do to make the other person feel better? For instance:

- making a picture;
- writing a note;
- talking about the mistake;
- fixing the mistake (erasing the pencil mark on the table);
- hugging the person.

1577

Mister Rogers shows a film about how books are made. He reads a book that has a mistake in it and says that some mistakes are easier to correct than others.

"A Book Factory" can help children:

- learn more about the world;
- recognize and use symbols.

A Book Factory

Materials

- paper
- carbon paper
- pencils
- felt-tipped markers
- heavy paper or lightweight cardboard
- scraps of fabric or paper
- shoelaces or heavy yarn

You and your children might want to make your own book factory in your home. Children can work on separate pages, and you can assemble a book for the group, or you can encourage each child to work on his or her own book. Using carbons and lightweight paper, children can make duplicates of their drawings. Here's the procedure you could use:

- For the cover, children can decorate pieces of cardboard or heavy paper with fabric scraps or felt-tipped markers.
- Each child can make one or more pages for the book. For younger children, the book could be a collection of drawings. If the children want to tell you about the drawings, you could write the words along the bottom of the pictures, or add a page after each drawing with the words about the picture printed on it along with the child's name.
- After assembling the books, poke holes along the left side and lace the pages together with a shoe lace or piece of heavy yarn.

Older children might appreciate some discussion about what to do when they make a mistake while making their books.

1578

Mister Rogers shows a film about how people make erasers to help children learn that some mistakes can be corrected. In the Neighborhood of Make-Believe, puppet Daniel Tiger wonders if he's a mistake. Lady Aberlin reassures him that he is just fine as he is.

"Now You See It, Now You Don't" can help children:

- develop healthy curiosity.

Now You See It, Now You Don't

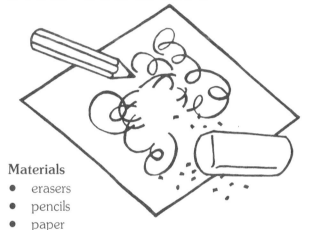

Materials

- erasers
- pencils
- paper

You might want to cover your work area with old newspapers to contain the pencil marks and the eraser "crumbs" while children are using these materials. Then give each child some paper, pencil, and an eraser. Can they tell you anything about the film on how erasers are made? Encourage them to play around with the pencil and eraser, making marks and then erasing them. What do they think happens to the pencil marks when they have been erased? You might show them the tiny pieces of eraser that are left on the paper. Often these pieces are darker than the original eraser so you can tell they have pencil marks on them. The children might want to talk about things that erase and things that don't erase. For instance, try erasing pen marks, erasable pen marks, crayons, markers, or paint.

This could be a good time for you and the children to look through the books you have to see if there are marks that can be erased to make the books look cleaner.

1579

Mister Rogers visits concert pianist André Watts, who plays some of his favorite compositions and talks about how making mistakes helps him be a better pianist.

"Listen to the Music" can help children:

- learn to listen carefully;
- talk about feelings.

Listen to the Music

Materials

- radio or record player or tape recorder
- piano music

If you have a record or tape of piano music, you could play it for the children. If not, you might be able to find some piano music on the radio — or ask the children if they can recognize the sound of a piano in the background music of songs on the radio.

Children might like to dance to the music, paint, or draw while the music is playing. Some of them might just want to sit quietly and listen. When the music is finished, you could ask the children to tell the group how the music made them feel (happy? sad? calm? sleepy? excited?). Children who have drawn or painted a picture might want to tell about it. Dancers might want to show others how they danced as you play the music again.

1580

Mister Rogers tells children that making mistakes is part of being human. He goes to Brockett's Bakery when Chef Brockett is having difficulty whipping some cream. In the Neighborhood of Make-Believe the castle is decorated for a Poetry Reading, and Prince Tuesday learns that even his father can make mistakes.

"Puppet Play" can help children:

- use play to work on feelings;
- develop creative play.

Puppet Play

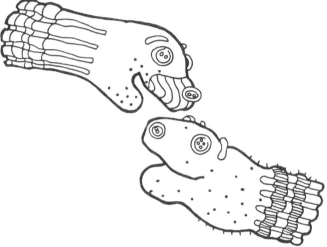

Materials

- hand puppets or materials to make sock puppets (See Program 1409)

If you are taking some time to make your own puppets, this can be a chance to talk about how children feel when they make a mistake on a project. What kind of things can they do when they make a mistake? What did they learn from a mistake?

Using one of the puppets yourself, you can ask another puppet character how he feels when he makes a mistake. Sometime children find it's easier to talk about their own feelings when they can pretend the feelings are the puppet's.

The children can use the puppets to talk about other important feelings, too. You might set aside time for them to play out a story of their own using the puppets. You could ask the children about the characters the puppets represent, and address the puppets by their character name to encourage pretending.

Thoughts For The Week

When young children begin to recognize likenesses and differences, they often focus on the differences and not the underlying sameness in people or objects. They sometimes think that being different means there is something wrong with them. Adults can help children see that there are human qualities that make all of us alike in many ways, even though we come in different shapes, sizes, colors and from different backgrounds.

Fred Rogers

Songs On The Programs This Week

1581   "Then Your Heart Is Full of Love"

1582   "Something To Do While We're Waiting"
        "I'm Glad I'm The Way I Am"
        "Everybody's Fancy"

1583   "I Love To Go To School"
        "The Truth Will Make Me Free"
        "You Are Special"

1584   "It's You I Like"
        "The Clown in Me"

Special Visits

1581   Antique Car Show

1582   Mister Rogers' Antique Car
        Television Programs from Other Countries

1583   Moth Turning into a Butterfly

1585   Circus

Your Notes For The Week

1581

Mister Rogers shows a videotape of himself in an old car. In the Neighborhood of Make-Believe, the neighbors are exchanging roles and clothes.

"How We Change and Grow" can help children:

- learn more about growing.

How We Change and Grow

Materials

- a set of pictures of babies and children of different ages
- a book about babies or about growing up

You could ask the children what they think about the changes that were going on in the Neighborhood of Make-Believe. What will be different? What will be the same? Have they ever switched rooms or beds at home? If they have, how did they feel about those changes? If they haven't, what do they think it would be like to make such changes?

Growing is a kind of changing, too. You can show pictures of babies, or read one of the stories about babies or about growing. Then ask the children how they are different now from when they were babies. You might ask questions like:

- What can babies do?
- What could you do when you were that little?
- What can you do *now* that you couldn't do then?

Try to help the children recognize their growing abilities, while allowing them to recall the pleasures and good feelings associated with being a baby.

1582

Mister Rogers talks about different languages and shows a film of children's television programs from other countries. In the Neighborhood of Make-Believe, Lady Aberlin helps Queen Sara with her new mayor clothes, and Mayor Maggie arrives in her new queen clothes.

"Am I Still Me?" can help children:

- try out different roles;
- develop creative play.

Am I Still Me?

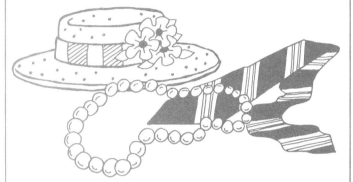

Materials

- dress-up clothes: hats, scarves, neckties, shoes, jackets, etc.
- mirror

Children sometimes think that changes in outside appearance will change who they are inside. You might begin by talking about the continued changes in the Neighborhood of Make-Believe. Then see if any of the children would like to try on some of the dress-up clothes that you have collected. If some of the children are hesitant, allow them to be onlookers as other children try on the hats and dress-up clothing. If you provide a mirror, the children can see how they look while you talk about differences they see. Be sure to point out similarities—the same eyes, the same smile—and assure children that *they* haven't changed, only their clothing has.

1583

Mister Rogers talks about similarities and differences between Rose, a real dog, and Bob Dog. In the Neighborhood of Make-Believe, Prince Tuesday is upset about all the changes—especially the switch between his mother and the mayor.

"What's Missing?" can help children:

- learn to look carefully;
- develop memory.

What's Missing?

Materials

- a collection of household items or small toys (e.g., a key, a spoon, a toy car, a ribbon, a block, a pencil)

You can talk with the children about changes and how they feel when something changes, and they have no control over it. For instance, how do they feel when:

- a new child comes to day care;
- the furniture has been changed around;
- you change the schedule;
- children go off to school.

You could play a game about changes where the children can control what is the same and what is different. Arrange five to ten small household items or toys on a tray and let the children tell you what the objects are. Then have the children close their eyes or leave the room while one child removes an item. When they come back, can they guess what is missing? Older children could rearrange the items *and* remove one, but younger children can probably manage better if the positions of the objects remain the same. You can repeat this game until all children have had a chance to make some changes.

1584

Mister Rogers talks about clowns and shows a clown mask. In the Neighborhood of Make-Believe, two clowns join the group of people who have switched roles. Everyone is happy when the changes are over!

"Clown Masks" can help children:

- try out different roles;
- develop creative play.

Clown Masks

Materials

- paper plates
- yarn
- felt-tipped markers
- large buttons
- assorted construction paper or bright stickers
- glue

You might begin by asking the children what they think about all the changes that have taken place in the Neighborhood of Make-Believe. You could ask if any of the children have ever seen a clown. Reassure them that clowns are people dressed up in a costume and suggest that they could make clown masks and pretend to be clowns.

After covering the work area with newspaper, spread out the materials children can use and give each child a paper plate. You might find that this activity goes more smoothly if you do it in groups of two or three at a time, especially if your children are at different age levels. You can talk with them about what clowns look like and help them select the materials they would like to use if they would like to do it. For instance, the children could:

- use yarn for brightly-colored hair;
- draw faces with markers;
- glue on buttons for noses;
- add stickers or small pieces of construction paper for decorations;
- cut holes for eyes.

With your help, the children can poke holes on each side of the mask and attach string to tie around their heads. If you have a mirror available, the children might want to look at themselves, first with their masks, then without them. (Infants and toddlers can be frightened by clown masks. This could be an activity for older children to do while the infants and toddlers are napping.)

1585

In the Neighborhood of Make-Believe, Daniel Tiger is afraid of a chicken costume. Lady Aberlin helps him talk about his feelings. Mister Rogers visits the circus where he sees elephants, lions, and a clown putting on his costume and make-up.

"Circus Day" can help children:

- develop creative play.

Circus Day

Materials

- rubber or plastic animals
- blocks or empty cardboard boxes
- fabric scraps
- string
- toy people and cars (optional)

How about a circus today? You can talk with the children about Mister Rogers' visit to the circus and the things they saw on the television program. What kinds of animals would they like to include in *their* circus? You can provide miniature animals or make some by cutting out pictures of animals from a magazine and taping them to pieces of wood or small cardboard boxes (See program 1499 "Animal Blocks").

You could help the children make a circus canopy for the toy animals by stretching a piece of fabric over the play area and fastening the corners to chair or table legs. Ask the children for their ideas on how to set up the circus and encourage them to play about the ideas they have. They could make clowns from wooden clothespins, yarn, and fabric swatches.

Thoughts For The Week

Nighttime can be a difficult time for children because having to go to sleep brings separation from the people they love. Children often wonder if everything will still be the same when they awake. They want to be sure that their parents (those who give them stability and comfort) will still be there. Most children have these concerns at one time or another, and talking about things that happen during the night can help children feel more secure when it's dark. Reassuring them that the people they love will be nearby to care for them at night— just like during the day—is a good way to help children learn that adults all over the world care for children in many different ways.

Fred Rogers

Songs On The Programs This Week

1587 "You Are Special"

1588 "You Can Never Go Down the Drain"

1589 "Welcome Song"

1590 "You Are Special"

Special Visits

1586 A Flashlight Factory

1587 A Russian Television Studio

1588 Mr. McFeely Brings Firefighter Gear

1589 A Matrouska Doll Factory
Tatiana Vedeneeva Comes from the Soviet Union

1590 People Who Work at Night

Your Notes For The Week

1586

Mister Rogers makes the room dark and uses a flashlight to look around. He shines the light under the bed to show no monsters are there. In the Neighborhood of Make-Believe, X the Owl becomes angry with Lady Elaine when she scares him by coming into his tree house without knocking, and Daniel is frightened because Lady Elaine told him that stars could fall. A lullaby helps calm Daniel.

"Shadow Dancers" can help children:

● express feelings through movement and dance;
● develop healthy curiosity.

Shadow Dancers

Materials

● large white sheet
● flashlight or high intensity lamp
● lullaby music (optional)
● familiar toys

What can the children tell you about shadows? If it is a sunny day, you might take them outside to see shadows of familiar objects in the play area. Or, you could take a walk around the house to discover shadows inside. You might talk with the children about the differences between shadows and the real person or thing.

The children can use a bright flashlight or high intensity lamp to make shadows with their bodies. A sheet suspended from a doorway makes a good screen for the shadows. You could use lullaby music or other background music and let the children take turns making their shadows dance. If they dance between the light and the sheet, the other children can watch the shadows from the other side of the screen. When the children finish dancing, they might enjoy a guessing game with you holding a familiar toy behind the screen and with them trying to tell what it is from its shadow.

1587

Mister Rogers shows a videotape about his trip to Moscow and his visit to GOOD NIGHT, LITTLE ONES, the Soviet Union's longest-running children's television program. In the Neighborhood of Make-Believe, Daniel Tiger is still worried about the possibility of falling stars.

"Star Mobiles" can help children:

- develop imagination;
- develop creative play.

Star Mobiles

Materials

- paper
- markers
- scissors
- string
- wooden dowel or clothes hanger
- glue
- glitter

Today the children could make hanging mobiles by cutting out star shapes, or moon shapes, or even plain round shapes, and attaching them to a wooden dowel or clothes hanger. (If you use a metal clothes hanger, it's a good idea to wrap the end of the hook with masking tape so the children won't get scratched.) To make sparkling stars for the mobile, the children could drizzle liquid glue on the shapes and sprinkle glitter on top. When the glue has dried, you can help them shake off the extra glitter, make holes in the shapes with a paper punch or pencil, and thread pieces of yarn or string through the holes. While you help the children tie the strings to the hanger, you might ask them what they think about the flying and falling stars in the Neighborhood of Make-Believe.

Younger children might want to have their own mobiles to take home, but older children could work together on a giant mobile that you can connect and display for parents to see. You might find that the youngest children aren't very interested in making mobiles at all. Instead of making mobiles, you could tie the decorated shapes to pieces of yarn and let the children dance around in a safe place while they pretend about flying stars.

1588

Mister Rogers talks about the darkness at the bottom of the ocean and shows a film about scuba divers. Mr. McFeely brings firefighter clothing for Mister Rogers to try on. Although the mask-like face gear is scary-looking, Mister Rogers reassures his viewers that it's for *protection,* and that firefighters who wear these masks are helpers who rescue people.

"Water Play" can help children:

- develop creative play;
- use play to work on feelings.

Water Play

Materials

- large basins
- plastic table cloth
- towels
- sea shells, stones
- toys: fish, people, boats
- squirt bottles

You can begin this activity by talking with the children about the underwater scenes from today's program. What did they see under the ocean? Some of the children might want to pretend about things that happen in the ocean by playing—in a basin—with water, sea shells, stones, and toys. You'll probably want to cover the play area with a plastic table cloth and have several towels available to clean up any spills. You could have the children take turns using the water, or provide more basins with additional toys.

1589

Tatiana Vedeneeva, host of the Soviet Union's longest-running children's television program, visits Mister Rogers today. She brings a videotape with her that shows how people in the Soviet Union make matrouska dolls—the wooden dolls that "nest" inside one another. Mister Rogers makes up a song for Mrs. Vedeneeva.

"Nesting Toys" can help children:

● use play to work on feelings;

● develop coordination;

● work on feelings about separation.

Nesting Toys

Materials

● an assortment of objects that fit inside one another (coin purse, cosmetic bag, purse, tote bag, shopping bag, and a small toy that fits inside the smallest one)

● paper envelopes of several different sizes

● paper

● scissors

● markers

● cardboard

● glue

You can make a set of nesting toys by hiding a small object inside a coin purse and putting it inside a cosmetic bag that will fit inside an old purse. The purse can go inside a tote bag, and finally the tote bag can fit inside a shopping bag. Children can try to find the object by opening each bag and removing what is inside until they come to the toy. You can help them put the nesting materials back together again for the next time.

Different size envelopes can make a nesting game, too: The children can draw a tiny picture or make a small shape on a piece of paper or cardboard, put it inside the smallest envelope, and then continue placing each envelope in a larger one, perhaps putting their name on the largest one of all.

Your children may want to make up a song about how they feel when they work and play—a song about anything.

1590

Mister Rogers shows a videotape of people who work at night. In the Neighborhood of Make-Believe, a creature from the night sky helps the neighbors learn that some feelings are shared by all.

"A Pretend Language" can help children:

● learn to listen carefully;

● learn different ways people communicate.

A Pretend Language

Materials

● globe or map of the world (optional)

You might want to talk with the children about different languages. Do any of the children speak or understand another language? If you know some words in another language, can you share them with the children?

Do they know what language children in the Soviet Union speak? (If you have a globe or map of the world, you might want to show the children the United States and the Soviet Union.) You can ask the children what they would do if they could not understand the language someone was using. Can they think of other ways they could communicate? How about facial expressions or gestures?

You could talk with the children in the me-thee-me-thee language they heard on the program today. Can they tell what you are saying to them? They might like to talk to you in this pretend language and see if you can guess what *they* are saying. Or, you could sing a favorite song using me-thee-me-thee talk—for instance, "Twinkle, Twinkle, Little Star."

Thoughts For The Week

It takes time for children to come to understand that they can affect other people's feelings by being kind or unkind. Adults can help children learn that being kind means trying to understand how other people feel.

Being kind to oneself is something people need to learn early in life, too. Exercising is one way to be kind to our bodies. Taking good care of ourselves is very important. Children learn to take good care of themselves when they know that someone is taking good care of them. As caregivers, you have the great opportunity of showing your kindness through the care you give to children each day.

Fred Rogers

Songs On The Programs This Week

1591   "You Are Special"
        "Mimus Polyglottos"
        "One and One Are Two"

1592   "O.C.S."
        "Sleep Little Baby Sleep"

1593   "O.C.S."
        "You've Got To Do It"
        "I'm Taking Care of You"

1594   "What Do You Think Is Important?"
        "Troglodytes Aedon"

1570   "Everybody's Fancy"
        "It's You I Like"

Special Visits

1591   *How People Make Garden Hoes*
        How People Make Harmonicas

1592   *The Luray Caverns*

1570   *How People Make Bicycle Helmets*

Your Notes For The Week

1591

Mister Rogers brings a harmonica to the Neighborhood. He begins to watch a videotape that is supposed to be about harmonicas, but he realizes he has the wrong tape. This one is about how hoes are made. He decides to watch it, even though it is not what he expected. Mr. McFeely brings the right videotape and Mister Rogers reassures him that everyone makes mistakes. In the Neighborhood of Make-Believe, King Friday is being unkind, and the neighbors are getting angry about it.

"Pocket Comb Harmonica" can help children:

- develop creative play;
- express feelings through music.

Pocket Comb Harmonica

Materials

- new or clean pocket combs
- waxed paper

Help the children fold a small piece of waxed paper over the comb and show them how to hum through the teeth of the comb to make a kazoo-like sound. You can encourage them to play music that expresses different feelings. For instance, ask them to:

- play music that makes them feel happy;
- play something that sounds sad;
- make angry music with the harmonica;
- show what it would sound like if they were lonely.

Then you might want to play a song together — one of Mister Rogers' songs, or another familiar tune they all know.

(Or, 1134 "Shoe Box Harp.")

1592

Jazz saxophonist, Eric Kloss, who is blind, and Betty Aberlin guide Mister Rogers through the Luray Caverns in Virginia. Deep in the limestone caverns, they play the song "Won't You Be My Neighbor?"

"Let's Explore" can help children:

- learn to look carefully;
- learn more about the world;
- recognize likeness and difference.

Let's Explore

Materials

- a role of wide masking tape or clear, self-adhesive paper
- paper bags

You and the children could take a nature walk around your neighborhood, gathering various interesting things along the way. You might talk with the children about the things they could look for, such as leaves, small sticks, a little acorn, tiny stones, or a feather.

You can give each child a paper bag to hold the collections during the walk and then make a nature hanging when you get back to the house. You could ask the children to close their eyes and try to identify the different objects by feeling them. Can they tell you which ones are smooth and which are rough? What other clues help them identify the objects?

One way to display the objects you've collected is to give each child a small sheet of clear, self-adhesive paper. Most light-weight objects will stick to the paper. Another way to make a nature collage is to give each child a small stick with strips of masking tape hanging from it. Here again, the tape will hold a variety of light-weight objects.

(Or, 1411 "Boxes Inside Boxes.")

1593

An exercise teacher and her students show Mister Rogers some jump-rope techniques. In the Neighborhood of Make-Believe, Prince Tuesday is unhappy because King Friday is taking him out of school and giving him a private tutor. Back in the real neighborhood, Mr. McFeely finds a lost kitten. He calls the telephone number on the collar tag and tells the owner that he will be right over with the kitten.

"Jump Over" can help children:

- develop coordination;
- develop muscle control.

Jump Over

Materials

- masking tape
- jump rope

After doing some warm-up exercises such as stretching as high as they can, jumping up and down, or bending down and touching their toes, the children might want to play a game of "Jump Over." There are many variations to this game, but basically the children try to jump over a rope without touching it. For very young children, you might just place a piece of masking tape on the floor and see if the children can jump over the tape without landing on it. Older children could first try to hop over a jump rope lying on the floor, then try to jump over it when you and another child hold it about an inch off the floor. Once the children become skillful at jumping over the rope, you could try holding it a little higher off the ground, or place two pieces of masking tape on the floor about six inches apart and see if the children can jump over both pieces with one jump.

(Or, 1170 "All Kinds of Exercise";
1248 "Magic Exercises.")

1594

Mr. McFeely brings a film about how people make bicycle safety helmets. Tap dancer Tommy Tune arrives in the Neighborhood to become Prince Tuesday's tutor.

"Keeping Yourself Safe" can help children:

- talk about feelings;
- learn about limits.

Keeping Yourself Safe

Materials

- none

You might talk with the children about the reasons people wear bicycle safety helmets. Can they tell you about things they do to help keep themselves safe? For instance:

- wearing car seat belts or riding in a car safety seat;
- holding a grownup's hand while crossing the street;
- staying in the yard while they're playing;
- picking up toys so people don't trip over them.

Children sometimes worry about being safe, so you can take this time to reassure them that you will help keep them safe. That's one thing adults are to do: help keep children safe. This might lead to a conversation about why you have to know where they are and what they are doing. You could end today's activity by talking with the children about the word "safe." What does it mean to be safe? Can they think of a game like tag or baseball where people are "safe" when they touch base? You could play a simple game of "safety tag" where you are the "safe base." Once children tag you, they are "safe." You may need to be sensitive to the children who have difficulty tagging someone. You might have to choose a new person to be "it," even if no one has been caught.

1595

Mister Rogers shows a paper crown that someone made for him and visits with a friend who plays an accordion. In the Neighborhood of Make-Believe, Tommy Tune enchants everyone with his dancing and his kindness—even King Friday who has been unkind all week long.

"Royal Dancing" can help children:

- express feelings through movement;
- develop creative play;
- try out different roles.

Royal Dancing

Materials

- dress-up clothes
- paper crowns
  (See program 1267 "Headbands That Fit")
- music

Do any of the children want to make paper crowns that they can wear while they're dancing? You can decorate them with "jewels" cut from shiny paper, or sprinkle glitter over a pattern made from liquid glue. (Be sure to shake off the excess glitter before the children wear their crowns.) If you have dress-up clothes that can be used as royal robes, your children might want to wear these as they prepare for their royal dance. (You may have to tape up the hems so the children won't trip while they're dancing.) You might suggest that one way to be kind is to help each other getting into the dress-up clothes. Can one child hold a "robe" while another person puts his or her arms in the sleeve?

Try to find some kind of "majestic" music, either from your record collection or from something on the radio, and encourage the children to dance along with the music. They might pretend to be kings and queens at a royal ball. Later the children might try to dance to other kinds of music. How were their dances similar? How were they different?

Thoughts For The Week

Children often think that the grown-up world is full of hidden secrets. Pretending about being grown-up can be a way for them to handle their curiosity about adults. Weddings, in particular, are fascinating for children. This is partly because of the ritual, ceremony, and festivities, and also because at one time or another, most children have fantasies about marrying their moms or dads. Encouraging play about weddings can be an important way to help children understand the realities of their relationships to their parents.

Secrets often hold a great appeal for children. One reason is that keeping a secret can give a child a very special feeling of holding something all to oneself. Yet there are some secrets that children should not keep, particularly when those secrets make a child feel uncomfortable. Those are the times when children need a trusting adult to confide in.

Fred Rogers

Songs On The Programs This Week

1597   *"Then Your Heart Is Full of Love"*
1599   *"The Truth Will Make Me Free"*
        "Sometimes"
1600   *"Birthday Song"*
        "There Are Many Ways"

Special Visits

1596   *An Underground House*
1598   *A Marble Sculptor, Allen Dwight*
1599   *A Blind Artist, Crist Delmonico*
1600   *How People Make Suitcases*

Your Notes For The Week

1596

Mister Rogers and Mr. McFeely visit an underground house, a home hidden from view because it's built in a hillside. In the Neighborhood of Make-Believe, Mr. McFeely delivers sand to Westwood for the building of a secret sandbox. Mister Rogers shows a plastic egg with a toy chick inside and says that it's no secret where human babies come from.

"An Underground House" can help children:

● develop creative play.

An Underground House

Materials

● wet sand or soil
● small boxes or cardboard tubes
● miniature life figures (optional)

You could begin this activity by talking about houses and homes. Can the children tell you how the underground home they saw on the program is similar to their own homes? How is it different? You might suggest that one of the unique aspects of the underground home is that it doesn't really look like a home because it is hidden under the earth. Can they tell you any advantages to having an underground house? For instance, the house stays warmer in the winter and cooler in the summer. What kinds of things wouldn't they like about living underground?

The children might want to make an underground house outdoors in the sandbox, or in an area where you allow them to dig in the soil. (If the weather is not suitable, you could substitute modeling dough and allow them to do this activity indoors.) Providing small cardboard boxes and tubes will enable them to make fairly sturdy houses that won't cave in. Younger children can use the cardboard boxes just as they are, but older children might want to connect several boxes and tubes together to make more elaborate homes. Once the houses are selected or assembled, the children can wet the sand or soil and mold it over the roof of the house. You could talk about leaving openings for light and doors for coming and going.

(Or, 1191 "Camouflage.")

1597

Mr. McFeely has planned a treasure hunt for Mister Rogers. The "treasure" is a visit from a balloon artist. In the Neighborhood of Make-Believe, Lady Elaine mistakes a ring balloon for an engagement ring.

"Treasure Hunt" can help children:

- develop healthy curiosity;
- learn to look carefully.

Treasure Hunt

Materials

- paper
- pencil

You could prepare secret messages for your own treasure hunt today and hide them around the house for the children to find. Each message should give a clue about where to find the next one. For younger children, you'll probably want to make the message straightforward, such as "Look under the record player," but for older children you can disguise the message in the form of a riddle. For instance, you could write, "Singing and dancing are great fun. Look for the music to find the next one." You'll have to read the messages to preschool children; and you may also have to help them think about what the riddle could mean.

There are several ways to organize the seeking and finding. You might assign one child to find the clue, encouraging him or her to ask for help when needed. Or, pair the children with a partner, and let each set of children look for a clue.

(Or, 1062 "Secret Envelopes.")

1598

Mister Rogers shows how an invisible-ink pen works. Mr. McFeely brings him a marble sculpture and a videotape of an artist sculpting a figure from a piece of marble. In the Neighborhood of Make-Believe, Lady Elaine makes secret plans, assuming that the balloon ring from Chuck Aber is an engagement ring.

"Secret Messages" can help children:

- develop healthy curiosity;
- learn more about the world.

Secret Messages

Materials

- a bar of white soap
- knife
- white paper
- soft lead pencils

Cut the bar of soap into chunky strips about an inch wide so the children can use pieces of it like crayons. With your help, older children can write actual messages with the soap. Younger children can draw symbols or use scribbles to write pretend messages. The soap does not show up on the white paper, so the message remains a secret until someone discovers it by rubbing across the paper with a soft lead pencil. If the messages don't appear at first, you may have to help the children press harder with the side of the pencil lead. Some children might want to decipher their own messages; others might like to trade messages to see what someone else has written.

1599

Mister Rogers plays the piano with his eyes closed. He visits a blind artist, Crist Delmonico, and watches him paint. In the Neighborhood of Make-Believe, Lady Elaine announces her plans to marry—much to the surprise of the prospective groom, Chuck Aber. Mister Rogers explains that children do not grow up and marry their parents.

"Cover Your Eyes" can help children:

- understand and accept individual differences;
- develop the ability to keep on trying.

Cover Your Eyes

Materials

- pencil
- paper
- box or grocery bag
- blindfold

Wearing a blindfold made from a scarf or piece of fabric, the children could try to complete several everyday tasks. (Younger children may prefer closing their eyes over wearing a blindfold.) Encourage the children to cover or close their eyes as they do one of the following:

- button a sweater;
- put on a hat;
- sweep the floor;
- work a puzzle.

Which things did they find easiest to do? Which ones were hardest? Take some time to talk with the children about the paintings Mr. Delmonico made even though he could not see what he was painting. Older children might want to try drawing a picture on a piece of paper that you have placed inside a box or paper bag. What do they find difficult about drawing when they can't see the paper? How can they tell where the edge of the paper is? You could talk about how difficult it is to do things without being able to see—but also talk about how people can learn to do many things by practicing and trying over and over again.

1600

Mister Rogers decodes an invisible-ink message from Mr. McFeely. In the Neighborhood of Make-Believe, Lady Elaine comes to realize that Chuck Aber was not asking her to marry him. She says that sometimes she only hears what she wants to hear. Mister Rogers discovers a hidden travel alarm clock that carries a message about a surprise party.

"Thank-You Messages" can help children:

- learn different ways people communicate;
- recognize and use symbols.

Thank-You Messages

Materials

- paper
- pencils, markers, or crayons
- envelopes

You might begin today's activity by talking with the children about messages. Can they tell you what a message is or give you some examples of messages they have received from someone? You can talk about telephone messages and other spoken messages (e.g., "Tell Grandma I said 'Hi!'.") as well as printed or written messages.

With your help, the children can write thank-you messages to someone who has done something special for them. These might include:

- thanking their parents for taking care of them;
- thanking the letter carrier for delivering mail each day;
- thanking the grocer for being friendly and helpful;
- thanking a crossing guard or police officer for helping the children in the neighborhood.

Younger children could dictate the words for you to write down; older children may be able to copy words or sign their own names. Some children might like to make small drawings to enclose with their messages.

(Or, 1336 "Find the Timer"; 1545 "A Pretend Wedding.")

Thoughts For The Week

Most games arise from an inner need—a need of our developing self. Peek-a-boo and hide and seek have always fascinated little children. That's because practicing little separations—and returns—makes the task of handling long ones more manageable. A game is often an important "growing" service.

*One parent I know got fed up at the way her daughter kept throwing her spoon off her high chair tray—until she realized her daughter was trying to initiate a **game** with her. Once she understood how important "drop and fetch" was to her daughter, she didn't feel so annoyed at having to retrieve that spoon again and again...another form of peek-a-boo and hide and seek.*

*As children get older, their games take more skill and practice. Self-confidence comes with success—by trying and practicing and getting better. Yet children also need to know that while most of us can become accomplished at something, no one can be good at **everything**. When it comes to helping children feel good about themselves, cheering their efforts is just as important as applauding their triumphs.*

Fred Rogers

Songs On The Programs This Week
1602   "It's You I Like"
1603   "You Are Special"

Special Visits
1601   Folksingers Andy Holiner and Alice Johnson

1602   Soccer Players at Practice

1603   Special Olympians

1604   Basketball Player, Suzie McConnell Dance Alloy Members

1605   Bowling Alley

Your Notes For The Week

1601

Mister Rogers and Mr. McFeely try on different hats today. Mister Rogers explains that hats can be fun to wear and to pretend with, nevertheless, the person underneath is still the same person with or without the hat. In the Neighborhood of Make-Believe, Queen Sara provides hats for everyone to wear just for fun, but King Friday says he doesn't feel like wearing one: He likes to have fun in other ways. Mister Rogers visits folk musicians Andy Holiner and Alice Johnson who are having a sing-along with a group of children.

"Paper Bag Hats" can help children:
* develop creative play.

Paper Bag Hats

Materials
* medium-sized paper bags
* scissors
* glue
* yarn
* construction paper
* markers
* mirror

A plain paper bag can serve as the basis for a variety of hats, and you might talk with the children about the kind of hats they'd like to make.

To make a wig-type hat, the bag needs to fit the child's head fairly snugly. Cut out the front of the bag to frame the child's face, leaving several inches along the top across the forehead. You can make "hair" by cutting the paper into thin strips all the way around. If a child wants to have curly hair, you can roll the strips of paper around a pencil to make them curl. Some children may want to add flowers, ribbon, bows, or other decorations.

A medium-sized paper bag turned inside out, with a cuff on the outside, can be the start for as fancy a hat as you like. You can scrunch the bags into any shape and fasten loops of yarn around it. If you want, you can decorate the hats with markers, or dab them with glue and stick on fabric scraps, buttons, or just about anything else.

When the hats are finished, the children might enjoy looking at themselves in a mirror. You might remind them that changing the way we look doesn't change the people we are inside.

1602

Mister Rogers visits a soccer team at practice and learns some of the basic rules of soccer. In the Neighborhood of Make-Believe, Daniel Tiger is feeling left out because he is not on a team.

"Kick Ball" can help children:

* develop coordination.

Kick Ball

Materials

* a large ball sturdy enough for kicking

How did the children think Daniel Tiger felt when everyone else was talking about the team? Can they think of a time when they felt left out? What helped them feel better? They might also want to talk about how Randy Caribou felt when he accidentally stepped on the cake for the soccer party. Can they think of a time when they accidentally knocked something over while playing? What did they do about it?

You'll probably want to do today's activity outdoors. You can explain that when people kick a ball, they can knock things over or break things, so they need to have a safe place to play. Older children might want to talk about teams and then divide into two groups so they can kick the ball back and forth. Younger children often find it hard to wait, so you might want to have several balls…or make sure they have something else to do until it's their turn.

(Or, 1332 "Hide and Seek.")

1603

Mister Rogers shows a group of baskets and talks about the uses of each one. He visits a practice session for the Special Olympics and watches the children doing the broad jump, walking the balance beam, and doing push-ups. In the Neighborhood of Make-Believe, King Friday tells why he doesn't like to play games: As a young prince, he was often left out.

"Walking the Line" can help children:

* develop coordination;
* develop the ability to keep on trying.

Walking the Line

Materials

* a long piece of string or masking tape
* tape to fasten the string
* chalk (optional)

You can make a type of balance beam for the children to practice walking on by taping a long piece of string or masking tape on the floor. (If you prefer, you could do this activity outdoors by drawing a line on a sidewalk.) Show the children how to go carefully along the line by placing your feet heel to toe as you walk. When they try, they might need to hold your hand at first. This activity takes some practice, so you might want to try it again from time to time. You'll probably find the children get better and better at it—something you could point out to them.

When the children seem ready, they might want to try walking backwards or sideways on the line, or you could make walking the line part of an obstacle course that might include jumping over a rope, hopping in a circle, throwing a ball in a basket, and crawling through a large box that is open at both ends.

(Or, 1398 "Bean Bag Toss"; 1448 "All About Baskets"; 1495 "Walk, Crawl, and Hop.")

1604

Mister Rogers demonstrates a game based on the Neighborhood of Make-Believe and explains that games don't play themselves: People have to play them. Olympic gold medalist Suzie McConnell visits Mister Rogers and gives him a basketball lesson in the back yard. In the Neighborhood of Make-Believe, the players realize that no one has asked X and Hen to be on the team, so they invite them to join in.

"Spin the Number" can help children:

- practice working cooperatively;
- practice taking turns.

Spin the Number

Materials

- cardboard or heavy paper
- markers
- scissors
- brass paper fastener

The directions for making a game spinner are in the "How To" section of your book (page B-1). Once you have a spinner, you and the children can make up any number of games using it. For instance:

- Spin a number and jump that number of times;
- Spin a number and find that number of toy cars;
- Bounce a ball or clap hands the number of times the spinner shows.

Do the children have other ideas for playing this game? Older children might want to make a type of board game to use with the spinner. They could draw a path of some sort on a large piece of cardboard and divide it into small sections (at least 25) and use toy cars or small blocks as playing pieces. They can take turns spinning a number and moving their tokens the number of times shown on the spinner.

1605

Mister Rogers and Mr. McFeely visit a bowling alley and practice bowling. Bob Trow shows them how the pins are set up, and they watch a bowling lesson. In the Neighborhood of Make-Believe, the players decide to play hide and seek. Lady Elaine declares herself the winner, but learns that they *all* are winners because everyone had fun.

"Bowling" can help children:

- practice working cooperatively;
- practice taking turns;
- develop coordination.

Bowling

Materials

- empty plastic soda bottles or clean milk cartons (an uneven number)
- plastic ball or sock ball
- masking tape

You can make your own set of bowling pins from empty plastic soda bottles or clean milk cartons. A small plastic ball makes a good bowling ball for young children. Or, you can make a softer ball by rolling old socks together and stuffing them inside one another until you get a ball the size you want. At first you'll probably have to help the children set up the bowling "pins." The game works best if you arrange the pins in a triangle, much the way regular bowling pins are arranged, because when children knock over one bottle in that arrangement, the others are more likely to fall down as well. It can help, too, to put a small piece of tape on the floor to show the children where to stand while rolling the ball toward the pins. Older children might want to keep score on a piece of paper. Do their scores change with practice?

Thoughts For The Week

There's a musical mini-series in the Neighborhood of Make-Believe this week. "Josephine the Short-Neck Giraffe" is the story of a young giraffe who is unhappy with her short neck and yearns for one that is long and graceful—the kind all other giraffes have. This story has special meaning for anyone—child or adult—who has ever felt unhappy about being "different."

Pretending is one of the ways children can come to feel comfortable about who they are. In play, they can "become" someone else for a while, someone else with different characteristics and motives. They can try out a variety of roles; and, with the help of a trusted adult, they can sort out reality from fantasy and perhaps come to feel better about who they really are.

Every one of us has characteristics that make us different from everyone else. We can all learn to value ourselves and each other as individuals, capable of finding fulfillment in life and capable of giving and receiving in very special ways. That's what Josephine the Short-Neck Giraffe finally does. She's finally able to sing "I'm Glad I'm The Way I Am."

Fred Rogers

Special Visits

1606   *"I'm Glad I'm The Way I Am"*
1607   *"Perfect Day"*
1608   *"For A Year and A Day"*
        "We Are Elephants"
        "Make Her Smile"
        "It's No Use"
1609   *"We Are Elephants"*
        "Promise"
        "You're Much More"
        "Attractive, Active Animals"
1610   *Songs from the musical mini-series*

Special Visits

1606   *San Diego Wild Animal Park*
1607   *A Lab Where People Develop Film*

Your Notes For The Week

1606

Mister Rogers visits the San Diego Wild Animal Park where a guide shows him live giraffes, elephants, tigers and other animals. In the Neighborhood of Make-Believe, the neighbors are preparing for a musical mini-series about a giraffe named Josephine who is unhappy with her short neck.

"Spool Animals" can help children:

● develop imagination;

● develop creative play.

Spool Animals

Materials

● spools

● pipe cleaners or yarn

● construction paper

● glue

Today the children might want to pretend about some of the animals they saw on the program. Here are a few suggestions for turning empty thread spools into toy animals that children can use in their play:

● Turn the spool sideways to suggest an animal's body and wrap it with pipe cleaners or yarn in colors suggested by the children.

● Wrap pipe cleaners around the spool, next to the front and back rims, twisting them underneath to keep them tight, then spreading them out to make legs and paws.

● You can make a tail and whiskers by pushing five pipe cleaners through the hole of a large spool. (If you make one of the pipe cleaners a red one, it can also serve as a tongue.) The pipe cleaners should stick out about an inch or so at one end for whiskers, with the rest sticking out at the other end for a tail. By twisting the long ends together, you'll have a tail. After drawing and cutting out the animal's head from paper, you can push the pipe cleaners through the paper about where the nose should be. The children can help you spread out the ends to make whiskers and loop one of the pipe cleaners to form a tongue.

Do any of the children want to make a giraffe for their play? You can help them draw a head and a long or short neck, attaching it to the spool with glue or the pipe cleaners.

1607

Mister Rogers visits a film-processing plant to learn how people turn an unexposed roll of film into finished photographs. In the Neighborhood of Make-Believe, the neighbors continue their preparations for the mini-series, "Josephine the Short-Neck Giraffe."

"A Photograph of Me" can help children:

- learn more about growing;
- recognize and accept individual differences.

A Photograph of Me

Materials

- photos of the children (either ones you have taken or ones they bring from home)
- camera (optional)

You'll probably want to plan for this activity ahead of time by asking parents to bring in some fairly recent photos of their children. Or, you may have photographs that you have taken while the children were in your care. You can begin by asking the children what they can remember about the film showing people developing photographs. (If you know someone who has a dark room, you might arrange a brief visit to actually see film being developed. You might also use a camera that takes photographs and develops them in a few minutes.)

Once you have a set of pictures, let the children look at them and tell you who they see in the pictures. Do all the children look the same now as they do in the pictures? If not, you might talk about some of the changes. For instance, someone may have had a haircut…or lost a tooth. You might want to display the photographs for a few days. It would help if the photographs include parents and other family members. The children might want to talk about where their parents and others are and what they might be doing.

You may want to hold each child's photo up at group time and ask, "Whose picture is this?"

1608

The neighbors of Make-Believe present "Josephine the Short-Neck Giraffe." Today Josephine is feeling sad because her neck is so short. Her friend, Hazel Elephant, suggests that Josephine might want to attend the School for Growing.

"Growing and Changing" can help children:

- learn more about growing;
- recognize and accept individual differences;
- feel proud of accomplishments.

Growing and Changing

Materials

- long strips of paper
- markers

You might begin today's discussion by talking about why Josephine is feeling sad. Can any of the children remember ever feeling sad about something? Your careful listening can help you learn more about that particular child. Can they tell you why they think Josephine was feeling sad?

You can continue by talking with the children about many different ways of growing. Can they tell you if they've grown taller than they were before? How do they know? Have they outgrown any clothing?

Maybe they can tell you about some "inside" ways of growing. For instance, they may have learned to do something new, such as:

- how to use the potty chair;
- how to dress themselves;
- how to ride a tricycle;
- how to use a fork;
- how to use a paint brush or how to glue a picture.

You might make a list of all the things they have learned to do recently. You could also start a record of the children's physical growth, by hanging strips of paper on the wall that show their height. They could take the strips home, or you could keep them for a record and measure them again in several months to see how they've grown. Through it all, it can be very helpful to stress the fact that inside growing is the most important of all.

Thursday

1609

In the Neighborhood of Make-Believe, the mini-series continues: Josephine and Hazel Elephant enroll in the School for Growing and encounter a snake who can't hiss, an elephant with stripes and a very shy boy giraffe named J.R.

"Animal Play" can help children:

- try out different roles;
- develop creative play;
- express feelings through movement and dance.

Animal Play

Materials

- records, tapes, or music from the radio

Do the children remember what kind of animals they have seen on the television program this week? See if they can show you how certain animals move. You might have them act out an animal and let the other children try to guess what the animal is. If you have records or tapes available, play some music and let the children pretend to be animals while they move to the music. Or, you could simply turn on the radio to find some appropriate music for this activity.

When the children are finished, see if they want to talk about the animals they pretended to be. What do they know about these animals? This could lead into other activities such as reading a story about animals, singing a song about animals, or playing with the spool animals that you made earlier in the week.

Friday

1610

The neighbors of Make-Believe continue to pretend about "Josephine the Short-Neck Giraffe." In their story, shy J.R. Giraffe helps Josephine learn to accept her neck the way it is, and Josephine helps J.R. feel more confident. The musical ends with everyone singing "I'm Glad I'm the Way I Am."

"I'm Glad I'm the Way I Am" can help children:

- understand and accept individual differences;
- feel proud of accomplishments;
- learn more about growing.

I'm Glad I'm The Way I Am

Materials

- paper
- markers

You might talk with the children about their reactions to today's program. You could ask questions such as:

- What did you think about that story?
- How do you think Josephine and J.R. felt at the end of the story?
- What do you think made them feel that way?

See if the children can tell you some things that they like about themselves and about others. How do those things make them feel? Can they tell you some reasons why they are glad they're the way they are and glad their friends are the way *they* are? You could write these down on a large piece of paper under each person's name…or, make a separate piece of paper for each child.

Thoughts for the Week

Wanting to be able to take good care of our children is a big part of why most parents leave them to go off to work. Of course, that can be hard for children to understand. They sometimes wonder why a person who loves them wouldn't want to be with them every minute. One of the things that caregivers can do is to assure children that their parents miss them when they are away from them and love them even when they can't be with them.

Part of growing is learning to cope with the strong feelings that come when a parent goes away. Sadness is one of those emotions, and that's the one we generally associate with partings. The other significant feeling at being left behind is anger. That one is not so often recognized or acknowledged, and it can have some delayed effects. Reunions often bring to the surface all the anger about their parents' having left them that children may have kept inside. Although adults tend to think of "hello" and "goodby" as opposites, children may treat them both as aspects of the same experience: being left behind by a loved one. A sensitive caregiver can help children handle the anger that comes with separation by talking with them about why people leave and what the feelings are that children have when parents leave—and come back again.

Fred Rogers

Songs On The Programs This Week

1611 *"Everybody's Fancy"*
     "There Are Many Ways"
     "We Are Elephants"
     "Nobody Likes It"

1612 *"There Are Many Ways"*
     "You Are Special"
     "When the Day Turns into Night"

1613 *"Something To Do While We're Waiting"*
     "I'm Taking Care of You"

1614 *"It's You I Like"*
     "You're Much More"
     "You Are Special"

1615 *"I Will Be Back"*

Special Visits

1613 *A Place Where People Make Peanut Butter*

1614 *Natasha, an Oboist*

1615 *Balloon Artist, Bruce Franco*

Your Notes For The Week

1611

At Negri's Music Shop, Joe's assistant, Helena, leaves to go home and care for her sick child. In the Neighborhood of Make-Believe, Prince Tuesday is angry because it seems like his parents are always going to work and never have much time to be with him.

"Telephone Talk" can help children:

• work on feelings about separation.

Telephone Talk

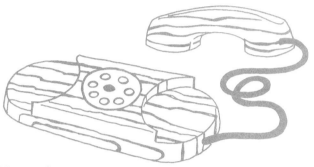

Materials

• one or two toy telephones
  (See 1270, "Telephones" for directions on how to make toy telephones.)

You might talk with the children about where their parents work and what kinds of things they do there. Can they think of a time when they felt the way Prince Tuesday feels—angry because their parents couldn't spend time with them? You could suggest that the children might have pretend telephone conversations with their parents. If you have several, you could provide toy telephones for their play. If not, you could demonstrate how to pretend that a wooden block can be a telephone receiver, and you could make a pretend call yourself. If you make the "phones" available on a regular basis, the children will be able to incorporate telephone play into their daily activities. Then, whenever children are missing their parents, they may want to pretend to talk with them and say how they're feeling.

1612

Mr. McFeely brings Mister Rogers some peanuts in their shells. They shell them and eat a few, then make a peanut butter treat. In the Neighborhood of Make-Believe, Princess Zelda arrives with a giant peanut and uses magic to make it disappear and reappear. Prince Tuesday wonders if the princess can make his mom and dad come back from work by magic.

"Where's The Peanut?" can help children:

- work on feelings about separation;
- develop memory.

Where's The Peanut

Materials

- three paper cups
- a bag of peanuts (in the shell)

You might begin today's activity by talking with the children again about how they feel when their parents go off to work. Recall the conversations from yesterday about where their parents work and what they do there. Once again, the children may need some reassurance that their parents will be coming back at the end of the day.

Then you can show the children the bag of peanuts and point out the different shapes and sizes of the peanuts. See if the children would like to play a game called "Where's the Peanut?" Ask them to close their eyes while you hide a peanut under one of the three paper cups, then see if the children can guess which cup is hiding the peanut. When the children have guessed correctly, let someone hide the peanut under a cup again. Playing peek-a-boo and hide-and-seek games give children a chance to control separations by being the ones to do the hiding and finding.

1613

Mr. McFeely brings a videotape that shows how people make peanut butter. In the Neighborhood of Make-Believe, Queen Sara is quite busy working to help hungry people. Prince Tuesday is still upset that his parents can't spend more time with him.

"Peanut Butter and Fruit" can help children:

- learn more about foods;
- practice working cooperatively.

Peanut Butter and Fruit

Materials

- peanut butter (see 1166 "Peanut Butter" for recipe)
- butter knives
- fruit (apples, bananas, pears)
- crackers

You might begin this activity by talking with the children about the different fruits you are using and helping them wash their hands since everyone will be handling the food. Let the children look at and hold the apples, pears or bananas and talk about how they look and feel and smell. Afterwards you can help the children decide how they want to divide the different jobs needed to make today's snack. For instance:

- one child can wash the apples or pears;
- another can dry the fruit or peel the bananas;
- a third can cut the banana into bite sized pieces while you slice the apple or pear;
- someone else can spread peanut butter on the fruit;
- other children can arrange the snack on a platter and serve it.

You might want to provide crackers along with the fruit for variety or just in case some children are hesitant to try peanut butter on fruit. The children might want to talk about the kinds of snacks they eat at home with their parents.

1614

Mister Rogers visits Joe Negri's Music Shop and talks with Natasha, an oboist who is also a parent. In the Neighborhood of Make-Believe, the neighbors are preparing for the Caring Center at Corney's factory.

"Working and Caring" can help children:

- work on feelings about separation;
- talk about feelings.

Working and Caring

Materials

- books or pictures showing various occupations
- paper
- markers
- assorted play props

You might begin by talking with the children about their parents' occupations or jobs. You can explain that sometimes parents have mixed feelings about their jobs—wanting to go to work, but also wanting to be with their children. You might mention that working is one of the ways that parents show they care about their children. You could tell them that you have a job as a day-care giver. If you have pictures of people working at various occupations, you can share those with the children. Then see if some of the children want to use the markers and paper to make pictures of their parents—either at work or at home— with them. Some of the children might want to pretend about the various jobs their parents hold. You could help the children gather or make the necessary props. For instance, you might put together a medical play box, or a restaurant kit, or a box containing office supplies that the children can use in their play.

(Or, 1380 "Going Down the Drain.")

1615

In the Neighborhood of Make-Believe, Prince Tuesday feels less angry with his working parents when he volunteers to help younger children at the factory's child-care center.

"The Caring Center" can help children:

- develop creative play;
- work on feelings about separation.

The Caring Center

Materials

- dolls, stuffed animals
- beds, blankets
- baby bottles

Today you could help the children make a Caring Center for the dolls and stuffed animals. You might talk with them about what children need when their parents are at work. What do they like to do at day care? How does the caregiver take care of them? What do parents do to show they care for their children?

You can let the children pretend to be caregivers for the stuffed animals or dolls. Ask them what they need to set up a Caring Center (beds, toys, blankets, baby bottles). Some of the children might want to talk about pets they have at home and ways they care for their pets. If you have a pet in your home, you might allow the children to help care for that animal, too.

Thoughts For The Week

Taking good care of the earth is one way children can learn to take good care of themselves, and there are so many ways they can help care for the earth and its resources. When children make toys from cast-offs around the house, for instance, they are actually recycling. Adults who spend time with children can, by example, help them learn about conserving resources. One of the best gifts we can give children is the experience of being in households where people use resources wisely. That's a gift that will never wear out.

Fred Rogers

Songs On The Programs This Week

1617   *"I Like to Take Care of You"*
1618   *"You Are Special"*
1619   *"Did You Know?"*
       "Come On and Wake Up"
       "Everybody's Fancy"
1620   *"I'm Proud of You"*

Special Visits

1617   *A Recycling Center*
1618   *Leo Sewell, A Sculptor*
1619   *Snorkling with Sylvia Earle*

Your Notes For The Week

Monday

1616

Mr. McFeely is worried that there's too much garbage in the community dump so, he reminds Mister Rogers to *think* before throwing anything away. Mister Rogers finds a clean paper bag on his sidewalk and uses it to play "bagball."

"Bagball" can help children:

- develop coordination;
- learn about conservation.

Bagball

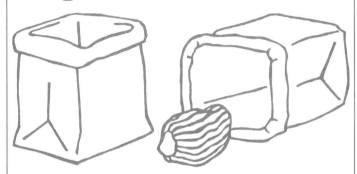

Materials

- an empty paper grocery bag
- soft stuffed ball

To make Mister Rogers' version of bagball, fold down the top edge of an empty grocery bag about one inch all around. That way, the bag will stand up fairly well by itself. The children can take turns tossing a lightweight stuffed ball into the bag. If the bag falls over they can bowl the ball into the bag. You could even use a pair of socks that have been rolled into a ball or a small plastic bag stuffed with clean rags. If you have several paper bags, each child could have a bag and ball.

You might want to talk with the children about other uses for an empty paper grocery bag. You could make a list of the ideas and ask each child to "recycle" a bag from home by bringing it in sometime this week to try out the different ideas.

1617

Mr. McFeely takes Mister Rogers to a recycling center where they see what happens to discarded bags, bottles, and cans. In the Neighborhood of Make-Believe, there's too much garbage, and the dump at Some Place Else is full. When the neighbors learn that the Westwood dump is also full, everyone becomes concerned about where to put the garbage.

"Milk Carton Haulers" can help children:

- develop creative play;
- learn more about conservation.

Milk Carton Haulers

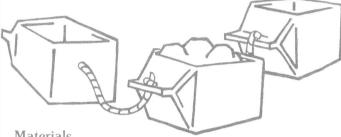

Materials

- clean, empty milk cartons
- heavy string or cord
- scissors
- stapler

Do the children know what recycling means? You might talk with them about things we can do to recycle some of the things we use. For instance, empty paper milk cartons can be washed and used to make toys for creative play. You can suggest making milk carton wagons that the children can use for hauling pretend trash (or anything else, for that matter). Here's the procedure:

- First, staple the top closed and attach a piece of heavy string or cord to the closed top portion.
- Then cut out one of the four side panels and turn the carton on its side to make an open wagon.

The children could use these wagons as part of their play today. Some of the children might choose to play about hauling discarded objects to a pretend dump. Younger children might simply use the haulers for filling and dumping an assortment of small toys.

1618

Mr. McFeely brings a film of his visit with Leo Sewell who makes sculptures from throw-away things people don't need anymore. In the Neighborhood of Make-Believe, the neighbors send a message to the Goats of Northwood, asking for help with their garbage problem.

"Recycling Projects" can help children:

- learn more about conservation;
- learn to do things independently.

Recycling Projects

Materials

- assorted discarded items such as paper towel rolls, plastic milk caps, string, ribbon, used wrapping paper, empty boxes
- glue
- scissors

You might begin this activity by talking with the children about ways they can reuse or recycle boxes, paper, and cardboard. What ideas do the children have? You can suggest that each child create something from the discarded objects you've collected. The children might want to try one of the following:

- making a collage by gluing objects onto heavy paper or cardboard;
- making a sculpture by gluing together boxes and tubes, then decorating it with ribbon, string, or pieces of scrap paper;
- turning empty paper milk cartons into toy vehicles or blocks (see 1617 or page B-1);
- using empty plastic milk cartons as bins for storing crayons or toys by cutting off the tops and covering the cut edges with masking tape.

When you talk with the parents about your recycling projects, you might want to ask for their help in collecting small, discarded things that you can use for future art or craft projects. The children could help set up a place where these things can be stored.

1619

Mister Rogers visits a deep-sea diver and talks about "dumping" things into the sea. In the Neighborhood of Make-Believe, everyone is still looking for a solution to the trash problem.

"Underwater Pictures" can help children:

● develop imagination;

● learn about conservation.

Underwater Pictures

Materials

● crayons

● paper

● watercolors and brushes

What do the children think about the problems people are having in the Neighborhood of Make-Believe? You might spend some time talking with them about their ideas for a solution. What do they think of Lady Elaine's idea of throwing things into the ocean? The children might want to talk about the deep-sea diver and the beautiful ocean scenery. They might even be able to show you how they would move if they were fish themselves.

How about making undersea pictures today? Some of the children may have very clear ideas about what they want to make. Others may need your assistance to recall some of the things they saw in the underwater scenes. Using crayons and paper, the children could draw whatever they want and then cover the picture with a watercolor wash. (A little food coloring in water will work, too.) The watercolor won't stick to the waxy crayon, and the colors and drawings will show through as if they are underwater.

(Or, 1534 "Aquarium Pictures.")

1620

Mister Rogers uses a discarded box as the basis for a television puppet stage for homemade puppets. In the Neighborhood of Make-Believe, the Goats of Northwood help the neighbors find a solution to the garbage problem.

"A Television Stage" can help children:

● develop creative play;

● learn more about conservation.

A Television Stage

Materials

● discarded cardboard box

● discarded spools, bottle caps, tubes, string

● puppets

● tape

● glue

● felt-tipped markers

● knife or heavy-duty scissors

You can show the discarded objects you've collected and talk with the children about how each thing might have been used before being discarded. Can they think of ways to reuse some of the objects?

Some of the children may want to help you turn an empty cardboard box into a television stage for the puppets. First turn the box on its side with the opening at the back. The children could help you draw a "screen" on one side, but you'd better be the one to cut the shape out with a sharp knife or heavy-duty scissors. Then let the children tape or glue discarded caps onto the box to serve as knobs and buttons. They can attach tubes to the top as "antennae" and decorate the box with markers if they wish.

You can either open the back of the box or cut a hole in the bottom of the television to insert the puppets. (In the latter case, you'll probably want to tape the back flaps closed.) If you want the children to be "on television," open the back of the box and let them kneel behind the screen as they talk to the audience.

Thoughts For The Week

Some children see their dads daily: it may even be their father who provides the primary care in their household. Other children see their fathers only occasionally, if at all, but even children who have had no contact with their fathers are likely to have fantasies about who that person is. In the programs this week, we focus on fathers as nurturers, and the ways that dads pass on values and interests, such as music. We can never tell how—or if—such interests as a love of music will pass down the generations, yet it's often those interests of fathers that leave lasting memories as children grow older. Helping children appreciate the many ways fathers give care is an important way of helping them understand what love is all about.

Fred Rogers

Songs On The Programs This Week

1621 *"Something To Do While We're Waiting"*
1622 *"I Like To Take Care of You"*
"Everybody's Fancy"
1624 *"Everybody's Shy Sometimes"*
1625 *"Ornithorynchus Anatinus"*
"Mimus Polyglottos"

Special Visits

1621 *Mister Rogers Visits with the Marsalis Family*
1622 *How People Make Bandages*
1625 *Mister Rogers Visits Yo-Yo Ma and his Son*
Mister Rogers' Son and Grandson Visit

Your Notes For The Week

1621

Mister Rogers remembers what it was like when he was a child and saw someone wearing a bandage: He wondered what was underneath the bandage. Sometimes when he got hurt, his father would put a bandage on him and let him look underneath the bandage to see what was there.

"What's Under The Bandage" can help children:

- learn more about body parts;
- develop creative play.

What's Under The Bandage?

Materials

- an old sheet or several old pillow cases
- scissors

Playing with pretend bandages is one way children can be reassured that bandages don't change what's underneath. To make a supply of play bandages, you can cut an old sheet or pillowcase into long strips about three inches wide and three feet long. The children can help hold the material, but you will probably have to cut the strips.

You can begin the activity by wrapping a strip of cloth around your own arm like a bandage and letting a child unwind it and take it off to see that your arm is still underneath. If the children feel comfortable about it, you could wrap a part of their body—an elbow, knee or foot—and let them unwrap the bandage. Or, give them the bandages and let them wrap up a leg or foot for themselves. They can wear the bandages for a while and have some pretending. When finished, you could help them unwind the bandages to see that their bodies are still intact. While you and the children are bandaging and unwrapping, it might be helpful for you to name the various body parts. For instance, you could say something like:

- I'm wrapping Jason's **knee.**
- Janie is bandaging her **elbow.**
- See, Jason's **heel** is still under the bandage.

(Or, 1311 "Talking about Waiting"; 1436 "What's Under the Scarf?")

1622

Mister Rogers brings a rag doll and talks about pretending with dolls. Later he makes a bed for the doll and pretends the doll isn't feeling well. In the Neighborhood of Make-Believe, Prince Tuesday and his father pretend that a doll comes to life. The neighbors are trying to cheer up Ana Platypus who is wearing a bandage on her sore paw.

"A Doll Hospital" can help children:

- develop creative play;
- use play to work on feelings.

A Doll Hospital

Materials
- dolls
- stuffed animals
- medical kit
- bandages
- boxes
- small pillows
- pieces of fabric or doll blankets

The children could use the bandages from yesterday's activity to pretend about having a doll hospital. You might begin this activity by talking with the children about what it feels like to be sick or to be hurt. Can any of them remember a time when they didn't feel well, or when they had a sore finger or leg? Can they tell you about it?

As you hold the doll or stuffed animal, you could see if any of the children want to pretend that the doll is hurt or sick. You could pass the doll around and ask the children to show how they would hold a sick baby. Can they tell you what they could do to help the doll get better? Other children might want to pretend the doll has a broken leg and bandage it. If you provide a few boxes, small pillows, and pieces of fabric, the children can create a hospital for their dolls and stuffed animals and continue playing on their own.

1623

Mister Rogers uses a vacuum sweeper to clean the rug and remembers how, when he was a boy, he wondered if the vacuum cleaner could sweep people up into it. He reassures his television friends that we can never go up the sweeper, just like we can never go down the drain. Later, Mister Rogers learns more about wolves when an animal lover and a wolf named Shaman stop by for a visit.

"Sweeping The Carpet" can help children:

- feel comfortable asking about things;
- talk about feelings.

Sweeping The Carpet

Materials
- vacuum cleaner
- empty vacuum cleaner bag

You might want to begin this activity by talking with the children about Mr. Rogers' boyhood fears. You can talk about the differences in size between a person and a small toy, and you could show them an empty vacuum cleaner bag, explaining that the bag holds the dirt or other little items that are swept into the cleaner until an adult empties or replaces the bag.

When it's time to clean up, you might let the children help you with the vacuuming. Having a chance to turn the sweeper on and off can make the machine less scary to them because they can control the sound that it makes. Very young children might just want to pretend about sweeping the floor by running the sweeper without turning on the motor, or by using a toy vacuum cleaner.

1624

In the Neighborhood of Make-Believe, Lady Elaine is upset that Prince Tuesday brought a doll to life through make-believe. She worries that pretend wolves might come to life, too. When Lady Elaine meets Chuck Aber dressed in a wolf costume, Lady Aberlin helps her learn that no one can turn you into something you don't want to become.

"A Make-Believe Wolf" can help children:

- use play to work on feelings;
- understand that wishing can't make things happen;
- understand the difference between real and pretend.

A Make-Believe Wolf

Materials

- none

You might begin by asking the children to tell you what they think about Lady Elaine's fears. Have they ever been frightened by stories about a big bad wolf? You might want to reassure them that stories such as Little Red Riding Hood and The Three Little Pigs are just stories. You could encourage them to make up a story about a shy wolf. What would he say? How would he act? Then let several of the children take turns acting out the role of a shy wolf. Can they take on the role of a good wolf? If some of the children really want to be a mean wolf, you could let them show you what its face would look like, but you'll have to let them know that mean wolves can be pretty scary to the other children. You might even have to confine scary wolf play to a safe area—for instance, behind a puppet-theatre box, or within a "cage" made of cardboard boxes. The children will welcome the limits you set for scary play even though they may say otherwise. Other safe ways to play about scary wolves might be to draw pictures of them, or to make them the subject of stories you could write down or tape-record.

1625

In the Neighborhood of Make-Believe, King Friday is feeling fatherly about his son, Prince Tuesday, as well as his two pet birds, Mimus Polyglottos and Troglodytes Aedon.

"Fatherly Care" can help children:

- use play to work on feelings;
- try out different roles.

Fatherly Care

Materials

- none

If you remember him and are comfortable talking with the children about your own father, you might want to share with them some ways your father cared for you. The children, for their part, might want to talk about experiences they have had with their fathers. Can the children tell you some ways that fathers can care for their children? Fathers might do things like:

- tucking them in at night;
- packing a lunch for them;
- reading a story;
- bandaging a cut.

Some children might want to pretend to be fathers to the stuffed animals or dolls. Others might want to pretend to be a different kind of caring adult—and that's fine, too. If children never knew their fathers or are missing their fathers, it's important to give them a chance to talk about how they feel. Can they tell you about the other people who care for them (grandfathers, uncles, mothers, aunts, neighbors, grandmothers, friends)?

Thoughts For The Week

When it comes to our development as human beings, our mouths are one of our most important body parts. When we're babies, our mouths bring us nourishment, comfort, information, and the means to communicate and express feelings. Our mouths also bring us one of our first experiences of persistent pain—the pain of teething! And of course biting becomes an early primitive way of expressing anger and frustration. Learning to control the urge to bite is a very important task of early childhood.

Because we have such strong feelings about our mouths, it can be particularly difficult when someone like a dentist wants to use strange equipment to look around and probe our teeth and gums. We hope one of this week's outcomes will be to help children know what to expect during a dental exam.

Fred Rogers

Songs On The Programs This Week

1626 *"You Are Special"*

1627 *"We Would Like to Welcome You"*

1628 *"Let's Think of Something to Do While We're Waiting"*
"I'm Still Myself Inside"

1629 *"It's The Style to Wear a Smile"*

Special Visits

1628 *How People Make Toothbrushes*

1629 *A Visit to the Dentist's Office*

1630 *How A Steam Shovel Moves Earth*
How People Make Toothpaste

Your Notes For The Week

1626

Mister Rogers visits Brockett's Bakery where Chef Brockett is making "Gingerbread Brocketts" with happy, sad, or bored expressions. In the Neighborhood of Make-Believe, Lady Aberlin is bored because she doesn't have a real job. King Friday appoints her Director of Research and assigns her a special project: to do research on laughing.

"Gingerbread Faces" can help children:

● learn more about food;

● talk about feelings;

● practice working cooperatively.

Gingerbread Faces

Materials

● mirror

● gingerbread recipe and ingredients
(See page C-4.)

● bowls, mixing spoons, cookie sheets

● measuring cups and spoons

● raisins

You might begin this activity by talking with the children about feelings. Can they think of a time when they felt happy? Sad? Bored? Encourage them to show you how their faces look when they have those feelings. How do they look when they feel surprised? If possible, let them see their own expressions in a mirror. Of course not everyone who smiles is happy way down deep. A particularly sensitive child may mention that or you may want to help the children recognize that the outside of a person's face doesn't always tell you how that person is really feeling inside!

Some of the children might want to help you make gingerbread cookies that show the different expressions. You can follow the recipe to make a gingerbread dough and use raisins to place eyes, noses, and mouths on the cookies. You might want to talk about feelings and facial expressions again at snack time or lunch when you serve the cookies.

(Or, 1298 "Mouth Puppets"; 1452 "Box Puppets.")

1627

Mister Rogers uses empty cardboard tubes to make tunnels for a toy car, then sings through one of the tubes as if it were a megaphone. In the Neighborhood of Make-Believe, Handyman Negri has cardboard tube scrolls with the names of all the kings, queens, princes, and princesses for Lady Aberlin, the Director of Research. She is conducting research with a laughing machine, and Robert Troll mistakenly believes that there is a tiny person inside the laughing machine.

"Tubes and Tunnels" can help children:

● develop creative play;

● work on feelings about separation.

Tunnels and Bridges

Materials

● empty cardboard tubes

● oatmeal boxes with both ends removed

● toy cars

● toy people or animals

● blocks or small cardboard boxes

You can pass around the cardboard tubes and oatmeal boxes and let children try out ways of using them. After they have had a chance to try out their own ideas, you can ask them if they remember how Mister Rogers used the tubes. If no one suggests using a tube as a tunnel, you could show them how. Some of the children might want to use blocks or small boxes to make a bridge over the tunnel. Others might want to use the tubes outdoors and cover them with sand or earth (leaving the ends open) to make tunnels for their cars.

If you have very young children, you might want to play a simple game of "hide and find" with the tubes and a toy car. As the children watch, you can hide the car inside the tube and let the children "find" it. Another way they might enjoy playing with the car is on a string—pulling it into and then out of the tunnel. You can "hide" the car by pulling it into the tunnel... and then let the children take turns pulling the string to make the car reappear.

1628

Mr. McFeely brings Mister Rogers a film showing how people make toothbrushes. In the Neighborhood of Make-Believe, Lady Aberlin turns into a tiger.

"Brushing Your Teeth" can help children:

● learn to do things independently;

● learn more about their bodies.

Brushing Your Teeth

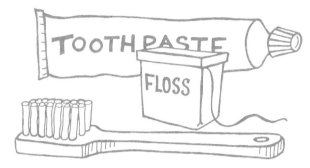

Materials

● toothbrush for each child

● toothpaste

● floss

● mirror

Making toothbrushing a part of your daily routine can help children learn to take care of their bodies. Perhaps the children can bring a toothbrush from home to leave with you for use every day. If not, you could check with your local dentist about getting a supply of free toothbrushes for the children in your care.

After meal and snack times, encourage the children to brush their teeth, using their own special toothbrushes. You might want to try the homemade toothpaste recipe, program 1129 in your book. Otherwise, you can give each child a small amount of commercial toothpaste for their brushes. You might also want to show the children how to floss their teeth. Having a mirror nearby will encourage children to look at their teeth afterwards to see if they look cleaner. Can they see or feel any difference after they brush?

(Or, 1129 "Making Toothpaste"; 1411 "Boxes Inside Boxes.".)

1629

Mister Rogers visits the dentist's office for a check-up. In the Neighborhood of Make-Believe, people are looking for Lady Aberlin, but they can't find her because she has turned into a make-believe tiger.

"A Pretend Dentist" can help children:

● try out different roles;
● use play to work on feelings.

A Pretend Dentist

Materials

● toothbrushes
● dental floss
● an old white shirt for a smock
● tongue depressor or popsicle stick for a dental instrument

You can begin by asking the children to tell you what they remember about Mister Rogers' visit to the dentist's office. Have they ever visited a dentist? What can they tell you about that visit?

You could ask if any of the children want to pretend about being a dentist. They could use dolls as patients and set up a dentist's office, wearing an old white shirt as a smock and using a popsicle stick as a dental instrument. This kind of play might also bring to mind concerns that children have about biting or being bitten. Having several mouth puppets available also can allow for other kinds of play about mouths and teeth.

1630

Mister Rogers plays with a small steam shovel and shows a film about earth movers with large "teeth" that scoop up earth and move it to another place. Mr. McFeely brings a film about how people make toothpaste. Mister Rogers talks about the things we can do with our mouths.

"A Cardboard Mouth" can help children:

● use play to work on feelings.

A Cardboard Mouth

Materials

● several pieces of lightweight cardboard, such as the backs from paper tablets

To prepare for this activity, you can cut the cardboard into 3″ x 5″ pieces and fold each piece in half to form a hinged shape that children can use for pretending about mouths. When you give the children the cardboard, you might just watch for a while how they play with the shapes. If they haven't already done so, you can ask them to pretend the hinged shapes are mouths. What kinds of things can we do with our mouths? The children might think of things like:

● eating;
● singing;
● yawning;
● whistling;
● humming;
● laughing;
● talking about how they feel.

The children can use the hinged shapes to pretend about doing some of these things. Do any of the children want to use the pretend mouths as puppets and talk about some of their feelings?

Thoughts For The Week

Growing is often a slow, invisible process, making children impatient at times that changes aren't happening more quickly. They must sometimes think they'll never be as big as their parents. They can even feel angry about not being able to make the kind of decisions that adults are always making about who's to do what. Feeling angry at an adult who cares for them can be scary for children: They wonder whether that adult might stop loving them if they let that anger out. When we encourage children to talk and play about their anger and their fears, those strong feelings often become more manageable through the talking and playing.

One way to show children that they are growing is to support their day-to-day "inside" growing that is often harder than outside growing to see or measure: learning to share their toys or learning to use words to let people know how they feel. Helping children feel proud about their inside growing can make it easier for them to wait for the time when they will be grownups, and make many decisions for themselves.

Fred Rogers

Songs On The Programs This Week

1631 "Speedy Delivery to You"
"Children Can"

1632 "I'm Taking Care of You"
"We're Not to Be Afraid"

1633 "You're Growing"
"Your Story Is Your History"

1634 "You Are Special"
"I'm Taking Care of You"

Special Visits

1631 How People Make Model Cars

1632 A Conservatory Where People Care for Plants

1634 Mister Rogers Visits his Barber for a Haircut

1635 Harlem Spiritual Ensemble, Directed by François Clemmons

Your Notes For The Week

1631

Mister Rogers builds a roadway for his model car and tells how he felt when he was little and wanted to grow up right away so that he could drive a real car like his father. In the Neighborhood of Make-Believe, Prince Tuesday is having a hard time waiting to be as big as his father, King Friday.

"Measuring Our Growth" can help children:

- learn more about growing;
- feel proud of accomplishments.

Measuring Our Growth

Materials

- long strips of paper (2-3 inches wide and 4-5 feet long; adding machine paper is fine)
- construction paper
- measuring tape or string
- glue
- scissors

You might begin by asking the children how they think Prince Tuesday felt on the program today. Can they remember a time when they felt impatient about not growing up fast enough? To begin keeping a record of their growing, you can cut a long strip of paper (4-5 feet long) for each child and tape it to the wall so it touches the floor. As each child stands against a strip of paper, you can mark his or her height with a line. If you have records of children's growth, you can measure and mark how tall they were when they started coming to child care, or how tall they were last year...or the year before.

Older children who are interested in measuring might want to use squares of paper to show how tall they are. You could cut assorted colors of construction paper into squares (2" x 2" or 3" x 3", depending on the width of your measuring strips) and let the children glue the squares onto their strips—from the floor to the line you have drawn. Some children may be able to count the number of squares. While they might not know what "inches" means, they can begin to see that height can be measured and recorded.

You could also keep a record of some of the "inside growing" that is taking place. For instance, you could list some of the accomplishments children talked about earlier and post them next to each child's chart.

1632

Mister Rogers wants to grow a bean plant, so he plants a bean seed in some potting soil. In the Neighborhood of Make-Believe, King Friday is trying to keep everyone calm about the mysterious "Big Thing" that was spotted in Westwood.

"Growing Takes Time" can help children:

● learn more about growing;

● learn more about the world.

Growing Takes Time

Materials

● potting soil

● stones

● seeds

● paper cups

● water (small pitcher)

● a mister (or clean spray bottle with water)

You might talk with the children about what they think will happen when they put the seeds into a cup of potting soil. How long do they think it will take for the seed to sprout? How long before they see leaves?

Before beginning this activity, you might want to cover the work area with newspaper, just the way Mister Rogers did, and talk with the children about why that makes it easier to clean up afterwards. Then you can give each child a cup, several stones for the bottom if you like (not essential), some potting soil, and two or three bean seeds (in case one doesn't sprout). If possible, you could let the children take their own soil from the bag and spoon it into their cups. When all the seeds have been planted, you could use a mister to moisten the soil, or help the children water the seeds carefully using a small pitcher. Older children might want to plant a bean seed every three of four days and make a chart showing the differences in growth for each of the plants. You could then talk about the things they observe. Which plants are the oldest? Are they always the tallest?

1633

Mister Rogers brings a cat for a visit. He shows a videotape of the cat when it was a young kitten and talks about the cat's "history." In the Neighborhood of Make-Believe, there is concern about the "Big Thing" that is rolling along from Westwood.

"Once We Were Babies" can help children:

● learn more about growing;

● talk about feelings;

● feel proud of accomplishments.

Once We Were Babies

Materials

● a set of pictures showing babies and children — maybe even those in your care — at different ages

● a book about babies or a book about growing up

As you show the children the book or pictures you have of younger children, you can ask if they remember what it was like to be younger than they are. You might ask questions such as:

● What kinds of things can these babies do?

● What could you do when you were that little?

● What can you do now that you couldn't do then?

As you help the children recall the good and not-so-good feelings associated with being a baby, you can help them recognize their own growing abilities. You might ask the children to tell you something they have recently learned to do that makes them feel more grown-up.

If you have some photos of yourself as a child, you could show them and remind the children that you were a child once, too. You can let them know that you remember what it's like to be a child and reassure them that children grow little by little to become adults.

Thursday

1634

Mister Rogers visits his barber, Nick Failla, and gets a haircut. In the Neighborhood of Make-Believe, the mysterious "Big Thing" begins to sprout.

"Cutting Pretend Hair" can help children:

● use play to work on feelings.

Cutting Pretend Hair

Materials
● paper plates
● markers
● glue
● yarn or ribbon
● scissors

You might begin this activity by talking with the children about getting a haircut. Can they tell you about a haircut they have had? You can emphasize that only adults should cut children's hair; children should only *pretend* about cutting hair. To give them a chance to pretend about hair-cutting, you can give each child a paper plate and help them draw a face on the plate. With your help, they can glue long pieces of ribbon or yarn onto the plates for hair, and then, when the glue has dried, pretend about giving the plate puppet a haircut.

Friday

1635

Mister Rogers brings a jack-in-the-box and talks about people going away and coming back. In the Neighborhood of Make-Believe, the "Big Thing" bursts open into a fancy flower.

"Popcorn" can help children:

● learn more about food;
● develop creative play.

Popcorn

Materials
● popcorn
● oil
● popper or heavy pan
● bowls

You might talk with the children about how the Big Thing sprouted a flower, or the way a jack-in-the-box pops open to reveal the figure inside. Then you can show them several popcorn kernels and ask them if they know what happens when the kernels are heated. They could help you measure the oil and popcorn, but you should do the actual popping of the corn. You might ask the children to listen to the sound the popcorn makes as it pops. While you wait for the popcorn to cool, the children might want to pretend about being a popcorn kernel—first curling into a ball, then popping open.

(Or, 1103 "Jack-in-the-Box.")

Thoughts For The Week

Pretending can take many different forms, but most of it seems to be a way of trying things out—whether trying out what it would be like to be a grownup, a princess or a pilot; what it would be like to be children without parents; or to be able to solve problems magically; or even what it would be like to be in control of everything. Dressing up can be a part of that pretending as children put on the outfits of those they pretend to be. But sometimes pretending can seem so real that children may wonder if dressing up as someone else could maybe change the person inside the costume. It's important for them to know that although we can pretend to be someone else, we can never be someone else. We will always be ourselves.

Fred Rogers

Songs On The Programs This Week

1636   *"I'm Still Myself Inside"*

1637   *"Everybody's Fancy"*

1638   *"It's the Style to Wear a Smile"*

1639   *"I'm Still Myself Inside"*

1640   *"It's You I Like"*
       "I'm Taking Care of You"

Special Visits

1637   *A Visit to the Library*

1638   *How People Make Sneakers*

1639   *Boys Choir of Harlem*

1640   *How People Make Sweaters*

Your Notes For The Week

1636

Mister Rogers tries on a raccoon eye mask and plays a simple game of peek-a-boo from underneath the mask. In the Neighborhood of Make-Believe, Ana wants to be a ballerina in the school play, and Daniel wants to be a raccoon. Mister Rogers shows how to make a paper bag mask that covers the eyes and hair.

"Paper Bag Mask" can help children:

●   understand the differences between real and pretend;

●   try out different roles;

●   develop creative play.

Paper Bag Mask

Materials

●   paper bags

●   blunt-nosed scissors

●   crayons or markers

●   yarn

●   construction paper

●   glue

If you cut off the bottom portion of the right-size paper bag, it can fit over a child's head, covering only the eyes and nose. You can help children cut out eyeholes so they can see, and then they can decorate the masks with yarn, markers or construction paper to represent anyone or anything they want to pretend to be. They will probably want to look in a mirror to see the final result, but some children may need your reassurance that they haven't changed inside: If they lift the masks, they'll still see their real faces. It's important for children to know that only *paper* bags should be used to make this kind of mask.

(Or, 1029 "Paper Plate Masks"; 1582 "Am I Still Me?")

1637

Mr. McFeely brings a set of fancy crowns and shows Mister Rogers how to use them as hoops for playing a type of basketball. In the Neighborhood of Make-Believe, Handyman Negri is supposed to polish King Friday's spare crown. He leaves it with Prince Tuesday while he looks for the polish, but when he returns, both Prince Tuesday and the crown are gone.

"Fancy Crowns" can help children:

*   try out different roles;
*   develop creative play.

Fancy Crowns

Materials

*   strips of construction paper or lightweight card-board about four inches wide
*   aluminum foil
*   used foil wrapping paper or metallic ribbon
*   sequins or glitter (optional)
*   scrap materials (feathers, yarn, buttons)
*   glue
*   blunt-nosed scissors
*   tape

Most children will need to tape two strips of paper together to make a crown that fits. It's easiest to leave the strips flat while the child decorates the crown; later you can fasten the headband to fit the child's head exactly.

Children may need your help in cutting points or a fringe along the top of the crowns. Then they can decorate the strips with scrap materials or markers. Small pieces of aluminum foil, foil wrapping paper, or metallic ribbon make shiny additions to the crowns. Children might also want to glue on sequins or sprinkle glitter over glue they have drizzled on the crowns. When the glue has dried, the children can use the crowns for their pretending.

(Or, 1616 "Bagball")

1638

Mister Rogers brings an assortment of wigs and eye-glasses to show that even though we can change our appearance, we don't change the person inside. In the Neighborhood of Make-Believe, people are searching for the missing crown.

"Paper Bag Wigs" can help children:

*   try out different roles;
*   develop creative play.

Paper Bag Wigs

Materials

*   medium-size paper bags
*   scissors
*   glue
*   yarn
*   markers
*   ribbons and bows
*   old sunglasses (optional)

To make a paper-bag wig, the bag ought to fit the child's head rather snugly. Cut out the front of the bag to frame the child's face, leaving several inches along the top across the forehead. You can make "hair" by cutting the paper into thin strips all the way around. If children want curly hair, they can roll the ends of the paper around a pencil to make them curl. Or, children could glue on yarn for the hair and decorate the wig with ribbons and bows.

1639

Mister Rogers brings a knitted cover and uses it to cover up familiar objects in the kitchen. He tells Mr. McFeely that it has a special purpose: It's a sweater costume for the Trolley.

"What's Under the Cover?" can help children:

- work on feelings about separation;
- learn more about objects in the world.

What's Under The Cover?

Materials

- several familiar toys
- a scarf or small lightweight blanket

Once you have selected several toys for this game, you can let the children see the toys and pass them around so they can feel them. Then let the children take turns selecting a toy to place under the cover, while other children close their eyes. See if they can guess what has been hidden. Some children may be able to tell from the shape of the object; others may have to feel through the cover to tell what it is; and some may have to reach under the cover to touch the toy before they know what it is. Some children have a hard time waiting and taking turns, so you might want to play this game with only two or three children at a time.

1640

It's the day for the school play in the Neighborhood of Make-Believe. Ana Platypus is pretending to be a ballerina, and Daniel Tiger is a baby raccoon. Prince Tuesday wants to be a giant king. In the real neighborhood, Maggie Stewart dresses up to look like Mr. McFeely and brings a film about how people make zipper sweaters.

"Dress-up Day" can help children:

- try out different roles;
- develop creative play.

Dress-Up Day

Materials

- an assortment of dress-up clothes
- dress-up shoes
- old jewelry
- paper-bag hats or wigs from earlier in the week (optional)

You may already have a selection of dress-up clothes for the children to use in their pretending, but if not, you could ask them to bring some pieces of discarded adult clothing from their homes. The children might want to talk about the roles they'd like to try out. Or, they might want to try on some of the clothing and then decide who they are pretending to be. If possible, let the children see themselves in a mirror once they are in full costume. Of course, you'll want to set aside some time for pretending when the children are dressed.

Thoughts For The Week

There are all kinds of artists in the world, and even very young children have the ability to express their ideas and feelings through some form of art. Often, the scribbles and lines that children draw don't mean much to us as adults, but, to the child, they represent something that is worth drawing, and these early "artistic" expressions need our interest and encouragement. As children grow, learning it's okay to express their feelings in their own ways is more important than learning to copy a pattern, color inside the lines, or draw a chair that looks like a chair. Of course if they feel they want to do that, it's up to them. Nevertheless, no matter what our age, it's the art that is inside *each one of us that counts.*

Fred Rogers

Songs On The Programs This Week

1641   "You've Got to Do It"
1642   "I Like to Take Care of You"
*   "Everybody's Fancy"*
1643   "There Are Many Ways"
1644   "What Do You Do?"

Special Visits

1642   Spanish Singing Bakers
1643   Skywriter, Suzanne Asbury-Oliver
1644   Bill Strickland, Potter
1645   Eric Hill, Author-Illustrator

Your Notes For The Week

Monday

1641

In the Neighborhood of Make-Believe, Robert Troll paints a portrait of King Friday XIII. The king is so pleased with the finished product that he wants *everyone* to make one just like it. Lady Aberlin explains that copying someone else's painting isn't really art. Real art comes from inside a person, and we all see things based on who we are inside.

"The Art That's Inside You" can help children:

● represent their thoughts and ideas through artwork;
● develop creativity.

The Art That's Inside You

Materials

● paper
● markers
● paints
● crayons

Mister Rogers reminds his neighborhood friends that there are many ways to show the art that's inside us. Today the children might want to draw or paint a picture to show the art that is inside them. You could talk about the kinds of things children often draw:

● a self-portrait;
● a portrait of family members;
● a drawing of a car, or bus, or house, or pet;
● a drawing of something they have seen (the bulldozer at a neighborhood construction site).

Young children seldom draw things the way they look to adults, but by asking children to tell you about what they have drawn, you can come to learn what the lines and curves and shapes mean to them. Some children might want you to write down the words they say about their pictures. You could write the words on the back or on a separate piece of paper and attach it to the child's work with tape or a paper clip so you don't alter their work. Older children might be able to "read" the words back to you as they begin to learn what letters mean.

1642

Mister Rogers shows several paintings by Picasso and talks about the different creative ways that people can do things. In the Neighborhood of Make-Believe, people are making many different kinds of portraits for King Friday. The Spanish Singing Bakers perform at Brockett's Bakery and invite Mister Rogers to play a rhythm instrument.

"Rhythm Rattles" can help children:

- develop creativity;
- express feelings through music.

Rhythm Rattles

Materials

- cardboard tubes from wrapping paper, aluminum foil, or paper towels
- waxed paper
- rubber bands
- dried beans or pebbles
- markers
- glue (optional)
- tissue paper (optional)
- yarn (optional)

You could begin this activity by letting the children play with the cardboard tubes and talk about the different ways they could use them. For instance, some children might:

- talk through the tubes;
- peek through them;
- roll a marble through them.

You could help the children make rhythm rattles similar to the one Mister Rogers made by following these directions:

- Cover one end of the tube with waxed paper and fasten it with a rubber band.
- Pour a handful of dried beans or pebbles into the tube.
- Cover the other end of the tube with waxed paper and fasten with a rubber band.

The children can use the shakers to make their own musical rhythms. If some of the children want to decorate their tubes, you can allow time for them to glue tissue paper or yarn on the tubes before you make the rhythm rattles. If you find that some of the children don't want to do this particular project, you could let them decorate the cardboard tubes or play with them in some other way. By accepting their ideas, you let the children know that there are many different ways to be creative.

1643

A sky-writer, Suzanne Asbury-Oliver, shows Mister Rogers and Mr. McFeely how people use airplanes and special equipment to write messages in the sky. In the Neighborhood of Make-Believe, Chuck Aber draws a portrait of King Friday with his sky-writing airplane.

"Chalk Skywriting" can help children:

- develop creativity;
- express ideas and feelings through art;
- develop their imaginations.

Chalk Skywriting

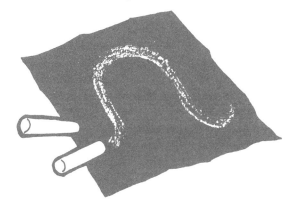

Materials

- blue, gray, or dark construction paper
- white chalk

You might begin by asking the children what they can tell you about skywriting. Some children may remember a great many details from the program; others may just recall that airplane pilots use special equipment to leave messages in the sky. You can ask the children to imagine they are pilots in a skywriting airplane. What kinds of drawings or messages would they leave in the sky? Using dark construction paper and chalk, the children can draw the patterns or messages they would leave if they were pilots. (Even if the children do not make actual "letters," they can often tell you what their messages say.)

1644

Mister Rogers uses homemade play clay as he sings the song, "What Do You Do (With the mad that you feel)?" He talks about different ways to use the play clay and then visits a potter who uses real clay and a potter's wheel to create plates, bowls, and other pottery. In the Neighborhood of Make-Believe, Lady Elaine is feeling jealous and makes a mess by putting play clay all over the portraits of King Friday.

"Play Clay" can help children:

* develop creativity;
* express feelings through art work;
* develop self-control.

Play Clay

Materials

* 2 cups flour
* 1 cup salt
* 1 cup water
* 1 teaspoon salad oil (optional)
* bowl
* spoon
* table covering or tray

Because this is often a messy activity, you might want to cover your work area with paper or plastic so that cleaning up will be easier. If you have small trays or plastic place mats for each child, you can ask the children to try to keep the play clay on the mats when they play with it. After the children help you combine all the ingredients, they can take turns kneading the play clay until it is smooth. Then divide the material among the children for them to use. You can remind them of the ways Mister Rogers pounded, rolled, and squeezed the play clay he made. Let the children get used to the "feel" of the material today. On another day, you might want to provide tools such as a rolling pin or cookie cutters for a different kind of play. If you store the play clay in an airtight container, it can last as long as two weeks.

Please Note: Toddlers might be tempted to eat modeling dough, so if there's a chance they may be around when the dough is used, it may be better to lower the salt content. The salt makes the texture coarse; otherwise, the flour and water mixture is like a paste. You may want to experiment to see how much salt is needed to get a consistency that works well for your needs.

1645

Mister Rogers shows slides of several different kinds of paintings and talks about the artists who made them. He says he enjoys visiting art galleries to see the real paintings up close. In the Neighborhood of Make-Believe, Lady Elaine uses her "boomerang-toomerang" to clean up the mess she made. Mister Rogers visits Eric Hill's studio to see the books and illustrations he creates.

"A Visit to an Art Gallery" can help children:

* learn to look carefully;
* learn more about art.

A Visit To An Art Gallery

Materials

* art books or postcards (optional)

You might want to arrange a visit to an art gallery where the children can see several paintings and sculptures. Encourage the children to tell you what they particularly like about the pictures they see. They might be attracted to the colors or patterns in a particular painting, or they might like particular representations of people or familiar objects.

If you are unable to arrange a visit, you could use a book containing reproductions of artwork as a basis for talking about the different ways people can paint or draw or sculpt. The children might want to create an art gallery containing their own works of art. You could frame and hang several of their paintings, or display other unique creations and arrange to have parents come early to view the gallery.

Thoughts For The Week

Many children have imaginary friends at one time or another. It sometimes makes adults a little uncomfortable when a child turns up with an imaginary friend, partly because this kind of friend can be controlled only by the child, and partly because adults may worry about a child's sense of real and pretend: Imaginary friends have a way of seeming all too real from time to time.

It may be helpful to remember that imaginary friends can play an important role in the lives of children, allowing them to fulfill wishes through their imaginations. Sometimes imaginary friends help children cope with loneliness by being the friend or sibling who isn't there. Other times, the imaginary friend becomes the scapegoat who makes messes or gets into trouble when the child doesn't want to face the consequences. Wise adults encourage both the child and the imaginary friend to clean up the mess or set things right again so that children come to take responsibility for the imaginary friend's behavior as well as their own. Imaginary friends usually play a brief role in a child's life. They usually go away as quickly as they arrive. But while they are there, they often provide the companionship and support many children feel they need.

Fred Rogers

Songs On The Programs This Week

1646 "You Are Special"
1647 "Pretending"
      "Please Don't Think It's Funny"
1648 "It's Raining in the Neighborhood"
1649 "There Are Many Ways"
1650 "Everything Grows Together"

Special Visits

1646 *How People Make Colored Markers*
1648 *Pittsburgh Ballet Theatre*
1650 *Folk Singer, Ella Jenkins*

Your Notes For The Week

Monday

1646

Mister Rogers uses felt-tipped markers to "draw a song." He talks about what he would do if he had no markers or paper or music, and he still wanted to "draw a song": He'd *imagine* that he had those things and make an imaginary picture in the air! Mr. McFeely brings a film about how people make colored markers. "Drawing with Colored Markers" can help children:

* develop creativity;
* develop their imaginations.

Drawing With Colored Markers

Materials
* paper
* felt-tipped colored markers
* music (optional)

You might begin by talking with the children about how people make colored markers. What do the children recall from the film? Do they have any questions or comments about what they saw? This might be a time for talking about favorite colors or the different colors of markers that are available for them to use. If you have tapes, records, or a radio in the room, you could play some music and let the children "draw a song." When the drawings are complete, see if the children want to tell you about their pictures. If you write down some of their comments, they might be able to "read" the words to their parents later on.

1647

Mister Rogers brings a telescope today. Bob Trow stops by with his imaginary dog and talks about the different ways he liked to pretend when he was a child. When his pretend dog becomes restless, Bob Trow says he has to leave.

"Imaginary Pets" can help children:

* develop their imaginations;
* develop creative play.

Imaginary Pets

Materials

You can begin by talking with the children about any *real* pets they have at home. If they have a real pet, they might want to pretend the pet is with them. Can they show you how they handle the animal or care for it? If they have no real pets, you can encourage them to create a pretend pet and tell you a little about it. Some of the children might want to draw a picture of their imaginary pets; others might want to take their imaginary pets for a walk, or have them become a part of their play today.

1648

Mister Rogers visits a dance studio where the dancers are using umbrellas and pretending to dance in the rain. In the Neighborhood of Make-Believe, Corney has created an umbrellarockit where people can sit and imagine whatever they want. Henrietta Pussycat uses X the Owl's I.V. (Imaginary Viewer) to pretend that she can see what Chuck Aber is imagining. Mister Rogers reassures children that no one can see the things you imagine.

"Imaginary Viewers" can help children:

* develop creative play;
* develop their imagination.

Imaginary Viewers

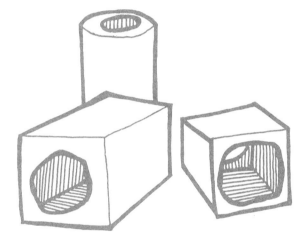

Materials

* assorted small boxes or cardboard tubes
* markers
* paper
* scissors (optional)

The children can create their own imaginary viewers with cardboard boxes or tubes. (If you are using boxes, you will need to cut a hole on two opposite sides for children to look through. Children can use the cardboard tubes as if they were telescopes). Encourage the children to imagine they can see something when they look into the viewers, and let them talk about the imaginary things they can see. You might want to reassure them that no one can see what they are thinking when they imagine; if they want you to know what they're thinking, they have to tell you. The children could use colored markers to decorate their I.V.'s Some children might want to use the markers and paper to draw pictures about the things they imagine.

1649

Mister Rogers brings a small chair and imagines that he is reading a story to a friend who is sitting in the chair. In the Neighborhood of Make-Believe, Prince Tuesday's doll, Tome (pronounced "Tommy"), becomes real—something that could, of course, happen only in the Neighborhood of Make-Believe.

"An Imaginary Book" can help children:

• develop their imaginations;
• develop their creativity.

An Imaginary Book

Materials
• paper
• stapler
• markers or pens
• construction paper

To prepare for this activity, you will need a blank booklet for each child. You can assemble these by stapling five or six sheets of paper together and writing each child's name, plus a title, on heavier paper to make a cover. For instance, you could write "*An Imaginary Book* by Johnny Smith." This activity might work best if you do it individually with each child, or perhaps with two children at a time, taking time to sit alone with them as they tell you their imaginary stories. (If you're comfortable having them on your lap, this might be a good time for that kind of closeness.) Encourage the children to turn the pages of the booklet as if it were a real book with words and pictures on each page. Some children might want to make up two or three different stories. Others may want to turn the imaginary books into real books by drawing on the pages and having you write down the words they say.

1650

Mister Rogers talks about the differences between real people and dolls or toys that come apart. He sings the song, "Everything Grows Together (because you're all one piece)" while Maggie Stewart signs the words. Folk singer Ella Jenkins visits Brockett's Bakery and sings while Maggie signs.

"Everything Grows Together" can help children:

• learn more about their bodies;
• learn the difference between real and pretend.

Everything Grows Together

Materials
mirror (optional)

If you and the children know the tune to "Everything Grows Together," you might sing it with the children and ask them to touch each body part as it is named. A variation could be a simple game of "Where's Your Nose?" By asking children to point to a particular body part as it is named, you help them become more aware of their own body image. If you are comfortable allowing the children to pass a hand mirror around, you can let them look at their faces as they point to their noses, eyebrows, eyelashes, mouths, ears, hair, cheeks, and chins. You might talk with children about the differences between real people and toys like dolls. What are some things that they can do that toys and dolls cannot do?

Thoughts For The Week

Most children are naturally eager to learn, right from the time they are born. For them, learning comes from the inside out as they try to make sense of the world through their feelings and experiences.

My grandfather was a person who loved to teach, and every time I was with him, he'd show me something about the world or something about myself that I hadn't even thought of. I loved him and wanted to please him, and I would have tried to learn anything he was interested in teaching me. Over the years, as I have grown and learned through my work, I've come to understand that learning does happen best when it comes through a caring relationship.

Fred Rogers

Songs On The Programs This Week

1651 *"There Are Many Ways"*
     "You're Growing"
1652 *"We Are Elephants"*
1653 *"You've Got to Do It"*
1654 *"Did You Know"*
     "I'm a Man Who Manufactures"
1655 *"It's the Style to Wear a Smile"*

Special Visits

1652 *Folk-singer, Ella Jenkins*
1653 *How People Make Colored Construction Paper*

Your Notes For The Week

1651

Mr. McFeely delivers a collection of whistles to Mister Rogers by mistake. (He is having difficulty learning the new computer delivery system.) In the Neighborhood of Make-Believe, Robert Troll is helping to take the Make-Believe world census and wants to know who has learned to whistle.

"Census Taking" can help children:

*   understand and accept individual differences;
*   recognize and use symbols.

Census Taking

Materials

*   large sheets of paper
*   markers
*   magazine pictures
*   scissors
*   tape or glue

You and the children could take a census of your own group today. First, you'll need a chart divided up into columns, with the children's names down the left-hand side. At the top of each column you could place a symbol for the answers to the questions you want to ask: A picture of a house could indicate the "address" column, a picture of crayons the "favorite color" column, and so forth. Once your group has decided on all the questions you want to ask, you can invite individual children throughout the day to tell you their answers, letting them know it's okay if there are questions they don't want to answer.

Older preschool children might want to interview family or friends at home and record the information on another chart. As you record your "census," you can talk with the children about similarities and differences among people's responses. Of course this is a good opportunity to remind children that each person is special!

1652

Mister Rogers brings the broken tube from the vacuum sweeper and uses it to pretend that he is an elephant with a long trunk. Then he shows how to pretend to be an elephant by using his arms for a trunk. Ella Jenkins visits Mister Rogers and teaches him a new song. In the Neighborhood of Make-Believe, Lady Aberlin is continuing her wind research.

"Learning to Pretend" can help children:

- develop imagination;
- express feelings through movement and dance;
- try out different roles.

Learning To Pretend

Materials

- music
- scarves

You can encourage children to pretend by asking them to imagine they are something else. For instance, they might want to imagine they are elephants today and pretend they have long trunks that swing as they walk. Some children might want to pretend to be the wind and move around the room, waving scarves or streamers. You can provide music and encourage children to change their movements to match the music. See if the children have other ideas about what they could pretend to be, and encourage them to act out the movements that represent the role.

1653

Mister Rogers brings a paper chain made from strips of construction paper. He explains that before he was able to use scissors, he would use torn paper for projects he was working on. He shows an example of torn paper strips in his paper chain. Mr. McFeely delivers a video-tape that shows how people make colored construction paper.

"Paper Chain Decorations" can help children:

- develop muscle control;
- develop fine motor coordination.

Paper Chain Decorations

Materials

- an assortment of colored construction paper
- blunt-nosed scissors
- glue

Learning to use scissors can be a difficult task for young children. One activity that allows children to practice simple cutting is to help them make paper chains or other decorations from strips of colored construction paper. Older children can cut strips from a standard sheet of construction paper, but you might have to help inexperienced cutters by providing longer strips and showing them how to use scissors to snip the strips in half. If using scissors is beyond the ability of the children in your care, you can encourage them to tear the strips of paper for this project. If children want to make paper chain decorations, you might also have to show them how to make a loop and glue it together. Threading a second strip of paper through the loop may require your assistance. Even the simple task of gluing the paper strips is something that children have to learn about. Children who do not want to make paper chains might want to glue their torn or cut paper strips onto background paper for a different kind of decoration. Your patient and caring attitude in teaching such seemingly simple tasks is what helps to make early learning an enjoyable experience for children, an experience they'll have inside of them for all their future learning.

1654

In the Neighborhood of Make-Believe, the children in Ms. Cow's class are planning a field trip. Mister Rogers says that a field trip does not have to be a trip to a "field," but can be any trip that is taken away from where you live or work.

"A Neighborhood Field Trip" can help children:

- learn more about their world;
- develop healthy curiosity.

A Neighborhood Field Trip

Materials

- paper
- pen or pencil

You and your children can plan a field trip around your own neighborhood today. As you talk with the children about places you all might visit, begin making a list on a large sheet of paper. For instance, you could suggest visiting:

- the grocery store;
- a construction site;
- the bus stop;
- a neighbor's house;
- a school, library, post office, or other community building.

You'll have to take into consideration the ages of your children as you begin to plan how many places to visit. With young children a simple trip to just one of these places may be all that you can manage. Older children may be able to handle a brief stop at more than one. Some caregivers prefer to take a walk through the neighborhood first, pointing out various places that they could plan to visit on other occasions.

1655

Mister Rogers brings an assortment of different-size batteries and a collection of objects needing batteries. He discovers which batteries fit in which objects. Then he closes the curtains to the room and uses a flashlight to explore the semi-darkened room.

"Flashlight Power" can help children:

- learn more about their world;
- develop healthy curiosity.

Flashlight Power

Materials

- flashlights
- batteries

If you have an assortment of batteries and flashlights, you could let the children discover which batteries belong to which flashlights. Then let the children take turns using the flashlights to explore a semi-darkened room. You can dim the lights or close the curtains. (If you have children who are afraid of the dark, you might want to keep the room fairly light, but still dark enough to see the beam of the flashlight.) Children might need to be reminded not to shine the light directly into anyone's eyes as they take turns with the flashlights. If you are comfortable allowing the children to play with the flashlights throughout the day, you can make them available in the pretend play area and see how many ways children use flashlights in their make-believe.

Thoughts For The Week

As adults, we often forget what it was like, in childhood, always to be looking up *at so much of the world. We looked* up *at the grownups who controlled so much that happened, and we looked* up *at the tables where so many interesting things seemed to be. If we climbed* up *on a chair to get a closer look at those curiosities, towering grownups would most likely put them* up *somewhere still higher—out of our reach. Having to look* up *at the world like that all the time must have made us feel small and powerless. How exciting it was when, from a parent's shoulders or some other safe perch, we could look* down *at things for a change!*

For children who have only recently mastered the ability to stand without falling, up and down can have extra special significance. Little wonder that children often like to build things up and knock them back down again: They're in control of what happens. It's easy for adults to become annoyed with this fascination for knocking things down, but sensitive caregivers soon find ways to support children's ways of learning and practicing more about up and down.

Fred Rogers

Songs On The Programs This Week

1656 *"Let's Think of Something to Do"*
"I'm a Man Who Manufactures"
"It's You I Like"

1657 *"Did You Know"*
"Then Your Heart Is Full of Love"

1658 *"I Love Someone Who Looks Like You"*

1659 *"When the Day Turns into Night"*
"There Are Many Ways to Say I Love You"

1660 *"You Are Special"*

Special Visits

1657 *Dominoes Display Artist, Bob Speca*

1658 *Exercise Specialist, Marilyn Barnett*

1659 *Clarinet Player, Richard Stoltzman*

1660 *Balloon Sculptor, Bruce Franco*

Your Notes For The Week

1656

Mister Rogers and Mr. McFeely take a ride on an elevator and escalator. In the Neighborhood of Make-Believe, Corney needs Handyman Negri's help to load a chair on an up and down pulley. Lady Elaine receives a special delivery for the Museum-Go-Round: a hydraulic platform that goes up and down.

"Up and Down Pulleys" can help children:

● learn more about their world;
● develop creative play.

Up And Down Pulleys

Materials

● a small basket with a handle
● heavy string
● wooden dowel
● toy animals, people, or furniture

The children in your care might want to experiment with up and down pulleys and perhaps use them later to develop their play ideas. To prepare a pulley-like contraption, you can tie string to the handle of a small basket and load toy animals, people, or furniture into the basket. Then use two chairs to support the ends of a wooden dowel (a broomstick works fine) and loop the string over the dowel. When children pull the string down on one side of the dowel, it will lift the basket with toys on the other side. With some experimenting, you may be able to set this up in the children's play area so they can use their up and down pulley as an elevator near the block buildings or doll house. Children could also hang the basket over a safe porch railing and lift toys from the ground to the porch; or, loop the pulley over a low tree branch and load toys in the basket for up and down play in the yard. You can ask what kind of ideas the children have for playing with the up and down pulley.

1657

Mister Rogers visits Negri's Music Shop and watches Bob Speca set up dominoes that fall down in a fancy pattern. In the Neighborhood of Make-Believe, Robert Troll inadvertently steps on Lady Elaine's new elevator. When it lifts him up, he thinks he's flying.

"Cardboard Blocks" can help children:

- use play to work on feelings;
- develop creative play.

Cardboard Blocks

Materials

- empty boxes in assorted sizes (cereal, pudding, cracker, or oatmeal boxes)
- clean, empty milk cartons

Lightweight boxes and clean milk cartons make good toys for children to build up and knock down without hurting anyone. You might want to let the children bring in boxes from their homes to add to your collection. You will probably want to set some rules about building up and knocking down. For instance, children should not be allowed to knock down another's creation without permission. The children can store the blocks in a large carton or on a shelf somewhere near their play area.

1658

In the Neighborhood of Make-Believe, King Friday gives Mayor Maggie and Neighbor Aber the task of finding someone to give dancing lessons to his two wooden birds, Mimus polyglottos and Troglodytes aedon. Mister Rogers shows how to make a bird on a straw.

"Bird on a Straw" can help children:

- develop creative play.

Bird On A Straw

Materials

- drinking straws
- magazine pictures of different kinds of birds
- construction paper
- markers
- glue
- tape

The children could make their own bird puppets by cutting out pictures of birds and mounting them on construction paper, then attaching them to a straw with tape. It's a good idea to let the children select their own pictures of birds. Or, they may prefer to draw a picture of a bird themselves and have you help them cut it out and mount it on a straw. It's important to see that each child's bird is special . . . and that no two are exactly alike.

Older children might want to make a set of bird puppets, to represent a family or friends. See what kinds of stories the children create with their new bird puppets.

1659

Mister Rogers plays some "up" and "down" music on his piano and visits with clarinet player Richard Stoltzman. In the Neighborhood of Make-Believe, King Friday's wooden birds are missing! The viewers know that Robert Troll took them for a walk, but their other neighbors in Make-Believe don't know where they've gone.

"Where's the Bird" can help children:

- use play to work on feelings;
- work on feelings about separation.

Where's The Bird?

Materials

- toy bird or small picture of a bird

Children often enjoy playing hide-and-find games. It can be a way of helping them work on feelings about being away from their parents and about being together again. You can begin this game by hiding the bird yourself while one child hides his or her eyes. The other children can give hints about where to look: up higher or down lower. When a child has found the bird, he or she can do the hiding for the next one's turn. It's best to play this game in small groups of three or four so that everyone has a chance to find the bird.

(Or, 1128 "Thumbprint Pies"; 1006 "Cardboard Trumpets"; 1196 "Birds in Flight.")

1660

Bruce Franco, who makes balloon animals, visits Mister Rogers and shows how he sculpts balloons into various figures. In the Neighborhood of Make-Believe, King Friday's birds are found and Lady Elaine's elevator stops going up and down on its own. Mr. McFeely tells Mister Rogers about a hot-air balloon ride he once went on with Maggie Stewart.

"Up in the Air" can help children:

- develop their imaginations.

Up In The Air

Materials

- none

If you take the children outside for a walk, you could pause from time to time to look up in the air. What can the children see? (Birds, airplanes, clouds, tree branches?) When you get back, you could ask them to recall what they saw. Can they imagine what it would look like if they were up in the air looking down? What kinds of things might they see down below? If any of the children have been on an airplane or up in a tall building, they might have some interesting observations. Some children might want to imagine what it would be like to be up in a hot-air balloon, to be birds, or to ride in a spaceship. When they've had a chance to think about being up in the air, they might want to tell you a story about what they imagined. Some children might want to make pictures and have you write down their stories to make books about being up in the air.

Thoughts For The Week

Children (as well as adults) sometimes think that people will stop loving them if they make mistakes or do things they shouldn't do. Parents and caregivers reassure children of their love when they acknowledge that everyone makes mistakes sometimes, and that even when we get angry with people, we can still love them. In fact, it's the people we love the most who can often make us feel maddest.

Fred Rogers

Songs On The Programs This Week

1661   *"I Love Someone Who Looks Like You"*
       "It's You I Like"

1662   *"You Are Special"*
       "I'm Taking Care of You"

1663   *"There Are Many Ways to Say I Love You"*
       "It's the People You Like the Most"
       "Alphabet Song"

1664   *"Darvo, Darvo, Darvo"*
       ("Tree, Tree, Tree" in Ukrainian)

1665   *"There Are Many Ways to Say I Love You"*

Special Visits

1661   *How People Make Stuffed Bears*

1662   *A Visit to an Aviary*

Your Notes For The Week

1661

Mister Rogers brings a stuffed bear and talks about people and things we love. When Mr. McFeely arrives, he brings a videotape showing how people make stuffed bears. In the Neighborhood of Make-Believe, Lady Aberlin dresses up in a bear costume.

"My Favorite Things" can help children:

- talk about feelings;
- work on feelings about separation.

My Favorite Things

Materials

- stuffed animals

You could begin this activity by showing the children a stuffed animal and talking with them about the videotape on how people make stuffed bears. Do any of the children have a favorite stuffed animal they would like to show the others? Some of the children may have a special toy that they take to bed or use to comfort themselves. See if they want to tell you about their favorite stuffed animal or toy. (It can be very hard to share these special toys, so if children have brought them along, you may have to reassure them that they are not toys they must share unless they want to.)

1662

Mister Rogers visits an aviary—a place where people take care of birds. In the Neighborhood of Make-Believe, King Friday is upset because his pet birds are not working hard enough. Lady Elaine is preparing exhibits for her Museum of Love.

"Museum of Love" can help children:

* express feelings through art work;
* develop creativity.

Museum of Love

Materials

* paper
* markers or crayons
* paint and brushes (optional)

The children could prepare their own exhibits for a Museum of Love today. They could either draw a picture of something they love or make a picture for someone they love: a picture of their parents, a pet, a favorite toy, or random designs on paper. Some children may want to tell you about their pictures or give the drawing a name. You can help them mount the pictures on construction paper to "frame" them and make name cards to show who made each picture. Then you and the children can decide where to hang the pictures for display. When parents come to pick up their children, they can take a few minutes to tour your Museum of Love.

1663

Mr. Rogers has been doing a lot of walking, and he soaks his feet in a tub of water to make them feel better. Officer Clemmons stops by for a visit and joins him. In the Neighborhood of Make-Believe, King Friday is concerned because people are playing and not working. Lady Elaine plans a soap opera called "As the Museum Turns."

"Soap Sculptures" can help children:

* develop creative play.

Soap Sculptures

Materials

* bar of soap
* vegetable peeler
* box of facial tissue
* large plastic or metal bowl
* water

With your help, the children can make a molding material from soap shavings and shredded facial tissues. (You'll need about thirty sheets of facial tissues, a bar of soap, and 3/4 cup of water to make enough for four children.) One or two children can tear the facial tissues into very small pieces. Others can take turns using the vegetable peeler to shave off bits of soap from the bar you have provided. Everyone can help mix the soap shavings and tissue pieces with a small amount of water. Add the water a few tablespoons at a time until the material is of molding consistency. (It should feel like mud when it's ready.) Children can then use the material to make clean "mud pies" or other kinds of sculptures. The molding material will hold its shape, but won't really harden. If it begins to dry out, you can add a few drops of water to make it pliable again. (As with any soap mixture, you'll want to be careful that children don't get the soap in their eyes.)

1664

Mister Rogers talks about shaving and looks at his reflection in the mirror. In the Neighborhood of Make-Believe, the plans for a soap opera continue.

"Shaving Cream Finger-Painting" can help children:

*   develop creative play.

Shaving Cream Finger-Painting

Materials

*   shaving cream
*   trays or washable surface
*   aprons

Give children trays or make sure they use a washable surface so the shaving cream will be easy to clean up. Children could wear aprons or old shirts to protect their clothing, too. You might want to remind them not to touch their eyes while they have shaving cream on their fingers. Give each child a small amount of shaving cream and let them spread it around on the tray or table. As they begin to experiment with the material, you could comment on the effects they make when they use the sides of their hands, one or two fingers only, or when they use their fingernails to make designs in the shaving cream. If the shaving cream becomes dry, you can add a little bit of water. When you are finished, the children can help you clean up the trays or table with warm water and sponges.

1665

Mister Rogers spends some time blowing soap bubbles on the program today. In the Neighborhood of Make-Believe, a bubble-making machine will be part of the soap opera.

"Soap Bubbles" can help children:

*   learn more about the world;
*   develop creative play.

Soap Bubbles

Materials

*   water
*   dishwashing liquid
*   glycerin (optional)
*   string or bubble wands
*   plastic dish pan
*   eggbeater

The children can use a hand eggbeater or a wire whisk to help you mix 2 cups of the dishwashing liquid to 1/2 cup of water. If you have bubble wands, you can give them to the children for blowing bubbles. If not, you can tie loops in pieces of heavy string and let children dip the loops into the soap mixture. Because this activity is messy, you might want to do it outside. If you are blowing bubbles indoors, you'll probably want to cover the floor with a sheet or newspapers.

Thoughts For The Week

Talking about "then" and "now" can help children think about all the ways they've grown and what they were like when they were younger. The day-by-day growing that children experience often goes unnoticed, unless we take the chance to help children see all the inside and outside ways they've grown.

Conversations about things that happened a while ago can also open the way for talking about losses that children may have experienced, such as the death of a pet or someone they knew. Such conversations give us a chance to help children begin to understand one of the most difficult facts of life—that all living things die. It's a fact that remains hard for many of us to face, no matter how old we are. When a pet dies, the understanding of what death means will come only little by little—as will a child's readiness to accept a replacement. Children need a lot of help understanding death, and, like all of us, need time to grieve.

Fred Rogers

Songs On The Programs This Week

1666   *"It's the Style to Wear a Smile"*
       "Look and Listen"
       "I'm Taking Care of You"

1667   *"Let's Think of Something to Do"*
       "Tree, Tree, Tree"

1668   *"One and One Are Two"*
       "There Are Many Ways to Say I Love You"

1669   *"You Are Special"*
       "It's You I Like"

1670   *"You're Growing"*

Special Visits

1667   *How People Make Light Bulbs*
       Shadow Artist, Jim West

1668   *Pantomime Artist, Motoko Dworkin*

1670   *Violinist, Itzhak Perlman*

Your Notes For The Week

Monday

1666

Mister Rogers experiments with food coloring and water and talks about the kind of science children learn at school. In the Neighborhood of Make-Believe, Robert Troll replaces the Trolley with a miniature one.

"Water Science" can help children:

- learn more about their world;
- develop curiosity;
- develop creative play.

Water Science

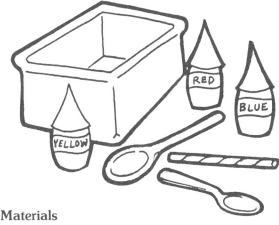

Materials

- dishpan or bowls
- water
- food coloring
- cooking utensils

Using a dishpan of water, experiment with different cooking utensils and food coloring to help children observe some scientific principles:

- that some objects sink and others float;
- that food coloring added to water creates changes they can see;
- that stirring water creates currents and swirls;
- that water left sitting out for several days will evaporate.

If you have many children in your care, you may want to use several bowls.

Tuesday

A shadow artist visits Mister Rogers and demonstrates his art. Mr. McFeely brings a videotape that shows how people make light bulbs. In the Neighborhood of Make-Believe, Robert Troll and Lady Aberlin are delivering shadows to their rightful owners.

"Hand Shadows" can help children:

- learn more about their bodies;
- learn more about the world around them.

Hand Shadows

Materials

- sunlight or high-intensity lamp
- black construction paper
- scissors
- pencil or pen
- glue
- colored construction paper

You can begin this activity by giving the children time to find ways to play with their own shadows. If it is a sunny day, they could look at their shadows outdoors and experiment with ways to make their shadows larger and smaller. If the weather doesn't permit, you can use a high intensity lamp or even a flashlight in a darkened room to create shadows on the wall. The children may want to make outlines of their hands on black construction paper to represent shadows. You could save these hand shadows to compare their hands at the end of the year to let them see how much they have grown.

Wednesday

A pantomime artist shows Mister Rogers actions that represent some of the characters in the Neighborhood of Make-Believe. In Make-Believe, Trolley has new tricks, showing pictures from times past and showing things upside-down.

"Then and Now" can help children:

- learn more about themselves;
- learn more about growing;
- learn more about their world.

Then and Now

Materials

- photos of the children at an earlier age (optional)

If you have any old photographs from when you were younger, you may want to share them with the children. You could ask parents to send in photos from when they were children. If you put the photographs in self-sticking album sheets, the children can handle them without bending or tearing them. If you don't have photographs, you can talk about something the children remember from when they were younger, like:

- starting child care;
- old and favorite toys;
- visits to grandparents or a special vacation.

You can help them recall things they could not do then that they can do now. Whatever they recall, you can help them develop a sense of pride in their growing accomplishments.

1669

Mr. McFeely has found a dead bird, and Mister Rogers remembers his pet cat, Sybil, who died some time ago. In the Neighborhood of Make-Believe, King Friday plays with his wooden birds on sticks and talks about his real bird, Cherry, who died.

"Remembering Pets that Died" can help children:

- talk about feelings;
- express strong feelings in appropriate ways.

Remembering Pets that Died

Materials

- stuffed animals or comfort toys
- a book about the death of a pet (optional)

If you, yourself, had a pet who died, you might begin by talking about how you felt when the animal died. Some of the children may have strong feelings about the death of their pet or someone they cared about, and they might want to snuggle close to you during these conversations or keep a favorite stuffed toy with them. The stuffed toys can give you the opportunity to talk about what it means to be living, and the difference between toys such as their stuffed animals and real animals that live and die. If you take your lead from the children's comments and questions, they'll let you know what they are concerned about. Some children may not want to join in the conversation, and it's okay if they just want to sit quietly nearby. Reading a story such as *The Dead Bird* by Margaret Wise Brown can also help you talk with the children about feelings that people have when a pet dies.

1670

Violinist Itzhak Perlman visits and talks about his music. He had polio and uses crutches and braces to walk. In the Neighborhood of Make-Believe, after seeing the Trolley's pictures of King Friday and others as children, the neighbors plan a Long Ago Party. Mister Rogers remembers some historical things from colonial times that he saw on a visit to Williamsburg, Virginia.

"A Long Ago Party" can help children:

- learn more about themselves;
- learn more about growing.

A Long Ago Party

Materials

- none

You can begin by helping the children talk about what they did long ago, when they were babies. It can help children to know it's okay, now and then, to wish they were babies. This pretend Long Ago Party can give them a chance to feel again some of the feelings they had when they were younger. When the party is over, you could ask them what are some good things about being a baby. . .and some good things about being as old as they are now. You can help them know you're proud of all the growing they're continuing to do.

Thoughts For The Week

During the preschool years, children may develop very specific ideas about what they will and will not wear. Naturally, those strong preferences will not always agree with what adults want them to wear. These times can be opportunities to work together on notions of "choice" and "control."

There are times when children must wear certain clothes, like when it's cold, but you may be able to let them choose, say between a coat or a sweater, or between their red or blue overalls. Making even small decisions can give children a sense that they can be in control of some things. That way, they may not have to struggle so much about things they cannot control.

Fred Rogers

Songs On The Programs This Week

1671   *"My Hat It Has Three Corners"*
       "Speedy Delivery"
       "It's You I Like"

1672   *"Let's Think of Something to Do"*
       "It's the Style to Wear a Smile"

1673   *"You Are Special"*

1674   *"Peace and Quiet"*
       "I'm Proud of You"

1675   *"You Are Special"*
       "My Hat It Has Three Corners"

Special Visits

1671   *A Bus Ride Through the Neighborhood*

1672   *How People Make Blue Jeans*

1673   *Organist, Alan Morrison*

1674   *How People Make Paper Bags*
       Flutist, Demarre McGill
       Clarinetist, Anthony McGill
       Pianist, Alan Morrison

1675   *The Millinery Shop in Colonial Williamsburg*

Your Notes For The Week

Monday

1671

Mister Rogers brings a three-cornered hat and sings "My Hat It Has Three Corners." He and Mr. McFeely take a bus ride through the neighborhood. In the Neighborhood of Make-Believe, Mayor Maggie brings three-cornered hats for King Friday and Queen Sara. King Friday makes a rule that everyone must wear one, but Lady Elaine chooses to wear something different.

"Three-Cornered Collages" can help children:
* learn about individual differences;
* develop creativity.

Three-Cornered Collages

Materials
* construction paper
* paste or glue
* a box of assorted paper cut into triangle shapes
* a box of assorted collage materials (paper shapes, ribbons, cotton balls, yarn)

You could begin this activity by talking with the children about triangles and other three-cornered objects. See if they can point out any three-cornered items in your home or center (a folded scarf, a three-legged stool, triangular blocks, folded paper napkins) and let them handle the triangle-shaped collage pieces. Children who would like to make three-cornered collages can glue the triangle shapes onto construction paper to make designs. You could even cut the background construction papers into triangles before the children begin making their collages. Some children may want to select collage items that are not triangles—and that's fine, too!

1672

In the Neighborhood of Make-Believe, nearly everyone is wearing a three-cornered hat—everyone but Lady Elaine, that is. She decided to spend time in the WN (Will Not) Room because she will not wear a three-cornered hat.

"Sometimes Isn't Always" can help children:

- talk about feelings;
- learn about individual differences.

Sometimes Isn't Always

Materials

- none

Here are some questions you might ask as you talk with the children about today's program:

- What did you think of Lady Elaine's hat?
- How was it different from everyone else's hat?
- How would you feel if you were living in the Neighborhood of Make-Believe and King Friday made a rule that everyone had to wear a three cornered hat?
- How do you think Lady Elaine felt about the King's rule?
- What do you think might happen next in the Neighborhood of Make-Believe?

Children can sometimes talk about times they felt like being different from other people and other times when they felt like doing exactly what everyone else was doing. You could talk about how they feel when they have to go along with rules, even if they don't want to. Can they think of times when it is all right not to go along with what other people are doing? Talking with trusted adults about their feelings can help children learn to manage those feelings better.

1673

Mister Rogers has two suitcases filled with shoes—one of each pair in each suitcase. He matches the shoes and talks about who might use them. He visits with an organist who wears special shoes for playing the pedals of the organ. In the Neighborhood of Make-Believe, Lady Elaine is squirting people who mention a three-cornered hat, and her neighbors hope that a friend can help resolve the dilemma.

"Shoe Match" can help children:

- learn to recognize likeness and difference.

Shoe Match

Materials

- assorted dress-up shoes or the children's shoes
- two boxes or baskets
- shoe boxes and tissue paper (optional)
- stool (optional)

To begin this game, place one shoe from each pair in one basket and the second shoe in another. Some children may not want others to touch their shoes, but if you have a supply of dress-up shoes, make these available so that everyone can have a pair of shoes. One at a time, the children take turns selecting a shoe from one container and then trying to find its match in the other basket. If you replace the shoes each time, the game will be just as challenging for each child. Talking with the children about differences in size, color, or shape can help them learn to recognize similarities and differences in objects. This might be a good day to add a few new pairs of shoes to the dress-up area. By adding shoe boxes, tissue paper, and a little stool, you could also set the stage for shoe-store play.

1674

Mister Rogers brings crutches, a cast, and a photograph of the time he wore that cast on his leg. Chef Brockett shows how he uses his crutches. Later, Mister Rogers listens to Alan Morrison, a friend who plays the piano, and two other young musicians, flutist Demarre McGill and clarinetist Anthony McGill, who are preparing for a concert. In the Neighborhood of Make-Believe, Lady Elaine agrees to wear a three-cornered scarf instead of a three-cornered hat.

"My Shape It Has Three Corners" can help children:

* learn to recognize likeness and difference;
* develop creative play.

My Shape It Has Three Corners

Materials

* fabric cut into triangle shapes, or
* scarves folded into triangles

See what ideas the children have for using the three-cornered fabric or scarves. They might think of things like:

* wearing it for dress-up play;
* using it as part of a dance;
* making a pretend bandage;
* wrapping a baby doll;
* making a cape for superhero play.

The three-cornered fabric and scarves can be stored with the dress-up clothes so that children can continue to think of ways to use them in their dramatic play.

1675

Mister Rogers brings a small sewing machine and shows a video about clothes people wore in colonial days. In the Neighborhood of Make-Believe, Lady Elaine and King Friday finally resolve their conflict and talk about their feelings.

"Three-Cornered Hats" can help children:

* develop creative play.

Three-Cornered Hats

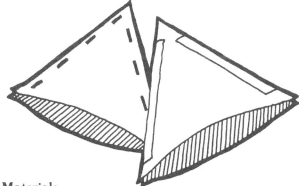

Materials

* heavy construction paper
* scissors
* staples or wide tape
* markers or crayons

Today you might want to help the children make three-cornered hats. You will need construction paper cut into sets of matching triangular shapes—one for the back and one for the front of each hat. Some children may want hats large enough to fit on their own heads; others might want to make smaller hats for their dolls or stuffed animals. You can use staples or wide tape to fasten two sides, leaving the bottom open. The children can decorate their three-cornered hats with crayons or markers.

Thoughts For The Week

As we think about difficult childhood experiences, so many of them include times when a child has to endure separation from an adult he or she loves and trusts. If that parting comes as a complete surprise, it can cause serious alarm. If, on the other hand, it's been talked about ahead of time, a child may be able to understand that the separation will last only for a while . . . and then the adult will be back. What's more, when the child sees that he or she is able to tolerate the short separation, that can build trust in his or her growing autonomy. (We feel good when we're able to tolerate hard times.)

*When children know ahead of time what's going to happen—and **not** happen—they have a chance to prepare themselves for what's coming. They can think about it and get used to their feelings about it. Encouraging children to do this kind of rehearsal through play is an important way to help them manage new experiences. Pretending about going away and coming back, for instance, can give children the chance to work on the feelings they may have about separation, whether it's the brief separation of a naptime or the longer separations that come with being away at a child-care program, or having to go to the hospital.*

Fred Rogers

Songs On The Programs This Week

1676 *"I'm Going Away"*
      "You've Got to Do It"

1677 *"I Like to Be Told"*

1678 *"Let's Think of Something to Do"*
      "It's You I Like"

1679 *"Did You Know?"*
      "Everything Grows Together"

1680 *"You Are Special"*

Special Visits

1676 *Mime, Dan Kamin*

1677 *An Ambulance Visit with Paramedics*

1678 *Wheelchair Basketball Players*

1679 *A Visit to the Car Wash*

1680 *How People Make Tortilla Chips*

Your Notes For The Week

Monday

1676

Mister Rogers brings a rolled-up map and talks about some ways people travel, going away and coming back. Mime Dan Kamin visits Mister Rogers and the Neighborhood of Make-Believe.

"Going Away and Coming Back" can help children:

- learn more about the world;
- develop creative play;
- develop symbolic play.

Going Away and Coming Back

Materials

- play furniture or pictures of furniture from catalogs or magazines
- toy people or figures drawn or cut from magazines

The children can use the play furniture to set up one model that represents the child-care setting and another one that represents home. Then, using the toy people (or figures that have been drawn or cut from magazines), they can pretend about going away from home to child care and returning back home at the end of the day. They might want to talk about any special routines they and their families have such as:

- saying good-by to a pet before leaving home;
- waving good-by to parents through a window at the child-care center;
- gathering their belongings just before parents come to get them.

1677

Mister Rogers visits with paramedics who show what an ambulance has on the inside and how they use the equipment to give caring help.

"An Ambulance for the Dolls" can help children:
- learn more about their world;
- use play to work out their feelings.

An Ambulance for the Dolls

Materials
- pillow case or towel
- toy medical kit
- strips of cloth that can be used as bandages
- medical dress-up clothes
- dolls or stuffed animals (optional)

Here are some ideas to talk about:
- Can they remember something about the ambulance on the program today?
- Does anyone remember hearing the siren noise?
- Have they ever been frightened by the sound?
- Can they tell you why we need ambulances?

The children can set up a pretend ambulance with the dolls or stuffed animals as the patients and themselves as the paramedics. A pillow case or towel can be the stretcher. The medical dress-up clothes and toy medical kit can be stored in a box so the children can get them out from time to time to continue their pretending about ambulances or other medical experiences.

1678

Mister Rogers plays basketball outside while he waits for a visit from exercise teacher, Marilyn Barnett. They visit a gymnasium to watch wheelchair basketball players during a practice session. In the Neighborhood of Make-Believe, people are looking for a secret tunnel.

"A Secret Tunnel" can help children:
- develop creative play;
- work on feelings about separation.

A Secret Tunnel

Materials
- card table or coffee table
- blanket or sheet
- cardboard tubes
- toy cars, trucks

You can make a tunnel by covering a card table or coffee table with a blanket or sheet, keeping both ends of the tunnel under the table open. Children can crawl in one side of the tunnel and then come out on the other side, creating a variation of the game of peek-a-boo. They may also want to make a tunnel for cars and toys, using cardboard tubes left over from paper towels or wrapping paper.

1679

Mister Rogers uses a cardboard tube as a tunnel for a toy car and Mr. McFeely brings a videotape of his visit to a car wash that seems something like a tunnel. In the Neighborhood of Make-Believe, the people find more clues that lead them to a secret tunnel.

"A Toy Car Wash" can help children:
- develop creative play;
- learn more about their world.

A Toy Car Wash

Materials
- clean milk cartons or cardboard tubes
- toy cars that will fit inside cartons or tubes

What can the children tell you about a car wash?
- Have they ever been through a car wash?
- Was it like the one Mr. McFeely visited?
- Can they imitate the sound of water in a car wash?
- What other ways do people wash cars?

If you are using empty milk cartons, open or cut off both ends so the toy cars can be driven through. Then let the children set up one or two car washes for their pretend play. They can pretend the car is being washed by imitating the sounds of a car wash. The children might like to use blocks or other cardboard cartons to make roads or to expand their play with cars.

1680

The people in the Neighborhood of Make-Believe find the secret tunnel! Mr. McFeely brings a videotape that shows how people make tortilla chips from blue corn.

"Salsa and Tortilla Chips" can help children:
- develop creative play;
- learn more about their world.

Salsa and Tortilla Chips

Materials
- 1 cup finely chopped tomatoes
- 1/2 tablespoon finely chopped green peppers
- 1 tablespoon lime juice
- 2 tablespoons water
- 1/2 tablespoon finely chopped onion
- bowl
- spoon
- tortilla chips, crackers, or pita bread
- serving plate

Let the children help you measure and mix the ingredients early in the day. Let the mixture sit for a while before serving. You can serve the salsa at snack time while you talk about how people make tortilla chips, or about other things that children remember from the program today.

Thoughts For The Week

We live in a society that seems so rushed. Parents have often told us how hard it can be to take time to relax and enjoy their children. They've also expressed concern about how they seem to be hurrying all the time, that they have to hurry their children—get them up and get them dressed, push them to eat faster, and move quickly through all the day's activities. Parents worry about how all the rushing around affects their children and themselves.

*Because adults are often in such a hurry, it may seem easier to do things **for** children rather than to give them time to do things for themselves. But it takes time to learn, to think, and to practice the important skills that can develop naturally during childhood. Whenever we do let children take their time to do things, we're giving them support for learning and growing.*

By letting children do things at their own pace as often as we can, we may also find that we're making it easier for them to accept those times when they do have to hurry. It can also help us adults to slow down and remember the most important things in life.

Fred Rogers

Songs On The Programs This Week

1681   *"I Like Someone, Do You Know Who?"*
       "You Are Special"
       "Peace and Quiet"

1682   *"Speedy Delivery Song"*
       "I'm Taking Care of You"

1683   *"Alphabet Song"*

1684   *"I'm Proud of You"*

1685   *"I Like to Take My Time"*
       "Everybody's Fancy"

Special Visits

1682   *How People Make Roller Skates*

1684   *World-Class Gymnast, Chainey Umphrey*

Your Notes For The Week

Monday

1681

Mister Rogers makes a game of dropping a small ball into tubes. In the Neighborhood of Make-Believe, Mayor Maggie discovers that the Trolley moves too slowly and then speeds up. She sings the song "Peace and Quiet" with slow and fast variations.

"Singing Fast and Slow" can help children:

- develop self-control;
- express themselves through music.

Singing Fast and Slow

Materials

- none

The children can choose one of their favorite songs and try singing the song fast and then slow. You might point out that some songs are easier to sing slow, and others seem like they should be sung fast. Some songs can be sung either fast or slow. Let the children sing several songs and then finish with a slow version of one of them to help the children calm down before going on to something else. "Peace and Quiet" might be a good choice to help some settle down.

1682

Mister Rogers has a pair of roller skates. He shows his safety gear and remembers a time when he went roller-skating with a friend. Mr. McFeely brings a videotape that shows how people make roller skates.

"Wheel Toys" can help children:

* learn more about the world;
* recognize likeness and difference.

Wheel Toys

Materials

* toys which have wheels
* riding wheel toys

You might begin this activity by letting the children each find a toy that has wheels and then bringing them together to show what they have found. Give them time to play with the wheels of the toys. Can they make the wheels go fast? Can they make them go slow? The children might want to go for a walk and point out the things they see that have wheels: cars, buses, trucks, bicycles. Are the vehicles moving fast or slow? When they play outside today, you can point out the wheel toys they can use (wagons, tricycles, and other riding toys).

1683

Mister Rogers looks at the Speedy Delivery Alphabet Book. In the Neighborhood of Make-Believe, Daniel is sad because he cannot say his ABC's fast, but Betty Aberlin shows him he can spell some important words, like his name, the word "tame," and the words, "I love you."

"Word Box" can help children:

* recognize and use symbols;
* develop the ability to read.

Word Box

Materials

* a box for each child (i.e., shoe box)
* marker or crayons
* glue
* paper

The children who know their ABC's might want a chance to show you that they can sing the alphabet song. Other children might want to point out letters that they recognize from things that are posted in the room or in a book. Then you can show the children that letters are put together to make words. Ask them what words they would like to see and write each word on a strip of paper. Then give each child a "word box" to store the words he or she would like to have. You will probably have to work with every child individually as you write each word on a separate piece of paper. If children want a phrase, like "I love you," you could help them see how to put the words together.

1684

Mister Rogers shows a wooden toy that is a gymnastics figure and visits with world-class gymnast Chainey Umphrey. In the Neighborhood of Make-Believe, the neighbors create scaffolding to try to catch the speeding Trolley and slow it down.

"Safe Gymnastics" can help children:
* learn to control their bodies;
* develop coordination.

Safe Gymnastics

Materials
* masking tape
* chairs or other objects for an obstacle course
* different sizes of pillows
* a box to crawl through (with both ends open)

You might begin by talking with the children about safe ways to play. Some children could show a safe way to do a somersault; others could show a safe way to balance on a low walking beam. Then you can arrange a variety of safe and easy gymnastics activities by:
* taping a line on the floor for a "tightrope";
* setting up an obstacle course of chairs or other objects for the children to go around;
* setting up a series of pillows to climb over;
* creating a tunnel to crawl through.

If any of the activities seem too difficult for some children, adjust them so that *everyone* can feel successful.

1685

Mister Rogers plays with a toy crane in the sandbox. In the Neighborhood of Make-Believe, the Trolley is going too fast, and the King has ordered it to stop. The Neighbors use a crane-like device to stop it and they discover a switch that slows it down.

"Fast and Slow, Then Stop" can help children:
* develop self-control;
* develop coordination

Fast and Slow, Then Stop

Materials
* tape recorder, record player, or radio
* musical tapes or records

Select fast and slow songs from a tape or record and let the children move to the music. Once the children have felt the difference between fast and slow, they can play a game by stopping when the music stops. First play the slow music and ask the children to stop. Then play fast music and let the children see how hard it can be to stop when you're doing something fast. If you end with the slow music, it could be easier for the children to calm down.

Thoughts For The Week

We're all so much alike...and yet we're all so different! A child's sense of identity grows slowly and for several years isn't likely to be very secure. As children grow, they need opportunities to express their uniqueness, whether in choosing the clothes they want to wear or in developing their unique art projects. There are always times when children need to do what everyone else is doing, but there are also many times when we can support children's self-esteem by helping them carry out their own ideas.

Fred Rogers

Songs On The Programs This Week

1686   *"You Are Special"*

1687   *"Then Your Heart Is Full of Love"*

1688   *"Look and Listen"*

1689   *"It's You I Like"*

1690   *"I Like To Take Care of You"*

Special Visits

1686   *How People Make Dinner Plates*

1687   *How People Make Wooden Shoes*

1688   *How People Make Guitars*

1690   *How People Make Kazoos*

Your Notes For The Week

1686

Mister Rogers looks in a mirror and talks about the fact that no two people are exactly alike. Chef Brockett prepares a birthday cake with raisins and nuts.

"Rice-Cake Faces" can help children:

- learn more about their bodies;

- learn more about foods.

Rice-Cake Face

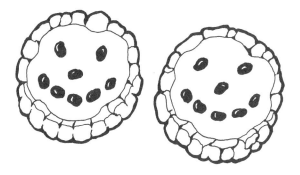

Materials

- rice cakes

- raisins

- peanut butter

You might begin this activity by letting the children look in a mirror to see their own faces. As the children take turns doing this, you can ask them to either point to or name facial features: nose, mouth, eyes, eyebrows. The children can help prepare snacks by making rice-cake or sandwich faces. Spread a rice cake or round piece of bread with a little bit of peanut butter and use raisins to make eyes, noses, and mouths. Encourage the children to do this any way they like and point out that no two have to be exactly the same.

1687

Mister Rogers shows pictures of twins who look almost exactly like one another. Even though they look alike, have the same parents and same birthday, each one is special.

"Mirror Play" can help children:

- learn more about their bodies;

- practice working cooperatively.

Mirror Play

Materials

- mirror

You can begin this activity by letting the children take turns looking in a mirror and making movements. Talk with them about the way the reflection moves when they move to introduce this game of mirror play. Children then get a partner and take turns being the leader and the reflection. As one child moves, the other child imitates the actions. Some children might want to touch fingertips to have a better sense of how and when the other person is moving.

Afterwards you can talk with them about how hard it is to move exactly like another person is moving. That's because no two people are exactly the same. Each one of us is special.

1688

Joe Negri plays music on his guitar as Mister Rogers shows pictures in a book of children dressed in animal costumes. Mister Rogers has fun with a cardboard guitar.

"An Air Band" can help children:

- develop creativity;

- express feelings through music.

An Air Band

Materials

- none

The children can create cardboard instruments for their own pretend play. Help the children draw guitar or banjo shapes on cardboard and cut them out for the children. Then let the children decorate the pretend instruments any way they would like. If you have a supply of cardboard tubes, the children could use them for trumpets, flutes, and other horns. Play the radio or taped music for the children's pretending.

1689

Mister Rogers makes a puppet, then shows how he does the voices of King Friday, Queen Sara and Corney. The puppeteer for Prince Tuesday comes to visit.

"Talking for the Toys" can help children:

*   express feelings through play;
*   develop creative play.

Talking for the Toys

Materials

*   toy dolls and animals

Using toy people or animals, let the children take turns "talking" for the different characters. Children can decide which "puppets" they want and how to talk for them. Some children may be able to switch roles and change voice tones as they pretend about being two different characters. You might even write down some of their words so that children can see how "plays" are developed.

1690

Corney has felt left out all week, thinking everyone forgot his birthday. His friends in Make-Believe surprise him with their celebration and help him know how important he is in their Neighborhood.

"Birthday Party Play" can help children:

*   develop creative play;
*   develop imagination.

Birthday Party Play

Materials

*   see below

You can set the stage for birthday party play by bringing in materials that children could use to pretend about birthdays. Here are some supplies to have on hand:

*   birthday party hats or materials to make them;
*   modeling dough to make pretend cakes;
*   popsicle sticks for pretend candles;
*   wrapped boxes or empty boxes and old wrapping paper and ribbon.

Let the children use their own ideas for pretending about birthdays. The children could pretend that one of the dolls or stuffed animals is having a birthday. Or, they might want to take turns pretending it's their birthday. If you keep these supplies stored in a bag or box, the children can take them out whenever they want to pretend about birthdays.

Thoughts For The Week

Learning to channel angry feelings into constructive activities is a hard task, but it's one of the most important things anybody can learn to do. Children's caregivers can help children learn that angry feelings can be expressed — as long as the children don't hurt themselves or others. We can help them to pound on clay, not on breakable toys; to kick a ball instead of kicking people or to throw a beanbag when they feel like throwing a toy. By setting firm limits, showing what's acceptable and what isn't about the expression of anger, you will be supporting them in some very important lifelong growing.

Fred Rogers

Songs On The Programs This Week

1691   *"What Do You Do With The Mad That You Feel?"*

1692   *"You Are Special"*

1693   *"Everything Grows Together"*

1694   *"You're Growing"*

1695   *"What Do You Do With The Mad That You Feel?"*

Special Visits

1691   *Artist Red Grooms*

1693   *How People Make Facial Tissues*

1694   *How People Make Steel Pans*

1695   *STOMP! Rythmic Percussion Performers*

Your Notes For The Week

1691

Artist Red Grooms shows Mister Rogers some of his whimsical sculptures and a Neighborhood picture he is painting. Mister Rogers talks about playing the piano when he felt frustrated as a child. In the Neighborhood of Make-Believe, Lady Elaine is feeling frustrated because she cannot draw as well as she wants.

"The Mad That You Feel" can help children:

• develop self-control;

• express feelings through play.

The Mad That You Feel

Materials

• none

You might want to begin this activity by giving an example of a time when you felt frustrated about something you were doing. Talk with the children about things you did that helped you feel better. Can the children remember a time when they felt angry or frustrated? They might be able to tell you some of the things they can do that make them feel better, such as:

• drawing about angry feelings;

• dancing to fast music;

• telling someone how they feel;

• pounding on modeling dough;

• running fast.

1692

Maggie Stewart tells Mister Rogers that swimming helps when she is feeling angry. Mister Rogers watches a video of Maggie swimming. In the Neighborhood of Make-Believe, Lady Elaine turns the Eiffel Tower upside-down because she is angry.

"Physical Exercise" can help children:

- develop coordination;
- learn to follow directions.

Physical Exercise

Materials

- none

You can begin by talking about angry feelings and asking if the children have ever felt the way Lady Elaine is feeling. Sometimes physical exercise can make people feel better when they are frustrated. See if the children can show you some exercises they could do at times like that. Put some active music on the radio, record or tape player and have the children follow your lead in doing some exercises. Let them follow you or encourage them to take turns being the leader. Some examples of exercise movements are:

- raising their hands over their heads;
- lifting their knees as if marching;
- making circular movements with their arms;
- touching their heads, shoulders and toes;
- twisting from side to side;
- jumping with one or two feet.

It can help calm the children at the end of this activity if you play softer, slower music as you are finishing.

1693

Mister Rogers talks about some things that people can do with their hands — things that don't hurt anyone. In the Neighborhood of Make-Believe, Lady Elaine is still upsetting people with the way she is handling her angry feelings.

"Hand Tracing" can help children:

- learn more about their bodies.

Hand Tracing

Materials

- paper
- crayons or markers

This activity is something that can be done on a one-to-one basis throughout the day. You might begin by talking with the group about all the many ways they can use their hands:

- drawing pictures;
- squeezing lemons;
- pounding dough;
- stirring food;
- reading books.

Then set aside time to trace each child's hand sometime during the day and talk with that particular child about things we can do with our hands. Write down some of the things the child tells you and attach the list to the hand tracing. When the children take the hand tracings home, you might encourage parents to talk with their children about other ways people can use their hands.

1694

Mister Rogers talks about safe things to pound. He has a recipe for making play clay for pounding. Mr. McFeely brings a book of musical instruments that shows a drum that is called a steel pan. He also has a video of Phil Solomon making a steel pan.

"Kneading Dough" can help children:

- develop self-control;
- express feelings through play.

Kneading Dough

Play Clay Recipe:

- 1 cup water
- 2 cups flour
- 1 cup salt
- 1 teaspoon vegetable oil

The children can help you mix these ingredients to make play clay for kneading and pounding. If you store the dough in an airtight container, you can keep it for times when children want to knead or pound something.

Please Note: Because of the salt content, it is recommended that children do not put this mixture in their mouths.

1695

An energetic group of performers of STOMP! show Mister Rogers how they make rhythms with their hands and feet, along with everyday things like brooms, pipes and pails. Mister Rogers has a sign that says CLAP on one side and STOMP on the other. He claps when the sign says CLAP and stomps when the sign says STOMP.

"Clap and Stomp Rhythms" can help children:

- develop self-control;
- express feelings through music.

Clap and Stomp Rhythms

Materials

- none

You could make a sign similar to the one Mister Rogers had and let the children make up rhythms by clapping and stomping. Begin by giving them a couple of rhythms, like:

- clap, clap, clap, stomp, stomp;
- clap, stomp, clap, stomp, clap;
- clap, clap, clap, stomp, stomp, stomp.

Then let children take turns making a pattern that everyone else follows.

Thoughts For The Week

Children experience many changes in their lives, from everyday transitions to major life adjustments, like when there's a new baby, a move, a parent's new job, or divorce. Along with helping children understand some of the changes in the world around them, we can also help them see that some things stay the same. For example, when we change the way we look on the outside, we're still the same person inside. Keeping routines consistent, helping children know what to expect, and offering extra comfort when a child is in need, can give children the stability to handle changes that come their way.

Fred Rogers

Songs On The Programs This Week

1696   "You Are Special"

1697   "Look and Listen"

1698   "Many Ways To Say I Love You"

1699   "I'm Taking Care of You"

1670   "Many Ways To Say I Love You"

Special Visits

1696   Storyteller Gay Ducey

1698   Setting Up Mister Rogers' Television House in the Studio

1699   How People Make Wagons

1700   Ducklings Hatching

Your Notes For The Week

1696

Mister Rogers experiments with colors and watches the changes that occur. In the Neighborhood of Make-Believe, Mayor Maggie has a package for Purple Panda. When she tosses it into the air, it changes color and flies away.

"Changing Colors" can help children:

- understand more about changes;
- learn to look carefully.

Changing Colors

Materials

- small margarine tubs or plastic bowls
- water
- food coloring
- plastic pitcher
- dishpan
- plastic spoons or stirrers

It would be a good idea to begin this activity by asking the children to help you cover the table with newspapers in case there are spills. Give each child a bowl that's about half full of water. Each child can then choose a food coloring and sprinkle a few drops onto the water. You might ask what the children think will happen to the water. Let them mix the coloring into the water and add a second color, if they'd like. What happens then? Encourage them to experiment with different colors and talk about what happens. You might have to get clean water from time to time, but save the old mixture in a larger bowl and talk about what happens when all the colors are mixed together.

1697

Mister Rogers visits with a teenager who juggles. In the Neighborhood of Make-Believe, everyone wonders what is in the package for Purple Panda. It has the words "Do Not Open" printed on it.

"Mystery Boxes" can help children:

*   develop healthy curiosity;

*   learn to listen carefully.

Mystery Boxes

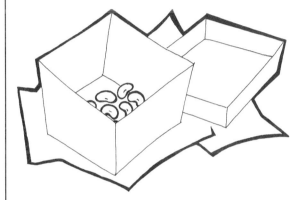

Materials

*   a small wrapped box with beans inside

*   several small jewelry boxes or plastic containers

*   used wrapping paper

*   tape

*   dried beans, rice, popcorn, birdseed, stones

You could begin by letting the children shake the wrapped box you have brought and see if they can guess what's inside. Then let the children make their own mystery boxes by putting a couple of spoonfuls of one item (rice, dried beans or birdseed) into each box, taping them up and wrapping them. As they shake the boxes, you can ask questions like: Which ones have soft sounds? Which are noisier? Do some of the boxes sound the same? Can they tell by the sound what might be inside? You might want to make a set of matching boxes that they can use as a listening game from time to time. Help them listen carefully and try to find the two boxes that sound the same.

1698

Mister Rogers brings sunglasses and a wig and tries them on. He says that he is still the same person, even when he looks different.

"Disguise" can help children:

*   understand more about changes;

*   recognize likeness and difference.

Disguise

Materials

*   sunglasses

*   scarf

*   hat or wig

*   mirror

You can begin this activity by disguising yourself in front of the children. First put on a scarf to cover your hair. Help them know it's still you. Then add sunglasses and a hat. Tell them what you are doing at each step and reassure them that you are still the same person. Then take off the disguise and let the children try on the scarf, hat and glasses. They might want to look at themselves in the mirror as they put on the things. Even though they look different, they are still the same under the disguise.

1699

Mister Rogers looks at the drains in the bathroom and sings, "You Can Never Go Down the Drain." Later, Mr. McFeely brings a video showing how people make children's wagons.

"Making a Wagon" can help children:

*   develop creative play;

*   develop imagination.

Making a Wagon

Materials

*   empty boxes

*   heavy cord

*   markers

*   scissors

The children might want to make their own wagons for carrying toys or toy people. You can help them make a simple wagon without wheels that they can drag across the floor. First punch two holes in the front of a box and help the children thread a piece of cord (about 3 feet long) through the holes. Tie the ends together. Let the children decorate their wagons with markers or construction paper. They can use these wagons at clean-up time to gather up the toys, or as part of their pretend play to give the stuffed animals or toy people a ride.

1700

In the Neighborhood of Make-Believe, Purple Panda's mysterious package hatches itself! It's a purple light that flashes the signal for "I love you." Mr. McFeely and Mister Rogers watch a videotape showing ducklings hatching from their eggs.

"Hatching Boxes" can help children:

*   learn more about size and shape;

*   work on feelings about separation.

Hatching Boxes

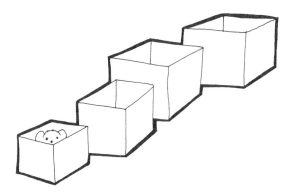

Materials

*   several different size boxes that fit inside each other

*   a small toy that fits into the smallest box

You can make a simple hide-and-find game by placing a toy inside a little box and putting it in the smallest of a series of boxes. Then put each box inside one that is larger. As the children open each box, they will find another box...until they get to the smallest box. Inside it, they will find the toy you have hidden.

Thoughts For The Week

Helping has two sides — asking for help from others and giving help to those around us. Children feel nourished when someone they love takes care of them by helping them. But it is just as nourishing for children to know that they can be helpful to others as well.

Fred Rogers

Songs On The Programs This Week

1701   *"You Are Special"*

1703   *"It's A Perfectly Beautiful Day"*

1704   *"Peace and Quiet"*

1705   *"It's You I Like"*

Special Visits

1702   *How People Make Vacuum Sweepers*
          African Musical Group, Jabali Afrika

1703   *Visit to B. Smith's Restaurant*

1704   *How People Make Chalk*
          Professor Wang, Chinese calligrapher

Your Notes For The Week

1701

Mister Rogers brings in a vacuum sweeper. In the Neighborhood of Make-Believe, Lady Elaine gets upset when Neighbor Aber uses an electric sweeper.

"Machines that Help" can help children:

• learn more about the world;

• develop healthy curiosity.

Machines That Help

Materials

• vacuum sweeper

• other appliances you have in the house

Ask the children if they think Lady Elaine might be afraid of the sweeper noise. Can they remember a time when the noise of an electric sweeper scared them? Are there other appliances in their homes that make a lot of noise, such as a blender, electric mixer, pressure cooker or washing machine? You could take a tour of your home or center to find some appliances that help people do work. You might be able to listen to the sounds the machines make while they are working. If there is an electric sweeper that the children can use, they might find it helpful to control the starting and stopping by pres-sing the buttons while you hold the handle. Older preschoolers can even help with the vacuuming.

1702

Mister Rogers shows a video about how people make vacuum sweepers. Jabali Afrika, a musical group from Kenya, rehearses in Negri's Music Shop.

"Talking About Things That Scare You" can help children:

- talk about fear;
- learn to manage feelings.

Talking About Things That Scare You

Materials

- none

Was there something that scared you as a child, like a vacuum sweeper, another machine, or thunder? Can you tell the children what you did when you were scared? What helped you overcome your fears? Share your experience with the children, then give them a chance to talk about things that scare them. What kinds of things can they do when they feel afraid? To whom can they go to for help and comfort? You might reassure them that talking or drawing about scary things can sometimes make them feel better.

1703

Mister Rogers visits B. Smith's restaurant kitchen. Mister Rogers and a young friend make a stove-less treat.

"Helping Grownups in the Kitchen" can help children:

- learn more about food;
- practice working cooperatively.

Helping Grownups in the Kitchen

Materials

- sandwich bread
- peanut butter
- raisins
- banana or apple slices
- plastic knives or spreaders

You can invite the children to help prepare peanut butter sandwiches today. Give each child two slices of bread. Let the children spread some peanut butter on one slice. See if any of them want to add banana slices, apples or raisins to their sandwiches before putting on the top slice of bread. Some of the children may want to talk about times they have helped their parents in the kitchen at home.

1704

Mister Rogers draws with colored chalk and sees how people make chalk. In the Neighborhood of Make-Believe, Purple Panda arrives to help solve the vacuum sweeper mystery. Mr. Wang helps Mister Rogers learn about Chinese calligraphy.

"Learning to Write with Chalk" can help children:

* develop fine motor control;
* recognize and use symbols.

Learning to Write With Chalk

Materials

* construction paper
* colored chalk (or crayons)

Children's earliest scribbles are their first attempts at writing. Encourage the children to make any kinds of marks they want on the paper. Some children may "write" all kinds of things that look like scribbles to us. You can ask them what these pretend words say while they "read" the scribbles back to you. Kindergarten children may want to practice the letters they already know or ask for your help in learning to write new letters.

1705

In the Neighborhood of Make-Believe, Lady Elaine learns that vacuum sweepers don't suck in people...only dirt.

"Straw Play" can help children:

* understand cause and effect;
* develop creative play.

Straw Play

Materials

* plastic straws
* one-inch squares of light-weight paper (2 or 3 times larger than the straw opening so they cannot be sucked into a child's mouth)

Let the children play with the straws and experiment with sucking in and blowing out. If they place their hands under the end of the straw, they can feel the air blowing out....and being sucked in. Then give each child a handful of paper squares and let them blow them around. If they place the straw against a piece of paper and suck in, the paper will stick to the straw.

Thoughts For The Week

There are two ways that we can be helpful to children when they face something new and difficult. The first is to let them know what to expect. When children know ahead of time what's going to happen — and not happen — they can prepare themselves for what's coming. They can think about it and get used to their feelings about it.

The second way that we can be helpful is by encouraging children to play about these events —both before and afterwards. Playing can give children a sense of control over scary feelings.

Fred Rogers

Songs On The Programs This Week

1706   *"It's You I Like"*

1707   *"Brave and Strong"*

1708   *"Please Don't Think It's Funny"*

1709   *"Are You Brave?"*

1710   *"Then Your Heart Is Full of Love"*

Special Visits

1706   *How People Make Cereal*

1707   *How People Make Socks*

1708   *How People Shear Sheep and Spin Wool Into Yarn*

1709   *Mister Rogers Gets an Immunization*

Your Notes For The Week

Monday

1706

Mister Rogers has snow globes. When he shakes them up, the pieces inside look like falling snow. Mister Rogers shows a video about how people make cereal. In the Neighborhood of Make-Believe, it's snowing cereal.

"Glitter Shakers" can help children:

- learn to look carefully;
- develop healthy curiosity;
- use play to work on feelings.

Glitter Shakers

Materials

- empty plastic soda bottles (one for each child, if possible)
- glitter
- water
- heavy masking tape

The children can help you make glitter shakers that resemble snow globes. Here's what to do:

- Fill each bottle about three-fourths full of water;
- Add two spoonfuls of glitter or foil confetti (more for larger bottles);
- Close tightly and tape the cap on.

The children can shake the bottles or turn them upside down to mix the glitter and then watch the glitter move as it settles to the bottom again. Sometimes children find it comforting to quietly watch the glitter patterns as they're settling down for a nap.

1707

Mister Rogers brings sticks and yarn. In the Neighborhood of Make-Believe, Daniel Tiger is afraid of the snowing cereal.

"Nature Collage Quilt" can help children:

- learn to look carefully;
- develop creativity;
- practice working cooperatively.

Nature Collage Quilt

Materials

- small zipper-close plastic bags
- yarn
- hole punch
- dowel or long stick

Weather permitting, you can take them for a short walk or do some exploring outside. Give each child a small plastic bag with a zipper closure to gather items from nature that they find interesting: stones, sticks, leaves, grass, moss. When you get back to your house or center, help the children zip the bags and punch a hole in each corner. Then see if the children can help connect the bags together to make a hanging "quilt" by threading the yarn through the holes and tying the bags together in rows. You can display the quilt by tying the top plastic bags to a wooden dowel or long stick.

1708

Mister Rogers brings a small baby blanket and talks about his sister's "Beankie" that made her feel more comfortable. Mr. and Mrs. McFeely have some lambs in their yard.

"Talking About Our Favorite Things" can help children:

- learn to manage feelings.

Talking About Our Favorite Things

Materials

- none

Did you have a favorite blanket or soft toy when you were a child? If so, you might tell the children what you remember about it. Then see if the children have a favorite item that they like to keep with them from time to time. Some children like to have these items when they are tired, afraid, away from home, or missing their parents.

Do any of the children have soft favorite toys with them to show the others? You might want to reassure children that you know these things are import-ant to them and that they won't have to share them with other children.

1709

Mister Rogers goes to the clinic for an immunization. In the Neighborhood of Make-Believe, Daniel Tiger's friends help him feel brave enough to stop the snow.

"Doctor Play" can help children:

- express feelings through play;
- learn more about the world;
- develop creative play.

Doctor Play

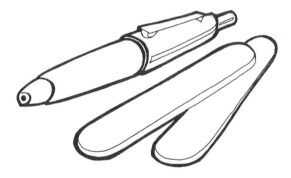

Materials

- ball point pen with retractable point
- strips of cloth
- tape for bandaging
- stuffed animals or dolls

The children might want to pretend about visiting the doctor or giving immunizations today. If you have an old ball point pen with a retractable point, you can remove the ink cartridge and let the children use the "clicker" end to pretend to give an immunization to their dolls or stuffed animals. Other children may want to bandage the dolls or pretend about doctor visits they have had. What kinds of things happen when they visit a doctor? You can ask them to help you make a list of other doctor play props that you can collect for their play.

1710

In the Neighborhood of Make-Believe, the neighbors decide what to do with all the boxes of cereal. Mister Rogers shows a video about how people make yogurt.

"Yogurt Cereal Mix" can help children:

- learn more about food;
- practice working cooperatively.

Yogurt Cereal Mix

Materials

- yogurt
- unsweetened cereal
- raisins
- bowl

Let the children help you mix together several types of unsweetened cereal and a cup of raisins. Give the children their own bowl of yogurt and let them sprinkle the cereal mixture over the yogurt.

Thoughts For The Week

Sharing isn't easy for children, and learning to share is a long process. Especially in a child-care setting, it can be hard for children to understand what's mine, yours and ours. Sharing grows little by little, as children develop the ability to see things from another person's point of view and to trust that what they share will be given back.

Fred Rogers

Songs On The Programs This Week

1712 *"Many Ways To Say I Love You"*

1713 *"It's You I Like"*

1714 *"Please Don't Think It's Funny"*

1715 *"What Do You Do With The Mad That You Feel?"*

Special Visits

1713 *How People Make Apple Juice*

1714 *How People Make Fig Bars*

1715 *Dump Trucks*

Your Notes For The Week

Monday

1711

In the Neighborhood of Make-Believe, King Friday's crown is missing. Some of the neighbors try to help him find it.

"Where's the Crown" can help children:

- work on feelings about separation;
- learn to look carefully;
- learn to listen carefully.

Where's the Crown?

Materials

- small paper crown

You might begin this activity by talking with the children about King Friday's missing crown. Can they think of a time when they have lost something? How do they go about trying to find it? You can play a simple hide-and-find game by hiding a small paper crown somewhere in the room and letting children take turns trying to find it. Giving clues such as "getting warmer" or "getting colder" can help narrow the area they are searching. Once a child finds the crown, he or she can hide it for the next person.

1712

Mister Rogers visits with artist Leonard Streckfus to see his collection of "found objects" sculptures.

"Found Object Collage" can help children:

- develop creative play;

- express feelings through art.

"Found Object" Collages

Materials

- construction paper

- assortment of "found objects"

- glue

The children could help you gather some of the "found objects." These might include milk bottle caps and rings, soda pop tabs, paper towel rolls, old newspapers or magazines, ribbon, string, or yarn, aluminum foil, cotton filling, or styrofoam packing material. "Found objects" from the yard or play area might include small stones, leaves, sticks, acorns, buckeyes, seed pods and other natural materials. Some of the children might want to arrange the items on the paper and then glue them all down. Other children prefer to select the items and glue as they go along. You might talk with the children about the many different ways that people create artwork. The children might want to display their work so parents can enjoy their creations.

1713

In the Neighborhood of Make-Believe, Lady Elaine thinks that sharing means taking things from other people when she wants them.

"Talking About Sharing" can help children:

- practice working cooperatively;

- practice taking turns.

Talking About Sharing

Materials

- none

You might begin this activity by talking about the situation in the Neighborhood of Make-Believe. What has been happening? Where do the children think the missing objects could be? See if the children can tell you what they think "sharing" means. You could ask questions such as:

- What does it mean to share something?

- Who decides that something is to be shared?

- What kinds of things have to be shared with other people?

- What can you say to someone who takes something without asking?

Sharing is sometimes hard for young children because they often think that playing with a toy means that the toy belongs to them. You might talk about how they can let someone know they are finished with a toy...or how to tell another child that they aren't finished using it yet. Many children need reassurance that they don't have to share special items they bring from home — such as a stuffed animal or blanket.

1714

Lady Elaine learns that she has to "ask before she takes." Mr. McFeely visits Mister Rogers and brings fig bars and a video that shows how people make fig bars.

"Sharing a Snack" can help children:

- practice working cooperatively;
- learn more about food.

Sharing a Snack

Materials

- bread
- jelly
- knife
- tray

Today the children could make a snack that they share with each other. Take several pieces of bread and cut off the crusts, saving them to make bread crumbs or to add to a casserole. Then let the children spread jelly on one slice of bread. Roll the bread into a "jelly roll" and cut it into several pieces. Each child can make a sandwich to share with others.....or all can work together by taking on different jobs: spreading the jelly, rolling the sandwich, cutting it into pinwheels, placing the pieces on a serving plate or tray.

1715

Bill Nye the Science Guy visits *Mister Rogers' Neighborhood*.

"Kitchen Science" can help children:

- learn to look carefully;
- learn more about changes;
- develop creative play.

Kitchen Science

Materials

- cornstarch
- water
- bowl
- tray
- cups
- spoons or popsicle sticks

Give each child a cup with a half-cup of cornstarch in it. Then add a half-cup of water to the cornstarch and let the children mix the ingredients with a spoon or stick. The substance will seem like liquid when poured from the cup onto a tray. But if the children try to pick up the substance, it begins to harden from the pressure of their hands. The children can trace letters or designs in the mixture and then watch it flow back together. If the mixture begins to dry out, add a few drops of water.

Thoughts For The Week

This week has two related messages — learning to stick with a task even when it may seem difficult...and recognizing that there are some things we cannot do, no matter how hard we try. All of us need to know that no matter what we're able to learn or what we're not able to learn, we're still lovable just the way we are.

Fred Rogers

Songs On The Programs This Week

1716   "You Are Special"

1717   "Peace and Quiet"

1718   "Look and Listen"

1719   "Let's Think of Something To Do While We're Waiting"

1720   "I'm Proud of You"

Special Visits

1716   Flying Karamazov Brothers
How People Make Macaroni

1717   Magician David Copperfield

1718   Uptown String Quartet

1719   How People Make Sleeping Bags

1720   Hula Hoop Expert Paul Tifford

Your Notes For The Week

1716

Mister Rogers meets world-famous jugglers, the Flying Karamazov Brothers. In the Neighborhood of Make-Believe, X the Owl wants to teach everyone how to fly.

"Juggling Scarves" can help children:

•   develop muscle control;

•   practice working cooperatively.

Juggling Scarves
Materials

•   scarves

One of the first steps in learning how to juggle is to toss and catch safely. Young children may not be able to learn how to juggle, but they can practice tossing and catching something like a scarf. Before you begin this activity, talk about the importance of throwing safely so that no one gets hurt. Then ask the children to find a partner and have them stand about two feet apart while they toss a scarf back and forth. If they have trouble catching the scarves, they can move closer together.

1717

Mister Rogers has some feathers and bird pictures. He shows beautiful feather art. In the Neighborhood of Make-Believe, X the Owl is trying to teach Prince Tuesday how to fly.

"Feather Collage" can help children:

*   develop creativity.

Feather Collage

Materials

*   craft feathers
*   construction paper
*   magazine pictures of birds
*   scraps of paper, cotton balls, yarn, ribbon
*   glue
*   scissors

Most craft stores carry bags of assorted feathers. Add these to a box of collage materials: scrap paper, yarn, cotton balls, ribbon, etc. If you don't have any craft feathers, you can cut out a few feather shapes to add to the collage materials or cut out some pictures of birds from a magazine. Give the children large pieces of construction paper and let them arrange and glue the materials however they wish.

1718

In the Neighborhood of Make-Believe, Prince Tuesday gets hurt and has to go to the hospital.

"Hospital Play" can help children:

*   develop creative play;
*   use play to work on feelings.

Hospital Play

Materials

*   play medical kit
*   long strips of cloth for bandages
*   white shirts or medical dress-up clothes
*   sofa or cot

The children might be concerned about Prince Tuesday's fall. It can help to talk with them about who helps them when they fall. Some of them may have gone to the hospital after a fall. Who were the people who took good care of them there? How did the people at the hospital help them feel better? Give the children time to use the medical props to pretend about going to the hospital. They can pretend that one of the stuffed animals or dolls fell and got hurt and that they're the hospital caregivers.

1719

Mister Rogers shows a video about how people make sleeping bags and talks about playing safely.

"Keeping Safe" can help children:

*   learn about limits.

Keeping Safe

Materials

*   none

You might want to talk with the children today about ways they can keep themselves safe. What are some of the rules you have about staying safe? You might mention things like:

*   walking rather than running;

*   not climbing on or jumping off the furniture;

*   staying on the sidewalk when walking outdoors;

*   not throwing things in a way that could hurt someone.

Children often find it easier to accept rules when they understand the reasons for them. See if they have any new rules they would like to add to your list.

1720

Mister Rogers brings a hula hoop and shows how to use it. He talks about how long it takes to learn to do something new. In the Neighborhood of Make-Believe, no one is trying to learn to fly anymore. Instead, they are trying things that are safe.

"Jump and Call" can help children:

*   develop muscle control;

*   develop coordination.

Jump and Call

Materials

*   hula hoop or piece of rope or tape

If you don't have a hula hoop, you can use a piece of rope or tape a large circle on the floor. This activity is meant for small groups of three or four children. They can imitate the "jump and call" activity on the program by jumping in place and making a fun calling sound. Then let the children take turns jumping into the circle of rope or hula hoop as they make the "call" sound. Then have them jump out.

Thoughts For The Week

For some children, being a generous giver and a gracious receiver are natural. But other children may need more time and more help from us — not because they're selfish, but because they have trouble letting go. When we show children we care about their feelings and that we enjoy giving and receiving, we help them understand how much we receive when we give and how much we give when we receive.

Fred Rogers

Songs On The Programs This Week

1721	"I'm Taking Care of You"
1723	"You Can Never Go Down The Drain"
1725	"Ways To Say I Love You"

Special Visits

1721	How People Make Fortune Cookies Eric Carle, Children's Author-Illustrator
1722	How People Make Bagels
1723	How People Make Toilets
1724	How People Make Merry-Go-Round Horses
1725	LeVar Burton Visits With Mister Rogers

Your Notes For The Week

Monday

1721

Mister Rogers gives fortune cookies to an appreciative Mr. McFeely, who has brought a video about how people make those cookies. Then he visits with author-illustrator Eric Carle, who shows how he did the artwork for his book *From Head to Toe*.

"A Gift for You" can help children:

- learn more about giving;
- recognize and use symbols.

A Gift for You

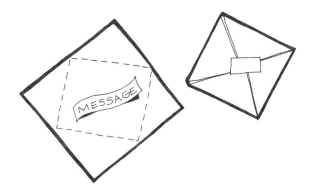

Materials

- paper
- markers or crayons
- tape
- fortune cookies (optional)

If you have any fortune cookies, you could let each child break one open to find the message inside. They might want to make something like that cookie by writing or dictating a message or drawing a small picture to enclose inside a gift envelope. While they are making their pictures or messages, cut paper into 6-inch squares. The children can fold up their messages or pictures and place them in the center of the square while you help by folding the opposite corners and taping them together. The children can fold in the last two corners and tape them into position. Ask the children to tell you whom the gift is for and write that person's name on the envelope.

If the children want to make several gifts, this might be a time to talk about gift-giving and how good it feels to give something to people we love.

1722

Today Mister Rogers puts on a batik vest instead of a sweater. He visits a workshop where artist Saihou Njie shows the process of creating his colorful batik fabric. Later, Mr. McFeely brings Mister Rogers a video about how people make bagels.

"Bagel Snacks" can help children:

• learn more about food.

Bagel Snacks

Materials
• bagels
• cream cheese
• jelly or peanut butter
• plastic knives
• paper plates
• napkins or paper towels

The children might want to make their own bagel snacks today. After you slice the bagels, you might want to toast them, but it's not necessary. Let the children place a small amount of jelly or peanut butter on their plates and then spread the toppings on their own bagels. While you are enjoying a snack with the children, you might ask what they remember about how people make bagels.

1723

Mister Rogers brings a small potty chair and shows a video about how people make toilets. He sings the song, "You Can Never Go Down the Drain."

"Playing With Water" can help children:

• develop self-control;
• use play to work on feelings.

Playing With Water
Materials
• basin or large dish pan
• towels
• colander
• tubes
• funnels
• plastic toys

Your children might want to play with water today and practice keeping it under control. Spread a large towel under the dish pan to absorb any spills and give the children a chance to play with one or two others at a time. You might want to show them how water goes through a funnel or colander...and that toys don't fit through the small holes that let water through.

1724

Mister Rogers uses paper plates to make a ring-toss game and a merry-go-round. Mr. McFeely brings him a video that shows how people make carousel horses.

"Paper Plate Merry-Go-Round" can help children:

*   develop creative play.

Paper Plate Merry-Go-Round

Materials

*   a paper plate for each child
*   magazines with pictures of toys or animals
*   glue
*   pencils
*   scissors

Give the children a chance to look through the magazines and choose small pictures of animals or toys they might want to use for their merry-go-rounds. Then help them tear or cut out the pictures and glue them around the edge of a paper plate. Punch a small hole in the center of each plate and put the point of a pencil through the hole. Children can twirl the pencils to make their merry-go-round spin.

1725

PBS *Reading Rainbow* neighbor, LeVar Burton, visits and shares his love of reading and books with Mister Rogers. In the Neighborhood of Make-Believe, King Friday becomes a gracious giver.

"Talking About Giving and Receiving" can help children:

*   learn more about giving;
*   learn to be considerate of others.

Talking About Giving and Receiving

Materials

*   none

You might begin by talking about a time when you received a gift that you really liked. Tell the children how you felt. Then ask them to talk about how they feel when they get something they really want. Ask them if they know what "disappointed" means? Have they ever been disappointed when a gift wasn't what they expected? What kinds of things could they do or say that wouldn't hurt the giver's feelings?

Thoughts For The Week

We all want children to respect people, including those who have disabilities. For a number of reasons, that can be a special challenge for preschoolers. When we model warm and caring acceptance of others — recognizing strengths and trying to understand limitations — we are helping children know that we appreciate all of who they are.

Fred Rogers

Songs On The Programs This Week

1726   *"Let's Be Together"*

1728   *"It's You I Like"*

1729   *"Many Ways To Say I Love You"*

1730   *"You Are Special"*

Special Visits

1726   *Wheelchair Lifts Installed in Vans*

1727   *Koko the Gorilla*
        How People Make Play Balls

1728   *Visit to the Eye Doctor*
        How People Make Eyeglasses

Your Notes For The Week

Monday

1726

Mister Rogers visits some neighbors who install wheelchair lifts in vans and buses. In the Neighborhood of Make-Believe, King Friday is worried that touching a wheelchair could make someone need one.

"Talking about Wheelchairs" can help children:

- learn more about disabilities;
- learn to be considerate of others.

Talking About Wheelchairs

Materials

- pictures of people in wheelchairs (optional)

You might begin by talking with the children about a time when you or someone you know used a wheelchair – when leaving the hospital, for instance. See if the children know anyone who uses a wheelchair on a regular basis. How do they know that person? Ask the children to tell you more about that person. Maybe they'd like to make up a story about people who are in wheelchairs — from the pictures you've cut out or from their imagination.

1727

A gorilla comes to the Neighborhood of Make-Believe, but doesn't feel very accepted there. Lady Elaine thinks the gorilla is a wild monster because the only ones she has seen are scary ones in movies. Mister Rogers shows a video about how people make balls.

"Feeling Left Out" can help children:

- recognize feelings;
- talk about feelings;
- express feelings through art.

Feeling Left Out

Materials

- paper
- markers

You might ask the children if they have ever been in a situation where they felt left out or excluded — times such as:

- when someone was building with blocks and wouldn't give them any;
- when older children were playing a game and wouldn't let them play;
- when they were new to the group and didn't know anyone.

What did they do? How did they feel? You could give children paper and markers to draw about those feelings. Some children might draw a picture of the actual experience; others might just draw scribbles and patterns that show their feelings.

1728

Mister Rogers visits an eye doctor and shows a videotape about how people make eyeglasses. In the Neighborhood, Lady Aberlin gets to know Kevin Wendell Gorilla, but some of the other neighbors are still afraid of him and run away when they see him.

"Making an Eye Chart" can help children:

- recognize and use symbols;
- learn more about the world.

Making an Eye Chart

Materials

- large paper or cardboard
- markers
- pictures from magazines of objects or animals
- large letters or symbols cut from magazines or newspapers
- tape or glue

Have some of the children ever had an eye exam? If so, let them tell the others about it. The children can make an eye chart by arranging pictures or letters and numbers in rows on a large piece of paper. They can take turns being doctor and patient while they "read" the names of the symbols on the eye chart. You might point out that there is a difference between not knowing the name of the symbol and not being able to see it. If they have an eye test and don't know the name of the letter the doctor is showing them, they should tell someone that they don't know its name.

1729

Mister Rogers talks about the importance of differences and plays a game with an assortment of different objects. In the Neighborhood of Make-Believe, some of the neighbors are getting to know Kevin Wendell Gorilla.

"Different and the Same Collage" can help children:

- recognize likeness and difference;
- develop creativity.

Different and the Same Collage

Materials

- construction paper
- glue
- identical sets of paper shapes: circles, strips, squares, triangles (one for each child; about 15-20 shapes in a set)
- plastic or paper bags or envelopes

You could begin by talking with the children about ways they are alike and ways they are different from one another. You might point out that even though they are alike in many ways, they have different ideas about how to play or what to draw. Give each child a bag or envelope with the same assortment of shapes to make a collage on construction paper. When they have finished their collages, talk about how each one is different from the others...even though all the children started with identical shapes.

1730

Mister Rogers makes a rainbow and talks about how beautiful it looks when more colors are added. In the Neighborhood of Make-Believe, Lady Elaine learns that Chuck Aber was pretending to be a gorilla to see if people would treat him the same, no matter what he looked like on the outside.

"Rainbow Containers" can help children:

- develop creativity;
- develop muscle control.

Rainbow Containers

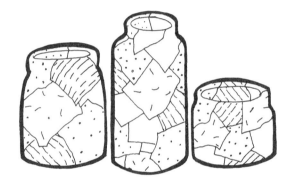

Materials

- tissue paper in rainbow colors
- glue
- water
- brushes
- jars or plastic containers

The children can cover a small jar or plastic container with tissue paper to make rainbow-colored gifts. Mix water into glue until it is the consistency of paint. Let the children tear or cut small mosaic-like pieces of paper and glue them onto the jars by "painting" over them with the glue mixture.

Thoughts For The Week

As children become more and more aware of themselves and their world, they become aware of how small they are, compared to people who take care of them. We adults can help young children feel good about who they are when we show that we value what they can do...and that we don't expect them to be more grownup than they are ready to be.

Fred Rogers

Songs On The Programs This Week

1733   *"Children Can"*

1734   *"You Are Special"*

Special Visits

1731   *How People Make Wooden Yo-Yos*

1732   *Helicopter Ride*

1733   *How People Make Grape Jelly*

1735   *Architect-Sculptor Maya Lin*

Your Notes For The Week

1731

Mister Rogers brings a small piano which he can play and a yo-yo that he has trouble making work. Marilyn Barnett visits and shows Mister Rogers exercises that have big movements and little movements.

"Little & Big Exercises" can help children:

• develop coordination;

• develop self-control.

Little & Big Exercises

Materials

• music from a radio or tape player (optional)

Encourage the children to make up exercises that have really big movements, like:

• making windmill arm movements;

• kicking as high as they can;

• lifting their knees and touching them with their hands.

Then see if they can show you some small movements, like:

• exercising their fingers only;

• opening and closing their jaws;

• moving only their toes while keeping their feet on the floor.

You could select music that encourages large movements and some music that suggests smaller movements (short, fast notes) and move to the music. Alternating big and small movements helps children develop self-control and the ability to manage body movements, contributing to their self-awareness and a sense of body boundaries.

1732

Mister Rogers shows big and little models of a helicopter, then watches Mr. McFeely take a ride in a real helicopter. In the Neighborhood of Make-Believe, Prince Tuesday can do tricks with a yo-yo, but King Friday bans yo-yos because he has trouble making one work.

"Little Books, Big Books" can help children:

* recognize likeness and difference;

* learn to sort and classify objects.

Little Books, Big Books

Materials

* large poster board (2 sheets about 18" x 24")

* large paper (8-10 sheets)

* paper punch

* shoestrings or notebook rings

* thin cardboard (2 pieces about 2" x 4" for each child)

* small paper (5 sheets for each child, 2" x 4")

You might want to begin today's activity by talking with the children about little and big. See if they can find toys that are models of bigger things they might see (doll beds, toy stove, toy cars and trucks). Then help the children make one big book for the class with enough blank pages for each child to make a picture. Fasten the pages between two sheets of poster board by punching holes in the pages and cover, and threading shoelaces or notebook rings through the holes. The children can each make a small book of their own by stapling together small sheets of paper between cardboard covers. They can draw a picture on each page of their small books and later today, or on another day, take turns making a picture on one page of the big book.

1733

Mister Rogers brings a little suitcase that has little hats and a big suitcase that has big hats. He tries on the big hats and talks about dress-up play. Maggie Stewart brings a videotape about how people make grape jelly. She and Mister Rogers share a grape jelly snack.

"Grapes, Grapes, Grapes" can help children:

* learn more about food.

Grapes, Grapes, Grapes

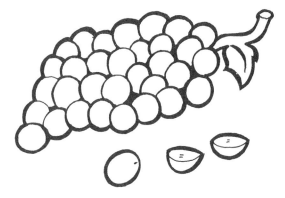

Materials

* different types of seedless grapes

* serving bowl

* grape jelly

* bread or crackers

* pictures of grapevines from a book or magazine (optional)

Do any of the children know how grapes grow? If you have pictures of grape vines, let the children take some time to look at the vines. Then show them several bunches of grapes so they can see the how they are attached to each other when they grow. After the children have washed their hands, they can help you pull the grapes off the stems and put them in a serving bowl. (If you have very young children, you might want to cut the grapes into halves.) After the children taste the grapes, let them spread grape jelly on bread or crackers for snack today.

1734

Mister Rogers brings an expandable sphere that can be made little or big.

"Talking About Little & Big" can help children:

* recognize likeness and difference;

* learn to sort and classify objects.

Talking About Little & Big

Materials

* little and big toys

* little and big baskets or boxes

* some middle-sized toys and baskets

The children might want to talk about things that seem big to them, such as construction trucks, houses, towers, airplanes. You might want to explain that the words little and big are relative words — that some things may seem big to one person and small to someone else. You could point out that they might seem big to their younger brothers or sisters, but feel small when compared to their parents. Have the children sort through a box of toys that have size differences to find things they would consider big to put in a big basket and those they would consider small for the smaller basket. You could add a middle-sized basket if the children have trouble deciding where to put the toys.

1735

Mister Rogers visits Maya Lin's studio to see how she uses models to plan her work.

"Drawing a Model" can help children:

* develop skills in planning;

* feel proud of accomplishments.

Drawing a Model

Materials

* blocks

* paper

* markers

Talk about the model that Mister Rogers had on the program and see if the children would like to create a model to plan for block-building. The plan could be as simple as drawing three or four blocks in a row and then making a replica of the drawing. When they are finished they can compare the buildings to their drawings. How are they alike? How are they different? Younger children may have more difficulty with this activity but you can be accepting of whatever they draw, remembering that children draw what they know, not what they see.

HOW TO'S

Modeling Dough I

Ingredients
- 2 cups flour
- 1 cup salt
- 1 cup water
- 1 teaspoon salad oil (optional)

Combine all ingredients and store in an air-tight container.

Modeling Dough II

Ingredients
- 1 cup flour
- ½ cup salt
- 2 teaspoons cream of tartar

Mix the above dry ingredients together. Then, in a separate bowl, mix the following wet ingredients:
- 1 cup water
- few drops of food coloring (optional)
- 1 tablespoon oil

Combine the two mixtures and cook over medium to low heat, stirring until combination is the consistency of mashed potatoes. Knead the mixture a little and let cool before handling. Store in a covered container.

Self-Hardening Modeling Dough

Ingredients
- 1½ cups salt
- 4 cups flour
- 1½ cups water

Mix the above ingredients and knead. Creations made from this mixture should harden overnight. You can also bake the dough in a slow oven until the creations harden. (Be careful not to burn them.) Baking and / or painting the final products will retard mold.

Corn Starch Modeling Dough

Ingredients
- 2 cups salt
- 1 cup cornstarch
- 1½ cups water

Cook the ingredients over medium heat until the mixture thickens. Cool before handling, then knead it like dough.

Please Note: Toddlers might be tempted to eat modeling dough, so if there's a chance they may be around when the dough is used, it may be better to lower the salt content. The salt makes the texture coarse; otherwise, the flour and water mixture is like a paste. You may want to experiment to see how much salt is needed to get a consistency that works well for your needs.

Homemade Pastes

Ingredients
- 1 cup flour
- 1 cup cold water
- 3 cups boiling water

Mix flour and cold water in a mixing bowl. Add this mixture to the three cups of boiling water and cook it for about ten minutes. Store in an airtight container. The paste will keep for several days.

Ingredients
- egg

Put an egg in a small mixing bowl and whip with a wire whisk, egg beater or mixer until thick and frothy. Use this as a substitute for glue or paste. If you don't want your mixture to have a yellow tint, use just the egg white.

Soapsuds Fingerpaint

Ingredients
- 1 cup mild soap flakes or soap powder
- ½ cup water
- food coloring or paint

Whip the soap and water until thick and frothy with a wire whisk, egg beater or mixer. Even though this is easy to clean up, you'll probably want to cover the table with a plastic tablecloth or an old shower curtain. You can add food coloring or a little paint for color variety.

Substitute
Instead of using soapsuds, try using pudding. Instant or cooked pudding works equally well.

Homemade Toothpaste

Ingredients
- 4 teaspoons baking soda
- 1 teaspoon salt
- 1 teaspoon flavoring: vanilla, almond or peppermint

Mix the ingredients well and store in airtight container.

PLAY PROPS

Game Spinner

Materials
- cardboard or heavy paper
- markers   • scissors
- brass paper fastener

Cut a five- or six-inch circle from cardboard or heavy paper and divide it into sections. Write a numeral in each section. Make a three-inch arrow from the left-over cardboard and attach it to the circle using a brass paper fastener. Loosen the arrow if necessary so it spins easily.

Milk Carton Blocks

Materials
- milk cartons
- scissors
- adhesive tape (optional)

Cut off the tops of two milk cartons and push the open end of one carton into another carton to make a sturdy block. If you want, you can cover the "blocks" with adhesive tape for a colorful appearance.

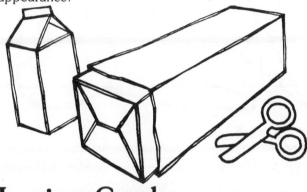

Lacing Cards

Materials
- heavy paper or cardboard
- pencil
- paper punch
- scissors
- shoelaces or string

Lacing cards can be made by drawing the outline of a shoe on heavy paper or cardboard. Make a rather large rectangle in the center of the shoe and cut it open down the center and across the top and bottom to resemble shoe flaps. Fold the flaps back and punch two or three holes along the center edges. Once the holes are punched, the children can practice lacing shoelaces through the cards.

Witch's Hat

Materials

- large sheet of black paper
- tape
- stapler
- scissors

Roll a large piece of black paper into a cone shape with a point at one end. Tape the pointed end together with several pieces of tape and staple the bottom edge to fit a child's head. Cut off the extra paper at the bottom to make a straight edge.

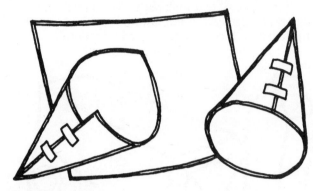

Top Hat

Materials

- two large sheets of construction paper (preferably black) or cardboard
- scissors
- tape

Roll and tape one sheet of paper to form a cylinder that fits a child's head. Cut a hole in the other sheet of paper the size of the cylinder and trim to form a three-inch brim for the hat. Place the brim on the cylinder so that approximately one inch shows through. Cut several slits in this one-inch band, fold back and tape to the underside of the brim. Use the circular piece of paper you cut from the brim portion of the hat to tape on top.

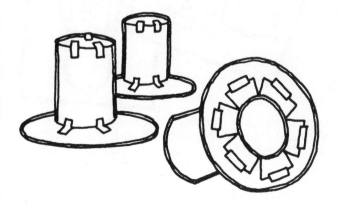

Chef's Hats

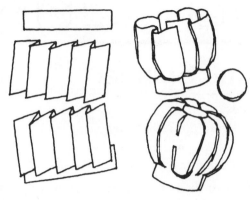

Materials

- strips of cardboard two inches wide and just a little larger than the size of each child's head
- tissue or crepe paper 20 inches by 30 inches (one piece for each hat)
- glue
- construction paper
- scissors

Pleat a piece of tissue or crepe paper and glue the pleated edge to the cardboard. Join the cardboard band and the pleated paper with glue. Close the top of the hat by gluing a three-inch circle of construction paper to the open ends of the crepe paper.

Parade Hats

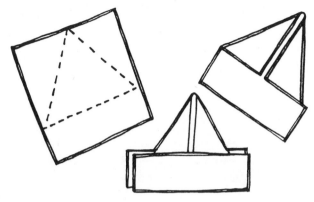

Materials

- newspaper (12-inch by 18-inch sheet)

Take a piece of newspaper and fold it in half to make a 12-inch by 9-inch piece. With the folded edge away from you, take the upper corners and fold them to the center. Fold the bottom edges up, one on each side.

Doll Furniture

Materials

- small cardboard boxes
- plastic margarine containers
- spools of thread (empty if possible)
- paper baking cups
- glue

Simple doll furniture can be made from small cardboard boxes or plastic containers. Use a margarine container with a lid for a table. Empty spools of thread can be used as end tables or lamps.
Two pudding boxes can be glued together for a chair. Two small boxes glued together can also make a bed. The children might want to:

- paint the furniture;
- cover it with cloth;
- make pillows and blankets from scrap material.

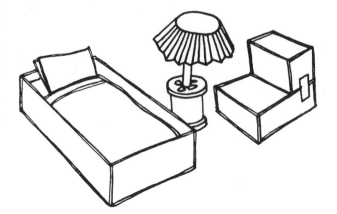

"McFeely" Box

Materials

- cardboard box with lid, at least 12 inches square and six inches deep
- cutting tool (one-sided razor or knife)
- six-inch square of heavy fabric (felt works well)
- glue
- scissors
- tape

Cut a hole in one side of the box, about five inches across. Cut a large "X" in the middle of the heavy fabric. Tape or glue the fabric over the hole you cut. Tape the lid to the box. The children might enjoy decorating the box with designs or scraps of paper. Now you can place small items in the box through the opening for such activities as "Guess What's in the Bag"—Program 1258.

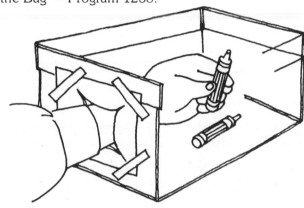

Play Money

Materials

- a set of coins (penny, nickle, dime, quarter)
- thin paper
- heavy paper or cardboard
- pencils
- paste
- scissors

Using thin paper and pencils, make rubbings of the coins and cut them out. Mounting them on cardboard or heavy paper will make them sturdier. The children can use them for pretend coins. Cut strips of paper and draw green designs on the paper to make dollar bills.

Make a pretend checkbook by stapling several strips of paper together. The children can draw lines on each paper to resemble checks.

RECIPES

Pound Cake

Ingredients
- 2 sticks butter or margarine
- 2 cups brown sugar
- vanilla, lemon, or almond extract
- 3 eggs
- 2 cups flour
- ¼ cup wheat germ (optional)
- ½ teaspoon baking soda
- 1 cup yogurt or buttermilk

Using an electric mixer, beat together the butter and brown sugar. Add the eggs and beat the mixture until smooth. In a separate bowl, mix the flour, wheat germ and baking soda. Then alternately add the dry ingredients and the yogurt a little at a time to the cake batter, mixing well after each addition. Stir in the flavoring of your choice and pour the batter into two well-greased loaf pans and bake at 325 degrees for one hour. Be sure to cool the cake before removing from pans.

Waffles Recipe

Ingredients
- 3 cups whole wheat flour
- 4 teaspoons baking powder
- ¾ teaspoon salt
- 1½ tablespoons sugar
- ½ teaspoon cinnamon
- 2 eggs
- 2¼ cups milk
- ½ cup oil

Combine flour, baking powder, salt, sugar, and cinnamon in a large bowl. Beat eggs in a separate bowl and add milk and oil. Pour the liquid into the dry mixture and mix with a large spoon until moistened. Cook the waffles on a heated waffle iron.

Whole Wheat Bread

Ingredients
- 2 packages of dry yeast
- 3 cups warm water
- ¼ cup oil
- ½ cup molasses
- 2 teaspoons salt
- 1 egg (beaten)
- 7 to 8 cups whole wheat flour (or 4 cups whole wheat and 4 cups white flour)

Dissolve the yeast in three cups of water. Add the oil, molasses, salt and beaten egg and mix well. Then add four cups of flour and beat until smooth. Add the remaining flour a little at a time. Knead the dough on a board or table five to ten minutes. Place the dough in an oiled bowl to rise (about one hour). Punch the dough to remove the air and knead it again. Form the dough into three loaves and place the loaves in greased pans. Let the loaves rise one hour before baking at 400 degrees for 45 minutes. Remove the bread from the pans and cool the loaves on racks.

Granola

Ingredients

- ½ cup honey
- 1 cup vegetable oil

Spread both on the bottom of a large pan.

- 3 cups of rolled oats
- 1 cup of dried milk
- 1 cup of shredded coconut
- 2 cups of untoasted wheat germ (if toasted, add later)

Distribute these dry ingredients on the bottom of the pan. Bake at 350 degrees for 40 minutes, stirring every 5 minutes until well toasted.

- 1 cup sesame seeds
- 1 cup sunflower seeds
- 1 cup crushed raw peanuts

Mix together and add to what came out of the oven, after it has cooled. Add raisins or other dried fruit as desired.

Daniel's Tiger Treat

Ingredients

- 2 cups apple juice
- 1 cup apricot juice
- 1 cup orange juice
- 1 cup pineapple juice
- 1 cup lemonade

Pour all the ingredients into a 2-quart pitcher, stir, chill and serve. Delicious at breakfast or anytime.

Mrs. McFeely's Old-Fashioned Popovers

Ingredients

- 1 egg
- ½ cup flour
- ½ cup milk
- Pinch salt
- Pinch nutmeg or mace
- Butter

Turn on the oven to 450 degrees. Beat the egg well. Add the flour, milk, salt and nutmeg or mace. Beat well again. Grease a six-holed muffin tin with butter that has come to room temperature. (Grease even if you're using a nonstick muffin tin.) Put two table-spoons of batter in each hole. Bake for 10 minutes at 450 degrees, then for 10 minutes at 400 degrees, then for 10 minutes at 350 degrees (30 minutes in all). Do not open the oven door during baking. Serve hot with butter, honey or jam.

Edgar Cooke's Maple Egg Custard

Ingredients

- 2 eggs
- 1¼ cups milk
- 3 tablespoons maple syrup
- ½ teaspoon vanilla
- ¼ teaspoon salt
- Dash cinnamon
- Dash nutmeg

Preheat the oven to 350 degrees. In a blender, whirl the eggs by themselves, then add the other ingredients and whirl again. Pour into floured small oven-proof custard cups. Bake in a deep pan with about an inch of water for 30 to 40 minutes. Remove the cups from the water right away after baking so that the custard doesn't continue to cook.

Donkey Hodie's Crunch Salad

Here are two zesty, crunchy salads that you can keep on inventing. They are pretty in a dessert dish or on a plate with a bed of lettuce.

No. 1 Salad
- Chunks of apple
- Slices of celery
- Sections of orange
- Cashew nuts
- Raisins

No. 2 Salad
- Chunks of apple
- Slices of celery
- Slices of carrot
- Walnuts
- Raisins

That's just the beginning. You can make more salad combinations by adding such things as:

- Green grapes
- Chunks of pineapple
- Sunflower seeds
- Miniature marshmallows
- Sliced pears
- Thawed frozen raspberries
- Flaked coconut
- Shredded red cabbage

For a delicious topping, combine about 1 tablespoon each (or equal parts) of cream cheese and marshmallow creme. Blend well with a fork. Or, combine the same amount of sour cream and mayonnaise, and add honey to taste.

Prince Tuesday's Mulled Apple Juice

Ingredients
- 3 cups apple juice
- 1 cup pineapple juice
- ¼ cup honey
- 3 tablespoons lemon juice
- 1 cinnamon stick (to flavor and stir)
- Dash nutmeg

Combine everything and simmer 10 minutes. Serve warm. A good drink to take to school in a thermos bottle on a cold day.

Chef Brockett's Best Baked Bananas

Ingredients
- 1 or more bananas (peeled)
- Butter
- Orange Juice
- Honey
- Graham cracker crumbs

Preheat oven to 375 degrees. Line a baking dish with foil, slice the bananas lengthwise and place in it. Dot with butter, drizzle with orange juice and honey, and sprinkle with graham cracker crumbs. Bake for 10 minutes, then broil for 2 minutes or until the banana is browned. They are delicious plain, or topped with vanilla or apricot yogurt, or whipped cream.

Robert Troll's Raw Vegetable Salad With Dill Dip

Ingredients

- Some of your favorite crisp raw vegetables (such as radishes, carrots, green peppers, celery, broccoli, cauliflower or zucchini)
- 2 tablespoons sour cream
- 2 tablespoons yogurt
- Pieces of chopped scallion (the green part)
- Sprinkle of dill weed

Cut the vegetables into dipping size pieces. Combine the sour cream, yogurt, scallion and dill weed in a small cup and mix well.

Speedy Delivery's Bugs On A Log

Ingredients

For a tasty fun snack, stuff a fresh stalk of celery with cream cheese or peanut butter, and stick some raisins on top. See the bugs sitting on the log? Try some peanuts or pumpkin seeds for some different bugs on a log.

Neighborhood Gingerbread Brocketts

Dry Ingredients

- 5 cups wheat pastry flour
- 1 teaspoon baking soda
- 1 teaspoon baking powder
- ½ teaspoon nutmeg
- 1½ teaspoon ginger

Wet Ingredients

- ¼ cup oil
- ¼ cup melted butter
- ½ cup molasses
- 1 cup honey
- ¼ cup milk

Combine the DRY ingredients in a bowl. Combine the WET ingredients in a separate bowl, and pour them into the dry ingredients. Mix well with a wooden spoon and your hands. Chill the dough 1 hour. Preheat the oven to 375 degrees. Roll out the dough, ¼ of it at a time, on a well-floured surface to a thickness of ¼" to ⅛". Cut into shapes. Cover cookie sheet with foil or baking parchment.
Bake 8-10 minutes.

Be careful with the baking time so the cookies don't burn.

SONGS

Children Can D-2
Clown in Me, The D-4
Did You Know? D-9
Everybody Has a History D-7
Everybody's Fancy D-3
Everything Grows Together D-5
I Like to be Told D-5
I Like to Take My Time D-5
I'll Think of You D-9
It's Such a Good Feeling D-8
It's You I Like D-7
Just for Once D-9
Let's Think of Something To Do D10
Lonely Kind of Thing, A D-8
Look and Listen D-1
One and One Are Two D-7
Peace and Quiet D-3
Parents Were Little Once Too D-9
Place of My Own, A D-7
Please Don't Think It's Funny D-6
Pretending D-4
Some Things I Don't Understand D10
Sometimes D-5
Sometimes People Are Good D10
Then Your Heart Is Full of Love D11
There are Many Ways to Say I Love You D-7
Truth Will Make Me Free, The D11
Weekend Song, The D-9
What Do You Do D-4
When a Baby Comes D-4
Wishes Don't Make Things Come True D-3
Won't You Be My Neighbor? D-3
You Are Special D-1
You Are You D-1
You Can Never Go Down the Drain D-2
You're Growing D-8
You've Go to Do It D-2

Look and Listen

©1970, Fred M. Rogers

If you will look carefully,
Listen carefully,
You will find a lot of things carefully.
Look…and listen.

It's good to
Look carefully.
Listen carefully.
That's the way you learn a lot of things carefully.
Look…look and listen.

Some things you see are confusing.
Some things you hear are strange.
But if you ask someone to explain one or two,
You'll begin to notice a change in you.

If you will
Look carefully.
Listen carefully.
That's a way to keep on growing carefully.
Look, look, look, and listen.

You Are You

©1972, Fred M. Rogers

VERSE
I eat and you do too.
You sleep and I do too.
I wake up and you do too.
So we two do so much the same,
But I'm Mister Rogers,
And you have your name.

CHORUS
You are you and I am I
And we will always be
Quite different to people who know us well
'Cause they're the ones who like us to be different.

You are you and I am I
And we will never be
Exactly like anybody else 'cause everybody else
  is different
Different, different, we are different.
Isn't it great to be different
You and I and he and she and isn't it great to be…
You…and I…and we will always be
Quite different to people who know us well,
'Cause they're the ones who like us,
They really want us
They're the ones who like us to be different.

You Are Special

©1968, Fred M. Rogers

You are my friend
You are special
You are my friend
You're special to me.
You are the only one like you.
Like you, my friend, I like you.

In the daytime
In the nighttime
Any time that you feel's the right time
For a friendship with me, you see
F-R-I-E-N-D special
You are my friend
You're special to me.
There's only one in this wonderful world
You are special.

Children Can
©1969, Fred M. Rogers

Who can crawl under a table?
Who can sit under a chair?
Who can fit their feet in little shoes
And sleep most anywhere?
Who can play very much longer,
Play much harder than grownups ever dare?
You're a child so you can do it.
You can do it anywhere.

Who can wake up every morning
And be ready right away?
Who can notice all the tiny things
That other people say?
Who can make the things they play with
Something different for every single day?
You're a child and you can do it.
You can do it any way.
Roll in the grass,
Squoosh in the mud.
Lick an ice cream cone,
Sing to a bass.
Splash in a flood
By a stepping stone, all alone.
Who can put your hand in my hand
And be ready to feel all safe and strong?
You're a child so you can do it.
Children do it all life long.

You Can Never Go Down the Drain
©1969, Fred M. Rogers

You can never go down
Can never go down
Can never go down the drain.
You can never go down
Can never go down
Can never go down the drain.
You're bigger than the water,
You're bigger than the soap,
You're much bigger than all the bubbles
And bigger than your telescope, so you see...
You can never go down
Can never go down
Can never go down the drain.
You can never go down
Can never go down
Can never go down the drain.
The rain may go down
But you can't go down
You're bigger than any bathroom drain.
You can never go down,
Can never go down,
You can never go down the drain.

You've Got to Do It
©1969, Fred M. Rogers

You can make-believe it happens,
    or pretend that something's true.
You can wish or hope or contemplate
    a thing you'd like to do,
But until you start to do it,
    you will never see it through
'Cause the make-believe
    pretending just won't do it for you.

CHORUS

You've got to do it.
Every little bit, you've got to do it, do it, do it, do it.
And when you're through, you can know who did it,
For you did it, you did it, you did it.

If you want to ride a bicycle
    and ride it straight and tall,
You can't simply sit and look at it
    'cause it won't move at all.
But it's you who have to try it,
    and it's you who have to fall (sometimes)
If you want to ride a bicycle
    and ride it straight and tall.

CHORUS

If you want to read a reading book
    and read the real words too,
You can't simply sit and ask
    the words to read themselves to you.
But you have to ask a person
    who can show you one or two
If you want to read a reading book
    and read the real words, too.

CHORUS

It's not easy to keep trying,
    but it's one good way to grow.
It's not easy to keep learning,
    but I know that this is so:
When you've tried and learned
    you're bigger than you were a day ago.
It's not easy to keep trying,
    but it's one way to grow.

CHORUS

Peace and Quiet

©1968, Fred M. Rogers

Peace and quiet.
Peace, peace, peace.
Peace and quiet.
Peace, peace, peace.

Peace and quiet.
Peace, peace, peace.
We all want peace;
We all want peace.

Won't You Be My Neighbor?

©1967, Fred M. Rogers

It's a beautiful day in this neighborhood,
A beautiful day for a neighbor.
Would you be mine?
Could you be mine?

It's a neighborly day in this beauty wood,
A neighborly day for a beauty,
Would you be mine?
Could you be mine?

I have always wanted to have a neighbor
    just like you!
I've always wanted to live in a neighborhood
    with you.
So let's make the most of this beautiful day,
Since we're together we might as well say,
Would you be mine?
Could you be mine?
Won't you be my neighbor?
Won't you please,
Won't you please?
Please won't you be my neighbor?

Everybody's Fancy

©1967, Fred M. Rogers

Some are fancy on the outside.
Some are fancy on the inside.
Everybody's fancy.
Everybody's fine.
Your body's fancy and so is mine.

Boys are boys from the beginning.
Girls are girls right from the start.
Everybody's fancy.
Everybody's fine.
Your body's fancy and so is mine.

Only girls can be the mommies.
Only boys can be the daddies.
Everybody's fancy.
Everybody's fine.
Your body's fancy and so is mine.

I think you're a special person
And I like your ins and outsides.
Everybody's fancy.
Everybody's fine.
Your body's fancy and so is mine.

Wishes Don't Make Things Come True

©1970, Fred M. Rogers

One time I wished a lion would come
And eat up my house and my street.
I was mad at the world
And I wished that the beast
Would stomp everything
With his big heavy feet,
And eat everything
With his big sharp teeth,
And eat everything
With his teeth.
But that wish certainly didn't come true
'Cause scary mad wishes don't make things
    come true.

One time I wished that a dragon would come
And burn up my Daddy's big store.
I was angry with him
'Cause I wanted to play
But my Daddy just went
To his store right away.
I wished that the dragon
Would burn his store.
I wished it would burn Daddy's store.
But that wish certainly didn't come true
'Cause scary, mad wishes don't make things
    come true.

Everyone wishes for scary, mad things.
I'd guess that you sometimes do, too.
I've wished for so many
And I can say
That all kinds of wishes
Are things just like play.
They're things
That our thinking had made—
So wish then
And don't be afraid.
I'm glad it's certainly that way, aren't you?
That scary, mad wishes don't make things
    come true.
No kinds of wishes make things come true.

The Clown in Me

©1968, Fred M. Rogers

A clown, a clown,
I think I'll be a clown.
I think I'll make the people laugh
  and laugh all over town.
A clown, that's what I'll be…a clown.

Sometimes I feel when I'm afraid,
That I will never make the grade.
So I pretend I'm someone else
and show the world my other self.
I'm not quite sure of me you see,
When I have to make a clown of me.

A clown, a clown,
I think I'll be a clown.
I think I'll make the people laugh
  and laugh all over town.
A clown, that's what I'll be…a clown.

Sometimes I feel all good inside
And haven't got a thing to hide.
My friends all tell me I'm the best;
They think I'm better than the rest.
It's times like this I act myself
And let the clown stay on the shelf.

Myself, Myself
I think I'll be myself.
I think I'll let the people see
  the comfortable inside of me.
Myself…I'll be myself.
It's only when I feel let down
I might be scared into a clown
But he can be himself
When I can be…
Myself, Myself
I think I'll be myself.

Pretending

©1972, Fred M. Rogers

Pretending you're a pilot or a princess!
Pretending you're a doctor or a king!
Pretending you're a mother or a father,
By pretending you can be
Most anything you want to think about
By pretending just pretending.

You can try out many things by pretending.
Your own makeup play can be different every day,
But it's your work, it's important, pretend.
You can try out life by pretending.
You can even say you're a baby today
By pretending, pretending.

When a Baby Comes to Your House

©1967, Fred M. Rogers

When a baby comes to your house,
It's a girl or it's a boy.
It's a sister or a brother,
But it's never just a toy.

It can cry and it can holler.
It can wet and it can coo.
But there's one thing it can never…
It can never be like you.

You were there before the baby.
Now the baby's always there.
Now you wait for special moments
With your mother in the chair.

You're a very special person,
You are special to your mom,
And your dad begins to say, "You'll
Always be the older one."

It's so good to know that always
There's a special place for you,
And a special place for baby
Right inside the family, too.
You've a place that no one else has.
There is only one like you.

What Do You Do?

©1968, Fred M. Rogers

What do you do with the mad that you feel
When you feel so mad you could bite?
When the whole wide world seems oh so wrong
And nothing you do seems very right?
What do you do? Do you punch a bag?
Do you pound some clay or some dough?
Do you round up friends for a game of tag?
Or see how fast you go?

It's great to be able to stop
When you've planned a thing that's wrong
And be able to do something else instead
And think this song:

I can stop when I want to,
Can stop when I wish,
Can stop, stop, stop any time.
And what a good feeling
To feel like this,
And know that the feeling is really mine.
Know that there's something deep inside
That helps us become what we can,
For a girl can be someday a woman
And a boy can be someday a man.

Sometimes

Sometimes I don't feel like combing my hair.
I don't feel like washing my face sometimes.
Sometimes I don't feel like saying "O.K."
But sometimes isn't always.

Sometimes I do feel like combing my hair.
I do feel like washing my face sometimes.
Sometimes I do feel like saying "O.K."
But sometimes isn't always.

Sometimes I don't feel like going to bed.
I don't feel like getting right up sometimes.
Sometimes I don't feel like wearing my shoes.
But sometimes isn't always.

Sometimes I don't feel like sometimes I do
I feel like I don't like to feel sometimes.
Sometimes I don't and sometimes I do.
But sometimes isn't always
Isn't always.
Isn't always.

I Like to Take
My Time

I like to take my time
I mean that when I want to do a thing
I like to take my time to do it right.

I mean I might just make mistakes
If I should have to hurry up and so
I like to take my time
To tie my shoes
To eat…
To get dressed
To go to sleep at night,
To sing a song for you and everything
I do
I like to take my time.
I mean that when I want to do a thing
I like to take my time to do it.

I mean I might just make mistakes if
I should have to hurry up and
So I like to
Take my time.

I Like to Be Told

I like to be told
When you're going away,
When you're going to come back,
And how long you will stay,
How long you will stay,
I like to be told.

I like to be told
If it's going to hurt,
If it's going to be hard,
If it's not going to hurt.
I like to be told.
I like to be told.

It helps me to get ready for all those things,
All those things that are new.
I trust you more and more
Each time that I'm
Finding those things to be true.

I like to be told
'Cause I'm trying to grow,
'Cause I'm trying to learn
And I'm trying to know.
I like to be told.
I like to be told.

Everything Grows
Together

Everything grows together
Because you're all one piece.
Your nose grows
As the rest of you grows
Because you're all one piece.

Everything grows together
Because you're all one piece.
Your ears grow
As your nose grows
As the rest of you grows
Because you're all one piece.

Everything grows together
Because you're all one piece.
Your arms grow
As your ears grow
As your nose grows
As the rest of you grows
Because you're all one piece.

(continued on next page)

Everything Grows Together *(Continued)*

Everything grows together
Because you're all one piece.
Your hands grow
As your arms grow
As your ears grow
As your nose grows
As the rest of you grows
Because you're all one piece.

Everything grows together
Because you're all one piece.
Your fingers grow
As your hands grow
As your arms grow
As your ears grow
As your nose grows
As the rest of you grows
Because you're all one piece.

Everything grows together
Because you're all one piece.
Your legs grow
As your fingers grow
As your hands grow
As your arms grow
As your ears grow
As your nose grows
As the rest of you grows
Because you're all one piece.

Everything grows together
Because you're all one piece.
Your feet grow
As your legs grow
As your fingers grow
As your hands grow
As your arms grow
As your ears grow
As your nose grows
As the rest of you grows
Because you're all one piece.

Everything grows together
Because you're all one piece.
Your toes grow
As your feet grow
As your legs grow
As your fingers grow
As your hands grow
As your arms grow
As your ears grow
As your nose grows
As the rest of you grows
Because you're all one piece.

Please Don't Think It's Funny

©1968, Fred M. Rogers

Sometimes you feel like holding your pillow
    all night long;
Sometimes you hug your teddy bear tightly,
He's old but he's still strong.
And sometimes you want to snuggle up closely with
    your own Mom and Dad
At night, you even need the light sometimes,
But that's not bad.

Please don't think it's funny,
When you want an extra kiss.
There are lots and lots of people
Who sometimes feel like this.

Please don't think it's funny
When you want the ones you miss.
There are lots and lots of people
Who sometimes feel like this.

It's great to know you're growing up bigger
    every day.
But somehow things you like to remember
Are often put away.
And sometimes you wonder over and over
If you should stay inside,
When you enjoy a younger toy...
You never need to hide.

In the long, long trip of growing
There are stops along the way,
For thoughts of all the soft things
And the look of yesterday.

For a chance to fill our feelings,
With comfort and with ease,
And then tell the new tomorrow,
"You can come now when you please."

So please don't think it's funny,
When you want an extra kiss;
There are lots and lots of people,
Who sometimes feel like this.

Please don't think it's funny,
When you want the ones you miss;
There are lots and lots of people
Who sometimes feel like this.

Everybody Has a History
©1972, Fred M. Rogers

Everybody has a history.
Everybody has a name.
Everybody has a story.
No one's story's just the same.

You see in the beginning…
I was born a baby and then
I grew and I grew and I grew and I grew
And I grew and now I can do
What a baby couldn't do.
My story is my history.

A Place Of My Own
©1970, Fred M. Rogers

I like to have a place of my own
A place where I can be by myself
When I want to think and play by myself.
I like to have a place of my own.

I like to have a place of my own
A step on a staircase, a drawer or a chair
A corner, a spot anywhere
A place I can call my own.

Dishes have places;
So do pots and pans,
Beds and bathtubs,
Shoes and socks.
Tables have places;
So do faces and hands.
Houses have places;
Keys have locks,
I like to have a place of my own.

I like to have a place of my own
A place where I can be by myself.
When I want to play and think by myself.
I like to have a place of my own.

There Are Many Ways
©1970, Fred M. Rogers

There are many ways to say I love you—
There are many ways to say I care about you.
Many ways, many ways, many ways to say
I love you.

There's the singing way to say I love you—
There's the singing something someone really likes
  to hear,
The singing way, the singing way,
  the singing way to say
I love you.

Cleaning up a room can say I love you.
Hanging up a coat before you're asked to—
Drawing special pictures for the holidays and
Making plays.

You'll find many ways to say I love you.
You'll find many ways to understand what love is.
Many ways, many ways, many ways to say
I love you.

Singing, cleaning,
Drawing, being
Understanding,
Love you.

It's You I Like
©1971, Fred M. Rogers

It's you I like,
It's not the things you wear,
It's not the way you do your hair—
But it's you I like
The way you are right now,
The way down deep inside you—
Not the things that hide you,
Not your toys—
They're just beside you.

But it's you I like—
Every part of you,
Your skin, your eyes, your feelings
Whether old or new.
I hope that you'll remember
Even when you're feeling blue
That it's you I like,
It's you yourself,
It's you, it's you I like.

One and One Are Two

1 + 1 = 2
2 + 2 = 4
4 + 4 = 8
8 + 2 = 10
1, 2, 3, 4, 5,
6, 7, 8, 9, 10.

You're Growing

©1967, Fred M. Rogers

You used to creep and crawl real well
But then you learned to walk real well.
There was a time you'd coo and cry
But then you learned to talk and, my!
You almost always try.
You almost always do your best.
I like the way you're growing up.
It's fun, that's all.

CHORUS

You're growing, you're growing,
You're growing in and out.
You're growing, you're growing,
You're growing all about.

Your hands are getting bigger now.
Your arms and legs are longer now.
You even sense your insides grow
When Mom and Dad refuse you. So
You're learning how to wait now.
It's great to hope and wait somehow.
I like the way you're growing up.
It's fun, that's all.

CHORUS

Your friends are getting better now.
They're better every day somehow.
You used to stay at home to play
But now you even play away.
You do important things now.
Your friends and you do big things now.
I like the way you're growing up.
It's fun, that's all.

CHORUS

Someday you'll be a grown-up, too
And have some children grow up, too.
Then you can love them in and out
And tell them stories all about
The times when you were their size,
The times when you found great surprise
In growing up. And they will sing
It's fun, that's all.

CHORUS

A Lonely Kind of Thing

©1970, Fred M. Rogers

It's a lonely thing to
Think you might
Do something
That might make someone very mad.

It's a lonely thing to
Think you might
Hurt someone,
And that someone
Might be your mom or dad,
Someone you like very much.

It's so lonely,
Lonely.
It's a very lonely, lonely
Kind of thing.
Lonely, it's so lonely
It's a very lonely, lonely
kind of thing.

It's Such a Good Feeling

©1970, Fred M. Rogers

It's such a good feeling
To know you're alive.
It's such a happy feeling:
You're growing inside.
And when you wake up ready to say,
"I think I'll make a snappy new day."
It's such a good feeling,
A very good feeling,
The feeling you know
You're alive.

It's such a good feeling
To know you're in tune.
It's such a happy feeling
To find you're in bloom.
And when you wake up ready to say
"I think I'll make a snappy new day,"
It's such a good feeling,
A very good feeling,
The feeling you know that we're friends.

The Weekend Song
©1970, Fred M. Rogers

I'll be back when the week is new
And I'll bring more ideas for you
And you'll have things you'll want to do
And I will, too.
I'll think of you when I'm not here
'Cause thinking of people makes them seem near.
The friends who know you love you cheerfully,
I do, too.

Did You Know?
©1979, Fred M. Rogers

Did you know? Did You know?
Did you know that it's all right to wonder?
Did you know that it's all right to wonder?
There are all kinds of wonderful things!

Did you know? Did you know?
Did you know that it's all right to marvel?
Did you know that it's all right to marvel?
There are all kinds of marvelous things!

You can ask a lot of questions about the world…
And your place in it.
You can ask about people's feelings;
You can learn the sky's the limit.

Did you know? Did you know?
Did you know when you wonder you're learning?
Did you know when you marvel you're learning?
About all kinds of wonderful,
About all kinds of marvelous,
Marvelously wonderful things?

I'll Think of You
©1990, Fred M. Rogers

When the day turns into night
And you're way beyond my sight,
I'll think of you, I'll think of you.

When the night turns into day
And you still are far away
I'll think of you, I'll think of you.

Even when I am not here
We still can be so very near
I want you to know my dear
I'll think of you.

Just for Once
©1969, Fred M. Rogers

Just for once, just for once,
Just for once,
I want you all to myself.
Just for once let's be alone
With nobody else to tell us
Do this, do that, sit down, get up,
Come back, no,
Nobody else but nobody else but you.

Just for once, just for once,
Just for once I want you all to myself.
Just for once let's play alone
With nobody else.
We'll build us a house with a garden…
And no, no, nobody else,
But nobody else but you.

Just for once, just for once
Just for once I want you all to myself.
Just for once let's stay alone
And I'll be the only one with you
And you'll be the only one with me.
You'll talk with me;
I'll talk with you,
Just we two.
Nobody else, but nobody else but you
Just for once, just for once.

Parents Were Little Once Too
©1968, Fred M. Rogers

It's great for me to remember
As I put away my toys,
That mothers were all little girls one time
And fathers were all little boys.

My daddy seems so big right now.
He must have grown a lot.
Imagine how he felt one day
When he was just a tot.

My mother's not so big as Dad
But bigger than my sister.
I wonder if she ever had
A little fever blister.

Daddy didn't even have
A real electric fan.
He had to wait a long time, too
'Til he became a man.

(continued on next page)

Parents Were Little Once Too (Continued)

My mother used an ironing board
And play irons that were colder.
She often wished for big folks' things
But she waited and got older.

So knives and plugs and hot things are
O.K. for Mom and Dad.
'Cause when they were a girl and boy
They played with what they had.

It's great for me to remember
As I put away my toys,
That mothers were all little girls one time
And fathers were all little boys.

Some Things I Don't Understand
©1968, Fred M. Rogers

Some things I don't understand.
Some things are scary and sad.
Sometimes I even get bad when I'm mad.
Sometimes I even get glad.

Why does a dog have to bark?
Why does an elephant die?
Why can't we play all the time in the park?
Why can't my pussycat fly?

Why, why, why, why, why, why
I wonder why.
Why, why, why, why, why, why,
I wonder why.

Why do big people say, "No!"?
Why are their voices so loud?
Why don't the witches and bad guys all go?
Why does the sky fly a cloud?

CHORUS

Why does it have to get dark?
Why can't the day always stay?
Let's say goodbye to the night time, Goodbye.
Let's send the dark time away.

Why do fire engines make noise?
Why is hot water so hot?
Why aren't live babies like my other toys?
Why do I wonder a lot?

Some day, oh some day, I'll know what to say.
Some day, oh some day, I'll not have to say
WHY?

Let's Think of Something To Do
©1982, Fred M. Rogers

Let's think of something to do while we're waiting
While we're waiting for something new to do.
Let's try to think up a song while we're waiting
That's liberating and will be true to you.

Let's think of something to do while we're waiting
While we're waiting 'til something's through.
You know it's really all right;
In fact, it's downright quite bright
To think of something to do
That's specific for you.
Let's think of something to do while we're waiting.

Sometimes People Are Good
©1967, Fred M. Rogers

Sometimes people are good
And they do just what they should.
But the very same people who are good sometimes
Are the very same people who are bad sometimes.
It's funny, but it's true.
It's the same, isn't it for me and…

Sometimes people get wet.
And their parents get upset.
But the very same people who get wet sometimes
Are the very same people who are dry sometimes.
It's funny, but it's true.
It's the same, isn't it for me and…

Sometimes people make noise
And they break each other's toys.
But the very same people who are noisy sometimes
Are the very same people who are quiet sometimes.
It's funny, but it's true.
It's the same, isn't it for me and…

Sometimes people get mad
And they feel like being bad.
But the very same people who are mad sometimes
Are the very same people who are glad sometimes.
It's funny, but it's true.
It's the same, isn't it for me and…

Sometimes people are good
And they do just what they should.
But the very same people who are good sometimes
Are the very same people who are bad sometimes.
It's funny, but it's true.
It's the same, isn't it for me…
Isn't it the same for you?

Then Your Heart is Full of Love

Lyrics: Josie Carey Franz
Music: Fred M. Rogers
©1984, Fred M. Rogers

When your heart has butterflies inside it,
Then your heart is full of love.
When your heart feels just like overflowing,
Then your heart is full of love.

Love is fragile as your tears.
Love is stronger than your fears.

When your heart can sing another's gladness,
Then your heart is full of love.
When your heart can cry another's sadness,
Then your heart is full of love.

Love is fragile as your tears.
Love is stronger than your fears.

When your heart beats for a special someone,
Then your heart is full of love.
When your heart has room for everybody,
Then your heart is full of love.

The Truth Will Make Me Free

©1970, Fred M. Rogers

What if I were very, very sad
And all I did was smile?
I wonder after a while
What might become of my sadness?

What if I were very, very angry,
And all I did was sit
And never think about it?
What might become of my anger?

Where would they go, and what would they do
If I couldn't let them out?
Maybe I'd fall, maybe get sick
Or doubt.

But what if I could know the truth
And say just how I feel?
I think I'd learn a lot that's real
About freedom.

I'm learning to sing a sad song when I'm sad.
I'm learning to say I'm angry when I'm very mad.
I'm learning to shout,
I'm getting it out,
I'm happy, learning
Exactly how I feel inside of me—
I'm learning to know the truth—
I'm learning to tell the truth—
Discovering truth will make me free.

Your Helpful

INDEX

We have included two indexes in this book. The first index lists all the activities according to the **type** of activity (art, music, play, etc.). The second index lists all the activities organized by the **topic** that is covered (biting, fears, real and pretend, etc.). We hope in this way to make the indexes helpful to you in choosing activites that meet the individual needs of the children in your care.

When using the index, it is important to know that the activities are listed by the **program number,** not the page number. As you look through the book, you can easily find the program number at the top of each activity.

TYPES OF ACTIVITIES

ART
1008— Painting Boxes
1011— Stick Designs
1017— Vegetable Prints
1027— How Do You Feel?
1028— String Painting
1029— Paper Plate Masks
1031— Picture Frames
1045— Tissue Paper Pictures
1048— Making a Book
1083— Salt Drawings
1098— Eggshell Pictures
1105— Draw a Song
1131— Construction Paper Mobiles
1140— Paint How You Feel
1149— Upside-Down Pictures
1151— Comparing Shoes and Feet
1161— Snake Pictures
1165— Bean Collage
1179— Decorating Pretend Cakes
1188— My Family and Me
1197— Invisible Pictures
1201— Styrofoam Sculptures
1204— Mixing Colors
1205— Let's Use It Again
1211— Kaleidoscope Patterns
1218— Connect-the-Dot Designs
1222— Coil Pots
1225— Making a Mural
1226— What's Behind the Fog?
1231— Leaf Rubbings
1233— Space Shapes
1237— Purple Paint
1240— Pole Dyeing
1241— Foam Painting
1242— Snow Pictures
1243— Multi-colored Snow
1251— Food Coloring Designs
1252— Drawing Pictures
1256— Soapsuds Fingerpainting
1262— Making Snow
1271— An Imaginary Person
1280— Shape Designs
1292— My Favorite Color
1298— Mouth Puppets
1317— Paper Collage
1319— Things That Are Fragile
1324— Nighttime Pictures
1327— My Special Box
1331— Paper Plate Pictures
1338— Sand Pictures
1341— Remember When
1342— An Handprint Mural
1352— Yarn Designs
1357— Purple Print Pictures
1362— Wooden Sculptures
1365— Recycle Collage
1366— All About Families
1369— Sparkle Paintings
1376— Fabric Cards
1382— Disappointments
1388— Things That Are Scary
1391— Where I Live
1394— Paint Blots
1420— Painting to Music
1423— Fingerpainting Designs
1434— Unhappy Feelings
1441— Crayon Window Hangings
1451— Clay Sculptures
1459— Torn Paper Pictures
1463— Chalk Drawings
1467— Dinosaur Models
1468— A Picture of a Dream
1474— Straw Painting
1475— Windstorm
1476— Different Kinds of Families
1481— Drawing the Neighborhood
1482— An Art Show
1485— A Rainbow for Everyone
1497— If I Had a Pet
1524— Marble Modeling Dough
1534— Aquarium Pictures
1541— Self-Portraits
1587— Star Mobiles
1601— Paper Bag Hats
1618— Recycling Projects
1619— Underwater Pictures
1641— The Art That's Inside You
1643— Chalk Skywriting
1646— Drawing with Colored Markers
1662— Museum of Love
1664— Shaving Cream Fingerpainting
1671— Three-Cornered Collages
1712— Found Object Collages
1717— Feather Collage
1729— Different and the Same Collage

COGNITIVE
1001— Things That Are Round
1041— Outline Match
1062— Secret Envelopes
1064— Sorting Buttons
1091— Wheel Toys
1100— Parents and Babies
1102— Matching Pairs
1108— Hide It, Find It
1147— In the Bag
1151— Comparing Shoes and Feet
1152— Supply Depot
1178— Key Match
1182— Hard and Soft
1184— Letter Rubbings
1258— Guess What's in the Bag
1260— Puzzles
1276— Name Cards
1279— Rubbings
1303— Making a Map
1306— What's Missing?
1318— What's Different?
1348— Sorting Shapes
1349— Alphabet Soup
1350— Matching Shoes
1360— Ways to Travel
1364— What Do You Hear?
1368— Front and Back
1371— Modeling Dough Letters
1373— Making Signs
1393— Comparing Sizes
1422— Which is Which?
1442— Same But Different
1447— Looking for Numbers
1462— Card Sorting
1465— Name Tags
1511— What's Under the Towel?
1513— Machine Collage
1577— A Book Fantasy
1583— What's Missing?
1612— Where's the Peanut?
1631— Measuring Our Growth
1651— Census Taking
1667— Hand Shadows
1673— Shoe Match
1682— Wheel Toys
1683— Word Box

FOOD
1015— A Wedding Cake
1020— Making Popsicles
1025— Oranges
1080— While You Wait
1090— Instant Pudding
1125— Pineapples and Tomatoes
1128— Thumbprint Pies
1155— Making Applesauce
1166— Peanut Butter
1199— Tasting New Foods
1203— Making Butter
1207— Homemade Soup
1220— Making Cookies
1230— Instant Oatmeal
1232— Animal Cookies
1255— Egg Salad Sandwiches
1265— Chef Brockett's Concoction
1305— Fruit Salad
1328— Making Pizza
1349— Alphabet Soup
1361— Pancakes or Waffles
1415— Egg Drop Soup
1433— Making Tacos
1455— Making Bread
1483— Cookie Decorating
1504— Making Popcorn
1508— Making Your Own Sandwich
1517— The Hoagie Factory
1520— Graham Cracker Treats
1527— Milk Shakes
1529— A Shopping List
1536— Dried Apple Rings
1537— Granola Gifts
1538— Chef Brockett's
         Nutritious Snack
1539— Vegetable Soup
1540— Homemade Noodles
1544— Arroz Con Leche
1613— Peanut Butter and Fruit
1626— Gingerbread Faces
1680— Salsa and Tortilla Chips
1686— Rice Cake Faces
1703— Helping Grownups in the
         Kitchen
1710— Yogurt Cereal Mix
1714— Sharing a Snack
1722— Bagel Snacks
1733— Grapes, Grapes, Grapes

GAMES
1034— It's Too Noisy
1041— Outline Match
1043— Questions
1092— Familiar Sounds
1093— Fishing
1103— Jack-in-the-Box
1108— Hide It, Find It
1146— Quiet Please
1147— In the Bag
1148— Guess Which Hand
1150— Use Your Breath
1181— Traffic Light Game
1258— Guess What's in the Bag
1284— I'm Thinking of a Child
1323— Games
1332— Hide and Seek
1333— Can You Find the Toy?
1336— Find the Timer
1343— Mirror, Mirror on the Wall
1377— Misunderstandings
1406— I Am Thinking of . . .
1427— Going Away and Coming Back
1478— Let Me Find You
1507— Simon Says
1512— Stop and Go Game
1514— Toss Game
1525— A Peaceful Solution
1597— Treasure Hunt
1598— Secret Messages
1599— Cover Your Eyes
1604— Spin the Number
1616— Bagball
1639— What's Under the Cover?
1659— Where's the Bird?
1685— Fast and Slow, Then Stop
1700— Hatching Boxes
1711— Where's the Crown?

LANGUAGE
1007— Open and Closed
1023— Looking for Letters
1033— Nonsense Rhymes
1043— Questions
1171— Nonsense Talk
1180— Our Newspaper
1189— Things I Like,
         Things I Don't Like
1198— Poetry Day
1235— Name Signs
1271— An Imaginary Person
1274— Animal Sounds
1276— Name Cards
1293— Talking Without Words
1372— Lip Reading
1373— Making Signs
1377— Misunderstandings
1405— Making Up Poems
1465— Name Tags
1488— Let's Imagine
1494— It Takes Practice
1523— Picture Stories
1590— A Pretend Language
1600— Thank-You Messages
1704— Learning to Write with Chalk

(books)
1048— Making a Book
1164— The Day Care Book
1188— My Family and Me
1192— What's Going On in the Picture
1732— Little Books, Big Books

(stories)
1067 — Three Magic Wishes
1288 — Making Up Stories
1340 — Tag Stories
1390 — Let's Tell a Story
1649 — An Imaginary Book

MAKING AND BUILDING
1010 — Making Doll Clothes
1014 — Making a House
1019 — Playing with Boats
1050 — Handprint Cards
1069 — Paper Towel Rolls
1070 — Paper Cup Containers
1077 — An Old Shoe Box
1095 — Paper Windows
1111 — Stone Paperweights
1117 — A Block Tower
1118 — Sanding Wood
1130 — Scented Balls
1139 — The Missing Pieces
1167 — Paper Mustache
1169 — Make a Birdfeeder
1174 — Flying Ghosts
1193 — Shoe-Box Trolley
1194 — Paper Chains
1195 — Fancy Eggs
1209 — Sand Clock
1217 — Spinning Circle
1227 — Parachutes
1229 — Rocket Ship
1238 — Paper Dolls
1249 — Your Own Make-Believe
1259 — Fixing Things
1267 — Headbands That Fit
1270 — Telephones
1278 — Look What I Built
1315 — Make a Pinata
1339 — Making Pillows
1345 — Body Outlines
1356 — My History
1397 — Pretending with Boxes
1400 — Bookmarks
1413 — Blockbuilding
1449 — Bean Bags
1492 — Newspaper Dolls
1496 — Softee
1499 — Animal Blocks
1518 — Balloon Faces
1521 — Coin Banks
1531 — Trolley Tracks
1606 — Spool Animals
1620 — A Television Stage
1627 — Tunnels and Bridges
1636 — Paper Bag Mask
1637 — Fancy Crowns
1638 — Paper Bag Wigs
1648 — Imaginary Viewers
1653 — Paper Chain Decorations
1658 — Bird on a Straw
1675 — Three-Cornered Hats
1699 — Making a Wagon
1706 — Glitter shakers
1721 — A Gift for You
1724 — Paper Plate Merry-Go-Round
1728 — Making an Eye Chart
1730 — Rainbow Containers
1735 — Drawing a Model

MISCELLANEOUS
1024 — You've Got To Do It
1046 — Something-To-Do Box
1069 — Paper Towel Rolls
1081 — Cutting Paper
1087 — Making Your Own Choice
1096 — Working Together
1109 — Cooperation
1281 — Variety Show

1283 — How You Are Growing
1320 — A Pounding Festival
1375 — Planning a Party
1411 — Boxes Inside Boxes
1412 — A Place of My Own
1429 — You Look Different
1425 — Flea Market
1436 — What's Under the Turban?
1440 — Expressing Feelings
1445 — Some Things Belong to
       Everyone
1448 — All About Baskets
1460 — Let's Do it Again
1489 — Safe Play
1490 — A Play Celebration
1491 — Everything in Its Place
1528 — Make Some Changes
1532 — Straws
1535 — Grandparents' Day
1607 — A Photograph of Me
1657 — Cardboard Blocks
1687 — Mirror Play
1693 — Hand Tracing

MUSIC
1035 — Clapping Rhythms
1066 — Making Up Songs
1105 — Draw a Song
1159 — Singing Instead of Saying
1239 — Rhythm Exercises
1266 — Loud and Quiet
1269 — Drum Rhythms
1325 — A Songfest
1334 — Animal Parade
1399 — A Pretend Orchestra
1420 — Painting to Music
1505 — Spoon Puppet Opera
1515 — Humming a Song
1579 — Listen to the Music
1591 — Pocket Comb Harmonica
1642 — Rhythm Rattles
1681 — Singing Fast and Slow
1688 — An Air Band
1693 — Hand Tracing

(dance and movement)
1076 — Dancing Day
1145 — Balloons
1196 — Birds in Flight
1264 — Seagulls
1363 — Friendship Dances
1430 — Let's Have a Parade
1444 — Caterpillars and Butterflies
1446 — Let's Dance
1475 — Windstorm
1484 — Dancers
1586 — Shadow Dancers
1595 — Royal Dancing

(making instruments)
1006 — Cardboard Trumpets
1134 — Shoebox Harp
1185 — Making Drums
1212 — Ringing Spoons
1213 — A Stringed Instrument
1404 — Sandpaper Blocks
1443 — Paper-Plate Shakers
1509 — Musical Jars

PANTOMIME
1013 — Getting Dressed
1026 — Messages
1084 — Giving a Clue
1085 — Can You See What
       I'm Thinking?
1107 — What's In the Suitcase?
1121 — Say It Without Words
1160 — Guess What I Am

1290 — Pantomime
1374 — Pantomime Feelings
1399 — A Pretend Orchestra
1668 — Then and Now

PHYSICAL EXERCISE
1021 — Digging a Hole
1032 — Tightrope Walking
1091 — Wheel Toys
1094 — Playing With Balls
1097 — Flying Discs
1137 — Rolling
1157 — Eye Exercises
1162 — Hopping
1170 — All Kinds of Exercise
1173 — Basketball
1202 — A Rag Ball
1223 — Ball Bounce
1228 — Jumping Over the Moon
1248 — Magic Exercises
1257 — Balancing Blocks
1323 — Games
1329 — Stop Sign Game
1334 — Animal Parade
1385 — Getting Permission
1398 — Bean Bag Toss
1486 — Stilts
1493 — Exercise Every Day
1495 — Walk, Crawl and Hop
1542 — Balance the Ring
1593 — Jump Over
1602 — Kick Ball
1603 — Walking the Line
1605 — Bowling
1684 — Safe Gymnastics
1692 — Physical Exercise
1716 — Juggling Scarves
1720 — Jump and Call
1731 — Little and Big Exercises

PLAY
(acting out a role)
1030 — Looking in the Mirror
1047 — Caring for Baby
1078 — Growing
1088 — Important Talk
1099 — An Award for Everyone
1110 — Pretend Animals
1115 — I'm Taking Care of You
1116 — Taking Care of Someone
1120 — Pretending about Bedtime
1121 — Say It Without Words
1122 — Sharing Someone's Time
1132 — Why is the Baby Crying?
1142 — Moms and Dads
1153 — Nursery Rhymes
1168 — Playing About Animals
1187 — A Caregiver
1214 — Occupations
1219 — A Cradle for the Dolls
1221 — The Clown in Me
1245 — Snow Statues
1247 — When Someone Goes Away
1250 — Funny Fast
1261 — Dress-up
1275 — Everybody Has a History
1378 — Trying on Hats
1381 — Pretending
1403 — Having Guests
1425 — An Imaginary Land
1426 — When Someone Goes Away
1461 — A Pretend School Bus
1464 — Take Something Along
1469 — Make-up
1480 — An Airplane Ride
1506 — Trying on Shoes
1522 — Shadow Play
1582 — Am I Still Me?

1584 — Clown Masks
1609 — Animal Play
1624 — A Make-Believe Wolf
1629 — A Pretend Dentist
1634 — Cutting Pretend Hair
1635 — Popcorn
1640 — Dress-up Day
1652 — Learning to Pretend
1698 — Disguise

(thematic play)
1002 — Moving Day
1004 — A New Doll House
1009 — Kings and Queens
1012 — Bathing the Dolls
1014 — Making a House
1068 — What Could I Be?
1104 — The Doctor's Office
1124 — A Telephone Conversation
1156 — Listen to Your Heart
1208 — Let's Go Shopping
1236 — A Pretend Tea Party
1272 — Making Doll Beds
1291 — A Birthday Party
1301 — A Pretend Store
1304 — A Hospital for Toys
1307 — Going on a Trip
1321 — I Have an Idea
1361 — Pancakes or Waffles
1367 — Washing Doll Clothes
1370 — Attending the Opera
1384 — A Television Program
1402 — Visiting
1416 — Playing Dentist
1424 — Keys
1438 — Playing with Ramps
1450 — Birthday Parties
1453 — Playing About Witches
1456 — Pretending About the Future
1466 — Super Capes
1500 — Let's Make a Zoo
1502 — Hospital Play
1503 — Going for a Ride
1510 — A Toy Village
1530 — There's Work to Do
1545 — A Pretend Wedding
1585 — Circus Day
1588 — Water Play
1589 — Nesting Toys
1611 — Telephone Talk
1615 — The Caring Center
1617 — Milk Carton Haulers
1621 — What's Under the Bandage?
1622 — A Doll Hospital
1670 — A Long-Ago Party
1676 — Going Away and Coming Back
1677 — An Ambulance for the Dolls
1678 — A Secret Tunnel
1679 — A Toy Car Wash
1690 — Birthday Party Play
1709 — Doctor Play
1718 — Hospital Play

PUPPETS
1172 — Meeting Someone New
1186 — Spoon Puppets
1285 — Stick Puppets
1286 — Puppet Play
1298 — Mouth Puppets
1389 — Paper Bag Puppets
1409 — Sock Puppets
1410 — Homemade Marionettes
1452 — Box Puppets
1505 — Spoon Puppet Opera
1578 — Making Mistakes
1630 — A Cardboard Mouth
1689 — Talking for the Toys

ROUTINES
1003 — A Job to Do
1183 — Safety First
1296 — Washing Clothes
1379 — Setting the Table
1458 — Cleaning Up a Mess
1623 — Sweeping the Carpet
1701 — Machines that Help

SCIENCE AND MATH
1005 — Things That Are Alive
1017 — Vegetable Prints
1020 — Making Popsicles
1044 — How Long?
1061 — Big and Little
1063 — Una Hoja
1079 — Watching Seeds Grow
1086 — Comparing Weights
1112 — Measuring Time
1113 — How Many Times?
1119 — What's Inside
1123 — A Vacuum Cleaner
1126 — Carrot Top Sprouts
1135 — Machines
1136 — Pouring Water
1138 — How Do Plants Eat?
1150 — Use Your Breath
1158 — A Close Look
1190 — Carbon Paper Printing
1191 — Camouflage
1197 — Invisible Pictures
1200 — Eggshell Garden
1215 — Plumbing and Drains
1224 — Magnets
1244 — Melting Ice Cubes
1273 — Planting Beans
1295 — Collecting Stones
1299 — Sweet Potato Plants
1310 — Looking at Seeds
1380 — Going Down the Drain
1418 — An Energy Crisis
1419 — People and Machines
1424 — Keys
1438 — Playing with Ramps
1442 — Same But Different
1447 — Looking for Numbers
1462 — Card Sorting
1471 — Bubble Play
1580 — Now You See It,
Now You Don't
1592 — Let's Explore
1632 — Growing Takes Time
1655 — Flashlight Power
1656 — Up and Down Pulleys
1660 — Up in the Air
1666 — Water Science
1674 — My Shape It Has Three Corners
1705 — Straw Play
1707 — Nature Collage Quilt
1715 — Kitchen Science

SELF-HELP SKILLS
1049 — All by Myself
1089 — Lacing Shoes
1114 — Hair Styles
1127 — Learning to Do New Things
1129 — Making Toothpaste
1289 — Practicing
1297 — Take Care of Your Teeth
1313 — Things I Can Do
1326 — Children Can
1387 — Help Me, Don't Help Me
1395 — Trying on Clothes
1401 — Buttoning
1501 — Using Silverware
1628 — Brushing Your Teeth

SENSORY EXPLORATION
1018 — Pouring Rice
1021 — Digging a Hole
1080 — While You Wait
1133 — Stick Sculptures
1136 — Pouring Water
1241 — Foam Painting
1254 — Making Modeling Dough
1256 — Soapsuds Fingerpainting
1312 — Making Pretend Cement
1351 — Blowing Bubbles
1353 — Water Play
1355 — Washing Toys
1367 — Washing Doll Clothes
1371 — Modeling-Dough Letters
1408 — Dough Play
1423 — Fingerpainting Designs
1449 — Bean Bags
1457 — Painting With Water
1471 — Bubble Play
1524 — Marble Modeling Dough
1644 — Play Clay
1662 — Soap Sculptures
1694 — Kneading Dough
1696 — Changing Colors
1697 — Mystery Boxes
1723 — Playing with Water

TALKING ABOUT . . .
1016 — My Home
1022 — Taking Turns
1042 — Some Place Else
1065 — Feelings Show
1082 — What Can Babies Do?
1101 — When a Pet Dies
1141 — Broken Toys
1143 — When Accidents Happen
1148 — Guess Which Hand
1154 — When We Were Little
1163 — Jobs and Occupations
1175 — Scary Sounds
1176 — My Inside Self
1177 — I Feel Jealous When
1210 — Rules and Limits
1216 — My Parents Take Care of Me
1246 — Caution
1253 — Talking about Feelings
1263 — Talking about Limits
1268 — Angry Feelings
1277 — Feeling Jealous
1282 — I Used to be Afraid
1294 — Thunder Noises
1300 — Alike and Different
1302 — Time to Myself
1308 — The Working Way
1309 — What is Love?
1311 — Talking About Waiting
1314 — Ways I'm Growing
1316 — Unexpected Changes
1322 — Talking About Disabilities
1326 — Children Can
1330 — Wishing and Doing
1335 — Saying Good-bye
1337 — Talking About Sharing
1341 — Remember When
1346 — How Would You Feel?
1347 — When Something Breaks
1354 — Why Do People Cry?
1358 — What Do You Call Me?
1359 — Winning and Losing
1382 — Disappointments
1383 — Pictures of Things
1385 — Getting Permission
1386 — Talking About School
1391 — Where I Live
1392 — Scary Things
1396 — Feeling Angry
1407 — Can Wishes Come True?

1414 — Missing Persons
1417 — Saying What You Feel
1421 — The Best of Whatever You Are
1428 — When You Have to Wait
1431 — Safety Rules
1432 — Giving Up Old Things
1439 — Take Your Time
1454 — Remembering
1472 — Ways to Say "I Love You"
1477 — Wanting and Needing
1479 — Working Out Problems
1487 — Safe Toys
1497 — If I Had a Pet
1516 — My First Day
1519 — Dreaming
1533 — I Wonder
1543 — Yes and No
1576 — Saying I'm Sorry
1581 — How We Change and Grow
1594 — Keeping Yourself Safe
1608 — Growing and Changing
1614 — Working and Caring
1625 — Fatherly Care
1633 — Once We Were Babies
1647 — Imaginary Pets
1650 — Everything Grows Together
1661 — My Favorite Things
1669 — Remembering Pets That Died
1672 — Sometimes Isn't Always
1691 — The Mad that You Feel
1702 — Talking About Things
that Scare You
1708 — Talking About Our Favorite
Things
1713 — Talking About Sharing
1719 — Keeping Safe
1725 — Talking About Giving and
Receiving
1726 — Talking About Wheelchairs
1734 — Talking About Big and Little

VISITORS AND OUTINGS
1206 — Making Choices
1287 — Buying Groceries
1402 — Visiting
1470 — Mechanical Monsters
1498 — An Animal Comes To Visit
1526 — Mail a Letter
1645 — A Visit to an Art Gallery

TOPICS

BITING
1007 — Open and Closed
1081 — Cutting Paper
1298 — Mouth Puppets
1452 — Box Puppets
1630 — A Cardboard Mouth

BODY AWARENESS
1013 — Getting Dressed
1114 — Hair Styles
1141 — Broken Toys
1260 — Puzzles
1319 — Things That Are Fragile
1342 — A Handprint Mural
1343 — Mirror, Mirror on the Wall
1345 — Body Outlines
1347 — When Something Breaks
1350 — Matching Shoes
1368 — Front and Back
1395 — Trying on Clothes
1436 — What's Under the Turban?
1492 — Newspaper Dolls
1507 — Simon Says
1518 — Balloon Faces
1541 — Self-Portraits

1621 — What's Under the Bandage?
1650 — Everything Grows Together
1667 — Hand Shadows
1686 — Rice Cake Faces
1693 — Hand Tracing

CELEBRATIONS
1375 — Planning a Party
1490 — A Play Celebration

(birthdays)
1291 — A Birthday Party
1450 — Birthday Parties
1690 — Birthday Party Play

(weddings)
1009 — Kings and Queens
1015 — A Wedding Cake
1545 — A Pretend Wedding

CHANGES
1114 — Hair Styles
1203 — Making Butter
1204 — Mixing Colors
1244 — Melting Ice Cubes
1255 — Egg Salad Sandwiches
1316 — Unexpected Changes
1318 — What's Different?
1429 — You Look Different
1455 — Making Bread
1469 — Make-Up
1504 — Making Popcorn
1528 — Make Some Changes
1583 — What's Missing?
1584 — Clown Masks
1635 — Popcorn
1699 — Changing Colors
1698 — Disguise

CHOICES
1155 — Making Applesauce
1206 — Making Choices
1287 — Buying Groceries
1359 — Winning and Losing
1508 — Making Your Own Sandwich
1529 — A Shopping List

CLASSIFICATION
1005 — Things That Are Alive
1064 — Sorting Buttons
1091 — Wheel Toys
1152 — Supply Depot
1442 — Same but Different
1462 — Card Sorting
1732 — Little Books, Big Books

(matching)
1041 — Outline Match
1100 — Parents and Babies
1102 — Matching Pairs
1178 — Key Match
1279 — Rubbings
1350 — Matching Shoes
1424 — Keys
1673 — Shoe Match

(shapes)
1001 — Things That Are Round
1062 — Secret Envelopes
1220 — Making Cookies
1348 — Sorting Shapes

(numbers)
1113 — How Many Times?
1447 — Looking for Numbers

(letters)
1023 — Looking for Letters

1184 — Letter Rubbings
1235 — Name Signs
1276 — Name Cards
1349 — Alphabet Soup
1373 — Making Signs
1465 — Name Tags
1683 — Word Box

(animals)
1110 — Pretend Animals
1168 — Playing about Animals
1232 — Animal Cookies
1274 — Animal Sounds
1334 — Animal Parade
1497 — If I Had a Pet
1498 — An Animal Comes to Visit
1499 — Animal Blocks
1500 — Let's Make a Zoo

(machines)
1123 — A Vacuum Cleaner
1135 — Machines
1296 — Washing Clothes
1367 — Washing Doll Clothes
1470 — Mechanical Monsters
1490 — People and Machines
1513 — Machine Collage
1682 — Wheel Toys

COMMUNICATION
1026 — Messages
1033 — Nonsense and Rhymes
1043 — Questions
1065 — Feelings Show
1084 — Giving a Clue
1085 — Can You See What I'm
　　　　Thinking?
1121 — Say It without Words
1124 — A Telephone Conversation
1132 — Why is the Baby Crying?
1159 — Singing Instead of Saying
1171 — Nonsense Talk
1192 — What's Going On in the Picture
1270 — Telephones
1274 — Pantomine Feelings
1479 — Working Out Problems
1505 — Spoon Puppet Opera
1523 — Picture Stories
1590 — A Pretend Language
1598 — Secret Messages
1600 — Thank-you Messages

COMPETENCE
1099 — An Award for Everyone
1127 — Learning to Do New Things
1221 — The Clown in Me
1249 — Your Own Make-Believe
1259 — Fixing Things
1278 — Look What I Built
1281 — Variety Show
1283 — How You Are Growing
1289 — Practicing
1312 — Making Pretend Cement
1313 — Things I Can Do
1314 — Ways I'm Growing
1326 — Children Can
1387 — Help Me, Don't Help Me
1401 — Buttoning
1413 — Blockbuilding
1421 — The Best of Whatever You Are
1433 — Making Tacos
1439 — Take Your Time
1458 — Cleaning Up a Mess
1482 — An Art Show
1491 — Everything in Its Place
1501 — Using Silverware
1704 — Learning to Write with Chalk

COOPERATION
1096 — Working Together
1109 — Cooperation
1128 — Thumbprint Pies
1164 — The Day Care Book
1166 — Peanut Butter
1180 — Our Newspaper
1225 — Making a Mural
1249 — Your Own Make-Believe
1254 — Making Modeling Dough
1315 — Making a Pinata
1328 — Making a Pizza
1336 — Find the Timer
1361 — Pancakes or Waffles
1375 — Planning a Party
1483 — Cookie Decorating
1485 — A Rainbow for Everyone
1496 — Softee
1517 — The Hoagie Factory
1525 — A Peaceful Solution
1527 — Milk Shakes
1540 — Homemade Noodles
1613 — Peanut Butter and Fruit
1680 — Salsa and Tortilla Chips
1710 — Yogurt Cereal Mix
1722 — Bagel Snacks

COORDINATION
1032 — Tightrope Walking
1094 — Playing with Balls
1097 — Flying Discs
1137 — Rolling
1150 — Use Your Breath
1162 — Hopping
1228 — Jumping Over the Moon
1239 — Rhythm Exercises
1250 — Funny Fast
1257 — Balancing Blocks
1323 — Games
1344 — Paper-Punch Designs
1352 — Yarn Designs
1398 — Bean Bag Toss
1401 — Buttoning
1404 — Sandpaper Blocks
1449 — Bean Bags
1486 — Stilts
1493 — Exercise Every Day
1495 — Walk, Crawl and Hop
1514 — Toss Game
1542 — Balance the Ring
1602 — Kick Ball
1603 — Walking the Line
1605 — Bowling
1616 — Bagball
1653 — Paper Chain Decorations
1692 — Physical Exercise
1716 — Juggling Scarves
1720 — Jump and Call
1731 — Little and Big Exercises

CREATIVITY
1008 — Painting Boxes
1010 — Making Doll Clothes
1011 — Stick Designs
1014 — Making a House
1028 — String Painting
1031 — Picture Frames
1045 — Tissue Paper Pictures
1046 — Something-To-Do Box
1069 — Paper Towel Rolls
1070 — Paper Cup Containers
1111 — Stone Paperweight
1117 — A Block Tower
1131 — Construction Paper Mobiles
1133 — Stick Sculptures
1161 — Snack Pictures
1165 — Bean Collage
1195 — Fancy Eggs

1201 — Styrofoam Sculptures
1211 — Kaleidoscope Patterns
1221 — Coil Pots
1240 — Pole Dyeing
1241 — Foam Painting
1243 — Multi-colored Snow
1267 — Headbands That Fit
1317 — Paper Collage
1362 — Wooden Sculptures
1369 — Sparkle Paintings
1400 — Bookmarks
1410 — Homemade Marionettes
1441 — Crayon Window Hangings
1531 — Trolley Tracks
1532 — Straws
1534 — Aquarium Pictures
1586 — Shadow Dancers
1596 — An Underground House
1601 — Paper Bag Hats
1609 — Animal Play
1637 — Fancy Crowns
1663 — Soap Sculptures
1674 — My Shape It Has Three Corners
1675 — Three-Cornered Hats
1699 — Making a Wagon
1717 — Feather Collage
1723 — Playing with Water
1724 — Paper Plate Merry-Go-Round
1735 — Drawing a Model

CURIOSITY
1017 — Vegetable Prints
1119 — What's Inside
1123 — A Vacuum Cleaner
1158 — A Close Look
1215 — Plumbing and Drains
1230 — Instant Oatmeal
1533 — I Wonder
1597 — Treasure Hunt
1654 — A Neighborhood Field Trip
1655 — Flashlight Power
1656 — Up and Down Pulleys
1665 — Soap Bubbles
1666 — Water Science
1697 — Mystery Boxes
1706 — Glitter Shakers

DISABILITIES
1293 — Talking Without Words
1322 — Talking About Disabilities
1372 — Lip Reading
1726 — Talking About Wheelchairs

EXPERIMENTS
1019 — Playing with Boats
1020 — Making Popsicles
1086 — Comparing Weights
1138 — How Do Plants Eat?
1150 — Use Your Breath
1190 — Carbon Paper Printing
1197 — Invisible Pictures
1224 — Magnets
1244 — Melting Ice Cubes
1299 — Sweet Potato Plants
1351 — Blowing Bubbles
1418 — An Energy Crisis
1419 — People and Machines
1471 — Bubble Play
1504 — Making Popcorn
1580 — Now You See It,
　　　　Now You Don't
1705 — Straw Play
1715 — Kitchen Science

FEARS
1282 — I Used to Be Afraid
1324 — Nighttime Pictures
1347 — When Something Breaks

1389 — Paper Bag Puppets
1522 — Shadow Play
1702 — Talking About Things
　　　　that Scare You

(ghosts)
1174 — Flying Ghosts

(sounds)
1175 — Scary Sounds

(thunder)
1294 — Thunder Noises

(drains)
1012 — Bathing the Dolls
1215 — Plumbing and Drains
1380 — Going Down the Drain

(dreams)
1468 — A Picture of a Dream
1519 — Dreaming

(giants)
1392 — Scary Things

(witches)
1388 — Things That Are Scary
1453 — Playing About Witches

(monsters)
1467 — Dinosaur Models
1470 — Mechanical Monsters
1624 — A Make-Believe Wolf

(machines)
1123 — A Vacuum Cleaner
1296 — Washing Clothes
1623 — Sweeping the Carpet

FEELINGS
1065 — Feelings Show
1085 — Can You See What I'm
　　　　Thinking?
1088 — Important Talk
1140 — Paint How You Feel
1143 — When Accidents Happen
1221 — The Clown in Me
1253 — Talking About Feelings
1286 — Puppet Play
1292 — My Favorite Color
1309 — What is Love?
1316 — Unexpected Changes
1346 — How Would You Feel?
1354 — Why Do People Cry?
1359 — Winning and Losing
1434 — Unhappy Feelings
1578 — Puppet Play
1626 — Gingerbread Faces
1672 — Sometimes Isn't Always
1708 — Talking About Our Favorite
　　　　Things
1727 — Feeling Left Out

(expressing feelings)
1006 — Cardboard Trumpets
1027 — How Do You Feel?
1076 — Dancing Day
1198 — Poetry Day
1440 — Expressing Feelings
1472 — Ways to Say "I Love You"
1576 — Saying I'm Sorry
1591 — Pocket Comb Harmonica

(anger)
1021 — Digging a Hole
1081 — Cutting Paper
1268 — Angry Feelings

1269— Drum Rhythms
1320— A Pounding Festival
1396— Feeling Angry
1408— Dough Play
1691— The Mad that You Feel

(jealousy)
1047— Caring for Baby
1122— Sharing Someone's Time
1177— I Feel Jealous When
1219— A Cradle for the Dolls
1277— Feeling Jealous
1403— Having Guests

(shyness)
1172— Meeting Someone New
1417— Saying What You Feel

FOLLOWING DIRECTIONS
1167— Paper Mustache
1217— Spinning Circle
1415— Egg Drop Soup
1443— Paper-plate Shakers

GIVING
1050— Handprint Cards
1070— Paper-cup Containers
1130— Scented Balls
1376— Fabric Cards
1537— Granola Gifts
1721— A Gift for You
1725— Talking About Giving and
          Receiving
1730— Rainbow Containers

GROWING
1078— Growing
1079— Watching Seeds Grow
1082— What Can Babies Do?
1126— Carrot Top Sprouts
1151— Comparing Shoes and Feet
1154— When We Were Little
1273— Planting Beans
1275— Everybody Has a History
1299— Sweet Potato Plants
1341— Remember When
1432— Giving Up Old Things
1444— Caterpillars and Butterflies
1454— Remembering
1581— How We Change and Grow
1607— A Photograph of Me
1608— Growing and Changing
1633— Once We Were Babies
1668— Then and Now
1670— A Long-Ago Party

IMAGINATION
1077— An Old Shoe Box
1107— What's in the Suitcase?
1142— Moms and Dads
1144— Speedy Delivery
1149— Upside-Down Pictures
1153— Nursery Rhymes
1179— Decorating Pretend Cakes
1186— Spoon Puppets
1193— Shoe-Box Trolley
1197— Invisible Pictures
1218— Connect-the-Dot Designs
1226— What's Behind the Fog?
1227— Parachutes
1229— Rocket Ship
1233— Space Ships
1236— A Pretend Tea Party
1242— Snow Pictures
1245— Snow Statues
1271— An Imaginary Person
1285— Stick Puppets
1288— Making Up Stories

1290— Pantomine
1321— I Have an Idea
1331— Paper Plate Pictures
1340— Tag Stories
1370— Attending the Opera
1378— Trying on Hats
1390— Let's Tell a Story
1394— Paint Blots
1397— Pretending with Boxes
1402— Visiting
1409— Sock Puppets
1425— An Imaginary Land
1430— Let's Have a Parade
1438— Playing with Ramps
1456— Pretending about the Future
1457— Painting with Water
1474— Straw Painting
1481— Drawing the Neighborhood
1488— Let's Imagine
1510— A Toy Village
1585— Circus Day
1587— Star Mobiles
1606— Spool Animals
1619— Underwater Pictures
1643— Chalk Skywriting
1646— Drawing with Colored Markers
1647— Imaginary Pets
1648— Imaginary Viewers
1649— An Imaginary Book
1660— Up in the Air
1688— An Air Band
1689— Talking for the Toys

INDEPENDENCE
1049— All by Myself
1087— Make Your Own Choice
1089— Lacing Shoes
1326— Children Can
1355— Washing Toys
1387— Help Me, Don't Help Me
1628— Brushing Your Teeth

INDIVIDUAL DIFFERENCES
1045— Tissue Paper Pictures
1189— Things I Like, Things I Don't
          Like
1234— There's No One Just Like You
1237— Purple Paint
1238— Paper Dolls
1251— Food Coloring Designs
1280— Shape Designs
1284— I'm Thinking of a Child
1300— Alike and Different
1357— Purple Print Pictures
1448— All about Baskets
1538— Chef Brockett's Nutritious
          Snack
1599— Cover Your Eyes
1610— I'm Glad I'm the Way I Am
1651— Census Taking
1658— Bird on a Straw
1729— Different and the Same Collage

LIMITS
1210— Rules and Limits
1263— Talking about Limits
1329— Stop Sign Game
1385— Getting Permission
1431— Safety Rules

LOSS
1139— The Missing Pieces
1336— Find the Timer
1148— Guess Which Hand
1359— Winning and Losing

MEASURING
1044— How Long?

1631— Measuring Our Growth

(time)
1112— Measuring Time
1209— Sand Clock

MEMORY
1147— In the Bag
1306— What's Missing?
1318— What's Different?
1325— A Songfest
1454— Remembering
1460— Let's Do It Again
1494— It Takes Practice

MONEY
1208— Let's Go Shopping
1287— Buying Groceries
1301— A Pretend Store
1435— Flea Market
1477— Wanting and Needing
1506— Trying on Shoes
1521— Coin Banks

NATURE
1063— Una Hoja
1106— Going for a Walk
1169— Make a Birdfeeder
1191— Camouflage
1200— An Eggshell Garden
1231— Leaf Rubbings
1295— Collecting Stones
1310— Looking at Seeds
1592— Let's Explore
1707— Nature Collage Quilt

NEW EXPERIENCES
1480— An Airplane Ride

(day care)
1516— My First Day

(school)
1386— Talking about School
1461— A Pretend School Bus
1464— Take Something Along

(hospital)
1304— A Hospital for Toys
1502— Hospital Play
1677— An Ambulance for the Dolls
1718— Hospital Play

(doctor)
1104— The Doctor's Office
1156— Listen to Your Heart
1157— Eye Exercises
1709— Doctor Play
1728— Making an Eye Chart

(dentist)
1129— Making Toothpaste
1297— Take Care of Your Teeth
1416— Playing Dentist
1629— A Pretend Dentist

(moving)
1002— Moving Day
1004— A New Doll House

(death)
1101— When a Pet Dies
1669— Remembering Pets That Died

(divorce)
1476— Different Kinds of Families
1477— Wanting and Needing

(haircut)
1114— Hair Styles
1262— Making Snow
1634— Cutting Pretend Hair

NURTURING
1047— Caring for Baby
1115— I'm Taking Care of You
1116— Taking Care of Someone
1187— A Caregiver
1216— My Parents Take Care of Me
1219— A Cradle for the Dolls
1247— When Someone Feels Tired
1615— The Caring Center
1622— A Doll Hospital
1625— Fatherly Care

OCCUPATIONS
1160— Guess What I Am
1163— Jobs and Occupations
1214— Occupations
1526— Mail a Letter
1530— There's Work to Do

OPPOSITES
1007— Open and Closed
1018— Pouring Rice
1061— Big and Little
1100— Parents and Babies
1118— Sanding Wood
1149— Upside-Down Pictures
1151— Comparing Shoes and Feet
1182— Hard and Soft
1189— Things I Like, Things I Don't
          Like
1266— Loud and Quiet
1393— Comparing Sizes
1734— Talking About Big and Little

PATIENCE
1093— Fishing
1103— Jack-in-the-Box
1273— Planting Beans
1311— Talking abut Waiting
1428— When You Have to Wait
1455— Making Bread
1536— Dried Apple Rings
1542— Balance the Ring
1632— Growing Takes Time

PRIVACY
1302— Time to Myself
1327— My Special Box
1337— Talking about Sharing
1339— Making Pillows
1406— I Am Thinking of . . .
1412— A Place of My Own

REAL & PRETEND
1024— You've Got to Do It
1067— Three Magic Wishes
1232— Animal Cookies
1248— Magic Exercises
1330— Wishing and Doing
1360— Ways to Travel
1381— Pretending
1382— Disappointments
1407— Can Wishes Come True?
1466— Super Capes
1539— Real and Pretend
1636— Paper Bag Mask
1640— Dress-up Day

RECYCLING
1205— Let's Use It Again
1365— Recycle Collage
1617— Milk Carton Haulers
1618— Recycling Projects

1712— Found Object Collage

RELATIONSHIPS
1703— Helping Grown-ups in the
      Kitchen

(families)
1188— My Family and Me
1366— All about Families
1476— Different Kinds of Families

(friends)
1363— Friendship Dances

(grandparents)
1534— Aquarium Pictures
1535— Grandparents' Day

RESPONSIBILITY
1003— A Job to Do
1379— Setting the Table

SAFETY
1183— Safety First
1246— Caution
1487— Safe Toys
1489— Safe Play
1503— Going for a Ride
1594— Keeping Yourself Safe
1684— Safe Gymnastics
1719— Keeping Safe

SELF-AWARENESS

(identity)
1029— Paper Plate Masks
1030— Looking in the Mirror
1176— My Inside Self
1234— There's No One Just Like You
1235— Name Signs
1275— Everybody Has a History
1276— Name Cards
1356— My History
1358— What Do You Call Me?
1395— Trying on Clothes
1465— Name Tags
1582— Am I Still Me?
1687— Mirror Play

SELF-CONTROL
1034— It's Too Noisy
1042— Some Place Else
1080— While You Wait
1136— Pouring Water
1146— Quiet Please
1181— Traffic Light Game
1239— Rhythm Exercises
1250— Funny Fast
1257— Balancing Blocks
1262— Making Snow
1266— Loud and Quiet
1320— A Pounding Festival
1329— Stop Sign Game
1353— Water Play
1512— Stop and Go Game
1543— Yes and No
1685— Fast and Slow, Then Stop
1694— Kneading Dough
1695— Clap and Stomp Rhythms

SELF-EXPRESSION
1048— Making a Book
1066— Making Up Songs
1083— Salt Drawings
1098— Eggshell Pictures
1105— Draw a Song
1140— Paint How You Feel
1145— Balloons

1196— Birds in Flight
1198— Poetry Day
1252— Drawing Pictures
1256— Soapsuds Fingerpainting
1264— Seagulls
1325— A Songfest
1338— Sand Pictures
1405— Making Up Poems
1420— Painting to Music
1423— Fingerpainting Designs
1444— Caterpillars and Butterflies
1446— Let's Dance
1451— Clay Sculptures
1459— Torn Paper Pictures
1463— Chalk Drawings
1475— Windstorm
1484— Dancers
1515— Humming a Song
1524— Marble Modeling Dough
1577— A Book Factory
1579— Listen to the Music
1595— Royal Dancing
1641— The Art That's Inside You
1642— Rhythm Rattles
1644— Play Clay
1645— A Visit to an Art Gallery
1652— Learning to Pretend
1657— Cardboard Blocks
1662— Museum of Love
1664— Shaving Cream Fingerpainting
1675— Three-Cornered Collages
1681— Singing Fast and Slow

SENSES

(taste)
1025— Oranges
1125— Pineapples and Tomatoes
1199— Tasting New Foods
1207— Homemade Soup
1265— Chef Brockett's Concoction
1305— Fruit Salad
1520— Graham Cracker Treats
1733— Grapes, Grapes, Grapes

(smell)
1025— Oranges
1130— Scented Balls

(touch)
1258— Guess What's in the Bag

(listening)
1035— Clapping Rhythms
1092— Familiar Sounds
1105— Draw a Song
1134— Shoe-Box Harp
1185— Making Drums
1212— Ringing Spoons
1213— A Stringed Instrument
1364— What Do You Hear?
1377— Misunderstandings
1390— Let's Tell a Story
1399— A Pretend Orchestra
1422— Which is Which?
1509— Musical Jars

SEPARATION
1016— My Home
1095— Paper Windows
1100— Parents and Babies
1103— Jack-in-the-Box
1108— Hide It, Find It
1120— Pretending about Bedtime
1124— A Telephone Conversation
1187— A Caregiver
1202— A Rag Ball
1224— Magnets

1272— Making Doll Beds
1303— Making a Map
1307— Going on a Trip
1308— The Working Way
1332— Hide and Seek
1333— Can You Find the Toy?
1335— Saying Good-bye
1336— Find the Timer
1391— Where I Live
1411— Boxes Inside Boxes
1414— Missing Persons
1426— When Someone Goes Away
1427— Going Away and Coming Back
1437— Peek-a-Boo
1478— Let Me Find You
1511— What's Under the Towel?
1526— Mail a Letter
1589— Nesting Toys
1611— Telephone Talk
1612— Where's the Peanut?
1627— Tunnels and Bridges
1639— What's Under the Cover?
1659— Where's the Bird?
1661— My Favorite Things
1676— Going Away and Coming Back
1678— A Secret Tunnel
1679— A Toy Car Wash
1700— Hatching Boxes
1711— Where's the Crown?

SHARING
1337— Talking About Sharing
1445— Some Things Belong to
      Everyone
1713— Talking About Sharing
1714— Sharing a Snack

(taking turns)
1022— Taking Turns
1090— Instant Pudding
1229— Rocket Ship
1544— Arroz Con Leche
1604— Spin the Number

TELEVISION
1383— Picture of Things
1384— A Television Program
1620— A Television Stage

WORK
1135— Machines
1308— The Working Way
1517— The Hoagie Factory
1526— Mail a Letter
1527— Milk Shakes
1528— Make Some Changes
1530— There's Work to Do
1614— Working and Caring
1701— Machines That Help